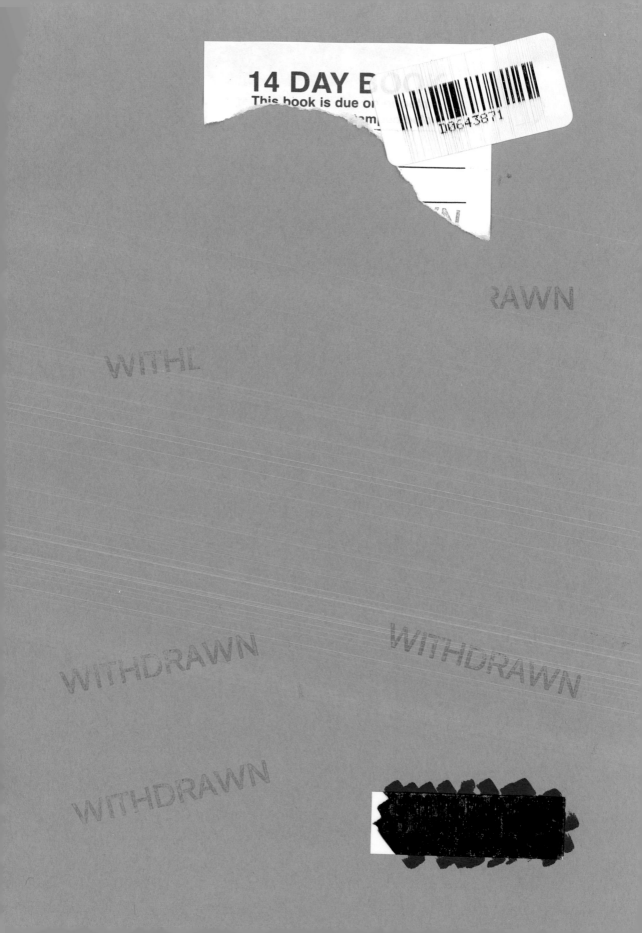

LETTERS FROM
THE
GRAND
TOUR

Edited by Slava Klima

McGILL – QUEEN'S UNIVERSITY PRESS

MONTREAL AND LONDON 1975

Joseph Spence: LETTERS FROM

THE GRAND TOUR

© 1975 McGill-Queen's University Press
International Standard Book Number 0 7735 0090 1
Library of Congress Catalog Card Number 73 79098
Legal Deposit first Quarter 1975
Bibliothèque nationale du Quebec

Designed by Susan McPhee
Printed in Great Britain by Robert Stockwell Ltd

This book has been published
with the help of a grant from
the Humanities Research Council of Canada,
using funds provided by
the Canada Council.

contents

acknowledgements

THE publication of this volume has been made possible by the financial grants I received from the Humanities Research Council of Canada and from the Committee on Research at McGill University. I wish to record my sincere thanks to both.

The bulk of the volume consists of hitherto unpublished manuscript material gathered from various sources. I want to thank the Keeper of the Department of Manuscripts in the British Museum for the permission to publish Spence's letters and travel notes contained in Egerton 2234 and 2235, as well as excerpts from Lord Lincoln's correspondence with his uncle in the Newcastle MSS (Add. MSS 33065). Count Enrico Baldasseroni has kindly allowed me to publish four of Spence's letters to Dr. Cocchi in his private collection. The curators of manuscripts at the Leicestershire Record Office and Nottingham University have generously placed at my disposal the Finch and Newcastle MSS, while the Manuscripts Division of the Henry E. Huntington Library, California, kindly allowed me to print the text of original letters from the extra-illustrated copy of Spence's *Anecdotes*. To the Keeper of Manuscripts at Trinity College I am much obliged for permission to reprint *Letter* 107 from Joseph Warton's transcript of Spence's correspondence with Christopher Pitt. Dr. Wilmarth Lewis of Yale University called my attention to Horace Walpole's annotated copy of *Polymetis* in his collection, and the curator of manuscripts at the Carregi Library at Florence allowed me to inspect Dr. Cocchi's unpublished *Effemeridi* notebooks.

I would also like to express thanks to my friends at Yale and McGill University. To the late George L. Lam for his erudite advice on Italian time in the eighteenth century, to Professors Frederick A. Pottle, Frank Brady, and George Mathewson for the reading of the early drafts of this volume, and to Professor Joyce Hemlow for her expert advice on indexing. I am also much indebted to the work of Spence's biographer, Austin Wright, to the editors of the Yale edition of Horace

Walpole's *Correspondence*, and to Robert Halsband's edition of *The Complete Letters of Lady Mary Wortley Montagu*.

My greatest debt, however, goes to Dr. James M. Osborn, editor of Spence's *Observations* and owner of the Spence Papers, whose invaluable collection of manuscripts is now deposited at the Yale Library. It was he who encouraged me to bring out this edition, and the years I spent in his learned and congenial company have greatly contributed to my love of the eighteenth century. It is to the memory of these years spent with him and his wife, Marie-Louise, which I count among the happiest in my life, that I would like to dedicate this volume of Spence's 'little *Tatlers*' from abroad.

abbreviations & short titles

Addison, *Remarks*	Joseph Addison, *Remarks on Several Parts of Italy, &c. in the years 1701, 1702, 1703* (1705).
Anecdotes	Joseph Spence, *Anecdotes, Observations, and Characters of Books and Men. Collected from the conversation of Mr. Pope, and other eminent persons of his time,* ed. Samuel Weller Singer (1820).
Crito	Sir Harry Beaumont [pseudonym of Spence], *Crito: or a Dialogue on Beauty* (1752).
Cust	Sir Lionel Henry Cust, *History of the Society of Dilettanti,* comp. Lionel Cust, . . . ed. Sidney Colvin (1898).
De Brosses	Charles de Brosses, *Lettres familières sur l'Italie,* ed. Yvonne Bezard, 2 vols. (Paris, 1931).
Foster	Joseph Foster, *Alumni Oxonienses; 1500–1714, 1715–1886* (Oxford, 1891–2, 1887–8).
Fugitive Pieces	*Fugitive Pieces on Various Subjects, By Several Authors,* ed. R. Dodsley, vol. I (1761).
G.E.C.	George Edward Cockayne, *The Complete Peerage* . . ., rev. Vicary Gibbs, 12 vols. (1910–59).
Gent. Mag.	*The Gentleman's Magazine* (1731–1907).
Gray, *Corresp.*	*Correspondence of Thomas Gray,* eds. Paget Toynbee and Leonard Whibley, 3 vols. (Oxford, 1935).
Hertford Corresp.	*Correspondence between Frances, Countess of Hartford, (afterwards Duchess of Somerset), and Henrietta Louisa, Countess of Pomfret, between the Years 1738 and 1741,* 3 vols. (1805).

From Joseph Spence, *Polymetis* (1747)

From Joseph Spence, *Polymetis* (1747)

introduction

JOSEPH Spence was thirty-one, Professor of Poetry at Oxford, and author of a reputable critical study of Pope's translation of Homer, when he embarked on a period in his life which he later spoke of as his 'Years of Travel'. Between 1730 and 1741 he made three tours of the continent, spending five and a half years in Italy, France, and Holland; and the experience, of which his letters are a partial record, left an indelible mark upon his further development and outlook.

The Grand Tour in the eighteenth century was a civilizing institution, whose primary purpose was to extend university education by travel. A young gentleman of birth and fashion, just graduated from Oxford or Cambridge, was reasonably assured of rounding off the academic knowledge he had acquired at college by setting out for two or three years on a tour of the continent. This was an extremely costly venture, which 'could easily run his father into three or four thousand pounds a year—in gold'.[1]

For a commoner like Spence, whose annual stipend at Oxford amounted to £180 (with an expected increase of £20), such expensive venture was clearly impossible. Yet a young don, especially one who had lectured on the *Aeneid* as a political poem, must have longed to enlarge his academic outlook by paying a personal homage to the 'Classick Ground', and no doubt would have concurred with Dr. Johnson that 'a man who has not been to Italy is always conscious of an inferiority, from not having seen what it is expected a man should see.'[2] To the imagination of the men of Pope's generation Italy was not the land *wo die Zitronen blühen*, but a place where an inscription S.P.Q.R., the ruin of an amphitheatre (which tourists like Spence diligently paced for measure), a milestone on the Appian or the Flaminian Way were things to jot down reverently in one's

1. J. H. Plumb, *Men and Places* (1963), p. 60.

2. Boswell, *Life of Johnson*, ed. Hill-Powell, II, 458.

memorandum book; where the eruption that buried Herculaneum and killed Pliny seemed closer than the recent one of 1737.[3] Metaphorically, and perhaps more than metaphorically, Augustan travellers considered themselves heirs of ancient Rome.

The problem for a man in Spence's predicament, however, was quite simply what he could do to satisfy his thirst to visit 'the country of the old Romans'. There was one way, or at least one possibility, open for the less fortunate, namely, to accompany the son of a rich nobleman as a tutor. The governor (or 'bear-leader' as he came to be known) had been long taken as an indispensable ingredient of a young aristocrat's travels abroad, and the profession included among its members such distinguished figures as Hobbes, Locke, Coxe, and others.

In the summer of 1730 Spence began to explore this possibility seriously. As a friend of Alexander Pope, England's greatest living poet, and as a critic and scholar of some note, he enjoyed an enviable reputation. Even the habitually sour Thomas Hearne grudgingly admitted that Spence was being much 'cryed up' at Oxford.[4] 'A man of letters, without pedantry, no bigot, nor violently attached to any party, but of a catholic spirit, and not unacquainted with natural philosophy and the mathematics',[5] Spence was obviously a desirable choice as a tutor. However, he lacked previous experience and knowledge of the necessary languages. His Latin and Greek were no doubt beyond reproach, but for going abroad French and Italian would be regarded as more practical qualifications.

Spence inquired among his friends for advice, and for a time at least seems to have considered the possibility of 'qualify[ing] himself for a larger tour' by making a short preliminary trip to France on his own to get the language. Francis Lockier, Dean of Peterborough, who had accompanied members of the Molesworth family on several journeys on the continent, gave him sound advice:

> If a person would travel for three months to get the French language and qualify himself for a larger tour, the whole expense need not be above £50. Orleans would be the best place, or Caen ⌐in Normandy—good for its nearness? —and you might see Paris for a fortnight to say you have been at it. They talk very good French in Orleans ¬.
>
> If you take a friend with you 'twill make you miss a thousand opportunities of following your end. You go to get French, and it would be best if you could avoid making an acquaintance with any one Englishman there. To converse with their learned men will be beside your purpose too, if you go only for so short a time. They talk the worst for conversation, and you should rather be with the ladies, who are the best for it.[6]

Though Spence on his later travels was to ignore much of the Dean's counsel, he seems to have taken to heart the last point (see *Letter 5*).

---

3. *Letter* 156.
4. *Remarks and Collections of Thomas Hearne*, ed. Salter (Oxford, 1915), X, 31.
5. John Duncome, *Letters by Several Eminent*

Persons Deceased (1773), II, 13 n. (quoted by Wright, p. 34).
6. *Obs.* No. 695 (Sept. 1–6, 1730).

An opportunity of going abroad presented itself to Spence a few days after this conversation with Lockier. On September 15 Lionel Cranfield Sackville, first Duke of Dorset and Lord Lieutenant of Ireland, was awarded an honorary D.C.L. at Oxford, while his son, styled Lord Middlesex, received his M.A. and was deemed ready to set out on a Grand Tour. Alexander Pope knew the Sackville family, and we have Joseph Warton's word for it that 'it was upon Pope's recommendation that [Spence] travelled with Lord Middlesex, which was the foundation of his future good fortune.'[7]

By the end of the following month his going abroad was settled, for on October 29 Spence wrote to his friend Pitt:

> I have an offer of attending a nobleman in his tour of France and Italy, and I believe we shall set out in a month's time. Never were the circumstances of any thing more happy than mine in this affair are at present. I had the honour of some intimacy with Lord Middlesex when in Oxford. He is a young gentleman of fine parts, of a very polite turn, and extremely good-natured and humane. I don't go as a tutor or with any charge, only as a companion: so that there's scarce any room for disobliging.[8]

Spence made hasty arrangement with his friend Edward Rolle to substitute for him as 'my deputy at Oxford' (*Letter* 5). This was a relatively easy matter at the time, for the Professorship of Poetry was a sinecure which, like the holding of a prebend, did not require permanent residence. Full of anticipation, he set out on his first tour shortly before Christmas.

LORD Middlesex was nineteen, Spence twelve years his senior, when they embarked on their first journey abroad. Both, for the first months at least, depended on the bond of common language, and this, in spite of differences in social rank and temper, created a spirit of easy camaraderie between them. Yet one can hardly imagine two more disparate characters. Spence, with an air of a scholar about him, remained deferential with a smile; Lord Middlesex displayed every characteristic of a budding Lord of Misrule, and his influence could be infectious. They drank together, and occasionally (as on the much vaunted excursion along the Brenta) became 'as merry as fiddlers'. It was during one bibulous session in May 1733 that his lordship had the following 'Recommendatory Verses for Giuseppi at Bologna' composed at Spence's expense:

> *Il Signor Giuseppe Spence, Poeta celebre tra gli Hoglandici*
> *A tutti i Cavalieri che viaggiano, o per le virtù;*
> *o per bere; o per dormire più profondamente:*

> *Voi Cavalieri, veramente Erranti,*
> *Siate Inglesi, o ben Tedeschi o Turchi,*
> *Ecco'l Giuseppin: mangiator tremendo:*

7. *Works of Pope* (1797), I, xxxvi (quoted by Wright, p. 41).   8. *Obs.* I, xxvii.

3

Scudier del Invincibile Appetito:
Che merita diventar sopra ogni altro,
E per la Gola sua e pel Inteletto
E per la Forza di sputar Sentenze,
Il SANCO PANCA di vostre Eccellenze.

(Qui seguita apposta l'Autorità del Signor Carlo Sacville,
Altro poeta tremendissimo, della Provincia di Lunghe Code:)

E per raccomandarlo più al vostro
Favore, O gentili Cavalieri:
Non solamente ha di Sanco i merti
Ma quelli ha ancor della sua Bestia;
Che soffriva, con santa pazienza,
I duri colpi ed i grandi lavori:
Prendete dunque questo: prendete insieme
Un fido SANCO ed un buon ASINELLO.[9]

Lord Middlesex, as a member of the Sackville family, could boast of at least two poetic ancestors: the Elizabethan Thomas Sackville, author of *Gorboduc*, and 'the witty Earl of Dorset', one of the Restoration rakes 'who wrote with ease'. Louis Marlow quotes an epigram, which amusingly comments on the prolific muse of the family's youngest scion:

So fast from S[ackville]e's mouth the verses fly,
You'd swear he had a Gleet of Poetry.
But Gleets the Back of strength and moisture drain,
And pray, do Verses fortifie the Brain?[10]

Spence, with his talent 'di sputar Sentenze', retaliated at Venice with 'A Heathenish copy of Verses, design'd to be address'd to the E. of Middlesex whenever he pleases to die'. If he buried his lordship alive, it was as a compliment *aere perennius*:

Here lies a Peer, whose look was form'd to move
In men Respect; and in each Woman Love:
An air of Majesty, and a pleasing Grace,
Was mixt in every feature of his face.
Free was his Soul; and warm'd with generous fire:
Bold to engage; and prudent to retire:
A temper'd courage which by years refin'd
Improv'd the first brisk Sparklings of his mind.
His Humour easy; and a natural Wit
Shone forth in all he said and all he writ.
Learn'd without Pride; without affecting bright;
Tho' studious, free; and modest, tho' polite.

9. Spence Papers.   10. *Sackville of Drayton* (1948), p. 268.

> *In all the offices of life severe,*
> *Yet gay; and chiefly to the Muses dear.*[11]

Dabbling in verse and a common friendship with Pope were bonds that linked their very different characters. Spence's admiration for Pope is well known; the young Earl, while at Oxford, composed an encomium in couplets on the 'great Bard', of which the following will serve as a specimen:

> *Attend, great Bard, who canst alike inspire*
> *With Waller's softness, and with Milton's fire,*
> *Whilst I, the meanest of the muses throng,*
> *To thy just praises tune th' adventurous song.*[12] ...

No wonder that Pope later gallantly ranged Lord Middlesex among the 'three poetical noblemen now'.[13]

Entirely in keeping with the nature of Lord Middlesex's 'free soul' and the 'brisk Sparklings of his mind', was his enthusiasm for freemasonry, and his tour had at least one historical consequence—the establishment of the first masonic lodge in Italy. The two travellers arrived in Florence on July 11, 1732; on August 4 Dr. Cocchi wrote in his diary, 'La sera fui ricevuto tra "*Free Masons*".'[14] If, as histories of freemasonry unanimously agree, Lord Middlesex founded the lodge in Florence, he certainly lost no time in doing so.

Actually there is some uncertainty about the origin of the lodge. Most histories give 1733 as the date of its foundation. But, as Cocchi's note shows, the lodge existed in the summer of 1732. Moreover, Cocchi says, 'Capo di essi era Mr. Shirly' (whom Spence had met at Milan in November 1731). 'Mild. Middlesex' and 'Capt. Spens'[15] are mentioned among 'gli altri'. It seems probable that a lodge of a sort existed before, but that in 1733 its status was either raised or made 'official'; that Lord Middlesex became its Master is clear, for he appears on Natter's medal, struck in his honour in 1733, as 'Magister Florentiae'.[16] 'C'était une manifestation de courtoisie', writes René Le Forestier, 'envers un jeune seigneur étranger, qui avait initié les Toscans aux usages pittoresques des clubs maçonniques anglais, que ses compatriotes faisaient connaître aux Parisiens à la même époque.'[17]

What is not clear is who authorized Lord Middlesex to assume this dignity. According to Le Forestier, two gentlemen, whom I have been unable to identify, appear to have been involved in the process. 'Alding, Eques ab Unione, élu Grand Maître [of the chapter of Aberdeen] en 1732 par les trois Provinces [Scotland, Auvergne, and Italy] avait nommé Robert Bedfort, lord écossais, Maître Provincial d'Italie et établi le Grand Chapitre d'Italie à Florence.'[18] Le Forestier's subsequent statement, however, that it was the Pretender who

11. Spence Papers.
12. Marlow, p. 268.
13. *Obs.* No. 506.
14. In his *Effemeridi*, MS diaries preserved at the Library of the Medical Faculty at Carregi, Florence. Volume headed '1732'.
15. Not our Spence, see *Letter* 37 n. 8.

16. Edward Hawkins, *Medallic Illustrations of the History of Great Britain* (1885), II, 504.
17. *La Franc-maçonnerie templière et occultiste aux XVIIIe et XIXe siècles* (Paris, Louvain, 1970), p. 163.
18. Ibid.

conferred 'la Maîtrise Provinciale d'Italie à lord Sackwill' is absurd, and stems no doubt from the Jacobite legend concocted later in the century.[19]

That Spence in his letters should have nothing to say of this event need not surprise us. Harpocrates, who was (wrongly) regarded by the Greeks and the Romans as the god of 'inviolate secrecy', presided over the masonic cult (indeed, he appears on Natter's medal),[20] and Spence, who was a diligent collector of conversational odds and ends, was no gossip. Yet *Letter* 112 shows that he was acquainted with masonic lore, and though there is no proof of his being a freemason, as a close friend of Lord Middlesex he must have assisted at the Saturday meetings, originally held at an inn kept by Monsiù Pasciò in the Via Maggio and later transferred to the house of John Collins.[21]

The Florence lodge soon counted some sixty members and consisted mostly of English grand tourists, though a number of Italian virtuosi, university professors, a senator, even abbés, were members. Among Spence's known Italian friends at Florence, there is only one, Sebastian Bianchi (the curator of the Grand Duke's gallery), of whom there is no record to prove that he was a freemason. The rest with whom Spence conversed, and whose informative scraps he jotted down in his *Observations*, were all members of the craft: the Marquis Niccolini, technically an abbé but a noted liberal and a friend of Montesquieu; Signor Buondelmonte, a wit and translator of Pope; Dr. Cocchi, the learned physician and host of English visitors at Florence; Vaneschi, one of the *improvvisatori*; the notorious Baron von Stosch; and the anti-clerical poet Tommaso Crudeli. To commemorate the pleasant evenings spent among the virtuosi and freemasons, Spence originally planned to call his *magnum opus*, in imitation of Aulus Gellius, *Noctes Florentinae*.

Lord Middlesex in the meanwhile discovered another passion on his tour—that for the Italian opera on which, later in London, he was to squander lavish sums of money. His interest was no doubt further stimulated by Francis Colman, British resident at Florence and a renowned enthusiast of the opera. Colman introduced Middlesex and Spence to the local *improvvisatori*, among them Signor Vaneschi, whom Lord Middlesex later invited to England as a librettist.

On his return to England, after two and a half years of touring, Lord Middlesex was duly elected a Member of Parliament for East Grinstead. Almost immediately ('having drank very plentifully') he became involved in a violent brawl with a mob that accused him of insulting the memory of Charles I. He breezily described

19. Lord Middlesex was, if anything, anti-Jacobite, as is shown by the disgraceful incident of desecrating the memory of Charles I, in which he became involved after his return to England. See n. 22.

20. Hawkins (see n. 16) describes the medal as follows: 'Bust of Sackville, *r.* hair short, in mantle fastened with brooch on the shoulder. *Leg.* CAROLVS . SACKVILLE . MAGISTER . FLO: Below, L. NATTER . F . 1733. *Rev.* Harpocrates, with fingers on his mouth, leans against a truncated column and holds a cornucopia. On one side, on the ground, are emblems of masonry; on the other, the mystic basket and thyrsus. *Leg.* AB . ORIGINE . *Ex.* L: NATTER . F . FLORENT.' A rare specimen of the medal is preserved in the Ashmolean Museum.

21. For information on the early history of the lodge, see F. Sbigoli, *Tommaso Crudeli, e i primi framassoni in Firenze* (Milan, 1884); Janet Ross, *Italian Sketches* (1887), pp. 137–51 (based on Sbigoli); Humphrey Johnson, 'Freemasonry in Italy', *Dublin Review* (spring 1949), pp. 98–108; and J. H. Leper, *The Earl of Middlesex and the English Lodge at Florence* (London, privately printed, 1945).

the incident in a letter to 'Dear Spanco'.[22] He also introduced Spence to the newly founded Society of Dilettanti, 'a club', says Horace Walpole, 'for which the nominal qualification is having been in Italy, and the real one, being drunk: the two chiefs are Lord Middlesex and Sir Francis Dashwood, who were seldom sober the whole time they were in Italy.'[23] Spence, comments his biographer in what sounds like a sly understatement, 'does not appear to have taken an active part in its proceedings.'[24] Instead, he edited, on Pope's suggestion, the tragedy of *Gorboduc* as a tribute to the Sackville family. The edition is prefaced with 'Some Account of the Lord Buckhurst, and his Writings: In a Letter to the Right Honourable the Earl of Middlesex'. One wonders if an edition of the Lord Buckhurst's deliciously bawdy Restoration verses would not have been more appropriate; but the decorous choice is characteristic of Spence, who once remarked, 'I have nothing to do with scandalous history' (*Letter* 149).

Iℕ striking contrast to the rakish Lord Middlesex, John Morley Trevor of Trevallyn, whom Spence accompanied on his second tour, remains a shadowy and one suspects rather dull figure. He was a relation of the Pelhams, with whom Spence became acquainted through Betty Spence, companion of the Duchess of Newcastle. One has the impression that Trevor's sole ambition after graduating from Christ Church, Oxford, was to qualify as an efficient cog in the Pelham political machine.

In May 1737 Trevor and Spence set out for The Hague to pay respects to Robert Hampden-Trevor, young Trevor's cousin, who acted as secretary at the British embassy and was later to become British minister at The Hague. After a short tour of Holland, they headed via Paris (which in July proved too hot to be enjoyed) for Blois, where Trevor applied himself assiduously to the study of French. Spence must have found Trevor's company thoroughly boring, and the lack of human stimulus, which he had found in the company of Lord Middlesex and later of Lord Lincoln, is reflected in his letters. Those written on the second tour exude a sense of tedium and are the least interesting of the lot.

Spence had undertaken the tour 'wholly owing to the respect' he had for his financial advancement (*Letter* 70), and was impatient to be in Italy. He did not get there this time. At Christmas Trevor was hastily recalled to England, having been nominated to succeed the recently deceased 'Turk' Pelham, M.P. for Lewes, in the forthcoming by-election. The tour, which started as fresh as a May morning ('we saw the milkmaids with their garlands and practising their feet to dance'), came to a premature end in January 1738. And though Spence collected an interesting anecdote from a local abbé on Addison's studious *séjour* at Blois,[25] one would have preferred to see him accompany the much more lively young Earl of Sandwich, 'that I had an offer of travelling with' (*Letter* 87) shortly after his return to England. Spence had declined the offer, not so much because he 'was not in a travelling humour', as that Lord Sandwich hankered

22. *Anecdotes*, ed. Singer, pp. 395–7.
23. *H. W. Corresp.* XVIII, 211.
24. Wright, p. 43.
25. *Obs.* No. 815.

after wider horizons—Greece, Turkey, Egypt—that lay outside the established pattern of the Grand Tour,[26] whereas Spence longed to visit the 'Classick Ground' of Italy in order to complete his research for *Polymetis*.

SPENCE's final opportunity for revisiting Italy came a year and a half later when he was asked to accompany Lord Lincoln on the third and perhaps most interesting tour. By then Spence had been twice on the continent and could be trusted as an experienced guide. The year 1740 was a vintage year for such scribbling travellers as Gray, Horace Walpole, whose life Spence saved at Reggio, Lady Pomfret, and Lady Mary Wortley Montagu, all of whom Spence encountered in various places. They often mention Spence in their letters and their comments in turn give an additional interest to his own.

Henry Fiennes Clinton was an orphan. His father, the seventh Earl of Lincoln, who had married a Pelham, died in 1728, when Henry was eight years old. Four of his sisters and two brothers were dead before he was ten, and his mother, who desperately tried to save her frail children by taking them to Provence for their health, died in 1736. At seventeen Lincoln and his younger sister were the only survivors of a family of ten.

After his father's death, Lincoln was adopted by his uncle. The childless Duke of Newcastle, Walpole's Secretary of State, was a brother of Lady Lucy, Lincoln's mother, and he bestowed upon the young boy during his years at Eton and Cambridge a profusion of wise saws and well-meant advice, including stern periodic reminders 'not to forget Dr. Hulse's powders'.[27] Spence's first task on the tour was to watch over the delicate youngster's health.

Armed with '3 pair of Pistols' and 'A Blunderbuss',[28] the two travellers set out for the continent in September 1739. This time, to avoid the frustration of another long stay in France, they headed straight for Italy, where Lincoln was to attend the Royal Academy at Turin for one year.

The academy was newly restored in 1713 as a military finishing school for young gentlemen. 'The nobility were eager to have their sons brought up there.' In its cosmopolitan atmosphere Lincoln 'was taught horse-riding, dance and the polite graces befitting a young nobleman'.[29] He was genuinely grateful to Spence for his easy, civilized attention, very different no doubt from that he had received from his former tutors, Mr. Hume, Mr. Wilcox, and Dr. Goddard (later Master of Clare Hall), who was deeply mortified that Spence and not he was appointed Lincoln's companion.[30]

The Duke of Newcastle believed that 'Linki' was an 'extremely well disposed' young man, but 'sometimes led away by company which he has not always the

26. When in 1740 he met Lord Sandwich, just back from the Middle East, at Turin, he questioned him extensively on his travels, and made his lordship's account the subject of several letters (*Letters* 87, 90, 92–3, 95, 98, 101–2, 104).

27. Their correspondence is preserved among the Newcastle Papers—the early part in the British Museum (Add. MSS 33065) and the more extensive latter part at the Nottingham University Library.

28. *Appendix* 8.

29. Modeste Paroletti, *Turin et ses curiosités* (Turin, 1819), pp. 240–2. For descriptions of the life at the academy, see *Letters* 78, 80.

30. J. Nichols, *Literary Anecdotes*, II, 374.

resolution to resist'. 'I do earnestly desire and must insist with you', he charged Lincoln's tutor at Cambridge, 'that you would send constant accounts of his behaviour.'[31] One of Spence's chief duties on the tour was to send regular reports to Andrew Stone, the Duke's secretary.[32] They must have done him credit, for the Duke writes: 'I am glad to find by all Mr. Spence's letters that your behaviour is so agreeable to him. He knows very well what it should be, and I dare say would not flatter me with saying it was what it was not' (*Letter* 91).

When Lincoln showed at one point an unhealthy interest in gambling, Spence, presuming on the efficient powers of the fictive muse, composed a gruesome 'Moral History' for his benefit, entitled 'Florio', which depicts a good-natured rake's progress from gambling through duelling to murder, and ends in a most melancholy way.[33] One suspects that it was Spence's conversational good sense rather than the story that made the young Earl change his mind.

In November 1739 Henry Pelham's two young sons and heirs died. Henry Pelham, Lincoln's other uncle, was the younger brother of the Duke of Newcastle, and the tragic event changed Lincoln's status overnight from that of an orphan nephew to that of his uncles' nearest male relative, and thus a factor to be counted with in the future of the vast Pelham estates.

If Spence managed to get the young Earl's health, both physical and moral, well under control, there was one unpredictable development that was to give him no end of headaches during the second half of the tour.

Lord Lincoln's affair with Lady Sophia, like one of those varnished bubbles punctured by the intrusion of the real world, has an amusingly Augustan air about it. Its progress can be followed in Lord Lincoln's letters, in those of Lady Pomfret and Lady Mary Wortley Montagu, but the fullest and wittiest account of it is given by Horace Walpole: 'The Duke of Grafton used to say that they put him in mind of a troop of Italian comedians; Lord Lincoln was Valere, Lady Sophia, Columbine, and my Lady [Pomfret], the old mother behind the scenes.'[34]

As Lord Lincoln's governor, Spence found himself in a delicate position. He had to satisfy the Pelhams, in whose view Lady Sophy simply had no fortune to equal her matchless beauty, and at the same time he had to avoid offending the sensibilities of his future patron. The bitter-sweet details of the dénouement, when on their return to England Valere married the fortune of his cousin Miss Pelham ('Lord! how ugly she is!'), while Columbine wedded a ripe widower of fifty-four (Lord Carteret) can be followed in Horace Walpole's correspondence. A contemporary wit made a wry jingle on the nuptials:

> *Her beauty like the scripture feast*
> *To which th' invited never came,*
> *Deprived of its intended guest,*
> *Was given to the old and lame.*[35]

As for Spence, who was of the opinion that 'some conversation with the ladies

---

31. Dec. 25, 1738. Add. MSS 33065 f. 322.
32. Only one of these (*Letter* 121) appears to to be extant.
33. See *Letter* 118 n. 1.
34. *H. W. Corresp.* XVIII, 103.
35. *Letters*, Toynbee edn., I, 115.

is necessary to smooth and sweeten the temper as well as the manners of a man, but too much of it is apt to effeminate and debilitate both',[36] so much is certain: that he must have sighed with profound relief when in November 1741 he landed at Dover. To have left English shores with a sickly youth and returned with a handsome young man in perfect health was commendable; to have delivered a love-sick peer to the Duke, his uncle, unharmed, uncommitted, unengaged, was an achievement.

Ten years later, unmindful of the fact that 'in the course of his last tour his own health had been considerably impaired',[37] Spence reflected with a smile on the affair: 'When I had the pleasure of being abroad with you,' he wrote to Lord Lincoln, 'I aimed at two things in particular, which I have since often reflected on with a great satisfaction. The first was my honest endeavours to prevent a match which you then seemed strongly inclined to, on the apprehension of its being likely to have proved very unfortunate to you; and the other was an endeavour of leading you into an inclination for planting and gardening. . . . The first, I thank God (though with much pain both to your Lordship and myself) I succeded in . . . .'[38] As for the second, Candide's wise commonplace requires no elucidation.

Dean Lockier had told young Spence, ready to embark on his years of travel: 'Let your great endeavour be, to get an independency.'[39] Spence listened to the advice. He probably (though this is by no means certain) earned the governor's usual remuneration of one hundred guineas for each year spent on the travels,[40] and by the end of the second tour expected to be worth a thousand 'pagodas' (*Letter* 70).[41] On his return he reaped some of the customary rewards of patronage. In 1737 the Earl of Middlesex's father offered him the Deanery of Clogher (which Spence, who had no intention of spending his life in Ireland, declined). In April 1742, five months after his return from the last tour, Lord Lincoln signed a contract in which he bound himself to pay Spence one hundred guineas annually until he procured him a preferment 'of the clear yearly value of two hundred and ten pounds or upwards'.[42] Since in May Spence was appointed Regius Professor of History at Oxford, this part of his contract was cancelled, but in 1747 Lord Lincoln furnished Spence with a comfortable house at Byfleet, two miles from his own seat at Oatlands. In 1754 Bishop Trevor, a relation of Spence's companion on the second tour, granted him a prebend at Durham.

The years abroad paid. Among the subscribers to *Polymetis* three names are significantly listed for twelve copies each: the Earl of Middlesex, John Morley Trevor, Esq., and the Earl of Lincoln.

---

36. *Obs.* No. 1187.
37. Rolle's Life of Spence (Spence Papers).
38. Apr. 28, 1751. Spence Papers.
39. *Obs.* No. 739.
40. When the Duke of Somerset asked Addison to be 'a companion in my son's travels', he stipulated that 'neither lodging, travelling, or diet shall cost him sixpence and over and above that, my son shall present him at the year's end with a hundred guineas'

(Smithers, *Life of Joseph Addison* [1954], p. 84). Though Addison considered the payment inadequate, I am inclined to believe that Spence accepted it.
41. This probably includes savings from Spence's Oxford stipend, his prebend, and the first tour.
42. Wright, p. 68.

*I*T would be idle to compare Spence as a letter-writer with Horace Walpole, Gray, or Boswell. He belongs to a group of minor but no less interesting devotees of the epistolary Muse, such as Lady Pomfret, and some of the blame (and praise) for the nature of his account of the Grand Tour must be laid at the door of the person to whom the letters were addressed. Mirabella Spence was at the time of Spence's travels an old lady in her fifties, mother of three sons and a daughter. Her little world at Winchester was bounded by Colebrook Street and her neighbours: Dean Wavell, with his discourses on predestination; the Pescods; Frank Riley, the local hunchback; and others, whose names like those in Gray's country churchyard, are barely rescued from oblivion by an entry in the local parish register.

One can imagine the old lady's flutter of anticipation as, with spectacles on her nose (her eyes were getting weak), she opened each missive from her son 'with that outlandish mark upon it', and proudly read to Mr. Morecroft or Dr. Kelley the character of the new Pope whom Spence had just seen at a consistory at Rome or his account of the wedding of the Prince of Carignan with one of the beautiful Hesse-Rheinfels sisters at Turin. Mrs. Spence was proud of her descent from the Neville family,[43] and obviously enjoyed the visits of her son's noble friends, such as Lord Middlesex, Lord Lincoln, or Horace Walpole.[44] She was delighted no doubt when Spence wrote to her: 'One of the greatest advantages in travelling, for a little man like me, is to make acquaintances with several persons of a higher rank than one could well get at in England, and to converse with them more on a foot, and with greater familiarity than one ever could have done, had one stayed always at home' (*Letter* 149).[45] Yet she would have been even more pleased if Spence's intrusion into the larger world had taken a more material turn. In one letter she urged him to apply for a vacant wardenship or a bishopric. Spence retorted, 'I have suspected you a little of an ambitious turn in your mind.' He was incorrigibly allergic to ecclesiastic advancements, 'or indeed any high dignity in the world' (*Letter* 119).

Naturally, Spence's selection of the topics in his letters depends to a very large extent on the character of the recipient. Mrs. Spence could be trusted to enjoy a lively account of the crossing of the horrid Mount Cenis, of an excursion to the top of Mount Vesuvius, of the 'famous voices' at the Venetian conservatorios, or of Lady Mary at Rome ('pertickeller fine'). Her comments were at times perceptive. When Spence read to her from Spenser, she shrewdly diagnosed the Elizabethan poet's descriptions as 'a collection of pictures'.[46] Her oddly spelled endorsements, written in a small seventeenth-century hand, often amusingly reveal her response: 'verrey pretey', 'merriest, & short', 'as dark as yᵉ joke aingells', and though her own letters are not known to be extant, we have Spence's word for it that they were 'very well wrote' and that Mrs. Spence had 'a particular good manner of writing letters' (*Letter* 84).

43. Ibid., pp. 3–4.

44. When in 1750 Spence introduced her to Horace Walpole, the latter wrote to Mann: 'The good old woman was mighty civil to me, and among other chat, said, she supposed I had a good neighbour in Mr Pope—"Lord! Madam, he has been dead these seven years!"—"Alas! Aye, Sir, I had forgot"' (*H. W. Corresp.* XX, 189).

45. See *App.* I for an extensive list of English travellers Spence met abroad.

46. *Obs.* No. 419.

No reader of the letters can fail to miss Spence's affection for the old lady, which runs through them. Horace Walpole said that Spence 'fondles an old mother in imitation of Pope'.[47] One has the impression that through her the Oxford don remained tied to his Winchester roots. To her he could unburden his soul of his concerns, to her pour out the impressions of the tour. His letters were, as Spence freely admits, a means of continuing conversation, a fireside chit-chat with her while abroad. Sometimes they verge almost embarrassingly on what perhaps can be best described as an old bachelor's sublimated love affair. How else explain his near panic at Rome when he had received no letters from her for six weeks, or his writing to her of Louis XIV's domestic idyll with Mme de Maintenon at the little Trianon when his own mind was full of elaborate plans to settle down with his mother to a comfortable old age in a large flat he hoped to rent in Queen's Street in London? To be sure, some of this prattle has very little to do with the Grand Tour as such. Mrs. Spence described such excursions into the private as 'home affaires' or 'not a reading letter', and Spence, when he later prepared his letters for a fair transcript, marked them 'not to be Copied'.

The majority of the letters, however, were meant to be what the *Spectators* and the *Tatlers* had been to the rising London middle class a generation earlier. Where Addison claimed to have 'brought Philosophy out of Closets and Libraries' to dwell 'at Tea-Tables and in Coffee Houses',[48] Spence's 'sort of *Tatlers*' (*Letter* 128) were intended to make his mother and her neighbours in Colebrook Street share at least some of his experience abroad: they offered vivid first-hand glimpses of that fabulous world of the Grand Tour, which 'their lot forbade' them to discover for themselves.

At this point it is only fair to say that the letters do not fully mirror the impact which the Grand Tour had on Joseph Spence. Interested as she must have been in her son's descriptions of the religious ceremony of making a nun, of spy-infested Venice at carnival time, of the Strong Man of Kent, of Vaucanson's mechanical duck, or of the grand opera at Rome (with the old Pretender sitting in one of the boxes), Mrs. Spence was hardly an ideal listener to discourses on a ravishing relievo representing the twelve labours of Hercules, and was not likely to appreciate Dr. Cocchi's views on Italian literature, Rosalba's on painting, or Bishop Foucquet's on Chinese figurism. She could hardly be expected to share Spence's interest in the *Crusca provenzale*, or the kind of virtuoso chit-chat that went on during the long *noctes florentinae* at Monsiù Pasciò's, or in the more sophisticated opinions of the Abbé Niccolini, Ficoroni, or the Chevalier Ramsay.

For Spence's interest in art and literature, which was one of his chief concerns on his tours, one must go outside the letters and consult the second volume of his *Observations* (in J. M. Osborn's edition) and such works as *Polymetis* and *Crito*, which reveal the Oxford don side of Spence's character. The remaining part of the introduction is meant to suggest something of this essential ingredient of Spence's travel experience, which is unfortunately missing in the letters to his mother.

47. *H. W. Corresp.* XX, 188–9. Horace Walpole himself was not exempt from this fate of 18th-century bachelors, as his tragedy *The Mysterious Mother* and his curious relationship with old Mme Du Deffand amply show.

48. *Spectator*, No. 10.

*P*olymetis, published in 1747, was perhaps the most significant scholarly result of Spence's years of travel. As one might expect from a professor of classical literature, it was not sculpture that drew Spence to Italy, but the love of the Roman poets. Once on the farther side of the Alps, however, he could hardly resist the fascination that the wealthy heirs of seventeenth-century Puritanism experienced amid the sheer Latin profusion of plastic arts, and that turned so many travellers into amateur collectors of gems, medals, cameos, or paintings. Some of them, Sir Andrew Fountaine or Baron von Stosch, for instance, became shrewd professionals capable of outwitting the Italian connoisseurs at their own game, but the great majority of milords remained amateurs, even if on their return some occasionally indulged in composing such virtuoso discourses as Addison's *Dialogues upon the Usefulness of Ancient Medals*.[49]

Spence belonged to the latter group of curious dabblers. He had purchased (no doubt from the persuasive Signor Ficoroni) 'an intaglio found in the mausoleum of Augustus' (*Letter* 42), which he used as a seal for his letters, but— in contrast to the majority of tourists who confined their hobby to the amassing of souvenirs—he discovered a virtuoso interest of his own, which soon developed into a veritable passion. 'I have often thought when in Italy, and at Rome in particular, that they enjoy there the convenience of a sort of contemporary comments on Virgil and Horace, in the nobler remains of the antient statuaries.'[50] In other words, it was his old (one might say 'professional') affection for the classics that awakened his attention to the potential usefulness of the plastic arts in the study of allegorical representation in the old Roman poets. Or, as he later stated it, *Polymetis* was 'the result of two very different scenes of life, in which I have happened to be engaged. The one, was my having been Professor of Poetry, in the University of Oxford, for ten Years; and the other, my being abroad, for above half that space of time. The former obliged me to deal in Poetical Criticism; as the latter, (and particularly the considerable stay that I made, both at Florence, and at Rome), led me naturally into some observation and love for the fine remains of the antient artists.'[51]

Rome's '10,600 pieces of ancient sculpture', vaunted by Signor Ficoroni,[52] may have aroused Spence's curiosity in the spring of 1732, but his project of 'comparing the mutual lights that the statues of the ancients, and their poetical descriptions of them, give to one another' did not mature till a few months later, after he had examined the treasures of the Grand Duke's gallery, which, 'though we stayed nine months in Florence and visited [it] above a hundred several times, was so far from being exhausted that I . . . could very willingly go and see it a hundred times more' (*Letter* 45). By winter 1732/3 he was fully engaged in work. 'My madness that way is gone so far', he writes to young Rolle, 'that were I to have another lease of the Poetry Lecture, I verily believe I could easily fill up the other five year [doing nothing else]. . . . You would then see that

49. 'Mr. Addison', Spence's learned cicerone at Rome suggested, 'did not go any depth in the study of medals. All the knowledge he had of that kind I believe he had from me, and I did not give him above twenty lessons upon that subject' (*Obs.* No. 816).
50. *Polymetis*, p. 3.
51. Ibid., p. iii.
52. For Signor Ficoroni's comments on the Roman antiquities, see *Obs.* Nos. 1365–98.

13

Lysippus often would explain a passage in Virgil with a stroke or two of his chisel better than a dozen commentators with all their lamps together' (*Letter* 42).

For the next fifteen years Spence devoted much patient labour to gathering material for his *magnum opus*. He re-read all the Roman poets from Ennius to Juvenal, took copious notes, and profited by much curious knowledge from the travelling Virgilian scholar Holdsworth.[53] He was befriended by the erudite curator of the Grand Duke's gallery, Sebastian Bianchi, who enlightened him on the mass of antiques collected there,[54] and Baron von Stosch occasionally advised him on medals. After Spence's return to England Dr. Cocchi could be counted on to check up on a relievo and send him a description or a sketched drawing of it.

Prints, especially good and accurate prints (apart from such as could be found in the monumental compilations of Graevius, Gronovius, Montfaucon, and some specialized monographs) were rare. Spence purchased many from Giacomo Frey, a naturalized Bavarian engraver, much esteemed in his time,[55] but as for out of the way originals, which photography makes so easily obtainable today, he had to ask Dr. Cocchi to 'get them drawn . . . by the best hand you have in Florence', or wherever the particular work might be (*Letter* 135).

'The large work I have on my hands', which Spence from time to time mentions in his letters, proceeded 'in a leisurely way'. In 1740 Gray saw part of it in manuscript at Florence, while Horace Walpole teased the Professor of Poetry about his single-minded absorption in 'gods and goddesses': 'Is Mr. Spence enough at liberty among his antiquities to think of me? I deserve it a little, for I have a vast esteem for him. Do you hear, Mr. Spence . . . I design to visit the Virgil you tell me of,[56] but for getting it, I have no hopes.'

THE violent contortions of the Laocoön group (which gives an impression of a *tour de force*, as if the artist, too conscious of his craftsmanship, would hammer the marble out of its grain) had to wait for a later generation to stir deeper response. In the 1730's one praised the group in an urbane phrase for its 'greater Variety of Expression'.[57] Spence was still close enough to the

---

53. Edward Holdsworth specialized in the geographical approach to Roman classics, comparing a passage in Virgil or Horace with the actual site—a branch of contemporary scholarship that the Grand Tour was particularly well suited to foster. During his conversations with Holdsworth, Spence not only 'took notes down on paper', but 'procured and interleaved Virgil . . . that I might not lose his thoughts' (see the Preface to *Remarks and Dissertations on Virgil* [1768] and *Obs.* Nos. 1416–30).

54. Bianchi compiled a detailed catalogue of the collection, now preserved in manuscript in the historical archives of the Uffizi Gallery.

55. A list of Frey's *stampe*, with Spence's notes on how much he paid for each, is preserved in Egerton 2235 f. 124. 'Why have you not done more of Raphael's?' Spence asked him. 'Because many of his are done already, and others are ill-placed. I wanted to have done the Transfiguration, but when I took a view of it with that design, I found I could not see it enough to do it.' Guido Reni's paintings were the best for prints 'from his disposition of the lights and shades' (*Obs.* Nos. 1431–2).

56. Spence apparently urged Horace Walpole to procure a medal representing young Virgil from Baron von Stosch's collection of gems and medals (*H. W. Corresp.* XXX, 10–12).

57. *Crito*, p. 27.

elegant reaction against the excesses of seventeenth-century baroque to be captivated by Laocoön; the antiques that pleased him most were, characteristically, the Venus of Medici ('her shape is the most exact and elegant imaginable; all soft, and full of tenderness')[58] or that 'most graceful Statue in the World', the Apollo Belvedere.

At the Palazzo Lancilotti in Rome Ficoroni remarked: 'You may know that Hercules to be Roman by its being so much over-wrought: the muscles look like lumps of flesh upon it. The Greek artists were more expressive without taking so much pains to express.'[59] By the time Spence reached Florence, he was a *cognoscente* in his own right. 'Is not the pleasure', he asked Sebastian Bianchi, 'in the face of that very pretty Bacchus, who holds up a cantharus in his left hand and regards it so fondly, too violently expressed for the ancient manner?' —'Tis modern', said the curator of the Grand Duke's gallery, 'and was made by Sansovino.'[60]

In *Polymetis* Spence was to conclude that 'the allegorical representations of the antients generally express what they mean directly, and easily; and often by a single circumstance . . . (Prudence . . . is marked out by her rule, pointing to a globe at her feet; Justice by her equal ballance; Fortitude, by a sword, and Temperance, by a bridle).' In contrast to this, the moderns, according to Spence, offer nothing but confusion: 'As propriety and simplicity are the distinguishable character of the antient artists, in their allegorical figures; so multiplicity and impropriety may almost be looked upon as the distinguishing character of the modern.'[61]

I F simplicity was Spence's touchstone for good classical art, in modern art he championed *helle nature*, the cult which was made fashionable by Abbé Batteux. In this Spence followed one of his rules for landscape gardening: on the one hand 'to hide from sight whatever is disagreeable', on the other '*to imitate Nature*': 'Not like the Dutch painters, who often choose to copy Nature in her lowest and most disagreeable works,[62] nor like Michael Angelo Caravaggio who takes to her indifferently as he finds her, nor like Guido Reni who often hides or disguises her with a profusion of grace and beauty, but like Raphael, who follows her always with a careful judgement and a happiness of choice.'[63]

These were Spence's preferences that lie behind the lengthy dry catalogues of paintings he records in his notebooks. Giotto and Francesco Francia are passed over in a word (Botticelli of course remained unnoticed until the following century); the painters that mattered ranged from Leonardo da Vinci to Domenico Guidi ('the last good painter we had'). As for earlier schools, one shuddered at

58. *Polymetis*, p. 66.
59. *Obs.* No. 1386.
60. Ibid., No. 1577.
61. *Polymetis*, p. 292.
62. Yet occasionally Spence would praise such paintings as 'Titian's "Old Woman with Eggs" that Wright calls the best piece of low

life he ever saw' (*Nbk.* 1 33ʳ–38ʳ) or the Flemish 'little figures' in a Carthusian monastery near Dijon as 'indeed extraordinary good for the time they were done in' (*Nbk.* 3 73ᵛ–74ʳ).
63. From a fragment of Spence's essay on gardening, quoted in *Obs.* No. 1069 n.

'the tawdry taste' of gilded ground inherited from Byzantine art, and believed that Leonardo's 'banishing of it ought most probably to be reckoned among the many very high merits of that extraordinary man.' Even Mantegna, 'much the best painter of all in Europe, till Leonardo da Vinci so greatly advanced that art', shows traces of this barbarianism. Otherwise his 'faces are very well, but the manner in general is still stiff and dry.'[64]

In Holland, Rembrandt, Hals, and Vermeer were ignored, while Vandyck's fine portraits of the Stuarts and other cavalier aristocrats virtually monopolized Spence's attention, together with the canvasses of Rubens, whose zest for life struck a sympathetic chord in English souls. In Italy Spence was told: 'All the best Artists in the noblest Age of Painting, about *Leo* the Tenth's Time, used this deeper and richer Kind of coloring; and I fear one might add, that the glaring Lights introduced by *Guido*, went a great Way toward the Declension of that Art; as the enfeebling of the Colors by *Carlo Marat* (or, if you please, by his Followers) hath since almost completed the Fall of it in *Italy*.'[65]

Yes, 'the arts are greatly fallen among us of late,' sighed Signor Ficoroni, as he showed Spence 'what they point out as the four most celebrated pictures' at Rome: 'Volterra's *Descent from the 'Cross*, Domenichino's *St. Jerome*, Andrea Sacchi's *Romualdo*', and of course, 'Raphael's *Transfiguation*'.[66] Although Dr. Cocchi told Spence 'that to my taste Correggio is the best of all our painters' ('His pieces are less pictures than those of Raphael himself'),[67] Spence remained unshaken in his preference, for 'the divine Raphael', one of whose *cartoons* (probably a fake) he bought for £5 17s. at Turin (*Letter* 97).

In the summer of 1741 at Venice Spence met Rosalba Carriera. Venice was already a *città museo*. The Carnival and refined courtezans excepted ('but I would have nothing to do with' them), one went to see its Titians, Correggios, and Veroneses. Rosalba, 'one of the most modest painters of the age', enjoyed great reputation in her time for her genteel pastels. Spence, Horace Walpole, and Lord Lincoln sat for portraits,[68] and Spence had with her one of his usual 'chit-chats'.

'The eyes are everything,' the old lady told him as they discussed the 'incomparable' Magdalen of Titian that he had seen at the Barberigo Palace. ''Tis not only her eyes that cry ... elle pleure jusq'aux bouts des doigts,' she added. Then, looking at Spence from behind her easel: 'I have been so long used to study features, and the expressions of the mind by them, that I know people's tempers by their faces.' To convince Spence (for her own portraits are not very expressive), 'she added as a proof of this, the characters of two of my friends [Lincoln and Walpole] whom she had seen but twice or thrice ... as justly ... [as] I could have done myself.'

'For God's sake,' asked Spence, more curious than alarmed, 'what is *my* temper?'

'Ni allegro, ni malinconico, ma un buonissimo misto.'[69]

64. Ibid., No. 1467.
65. *Crito*, p. 11.
66. *Obs*. No. 1368. 'The four most celebrated works of the modern sculptors' were 'Michelangelo's *Moses*, Algardi's *Story of Attila*, Fiamingo's *Susanna*, and Bernini's *Bibbiana*' (ibid., No. 1372).
67. Ibid., No. 1496.
68. See the portrait in *Obs*., facing p. 604.
69. Ibid., Nos. 1609–14.

The best expression of Spence's 'genteel' aesthetics will be found in his little 'Dialogue on Beauty' called *Crito*, which, though written in 1752, not only takes 'a good deal of the illustrations in it . . . from Italy',[70] but probably owes its germinal idea to a conversation he had in February 1741 at Rome with Lady Mary Wortley Montagu. Lady Mary remarked that 'Lord Bacon makes beauty to consist in grace and motion.' Spence replied that 'Mr. Locke makes it consist in colour and figure.' So, he reflected, 'Perhaps the two definitions joined together would make one much better than either of them is apart.'[71]

Spence's formulation of the concept of 'grace in motion', though not entirely original, gives him an honourable place in the history of eighteenth-century aesthetics.[72] But what makes *Crito* appeal more than its theoretical content is an occasional freshness of perception such as, in a passing remark on Rubens, 'His very Graces are fat', or again that 'the Mouth is the chief Seat of Grace' (the 'something not quite enough to be called a Smile, but an approach toward one'). We need not subscribe to the aesthetics of *belle nature* which made rather too much of 'a set of Features full of the greatest Sweetness', yet whenever we come up against a sculptured visage that, before all else, strikes us as transfigured by grace, we may be sure that the 'something not quite enough to be called a Smile' is there.

F EW persons travel 'for literature', but each of us carries in him a bit of his métier. If the traveller happens to be a Professor of Poetry, he can hardly avoid it. 'I should be delighted', wrote Spence to Dr. Cocchi à propos *Crito*, 'to see it in your most beautiful language, and if you did not think it unworthy of you, and so much trouble, I dare say you might translate it in a few mornings.'[73] In 1732 at Florence Cocchi and Spence had discussed 'postulata' for translating (*Letter* 36), so the 1752 letter appealed to an established interest. Spence himself was sufficiently intrigued by Cocchi's letter on ethics to turn it into English,[74] while Dr. Cocchi (who early in his life had made an elegant translation of Xenophon's *Ephesiaca*) may have obliged Spence by translating into his 'most beautiful language' a little treatise 'sul Rinascimento della Letteratura'.[75] In Spence's time literature, like occasional verse, could be an exchange of *savoir faire*.

The treatise also exists in French ('after the scole of Stratford atte Bowe') and was evidently written at Dijon or Lyons as an exercise in 'getting the language'. The fact that there are two other such essays among the Spence Papers, one 'sur

70. Spence's undated letter to Dr. Cocchi, written in 1752, in the collection of Count Enrico Baldasseroni at Florence.

71. *Obs.* No. 761.

72. It is not unlikely that Lessing, who was so fruitfully rude to *Polymetis*, derived his idea of *Reitz in Bewegung* from Spence. See Wright, pp. 128–30.

73. An undated letter written from 'Mr. Dodsley's' in 1752 (see n. 70).

74. Spence Papers.

75. Ibid. Though there is no evidence to prove that the translation is by Dr. Cocchi, the Italian is too good to be Spence's own, and Cocchi (who had the reputation of a fine stylist) was the most intimate of his Italian friends.

les Poëtes Anglois',[76] and another entitled 'Quelques Remarques sur la Renaissance de la Pöesie', suggests that before Spence discovered the antique in Italy, he probably set out on his first tour with the intention of investigating the influence of 'the Provençal [i.e., French mediaeval] poets' on the Renaissance[77] and of collecting material for a projected poetical dictionary.[78]

While continuing his French exercises at Lyons,[79] Spence thought a good way of preparing for his travels in Italy might be to read Italian plays. But 'that kind of reading', the Chevalier Ramsay advised him, was not 'the properest for learning the beauties of their amiable language'.[80] Spence certainly read Machiavelli's and Villani's histories of Florence. One would like to think that, with his professional interest in 'Poetical Criticism', he had a look at Crescimbeni's *Istoria della Volgar Poesia* in the edition printed at Venice in 1730, which 'in a great measure remedied' the critic's early 'huddled method', and that he perhaps read an essay or two by Muratori, 'one of the most learned men at present in Italy'.[81] In any case, with his unostentatious good sense, his modest display of learning, and his gift of turning out on occasion neat little Latin verses, Spence managed to impress his friends on the continent. Preserved among the Spence Papers is a wild Latin panegyric *in ejusdem laude*, which may have tickled the little vanity Spence had, when he reflected how these Italians give 'every word . . . more . . . noise than any of our people on the stage' (*Letter* 27). It begins:

> SPENCE, *decus Pindi, nulliq: Poeta secundus*
> *Quem velit esse suum Grecia, Roma suum;*
> . . .
> *Musa latina tua est nitidissima, cumq: latinis*
> *Egregie Argolicos scis sociare modos*
> . . .
> *Virtutem quamvis habeas, moresq: Catonis,*
> *Non tamen ora rudis torva Catonis habes.*

76. See J. M. Osborn, 'The First History of English Poetry', in *Pope and His Contemporaries: Essays Presented to George Sherburn* (1949), pp. 23–50.

77. In 1728 Bolingbroke told him that his wife, the Marquise de Vilette, 'can help you to several particulars (about the Provençal and French poets)'. Later, at Florence, Baron von Stosch informed Spence that 'Signor Recanati, a nobleman of Venice, has the best collection of the Provençal poets' which he acquired in 1708 'when the Duke of Mantua's library was sold', and recommended 'a book of immense erudition . . . called *La Crusca Provenzale e Catalana*' as well as Polycarpus Leyser, Professor of Poetry at the Helmstadt Academy, whose *Historia Poetarum & Poematum Medii aevi* Spence marked as 'A book that may be very useful' for his project (*Obs.* Nos. 886, 1548–50, and Spence Papers).

78. The fragmentary notes for the English portion of the work have recently come to light and were purchased by Harvard University. For an account of them by James M. Osborn, see the *Harvard Library Bulletin* (spring 1968).

79. Among several *thèmes* in the Spence Papers, heavily corrected by his Jesuit French master, there is one on Molière's *Le Malade imaginaire*: 'Vous voulez que je vous dise, ce que je pense du Malade de Molière. . . .' For his beauties Spence allows Molière to be 'redevable à son naturel, peut-être le mieux porté à la Comédie qu'on ait vû', after which, in his usual manner of 'finding like a friend, something to blame, and something to commend' (he had earlier practised it in discussing Pope's Homer), Spence blames Molière for sometimes turning into a mere *farceur*: 'Pour les Fautes, elles sont ordinairement faites exprès pour plaire à la foule.'

80. *Obs.* No. 1292, taken from Ramsay's letter to Spence.

81. Ibid., No. 1528.

Nil dant Te melius, nil doctius astra Britannis;
Perpaucos Tibi habet Terra Britanna pares. . . .

When it comes to addressing Spence as 'Arge oculate' and to such lines in compliment to his critical powers as 'Terres Scriptores, Censor acute, malos', the author himself, one feels, ought to have feigned a little polite trembling.

Italy in the 1730's was dominated by the academies: Della Crusca was bringing out the fourth edition of its dictionary ('The gentlemen', said Crudeli, 'study words more than things, and therefore the definitions . . . are often extremely absurd'),[82] and the chief effort of the dozens of Arcadian academies, under such men as Crescimbeni, Gravina, and later Salvini and Muratori, was to stem the tide of the seventeenth-century baroque by urging a return to classic simplicity. Erudition flourished to the point that even exceptionally learned women were 'admitted to . . . degrees as well as the men',[83] but the Italian Parnassus resembled, to use a simile which Spence applied in another context, 'un fils qui tettant trop vigoureusement sa mère la desèche jusqu'à la consomption'.[84] Among the creative writers in Italy there was no one of the stature of a Swift or a Pope, and though Cocchi called the erudite Signor Manfredi at Bologna 'the best poet we have now in Italy', he hastily added, 'If you look for a *right good* poet among us, 'tis a thing that you must look for in vain.'[85]

In such a predicament it was natural that cultivated Italians should look, with a certain nostalgia, toward the great artists of the past—Dante, Petrarch, Ariosto, Tasso, Machiavelli—as well as to the writers of the 'last age'. Spence duly recorded this state in his collection of anecdotes, especially those he gathered from his friend Dr. Cocchi at Florence,[86] and his conversations are valuable as evidence of a continuity of English interest in Italian letters at a period when Italian literary (in contrast to musical) influence in England reached its lowest ebb.[87]

But it is, of course, first-hand experience that counts most, and here the grand tourist was perhaps in a better position than the scholar to give us a vivid glance at the contemporary scene: 'When we were at Venice, there was a common gondolier that could repeat all Tasso's *Gerusalemme Liberata* [to the accompaniment of music]. Dip where you pleased, and show him the top of the page, and he'd sing three or four stanzas on immediately.'[88] The gondolier sang them to a tune called *il passa gallo* ('sounds something like church music') which was also used by the *improvvisatori* whose art of extempore versifying was as much in style in the 1730's as certain manifestations of pop art in more recent days. Spence at least thought that 'the impromptu way had prevailed all over Italy, and was regarded as the highest excellence of poetry at present.'[89]

This popular mixed genre relied chiefly on the resources of quick inventiveness and a certain 'be-in' immediacy of its effect (the verse itself is usually

82. *Obs.* No. 1540.
83. Ibid., No. 1505.
84. 'Quelques Remarques sur la Renaissance de la Poësie' (Spence Papers).
85. *Obs.* Nos. 1518, 1488.

86. Ibid., Nos. 1469–92.
87. R. Marshall, *Italy in English Literature 1755–1815* (1934), pp. 8–16.
88. *Obs.* No. 1536.
89. Ibid., No. 1518.

negligible). It was performed 'with great emulation and warmth', and 'generally in octaves, in which the answerer is obliged to form his octave to the concluding rhyme of the challenger, so that all the octaves after the first must be extempore, unless they act in concert together'.[90] Spence met two of the Tuscan school at Florence, the pious Cavalier Perfetti of Siena, who considered himself blessed with divine afflatus and in 1728 was 'crowned in the Capitol . . . by order of the Pope',[91] and the very much less pious Signor Vaneschi, 'an Abbé of Florence, and very ready in that sort of poetry', who gave Spence the following account of the art:

> Our method is to create our thought at the enemy's seventh verse. Then we have the idea, the rhymes, the words, and the verse to think of only whilst our opponent is repeating his last line, which we take no manner of notice of at all. We almost always do better the second half hour than first, because one grows warmer and warmer, to such a degree at last that when I have improviso-ed a whole evening, I can never get a wink of sleep all the night after.[92]

Spence who 'thought it impossible for them to go on so readily as they did', and suspecting there might be some trick of their acting 'in concert', 'having agreed things together beforehand', decided to try one of them out.

> It was at Florence at our resident's, Mr. Colman's, and when that gentleman asked me what I thought of it, I told him that I could not conceive how they could go on so readily, and so evenly, without some collusion between them. He said that it amazed everybody at first, that he had no doubt of its being all fair, and desired me, to be satisfied of it, to give them some subject myself, as much out of the way as I could think of. As he insisted upon my doing so, I offered a subject which must be new to them and on which they could not well be prepared. It was but a day or two before that a band of musicians and actors set out from Florence to introduce operas for the first time in the Empress of Russia's court. This advance of music and that sort of dramatic poetry (which the Italians at present look upon as the most capital parts of what they call *virtù*) so much farther north than ever they had been, under the auspices of the then Great Duke, was the subject I offered for them.
>
> They shook their heads a little and said it was a very difficult one. However, in two or three minutes' time one of them began with his octave upon it, another answered him immediately, and they went on for five or six stanzas alternately, without any pause, except that very short one which is always allowed them by the going off of the tune on the guitar at the end of each stanza. They always improviso to music.[93] . . .

Their lively peripheral art ('admired so much by the little and great vulgar', growled Dr. Cocchi) was no doubt greatly encouraged by the vast numbers of

---

90. Ibid., No. 1520. See also ibid., pp. 680–1, for 'Examples of Improvised Verses' among the Spence Papers.

91. Ibid., No. 1522.
92. Ibid., No. 1520.
93. Ibid., No. 1519.

mesmerized grand tourists,[94] while the purses of English milords (as potential patrons) were courted with exceptional zeal, if we are to judge by a sonnet addressed to Spence by one of the *confraternità*, evidently short of cash: 'In umilissima richiesta dell'autorevole Protezione del celebre, ed erud^mo Sig^e SPENCE, Degnissimo Professor di Poesia nell' Alma Università d'Oxford.' In it the needy bard pathetically pictures himself fallen on evil days,

> *E, per alzarmi, in van più sforzi io faccio*
> *Ch'al furor di fortuna, a cui soggiaccio*
> ...
> *Inclito SPENCE, ah! porgi a me la pia*
> *Tua destra, e di la m'ergi, ov'ora io giaccio;*
> *No isdegnar che'l tuo possente Braccio*
> *Sia mi sostegno, e difensor mi sia.*
> *Noto farotti all'uno, e all'alovo Polo*
> *Se cogli Auspizij tuoi me rizzo in piede,*
> *Ed il fianco abbatuto alzo dal suolo.*
> *Cederatti'l Destin ch'aspro me siede,*
> *Se stendi in mio soccorso un dito solo;*
> *Che'l tuo Favor l'ire del Fato eccede.*[95]

Serious people were concerned about this situation. 'Our not having any settled stage for tragedies in Italy', sighed Dr. Cocchi, 'is a great blow to our dramatic poetry. The actors indeed that stroll about from city to city do now and then act a tragedy, but even when that happens, and the king of the play is seated in his throne, 'tis ten to one but in a few minutes you shall see a harlequin come in upon the stage and place himself just by him.'[96] Spence saw at least two such 'strolling tragedies', and the results were hilarious. One was a performance of *Don Juan* at Leghorn (*Letter* 35) in which the harlequin and flame-coloured devils usurped the centre of the stage in the last act. The other was a late survival of a *sacra rappresentazione*, or morality play, about *The Damned Soul* at Turin, which he describes at great length in *Letter* 81.

At Verona Spence met the Marquis Maffei; and though the gallant marquis was celebrated as author of a neo-classical tragedy called *Merope* (an Italian equivalent of Addison's *Cato*) there was an air of a *settecento* comedy of manners about the encounter. The aristocratic virtuoso and littérateur was giving the last touches to the graceful porticos of his newly constructed Teatro Filarmonico, which was to open a few weeks later with a performance of his early piece *Fida Ninfa*. The play, for which Vivaldi composed the music, apparently was then in rehearsal, for the marquis whispered in great secret to Spence: 'When I was young I published a piece called *Ninfa Fidele*. Was I to write anything of that nature now, it would be *Ninfa Infida*. That title should have been the more just —at least I am sure I have found them so!'[97]

In 1741, shortly before his final return to England, Spence visited Le Sage.

---

94. Lady Pomfret and the Président De Brosses give detailed accounts of other performances.

95. Spence Papers.

96. *Obs.* No. 1494. Contemporary English tragedies were not much better, though for different reasons.

97. Ibid., No. 1361.

The aging veteran of the picaresque novel lived 'in the suburbs of St. Jaques' at Paris, supported by his son, and gruffly reconciled to an old man's lot. 'Je suis mort', he moaned (with an air of 'complacency in his looks'), 'il n'y a [pas si] long temps que je vivais, mais tout est fini!' 'I thank God,' he added, 'I don't wish for any one thing that I could not pray aloud for.'[98] He was 'extremely deaf', but as he loved to crack jokes, he managed to keep himself 'gay in company by the help of a *cornette*'.[99] This bothersome contraption, as there is some good in every ill, proved useful in keeping off bores: when one threatened him, he simply removed it.

Le Sage spoke with a touch of sarcasm of *Gil Blas* and *Le Diable boiteux* as 'mes deux enfants perdus', and while he showed Spence his house and garden (''twas in this room that I wrote most of *Gil Blas*') grumbled: 'They have made my Hidalgo a Lord in the English translation and a Burgomaster in the Dutch.' He feigned grave surprise that men across the Channel should be disposed to grumble too: 'Surely, the people of England are the most unhappy people on the face of the earth—with liberty and property and three meals a day.' Spence's visit added to the few biographical details we have of Le Sage, a pleasant *vignette* of his house ('an extreme pretty place to write in') and of the little garden in front, with its elegantly 'raised square parterre, planted with a variety of the prettiest flowers' and two berceaux 'covered with vines and honeysuckle'.[100]

Spence, who brought Pope as a souvenir from his travels for his grotto at Twickenham 'Several fine Pieces of the Eruption of Mount *Vesuvius* and a fine Piece of Marble from the Grotto of *Egeria* near *Rome*',[101] must have been flattered both as a member of the republic of letters and as an Englishman to find out at first hand 'what a regard they have even so far from home as Italy for our English writers, and that Mr. Pope is talked of there almost with more applause than here among us' (*Letter* 26). He mentioned 'several people of fashion in a good many of the towns he hath passed through, who are now actually learning our language to be able to read his [Pope's] and some other writings of our nation'. But few statements would have pleased Spence more than that of the Chevalier Ramsay, the colourful biographer of Fénelon, whom Spence had met and interviewed in England in 1729,[102] and whom he went to see each time he visited Paris. They talked of modern poets. Boileau and Pope were, of course, considered the best, 'but', said Ramsay, 'I should prefer Pope to Boileau because he excels in what is most material in the character of a poet. Boileau writes more correctly and better than Pope, but Pope thinks more nobly and has much more of the true spirit of poetry than Boileau.' 'This', added Spence (who had no doubt about the judgement but who thought that his being an Englishman and his friendship with Pope might colour his own views), 'had the more weight with one because Dr. Cocchi and some other good judges that I met with, both in France and Italy, agreed exactly in the same sentiments throughout, though they might express themselves in other words.'[103] It was the kind of information that a critic, on his return, could claim to have travelled for.

98. Ibid., Nos. 1351–2.
99. Ibid., No. 1348.
100. Ibid., No. 1354.

101. J. Serle, *A Plan of Mr. Pope's Garden, As it was left at his Death* (1745), p. 7.
102. *Obs.*, Nos. 1206–1301.
103. Ibid., Nos. 528, 1294.

notes on the text

SPENCE evidently had some thoughts of publishing the travel letters: 'When they are in print,' he wrote to Mrs. Spence on December 17, 1740, 'they will be well worth your reading.' After his return he did some preliminary work, the details of which reveal something about the practice in Pope's day of editing one's correspondence.

In re-reading the letters that had been previously endorsed by Mrs. Spence (date and brief account of the contents), he numbered some of them and added his own endorsements. He changed 'Dear Mother' to 'Dear Madam' or 'To Mrs. —— —' and cut out the closing formula and signature. He also crossed out large sections relating to Winchester 'home affairs', and for the same reason marked 35 (out of the 154) letters 'not to be transcribed'.[1] In correcting the style he altered a number of words or colloquial expressions. The changes were, for the most part, stylistic improvements,[2] although in some cases the original reading is much racier.[3] In only two or three instances do the revisions involve a significant change of meaning. In general, as the change of 'Dear Mother' to 'Dear Madam' indicates, Spence's aim was to give his selections a more urbane Augustan air.

Sometime in the 1750's Spence had this edited material transcribed by Edward Hercules, who was preparing the Newcastle transcript of the *Observations*.[4] This fair copy entitled 'Travelling Letters', a handsome quarto of 479 pages, bound in brown leather, is now among the Spence Papers. Whatever Spence's later intention about publishing this volume might have been, these 'Travelling Letters' (with the exception of the six specimens published by Singer in his edition of the *Anecdotes*) never reached print.

---

1. He also marked for omission *Letter* 163 (on Horace Walpole's dangerous illness at Reggio) presumably because the subject was too personal to be published in Horace Walpole's lifetime; and he evidently used another letter as a rough draft for 'FLORIO: a Moral History', which he later printed in *The Museum* (see *Letters* 114 n. 1 and 118 n. 1).

2. For example, he changed 'set them all crying' into 'made them all cry', 'these seats' into 'this ring of seats', 'officious' into 'tender and officious', etc.

3. Thus 'we were merry as fiddlers' is hardly improved when changed into 'we were very cheerful', 'naughty jade' into 'naughty woman', 'bastards' into 'foundlings', or 'more talkative than seventeen parrots' into 'talkative'. Similarly, reference to an Italian guide who 'often called on Signor Diavolo while we were drinking some very good Lachrimae Christi that grows on the mountain' is deleted.

4. See *Obs.* pp. lxvii–lxviii.

A modern editor might, of course, be tempted to offer his own selection, which would appreciably differ from Spence's, for he would probably include a number of letters and passages that Spence had cut out and omit others. I have decided to sin on the side of inclusiveness, and have adopted as the two guiding principles completeness and modernization of text.

The present edition is based on material gathered from several sources. The most important of these is the collection of Spence's *original letters* preserved in the British Museum, Egerton 2234 ff. 1–299, which contains 151 letters (142 by Spence to his mother). One of these has been omitted,[5] because it is not by Spence himself and merely repeats information about the Low Countries given in Spence's earlier account. On the other hand, Spence's four letters to Henry Rolle (*Letters* 45–8) included at the end of this manuscript volume (ff. 292–9), though written from Oxford after his return to England, have been incorporated into the Florence section, because they give an interesting account of a tour of the Grand Duke's gallery. In three or four letters written from Venice, chronological sequence has been sacrificed to preserve the geographical continuity of the tour.[6] The letters that were transcribed by Edward Hercules, and so possibly intended by Spence for publication, are marked with an asterisk (the parts deleted by Spence being enclosed in angle brackets). The thirty-one of his own letters Spence desired 'to be omitted' or 'not to be copied', and that consequently do not appear in the fair transcript, as well as the additional material, are not marked with an asterisk.

In addition to these 154 letters, the present edition includes supplemental material that falls into four groups: Spence's travel notes, additional letters by or to Spence, un-Spencean letters relating to Lord Lincoln on the last tour, and miscellaneous items gathered in the Appendices.

1. Spence's travel notes or notebook (Egerton 2235), which nearly equals in bulk the companion volume of the original letters in the British Museum—191 large folio pages—may be divided into two parts.

The first part (ff. 1ʳ–83ᵛ) consists of large folio leaves, vertically divided: the text appears on the left-hand side, the right-hand side being used for additions, annotations, and corrections.[7] This part contains Spence's antiquarian notes on the cities and places visited, lists of curiosities or collections of pictures and statues, itinerary, brief sketches of the governments of Geneva, Turin, Naples, Venice, Lucca, etc. They served Spence occasionally as memoranda for some of his letters and anecdotes, and may be profitably compared with Gray's travel notes.[8]

The notes taken on the first tour are subdivided into two sections: ff. 1ʳ–22ᵛ contain the original rough notes hastily jotted down on the tour in a highly abbreviated form; the right-hand side is thickly filled with additional comments, often difficult to decipher. Later Spence had this section transcribed by E. Hercules (ff. 23ʳ–60ʳ), incorporating the various additional jottings, expanding the

5. Richard Spence to Mrs. Spence, London, August 6, 1737 O.S. (ff. 102–3).
6. See *Letters* 21–4 and notes; also *Letters* 32 and 45–8.
7. See *Obs.* pp. lxix–lxx.
8. D. C. Tovey, *Gray and his Friends* (1890), pp. 201–60.

24

abbreviations, and turning the whole into a readable account of the first tour, reminiscent of a fashionable travel guide. Perhaps he originally intended to publish it. He never got around to transcribing the rough notes taken on the second and third tours. It is this fair transcript that is designated here as *Notebook* 1; a few of the original rough notes from ff. 1ʳ–22ᵛ that Hercules failed to transcribe into the fair copy have been incorporated in angle brackets.

Folios 61ʳ–72ʳ consist of notes taken on the second tour, and are referred to as *Notebook* 2; ff. 73ʳ–83ᵛ are notes taken on the third tour, and are referred to as *Notebook* 3. Spence's internal pagination of ff. 61ʳ–75ᵛ is in roman numerals, i–xxvi; of ff. 76ʳ–83ᵛ, in arabic numbers, 27–42.

I have used Spence's notebooks extensively to supplement the letters by including brief excerpts in footnotes as Spence's own comments on certain passages in the letters, and by interpolating larger extracts at appropriate pages between the letters. Unlike the letters, however, these larger extracts have not been annotated.[9]

The remaining part of Egerton 2235 (ff. 94ʳ–191ʳ) contains various items and documents relating to the Grand Tour. The more interesting among these have been included in the Appendices.

2. Additional letters by or to Spence, not in Egerton 2234. These are twelve in number. Only six of them have been previously published: *Letter* 32 appeared in 1813 in *The Gentleman's Magazine* and was reprinted by Singer in 1820, together with five other letters, in his edition of the *Anecdotes*, but the text printed here is based on the originals preserved in the extra-illustrated copy of the *Anecdotes* in the Huntington Library (RB 131213).[10] Four of Spence's letters to Dr. Cocchi (*Letters* 36, 135, 139, 146) come from Count Baldasseroni's private collection; *Letter* 121 to Stone from the Newcastle MSS in the British Museum (Add. MSS 33065); and *Letter* 107 from Joseph Warton's transcript of Spence's correspondence with Christopher Pitt in the Trinity College Library.

3. Lincoln letters. These are seventeen letters relating to Lord Lincoln, Spence's pupil and companion on the last tour. They have been included in this edition because they often mention Spence by name and throw additional light on this tour. Fifteen of these were exchanged between Lord Lincoln and his uncle, the Duke of Newcastle; *Letter* 154 was written by Henry Pelham to Lincoln.[11] An unpublished letter by Lady Sophia Fermor (*Letter* 164) in the Finch MSS (deposited at the Leicestershire Record Office) alludes to 'The Affair', which had given Spence such headaches on the last tour. These non-Spencean letters, unlike Spence's own, have sometimes been slightly abridged.

4. The Appendices are mostly taken from the second part of Egerton 2235,[12] with additional items from the Spence Papers, and from the extra-illustrated copy of the *Anecdotes* at Huntington Library.

9. As the notebooks are themselves often 'notes', that is, lists of paintings and curiosities, or factual records of events, annotations would have been pedantic.

10. *Letters* 15, 81, 117, 118, 148. Three of these at least (81, 117, 118) must have been originally part of Egerton 2234, for they were transcribed by E. Hercules in the fair copy of Spence's selection of his 'Travelling Letters'.

11. The originals are among the Newcastle MSS in the British Museum and in the Nottingham University Library.

12. *Appendix* 16 gives a list of those items in Egerton 2235 not included in this edition.

*T*HE text of the letters and notebooks has been normalized in conformity with the practice adopted by J. M. Osborn in his edition of the *Observations*[13] and that of the Yale edition of *Horace Walpole's Correspondence*. Ampersands and contractions have been expanded, punctuation lightened, capitalization and spelling normalized—except in a few cases of proper names and names of places, where it seemed advisable to retain characteristic eighteenth-century usage ('Guerchin' or 'Guercin' for 'Guercino', 'Laneburg' for Lanslebourg') or where the correct spelling is given in the explanatory footnote (e.g., 'Wavil' for 'Wavell'). Also Spence's use of 'beside' and 'mile' for 'besides' and 'miles', 'this side the Alps', etc., has been retained. Both letters and excerpts from the notebooks have been silently divided into paragraphs.

Dates, which often occur at the end of the original letter, have been placed uniformly at the head, and are given in the continental New Style, eleven days ahead of the English Old Style, except in the few letters written from England, which are specifically designated O.S. Because the arrangement is chronological, Newcastle's letter of April 27, 1741 O.S., follows Lincoln's letters from Rome dated April 29 and May 6 N.S. In the notes, dates referring to events in England are marked O.S., other dates are assumed to be New Style.

Passages crossed out by Spence have been placed in angle brackets.[14] Spence's later emendations have been silently accepted; in the few cases where the original reading was given preference to Spence's later correction, the word or phrase appears in half brackets. Square brackets in the text indicate editorial insertions, mutilated margins of letters, passages left blank by Spence, or passages difficult to decipher.

Headnotes include address, postmark, and two endorsements. The first (*a*) was originally made by Mrs. Spence on receiving each letter; the second (*b*) was later added by Spence when revising the letters. The spelling of the endorsements has not been normalized in order to preserve the quaintness of Mrs. Spence's orthography. Dates, however (except in the very rare case where Mrs. Spence put down the date of reception), have been omitted from the headnotes, for both endorsements simply repeat the date given in the letter.

All the quotations from the *Notebooks* are taken from Egerton 2235.

13. See *Obs.* pp. xxxix–xl.

14. The reader who wishes to know what Spence's own selection in his 'Travelling Letters' was may read the asterisked letters alone, omitting passages in angle brackets. At least he should not hold Spence responsible for the sort of Winchester chit-chat he desired to withhold from the public.

The
first tour

Source:	Egerton 2234 ff. 1–2
Addressed:	To/Mr Spence/at Mrs Gregories/near Chancery Lane
Numbered:	(1st Tour) N°. 1 A
Endorsed:	*b.* safe arriv'd/[arrival to France]/40 Let^rs. o (Not transcribd)

[Calais,]
Thursday, December 24, 1730 [O.S.]

⟨Dear Mother,⟩

—I believe that last night you received a letter to let you know that we should not leave England in six or seven days. This comes to tell you that I was then at Dover, where we had waited a day or two for a good wind, and am now at Calais, where we came this morning with a very pleasant passage in three hours. We have been since ⟨beside a hearty dinner⟩ all over the fortifications of this place, at a Roman Catholic church service, in two religious houses and one nunnery. Tomorrow we get into the chaise for Dunkirk. I was very sea-sick for about half an hour, which was so far from doing me any harm that it made me eat an unreasonable ⟨good⟩ dinner. The captain of the vessel now stays for our packet. My next shall be longer. ⟨I am ever

Your dutiful and affectionate

Jo· Spence⟩

MIRABELLA SPENCE (1670?–1755?), dau. of 'Thomas Collyer, Brewer, of Shoe-Lane, London' and Maria Lunsford; Maria's mother, Katherine Neville, was dau. of Sir Henry Neville of Billingbear, Berks., Queen Elizabeth's ambassador to France (Wright, pp. 3–4, *Obs.* Nos. 1203–5). Two of Mrs. Spence's sons, John (b. 1700) and Richard, were employed in London. She lived with her daughter at Mr. Morecroft's in Colebrook Street, Winchester.

Notebook 1

Egerton 2235 ff. (1–4) 24^r–25^v

We went from London to Dover through Rochester and Canterbury. Rochester bridge is 245 of my ⟨common⟩ paces, about two feet each. The Medway makes a fine show on each side of it. The Cathedral at Canterbury 512 f. long ⟨*Bishop of Ossory*⟩; the *sanctum sanctorum* has something pretty in it.

The Castle at Dover has thirty acres of pasture within the walls. The great piece of cannon there 24 f. 2 inches long. It was cast at Utrecht in 1544, carries 7¼ miles. (Mr. Henshaw's vast vault there 184 yards (?) long.)

The fortifications at Calais are very extensive, and much assisted by the sea: the piers run out almost a mile (?) into the sea. Those of Gravelines neat and of stone. Nieuport, Ostend [Jan. 6], ramparts of earth, etc. For two leagues before and four after Ostend the chaise ran all upon the sand (with one wheel often in the sea) to Blankenburg, a town of fishermen, to which we drove through a street of boats. We saw some people that day fishing with a three-wheeled car and two horses, and men a horseback above hundred yards before them off at sea, the descent of the shore was so gentle, and most of the rest of the way was by the new canal from Dunkirk to Ghent [Jan. 7]. The road from Ghent to Namur is all paved, and from Ghent to Brussels every turn in it looked like the large avenues to our noblemen's houses: all the way a row of trees on each side. (The three kings at Bruges, with their star-paper lanthorn.)

The large towns grew still better and better from Calais on to Bruxelles [Jan. 8]. Their streets are better than ours, generally wide and very regular, but their houses (some extremely high) are generally false ornamented, run up in three or four points,[1] and make a worse and more tawdry appearance than ours. They are often ornamented on the points, particularly at Ostend, with birds, beasts, Neptunes, etc.

The parades, generally large, particularly at the latter. The Town House there very large: the Bedford stairs to the entrance, yet irregular: the range of windows—nine on one side, seven on the other.

The fine hangings in the Town House of Brussels, hung as pictures in gilt frames and, after touching, scarce to be distinguished from paintings by the eye (indeed but two window-shuts open).

The inmost room, and in that the last picture 'Laetus introitus Philippi Boni'. The two river-gods in the court, ibid. The rooms we saw—all painting, hangings and gilding. In the Arsenal the helmet and shield of Charles V seem fine work: his cradle there (Tu qui tam laxè curabas, addressing to the Deity), and the Roman shield engraved so as to have a smooth superficies to the touch (Fabricium frustra, Rex Pyrrhe, Proboscide terres).

The heathenish images appear at the entrance of their towns, on their bridges, in the streets, and even (all the way) are frequent on their highroads. Some of these in a little sort of wooden covers, scarce a foot square (the Lady in the lobster, gilded gingerbread). Some with lanthorns before them and some with candles burning.

The first look of Namur [Jan. 9–17] very striking: the fine country for two leagues before you see it preferable to Dorsetshire, and the rockiness when you do. The strong site of the citadel, all on rock, with the Maese on one side of the town and the Sambre on the other, and the rest all fortified or inaccessible rock. 'Now between four and five thousand men in it,' [said] the deputy governor. With 15,000 men furnished with all necessaries and £20,000 laid out previously, would be impregnable. 'The (Imperial) governor of the citadel is inferior to the (Dutch) governor of the town, nor are any orders from the Emperor to him valid without the conjunction of the States of Holland. The town [is] the Emperor's, but the soldiers all in the Dutch service. So with all the barriers' (*General Collier*). The garden and shell summerhouse in the citadel. Taken by the French in —92, and retaken by King William in —95.

All subsequent excerpts from *Notebook* I are taken from Egerton 2235.
  1. Here Spence sketched an outline of the façade.

2

Source: Egerton 2234 ff. 2–4
Addressed: Pass this/To/Mrs Spence/at Winchester
Endorsed: *b.* Mr Rolle/Citadel at Namur / o.

EDW. ROLLE TO MRS. SPENCE

New College,
January 19, 1731 [O.S.]

Madam,

I take it for granted I have leave to trouble you every time I hear from Mr.
Spence. I have just received a letter from him in which he is so obliging as
to be particular in the accounts of what he hath met with, and withal
desires I would inform you of what I know, which was unnecessary, since I
think it my duty to acquaint you with his welfare which must be so
agreeable to you, and shall hope by so doing to merit learning what you
know of his motions, by which means we shall each in some sort have the
pleasure of those letters which are sent to either.

I don't know whether I may not be late in my accounts that he got to
Calais in three hours' sail, which place looked more beautiful, he says, by
the sunbeams playing upon the town as he first saw it, and made him
forget his sickness at sea. If there were anything to a man of sense more in
Christmas than any other ordinary time, one would condole with him, for
it seems he lost Christmas Day, for by setting out on the twenty-fourth of
December, and next day coming to a place where their accounts are eleven
days before us, he found himself next morning got to the fourth of January.[1]

There is nothing at present more disturbs him than the language, I find
(which difficulty, however, I dare say he will as easily wind himself out of
as anyone). The pain of talking French is not the worst it seems, because
what would make him understood at one stage, in a day's riding farther
would be almost unintelligible. So that 'twould be almost useless for him to
get a capacity of speaking which would serve only today, and must be
altered in a few miles' riding; at Dijon, where he thinks to make some stay,
he hopes to master the language when it will be more certain. Nothing is
more agreeable than his climbing up rocks, etc. for a vast height, and of a
sudden finding himself in the deputy governor's garden with a summerhouse wainscoted with fine shells.

31

You will pardon me if you should have heard of most of this before, but I concluded nothing would be more agreeable [to you] than to hear even the least circumstances relating to my friend. [   ] the reading over his letter again to give you a transcript of it, is a fresh [   ] to Madam,

Your affectionate humble servant

Edw. Rolle

EDWARD ROLLE (1703–91), Fellow of New College, acted as Spence's 'deputy at Oxford'. From 1732 to 1755 he held a living at Monk Okehampton, Devon., later Rector of Berwick St. John, Wilts. Spence had written to him from Namur (see *Letter* 4).

1. The Gregorian calendar (New Style) was eleven days ahead of the Julian (Old Style) kept in England until 1752.

Notebook 1
(4–5) 25ᵛ–26ʳ

Rheims [Jan. 19] makes a better appearance at a distance than when you come into it. Scarce anything handsome in it, except churches and ecclesiastical houses. Both the convents of [the] Benedictines have something grand in them. At their church of St. Nicaise is the trembling pillar: when the bell strikes or is only moved about. 'Tis in one of the front turrets. The pillar is one of the buttresses of which there is a range to the east, the higher part of them more detached from the body of the church. *This* is what trembles most sensibly. They say the three next to the bell tremble, the first most and the second least. I did not observe any motion but in the first.

At their other church of St. Rémy we saw the sacred ampoule. The good priest who showed it behaved as if it had really come from heaven. When he was to go in to the wicket, he put on his cope, kneeled down and paid his devotions, and took it out with great reverence. The body of St. Rémy lies behind it, as they said, still entire and incorruptible. He showed the vast candlestick (with seven branches) as all of Corinthian brass. The precious stones about the ampoule, its receptacle, and the face of the altar, very numerous and large. (Q. whether this of solid gold, as that of the church of Notre Dame where the kings are crowned?)

The monks of this convent seem to be great lovers of champagne. I counted forty-five hogsheads flung by in one of their back-courts by the church of St. Rémy. Their library is large and handsome: one whole class in it of concinnatores only (*Nescitis diem, neque horam*, the motto on their new dial).

The fine walk, even at such a moderate town as Châlons [Jan. 23], is continued for a league to a nobleman's house.

Source:	Egerton 2234 ff. 4–5
Addressed:	To/Mrs Spence/at Winchester/in Hamshire/ *Angleterre*
Postmarked:	IA 25
Franked:	*franco Paris*
Endorsed:	*a.* Rec'd Jan. 20
	b. Route frō Calais to Dijon./o.

*3

[Dijon,]
January 26 ⟨here, with you the 15th⟩, 1731

⟨Dear Mother,⟩

We are at last got safe to Dijon, the place where Lord M[iddlesex] is to
pass all the rest of the winter. 'Twas a long and tedious journey hither—I
mean as to the time of year and, generally, the badness of the roads; but a
chaise made both less troublesome.[1] Generally speaking, we sat so easy in
it that we could sleep or read. We had a perfect study of books round us,
in books contrived on each side within the chaise, and every day we read a
play or two of Shakespeare, or two or three poems of Mr. Pope's. Sometimes
the prospects took us off from our books, which even in this season are
sometimes agreeable.

The first part from Calais we came 140 miles, without seeing any such
thing as a hill even anywhere at a distance, often by the sea-side and more
by the side of a large canal. Since Namur, the three or four last days hither
have been through vineyards or between a variety of little hills on each
side, covered with woods, here and there rocks, and now [and] then an old
castle on the top of them. We went on a raised causeway which runs all
through the vale between these hills, with a river all the way on the left
hand, which winds along the vale and falls often in the oddest little cascades
that ever I saw.[2] I thank heaven I have been all the way, and am now, in
perfect good health, and we are now settled for four or five months.

A house is taking for my Lord here where I shall have a servant and a
separate apartment, and may live just as if I were at Oxford. Only we can have
more diversions here in the afternoons and evenings, ⟨and I am all the while
with a gentleman of so much good sense and good nature as Lord Middlesex,[3]
who excels most people in both. I hope you and my sister[4] and all friends
are very well. I sent a letter from Namur to Mr. Rolle, which I hope came
safe to you; as yet I have received none, but hope to do it when we are
settled at a place. I find that the bringing about a year will not be near so
expensive to me here as it was in England. The [   ] elow.
I am ever

Your dutiful and affectionate

Jo: Spence

Pray let Mr. Rolle know of this, and how to direct to me.⟩

1. They had left Rheims Jan. 20, and travelling through Châlons (21), Joinville (22), Vignory, Chaumont, Langres (23), arrived at Dijon on Jan. 24.

2. The Marne.

3. Charles Sackville (1711–69), styled Lord Buckhurst till 1720, E. of Middlesex 1720–65. Educ. at Westminster School, matric. at Christ Church, Oxford, Nov. 27, 1728, M.A. Sept. 15, 1730. After his return from the Grand Tour,

M.P. for East Grinstead (1734–41), Sussex (1742–7), Old Sarum (1747–54), East Grinstead (1761–5); Ld. of Treasury 1743–7; Master of the Horse to Prince of Wales 1747–51; suc. father as 2d D. of Dorset Oct. 10, 1765; P.C. Feb. 10, 1766; Ld. Lt. Kent 1766–9.

4. 'Of whom almost nothing is known' (Wright, p. 5). Spence calls her 'Belle' in his letters, and she lived at this time with her mother in Colebrook Street.

Notebook 1

(5–6) 26^{r-v}

Dijon [Jan. 24–May 14] a handsome city, the streets broad and well paved. The river Suzon passes through the town, concealed under arches. The Palace Royal with the statue of Louis XIV, the Maison du Roi at the end of the half moon and the Rue de Condé make the handsomest part of it. The walks (they say of a league long) are grand, and those on the ramparts very agreeable. I don't know how they came to commend the front of St. Michael's: 'tis gothic, with false modern pillars. The front of St. Stephen's is a neat new one. At the Sainte Chapelle is the old *hostie* that has kept entire so long. Notre Dame has some very bad copies of very good pictures. St. John's is a large cross without pillars to support the roof, and the pictures in it look less insufferable than those in the other churches.

The hospital has eighty women and fifty men on the foundation. There's a hall for the sick men, another for the women, and another for the daughters of people that can't keep them; and another for passengers. In all, Cotheret, when one of the directors, has numbered 990 at a time in their hospital. The settled revenue is 45,000 livres, and the accidental, one year with another, 55,000. This is without the walls, and there is a house for the *enfants trouvés* in the city.

The university is not above five or six years old, 'tis rather a school to study the law in, not above forty scholars as yet. The schools of the Jesuits look more like an university and have almost ten times the number of scholars.

'The English abroad', Dean Lockier told Spence shortly before his departure, 'can never get to look as if they were at home. The Irish and [the] Scotch, after being some time in a place, get the air of the natives, but an Englishman in any foreign court looks about him as if he were going to steal a tankard' (Obs. No. 697).

*4

Source:	Egerton 2234 ff. 6–7
Addressed:	To/Mrs Spence/at Mr Morecrofts; in/ Winchester:/en Angleterr
Franked:	*Franco Paris*
Endorsed:	*b.* Walks, & Concert at Dijon *red wafer*

Dijon,
February 16 ⟨5⟩, 1731

⟨Dear Mother,

I have written to you from Calais and this place, and to Mr. Rolle—which I reckon much the same thing—from Namur. We have not yet received a single letter from anybody.⟩

We are now above three weeks old at Dijon. The situation of it is very agreeable, and has in some parts of the prospect just resemblance enough to put one in mind of Oxford. Almost ever since we have been here, there has been the deepest snow that has been seen in these parts these fifteen years—the common depth of it has been two foot. Towards our first coming there was a thaw of two or three days. I took the advantage of it to see the public walks which are just without the east gate of the city. They are extremely handsome: a full mile in length, the middle walk twenty yards over, and those on each side ten yards. In the midst they all widen into a circle which serves here, in proper weather, as the Ring in Hyde Park.[1] At the farther end of the walks is a public park where the walks are all star-fashion, and at the end of that is half a circle planted entirely with firs, pines, and evergreens: all along this runs an open walk, and that is bounded by a very wide and very particular canal. The first time of finding out all this, one piece after another, was extremely agreeable, and I have not yet had any room for a second view, the snow being still knee-deep, as we call it in the country. However, I don't lose my morning walks, for in the town they clear away the snow in a good degree every time after it falls, and my favourite walk now is upon the walls or ramparts on the sunny side of the town.[2]

⟨Though I used to have eight or ten colds every winter at Oxford, both in our journey hither and ever since we have been here I have not had any such thing, and am, I thank heaven, in all respects entirely well at this present writing. I should be very happy in hearing that you and my sister etc. are so too.⟩

35

This place does not at all want for company: at our concerts of music and our masquerades, which all the carnival time were every Sunday night, I have seen above 150 people of fashion. Though 'tis Lent, the concerts continue still at the same time, for Sunday here is the high day of diversion. Their music, at least to us, is not near so agreeable as the English. They have above thirty hands and voices: in the front of them are six women who all sing, but to me in the most howling manner that ever I heard. Indeed all except one (who is the governor's mistress)[3] are extremely ugly and without any exception painted to a gross degree, both the red and the white. In the midst of these is a desk raised on which stands the master of the music: he has a roll of paper in his hand with which, his head, and his whole body, he is continually keeping time in so violent a manner that I can hardly think of him without laughing.

I believe all the great cities here abound in a little sort of noblemen, of all sorts of titles. With the benefit of being my Lord's shadow (and following him everywhere) I am now as well acquainted as the strangeness of the language will permit with one comtesse, two comtes, a marquis, and four barons. If I have forgot any of my new quality friends in this calculation, I hope they will have the goodness to forgive me. ⟨Three of my barons are strangers—Germans who are now in this place, and the fourth is (God bless him) an Englishman.[4] Both he and his lady talk English very well, so that 'tis the most comfortable thing in the world to go and see them.

We begin all to long very much to hear from England. Pray how does Mr. Wavil[5] do and all his good family? And Mrs. Kelley[6] and her fireside? The nun letters lie still as quiet as lambs,[7] and as we seem inclined, I don't know whether Paris will not be the very last place we shall be at. Next October we are for Italy. When you write any letter for me, please not to send it to my brother[8] as I first desired. The best way will be to direct it as below, and to put it as you would any other letter into your post. Never but half a sheet, but in that pray let me have as much as you can. My service to Mr. and Mrs. Morecroft[9] and all friends. I am ever

Your dutiful and affectionate

J. Spence

à Monsieur / Monsieur Spence, chez Mr. Cotheret,[10] / proche la Place Royale / à / Dijon. / *Par Paris.*⟩

1. A circle for fashionable *tours en chaise*, constructed under Charles I and partly destroyed in George II's reign when Queen Caroline had it replaced by the Serpentine.

2. A contemporary engraving of the 13th-century fortifications may be found in Claude Fyot de la Marche, *Histoire de l'église abbatiale et collégiale de Saint Estienne de Dijon* (Dijon, 1696), pp. 6–7. 'Le boulevard qui les domine est le rendez-vous des plaisirs' (C. X. Girault, *Essais . . . sur Dijon* [1814], pp. 81–3).

3. Louis-Henri, D. of Bourbon (1692–1740), 4th governor of Burgundy, was at this time himself in danger of horns (see *Letter* 30 n. 9), but no records I have seen attribute a mistress to him at this period.

4. Probably Sir George Colgrave (see *App.* 1), a Jacobite who had served as captain in Lee's regiment and was knighted Nov. 12, 1710 (Ruvigny, *Jacobite Peerage* [1904], p. 191). Two of his petitions addressed to the Pretender and the Earl of Mar in 1718 appear in *HMC*, Stuart Papers, VII, 66. 'Lady Colgrave' has not been identified.

5. Daniel Wavell (b. 1676), Vicar of South Hayling, Rector of St. Maurice and St. Mary Calendar at Winchester, 1721, Vicar of Warenham, Hants, 1722. Spence calls him 'my old friend the apostle' who often talked in his garden 'about predestination' (*Letter* 27 and

Obs. Nos. 1017–19).

6. Perhaps wife of Dr. George Kelley, another Winchester neighbour, whose son is mentioned in *Letter* 66.

7. Addressed to Miss Belson (see *Letter* 6) who was to enter a nunnery in Paris. Perhaps Frances Belson, dau. of Thomas and Anna Belson, who married Richard Layton three years later ('The Registers of the Catholic Mission of Winchester, 1721–1826' in *Cath. Rec. Soc.* [1905], I, 154).

8. Richard (b. 1701, still living 1757) who worked for the African Company and lived, with his wife, at the African House in Leadenhall Street, London.

9. Mrs. Spence stayed at their house in Colebrook Street.

10. A merchant, formerly 'one of the directors' of the hospital at Dijon.

---

*5

Source:	Egerton 2234 ff. 8–9
Addressed:	To/Mrs Spence/near Colebrook-Street/in/ Winton
Endorsed:	*a.* ye desripshon of/ye frensh Ladys/dressing *b.* Dress, &c.

Dijon,
March 1 ⟨February 17 O.S.

I wrote to you from Calais, but know not whether it came to hand.⟩

⟨Dear Mother,

Today morning, just as the servant had lighted the fire in my chamber, and before I cared for stirring out of my bed, in came the postmaster with an armful of letters. Among the rest I had the pleasure of receiving one of yours (dated January 30), one from my brother Dick, and another from my brother Rolle. I'm so particular because they are the first packet I have received from England, and to see your hand, after longing for it so long, was an extreme pleasure to me. I'm overjoyed to find you are all well, and beg you'd return my services to everybody, and particularly to Mr. Wavil. Your being acquainted so well with my dear deputy at Oxford (Cap. Rolle) and owning him for your son in my absence is just what I wished.[1] I beg you'd write to him on all occasions, for you know what, just as you would to me if I were at Oxford. I thank God I am in a better situation than I could be there. My dear Lord has everything in him that is agreeable—the finest sense and the best nature.⟩

I have talked to you as yet only of the roads and walks. 'Tis proper one should let you know a word or two about the people. In deference to the fair sex I shall begin with them. One may say it safely, for 'tis owned even here, that the French women are not so beautiful as the English, but then they make it up in a sprightliness and freedom of behaviour that is universal among them. Their head-dress here for the people of fashion is called 'Tête des Muttons';[2] 'tis a very small head just on the top, without flaps or anything coming down on the sides. Their hair is short and formed all into little curls, row after row, quite down to the neck, every way. They wear a sort of sultanas,[3] or at least a vest of silk, that comes up almost quite to the neck and falls loose every way down to the feet. The breast is invisible, and there is no pretence to a waist in this dress[4]—but yet I must say it has something very graceful in it.

One thing that I was surprised at was a compliment that is very common both here and at Namur. You have heard of the Dutch women's sitting at market with a pan of coals under them. There's a great many of these pans here, and at an assembly you'll frequently see a gentleman scuttle along with a pan of coals and put it himself under a lady's petticoats, who bows kindly in her seat, and plays on her cards at quadrille all the while, with great serenity and satisfaction.[5]

We have had an extreme hard winter here, snow two feet deep for these five weeks. 'Tis now almost gone, and this afternoon I had a very dry and pleasant walk half round the town upon the ramparts. But to return: my Lord lives in part of a merchant's house,[6] whose wife and I are grown extremely acquainted. I believe I might make a cuckold of my landlord whenever I had a mind to it—but such a villainy is not in my nature. She is sometimes half the day together in my chamber, and as she is eternally talking French and I always endeavouring to answer her, she has really done me more good that way than my French master.[7] She is about five and thirty, or, by our Lady, forty years old, but forever brisk and ⌐more talkative than seventeen parrots⌐.[8] When I don't understand what she says, or she does not understand what I say, we always fall a laughing: so that 'tis a very merry method of learning a language. ⟨I laugh till I hold my sides, and then we talk again.

I told Capt. Rolle in my last [of] my top dress here,[9] but I must repeat it to you for fear his should miscarry. 'Tis a black velvet coat lined with red silk, a black silk waistcoat lined with white, black velvet breeches, and black silk stockings, a sword always tucked to my side, and a cane never out of my hands; and, to crown all, a French wig in a bag, with two large black pieces of silk that come on each side under my chin, and are lost in the buttoning of the breast. Beside this I have just begun to learn to dance, and I believe verily shall come home very much a gentleman.—My hearty service to my sister. I hope she and you and all friends are well, and am ever

Your most affectionate

Jo: Spence

I find by our letters that 'tis but ten days from hence to London, and twelve to Winton.[10] Rather less than more.⟩

1. Spence had been elected Professor of Poetry July 11, 1728, and held the office for the usual period of ten years. During his absence Edward Rolle acted as his deputy.

2. Or 'moutonne': 'Coiffure de femmes ... qui consistait dans une tresse de cheveux frisés et fort touffus, qu'elles se mettaient sur le front' (Littré).

3. Rich gowns trimmed with buttons and loops.

4. In contrast to the current English fashion which was to 'go always with ... bosom uncovered' (*Obs.* No. 763) and to cultivate a 'fine and taper' waist; although Spence thought that 'our beauties in England carry ... this nicety generally too far' (*Polymetis,* p. 66).

5. Horace Walpole also laughed at these continental 'portable stoves', *réchauffe-pieds* (or *scaldini,* as they were called in Italy). *Corresp.* XIII, 204–5.

6. M. Cotheret's.

7. A Jesuit priest who corrected Spence's exercises. See *Letters* 6 and 7.

8. Emended to 'for ever talkative'.

9. This letter, dated before March 1, does not appear to be extant.

10. *Letter* 3 dated Jan. 26 [N.S.] is marked in Mrs. Spence's hand: 'Rec'd Jan 27' [O.S.]. There was a difference of eleven days between the Old and the New Style. The first letter from Winchester to Dijon took eighteen days, but subsequent letters only five to eight days.

*6

Source: Egerton 2234 ff. 10–11
Addressed: Mrs Spence
Endorsed: b. Account of/the Carthusians/near Dijon.

Dijon,

March 27 (16 old style)

⟨Dear Mother,

I have had the pleasure of receiving a whole covey of your letters together. There were four of them, the first dated December 20 and the last February 21. I am very glad you did not think time enough of writing to Dick to curtail them, for I would not have had them otherwise than they are for twice the postage. Indeed, the post hither is very tolerable as well as very expeditious: all four, together with Dick's, did not cost me above eighteen pence and they got hither from Dick in eight days.[1]

I'm glad my cheat succeeded so well to let you know that I was at Calais before you thought I had left England. I wish Mr. Wavil all the health that is necessary to hold him out twenty years longer, though I hope to see him in two. I wrote to him the thirteenth of this month N.S. I am very glad Miss Belson[2] is to be in England again, for a nunnery here would be a terrible thing for a lady of her constitution. I'll bring the letters very gladly back with me.⟩

I just came home from a walk when I received your letters, and am now just returned from another, when I sat down to write this. Our weather here has been almost this fortnight as warm as May in England; nothing can be more delicious than the air, and abroad all round us they are busy in their vineyards setting up the sticks and tying the vines to them. They don't seem to make half the figure that I expected: the sticks (or hop-poles in miniature) are not above breast-high, and a whole vineyard, when the poles are set, looks only like a large regular plantation of raspberries.

About a fortnight ago we walked out to see a college of the Chartreux, about half a mile without the walls.[3] These are, generally speaking, some of the strictest religious people among the Roman Catholics. Our English friend[4] conducted us thither, as he does almost everywhere. He led us directly to the governor of the college, who was a plump, good-natured, arch, bald-pated old gentleman ⌐'for God's sake don't let us talk of the devil'¬.[5] After staying the time of a civil visit with him, we had leave to speak with one of the Society, or rather we carried him leave to answer us when we spoke to him, for they are all under an oath of silence.

The Society consists of twenty-four beside Mr. Abbot. There is a little hole in the wall, about a foot square, belonging to each chamber. The cook keeps the key of it, and puts in their dinner without speaking a word. Of each twenty-four hours they have eight set apart for public prayer, eight for sleep, and eight for their business, reading or working in their little gardens. They go to bed at six, winter and summer, rise at ten at night, pray till two, then in bed again till six, and then pray again till ten. From that to six in the evening is their eight hours at their own disposal. The Brother we saw had very neat little lodgings and a pretty garden, and the rest have all the same. They never speak but for two hours on two days in the week, nor stir out of their foredoor, even into their own cloisters, but for an hour or two on stated days. Then they walk each singly, and if one happens to cross another, all he is allowed to say is 'Remember your death-bed' in Latin.[6] They keep a fast for life and never taste anything but fish or herbs.

I was mightily pleased with one thing. A bird here, something like our moorhens, that lives chiefly on the water, they will have to be a fish: I mean they always eat it as a water creature. They do the same by otters which, the abbot assured us, were excellent good when well dressed. For their eight hours of diversion each has some employment or handicraft, as painting, making of statues, music, etc. The Brother we visited was a turner, and made little Tunbridge ware things. After I came home I could not help being really concerned to think that religion, which was designed to make men good-natured and sociable, should ever be perverted so very far from its original intent as to make people plant themselves, one by one, like orange-trees, in their particular boxes, and even forswear the use of their tongues, which I have a strong notion were given them to talk with.[7]

⟨I begin myself to come by little and little to the use of my tongue again, and (heaven be praised) have taken no oath as yet of silence. I have a priest that comes to me every day to teach me the language, and after Easter he is to come twice a day. I can now hold a little sort of a broken conversation with anybody I meet, and every day it will grow easier and easier. We dine generally at a large inn where there is an ordinary kept every day for all strangers to help on learning the language, and yesterday we had the pleasure of having no less a man than a Knight of Malta for one of the company.

I desire my hearty service to nurse Page,[8] and tell her 'twas a fine day the twenty-fourth of December on the sea between England and France as well as in Culver's Close. My very hearty service to my sister, Mr. Wavil, and all friends round the Reking.[9] I am, thank heaven, very well and ever

Your most affectionate and dutiful

Jo: Spence⟩

1. The usual postage, paid by the recipient, was a shilling per letter. Dick is Spence's brother Richard.

2. To whom Spence was bringing 'nun letters' (*Letter* 4).

3. In the 'Faubourg d'Ouche' (*Nbk.* 3 74r). Founded 1383 by Philippe-le-Hardi and enriched by the Dukes of Burgundy who desired to be buried there, it was destroyed during the Revolution. Spence revisited the place in 1739.

4. Probably Sir George Colgrave (*Letter* 4 n. 4).

5. Inserted from *Notebook* 1 26v; not in the original letter.

6. 'The hair-shirt they showed us [was] not above four or five inches square' (*Nbk.* 1 26v).

7. 'The Religious of the severer orders abroad,' Spence commented later, 'instead of summer-houses, and places of pleasure, have often a sort of penitential caves in their gardens; contrived so as to cast gloom over the mind: with a single taper in its inmost recess; that shews you the figure of a Magdalen weeping over a death's head, or some such melancholy object' (*Polymetis*, p. 3).

8. Not identified. Perhaps a relation of Richard Page (b. 1705), Winchester scholar in 1716 (Kirby, p. 226).

9. The Wrekin in Shropshire.

*7

Source: Egerton 2234 ff. 12–13

Endorsed: *b.* Some of yᵉ Easter Ceremonies; & Penances/
[Palm-Sunday Procession: Eas-/ter: Pennance
&c.]

Dijon,
April 12 ⟨1st⟩, 1731

⟨Dear Mother,⟩

In my last I was got into a very religious strain by talking of the grave
Brethren of the Chartreux. As I have nothing else to say, I thank heaven
(but what I have said so often) that 'I am very well and very happy', I
don't see why you and I should not sit down and talk a little more about
the religion. The common things you know. I must only add that the lower
people are very devout and very much in earnest in all the formalities of
their religion.

On Palm Sunday we had a grand procession of the clergy through the
streets. They went by our window, with the silver crosses etc. before them,
to the great prison of the town, to deliver one prisoner. This they do every
year on this day in memory of that very worthy gentleman, Mr. Barabbas.
On Good Friday in the morning I was surprised with a strange rumbling
in the streets before I was up. 'Twas repeated several times, and everything
else was particularly still and hush. At breakfast the rumbling came about
again, and then we could see 'twas a boy with an odd sort of wheelbarrow
that made more noise than half a dozen common wheelbarrows could have
made. This is a custom I think peculiar to this place.[1] Always on Good
Friday, and till Saturday noon, all the clocks and bells are speechless, and
the wheelbarrow comes to tell the people the different hours for prayers.
In giving the reason of this, my priest had not his story quite perfect. He
said only that anciently wheelbarrows were used here instead of bells, and
that for those most solemn days in the year it was still kept up—I suppose
out of a particular veneration to their rumbling, which has indeed something
[ve]ry edifying in it.

On Easter day I was at no less than three of their churches in the height
of their ceremonies. I planted myself very near the holy water, and by
leaning against the pillar seemed half to kneel when there was any occasion
for kneeling. Everything was pompous beyond what I had ever imagined
for worship, and if they are not in earnest, they are at a great deal of pains

42

to seem so. The next day I got to church half an hour before public prayers
—you see I am grown very devout—just by a side altar where the statue
of the Virgin Anne was teaching her daughter, the Virgin Mary, her ABC.
As it happened, this altar had a great deal of custom that day. Several good
women dropt in, one by one, before the public service, and told their beads
at it very heartily, till by degrees the sides and the steps were all full.
'Twas the time for the little penances for the breach of Lent which was
just past. I observed one woman in particular who sat upon one of the steps
to pray, and continued so all the time. As I had a great deal of reason to
think (and I observed her very narrowly) she sat all the time on the cold
marble, quite bare, which I suppose was her penance. Though she sometimes
looked very sour, she had generally a philosophical steadiness in her face
that appeared quite heroic for a lady in her situation. These penances are
sometimes little slight things that are very convenient for people that
delight in sin. A servant of my Lord's, for his breaches of the last Lent, and
for perhaps a thousand other crimes, was ordered only to go to church so
often every day the next week, and to give away sixpence to the poor each
time he went into a tavern for the month ensuing. ⟨My priest and master
of language is just come. I hope you are all well, and am

Your most affectionate

J. S.

Service to Mr. Wavil in particular, and thanks for his kind letter.⟩

---

1. It has survived in many parts of France, except that the 'kind of wheelbarrow' (*brussoir*) has been replaced by various kinds of rattles (*crécelles*). A. Van Gennep, *Manuel de folklore français contemporain* (Paris, 1947), I, iii, 1206–39.

❋8

Source: Egerton 2234 ff. 14–15
Endorsed: *b.* Old Temple there./Old Temple, at Dijon.

Dijon,

April 19 ⟨8⟩, [1731]

⟨Dear Mother,⟩

Heaven forbid that you should have your son come home a Roman
Catholic, but he is very well acquainted with the Jesuits, I can assure you.
'Tis but this very afternoon that he was writing things out in their library,

and was very kindly received by one of their superiors.[1]

The day before yesterday I was at a church here where are yet the remains of an old heathen temple.[2] In the middle 'tis a round composed of pillars, three story high: two above ground and one under. Each story consists of eight pillars; at the top of this round is a dome, open in the middle, and contrived so as to fling a strong light to the bottom. All the rest of the church is very low, filled all with rows of pillars and with scarce any window to give any light to it. I never saw a place so solemn, or rather so dark: it seems to have been an excellent place formerly for the old heathens to worship the devil in.

To this old piece of the church the Papists here have added a good handsome new one,[3] which is dedicated to St. Bénigne, the first person that preached the Gospel at Dijon.[4] I liked it because 'twas less stuffed with ornaments than the churches here generally are. St. Bénigne was martyred for the Gospel. They keep his ⌜old dry⌝ skull here,[5] and have also a wooden great chair in which he used to sit in days of yore and preach or sleep, as the fit took him. What this chair is at present remarkable for (beside its being very old and very worm-eaten) is the curing of mad people. They ⌜take and⌝ set them in this chair, clap the saint's skull upon their heads, say a few prayers, and up they rise perfectly restored to their senses. 'Twould be of excellent use if we could transport it once a year to Bedlam, or perhaps to any other quarter that you please in our great metropolis.

⟨I am glad to hear my old friend the apostle[6] is well. I wrote to him the 13/2 of March, so that I wonder he had not received it when you saw him. I would not have had my cousin Lowth suffer in my room for all the world, and am mighty glad to hear that he prevented the villain.[7] When you see them next, I beg my most humble service to all the good family.

As to the use of my tongue, now I have crossed the salt seas into these foreign parts, I can tell you that I begin at present to move it pretty well and keep it entirely from being mouldy. I believe we shall leave this place in a fortnight, I don't yet know certainly for what place. When I do, I'll take care to inform you how to direct. However, you need not at all defer writing on that account, for my Lord will have packets come hither that will be sent safe after him. The post really grows more expeditious than it was, and I received one letter from London in five days and a half, but I believe that was its utmost speed that it ever did make.

I wish I had been with you up in the High Chamber to have overlooked Count Hyems, and to have given her one volley of small shot. I beg you'd carry up a lapful of pebblestones with you next time, and you'd oblige me infinitely if you would give her four or five thumps with them particularly in my name and on my account. I am very glad to hear Belle is well, and with my hearty humble service to her and all friends (Mr. Wavil in particular) am ever

Your dutiful and affectionate

J. Spence⟩

1. Spence may have been introduced to the Jesuits by the Chevalier Ramsay.

2. The original crypt of St. Bénigne, constructed in the 6th century. For a detailed account, see Abbé L. Chomton, *Histoire de l'église Saint Bénigne* (Dijon, 1900).

3. 'Just behind the Rotonda, which was laid in a line to the East, if this altar stands right' (*Nbk.* 1 27ʳ).

4. St. Bénigne, the patron of Dijon, was martyred after A.D. 270. The basilica and monastery were built over his sepulchre.

5. Emended to 'Saint's skull'. 'His bones were kept in the vault of the Rotonda, but are now over the altar of his own church' (*Nbk.* 1 27ʳ). Most of the relics had been sent to Germany in 1073 and the rest dispersed in 1793.

6. Dean Wavell.

7. Robert Lowth (1710–87), later a noted Hebrew scholar and from 1777 Bp. of London, was at this time a New College undergraduate. In 1741 he became Spence's successor as Professor of Poetry at Oxford. The allusion is probably to the circumstances surrounding the publication of Spence's pamphlet on Stephen Duck, the Thresher-Poet, which came out in Mar. 1731 under the title, *A full and Authentick Account of Stephen Duck, the Wiltshire Poet.* Spence had left the manuscript 'in the hands of his friend Mr. Lowth', 'to be published', says Lowth, 'as soon as Spence had left England, with a Grub-Street title, which he had drawn up merely for a disguise, not choosing to have it thought that he published it himself' (Nichols, *Literary Anecdotes* [1812], II, 373 n. and I, 643 n.). The 'villain' was probably the publisher, who may have wished to use Lowth's name as authorizing the publication. See also *Letter* 12.

9

Source:	Egerton 2234 ff. 16–17
Addressed:	To/Mʳˢ Spence/at Mʳ Morecroft's/in Colebrook-Street/Winchester
Postmarked:	13 MA
Endorsed:	*b.* Way of Eating in France *red wafer*

Dijon,
May 12 ⟨1⟩, 1731

⟨Dear Mother,

I'm very glad you mentioned Mr. Wavil in your last, for I expected a letter from him and forgot to write to him in answer to what he mentioned of his son.[1] I have now made amends for it, and sent to him by this post. Mr. Rolle is got to Oxford again as I take it, for Dick has wrote to him and received an answer. I'll answer for him, he will be always glad of receiving your letters and in writing to you again.⟩

Among all the chat we have had together across the water I don't know that I have once mentioned our eating here. They delight mightily in fowl in particular, and I don't know that I have once, either on the road or here, sat down to dinner or supper without a pullet or capon on the table. At present we never miss of that and pigeons, with two plates of sparagrass—one dressed with oil and vinegar for the good people of the country, and another with ⟨honest⟩ butter for us poor Englishmen. The dinner always begins with a *soupe*, and both that and the supper end with a dessert. As soon as this is set on the table, the servants place a glass for each person and a bottle of Burgundy at each end of the table, make their bows, and retire. The dessert and cloth stay as long as you do—which keeps the table dry and gives you sweetmeats whenever you have a mind for them. In the winter we never missed of grapes, preserved in the bunches as they grow, and a plate of almonds in their neighbourhood. At present we have generally a preserve which is very much my favourite: 'tis made of barberries in which there is a mixture of sharpness and sweetness that is extremely agreeable. They have now, too, curds and cream in the dessert, but 'tis always sour. The best Burgundy at the taverns costs but eight pence a bottle, and from the finest cellars of the great merchants here but sixteen pence.[2] The common people buy worse sorts cheaper and cheaper, and 'tis matter of fact that the lowest of all is but a halfpenny a bottle. I had almost forgot to tell you that about the beginning of last month I had the pleasure of tasting a fricassee of frogs for the first time. ⟨It had a sort of a chickeny taste, but something of an odd sourness at the bottom that I did not quite like.

This week two gentlemen of Oxford came hither: one of them is son of Mr. Shuttleworth, Knight of the Shire (I think for Lancashire) and the other a very sensible pretty gentleman, one Mr. Denny.[3] They stay here for some time, but we are going next week for Lyons, more towards Italy. I expect to be there for three or four months. The other gentlemen are for Italy too, and I believe will probably follow us to Lyons in four or five weeks. The next direction to me is in all its form, according to the French fashion, as follows: à Monsieur / Monsieur Spence, / avec Milord Middlesex, / au Palais Royal / à / Lyon / *Par Paris*. 'Tis a very pleasant place by the pictures of it. I hope to give you an account of it in my next, and am

Your most affectionate and dutiful son,

Mr. Mr. Spence⟩[4]

---

1. Richard Wavell (bapt. Dec. 5, 1717) was to become Winchester scholar next year (Kirby, p. 238). Five months later Spence was 'extremely glad to hear Mr. Wavill's son goes on so well in the college' (*Letter* 21).

2. Whereas in England 'a bottle of wine [cost] two shillings' (*Obs*. No. 127).

3. Richard Shuttleworth, son of Sir Richard Shuttleworth (1683–1749) of Gilling, Yorks., b. 1709, matric. at Christ Church Mar. 14, 1725–6. Lord Middlesex composed the following 'epitaph' on him:

And is it true that Shuttleworth's no more?
Why Hell, I thought, had fire enough before.

(Spence Papers)

William Denny (1709–ca. 1770), matric. at Oriel Coll. 1726, B.A. Jan. 20, 1730. A noted man of fashion; Capt., later Col. in the army; one of the original members of the Soc. of Dilettanti (1736). Deputy Governor of Pennsylvania 1756–9. For Knapton's portrait of him (1744) 'as a Roman standard-bearer', see Cust, p. 218.

4. The letter passed through Dick's hand at London, who added a note at the end: 'Dear Mother. The bacon is come to hand and brother John is very well as is your dutiful son R.S.' John was the eldest of Mrs. Spence's three sons.

---

*10

Source:	Egerton 2234 ff. 18–19
Addressed:	*as in* 9
Postmarked:	18 MA
Endorsed:	*b.* Journey frō Dijon/to Lyons./Road to Lyons.

Lyons,
May 17 ⟨6⟩, 1731

⟨Dear Mother,

We set out from Dijon on Monday morning and came here to Lyons time enough to dine on Tuesday, that is a hundred and twenty miles. We had not been here above five minutes when the post-woman came in with the letters, one for my Lord, and, as good luck would have it, another for me. My brother had been with the Duke's secretary, and so had learned how to direct to me here, sooner than I expected.⟩[1]

We came out of Dijon a little after the rising of the sun. You know the post-chaise is as easy as a great chair, so that we could sit and enjoy all the prospects at leisure. The first four and twenty miles was all through vineyards, the leaves as yet only beginning to come out, but the variety and neatness of them still made it agreeable enough. After that the country mended much to the eye.

There are two towns in the way called Chalon and Mâcon, about thirty miles apart: all the way between I never yet saw so fine a prospect in my life. On the left hand was a continual rising and chain of hills of a moderate height, or rather one hill rising and sinking at least every quarter of a mile unequally. This was generally about a mile or two off from us: on the right hand, about the same distance commonly, was a river not much inferior to the Thames. Beyond that the country spread every way for a vast length, first in delicious meadows, then in cornfields, and then in woodlands. At the end of all, almost all the way, we could see the mountains of Switzerland, all covered with snow, whilst we were sometimes sweating with heat in the chaise. Our prospect on that side was almost always above sixty mile, for those mountains were generally about that distance from us. In spite of the prospect I wished to be nearer to them, for as we were, we could not discern the snow so plain as I could have desired. 'Twas so indistinct that 'twas difficult to distinguish their tops from clouds gilded a little with the sun. All the country on, quite to Lyons, was I think verily more beautiful to see than Dorsetshire, but by no means equal to the thirty miles I have been speaking of.

There was one thing that added a good deal to the pleasure of the journey. The two days we were upon the road happened to be Whitsun Monday and Tuesday with us here. In a hundred places the roads were full of country people, dressed all in their best, and in their different fashions. I think all the women had hats, some like men's, some odd high crowns, some neat straw hats, very wide-brimmed and with little steeples upon them, like the black high-crowned hats in England. For one part of the course all the women wore odd black things on their heads, of wool and fashioned like Turkish turbans. We had the pleasure too, as 'twas a great holy day, of seeing two country processions of the priests and poor people, one of which had the cross carried before them and the picture of their favourite saint swinging on a banner in the air. The other had all this with kettle-drums and music and the militia on horseback, and so was much finer and much more pleasing to heavens no doubt.—I did not think of lengthening out my letter at this rate, but as I have no room left to tell you anything of Lyons at present I must keep that for my next, ⟨and am

Your dutiful and affectionate

Jo: Spence⟩

1. A postscript in Richard's hand reads: 'You must know that Jo tells me he read my letter at Lyons in only eight days after the date. He says they are above a hundred miles farther from Paris than at Dijon, but it make[s] no more than a day with the post. Jack and I are well, thank God—the 18 May, 1731 [O.S.].'

Notebook 1
(7–11) 27ʳ–29ʳ

Lyons [May 15–Sept. 29] the first town in France for trade and called the second in size, but then all the farther side of the hill of Fourvière is only sprinkled with villas like the country. There is a great deal of apparent industry in all the streets, and yet in some even there a great number of children etc. without shoes and stockings. ('That, not only for poverty, for in hot countries they can and choose to do it more than in cold'—*Legris?*) The method of thinning the gold for lace is by drawing the ingot through a succession of holes, less and less, till two ounces would reach ten leagues. These and the silk manufactures are very numerous here. There is one of the latter with a stable five story high and two horses kept in the air. . . .

The church of Aisnay where the temple of Augustus stood, the speech of Claudius, the tauribole, the reservoir for water in the Ursulines' garden, the church under Mount Calvary (the good thief a saint there), and the remains of the 19,000 martyrs are the most remarkable antiquities there. Guerchin's St. Teresa at the Carmes déchaussés and Salviati's St. Thomas at the Jacobins' church the best pictures.

The town is governed by a provost, chosen for two years and continued sometimes to four, six or eight, four *écrivains* (anciently called consuls, and now so in the Latin inscriptions). The intendant is there on the part of the king: he represents him, sees all his orders executed, and governs all the affair of taxes, imposts, etc. . . .

'Tis surprising how the Rhône and Saône could overflow the place, considering its height above them and the lowness of the grounds (farther on the left hand) in Dauphiné. ⟨In 1711. The year before the two hundred (?) people were killed by that strange stoppage of the crowd on the bridge over the Rhône.⟩ The last bridge over the Saône is 228 paces, and the river is considerably broader in the middle of the town; that over the Rhône 808, but not half over water in the summer (eight arches of seventeen?).

The library at the great college of the Jesuits is a good room and finely situated; among the books there seems to be a good collection of antiquity writers. ⟨Henry V's mass-book there.⟩ The buildings in general poor ⟨Pierre-Lize, or the prison: what a terrible air it has!⟩, the streets narrow (for the heat) and ill paved, and the paper-windows give the town a very mean look. ⟨P. Kelley: 'La politique, comme il me semble, fait son caractère particulier avec un[e] douceur qui peut-être n'est pas moins politique.'⟩[1]

The variety of vineyards, churches, convents, water-houses—delightful. The environs are delicious, extremely cultivated to the tops of the little hills and well inhabited. Country-houses for the merchants very thick. The walk, after the rivers are joined, is delightful: you see Dauphiné spreading along to the hills, and behind them others covered with snow. There are wild mulberry-trees all along the roadside from Pillotière. (Walnut-tree grot, shower grotto, Pope's mount, the two goats and Hinksey.) To the north is the Mont d'Or (from its fertility) and to the south Mont de Pilate, whence almost all their bad weather. In the Place du Concert is the large church to St. Bonaventura, who died at the council at Lyons: his chamber and picture there.

The celebrated puppet-show clock: the angel and Virgin bowing, the little Holy Ghost descending, and the Bon Dieu moving his hand. The cock crows thrice at the beginning of the ceremony. There are very few pictures in the church: one in which God the Father is the principal figure and the angel turning away his face, and two statues at the entrance of choir, which is plain. There are above thirty county cannons. The Town House and royal convent is in the Place des Terreaux. The inscription is by Scaliger (?) on the former, and the only good couplet from Seneca. There the old speech of Claudius on brass.

The hospital is kept extremely neat; 2000 (?) people in it (the *religieuse*). The Charité, nine quadrangles—they have 1800 people in it now, enfants trouvés and all, and their revenue is at a medium 300,000 francs a year (of which 11,000

constant from the king, [the rest?] from the imposts on wine. The silk-works
and machines for making stockings there (the latter from England).

1. 'Fifty years without seeing any one of your relations!' said Spence. 'Yes, but relations, you know, are generally a good for nothing sort of people.'

11

Source: Egerton 2234 ff. 22–23

Addressed: To/Henry Rolle Esqr./Member of Parliament/ at Stevenston, near great Torrington,/in Devonshire,/England

Postmarked: IV 21

Franked: Franco Paris

Endorsed: b. To Coll: Rolle./Of ye old Temple at Dijon: red wafer E.

TO HENRY ROLLE

Lyons,
June 21, 1731

Dear Sir,

I wrote, the Lord knows how long ago, to know how to direct to you in
London by your cousin of New College and my good deputy to the
University of Oxford. The beginning of this month I received a letter from
him by which I found mine had miscarried. You see, Sir, the reason of so
long a silence which I assure you has been disagreeable to me, though it
may have saved you the trouble of a long letter so much sooner than it is
now likely to get to you. Because I don't know how to direct to you in
town I must venture to send this for Stevenston, where I hope it may find
you with all the health and happiness about you that I sincerely wish you.

   We have left Dijon some time, and are got to Lyons. In hopes of a letter
I shall trouble you with the directions below. Dijon was a good handsome
town, but had I been a man of curiosity I should have been terribly baulked
there, for it affords very few things worth observing. I think the most
material is an heathen temple, or rather half a one, for part of it is destroyed
and a good Christian church built in its room. They say 'twas a Pantheon,
and swear till they are black in the face that 'tis like the Rotonda at Rome.
That it is a Rotonda in general is very true. There is scarce any light in
it but what falls from the top of the dome, which is raised on three rows of
pillars, two above ground and one in the vault.[1] All the rest of the temple
is full of pillars—it seems a confusion of them when you first come in, but
after minding them, you find that they all stand very regularly and all
humour the little circle of them in the middle under the dome. That is a

circle of eight only, and managed so that the rising up to the dome on the inside is all an octagon. I have taken down the ichnography of all of them, and, when we come back, may have an opportunity of showing it to you some time or other, if you should ever think it worth while.[2] For my part, I have not so much regard for the old Gauls, and am very glad that we are got into a place where there are a great many marks of the old Romans still left, which I may trouble you with another time.

I'm particularly obliged to you, good Sir, for your account of our parliamentary duels etc. 'Tis what we know little of here and 'tis extremely agreeable at present to hear the news of one's dear country. For my part, I'm here in a great deal of ignorance as to what passes among you. Some time ago they told us that everything was assuredly made up, and that 'twould be peace all round. Now we hear of twenty men of war and expeditions again.[3] I should never care to be a politician, but methinks I should be very glad to know what you are about. I beg my most hearty humble services to your brother[4] and cousin when you see them, and am

Your most obliged humble servant

J. Spence

À Monsieur / Monsieur Spence / avec Milord Middlesex / au Palais Royal / à Lyon / Par Paris

HENRY ROLLE (1708–50) of Stevenstone in St. Giles-in-the-Wood, Devon., educ. at Winchester (1723), matric. New College, Oxford (1725), on Apr. 30, 1731, cr. D.C.L. at Oxford. 1730–41 Tory M.P. for Devonshire, 1741–8 for Barnstaple. In 1730 he succeeded his father in the Stevenstone estate, 1748 cr. Lord Rolle, Baron of Stevenstone. He was cousin and patron of Edward Rolle. Spence's letters to him are chiefly on antiquarian subjects.

1. 'The baptistery in the vault said to be of the sixth century. 'Tis the figure of a person standing half way as in water (?) in a large round pelvis like the top of a large well: he seems about fifteen or sixteen years old. One pours the water on him and another lays his hand on his breast' (*Nbk.* 1 27ʳ). It was des-

troyed about 1750.

2. A crude sketch of the crypt appears in Spence's *Notebook* 1 27ʳ.

3. Friction with France increased during the early part of 1731. 'Letters from *Dunkirk* advise, that on the Report of the *English* having fitted out a large Squadron for the Sea, several Troops were arrived there to garrison or fortify that Place' (*Gent. Mag.,* June, p. 270).

4. John Rolle Walter (1714?–79), educ. New College, Oxford. On Sept. 2, 1729, aged fifteen, suc. to estates of his uncle Sir Robert Walter, and took the name of Walter; to the estates of his brother Henry, 1750. M.P. for Exeter 1754–76, Devon. 1776–9 (Namier and Brooke, *The Commons 1754–1790* [1964], III, 605).

12

Source: Egerton 2234 ff. 20–21

Addressed: To/Mrs Spence/near Colebrook Street/in Winton/Hants.

Postmarked: 1[ ]/IV

Endorsed: b. Acc^t^ of our Terrace/by the water; &c./ Description of Lyons.

Lyons,
June 16 ⟨5⟩, 1731

⟨Dear Mother,

I received yours safe here at⟩ Lyons ⟨which⟩ is a much more agreeable city than any I ever saw as to its views. The people are chiefly merchants, and so we see very little of them. However, the place does not want for its diversions. We have a very good play-house, and the opera (which had failed for some time) is just going to be revived.

The river Saône, that attended us great part of our way hither, runs quite through the town, and my chamber opens upon a terrace on the banks of it. The city is built in a very particular and very pleasing manner: one part of it rises all along a hill on the other side the Saône, the other (which is the greater) lies on this side, between my river and the Rhône, which latter runs as violently as the other does slowly till they meet together about a quarter of a mile below our house. Just before my chamber-door, over the terrace, is a shed covered all with vines, and looks over the river on the houses rising up the hill on the other side quite to the top. The houses are intermixed with gardens and little vineyards and regular walks of trees which all together make a prospect that is extremely delightful. The river is full of fish, and we have always angles in my room to fish from the terrace, which is a story high above the water. With all these advantages you won't be surprised to hear that your son is turned a fisher, though I assure you he can't brag much of any great feats he has done that way as yet.

⟨If John North knew how I was situated, he would hardly be so much concerned for me.[1] 'Tis, however, vexation enough to me that I lost the pleasure of his company, [on] the last return of money, and indeed he and I were in a fair way of growing as dear friends as ever I knew in my life. My hearty service to him, wherever you see him or hear of him again.

I'm sorry to hear that my mistress is so absolutely lost to me; but now Hetty by the death of her second brother is grown an heiress; I suppose she will soon see herself at the head of seven or eight hundred pound a year, a family coach, two old horses and a country squire. 'Tis a great concern to me that I must wear the willow so soon, but I'm resolved to fall deeply in love with somebody else as soon as ever I get five miles on the other side of Dover, for I don't care much to bring home a wife from France or Italy, though I were sure of your consent to the match.

Any bookseller is certainly a rascal that pretends to fling out things of any kind about my old friend Stephen Duck in my name.[2] I don't know what those people that deal in spoiling of paper are doing in England, but whatever 'tis I wash my hands of it. Whoever did it, if it can be of any service to honest Stephen any way, I should not be sorry for the scandal that I may undergo for it.⟩

We have just by us here a noble square, which in these towns is usually called the Place Royale. There are two very fine sides to it: on the third are the public walks[3] ⟨not unlike ours by the churchyard at Winchester⟩ and the other consists of merchants' houses. In the middle is a fine statue of Louis XIV on horseback.[4] The pedestal is all of marble: on one side of it is the figure of a river goddess representing ⟨my favourite river⟩ the Saône, and on the other that of a river god for her husband, the Rhône.[5] They often put me in mind of the Thames and Isis.

⟨Though we are not much acquainted in the town, we make it up with English all in the same house. The Duke of Kingston was here with a large retinue when we came, and continues here still.[6] A week after us we had Mr. Denny and a grandson of your friend Lady Shuttleworth[7] came hither from Dijon. Yesterday, as we were taking the air, we met with two coaches full of English—a lady and three or four of her little children, two of which were cuddled under her wings in the same coach. I suppose they had been at Montpellier for their health. The highroad we were then passing had mulberry-trees growing on each side of the road like rows of elms with us. This is a great place for the silk manufacture, and mulberry-trees are very welcome here. My hearty service to my sister and all friends. I am ever

Your dutiful and affectionate

J: Spence.

I received Mr. Wavil's before I had finished this. I beg my thanks to him and my particular service to him and his. I have received no letter from Mr. Cheyney or Mr. Barton since the beginning of April.⟩[8]

---

1. Neither he nor 'my mistress ... Hetty' has been identified.

2. This refers to the recently published *Account of Stephen Duck* (see *Letter* 8 n. 7). The publisher says in the preface: "'Tis not material to tell you very minutely how the following Letter came into my hands: As to what is necessary, I can take upon me to say, that it was really written by Mr. *Spence*, and that this is a true Copy of it. The Author, who is now Abroad, I hope will pardon me, for Endeavouring to make us able still to enjoy thus much of his

Conversation here at Home.' Austin Wright (pp. 45–7) has shown that, despite this disingenuous denial, the *Account* was written by Spence.

3. The much-admired Bellecour. 'There is to be a fountain in each of the square grass-plats on each side of it. It should have faced the street to the Place of the Jacobins more exactly' (*Nbk.* 1 28ʳ). For a contemporary account, see André Clapasson, *Description de la ville de Lyon* (Lyon, 1741), pp. 4–6.

4. Designed by Desjardins and cast in bronze (1674) by the Kellers, the statue was formally installed at Lyons in 1715.

5. The two river-statues by the brothers Coustou are now in front of the Hôtel de Ville.

6. Evelyn Pierrepont (1711–73), D. of Kings-ton-upon-Hull, M. of Dorchester, travelled with his tutor, Dr. Nathan Hickman.

7. Catherine Clarke (1667–1727), dau. of Henry Clarke, President of Magdalen College, m. in 1682 Sir Richard Shuttleworth (1666–87) of Gawthorpe (Foster, *Pedigrees . . . Lancashire*, 1873). On Mr. Denny and young Shuttleworth, see *Letter* 9 n. 3.

8. Thomas Cheyney (1694–1760) of Wells, Winchester Fellow (1711–19), M.A. New College 1718, D.D. 1732; later Dean of Lincoln (1744) and of Winchester (1747). 'Barton' was probably Philip Barton (b. 1696), L.L.D., Fellow of Winchester College 1724–65, who married Warden Bigg's widow in 1740 (A. K. Cook, *About Winchester College* [1917], p. 220), or Stephen Barton (b. 1701), Winchester scholar in 1712 (Kirby, pp. 221, 224).

---

*13

Source: Egerton 2234 ff. 24–25

Addressed: To/Mʳˢ Spence

Endorsed: *b.* The Ceremony of ma-/king a Nun./ Making of a Nun, at Lyons.

Lyons,
⟨Friday⟩ July 13 ⟨2⟩, 1731

⟨Dear Mother,⟩

The difference of receiving letters hither or at Dijon is so small that I hope we may keep up our correspondence as brisk as ever. This is a very agreeable place, and is made more so ⌈by the number of English in it. ⟨In the next best house in the town—for you must know we are in the best— is at present an Irish nobleman with his company[1] and a Scotch baronet, one Sir William Stuart, with his.[2] In our street is arrived Mr. Solicitor Talbot's son⌉ and Mr. Thomson, the poet.⟩[3]

Wednesday last, just after dinner, a messenger came in and said that a nun was to profess that afternoon. Though 'twas then the hour appointed, I had the good luck to get a ticket for two. I ran immediately to Mr. Talbot ⟨for we are got greatly acquainted here⟩ and offered to introduce him. The ceremony was quite on the other end of the town. However, we flung ourselves immediately into a boat, and bid the woman—for, as an Irishman might say, we are served here almost wholly by she-watermen—row with all the haste she could for the monastery. We had the good luck to get there half a quarter of an hour before the affair began. The chapel was all filled with rows of chairs, a great number of ladies were ranged very regularly in several of them to see the sight, and we were showed to seats in the best part of the good company. They are infinitely civil to strangers in France, and we had room made for us to see everything to the best advantage.

The lady who professed was not in the chapel, but behind a grate that looked into it. The ceremony opened with a long dull sermon spoke with as much action and affectation as would furnish out a whole company of strollers in England. The preacher talked of the vanity of life and the vanity of the world, and called the young lady who was all this while invisible to us (for she was behind a terrible grate and we all turned toward the preacher) 'the new spouse of Jesus Christ'—though to me everything looked very dull for a wedding day.

After the sermon three other priests moved toward the grate, and sat in seats prepared close by it for them. The middle one was dressed in a rich cope of cloth of gold, the other two on each side of him in their surplices. All three had ruffles and laced bosoms, which is much the fashion among the clergy here. I was close by the priests and leaned with one hand on the grate. The room behind it was a sort of private chapel for the nuns. The poor lady that was to be sacrificed stood on a step within the grate, with only a white dress on her head and a vast taper lighted in her hand, and two nuns on each side of her. The other nuns were all ranged round the walls, each with a less taper and their black veils hanging quite over their faces, on each side, quite down to the lady abbess, who sat in the middle at the bottom of the room. There were several regular questions and answers passed between the middle priest in his fine cope and the poor young lady who kept her eyes wholly on the ground and answered always in a very melancholy tone. When she had sufficiently assured him of her being resolved to quit the world, she knelt down, and then laid herself on a thing like a coffin, and the two nuns on each side of her, with two others, flung the pall over her. Then all the nuns sang a hymn, after which she rose, made some few promises to the priest, had the veil, a crucifix etc. fixed to her, and was led out of the room.

When she returned 'twas with a very brisk air, without her face being hid, and a coronet of flowers on her head. She kneeled down before the grate for some time, then rose and made three very low bows to the priests: went bowing with her taper all down the room, bowed to the lady abbess and kissed her, and then each of the sisters with a low bow first to each. She then returned toward the grate: the nuns went out two and two, bowing and bending their tapers, and last of all she and her two assistants followed in the same manner, bowing half way to the ground and sinking their tapers. This concluded the ceremony, and though I was so eager to see it I left the place with more melancholy and a greater oppression upon my spirits than I have felt ever since I left you.

⟨Here I thought the ceremony was over, but the best thing belonging to it was to come, for, as we were strangers, the father of the young lady came up to us, begged us to go into the monastery with him to wish the young lady joy and to eat some sweetmeats. When we came in, he desired me to drink some of their wine and assured us 'twas some of the best of that country, for (says he) 'tis what the ladies keep for their own drinking. 'Twas fit for them, for 'twas extremely good. I was willing to give you the whole account, even to trifles, because 'tis a thing you might have more curiosity than ordinary to hear. I have wrote to my brother Rolle. I beg my love to my sister and service to all friends, and am

Your most dutiful and affectionate

Jo: Spence⟩

1. Probably Sir Edward Bellew (d. Oct. 1741) of Bermeath and of Castle Bellew, who was to succeed Sir John Bellew, his father, on July 23, 1734, as 3d baronet. He died 'in Flanders, on his road from Paris to Ireland' (W. Playfair, *Baronetage of Ireland* [1811], App. lvi–lvii).

2. Probably Sir William Stuart (d. 1777) of Colinton, co. Edinburgh; succeeded to the baronetcy on the death of his maternal grandfather (1722?). He resided chiefly at Venice, married a Venetian lady, and died *s.p.* at Paris, Dec. 6, 1777 (*Complete Baronetage*, IV, 436–7).

3. William Talbot (1710–82), 2d son of Sir Charles Talbot (1685–1737), Solicitor-General; 1733 Lord Chancellor. In 1734 young Talbot was raised to the peerage as Baron Talbot of Hensoe, Glamorganshire. The bracketed passage has been emended to 'to me by some friends of mine who arrived lately; and in particular Mr. Talbot (son of the Solicitor-General'. James Thomson (1700–48) accompanied young Talbot as a tutor. They had left England about the same time as Spence, but spent the winter and spring at Paris, and were on their way through Avignon to Rome (L. Morel, *James Thomson* [Paris, 1895], pp. 97–8). 'When Thomson published his Winter in 1726,' writes Joseph Warton, 'it lay a long time neglected, till Mr. Spence made honourable mention of it in his Essay on the Odyssey ... from this circumstance, an intimacy commenced between the critic and the poet' (*Works of Pope* [1797], I, 236).

*14

Source:	Egerton 2234 ff. 26–27
Addressed:	To/Mrs Spence
Endorsed:	*b.* Of ye River there; &/the Ladies bathing in it./Ladies at ye Bridge.

Lyons,
August 10 ⟨July 30⟩, 1731

⟨Dear Mother,

I received your letter yesterday, and this I hope will set out for you tomorrow. Beside being a very good boy, I write this with the more dispatch and beg you would answer it as soon after receiving it as you can, because we shall set out for Italy about the middle of next month. I hope to let you know in my next what particular route we are to take, which is not yet fixed.⟩

The poor nun, whose execution we were at, looked very much like a dying creature. She was extremely pale and had a face that was neither handsome nor agreeable. My acquaintance as yet in the nunneries does not reach far enough to say whether they are generally pretty. I believe for the most part they are not. If there are two daughters in a family and one of them to be a nun, the parents generally choose out the least handsome, because the other will be more ⌜fit to scuffle in the world for⌝[1] a husband. What may make people generally think that nuns are pretty may be this. In most of their houses they have needlework and little trinkets to sell, and when strangers come to the grate they always send the prettiest noviciate they have to offer their ware: there she stands like a milliner, and the prettiest milliners, you know, have always the best custom.

I ought to let you know the progress of my dress and by what degrees I creep into the habit of a gentleman. Ever since we have been at Lyons, my hair (which had six weeks' growth on my forehead and temples at Dijon) has been combed back on a light brown natural wig. It did not comply so well with the mode at first, but every day my barber persecutes it with an ounce of pomatum and then plasters it down with half a pound of powder. After the operation I walk out with what passes for a head of hair very well frosted. My coat is a light camlet[2] with silver buttons, a green silk waistcoat sufficiently daubed with silver lace, and I seem upon the brink of having a pair of stockings to it with silver clocks. With all this, I shall look upon myself to be as much a gentleman as that half of the gentlemen in England who are only so from the clothes they wear.

I have often told you of the fine river that runs under my window. Between my writing and reading in the morning it furnishes me with perpetual diversion. Beside the river itself, which has always boats upon it going and coming, just on my right hand, is a bridge over it that wants but very few yards of being as long as our famous bridge at Rochester, and there is always a flux of people and carriages upon it. On the river we have often a larger sort of boats which go and come weekly from the cities that lie up or down the Saône. They call them water-coaches, and indeed they use them just as we do our stagecoaches in England. They bring sometimes thirty or forty passengers at a time and they are such an odd mixture of people that 'tis very agreeable to be at their arrival. For the little boats and scullers, they are almost always rowed by women, and yet we don't abound so much with water-language here as on the Thames, which, considering the difference of the sexes as to the faculty of talking, surprises me very much.

The other day we saw a boy fishing for swallows on my bridge. Perhaps you may think I have got the knack of a traveller, but 'tis literally true. They bait for them not with meat but feathers: 'tis at the time the [pretty?] creatures make their nests; the feather waves about in the air, three or four of the swallows will sometimes skim at it after one another, and if either of them has the luck of snapping the feather 'tis ten to one but she snaps the hook too, and so is flung up on the top of the bridge.

The boats are not so neat and good as ours, and sometimes they use only a single board to pass the water. I have seen three men go down the stream on one. They stood on it very steady, two of them helped to row and guide it, and the middle man was playing upon a flute, very much at his ease. Their boys use these boards too, particularly when they first learn to swim. You will sometimes see five or six of them swimming round one, and as either of them is tired, he gets [up] and rests upon the board. 'Tis a little floating island for them that attends them wherever they please.[3]

About a month ago, as I was passing in a boat to a bridge beyond us, where the water is not above breast-high under the arches, and you may imagine how much I was surprised (for I had heard nothing of the custom) to see the arch I was going under one half full of boats, and the other almost full of ladies up to the chin in water.[4] When the weather is hot they do it to cool themselves; they have alway[s some]thing on, like our women at the bath, but they don't at all shriek to have men among them. Some of them sit on great stones that are in the water ⟨up to the chin all⟩. You see them in little parties: here three or four heads chatting together, and a gentleman perhaps in the circle with them; others in couples or threes; and there perhaps two or three holding their children in their arms, with only their

little heads and a silk cap and feather above water. They all look mighty
serene and well pleased, and 'tis no manner of affront to pass close by them
or to stop the boat to look upon them. ⟨'Tis really a very odd and very
agreeable sight.

⟨Your most dutiful⟩

1. Emended to 'more likely to get'.

2. 'A kind of stuff originally made by a
mixture of silk and camel's hair; it is now made
with wool and silk' (Johnson's *Dictionary*).

3. 'At *Lions* in *France*' Spence also saw a 'Sort
of Justs upon the Water. The Champions stand
as firmly as they are able, on the Prows of two
Boats, with a Shield in their left Hands, and a
blunted Spear in their right. There is an equal
Number of Rowers in each of the Boats, who
drive them on with Impetuosity. The two
Combatants charge each other with their

Spears; and often both, but almost always one
of them is driven backward on the Shock;
either down into his Boat, or (which often
happens) into the Water; which latter makes
one of the principal Parts in this odd Sort of
Diversion' (Dodsley, *Fugitive Pieces* [1761], I,
74 n.).

4. In 1729 Penton had drawn Spence's
attention to this continental curiosity: 'The
women at Geneva go into the lake publicly: in
one particular like the French ladies' (*Obs.* No.
1313).

15

Source: Extra-illustrated copy of *Anecdotes*, ed.
Singer, 1820, Huntington Library (RB
131213). Printed by Singer, pp. 441–2

Endorsed: (*by Singer*) No 25. Mr E. Rolle to Mr. Spence

EDWARD ROLLE TO SPENCE

August 12 [1731 O.S.]

You can't imagine, dear Jo, what a figure it gives one in Devonshire, where
I now am, to receive a letter with that outlandish mark upon it.[1] I am
vastly obliged to the good old lady for having our correspondence so much
at heart, and to yourself for so readily complying with her. An epitome of
Oxford do you call what you have with you? I could hardly have thought
Alma Mater had so many children abroad, take all Europe together. Don't
so many English faces tempt you sometimes to an English conversation? I
can hardly conceive a dozen true Britons abroad together, without their
allowing themselves now and then an hour's chat in a language they are at
no pain to talk in. Is it not *timide verba intermissa*, etc.?[2] You must certainly
relapse sometimes by stealth into a few snatches of English.

I am with Mr. Rolle now, who desires his services to you.[3] The sight of
your letter revived in him for a time his old affection for travelling: his last
resolves were to spend a month or two next spring in France, and he hath

promised I should be with him. *Est-il-possible*, I should be able to think with the least probability of a thing I never durst do more than admire before! As incredible things have happened, and perhaps some years since you as little thought of it yourself. What think you of the old gypsy? The seeing one of that order lately put me in mind of the intercourse you had with one at Oxford once: don't you remember, she foretold your going abroad precisely! One would almost really be inclined to think they did not always talk at hazard. For my part, I don't think it unlikely I shall live to see you a Mediagoras (was not that the hard word she gave your preferment?).[4] You won't be so unmerciful as to expect any account of new books from hence, where the talk never rises above the common country topics, and where I never see a book beyond two or three little travelling authors I brought with me, wrote every one of them the t'other side of Anno Domini.

I forgot to mention in my last that of the £200 per annum left to the university, £20 per annum is added to the Poetry Professorship.[5] I don't suppose it will be any advantage to it in your time, though I don't know whether the estate hangs upon more than one life.

New College, a month since, was worth four Gentlemen Commoners and Sir William Fitch under Mr. Price.[6] Mr. Brideoake hath one Gentleman Commoner and the others are with Mr. Morrison. He will in all probability be well stocked soon, he is in favour with Dr. Burton and the Warden,[7] 'tis thought rather in his interest. There were rooms taken for two more, and it does not seem unlikely from such a sudden flow that we should have our share again.

⟨For God's sake, how came you to think of taking such an affection to a bog-house? . . .[8] Farewell, dear Jo,

Yours affectionately

E. Rolle⟩

1. Spence wrote to young Rolle before July 13. The letter is not known to be extant. The 'old lady' is Mrs. Spence.

2. Ovid *Met.* i. 746.

3. Henry Rolle, his cousin and patron, from whose estate at Stevenstone the letter was evidently written. 'Your letter' refers to *Letter* 11.

4. Perhaps derived from 'me' 'de' 'agor', 'I strike a beginning.'

5. This would have increased Spence's stipend of £180 to £200. His ten-year term expired in 1738.

6. William Fytch (ca. 1714–36) of Kent, suc. to the baronetcy 1720; matric. at New College June 2, 1731, M.A. 1733. 'Mr. Price', 'Mr. Brideoake', and 'Mr. Morrison' no doubt kept boarders.

7. John Burton, Headmaster of Winchester College 1724–66. In 1727 he opened a new dormitory and later, not content with his boarding-house, founded the 'Commoners'. He apparently never got a sufficient number of boarders to compensate him for his outlay (T. F. Kirby, *Annals of Winchester College* [1892], pp. 132–4). Dr. Henry Bigg, of Chilton Foliat in Wiltshire, was Warden 1729–40.

8. There follows Rolle's advice to Spence to 'write verses on horseback' and a poetical 'smattering of your distemper' in sixty-two lines, entitled 'To Mr. Spence with Virgil's *Georgics*'. Singer crossed out this part of Rolle's letter in pencil, with a note: 'All to be omitted.'

Source:	Egerton 2234 ff. 28–29
Addressed:	To/Henry Rolle Esqʳ./Member of Parliament,/ at Stevenston, near great Torrington,/ Devon./en Angleterre
Postmarked:	SE 1
Franked:	*Franco Paris*
Endorsed:	*b.* To Col: Rolle. Of the Tauribolium at Lyons. *red wafer*

16

TO HENRY ROLLE

Lyons,
September 3, [1731]

Dear Sir,

Lyons, though a very agreeable place otherwise, has been very fatal to me for letters. I have scarce received any here, except from my mother and my good deputy. I designed to have troubled you with one long ago if the post was so good as to let it pass. 'Twas dated the 16ᵗʰ of June,[1] and was an account of an antiquity, the most famous thing we had to see at Dijon. I shall venture, whatever luck that might have, to give you now an account of our most entire piece of antiquity here at Lyons. 'Tis what we call a 'tauribole'. The most learned man in this good city is a Jesuit who has printed an account of it, and to whom I have been introduced.[2]

There was a particular ceremony of old (he tells me) of making a priest very terrible and very venerable. A pit was dug in the earth, the priest went into it, and then it was covered with boards bored full of holes. Over this they killed a bull, so that his blood might fall chiefly on the middle of the boards. As it ran through, the priest did his utmost to catch as much of the blood as he could on his robes, his breast, his face, in his mouth and in his ears, and when he was well soaked he came out, walked majestically through the people and went off sanctified for the space of twenty years. This was not the only good effect of it, for through him they often used to bless at the same time the emperor and perhaps one of the colonies of Rome. In such a case, if the ceremony was performed at Rome, they sent ⟨a messenger with⟩ an account of it and the *head* of the bull to the colony—I suppose *actually* to convey the benefit of the sacrifice to them. Such is the thing I speak of: 'tis the memorial of the tauribole engraved on stone found here, with the bull's skull and horns, about twenty-seven years ago. This account, I own, is pretty tedious, but 'twill be more so before I have done, for I am just going to give you the inscription all at large. 'Tis this:

TAURIBOLIO MATRIS D. M. ID.
QUOD FACTUM EST EX IMPERIO MATRIS D.
DEUM.
PRO SALUTE IMPERATORIS CAES. T. AELI
HADRIANI ANTONINI AUG. PII P. P. +
LIBERORUMQ EJUS;
ET STATÛS COLONIAE LUGDUN.
L. AEMILIUS CARPUS IIIIII VIR AUG. ITEM
DENDROPHORUS
VIRES EXCEPIT ET A VATICANO TRANS-
TULIT. ARA & BUCRANIUM
SUO IMPENDIO CONSECRAVIT.
SACERDOTE
Q. SAMNIO SECUNDO AB XV. VIRIS
OCCABO & CORONÂ EXORNATO.
CUI SANCTISSIMUS ORDO LUGDUNENS:
PERPETUITATEM SACERDOTI DECREVIT
APP: ANNIO ATILIO BRADUA T. CLODIO VIBIO
VARO COS.
L.D.D.D.

Between the lines 'Dendrophorus' and 'Vires excepit' etc. is the figure of a bull's head in mezzo-relievo, a ram's head on the left side (for 'tis on a stone in the shape of an altar), and the sacrificing knife on the right with this inscription: CUJUS MESONYCTIUM FACTUM EST V. ID. DEC.

The ceremony this inscription relates was performed A.D. 160, and my friend Père Colonia pretends it to be the most ancient of the kind that we have any account of. He has quoted in his treatise of it a very particular account of the whole ceremony from one of the Latin poets about the fourth century, but just now I have forgot his name.[3] I could plague you on at this rate through a quire or two of paper, but I believe you will excuse me for this haste, and so I beg to be ever / Sir,

Your most obedient

J. Spence

I beg my very humble service to your brother and the Captain, if with you. I wrote to him the 19th of July, but directed to Oxford. You will pardon my enclosing one for him now, because this is so sure a method of finding him. I heartily wish you joy of your first sessions in Parliament,[4] and had I been among the clergy of Devonshire I should have been very glad to have saluted you on your return from the Senate as a P.P.+[5]

1. Spence's *Letter* 11 is dated 'June 21'.

2. Père Dominique de Colonia (1660–1741), the learned librarian of the Jesuits' College at Lyons, author of several anti-Jansenist treatises and archeological studies, among them *Dissertation sur un monument taurobolique découvert à Lyon* (1705), later incorporated into the first volume of his *Histoire littéraire de la ville de Lyon* (1728–30).

3. Prudentius *Peristephanon liber* X. 1008–50.

4. Henry Rolle was Tory M.P. for Devonshire. The Parliament was to meet on Aug. 26, but was twice prorogued. Next sessions were held on Jan. 13, 1731/2.

5. An allusion to the P.P. (*pater patriae*) in the inscription.

*17

Source: Egerton 2234 ff. 30–31

Lyons,
September 4 ⟨August 24⟩, 1731

⟨Dear Mother,

I don't know whether we may not stay here long enough to receive another letter; at least the best way will be to direct your next hither as usual, and if we go, orders will be left here how to send it after us.⟩ The violence of the heats in Sicily need not have alarmed you for us: we have had very good luck here, and indeed at times (I dare say) a much cooler summer than yours at Winchester. We came hither about the middle of May: the last week of that month and the first of June were so extreme hot that, if it had gone on increasing in proportion, we must have kept in entirely all day, or been roasted to death. But the convenience is that we have a northerly wind, which we call the *bise* that travels through the snow on the top of the Alps and cools the air here and keeps it from taking fire. These cold breezes have their inconvenience too, for sometimes after a day that has been much hotter than any I ever felt in England, the next day comes a wind that puts us all at once in the middle of December. We actually had a great Christmas fire one day in the dining room at the end of June, and I had one here in my chamber the 24th of August. At present neither the cold nor the heats are so extreme. In all this trial of one's constitution I thank heaven I have not been out of order any one day since I came to this place.

The ladies here would really frighten you to see how very unconcerned they are in their watery situation. The same ⌈impudence⌉[1] runs through them all. If they were prettier, this would take away a great deal from their agreeableness, but the misfortune is that Lyons is not a city of fine faces.

Though 'tis reckoned the second city for size in France, and is certainly one of the best peopled, I dare say that Winchester could beat them for beauties. I own I have a great regard for my own dear country, but I believe I may say this without any manner of partiality for the fair ladies of the capital of Hampshire.

The cool days that we have had intermixed with our hot have given me, beside our other expeditions, very often the opportunity of taking my walks. One day in particular I was resolved for a long one, to see the aquaeducts that in the time of the Romans brought fine water from above twenty miles distant hence, quite to the city. 'Twas a channel for water raised up into the air on vast arches of stonework. The remains of them are still considerable.

I set out at six o'clock in the morning with a priest. As soon as we got out of town we met with a great piece of it of ten or twelve arches, then it ceased, and at intervals we found traces of it again. About four miles from the town we came to a place that seemed formerly to have been the channel of a vast river, but there was not any water left in it. This the arches crossed, and remained all along the channel of it very thick and very high.[2] On farther, about half a mile off on the hill, we could see another range of it that seemed to consist of seventy or eighty arches all together.[3] However, we thought it time to turn for Lyons again, but as we were for making new discoveries we took a round on the left hand towards an old Roman castle that appeared on a hill. We walked all along through the bed of the river for a great way and then through meads that led us to some odd dark walks, the most romantic I think I ever saw in my life. The place was so agreeable that we wandered about and lost our great path. At last we found out a meadow at the back of a gentleman's house.

Everybody is obliging in France, so we knocked without any scruple at the gates to pass through and to be put into the right way. When the gate opened, it discovered an odd figure of a man, very much like our country squires, with five dogs about him and a hunting pole in his hand. He was the master of the castle. We told him our case, and he was so obliging that he would make us enter the palace and take a refreshment with him. His servants were all abroad, some at work and some at mass, and so he was forced to take care of us himself. Never was a man more bustling or more obliging. 'Twas between nine and ten in the morning, a very good time for people to breakfast that had taken so long a walk. Our good gentleman brought us everything as fast as he could, by degrees. He spread the table himself and laid the napkins. After that he disappeared for a considerable time ⟨for indeed the poor man had enough to do⟩. At last he returned with a very large plate of ham that he had cut very nicely into slices, and another of Bologna sausages: they were set off with pickles and anchovies. His next journey produced a bottle of very good Burgundy. He set us each a glass, and then we had nothing to do but to fall to eating and drinking, which we did very much in earnest.

After the first heat we began to come a little into a more regular conversation, and 'twas then that we found out that our friend was an old officer. He had served almost all the war, and both against King William and the Duke of Marlborough. Beside a number of wounds, which he showed us, he had twice been taken prisoner and had once been set out to be sent as such to London, but met the day before he was to go with a lucky exchange of one of our officers for him. He got enough by the war to purchase a very pretty estate, and now lives in that delicious old place where, as he told us, he passes almost all his time in walking or reading. He is a very sensible man, speaks very honourably of the English, and when our bottle of Burgundy was out, gave us another, so that we came off very chippant and very much in love with him and his dwelling place. He was very pressing that we should stay and dine with him; but his breakfast (though 'tis a very common one in France) was so new to me that I thought it might pass for breakfast and dinner too. So we took our leave with many thanks and arrived safe here by twelve o'clock.

---

1. Emended to 'boldness'.
2. From Mt. Pilatus to Fourvière, where the Forum and Trajan's palace had been situated.

3. 'That built by Marc Antony [runs] from the Gate of St. Irénée over the pretended old bed of the Saône and up the hill' (*Nbk.* 1 27ᵛ).

18

Source: Egerton 2234 ff. 32–33
Addressed: To/Mr Spence/att the African House,/in Leaden-Hall-Street/London/en Angleterre
Postmarked: SE 27
Franked: Franco Paris
Endorsed: b. Eagerness to go into I-/taly./Going for Geneva:

Lyon,
September 25 ⟨14⟩, 1731

⟨Dear Mother,

Yesterday the Duke of Kingston parted from hence for Geneva, today some of our gentlemen of this house are to set out for Marseilles, and in a few days Lord Middlesex will leave the place too. My Lord's next brother is come abroad since we left England, and is at present at Lausanne in Switzerland.¹ So we intend for Geneva, and are to go thence to Lausanne (which is but thirty mile) to pay him a two or three days' visit. He is one of the best-natured creatures in the world. I had the pleasure of being with him at London, and 'twill be a greater pleasure to see him here, for there never was any Lord I believe more humble and obliging than Lord John.[2] We only touch upon Switzerland and shall not stay in that country above three weeks in all, and are to go thence to Turin, where the King of Sardinia has a very polite court. The way we shall take afterwards is yet uncertain, for we don't yet know whether we shall go to Rome before Christmas or not. After Christmas my Lord is determined to be all the carnival at Venice. As we shall be wandering about Italy till we fix either there or at Rome, it will be necessary to settle one place for my friends in England to direct to me at, and we shall send notice there and orders to have them sent to us in our different stages. Venice is as yet the best I can think of, and your next letter please to direct à Monsieur / Monsieur Spence / avec Milord Middlesex / recommandé à Monsr. John Pommer / Banquier / à Venise en Italie.⟩ Not one word of any kind relating either to religion or politics ought to be in any letter sent me into Italy.[3] Travellers, if they are silent in those two respects, are perfectly well received there in all others. We go there to see the people, their different governments, their buildings, statues, pictures, antiquities, and country, and 'tis a happiness that I long for with the earnestness of a great boy.

As I never quarrelled with anybody in my life for being of a different religion from me and never pretended to be anything like a politician, I can be absolutely reserved on both those heads without any balk to my inclinations. ⟨One of my best acquaintance here was a Jesuit,[4] and a very agreeable man he is, and I am recommended to another at Rome[5] by Mr. Ramsay who wrote the *Travels of Cyrus* that I left with you.[6] I have had several letters from him (Mr. Ramsay) of late; he is particularly obliging to me.[7] He lives at Paris, and perhaps you will be glad to hear that he is lately made governor to a young French Duke there and has a good pension settled on him for life.[8]

I have just brought in to me a picture of the town of Lyons, very large, in black and white. I got another of Dijon while there and intend to do the same at Venice, Rome and all the considerable places where we make any considerable stay, on purpose to bring them home to you, and to talk over the places together.⟩ About five weeks hence we shall pass the Alps. 'Tis a thing made ten times more of in England than it is in reality. Travellers love to look big and talk extravagantly of the things they have done. To pass the largest mountain we go over will take up but four hours, and we are carried there all the way in chairs by men ⟨as we intend to be, two to each, like your London chairmen, and we set jog-it-a-jog all the way without trouble or danger, for⟩ we shall pass it before the time of the snows

[fa]lling, which is the chief thing that makes that road so dangerous in the depth of the winter.

⟨P.S. Sept. 27, Thursday. Saturday we set out [for] Geneva. Today the French ambassador for Rome[9] is expected here in his way to Italy; 'tis very likely we shall have the pleasure of seeing him at the play tonight. I beg my service to my sister and all friends, and am ever

Your affectionate and dutiful

J. Spence

Please to get Mr. Wavil to take a copy of the directions to me. I hope he and all his good family are well. If he would communicate the direction to Mr. Cheyney, Mr. Barton, and the schoolmaster, as he happens to see them, it would be very obliging.⟩

1. John Philip Sackville (1713–65), 2d son of Lionel Sackville, 1st D. of Dorset; equerry to the Queen; M.P. for Tamworth 1734, 1741.

2. Lord Middlesex characterized his brother in an 'epitaph' preserved in the Spence Papers:

> Beneath this Stone
> Lies restless John;
> The second Hopes of Sackville's Race:
> How strange that he
> Should ever be
> Confin'd three minutes to a place!

Later in life he was 'plongé périodiquement dans une tristesse accablante' (L. Marlow, *Sackville of Drayton* [1948], pp. 75–6).

3. After the sudden arrest of Victor Amadeus (see *Letters* 19, 21) there may have been grounds for caution.

4. Père Colonia (see *Letter* 16).

5. Jean-François Foucquet (1663–1740) who had returned to Rome from a mission in China. See *Obs.* Nos. 1406–15a.

6. Spence had met the Chevalier Andrew Michael Ramsay (1686?–1743) in 1729, when Ramsay was in England on several errands, including the promotion of his successful romance *The Travels of Cyrus* (*Obs.* Nos. 1206–1301).

7. Ramsay's letters to Spence are not known to be extant, except for one fragment, dated Sept. 14, 1731: 'I have read most of the Italian dramatic compositions, but am no great admirer of their stage; neither is that kind of reading the properest for learning the beauties of their amiable language. Boccaccio, Bembo, and Monsignor della Casa ought to be your particular study, and by all means don't begin with Bentivoglio. His language is altogether frenchified by his stay at Brussels and Paris, and though beautiful in its kind, yet far inferior to the others who are all of the true Tuscan dialect. After the three above-mentioned, Guicciardini's history, then Bentivoglio, and then their poets, who are full of beauties mixed with a terrible contrast of concetti, epigrams, etc. Dante, Petrarch, and Ariosto themselves are full of surprisingly great and little things' (*Obs.* No. 1292).

8. On his return to Paris in 1730, Ramsay befriended the family of the Duc de Bouillon and became tutor to his nephew, Godefroi Géraud, Duc de Château-Thierry. The boy died in March 1732, aged thirteen (G. D. Henderson, *Chevalier Ramsay* [1952], pp. 152–3).

9. Paul-Hippolyte de Beauvillier, Duc de Saint-Aignan (1684–1776).

*19

Source: Egerton 2234 ff. 34–35
Addressed: as in 18
Postmarked: OC [2?]
Franked: Franco ~ Paris ~
Numbered: 1st.*
Endorsed: a. yͤ passage of yͤ hills/going to gineva
b. First passage of the Alps;/from Lyons to Geneva.

Geneva,
October 3 ⟨September 22⟩, 1731
⟨Sent away October 5⟩

⟨Dear Mother,⟩

We made three days of it in coming from Lyons hither.[1] In most parts of France the posts are so managed that you have generally a change of horses every six mile, in some places at nine, and in others at twelve; but for this journey we were forced to take one set of horses for the whole and to pass a good deal of hilly country into the bargain.

At our first setting out we went by the course of the Rhône. Before us at a distance lay a whole range of hills that we thought all along we were to pass, but when we came to them were agreeably enough surprised to find that there was a double range of them, and that we passed between both. 'Twas a very odd and uncommon sight all the way: the plain between them was generally not above three or four hundred yards wide, then the ground rose with little vineyards and fields—the rising was often full of woods which went sometimes up to the top of the ground. The highest part of the hills on each side was all solid rock, which came down straight to the woods and fields, like your great quarry at Giles' Hill.[2]

This sort of road continued for about fifteen miles, and though 'twas in general like what I have mentioned, there were several varieties in it that made it still new and surprising. In one place the stone at top had formed the ruins of a castle, and though there were several real ones in the way which we had just seen, we were a good while before we could distinguish whether this was real or natural stonework. Sometimes the meadows and rising fields took a greater stretch, and in one place made a view exactly like the picture of Tempe which I left with you and which was reckoned the most agreeable spot in the world.[3]

In one place we had a fall of water in a straight line from the top of the rock to the bottom, and in another the stones on each side formed a street of ruined houses which, the more you looked upon it, looked the more like a town with broken pillars and arched windows in a thousand parts of it. The cathedral of this town that was built by nature (possibly at the time of the deluge) was very distinguishable, and we passed close by the front of it. It was an old Gothic building (as your cathedral is at Winton), and looked grand, though irregular. There was a real house or two sometimes stuck up against the side of the hills, a few more about the middle of the plain, and two villages—one of which was the oddest dark street I ever saw. There was a slanting shed came from over all the first windows which shelved down for half the height of the houses, then began another that came down quite to the ground. 'Twas so on both sides the way, and between them was nothing but a little stream of water that a frog might jump over without straining himself. The people walk on both sides under the ugliest penthouse in the world, and I can't imagine why they are so covered, except it be to save them from the snows, especially those heaps that might fall from the tops of the hills over them in the beginning of the summer, and knock the citizens on the head.

Geneva is a very neat place, and there is an air of liberty and happiness all over it.[4] I have not yet seen a beggar in the streets, though I have walked them considerably for the time we have been here. Yesterday morning I took one of my Lord's footmen with me to show me to the Great Church. Just before we came to it I saw the head of the professors here, old Turretin,[5] reading a lecture in the German church, and as I was willing to hear so famous a man I bid the servant stay at the door and entered and took my seat in the circle of students. After I had satisfied my curiosity and was coming out I found the servant was gone, and should have been much at a loss if it had not been for a worthy old gentleman whom I took by his dress to be a lawyer. He offered his service to me to show me all about the town and all over their fortifications, and, whatever I could say to the contrary, forced me at least to take his servant with me to the places I was to see and left me with half a dozen compliments on each side. As soon as I was got some distance from him I asked the servant who was that very obliging gentleman his master, and who should it be but the head magistrate at present of all the state of Geneva![6] I mention this only as one instance of the politeness and obligingness of the people of this city, of which indeed one could not say too much. ⟨'Tis confidently reported here that the King of Sardinia, our neighbour at present, has put his father, the Duke of Savoy, in prison for attempting to resume the crown.[7] I am

Your dutiful son,

J. Spence⟩

1. They set out from Lyons on Sept. 29, and arrived in Geneva Oct. 1.

2. On the east side of Winchester.

3. Spence considered 'Tempe' as a title for his projected work on gardening.

4. Spence versified on the subject in *An Epistle from a Swiss Officer to his Friend at Rome*. The Swiss 'Happy in Freedom and Laborious Swains' are contrasted with 'What signs of Roman grandeur still remain' ('Fine pageants for Slaves'). *Museum* (1746), II, 259–61.

5. Jean Alphonse Turretini (1671–1737), the prominent Swiss theologian. In 1701–2 Addison 'conversed with Mr. Turretin', then Professor of Ecclesiastical History and Rector of the College at Geneva and retained 'a very great Honour and Esteem' for him (*Letters*, ed. Graham [1941], pp. 54–5). Spence heard him 'examining (about little quarrels and scuffles between the Protestants and Catholics)'. *Nbk.* 1 4ʳ.

6. 'The Premier Syndic (in 1731) Monsieur Galotin, Father to the Professor of that name' (*Nbk.* 1 4ʳ). Barthelémy Gallatin (1662–1748), of the Conseil de Deux-Cent in 1688, was syndic every fourth year between 1723 and 1735, premier syndic 1739. His son Ezechiel Gallatin (1685–1734) was Professor of Philosophy and Rector of the Academy (*Dict. hist. et biogr. de la Suisse* [Neuchâtel, 1926], III, 311).

7. Victor Amadeus II (1666–1732) was arrested on Sept. 28, as he attempted to regain the throne, which he had renounced in 1730 in favour of his son Charles Emmanuel III. See *Letter* 21.

Notebook 1

(11–12) 29ʳ⁻ᵛ

The first view of Geneva is fine, the best houses lying on the Savoy side of the Rhône. They are all busy at the fortifications on that side and have done almost all the new works there within these ten years. It wanted it much. The chief citizens' houses are on that side. There are the garden promenade, Monsieur [le] Ministre Lullin's house, and farther on to the right the casemates. The fortifications from the mount look extremely neat and the earthworks are like Bridgeman's slopes. They intend to fortify the other side of the town when they have done this. They hire a garrison of 200 (?), and all the bourgeois from sixteen to sixty are soldiers (about 1600?). The troops of Bern, in a case of necessity, would be with them in twenty-four hours: there is a suite of beacons, which are so many pyramids of faggots. We passed two or three of them in going to Lausanne.

The island and part of the town beyond the Rhône generally bad, the other has very good houses, the Great Church, Hôtel de Ville and hospital. ('Oh, we have two thousand belonging to it too.' *Mr. Cramer.*) In an inscription on the Town House they call themselves S.P.Q.G.

The works they are upon seem to be of great expense, but they say it does not cost them a third part of what it would cost a monarch: a great many give them their labour, and they look all as busy as a nest of emmets. They are rich, though they have so small a territory as would make (according to Chopy's map of the Lake of Geneva) a circle scarce one league in diameter.[1] It lies in a half moon to the lake.

The Lake of Geneva is fifty-four miles long and about twelve broad: we passed about thirty-six of them in going to Lausanne [Oct. 5–10] and saw the beginning of the lake from the three ranges of mountains. ⟨You pass the Pays de Genève and go there in little pieces that belong to the P[ie]d[montes]e. The division of the countries there is only a little pillar, no more than the mark between Hampshire and Berkshire: but there's no need of fences, because the

French have so frequent occasion of Swiss troops.⟩ The Great Church at Lausanne has paintings in the windows as well as that of Geneva. The faces of some relievos not cut off there as in that of Geneva. The people of Geneva seemed to keep the Sunday too with more decency than the Lausannois (though perhaps no people, [said] Monsieur Soyer, are so strict in that particular as the English).

1. 'When I was at Geneva,' Spence wrote in 1751, 'a mathematician of their university at my desire was so good as to reduce a map of their city and the ground about it belonging to them into a regular figure, and it made a circle of but three mile in diameter' (*Obs.* p. 652).

---

*20

Source: Egerton 2234 ff. 36–37
Addressed: as in 18
Postmarked: OC 25 DE TURIN
Numbered: 2ᵈ.
Endorsed: a. Italie/the descripshon/of the alps
              b. Passage of the Alps; &/Mount Cenis.

Turin,
October 24 ⟨13⟩, 1731

⟨Dear Mother,⟩

I wrote to you a long letter from Geneva ⟨Oct. 5—September 24 with you⟩ without an account of the road thither ⟨and the most remarkable of our adventures in our present state of knight-errantry⟩.[1] I then talked to you of hills, and I really thought they had been pretty handsome ones then because they were as big again as any I had ever seen in my life, but now I can fairly look upon them as pigmies. In short we have now entirely passed the Alps.

All the way from Geneva for five days we kept rising higher and higher. The first day we were in a confusion of hills, and the rest between two ranges of them again, with a line of fields and meadows between, which grew each day narrower and narrower, and more and more barren. The fifth day brought us to a stop. It was the vast Mount Cenis, the most usual passage from France into Italy. We had for a good while before travelled through a road where each side of us was generally a wild face of nature quite untaught and unmanaged by man. Rock above rock, with vast wild quarries of loose stone, the tops of the hills covered often with snow, and often hid part in the clouds, and sometimes partly appearing above them: little streams of water breaking down the hills, sometimes falls of water all at once that at a distance looked like white smoke tumbling downward, a river at the bottom that was almost all the way labouring over a bed of broken pieces of the rocks and looked often more like a stream of boiling than running water. Nothing that looked human or agreeable, except sometimes great woods of firs and pine-trees that grew all up some of the hills and rocks where one would think it impossible for them to grow, and a little village now and then in the bottom with people in it, with swelled necks, and such shapes and faces as made them look very little like men and women in spite of their having something of clothes on.[2]

Whatever they are, they live to a great age, and in one of these little villages[3] we passed in the last twelve miles toward Mount Cenis they say scarce anyone dies before they are a hundred years old. They live upon nothing but milk, indeed, and the water there which, though it gives them vast swellings in their necks, is (they say) otherwise very wholesome. We lay at a village just at the foot of Mount Cenis where the people seemed to be much of the same kind: they can say 'yes' or 'no', laugh when you speak to them, and I suppose eat and drink when they can get anything. I asked the moderate-aged woman who lighted our fire how old she was: she said she did not know, but that she was young. 'Perhaps you are past thirty?' 'Yes, yes, I'm past thirty.' 'Forty, perhaps?' 'Ay, that I am.' 'Perhaps fifty?' 'I believe I may.' This is a true history of our dialogue, and I did not carry it any farther for fear three more questions should make her fourscore.

This wild road I have been talking of was all in our last day and a half to Mount Cenis—we lay at the foot of that monster.[4] The next day was designed wholly for passing it. We had often seen the clouds on each side of us lower than the tops of the mountains, but that day was the first that we were to take a journey into them. Over night one of the prime ministers of the King of Sardinia for that village came to take measure of us, I mean ⟨one of the head porters came⟩ to view each person and see how many men would be necessary to carry him up the hill. Lord Middlesex had four assigned him, the Duke of Kingston six, and his governor,[5] who is a portly plump gentleman, no less than eight.[6] For my part, when I compared my own size with his, I was under terrible apprehensions that they would allow me only two,[7] but was overjoyed when the manager said that my little Lord (for we English are all lorded abroad) must have four too.

The morning came, and the moment we came out of doors we were each placed immediately in our chairs, with our feet in a bag of bear's skin, and our honest carriers began to move upward in a good round trot. 'Tis surprising with what dispatch they shuffle with you up the hill. They call the ascent itself three miles,[8] and yet in comparison to the length, we seemed to be up immediately. Half way up we passed through a grove of pine-trees on each side, for a good way like the avenue to a gentleman's house, only the road serpentizes through them, running up generally in the shape of an S. We were so many in company (porters, servants, and all

72

above fourscore men, and I believe at least fifty horse and mules with baggage) that sometimes you would see one of these great *S*'s all full of company, moving up together against the steep.

When we conquered the ascent, we found ourselves in a great plain on a level with the clouds, the hill rising in pieces all round us and the clouds rolling against their sides. This plain we passed for above three miles. We went by a lake there (of above a mile long, as they say) well stocked with fish, and a religious house built in the clouds to the beginning of the descent. The descent is about six miles, and I'm glad that I am got to the end of my letter, for 'tis in some places so rough and so wild that it would be very difficult to describe it. ⟨We are all very well, and I am

Your dutiful and affectionate

J. Spence⟩

1. They left Geneva Oct. 16, and via Aix, Chambéry (18), Montmélian (19), Mount Cenis (21), 'Susa and the Castle', arrived in Turin Oct. 22.

2. Spence relates in *Crito* (p. 49) the following anecdote: 'One of our own Countrymen (who was a particularly handsome Man), in his travelling over the *Alps*, was detained by a Fever in one of those Villages, where every grown Person has that sort of Swellings in the Neck, which they call *Goters*; and of which I have seen some, very near as big as their Heads. The first *Sunday* that he was able, he went to their Church (for he was a *Roman* Catholic) to return Thanks to Heaven for his Recovery. A Man of so good a Figure, and so well drest, had probably never before been within the Walls of that Chapel. Every body's Eyes were fixt upon him; and as they went out, they cried out, loud enough for him to hear them: "O how completely handsome would that Man be, if he had but a *Goter*!" '

3. Lanslebourg, called 'Laneburg' by English travellers.

4. 'The day and half before Mount Cenis, very bad' (*Nbk.* I 29ᵛ).

5. Dr. Nathan Hickman (1695–1746), Fellow of Merton College, Oxford, Dr. Radcliffe's travelling fellow 1731–5 from University College. (Some of his letters concerning the Duke of Kingston's stay in France are among the Cheyne Papers, *HMC*, 11th Rep., VII, 152.) On D. of Kingston, see *Letter* 12 n. 6.

6. 'Though it be the work of two men only to carry you,' writes Samuel Sharp, 'six, and sometimes eight attend, in order to relieve one another ... when the person carried is corpulent, it is necessary to employ ten porters' (*Letters from Italy* [1766], pp. 290–1).

7. Spence was thin and short (about five foot, *Nbk.* 3, xxxvi). Horace Walpole called him 'little Spence' and a friend referred to his 'trama figurae' (Wright, p. 5).

8. '4 leagues', 'or 12 miles the whole way, (½ ascent, 1¼ plateau, 2 descent)' according to *Nbk.* I 30ʳ, 4ᵛ.

21

Source: Egerton 2234 f. 39

Numbered: 3ᵈ.

Endorsed: Turin [*crossed out*]

Date: *The original date at end of letter:* Venice, Dec: 10/21 1731 *crossed out, and replaced at the head by:* Milan Turin; Oct: 27, —31. *Also crossed out:* No date to this; but to be placed next after that of Oct: 24, —31.

Milan Turin,
October 27, 1731[1]

⟨Dear Mother,⟩

I am mighty glad that you are got over the Alps with me, because you were before so much concerned about that part of our passage. Though there was no great danger in it there were a thousand things that looked horrible enough, and you may imagine that after the descent (which looked the most rude of any part of it) we were very glad to find ourselves on common footing with the world and going upon a plain country which is very beautiful and fruitful, and which widens itself continually, more and more, till you come to Turin.

I don't know whether I mentioned to you the neatness and beauty of that city, which is the capital of Piedmont (the first country we came to in Italy) and the seat of the King of Sardinia. About nine miles before you come to the city we passed a castle where the old king, [the] famous Duke of Savoy in the late wars, had then been imprisoned about five weeks by his son.[2] The old gentleman, about a year before, had resigned his crown to him; he wanted [it a]gain, was laying some plots for it. As it happens in [so much] mischief, a woman was at the bottom of it,[3] but all their [de]signs were broke by the poor old gentleman's being seized one night in his bed and carried to this castle with [a] good deal of roughness: where, when we were at Turin, [he] was allowed four rooms to walk in, but was guarded always in sight. From this castle we fell into a wide noble walk of trees which leads in a line and continues quite on to Turin.

In Turin all the streets are laid exactly as with a line. I never saw anything in my life so regular,[4] and there's a genteel air runs through the people. The court is reckoned one of the politest in Europe. I saw some of the ladies of it who are dressed in the manner of the Spanish ladies, and that way has something great and very graceful in it. I saw the young prince[5] in one of their arms, who is a beautiful child and ought to be so, for his mother[6] is of the most beautiful family perhaps in Europe. 'Tis ⟨something⟩ particular enough that this lady and her sisters have got the best share of beauty in the world in their own possession.[7] Their father is a German prince,[8] but with so small revenues that he was not able to give them any considerable fortune. Nature made this fault up to them in their persons. They were so eminent this way that one of them is married to the Duke of Bourbon and is reckoned the first beauty of France, another to the King of Sardinia, and is allowed to be one of the finest women in Italy, and a third is to be married to a prince of the Empire and, they say, will be the greatest beauty in Germany.

At Turin I first saw the river Po, the Thames of Italy. From a hill just beyond it you have a full view of the town and a noble prospect of all the country round it. On the left hand, about forty miles off, appears a very high hill which runs up like a sugar-loaf, with its point (very sharp to appearance) above the clouds: this is Mount Viso, from whence begins the course of the Po. On the right hand, above a range of hills—that are all vast ones— appears Mount St. Bernard, one of the largest in Switzerland, like a vast iced cake, broad and all covered with snow. Between each, about the middle, I had the pleasure to look back on Mount Cenis which spreads before the eye and makes the greatest figure of any of them, and could not help thinking of th[ose] poor honest fellows that carried us over it, and who live [en]tirely on such sort of jobs. These hills, with the numbers of less ones that spread on each side between them, take up three parts of the circle of the prospect from the little hill that I was upon,[9] and the fourth part is an open country th[at] continues still widening on to Milan.

⟨I am forced to go back in my journey because—though I should have nothing to say of concern—yet 'tis not best to speak of Venice till we are got from it.[10] I heartily wish Nanny Rhimes[11] joy, and desired my brother in my last to pay her [   ] what she demanded. I'm extremely glad to hear Mr. Wavill's son goes on so well in the college.[12] His being raised in the school will be such an encouragement that it must probably make him go on with twice the earnestness that he ever had, and I hope it will not make him any enemies in the school, or none at least to give him any trouble. I hope you and Belle are in stout health, and with all services to friends am ever

Your dutiful and affectionate

Jo: Spence⟩

1. The letter was actually posted Dec. 21 N.S. from Venice, where Spence arrived Nov. 15. In order to give his mother a consecutive account of his travels, Spence writes about Turin when he is in Venice, about Venice when he is already at Rome, etc. Similarly *Letters* 22 and 23 are written from Venice and antedated.

2. The castle of Rivoli was lately rebuilt according to the designs of Juvarra by Victor Amadeus II. The arrest occurred on Sept. 28. For a full account of this pathetic affair, see *The History of the Abdication of Victor Amedeus II . . . In a Letter from the Marquis de T*** a Piemontois, now at the Court of Poland; to the Count de C*** in London* (1732).

3. The ambitious Marchioness of Spino (d. 1733), dau. of the D. of Nemours, and King Victor's mistress, whom he secretly married a month before his abdication (Sept. 3, 1730). She entertained thoughts of becoming, on Victor's restoration, Queen of Sardinia.

4. After the destructions of the 1706 siege, Turin was rebuilt according to a planned design.

5. The five-year-old Duke of Savoy (b. June 26, 1726), later (1773) King Victor Amadeus III.

6. Polyxena of Hesse-Rheinfels-Rothenburg (1706–35), 2d wife of Charles Emmanuel. She was the eldest of four sisters.

7. Her sister Caroline (1714–41) married Louis-Henri, D. of Bourbon; and Eleonora-Philippina (b. 1712), the Prince of Sulzbach (La Chenaye-Desbois Badier, *Dictionnaire de la noblesse* [Paris, 1861], X, 606–7). See *Letter* 110.

8. Ernest-Leopold, Landgrave of Hesse-Rheinfels-Rothenburg (1684–1731).

9. 'The Hill of the Capuchins ... ⟨'Twas thence that the French were beat [in 1706] by Prince Eugene, who lay on the hill where the new church is building ex voto⟩.' *Nbk.* I 4ᵛ.

10. See note I.

11. Not identified.

12. Dick Wavell (see *Letter* 9 n. I).

---

*22

Source: Egerton 2234 f. 38

Numbered: 4ᵗʰ.

Date: Venice. Jan: 4, 1732. N.S. No dates, but is to be placed next but one after Oct: 24,—31, *crossed out, and replaced by:* Milan. Nov: 5. —31.

Milan,
November 5, 1731[1]

⟨Dear Mother,⟩

I hope you are furnished with a good map of Italy ⟨and a pair of jackboots⟩ to travel through it with me. I left you in my last at Turin. After the pleasures of that delicious city we went to Milan.[2] You shall seldom find so large a town so very ill inhabited. They call it ten miles about, and when we entered it, it looked almost like a desert. It is really very thin of people, and as the women never walk the streets (but to go to church) it seems much less inhabited than it is.[3]

Here we began to see the care of the Italian husbands very sensibly. The women do not only keep generally within, but appear too very rarely in the shops or any public part of their own houses. They keep mostly in their own chamber, and their chief diversion is looking out of [the] window. Even when they do that, you must not expect to see their faces: there's a sort of wooden lattice (they call them 'jealousies') that generally hangs down all over the outside of the window, 'tis made movable to about half a foot before them; there they poke out their heads and see about them without being fairly seen. By what one could discover of them, I believe there were several faces among them that deserved better usage.

The dress of the head especially is very becoming. The common people wear nothing upon their heads: their hair is twisted in two long braids behind. These braids are then drawn round and round a silver bodkin on the top of their heads and looks like a natural crown of hair—the rest they set very prettily to the face, and if they have any ornament at all on the head 'tis two or three real rose-buds or a sprig of jessamin. The ladies come very often near this, or if they go farther 'tis often nothing but a little cap, all of short red ribbons, and for the graver gentry black. In assemblies they dress pretty much in the French fashion, in the churches and streets you lose most of their head-dress by a veil that covers that and most all of their face.

One of the things that I have seen with the greatest pleasure at Milan was the Grand Hospital.[4] There is one large court and four less on each side of it. Each court has a canal of clear water running round it. They are served with all conveniences and everything looks neat about them. In one square are religious women, in another the sick, in another the decrepit, and in a fourth children that come by chance into the world, etc. The latter, if boys, they prentice out when about fourteen years old, and the girls are kept there till they can get husbands or some method of living out of it, if they choose it. The income for the maintenance of the hospital is very great, and they are all kept very well. The number of the ⌜bastards⌝[5] upon the spot there, or now prenticed with the hospital money, amounts to between eleven or twelve thousand. In a modest computation they have about ten fresh ones come in every week. We were in the chamber of infants, and I never saw anything that pleased me more. There were between fifty and sixty little creatures perhaps, all from a day or two to seven or eight weeks old, and about ten neat nurses in the room that seemed as busy and as pleased in taking care of them as could be. Above half the chits were asleep in little long beds with bolsters at both ends, and sometimes you'd see two little heads together at each end. Some were feeding and scarce anyone whimpering, for they manage them extremely carefully and well. I believe most of the nurses had been of the same breed themselves, and as they grew up were taught to take care of their new little cousins as they came in. We have something of this kind in all the great cities where I have been: there is a noble one in particular at Venice, and before it was established they said they used to find numbers of little children floating in their canals, some every morning: horrible sight, which is now put an end to. Though the hospital at Milan ⟨where we saw the little nursery I have been talking of⟩ is so rich, there are still people continually leaving money to it. They have a great hall with the pictures of their benefactors in it, among which there is one in a shabby dress who was a small coalman, but managed his gains so well that he died worth a hundred thousand crowns, and left them all to the hospital. ⟨With hearty services to all friends, I wish you and Belle a happy New Year, and am ever

Your affectionate and dutiful

Jo: Spence⟩

1. The letter was actually written Jan. 4 from Venice. See *Letter* 21 n. 1.

2. They stayed at Turin Oct. 22–27, Vercelli (28), Novarra (29), Milan Oct. 30 to Nov. 6.

3. 'They say the inhabitants of Milan are at present 80,000' (*Nbk.* I 31ᵛ).

4. Originally ducal palace designed by Antonio Filarete, donated to the city (1456) by Duke Francesco I Sforza, to serve as a hospital. It was considerably enlarged in the 17th century.

5. Emended to 'foundlings'.

Notebook 1
(14–16) 30ᵛ–31ᵛ

Milan [Oct. 30–Nov. 6] is very large. They call it ten miles, and it lies pretty near in a round, in an half moon when you view it from the castle. It seems thinly inhabited (unless on holy days). The Great Church is not, and is not likely to be, finished.

Proportions of the dome at Milan:

Length   250 braccia[1]   —500 Engl. feet
Breadth 150   „   300   „   „
Height   200   „   400   „   „

No church has so many statues about it, especially the south side, and there the saints tied to trees, etc. The number of statues, good, by Biffi, etc. The St. Bartholomew is like a print in a book of anatomy, and as such is exquisite (the hanging of the skin, especially the thick leg and full head behind, very unnatural. Why a book in his hand?). 'Tis not historical; the head is a little like Seneca's, and is perfectly philosophical, for it expresses no passion. St. Ch. Borromeo lies very fine, in rock crystal: his history in eight compartments (silver bas-reliefs) round him. . . .

The Count d'Arese's gallery ⟨of the Borromean family: the view into his little garden, shaped like a Venetian window; the door in the middle opening, all one eagle in iron-work; the vines hanging wild all over⟩ [contains] the best collection of pictures we met with: Laura by Leonardo da Vinci, the Horatii and Curiatii— a battle, and an Andromeda (?) by Arpino. St. Francis by Guido ⟨and among the little statues Nero (?) enjoying the wound of the dying gladiator he has just stabbed⟩. The front of St. Celso was the prettiest we saw (by Fontana?). The basso-relievos upon it in compartments and, between each, statues as big as life (by Jean de Bologna?). . . .

Milan is taken and retaken so often that they don't so much as efface the names of those who have lost it. On the castle Philip is still called 'rex maximus' (the Emperor pretends to be his successor for Spain) and over the gate ditto and 'defensor fidei'. The Emperor has now, as they say, 40,000 men in the

Milanese and Mantuan, 16,000 in the kingdom of Naples and ditto in Sicily. . . . Purgatory pictures in the streets of Milan: that, and begging for the souls, common after.

1. '60 braccia milanesi = a 100 pieds du Roi. The French foot one inch more than the English, so that 60 braccia milanesi are equal to 120f. English, and one braccia to two feet English.' [Spence's note]

---

*23

Source: Egerton 2234 ff. 40 41
Addressed: as in 18 (without en Angleterre)
Numbered: 5th.
Endorsed: a. venice still: this come tonight/feb: ye 21: 1731-2: not to be/shard?: but redd to a frind:/an entertaining Leter
             b. Feb: 21, 1732. crossed out/Milan, & Verona; Maffei/Ambrosian Library, &c.

Verona,
November 10, 1731[1]

⟨Dear Mother,
I'm mighty glad to find by yours that Dick has received my letter about the money affair. I was uneasy for fear one might miscarry, and so sent him two, one of the 22nd Nov. and another the 31 of Decr. Now I hope the business is done, and so I am at ease.⟩

I think I left you in my last at Milan. There's one particular I forgot to mention to you. One of the most famous libraries in Italy is at Milan. You must know our libraries here are places that a lady might see with pleasure. They are not wholly all stuffed up with musty books and old authors: half of them at least is taken up with ornaments that are very agreeable. In that at Milan there is one room full of statues and curiosities,[2] and another of fine pictures.[3] In the curiosity room is the thing that I mention this for. There was formerly a lady of Milan that was extremely beautiful: she had not only one of the finest faces in the world, but her shape was absolutely the most perfect that ever was seen. You must excuse her if she was a little proud with all this. However that be, when she came to die (as she did very young), and they opened her will, they found that she had left her body to the surgeons to be anatomized and desired that her skeleton, prepared in the neatest manner that could be, should be set up in this room belonging to the Ambrosian Library, that all strangers and all curious people that came thither might be witness to the fineness of her shape. Her will was executed punctually, and there we saw her ladyship with an inscription on the pedestal on which she stands, which says that it was done to put all fine ladies that may see it in mind of the frailty of beauty, and that in spite of their charms they must soon come to be just what she is. And indeed, considering she has neither any eyes nor cheeks, it must be owned that her appearance is none of the most charming at present.[4]

After Milan, the next great city we came to was Verona.[5] Here ⟨you must know⟩ lives the famous Scipio Maffei.[6] He is by title a Marquis, and for learning one of the most eminent men now in Italy. He is an old bachelor, and talks as if the ladies had played him some scurvy tricks in his youth. Among other things he introduced us to a ball ⟨where I was most horribly afraid of being asked to dance⟩, and you cannot conceive how busy and officious the good old gentleman was among all the ladies, from the eldest to the youngest. He'd whisper each as soon as ever she stood still, and was sometimes so entangled in the ranks that he'd put the whole dance into confusion. However, everybody is fond of him, for he is a mighty good man, and has just built an opera house for them at Verona, which is a very pretty one.[7] Round it are separate rooms for dancing, conversation, concerts, etc., all contrived and carried on by this good gentleman, who into the bargain in his time has himself written operas[8] and one of the best tragedies that ever were written in their language.[9] So that, you see, he is a great scholar, a nobleman, a poet, and a spoiler of dances, all at one and the same time.

⟨I'm mighty sorry to hear that Mrs. Nichollsis again disappointed of presenting her husband with an heir to his estate.[10] She has need now surely of all her good temper and life to get over such repeated ill luck. I hope heaven will bless them before I come into Hampshire again, which is likely to be just about the time you mention.

I beg Mr. Wavil would be at ease, for if a red hat be to be gotten for his son he shall certainly have it.[11] We are to go for Rome about a month hence, and I begin to smell gun-powder already, though I own I should long to see it more than a[ny] place in the world, if it were not so full of your Papishes. Letters may still be directed hither as usual, and I believe that will be our method all the while we are in Italy. You know that there's a way of going out of Italy and missing the great mountains: 'tis into Germany and so down the Rhine to Holland, which very probably will be our route after the summer is pretty well over. I beg my hearty service to Belle and all friends, and am ever

Your dutiful and affectionate

J. Spence⟩

1. Again an antedated letter, written from Venice, and posted after Feb 21, 1732.

2. 'Among the heads: Sir Thomas More, Fisher, Colvil, Duns Scotus, etc. . . . There too is the celebrated "School of Athens" by Raphael, the original sketch' (*Nbk.* 1 30ᵛ).

3. With 'several pieces by Titian, Mantegna's poor hard figures, copy of Vinci's "Last

Supper" (we saw the original at the Office of the Inquisition), Breughel's sweet pieces, particularly his "Elements", and the work he lost his sight in finishing.—Vinci's book of fortifications (in which is the design of bombs as they are now used) is entitled "Dell'arti segreti & dell'altre cose". The inscription over the place where 'tis kept, dated 1637, says that a king of England offered *aureos ter mille Hispanios* for it. Among the manuscripts we saw the Latin Josephus, on paper made of bark, as ours is of rags, which they call fourteen hundred years old; the epistles of Paul in five Oriental languages—about six hundred, and the illuminations in an old Bible, about four hundred [years old] (good colours [but] an horrible uniformity; something of perspective: on the whole not so good as some with us).' *Nbk.* I 31ʳ.

4. The only other mention of this skeleton was made in 1739 by De Brosses: 'un squelette effectif posé sur un piédestal et couronné de lauriers; c'est celui d'une femme docteur.' Unfortunately De Brosses adds: 'j'ai oublié le nom de la fille' (I, 100). There is no record of it in the Ambrosian Library at present.

5. They left Milan Nov. 6, passed through Brescia (Nov. 7), and arrived in Verona Nov. 8.

6. The Marquis Scipione Maffei (1675–1755), an erudite virtuoso and man of letters; member of the Académie des Inscriptions; in 1736 he received an honorary degree at Oxford. His works in twenty-one volumes were published in 1790.

7. The Teatro Filarmonico, built 1715–29, 'by Bibiena *sub auspiciis* of Maffei and three other noblemen', was to be opened on Jan. 6, 1731/2, with *La Fida Ninfa*, which was at the time probably in rehearsal. Maffei himself acted as impressario and Vivaldi composed the musical score.

8. *Il Sansone, oratorio, per la musica* (1699) and *Ninfa Fidele* were exercises in the fashionable 'conclusioni d'amore'.

9. *Merope*, first acted Aug. 12, 1712.

10. Perhaps the wife of John Nicholls (b. 1692) of St. James, Shaftesbury; Winchester Fellow in 1703. If so, Mrs. Nicholls satisfied her husband four years later, for one Thomas Nicholls, scholar of New College in 1748, was baptized Oct. 13, 1735 (Kirby, pp. 218, 248).

11. Dean Wavell apparently asked Spence to use his influence in behalf of young Richard who was to become a commoner at Winchester College (see *Letters* 9, 25).

24

Source: Egerton 2234 ff. 44–45

Addressed: as in 11

Postmarked: 22 FE

Endorsed: *b.* To Col: Rolle. Of the Amphitheater/at Verona, &c.
red wafer

TO HENRY ROLLE

Venice,
February 15, 1732[1]

Dear Sir,

I received the favour of yours at Geneva, so that I was too late for P. Colonia's book which I should otherwise have gotten for you with pleasure.[2] From Geneva we had seven days' journey, mostly through the Alps, to Turin. We came there a little after the late King of Sardinia was confined. It was then all the conversation of the place, and yet people seemed very quiet and calm on so particular an event. Whether that stillness hid something the more deep under it I can't say. They have a new university set up at Turin.[3] The building looks handsome, and the ground court, when you enter it, is set round with old marbles and pieces of antiquity presented to them by the Marquis Scipio Maffei (whose name you see so often in Montfaucon) of Verona.[4]

I had the pleasure to meet with several pieces there that had been my old acquaintance in New College library, but what exceeded it much was being afterwards with the old Marquis himself the greatest part of the four days we were at Verona. He is an old bachelor, quite gay between whiles and always very obliging. He contributes much to the pleasures of the place, and 'tis he principally who has built them a new theatre, which is one of the prettiest and best contrived I ever saw.[5] There's a square court before it with a wall round, which is already half wainscoted with antiquities given by Maffei, and the other half is to be so when finished.

Beautiful as this is, it looks like a house of cards when compared with the old amphitheatre, which is not far from it. The greatest length of the amphitheatre is 450 Veronese feet, the greatest breadth 360, and the circumference 1290.[6] The length of the area within the lowest seats is 218 and the breadth 129. The area at present is all filled up to the lowest seat, though it was formerly, as the Marquis conjectures, eighteen feet deep.[7] After all 'tis not the great length and breadth that make the grandeur of it, but something that depends on the proportioning every length and breadth about you. Whatever 'tis, the first sight of it strikes one with such an admiration that one does not care to speak for four or five minutes. A poet would say that its grandeur strikes you mute with admiration, but I choose to tell it you in plain prose, just as I felt it.

There are two or three fine collections of antique statues at Verona, which the Marquis was so good as to introduce us to.[8] At the Bishop's Palace is one of Grecian ladies, which they call the best of the sort in Italy. One can't walk through the whole row of them without perceiving plainly the superior grandeur of the Greek statues when compared to the Roman.[9] There are some male statues in the house too, and I observed one particularly [with?] horns, inscribed 'Divus Lunus', which was [a] new thing to me, though probably not to you.

We are at present at Venice, and if you favour me with any letter all the while we stay in Italy, a direction à Monsieur Spence, avec Milord Middlesex, recommandé à Monsieur John Pommer, Banquier, à Venise will find me out wherever we are. If you have any particular commands for me at Rome or elsewhere 'twill be a pleasure to execute them to

Your most humble servant

J. Spence

1. The letter is placed here to conform to the geographic, not to a strictly chronological, continuity of the tour. See *Letter* 21 n. 1.

2. *Dissertation sur un monument taurobolique découvert à Lyon* (1705). See *Letter* 16 n. 2.

3. The old university of Turin (founded 1406), once famous for the study of law, lost its reputation in the 17th century. In 1720 Victor Amadeus II, in his attempt to reorganize higher education, gave orders to erect 'le superbe Palais de l'Université' (Modeste Paroletti, *Turin et ses curiosités* [Turin, 1819], p. 221).

4. In his *Museum Veronese* (1749) Maffei gives a lengthy account of the work he had performed in Turin at the King's request.

5. You see 'five demi-ellipses of seats rising gently above and coming out each a little farther than [the] other: the front of the stage handsome. About it are different apartments for the conversazione, Académia Filarmonica, etc.' (*Nbk.* 1 32ʳ). See also *Letter* 23 n. 7.

6. 'Il pie Veronese cresce per l'appunto un terzo del palma Romana degli architetti. Maffei's book' (*Nbk.* 1 32ʳ). Maffei's *Verona illustrata* appeared in 1731/2.

7. 'The lowest step ... eighteen foot above the beasts, and defended too. In the surrounding wall there were four ows of pillars: first row Doric, without pedestals, second Ionic, third Corinthian, fourth composite. Next to the wall 'tis all full of shops now, except at the entrance and exit. ... The seats all round are entire. They were much damaged in the disturbances of the Guelphs and Ghibellines, but repaired in the old manner, *pluribus vicibus* (except perhaps the two balconies over the entrance and exit) from 1517 to 1572. [There are] forty rows of steps, four of vomitoria, sixteen in each row' (*Nbk.* 1 32ʳ).

8. 'The Marquis Maffei had us to the house of Bevilaqua. The chief things he pointed out was a Venus (sister to that of Medicis), a sleeping statue, Bacchus with the true thyrsus, Hadrian (the hair and beard), and young Augustus with the civic crown' (ibid., 32ʳ⁻ᵛ).

9. 'Pray observe,' said Maffei, 'with what ease the passions are expressed in that face! Our statuaries now are forced to distort the features to show a passion, their strokes are all violent and forced. This will help you as much as anything to see the superiority of the best ancient sculptors over the modern. We have no one except Michelangelo that comes near them' (*Obs.* No. 1364).

---

* *25*

Source: Egerton 2234 ff. 42–43
Addressed: To/Mʳˢ Spence.
Numbered: 6ᵗʰ.
Endorsed: *a.* Venice/& a descripshon/of his passage theather
b. Passage to Venice; & some/accᵗ of yᵉ Place.

Venice,
November 22, 1731[1]

⟨Dear Mother,

I am now by a good fireside, with the sea all round me—for the middle of our streets here at Venice are paved with nothing but water—and two of your letters before me. I'm very sorry to find that your eyes trouble you again, and beg you would spare them as much as possible. If my sister will be so good as to write for you, it will be a great satisfaction to me, for then I shall be sure you take care of them. When I hear from you, which can't be too often, I should be glad always of your Winchester news, who is married and who dead, for I would willingly know all the terrible accidents

83

there. As for the length of my letters, you need never fear them: the only danger is that they should be too long.

My last letter to you (October 24)[2] brought us safe over the Alps to Turin. From thence we came with the Duke of Kingston to Milan, where we stayed about a week. There we changed companies: the Duke with his attendance went for Genoa, and Lord Middlesex with a brother of the Duke of Manchester[3] and Lord Ferrers's brother[4] (two of the best-natured gentlemen in the world) for Venice. We stopped on the road four or five days at Verona and two at Padua.⟩[5] We came to this place from Padua in a day by water, and I think 'twas one of the most agreeable days I ever passed in my life. The river Brenta, by which we came into the sea, is a great passage: we met with boats perpetually, the weather was of a right temperature, neither too warm nor too cold, the side of the river is full of gentlemen's and noblemen's seats, we ate and drank with a particular good appetite and were all ⌈as merry as fiddlers⌉.[6] When first you fall in upon the sea, you discover Venice before you: a fine city, spreading very much each way and, as it were, floating upon the waters. You see nothing but buildings and ocean.

If ever there was an agreeable place in the world to live in for two or three months, it must be Venice, especially at this time of year. It looks like nothing else in the world. The streets are all full of sea, and instead of a coach you have always a boat (they call them gondolas here) waiting for you. They are the best contrived for swiftness and the snuggest things to be in that can be imagined. We have three always at the door, and if you want to go a mile or two in the town 'tis but stepping into one of them, and away they go with you, either concealed or with the windows open if you please. And there you are carried on in the most agreeable—or at least the most indolent—manner in the world.

We live in a very good house, in the great street just in sight of the Rialto ⟨the picture of which if I don't mistake is at Mrs. Kelley's, to whom and all her good family I beg my humble service⟩. After dinner we never go out without our masking habits, for though 'tis not yet carnival, in the public places there is not one in ten but what is masked. The best opera house is just by us, and we can go to it afoot, which is particular enough in this place. You'd be charmed with their singing. Faustina and Bernacchi, who were both in England last winter, I heard there last night, and the former of them sings certainly most exquisitely well.[7] You know I am a judge—but I speak rather from others that are so than from myself.[8] There's nowhere perhaps a greater number of fine-looking pictures than in Venice. The collections of them are very numerous, and the going to see one or other of these collections is the business of the morning.[9] When you are once got into your boat you are surprised to find yourself so soon at the place you designed for—they shoot along like arrows, and though there are such multitudes going and coming in every street, they are so dexterous in the management of them that you scarce ever see any two hindering one another. ⟨We shall stay here for two or three months, and then for Rome. I believe I have told you that if you have any commands to the Pope I shall be very ready to execute them.

I'm very much obliged to Mr. Wavil for giving my direction to Mr. Cheyney, and am glad to hear his son Dicky is a commoner at the college. That will be a trial to him, and in my mind I should not fear to put him in upon the foundation afterwards if he goes on well there, especially as he is pretty high in the school, and will grow more so daily and consequently more considerable in that commonwealth. I hear the praises of the school even here as I am wandering about the world, and this day am told that the Duke of Queensborough waits for a place in the schoolmaster's lodgings for his son.[10] 'Tis a particular happiness to me ever to hear of the success of things there, and more so in regard to the schoolmaster who has been so particularly a friend to me.

I should be glad to know whether you are entirely with Mr. Morecroft again or whether you are in Sestos' tower[11] only by the by. I could go and see the original Sestos' tower if you please, for as we are upon the Mediterranean at present, we are upon the high road to it. I beg my humble service to my sister and all friends, and am ever

Your dutiful and affectionate

Jo: Spence⟩

1. The date is correct. It is probably Spence's first letter from Venice, where he arrived Nov. 15. See *Letter* 21 n. 1.

2. *Letter* 20. Date crossed out.

3. Robert Montagu (ca. 1710–62) was M.P. for Huntingdon 1734–9. In 1739, on his brother William's death, he became the 3d D. of Manchester.

4. Hon. Sewallis Shirley (1709–65), 4th son of the 1st E. Ferrers; M.P. for Brackley 1742–54, Collington 1754–61. Comptroller of the Household to Queen Charlotte, 1762–5. He was a freemason and, like Robert Montagu, one of the original members of the Soc. of Dilettanti (1736). His affair with Lady Vane is recorded by Smollett in *Peregrine Pickle*. For his portrait, see Cust, p. 14.

5. They left Verona Nov. 12, stopped at Vicenza ('At Vicenza we saw a theatre, the building by Palladio, and the perspective decoration by Sansovin' [*Nbk.* 1 32ᵛ]), spent Nov. 13–14 at Padua, and Nov. 15 arrived in Venice.

6. Emended to 'extremely cheerful'.

7. Faustina Bordoni Hasse (1693–1781), famous soprano, made her debut in London in 1726 and stayed for two seasons with a salary fixed at £2000. In 1730 she married the composer Johann Adolph Hasse. Dr. Burney says that 'she in a manner, invented a new kind of singing, by running divisions with a neatness and velocity which astonished all who heard her ... sustaining a note longer ... than any other singer' (*A General History of Music*, ed. F. Mercer [1935], II, 738). Antonio Bernacchi (1685–1756), famous castrato, sang in London in 1716–17 and again in 1729.

8. The true *cognoscente* was Lord Middlesex.

9. For a lengthy catalogue of those Spence visited, see *Notebook* following *Letter* 26.

10. Henry Douglas (1722–56), styled E. of Drumlanrig, elder son of Charles (1698–1778), 3d D. of Queensberry and Dover, was educated at Winchester 1731–9, matric. Jan. 28, 1739/40, at Christ Church, Oxford. On Dr. Burton, the schoolmaster of Winchester College, see *Letter* 15 n. 7.

From which Hero supervised Leander's amorous swims across the Hellespont; here no doubt applied to the 15th-century tower of the Church of St. Maurice at Winchester, and probably identical with the 'High Chamber' and 'Trinity Tower' (*Letters* 8 and 76). Mr. Wavell was Rector at St. Maurice. Mrs. Spence lived at Mr. Morecroft's house in Colebrook Street.

Notebook 1

(19, 21–22, 29–31, 27) 33^r, 34^{r-v}, 38^r–39^r, 37^r

Venice was built toward the beginning of the fifth century in the marshes of the Adriatic.[1] The devastations of Italy by the Goths drove people to live here, and its being so well inhabited has made the air tolerably wholesome. At low water you see the channels that lead to it and the badness of its situation. Formerly it has often changed its government, but flourished longest under that of a Doge and the nobility. They are said to keep the people of the *terra firma* extremely under—possibly some particular may one time or other get the power into his hands, now they are in their decay. There is one of the Pisani at present who is popular to a great degree.

The Doge is but a lodger in his palace at best. He has but three rooms in it. The office of the state, the courts of justice, and the council and senate rooms, etc. take up almost all the palace. The meanest of the people are about the court and in the galleries. I have seen them playing at ball there, and there's a day when they bait a bull in the middle of the court, not to mention some nastier liberties that they take all over the palace. They are satisfied with this, though at the same time there are places open in every corner to take in secret informations against their lives. The palace itself has a mean look; the east side is better than the rest of it, and the staircase there to the gallery is of handsome fresh marble.

Their trade is quite sunk with their power, or rather their power with their trade. The nobility's aiming to get possession of the *terra firma* has been a great reason of their sinking thus. The politics, too, are good to make slaves of the people, but not to make the nobility considerable to other states. Pleasure and vice are not only allowed but managed and promoted politically among them: 'tis one of the main hinges of their government. They have a mast by the Arsenal on which is a *basso-relievo* of a Doge in a shell and four horses, and Neptune coming to pay his respects to him on one. The three masts in the Place of St. Mark support (as they say) the crowns of the Morea, Cyprus, and Candia. These and the former are perhaps equally modest, for as neither of the three crowns belong to them, the Doge seems not [to] be master of the sea. Of all their islands and domains to the east they have nothing now to defend them from the Turks but Corfu which, though extremely well fortified for those times in which it was done, could scarce hold out against the enemy for any long time. That lost, the Turks could easily deluge the Venetian state, and after them the Pope's.

In the Arsenal we saw their galleys and galleasses (the cannons are the best part of their stores). There's the machine to help ships off a shallow, the chair they carry the Doge in after his election (like our parliamenteerers) and the Bucentaur, which is very beautiful.

They reckon about 1500 voting nobles; they vote at twenty-five. When one man is ennobled it holds for all his relations, 'tis saleable at a certain price, and yet the number does not increase as one would at first expect. Generally there is but one brother in a family marries, the rest keep, and if they happen to have children don't increase their nobility—the rest in general are too vicious and luxurious to have much health or many children.

The Great Council makes but a poor appearance: there are nine to one in it that look very meanly; the Senate looks better and is much more regular. One of the chief officers takes the oath before ballotting there and then administers it to all the rest; little charity-boys collect the ballots. 'Tis the civillest oath, if it is an oath, that ever I saw in my life: he has a paper in his hand, which he shows with a bow to each senator as he passes them, each bows to him in his turn, and that's all.

The senators in the streets seem much more numerous than they are, for all the nobles, physicians and lawyers have habits alike: their robes are black silk for the summer, black cloth autumn and spring, and the same with furs for the winter. They have an odd black cap which they very seldom wear, yet 'tis of very good service to them: many of them choose to walk, and . . . even cater for themselves often in the markets and bring home things (as far as their caps will allow) themselves.

There's a strange spirit of inquisitiveness reigns among the Venetians: they know every little trifle. Perhaps in hearing a thousand frivolous things, they meet with one that may be of some concern to them. The great channel that secrets are discovered by is the gondoliers, and this may be one reason why the nobles walk so much (without servants, for privacy). A foreigner's gondoliers there tell everything they do, and I believe the servants you hire to attend you there too often understand more languages than they pretend to.

The nuns in Venice seem to have a very different air from those we saw in France. Their convents are light, the parlatorios of more extent and more open, the ladies have a gay air, fresher complexions and a great deal of freedom in their behaviour and manner of talking. I have seen a nun professing at Venice that laughed almost all the time of the ceremony, and one at Lyons that looked as if she was leaving this life in good earnest. I need not add what is said of some greater liberties of the Venetian nuns than we saw.

---

1. Félibien.—'The twenty-four houses were all in the quarter of the Rialto and the town was at first called by that name. Near the bridge of the Rialto was formerly the Doge's Palace. . . .' [Spence's note]

26

Source:	Egerton 2234 ff. 46–47
Addressed:	To/Mrs Spence/at Winchester
Numbered:	(betw: 6th, & 7th)
Endorsed:	*a.* there dress at venice/from mr Rolle—merryest
	b. Rolle./some acct of the/people at Venice/Pass this. not to be Copied.

EDW. ROLLE TO MRS. SPENCE

New College,
February 18, 1732 [O.S.][1]

Well, I have had another letter, Madam, from Venice. It came last week, but not time enough for me to be able [to] give you an account of it then conveniently. I had been telling him in my last that I almost envied him the warmth of Italy as I imagined at the then cold and dead time of year, but it seems I was mistaken. Jo. tells me Venice is as cold as he ever remembered it in England, which is occasioned by its lying open to the sea. Their clothes are the most comfortable, as he describes them, that can be: they are all the days wrapped round in furs and their shoes and stockings lined with squirrels' skins. This is all his news touching the manners of them, for which I find I must receive the greatest lights from you. The rest of his letter, which is yet a very honest one for length, is taken up in telling me what a regard they have even so far from home as Italy for our English writers, and that Mr. Pope is talked of there almost with more applause than here among us. He goes so far as to say there are several people of fashion in a good many of the towns he hath passed through, who are now actually learning our language to be able to read his and some other writings of our nation. As Jo. is a very good patriot, I dare say he is not a little pleased with the honour done Old England.

I am, Madam, etc.

E. Rolle

1. In preparing the letters for a fair transcript, Spence misdated this one: 'Venice, Feb. 18, 1732'. His letter to Rolle was probably written toward the end of January.

The most striking things [at Venice] are the oddness of the carnival and the pictures, for which they are reckoned the third or fourth place in Italy.

The famous *Place of St. Mark* is irregular in every part of it: its length, from the three masts to S. Geminiano, is 222 paces, its breadth, by the three masts, 126 in front and at bottom, by S. Geminiano, 85. The front of St. Mark's, too, slants from it toward the clock ('tis 38 paces from the line of the masts, and toward the palace 26). The Campanile is a botch between them and the Library, and as for the Piazzetta, the hither part of the Broglio side is a good deal wider than the lower toward the sea. The sea side of the Place is by Sansovin and Scamozzi, built in a much better manner than its opposite, and the Library side to the Piazzetta just the contrary. The church of Geminiano is commended very deservedly, and the Palace turns its worst side to the Piazzetta, so that 'tis not its own beauty but the view to the sea and the diversions there that make it look agreeable. ⟨They were going to rebuild the whole palace, but only finished the side next the Ponte de' Sospiri.⟩

Of all the celebrated buildings one of the most ugly is the *Church of St. Mark*. 'Twas built by the Greeks in the Greek manner.[1] The top of it is heaped with domes and the inside is dark and ill-contrived. The best things in it are the mosaic pictures, several of which are after designs of Titian and done by the best hands. They pass absolutely for paintings at the first sight and at a tolerable distance. Those we came near were all in little squares of glass (a sort of paste, etc., and then the colouring or gilding).—The two mezzolanes at first coming in were done by two Venetian brothers, Francesco and Valerio Zuccati, in 1545. On the outside, the first mezzolane (on the left hand in entering) was lately done by Leopoldo Pozzo (in 1729) and is of very strong colours.—Over the great mezzolane at the entrance stand the four beautiful horses, said to be cast by Lysippus[2] (two hold up the off leg and two the in leg: two turn their heads outward and two inward—misplaced?—the second and third hold their heads outward).—The two great granite pillars toward the sea are topped with two pitiful figures: St. Mark's winged lion and the former patron of Venice (St. Theodore) with his shield in his right hand.

In the room before the library is the Ganymede with the old Phrygian bonnet (the look of the eagle), and Leda and the Swan, a fine basso-relievo of suovetaurilia, etc. The library is small and the librarian knows nothing of it. One side is entirely taken up with the books Bessarion left them.

In the *Great Council Hall* is Tintoret's 'Paradise' [or] 'Heaven' (the Virgin Mary, the second principal figure in it, is in a posture as kneeling to our Saviour; the Evangelist St. Mark is distinguished lower on the right hand and St. John on the left; farther to the right is a Moses with horns of light.—In the same hall is a suite of pieces by different hands, relating to the history of Pope Alexander III. There are at least ten of them. The seventh and eighth is the submission of the Emperor (Frederic Barbarossa) to that Pope: the Emperor is almost prostrate and the Pope sets his foot on his right shoulder. 'Tis by Zuccaro, and by the inscription ('F. Zucara, F. 1582. perf. 1603') he seems to have been above twenty years about it.—The other side of that room is full of Venetian victories. There is in particular a city besieged partly by sea by them, of Tintoret: some of the galleys are close to the walls, the cross-yard is sunk horizontally, and several are getting by it on the enemies' walls (perhaps 'tis rather a mad compliment to his countrymen than what was ever practised by any of them in reality). —Several of the compartments on the roof seem to be finer than the side pictures, but you must almost break your neck to look upon them sufficiently.—In one of the staircases is a vast St. Christopher that almost sinks under the weight of the little Jesus, according to the legend.

Some of the best churches are St. George's, St. Peter's, and the Redentore—all by Palladio (?).

In the *Church of St. George* are several pictures by Tintoret, in particular two or three martyrdoms in which the dying saints seem to feel no pain at all. He certainly overdoes the calmness of them. There's one with a great nail driven into his skull, perfectly unconcerned at it, and a St. Stephen stoning to death, very much at his ease.—The two courts in the convent there are by Sansovin and Palladio, the latter on double ranges of pillars and of a fine air in the whole.

The *Church of the Redentore* looks like that of St. Justin at Padua: beside that it is a perfect orangery and placed on the Great Canal of the Giudecca.—Almost opposite to the Redentore is the *Madonna della Salute,* both of which were built ex voto on deliverances from the plague.—At the *Jesuits'* is a good St. Lawrence and St. John Baptist, but what they are most famous for is their marble (the prevailing colour is greenish) of which inlaid are the long pieces like painted calico, the marble carpet for the steps of the altar, and the marble curtains to the pulpit. The great altar is of fine marble and several of the side-altars of grey and other sorts, extremely beautiful.

It was in this city that I first observed that the taste of the artists for allegory increased greatly upon us as we advanced more toward the East. Even the signs to their shops are full of it.[3]

In the *refectoire of St. George's* is the famous 'Marriage of Cana' by Paul Veronese. Félibien talks of 120 finished persons in it; he must reckon in every the least and obscurest head, for after reckoning in the most inconsiderable, I told but 118, some of them of so little appearance that one might very well miss two more in counting. 'Tis in his usual way, magnificent instead of proper. The architecture part is grand and the feast and attendants all for a person of the first rank. The figures are many of them excellent: the person tasting the wine is Paul Veronese's brother and the person playing on the bass-viol himself, with a group of brother painters under the characters of musicians.

At *St. John's and St. Paul's* is the famous 'St. Peter the Martyr', which Vasari calls the best of all Titian's works, but so ill kept that we, who are no connoisseurs, should take it for a wretched piece of daubing.—A little beyond it is the history-piece of St. Dominic with the hostie and the ass worshipping it (a good emblem for the Roman Catholics).—'Tis a mighty common thing in most of the churches of Venice to have honorary monuments for their great men. The senate, who love to depress any dangerous merit in the living, make it up in their gratitude to the dead. This church is particularly full of these monuments. Valerio's tomb is the most distinguished among them (the middle statue by J. Bonazzo), and before the church is an equestrian statue set up S. C. to Bartolomeo Colleoni, just after they had taken care to have him poisoned.—Over one of the tombs in the church, in an urn, is the skin of Bradeniga [?] ransomed from the

Turks. There is a good statue in the church (on the right hand of the high altar) said to be of Sansovin.—At the *Frari* is St. Antony (?) restoring his father to life.

Just by St. John's and St. Paul's is the *School of St. Mark*. The pictures at the altar-piece by Palma (?) and that at the bottom by Tintoret: the latter is a worshipper of St. Mark, delivered from death by a sudden storm of hail and rain.—The large naked piece, endeavouring to cover himself, is greatly esteemed (what's the meaning of the man on horseback galloping off the Palace of St. Mark as fast as he can drive?).—In the albergo just by is 'The Storm' by Giorgione (a sea as dark all as ink and the three saints on it going to sink the devils) and 'The Ring Delivered' in another piece, by Paris Bordone.

At *St. Roc's* is the swift piece by which Tintoret got to be employed for the whole. 'Tis a St. Roc in the air, an oval, not large, on the roof of the albergo. In the same room is the best piece Tintoret did for that School, his 'Crucifixion' which is engraved by Aug. Carracci and is one of the three only plates that he ever set his name to.—On the staircase is 'The Plague' and 'Deliverance'.—The great room is full of Tintoret too: there is a 'Salutation' in particular of his, in which a chair is exactly expressed and the Virgin's face altogether as horridly done.

At the *Carità* is Titian's 'Old Woman with Eggs' that Wright calls the best piece of low life he ever saw.—In the *Dominicans*, near the School of St. Mark, is 'Our Saviour with the Publicans', one of Paul Veronese's famous feast pieces. We only saw the copy of it by a German in their refectoire for meagre days.— At the monastery of *St. Daniel* (by Palladio's St. Peter's) are some pretty little pieces, and at the nunnery of *Maria delle Virgini* a Madonna by Raphael. The latter receives none but ladies of quality, the obliging portress that day was of the Contarini family. . . .

In the *palace of* one of *the Pisani* ⟨the descendant, I believe, of him who bought up the MSS of the Aldus family⟩ is a library open to all the studious three whole mornings each week. The Corinthian pillars between the ranges of books are all cheats: they are hollow and full of books that might not become the Italian gravity in public. 'Tis not for anything farther, for he has a license from the Pope to entertain any heretical authors in his library. We saw there the first product of the press lately set up at Constantinople. 'Tis a sort of dictionary, very handsomely printed.—At another of the Pisani's is the family of Darius addressing the conqueror, by Paul Veronese.

At Sʳᵉ *Barberigo's* is a good collection, especially of Titians. There is the first piece he ever did, a 'St. Jerome in the Wilderness' (the *paysage* even then good, but with very bad beasts) and his last, a St. Sebastian, unfinished. There's another whole room with nothing but Titians, particularly a Venus viewing her face in a glass (her hair is milk-white and her eyebrows black) and opposite to the Venus a Magdalen in which the flesh of the face and look of the eyes and cheeks after weeping is incomparable. The French King had the fellow of this, and upon its being burnt, offered, as they say, 40,000 crowns for this.

At the *Grimani's*, near the Servi, there is in one room two very good Bassans with a Titian (?) between them, and two Veroneses with a Vinci (?) between them. The brass and copper in Bassan's and the Pharaoh's daughter in Paul Veronese's particularly good.

The form of what we call a Venetian window is used for several other things. Often, with double rows of pillars, it makes the entrance to a house and, without them, a gate to a garden (then perhaps nearest its original: a triumphal arch?).—The great altar with the two side-chapels is of the same form at the Nuns of St. Bennet in the Giudecca.—In the Giudecca is a range of storehouses that seem now almost useless. The Dogana is prettily placed, and the Arsenal but moderately furnished at best.

1. ' 'Tis the Greek cross, a duomo over each of the five partitions, and four arches to each dome—only the entrance arch is lengthened out by what one sees of the top of the portico, and the back arch to the great altar is half a dome. The whole ceiling is histories in mosaic on a gold bottom, and the floor common mosaic.' [Spence's note]

2. 'Presented to Nero by Tiridates, King of Armenia, placed on his triumphal arch at Rome, removed by Constantine to Constantinople, and recovered thence in 1206 when the Venetians and other Christian powers took that city'—*Wright*. [Spence's note, referring to Edward Wright's *Some Observations made in travelling through France, Italy, &c., in the years 1720, 1721 & 1722* (1730), 2 vols.]

3. 'Among these are Il Paradiso, F[ather] S[on] H[oly] G[host] and V[irgi]n—Volontà di Dio, naked woman descending from God the Father—Il Padre Eterno—Il Secolo d'oro, gilt old man with bird in his hand—La Trinità—Bologna, a lady like Pallas—Providenza, with a rudder—Madonna de Lotto—The Assumption, Redeemer and Holy Ghost, more than once each; the latter God the Father and a dove—Secolo delle Lettere, old man with phoenix rising from the flames—Felicità delle Lettere, genius holding up a book—Innocence, a brunette beauty in white, stroking a lamb in her lap—Justice and Peace, in a fondling posture—The Judgement of Paris—(God the Father nine times from St. Chrysostom's to the Piazza)—Il Pensiero, a man with wings to his head, holding his hand to his forehead, as considering—La Dea, Venus.' [Spence's note]

---

*27

Source: Egerton 2234 ff. 48–49
Addressed: *as in* 18
Numbered: 7th
Endorsed: *a.* at wint mar: 13/y[e] act of padua: & as/ dark as y[e] joke aingells
            b. Padua; & way of/preaching in Italy

Venice,
February 29, 1732

⟨Dear Mother,⟩

We are now preparing to leave Venice,[1] and in all probability shall have the pleasure of being in Rome before this comes to your hands. They tell me that we are going to meet the spring, and I'm the more apt to believe it because (though we have no spring yet in Venice itself) I see every day the flowers that are brought from the continent, and which are ranged in several of the markets here for the ladies, who buy them to put them in their head-dresses. The carnival died last Tuesday, and everybody now is got into mourning for it. Instead of the multitudes of fine dresses we used to see everywhere, one can now only meet with old women, and now and then a young one buried alive in a black veil. But I must not forestall things. I hope to give you an account of what we have seen here from Rome, and 'tis proper to tell you something of the life of the carnival before I talk to you of the death of it.

The last considerable place before we came to Venice was Padua. 'Tis a large city,[2] and the number and situation of the spires, which lay in a line before the eye, put us very much in mind of Oxford: we began to expect very fine things of it, but upon our entrance were very much disappointed. 'Tis much less inhabited than Milan,[3] and in reality the grass gets the better of them in several of the streets for want of feet enough to tread it down. In short, it looks like the ghost of a great city, and is rather famous for what it has been than what it is. We saw there the stone that Mr. Addison speaks of, which debtors for a moderate sum are to sit upon in a pretty scandalous manner instead of paying what they owe.[4] 'Tis come in play again lately, and last year there were three or four that caught colds upon it.

In going through the university[5] there we saw a famous doctor[6] that was instructing the young gentlemen. His subject and style were both as plain as the calmest chapter in the Bible,[7] and yet he spoke every word with more action and noise than any of our people on the stage in the most violent of tragedies. ⟨I thought he would have talked his wig off, though that would have been no great misfortune, for 'twas so bad that nobody would have stooped to take it up again, though they might have had it for their pains.⟩ 'Tis the same with the Italian preachers; those I have seen make a terrible noise and hubbub in their pulpits, but 'tis more excusable in them, for they talk there prodigiously often of the devil. One observation I have made in my travels, which is, that 'tis much more wholesome to be a parson in Italy than in England, for preaching here is really a very strong exercise and must conduce very much to their continuing in a good state of health. Beside that, they have very much the advantage of us on frosty mornings, for, let the weather be as cold as it will, they are sure to bawl till they are all over in a sweat. You see that I am not prejudiced in my religion, but would give the papists the preference where they really deserve it.[8]

⟨As the smallpox is very much in Winchester, I shall pray heartily for the preservation of the many pretty faces in it, and am very glad to hear 'tis so favourable a sort.[9] Pray who is it that is going to marry somebody at Southampton? For I can't recollect who you should mean.—The papers from England tell us that Mr. Nicholls is made a Knight of the Bath;[10] I was extremely glad to hear it, and have some reasons to hope 'tis true.—I am glad to hear the happinesses of Mr. Wavil's family, and long often to be in the Dean's garden with him talking about predestination. Hearty services to my sister and all friends from your

Dutiful and affectionate

Jo: Spence⟩

1. They left Mar. 3.

2. 'They call [it] eight mile about' (*Nbk.* 1 32ᵛ). Spence and Lord Middlesex stopped at Padua Nov. 13–14.

3. Our 'English Consul at Venice' told us that 'there are about twenty-five thousand inhabitants' (ibid.).

4. 'In the great Town-Hall of *Padua* stands a Stone superscrib'd *Lapis Vituperii.* Any Debtor that will swear himself not worth Five Pound, and is set by the Bailiffs thrice with his bare Buttocks on this Stone in a full Hall, clears himself of any farther Prosecution from his Creditors; but this is a Punishment that no Body has submitted to these Four and Twenty Years' (*Remarks on Italy,* p. 77).

5. 'Our cicerone' said that there were 'not above five or six hundred students belonging to the university, and yet 'tis the largest in Italy' (*Nbk.* 1 32ᵛ).

6. 'A Spanish count, a professor there' (ibid.).

7. 'Whether the *aediles curules* (?) were magistrates of the higher order or not' (ibid.).

8. Spence also saw at Padua 'St. Antony's tomb: the people smelling and kissing it ('Tis set around with nine relievos of his miracles by Lombardi, Sansovin, etc.)—Picture of the fishes, all with their heads poked out of the water like a simple congregation. The church of Justina, extremely neat and beautiful, and in the library by it Alfordi (alias Griffith) *Anglia Sacra,* four volumes folio' (ibid.).

9. On Mar. 13 O.S. the Duchess of Queensberry 'set out all on a sudden to take care of [her son] Lord Drumlanrig, who was taken ill of the Small pox at Winchester School. He is now perfectly well recover'd (for he had a favourable kind)' (Gay to Swift, May 16, 1732, *Swift Corresp.,* ed. H. Williams, IV, 22). On Lord Drumlanrig see *Letter* 25 n. 10.

10. Charles Gunter Nicol was made Knight of the Bath on Jan. 17, 1731/2 O.S. (*Haydn's Book of Dignities* [1894], p. 764).

*28

Source: Egerton 2234 ff. 50–51

[Rome,]
March 15 ⟨4⟩, 1732

⟨Dear Mother,⟩

Yesterday we arrived safe at the city of Rome,[1] and in this morning only I have already seen enough to make one most sincerely amazed at the magnificence of it. All the time we stayed at Venice I did not care to mention anything relating [to] that people; now we are four hundred miles out of their dominions I think I may do it with some safety.

The situation of their city is not more particular than their manners. They seem wholly to be divided between debauchery and devotion, and of course 'tis the most melancholy and the most gay place in the world. In the carnival they give a loose to all their passions, and 'twould be a modest thing to say they are only half mad.

The chief diversion is appearing in the great square, which is called the Place of St. Mark, in all the odd habits they can invent: their faces are hid, and in short 'tis a *mascarade* of six weeks' continuance. The pleasure of foreigners ⟨there⟩ is to see them act over their parts, for it requires a good deal more practice than we generally have had to behave so properly as they do, and the Venetians are grown the most eminent of all nations for the noble art of mimicking. You see always after dinner numbers of all sorts of people flocking to the Place of St. Mark. An odd blundering harlequin pushes you on one side as you are walking the streets, and while you are recovering yourself you stumble perhaps against a milkmaid who, ten to one, is a lady of the first quality. There are great numbers of gentlemen dressed up like country fellows, with wooden shoes, and I have seen one of them all covered with sheepskin and playing upon a bagpipe before thirty couple at least of people of fashion dressed up like country people. There are others like Turks, Indians, Sclavonians, etc.

The character[s] that gave me the most pleasure were the lawyers. You'd always have five or six of them together with very scurvy black gowns and weather-beaten wigs. They were always in a hurry, and the noisiest people upon the place. They catch people as they bustle along in the crowd and swear they have a lawsuit against some of their neighbours. Upon these occasions every moment the dispute grows louder and louder, and the poor occasional client has a very bad time of it. I once saw six of these lawyers mounted on some rails near the church of St. Mark and disputing with much impetuosity, when—as heaven would have it—in the perfection of their bawling in comes a company of harlequins upon them, a dozen at least in number, who scampered up at them all at once, drew their wooden daggers, set upon the disputants and beat them all off their higher station, and then mounted in their places and chattered at one another like so many monkeys.

One day there was two excellent wild Indians, a male and a female, walked up and down very sagely through the crowd. The female one was a little polished for an Indian, for she had a muff made of a hollow piece of a mossy oak that became her extremely. Another time there was a great fat fellow dressed up like a nurse, and one of the tallest gentlemen in Venice like an infant in swaddling-clothes: the poor child bawled out every minute as loud as it could roar for more pap, and as fast as the nurse fed him sputtered it out again, very much to the diversion of the spectators. I was by him at the instant that an unfortunate English sailor, who had ventured from the port (which is just by) to the Place, stood to gape upon him, and the great child was so mischievous and aimed so well as to give him a mouthful he did not care for. My countryman took it very ill and clenched his fist very furiously at him, and I believe verily, if we had not interceded with him, would have beat the baby's teeth down his throat.

Between the port and the Place is an opening from the great square where

I have gaped away many a good hour. 'Tis the region of the mountebanks, ballad singers, rope-dancers and conjurers. There were never less than three mountebanks' stages, the gentlemen on them all haranguing together, and at least seven seats of conjurers. One conjurer was a gentleman dressed in scarlet trimmed with gold, and his wife by him, a lady of the same profession. They sit in chairs on a table; they have their books by them and a long trumpet in their laps. When the curious come to be informed of their future fortunes, they apply the little end of the trumpet to their ear and speak down the great end of it. The patients listen at bottom with much anxiety in their countenances. 'Tis surprising how many customers they have. I have observed my friend in scarlet for an hour together on purpose, and in all that time he has not been a minute together without some new fool at the end of his trumpet. ⟨I have no more room, and am

Your dutiful and affectionate

Jo: Spence.⟩

1. The ten days' journey from Venice to Rome is described in *Letters* 29 and 30.

Notebook 1
(31–32) 39^{r-v}

The carnival seems at first a mighty foolish thing, but in eight or ten days you find it pleases you insensibly more and more, and anybody that has sense enough may easily grow as great a fool as the rest. The air is even infectious, and you have nothing to do but not to be too wise. The masks are not in so great a variety as might be expected: harlequins, pleaders, *paysans* and *paysannes*, squeaking fellows with high hats and a foolish sort of women with turn-up noses are perpetual characters. ... I remember one noble Venetian and one priest, the long cavalcades with rustics playing and bagpiping, and the little children (especially the *coviello* that could but just walk) and others, even in arms, are dressed in characters. Whatever this masquerading is, you find yourself dissatisfied when 'tis over, and though you don't like it perhaps at the beginning, you are sure to be sorry for the loss of it when it ends.

*29

Source:	Egerton 2234 ff. 52–53
Addressed:	To/Mr Spence/att the African House/in Leaden-Hall-Street/London/*Inghilterra/ Angleterre*
Postmarked:	AP 26 ROME
Endorsed:	*a.* came here/aprill 28/ye descripshon of Loretto & Route/frō Venice to that place *b.* Route frō Venice/to Loretto *red wafer*

Rome,
April 16 ⟨5⟩, 1732

⟨Dear Mother,⟩

My last of the 15th of March I wrote to you from Rome; we stayed there for the present only two days, to take a little breath, and then went on hundred and fifty miles farther, to Naples.[1] Naples is the very farthest point we were to go to from England, and the morning we set out to return from thence hither, 'twas a common observation among us all that we were then first returning homeward again. As much as I long to see you, I should not care to forward our journey on homeward till we have enjoyed some months in this city. 'Tis the place I always had such an eager longing to see, and I assure you that in many things it more than answers my expectations. I long to talk more of it at present, but I must follow my old way, and let you travel on with me regularly as we used to do.

From Venice we set out in a large covered boat for Ferrara. We were two days and a night upon the Adriatic Sea, or rather coasting along the marshes that border on it.[2] The first night was the first time I had ever seen the sun set on the sea: 'twas really a very beautiful sight. Our vessel followed a great channel: the earth between us and the mainland is very high for five or six miles length: at low water it appears, and at high is all floated and looks like the ocean. 'Twas a very odd sight to us that evening to see hundreds of fisherboys walking upon the water. They were fishing for cockles, and had left their boats at a good distance from them: the water did not come up above their ankles, and at the distance we were they seemed to tread the surface of the sea. They trod the shallows for the fish, and as fast as they caught any, put them into little wicker-baskets they had fastened about their middle.

Though we were a good jovial company, seven (beside the servants and sailors), the night did not pass on so agreeably. In the morning we found ourselves gaining toward the mouth of the Po, the largest river in Italy, and came up it ⟨the rest of the day⟩ to the first town where we were to stay for a day or two. This was Ferrara.[3] It lies quite in a flat, and when you take a view of it from the top of the cardinal's house[4] there is not a hill to be seen in the whole circle round the city. ⌜Was it absolutely clear?⌝[5] The streets are prodigiously straight and regular, but as for the people, they are departed, and 'tis more the ghost of a town than Padua itself.[6]

Bologna makes up for it, the most populous town in the Pope's dominions,[7] in which almost all the streets are built with piazzas on each side, so that the people have everywhere dry walking in winter and cool in summer.[8] In going on toward Loreto we ran sometimes twelve miles together on the sea-shore, one wheel often in the water, like one of the days we had in Flanders. We often passed straggling pilgrims, and the nearer we came the thicker they grew: for the last five or six miles the road was extremely well stocked with them. The Holy House ⟨or rather room⟩ is cased ⟨all⟩ with a marble cover to secure it from the devotion of the pilgrims, who would else have carried it away, piece by piece, by way of reliques. There's a good handsome church built over it, and it stands in its marble doublet just under the dome.[9] Loreto is a little town, poorly walled and of no strength though on a hill. We came to it on a Sunday night while the people were at vespers: 'tis incredible what numbers streamed from the church after the service was over, we thought the run of them would never have ended.

Next day we went all to pay a visit to the Holy House. The first thing they show you is the image of the Virgin,[10] some of her clothes that always keep their colour as fresh as when she first bought them out of the shop, and a little dish out of which she used to breakfast ⟨etc.⟩. This image is covered all over with gold, diamonds, and precious stones. On one side of her is an angel of gold, given by James the Second's Queen towards a birth, and opposite to it one in silver, given by her mother, to help on that same great affair.[11] The riches of the House and of the treasury just by are beyond all expectation. Out of many gold lamps that hang up before the image there's one only which is valued at twenty thousand pound,[12] and that whole room is perfectly wainscoted with gold and silver,[13] and yet all the silver and gold together would be inconsiderable in comparison of the value of the jewels, if they are all or only one half of them real ones. How many millions of poor people might be made happy with what is now made useless out of piety and religion.[14] ⟨I should be very glad to receive a letter from Mr. Wavil. Services to my sister and all friends. I am ever

Your dutiful and affectionate

J. Spence.⟩

1. They left Rome on Mar. 16, spent ten days at Naples (17–27), and returned to Rome for a three months' stay (Mar. 30–June 30).

2. 'We passed the port of Malamocco, Chioggia, the mouth where the Adige falls into the sea, and so came up the Po to the little channel of Ferrara;' saw 'nasty shallows' (*Nbk.* 1 39ᵛ).

3. They stopped at Ferrara Mar. 4–5.

4. 'Cardinal Rufus' Palace' (*Nbk.* 1 40ʳ).

5. Inserted from *Notebook* 1 40ʳ.

6. At Ferrara they 'saw the tomb of Ariosto at the Benedictines, [and] some pictures that were not bad at the Carthusians. . . . The whole town is surrounded with water, and the Arsenal is in so good order and so well stored that they seem fond of shewing it.

'When you come toward Bologna, you first see a range of hills: they are the beginning of the Apennines that way that lie very prettily behind the town. . . . 'Tis the finest and most fertile country in the States of the Church: their fields are well manured and, some of them, like those in Lombardy. They say there are forty thousand farm-houses in the Bolognese, though its circuit is not above 180 miles' (ibid., 39ᵛ–40ʳ).

7. 'They talk of 120,000 souls in the city' (ibid.).

8. 'It was here [Mar. 6] we first saw the races of horses without riders—they have spurns near their rumps, they start in the great place from the statue of Neptune before the legate's palace' (ibid.).

9. 'I could never find anyone that could give me any account of Crashaw's epitaph at Loreto,' said Holdsworth. 'I hunted the church all over and read all the epitaphs, and enquired

of an English Jesuit whom I saw there, but could find nor hear of no such thing' (*Obs.* No. 777).

10. 'Done by St. Luke' (*Nbk.* 1 41ʳ).

11. The circumstances attending the Pretender's birth in 1684 gave rise to scandalous rumours. Among the Spence Papers is a copy of a ballad called 'The Miracle; how the Dutchess of Modena (being in Heaven) pray'd to the Blessed Virgin that the Queen might have a Son, and how our Lady sent the Angel Gabriel with her Smock, upon which the Queen was with Child'. In the margin Spence identified the 'Angel Gabriel' as 'The French Embassador to our Court'.

12. 'Given by the State of Venice for their deliverance from the plague' (*Nbk.* 1 41ʳ).

13. 'Very ill kept and blackened all over with the smoke of the lamps . . . two or three ships in silver, etc. by persons that had escaped shipwreck, a rock of rude emerald (I believe artificial)', etc. (ibid., 41ᵛ).

14. 'If these Riches were all Turn'd into Current Coin, and employ'd in Commerce, they would make *Italy* the most flourishing Country in *Europe*,' wrote Addison, and thought of an expedient solution: 'It would indeed be an easie thing . . . to surprize it . . . especially if [one] had a Party in the Town, disguis'd like Pilgrims, to secure a Gate for him' (*Remarks on Italy*, pp. 145–8). Spence, who remembered Addison's passage, questioned Father Atkinson, a Scots Jesuit in 'a college of priests just by the Church of Loreto' about it: 'His answer as to their strength if the Turks or any other potent enemy should fall upon them, was that "God would be in their defence, for they had no other to trust to" ' (*Nbk.* 1 41ᵛ–42ʳ).

Notebook 1
(33–36) 40ʳ–41ᵛ

Soon after we left Bologna we came to the Emilian way, so well peopled with beggars. *Imola* [March 7] is in the Romagna. At *Forli* there is a triumphal arch and a column erected in honour to the Virgin Mary. Between Forli and Rimini we passed what is called the Rubicon on the maps. The bridge at *Rimini* (begun by Augustus and finished by Tiberius) looks strong and heavy at present: the triumphal arch to Augustus has an air that strikes one more, though mixed with what they have built on it.

In the morning, after leaving Rimini [March 8], we saw the little republic of [*San*] *Marino* on the right hand: 'tis a high hill with three risings on it, beyond it lies a ridge of hills, then covered with snow. All the towns and villages have their fountains—that at *Pesara* the prettiest on this road. (There's a pretty little church dedicated to St. Peter at *Fano*, with some pictures, not bad, in it.

The priest who showed it us, upon our commending it, said that 'as we were going to Rome we should see a church there dedicated to St. Peter too, which, as all travellers assured him, was still better than his.') There's a triumphal arch to Augustus, too, at Fano, lined out as when entire on the wall just by.

From Rimini to *Senigaglia* you come into the Marca di Ancona. We ran often along the sea, sometimes whole posts together, [however, we] only went by the walls of that city and so could see nothing of the port.

Loreto [March 9–10] is placed on a steep ascent: I fancy the first approach of it must have something very venerable to minds really possessed with a great notion of the thing:

> *Aurea nunc, olim silvestribus horrida dumis.*
> *Jam tum religio pavidos terrebat agrestis*
> *Dira loci: jam tum silvam saxumque tremebant.*
>   (Virgil, on the Capitol Hill [*Aen.* viii. 348])

It looks down on the sea, which is about a mile and a half from it. The history of the Holy House is engraved on the left (soon after you enter the church) in Scotch and on the right in English. There are thirteen inscriptions in different languages all. The House stands under a dome: 'tis all cased in marble. The case is worked in *basso-relievos* ⟨by Sangallo, Sansovin and Bandinelli⟩, in the front is the 'Salutation of the Virgin'. 'Tis a common absurdity to represent her as in a grand house, with Corinthian pillars, etc., but sure that absurdity was never so ill placed as here. Behind, is represented the several stations of the Holy House in its travels: you see it bringing o'er the Adriatic, in Laureta's wood, on the hill of the two brothers and in its present situation, all in one piece. The prophets (large figures) are disposed in niches round the case, and the sibyls (much less, but better) all round them. Within, . . . the roof of the treasury and the crucifixion at the altar are painted very well by Pomerancio. There's an excellent picture (the meeting of the Virgin and Elizabeth) by Hannibal Carracci, and an incomparable one of the Virgin showing the little Jesus to Joseph by Raphael, which they value above 11,000 crowns. Round the Holy House are confessionals marked for the several nations and languages. From the church we were escorted by a very large regiment of beggars, the most impertinent and the most impudent in the world, quite to the inn door where we were received (by another sort of beggars) with drums and trumpets.

In 1743, after his return from the last tour, Spence paid another visit to Pope. 'When I was looking over some things I had brought from Italy to pick out what might be of use to his grotto, and came among the rest to some beads and medals that had been blessed at Loreto, he laid them gently aside and said, "Those would be good presents for a Papist"' (Obs. *No. 353*).

*30   Source: Egerton 2234 ff. 54–55
       Addressed: as in 29
       Postmarked: M[ ] 10 ROME
       Endorsed: a. this came to me/may: yᵉ 18: 1732/an acᵗ
                   of yᵉ fine cascade/of Terni, yᵉ River falls/
                   down from a precipice of/a hundred yards high
                   b. Road frõ Loretto to Rome./Waterfall at
                   Terni.

Rome,
May 1 ⟨Apr. 20⟩, 1732

⟨Dear Mother,⟩

My last I think left us at Loreto: all our journey from thence to Rome was hilly or mountainous.[1] We passed the Apennines, where we sometimes had snow lying close by the chaise wheels and sometimes the road all strewed with violets. 'Tis in this part of his travels that Mr. Addison says he saw the four seasons of the year, all in six days.[2] We came farther up toward the spring than he did, and travelled the same ground from Loreto to Rome (almost all across Italy) in three days[3]—which would have made such a sight the more surprising; however, we had not the good luck to see all those seasons. We had then ⟨really⟩ the spring about as forward as it may be in England now, and as Italy abounds in evergreens of many sorts, it sometimes looked much forwarder. On the tops of the highest hills all was snow above us at a distance, and we were as cold as in December for an hour now and then, and in the sunny vales sometimes as hot as [in] summer. Thus far we had a shifting of the seasons, and no farther ⟨for I would not tell fibs to my mother for all the world⟩.

Between Spoleto and Terni (you may trace the places as we go on in your map) we went out of our way to see one of the finest sights in Italy for a natural curiosity. 'Tis a good sizeable river ⟨as broad as the Wares at Winchester⟩ which falls all at once down a precipice of hundred yards high.[4] It tumbles into a vast hollow between two rocks which are separated from each other in the middle and rises again with a rebound all in a vast arch of mist about fifty yards high: the rest of the river rolls out at the bottom between the two rocks, roars and froths unequally over the stones and broken pieces of rock, has forced a broken course for itself through the vale, and then gathering into a regular stream again runs into the river Nar, and so goes on with it to the city of Narni.

The fall itself is a very striking and beautiful sight. The brow of the precipice is worn into hollows by the mist and vapours that rise from it, the descent and slopes on each side are covered chiefly with olive trees and other evergreens, the leaves of which for a good way on each side are tarnished from the same cause. This, and the sudden fall make it terrible,[5] but the rising again of the water in that scattered pretty manner—like a plume of feathers gilded with the sun—is very pretty. I don't doubt but in a proper situation you might see rainbows in this mist; but we were just opposite to it, and the sun on our right hand. This is called the cascade of Terni: of old the river was called Velino. There were some parts of the Apennines that put us in mind of the Alps, but 'twas only a faint resemblance and a picture of them in miniature. They can't compare to them for rudeness, natural ruins or height, and when you think of them together these seem only to be like the son of a vast giant, about seven or eight years old; however, a pretty sturdy one, and gross enough for his age.

⟨I have had the pleasure of meeting Mr. Holdsworth, the poet,[6] here at Rome and talking with him of Hampshire and Nurse Page.[7] He has now left us. About three weeks ago he was robbed of his clothes, watch, a diamond ring and some money by a fellow that got into his chamber at midnight. He slept all the while. The villain came into his room with a lighted candle which he left behind him, so that 'tis concluded that if he had stirred the fellow was prepared to murder him. The rogue is since taken, and is to be put to the torture to confess. He pawned the clothes, and the pawnbroker appears against him. 'Tis probable he will be sent to the galleys. As for his life, Mr. Holdsworth was unwilling that he should lose that, because he had spared his when 'twas evident he might easily have taken it away. Such a robbery as this makes the more noise here because 'tis a very uncommon thing. The Italians love to pick pockets and pilfer everything they can steal slyly, but seldom rise to such a robbery as this.

The Queen of Sardinia's [fa]ther is a poor prince of Germany (as there are thousands of poor princes there) called the prince of Hesse-Rheinfields.[8] I wish I may see the old gentleman to [give] your service to him. However, we are pretty likely to see one of his daughters, the Duchess of Bourbon, the first beauty of France, and not cared one farthing for by her husband, who is so civil generally as to let her have a bed all to herself.[9]

Last week I sent Capt. Rolle a full and true account of the delightful spot we live in here, and shan't trouble you with anything of it at present because, ten to one, he will be so dutiful a child as to send his mother word of it. Nothing pleases me so much as that you have been able to write all your letters yourself the whole winter. I was terribly frightened at what you said about your eyes the beginning of it, but now hope they are pretty well. Ten thousand services to all friends from

Your dutiful and affectionate

J. Spence.⟩

1. They left Loreto Mar. 10. 'A day brought us from Loreto to Foligno [Mar. 11] where we saw an altar-piece by Raphael at a convent of nuns: The old saint's face in it excellent. Near Loreto we saw the very high Gothic bridge with such narrow arches at a distance' (*Nbk.* 1 42ʳ).

2. *Remarks*, p. 165.

3. The second day they travelled from Foligno through Spoleto, Terni, Narni to Otricoli, and the last (Mar. 12) via Città Castellana to Rome.

4. The cascade of Terni was constructed 271 B.C. to prevent the waters of Velino from flooding the plain of Rieti.

5. Addison in his *Remarks on Italy* (pp. 157–8) argues 'notwithstanding the opinion of some learned Men to the contrary, but this is the Gulf thro' which Virgil's *Alecto* shoots herself into hell' (*Aen.* vii. 511–68). Spence disagrees: 'I took a view of the whole with a particular eye to Mr. Addison's conjecture that this was the very descent for Virgil's Fury: it would certainly not be unfit for it, and in a day less beautiful would have appeared more so. Addison saw it from above (for he went from Terni to it and speaks of its course before its fall) so that he must answer for its channel

being shaded with woods there, as anyone who had seen it from below may, for its being called "specus horrendum et saevi spiracula Ditis" ' (*Nbk.* 1 42ʳ⁻ᵛ). In an earlier draft (ibid., 11ᵛ) Spence stated emphatically in the margin: ''Tis not the descent of that Fury.'

6. Edward Holdsworth (1684–1746) gained his reputation as a poet by his Latin mock-heroic *Muscipula* (1709). Because of his Jacobite sympathies Holdsworth refused a fellowship at Magdalen College, and the rest of his life acted as travelling tutor.

7. Not identified. For another reference to her, see *Letter 6*.

8. Ernest-Leopold, Landgrave of Hesse-Rheinfels-Rothenburg (1684–1731). Mrs. Spence evidently had some queries on *Letter 21*.

9. Louis-Henri, D. of Bourbon (1692–1740), married Caroline, the third of the Hesse-Rheinfels sisters in 1728, when she was only fourteen. She appears to have charmed all Paris, except the Duke. By 1738/9 there were rumours that Louis XV had an intrigue with her and that 'M. le Duc voulait la répudier, la renvoyer en Allemagne' (L. M. G. Philpin de Piépage, *Histoire des Princes de Condé* [Paris, 1911], pp. 357–63). Spence did see her on his way back in Paris.

Notebook 1
(38–39) 42ᵛ–43ʳ

After you get into your road again, the descent to *Terni* is very agreeable, and 'tis a plain till you come toward *Narni* [March 12]. Narni is itself on a hill: it lies up against the side of it like the map of a town against a wall. *Otricoli* too is on a rising. . . . The way is generally smooth and broad, as particularly over the Monte dei Popoli, and even down the Somma, the highest though not the largest hill of the Apennines we passed. (How swift we went, turning down!) . . . After coming through Otricoli we first saw the Tiber, went all along by *San Oreste* (Soracte of old), a barren mountain with a church and three or four houses quite toward its top, came forty times on and off the Flaminian way, passed the Ponte Molle, and so entered by the Porta del Popolo into Rome.

*31

Source:	Egerton 2234 ff. 56–57
Addressed:	*as in 29*
Postmarked:	MA 31 ROME
Endorsed:	*a.* come to me/may yᵉ 18 actᵗ of vesuvius: virgils tomb/yᵉ sibils chamber: & a descripshon/of yᵉ town of naples/& fine throughout *b.* Some Accᵗ of Naples, Virgil's Tomb, Sibills/Grott: &c.

Rome,
May 22 ⟨11⟩, 1732

⟨Dear Mother,⟩

When we got first from Loreto to Rome we only stayed three days to take breath (in which I wrote you my first from Rome) and went on for Naples. In going to Naples we often passed old Roman roads, in many places all laid with large smooth stone and as entire still as the pavement of a great hall, though near two thousand years old.[1] 'Tis to me the most surprising thing of art which we have seen abroad. This noble pavement, sometimes for miles together is bordered with myrtles and a hundred other evergreens,[2] and on each side of it you see perpetually the ruins of old tombs and monuments, for the Romans always buried by great roads (perhaps to put people in mind that this life is but a journey, and that in this world we are not properly at home).

There are sometimes orange-trees in the road, and at Mola,[3] a little seaport in the way to Naples, all the orchards were full of them just like apple-trees with us. Within about thirty miles of Naples we came into a vast plain, the richest soil and the best cultivated in Italy: whence the Italians call it 'Campagna Felice' or 'the happy country'. It was soon after that we discerned the top of the famous Mount Vesuvius, and the smoke which it perpetually flings out looked at that distance like a cloud gilded with the sun.[4]

Naples is one of the most delicious sea-ports in the world: it lies down a sloping ground, all in a large half moon to the sea. The shore on for a great way humours the same shape of a half moon. In one side of it, about six miles on the left hand from Naples, is Vesuvius, and on the right the grotto of Pausilippo and the tomb of Virgil.

The grotto of Pausilippo is a road made in a straight line quite through the bottom of a hill, broad enough everywhere for two coaches to pass, and the lowest part fifteen foot high.[5] At the entrance 'tis eighty, but the arched top goes sloping down to fling the light in towards the midst of it.

'Tis near half a mile long,[6] and when you are in some part of it 'tis absolutely dark. I passed it twice, and 'tis certainly one of the oddest and most disagreeable sorts of travelling that can be. You are for some minutes without seeing anything except a gloomy light at a distance, at each end: you can there discern people entering and going out (for 'tis a great road) who amidst the dust they raise and the odd light look like a stream of ghosts flitting backward and forward, and hear coaches running by you and confused voices without seeing anything about you.

At the entrance of this gloomy passage, on the side of a high rock, is the tomb of Virgil, the greatest poet old Rome ever produced.[7] It stands like a little round temple, and on the top of it grow three or four laurel-trees ⌜of which I have sent a leaf to Kit Pitt, enclosed in a letter⌝[8] and the ground where he lies I have kissed three times, ⟨so that⟩ I think his ghost ⟨very⟩ much obliged to me.

The dark hollow road below leads to a country full of curiosities. A little way beyond it is a grotto ⌜Grotto del Cane⌝, the air in which is so poisonous that most creatures, when held down in it, are killed in a few minutes;[9] just by is a lake ⌜Agnano⌝ the water of which boils up in several places ⟨like the water in your tea-kettle⟩. Indeed 'tis not only Vesuvius but all the ground (perhaps for hundreds of miles about Naples) has a bed of sulphur all under it, which makes a number of hot baths thereabouts and sometimes breaks out in eruptions of fire, as now often in Mount Vesuvius and formerly in a vast basin twelve miles on the other side.[10] This horror and beauty of the country, so oddly mixed together, made the old poets perhaps place their hell and Elysian Fields both in the neighbourhood of Naples.

⟨Don't be frightened if I tell you that I have seen both. We were in hell on a very fine morning. Only crossing a league or two of the Mediterranean Sea brought us to the Lake of Avernus, one of the rivers of the old heathen hell:[11] by it is a deep passage under ground to the Grotto of a Sibyl, into whose chamber at the end we rode on the backs of our guides, who were up to the knees in water. This letter will look most like a traveller's to you, but I have several noble witnesses to the truth of every word of it. I have not time now to tell you the particulars of our journey up Mount Vesuvius; that for my next. With services etc. I am

Your dutiful and affectionate

J. Spence

I am particularly obliged to Mrs. Pitt for her visit to you and her kindness to me.⟩

1. 'As the Flaminian way brought us first into Rome, at our first going out of it for Naples we fell upon the Latin (Quorum Flaminia tegitur cinis atque Latina). . . . A mile or two before you come to Terracina (Anxur) you fall in with the Appian road' (*Nbk.* 1 43ʳ).

2. 'A little beyond Piperno is the fine wood of cork-trees which we passed by moonshine, between that and Sermonetta is the noble wood of oaks. . . . There are great numbers of buffaloes about the country here' (ibid.).

3. The boundary between 'the Pope's dominions' and the Kingdom of Naples.

4. 'We were three posts from Naples when we first observed it. The next was Capua (two mile from the old) into which we entered by passing the Vulturno, low and not so rapid as 'tis called' (ibid., 44ʳ).

5. ' 'Tis a soft sort of stone ⟨so soft that in one place they are forced to [prop?] it with a sort of wall, in many others cut like butter, smooth, [says] Mr. Holdsworth⟩ and an inscription there pretends that it was done by a hundred thousand (?) men in fifteen days' (ibid., 46ᵛ and 13ᵛ).

6. '2200 feet' according to Holdsworth (ibid.).

7. 'The people of Naples think Virgil was a schoolmaster, a conjurer or a saint. The Temple di Fortuna beyond Mergilline is showed by some for his school ('Tempio della Fortuna, or[a]

chiamata scuola di Virgilio . . .); the making [of] the grotto of Pausilippo is attributed to him as a magician, and his horse cured all his infirm brethren by virtue of his saintship.' [On the popular tradition in Naples, regarding Virgil as a sorcerer, see D. Comparetti, *Vergil in the Middle Ages* (1895), pp. 253–89, 348–9.] 'As for his being a poet, that's but little known there. They say indeed that he wrote a book formerly ("What language was it wrote in?"—"In English to be sure" [said] the gardener) and that there have been Englishmen who in the memory of [this] man have brought his book quite from England with them to the place' (*Nbk.* 1 46ᵛ).

8. See *Letter* 32 below. Emended to 'some of which I shall bring home with me'.

9 'We tortured two toads that were very loving together and gallantly killed our dog. 'Twas in vain that they flung him into the lake just by' (*Nbk.* 1 47ʳ).

10. 'Down the brims of the basin grow little shrubs of evergreens, in particular myrtles and something like jessamin, and there are several sweet herbs growing among them that put one strongly in mind of a verse of Mr. Addison's— "And trodden weeds send out a rich perfume" ' (ibid.).

11. 'The view of which is now far from disagreeable. . . . The banks abound with violets' (ibid., 47ᵛ).

Notebook 1

(39–45) 43ʳ–46ʳ

Velletri [March 16] pretends to be the birthplace of Augustus. Toward the top of the great hill near Velletri (in our return) we saw that odd sight of the country below, fine and gilded with the sun, while we were in dark clouds and rain above. The towns in the road to Naples lie mightily on hills. We passed under *Sermonetta*, the town of the Prince of Caserta (?). The post before, we saw the refuged banditti, and the post just after was the fighting one. A little beyond this post-house is a stream of sulphur, and two or three mile farther the remains of the three taverns. *Piperno* is on a hill, and when you take the whole view there you see nothing but two more towns and a castle, all of the same situation, flat upon the tops of hills. . . .

In the first post from [the Appian road] you enter the Kingdom of Naples. The old rock with the wall and windows forty or fifty yards high in it, and the winding way by the sea. Afterwards the country good to *Fondi* [March 17]. . . . We crossed the water to [*Gaeta*] in our return and saw the vase with Bacchus' birth on it (the satyr with two pipes and the odd thyrsus). 'Tis a very fine piece, but damaged in some of the figures. 'Twas too wet to go up to the round tomb of Munatius Plancus, and I missed the split rock with the view of the sea through it and the chapel half way up.

Mola is the Formiae of the ancients, the seat of Antiphates and the Man-eaters in Homer's *Odyssey*. They show there Cicero's house and gardens, and say that he was an excellent schoolmaster. Before *Garigliano* lie several ruins (a very considerable run of an aquaeduct on the left hand, and a piece of a theatre and the remains of a great tomb on the right). Never did anything hit a description more exactly than the Garigliano does that of Horace: 'Et rura quae Liris quieta Mordet aqua taciturnus amnis . . .' [*Carm.* I. 31. 8].

Naples [March 17–27] . . . the mole with a little pharos, and another arm with the Jesuits' College . . . between them lie their galleys with the slaves, etc. Beyond the mole runs a corso all along the water-side . . . called in an inscription there 'Viam Olympiam' . . . (they had formerly Olympic games there). 'Tis very well stocked with fountains and bad Latin inscriptions of Spanish growth. It leads to the Grotto of Pausilippo, over the entrance to which, on the left, appears what they call Virgil's tomb, and a little further on the shore is Mergillina, the seat, church and burial place of Sannazarius. Six miles from Naples, on the other side, begins the Somma, and 'tis called two miles from thence to the top. Out in the sea beyond the point of that half of the moon, you see the island of Capri (Caprea), thirty miles from Naples. You have a fine view of this and the whole town from the convent of San Martino.

The Carthusians there are very rich. They have a court surrounded with Corinthian pillars of fine marble, the arcades are of a good taste in architecture (which is not very common at Naples) and in their church is the best collection of pictures in Naples. There's a dead Saviour at the end of the treasury, by Spagnolet, which seems an excellent piece, and in the church the prophets (very good) by the same. Over the door of the treasury are two pieces, one by Michelangelo Caravaggio, and the other of the crucifixion by Arpino, in one view: Caravaggio's is a St. Peter denying our Saviour, and the face of St. Peter is very strongly expressed. In the church is the lost piece of Carlo Marat: a St. John baptizing our Saviour. There are several other pieces too of Lanfranc, Solimena, Paolo de Mattei etc. One of their best pieces is a 'Natività' by Guido, unfinished.

Neither the pictures nor the churches [at Naples] seem extraordinary. . . . We saw a pretty palace of the Marquis Marino's, and in the court of Caraffa's (?) several antiquities (in particular a *basso-relievo* where is a man playing on two pipes at once). The head of the horse, called Virgil's, so famous for sick horses coming on pilgrimage to it, sticks out of the wall and does now neither any good nor harm. The palace of the viceroy has a good front and court within and you go up a very grand staircase in it, but the rooms, what with want of furniture and what with German ornaments, make a horrible figure. Just by this palace stands the old Jupiter Terminalis, a colossal statue of fine marble, found at Cumae.[1]

On the back of the town, up the hill, are the catacombs. They are of a large extent now, and they show you the place whence they say they ran on three mile farther. 'Tis now stopped up, because there used to be frequent murders when people ventured on in those secret windings of it. 'Tis generally of a good height, often turned on arches, and the holes for bones five or six ranges on each side. (Sometimes you have four of those arches regularly in a square and an alley into each of them.) They show some bits of very bad paintings and mosaic work up and down, which they call as old as the primitive Christians, and point you out the sepulchres of particular saints and good men positively enough. . . .

Mergillina is a very odd and pretty situation: the stone-seats round it have an inscription that perhaps refers to the old name of that coast (Pausilippo). The court to the house is the solid rock levelled. Sannazarius's tomb is a handsome one, and there are two good modern statues, one on each side of it (the sculptor, Fra Joan. Angelo Fiorentino. Ord. Serv. F.): they are an Apollo and Minerva. The Viceroy of Naples had a great mind to them, and was very near getting orders for taking them away as things too heathenish for a Christian church. The *Serviles*, [however], were too cunning for him: they got the names of David and Judith inscribed on the base, and ever since they have been very good orthodox figures. (There is a *basso-relievo* on the tomb between them that wants new naming or altering more than either of them. There's a Priapus like Pan, a lascivious faun, etc.)

1. 'Perhaps a good deal refitted. The head, breast, etc. ad umbilicum old and good. The terminal part is square equally (or very near equally) all down, covered behind and on the sides with a robe or carpet, fringed (modern inscription). Flat eagle's head above the inscription, tail below it, and feet hanging down the sides. His hands are made to hold two coats of arms, his feet appear under the tail, the wings appear rounded before and their points behind, a little below his elbow on each side. Siste Viator / Et vetustum Jovis Terminalis bustum / Contemplare / Quod caenoso loco eductum / Petrus Antonius Aragon / Hujus Regni Prorex / Hic transferri jussit / Anno 1670.' [Spence's note]

32

Source: *The Gentleman's Magazine*, vol. LXXXIII, pt. I (1813), pp. 538-9

Addressed: To the Rev. Mr. Pitt,/Rector of Pimperne, near Blandford,/in Dorsetshire./Inghilterra/ en Angleterre

SPENCE TO CHRISTOPHER PITT

Naples,
March 19, 1732
(in sight of Mount Vesuvius)

I believe, dear Kit, you would be at some difficulty to guess where I have been this morning. 'Tis not St. Peter's at Rome, nor the Louvre at Paris; but a place that I respect more than either—the Tomb of Virgil, here at Naples. 'Tis necessary for us gentlemen-travellers, more than any people in the world, to endeavour to be fools as much as we can. When we go to see a thing that is shewed as something very remarkable, 'tis not our business to enquire what reasons are to be offered for and against, but to resolve to believe strongly and to gape and admire as much as we can.[1] Full of these resolutions, I went this morning along the Bay of Naples (which is one of the finest in the world), and mounted up the side of a hill, over the Grotto of Pausilippo, to pay my devotions at the Tomb of the great Virgil. After winding round the side of the hill, with some difficulty, you come to the repository of this great man. The first sight of the ruins look venerable to you; and when you are to enter the sacred place, something like a religious horror seizes you. There lies the body of that vast genius, the greatest that Rome in all its glory could produce. Over those rocks and through this shady gloom has wandered that great soul, separated from its body and— from pens and ink. So I am now recovered again, and can ask you very sensibly and gravely, why you don't go on in doing justice to the gentleman I have been talking of?[2] If you don't, I assure you I'll go once more to his tomb to inform him what you have done in his favour, and how long you have stayed to complete the obligation. O, I had almost forgot that 'tis very true that there are laurels, or rather bays, growing upon and round the tomb:[3] a leaf of which, as his truest successor, I send you herein inclosed.[4]

Beside other letters, I sent you one from Dijon in France, in which I promised to write to you when we should get to this place.[5] I am now as good as my word, and have discharged my conscience. To grow serious, I must assure you that the account our news mentioned of the fire at Blandford concerned me very much: 'tis the settled misfortune of that poor town: I hope by this time it begins to recover from it.[6] I should be particularly glad to hear of the health of all your good family, both there and at Pimperne, and, when I come to England, begin to flatter myself already with the hopes of seeing Dorsetshire once more. We are now at the very farthest step we are to go; and when we go back from Naples for Rome again, I shall look upon myself as coming home again. How does Mr. and Mrs. Riley[7] after this misfortune? I beg my humble services to them: and with my heartiest respects to all your good family, am ever, yours affectionately,

Jo. Spence.

P.S. This morning, March 20, we have been on the top of the aforesaid mountain; but I might as well not have mentioned it, for 'tis a sight not to be described.

CHRISTOPHER PITT (1699–1748), Spence's fellow student at Winchester and New College, was presented in 1722 with the rectory at Pimperne, Dorset, where he spent the rest of his life. In 1725 he translated Vida's *Art of Poetry*, in 1728 the twenty-third book of the *Odyssey*; at this time Pitt was engaged in translating the *Aeneid*.

1. In *Notebook* 1 46^r-v Spence discusses at length why 'Virgil's tomb wants yet a more particular proof than what is commonly produced for it'. See also 'Dissertation on the Tomb of Virgil' in Spence's and Holdsworth's *Remarks and Dissertations on Virgil*, 1768.

2. In 1728 Pitt had published his *Essay on Virgil's Aeneid, Being a Translation of the first Book*. Spence, who considered Pitt's version superior to Dryden's, encouraged him to go on with it. Pitt did not complete his translation till 1738; it was published in 1740.

3. 'It has two or three bay-trees upon it, and the honest gardener has a notion that they increase as fast as he cuts from them' (*Nbk.* 1 46ᵛ).

4. T. A. Salmon writes: 'A small relick of this very leaf is yet carefully and religiously preserved in the letter itself; but has long since been wrapped up, for the sake of greater security, in a separate piece of paper, superscribed in the hand-writing, apparently, of one of its former protectors, "*A Bay Leafe gather'd from Virgil's Tombe*, 1732".' In 1813 the leaf was 'nearly reduced to dust'.

5. Not known to be extant. This is Spence's only preserved letter to Pitt from this tour.

6. For an account of the fire, which broke out June 4, 1731 O.S., and 'consumed the whole Town (except 26 Houses) together with the Church', see *Gent. Mag.*, 1731, p. 269.

7. Not identified.

---

*33

Source:	Egerton 2234 ff. 58–59
Addressed:	as in 29
Postmarked:	IV 14 ROME
Endorsed:	*a.* a further acᵗ: of/vesuvius only
	b. Accᵗ of our going up/Mount Vesuvio.

Rome,
June 5 ⟨May 24⟩, 1732

⟨Dear Mother,⟩

It was with a great deal of impatience that I waited for the morning when we were to go up Mount Vesuvius, which was heightened by my seeing it every morning. The tops of the houses are all flat at Naples and as smooth as a floor; they often set them out with flower-pots or orange-trees, and 'tis their usual place for diversion on summer evenings. From the top of our house we had a most distinct view of Vesuvius, and I used to run up there every morning the first thing I did, to see whether he increased in his smoking or not.

At last the morning came:[1] four mile we went along the beautiful shore of Naples in chaises, which we were then to quit from the rising and badness of the way, for horses. These carried us two mile more, and then the way is so steep and bad that you are forced to quit even them and be dragged up the two last mile by men who make a trade of it, and so are the more ready in helping you. A mile before you come to them, you pass a dry stream of black earth for a great way together. This is the way that the mountain formerly has boiled over into the sea: 'tis melted brass, lead, brimstone and earth, all mixed together, which after the fury of the eruption, as it grew cold, settled and hardened all along to the earth.

After passing this a' horseback and creeping up along the hill, you come to the place where the men are to help you. This is at the foot of the part they call the sugar-loaf: 'tis much like it in its make, having been flung up in an eruption[2] and increased by several other since (for the great vent for the fire is in the midst of it) by the earth's pouring down on each side of it, like the lower sand in an hourglass. However, if 'tis a sugar-loaf, 'tis a pretty sizeable one, for 'tis two mile up to the very top of it. At the bottom of it, when we came all together (for we were a large company)[3] there were I believe a hundred and fifty fellows stripped to their waistcoats ready to help us up. Two of these honest men get just before you, with strong girdles on; you take hold of the girdles, and then they draw, and you climb up as fast as you can. Both they and we are forced to rest very often, and then ⌐tug and trudge¬[4] up again.

The first two stages were pretty tolerable; then we got up over a vast solid river of what had been all running fire formerly: it lies now all in ragged pieces, in colour and make like the cinders of a smith's forge, only larger and spread for a vast way. In some of the resting places here we felt the earth hot under us as we sat down, in others the smoke and vapours burst out here and there so hot that you can't suffer your hand two instants in it.

The last stage is infinitely the worst. 'Tis all a loose crumbled earth in which your two draggers and you sink every step almost up to the knees, beside which it often yields under you, and 'tis often impossible not to slip back half a yard or a yard with it together—but the eagerness to get to the top when so near makes it the less troublesome. When there, you have a ragged rocky edge all round a vast cauldron of perhaps half a mile deep and a mile round, all full of smoke. The wind every three or four minutes clears away the smoke, and then you have a view of it. It sinks irregularly and raggedly all down on the inside. There are several places in it that look of a fire-colour, blueish, greenish and principally yellow. Paper held to it lights, though it looks rather of a flame-colour than as actual flames. A stone is a vast time rattling down the hole, and sometimes sounds as if 'twas dashing through melted metal. The smoke often fills up the whole hollow, and by fits the wind clears it that you see the sides distinctly and the bottom. In a minute or two you are all clouded again. There seemed to be something like a regular pulse in its venting smoke.

One of my guides was an extraordinary honest fellow; I was got very intimately acquainted with him in our journey up. He told me that 'to be sure the devil lived in that hill',[5] and wished very heartily that all the Frenchmen were in there with him. Upon my telling him that we were all Frenchmen, he said he was sorry for it, but it could not be helped.[6] Our descent from this devilish place (which I was very sorry to leave) was rather flying than walking: we were down I think in fifteen minutes, which is pretty swift for two mile.

I forgot to mention one part of the sight: when the wind blew away the smoke from between the crags of the opposite side of the cauldron, we had a view of a beautiful piece of country, green fields, meadow-grounds, etc. thick set with houses; on the right hand appeared a part of the delicious bay of Naples: 'twas but turning the head, and we had a full view of all the city and bay. This mixture of the most beautiful things with the most horrid that can well be imagined, had a very particular effect, and struck one in a manner that I never felt upon any other occasion.[7] ⟨I could wish myself there again, was not I now a hundred and fifty miles nearer Winchester. We have almost finished our affairs at Rome and shall not stay here much longer.[8] In nine or ten months (which is about the time I used to stay at Oxford together) I hope to see how you do in Hampshire, and to walk up Giles' Hill instead of Vesuvius. In the meantime with all the services to all friends I am

Your dutiful and affectionate son

J: Spence⟩

1. On Mar. 20.

2. The terrible eruption of Dec. 16, 1631, which took 18,000 lives and considerably changed the shape of Vesuvius.

3. 'And the cicerones had a very good day of it' (Nbk. 1 45ᵛ).

4. Emended to 'draw and climb'.

5. 'This the common opinion at Naples, as that of the Solfatara's being Purgatory' (ibid., 13ʳ).

6. 'He often called out on Signor Diavolo while we were drinking some very good

Lachrimae Christi that grows on the mountain' (ibid., deleted by Spence).

7. 'I missed Dr. Hay's Well (the place from whence they first, and then, crept into the ruins of Herculaneum), they say 'tis as yet more troublesome than curious. We did not go to Capri on the same account' (ibid., 46ʳ). Large-scale excavations at Herculaneum did not begin till 1738. See Letter 156 from Spence's last tour.

8. They left June 30.

Notebook 1

(47–50) 47ʳ–48ᵛ

Solfatara is a worn-out, more peaceable kind of Vesuvius ('was', [says] Mr. Holdsworth, 'just as it is now, in Strabo's time'). The risings round it form a basin, and all the middle or 'area' is a white solid lake of bitumen. There are two or three small vents for smoke still, into which if you fling anything 'tis returned with a whirl of the stones and dirt round the vent. (On the other side, the rising water that boils violently with a vast smoke: Holdsworth ... imagines the whirl in it is occasioned by water, as much of the smoke too in Mount Vesuvius. A mattock held down in it has drops of water running from it in less than a minute.) There's a good part of it hollow beneath, as you find by the sound. ... In turning hence to *Puzzuoli* we saw the ruins of a theatre (?); from Puzzuoli we crossed the water to the *Lucrine Lake*, which has been little better than a puddle ever since the violent birth of Monte Nuovo [in 1631]. ...

[*The Sibyl's Grotto:*] This is a very deep passage cut into the hill; it is very narrow at the entrance, but afterwards of a reasonable height. It turns, after you are in, a pretty way and leads to an odd room, where your guides are knee-deep in water, and which seems to have been a bath. Its face does not appear to the lake, and there was formerly a wall to the right as you go to it. (Q: what it was, for it cannot be either the Sibyl's grot, nor even the entrance to hell, according to Virgil's account of them.) Opposite to the entrance of the grot, on the other side of the lake, are the remains of a temple which they call Apollo's. The antiquarians give it to some other god (more likely Diana's). At *Cumae* they show another Sibyl's grot, and they say there's a communication between the two.

All the coast to Baiae (quite to the castle at present) is a soil of antiquities. There are considerable remains of baths (Nero's, etc.) and temples (Mercury's, Diana's, Venus' . . .). We coasted thence to *Bauli*, saw the Lago Morto and the Elysian Fields, went down into the 'piscina mirabilis' supported by 48 (?) large pillars (12 by 4) joined at the top with arches, and the 'centum camerae Neronis'. *Baiae* at present is only four cottages straggling about these great ruins. From Bauli we passed the water again to Puzzuoli, saw the pedestal with *basso-relievos*, passed by the seaside ⟨over a continuation of the Appian way into a fine road⟩, and so returned through the Grotto of Pausilippo to Naples.

The new theatre at *Naples* is one of the finest and most spacious I have seen. Six rows of boxes, thirty in a row (where the King's box in front does not interfere) and room for four persons in the front of each box. (They are about 12 f. by 12 f. The parterre is about 60 f. deep and 68 wide to the orchestra, the stage about 152 f. in front, where 'tis most narrow, and 130 (?) deep.)

The people of Naples lie under a bad name. The Germans keep them a good deal under. There are numbers of patrols marching about the city all day long, to keep the people in order. Naples is extremely populous: they say 'tis twelve mile round (eighteen with the suburbs) and in all they talk of 500,000 inhabitants. They will tell you that they have 300 princes belonging to the city (I suppose all in the kingdom of Naples have seats there). 'And dukes?' 'Senza numero.' My Lord's banker there was a Duke of Carignani, and with them a duke is above a prince, because every duke is a prince but not every prince a duke. There are hot parties between the old and the new nobility, and each party is subdivided again by particular feuds.

The Viceroy of Naples at present is a worthy man, the Count de Harrach. Like all German governors, he never stirs out without a great deal of attendance and state. We saw him go to church (?) with a suite of fifteen or sixteen coaches, and he eats very soldierly to the sound of trumpets and kettle-drums. The Neapolitans, they say, love the Spaniards more than the Germans,[1] and their affairs are administered at present chiefly by a Spanish council at Vienna, under Prince Eugene. The Germans are more just upon the *great* men that oppress the people than the Spaniards, and therefore the Spaniards are more liked by *them*. Even as it is, justice is a very difficult thing to be got there: the privileges of the Church are much insisted on, and murderers have refuge in abundance. The Emperor, about twenty years ago, wanted to punish some particular murderers. The soldiers were ordered to kill them at the altar. The Bishop of Benevento (afterwards Pope Benedict XIII) immediately laid the Emperor and the whole Kingdom of Naples under an interdict. The then Pope hushed it up. This shows how fierce the best men may be for the worst privileges. They now murder on, with too much impunity. ⟨Those who murdered the Irish officer a little before we came there were betrayed, though not given up in form, by the monks.⟩

1. 'When [I was] there in 1741, they fed the Germans more than the Spaniards: this reconcilable enough: they hate their present masters most.' [Spence's note]

*34

Source: Egerton 2234 ff. 60–61
Addressed: as in 29
Postmarked: AV [3?]
Endorsed: a. a descripshon/of Rome
             b. Some Acc^t of Rome.
             red wafer

Florence,
August 2 ⟨July 22⟩, 1732

⟨Dear Mother,⟩

We are at last got to this city, from whence I should rather choose to write to you about Rome than to have done it from that capital itself.[1] ⟨I did not care to talk much to you about Rome till now, that I can assure you I have left the Pope's town without turning papist. We are now got safe to Florence, and so I may now talk my bellyful of it.⟩

Rome is above thirteen miles round the walls, but not a third of the inside of it is fairly inhabited. There are several vineyards within the walls ⟨as there are hop-gardens in Winchester⟩, and several of the nobler palaces have gardens to them as large as if they were in the country. 'Tis common for the first noblemen to have a palace in the heart of the town, and a house and gardens (which they call their country-seat) within the walls, but in the less inhabited parts of the city. I have taken a walk of a mile in a straight line to one of the gates, with hedges and not one house on either side of me. This mixture of city, country and gardens, with the inequalities of the ground (for Rome is built on above seven hills and in many other places is made strangely unequal by successive ruins) gives several views of an uncommon sort, and more beautiful than are to be met with in most other cities.

In many parts you have little groves of pine-trees rising above the houses, here you see a long garden with statues and fountains sloping down half the side of a hill, and the other half full of buildings and regular streets, and there a dark wood running along the side of a market-place. St. Peter's and the vast palace of the Vatican lie at distance in a line before our house, and between that and our part of the town is a pretty run of meadow-ground and the river Tiber. It was from this very meadow that the Romans formerly took an honest man from the plough to be general of their armies and sole governor of the state. He beat their enemies, settled everything extremely well in the government, and then retired again to his four or five acres of land which he ploughed and managed all himself to the best advantage to get bread for his wife and children. His name was Quinctius Cincinnatus, and the meadow I'm talking of is called the meadow of Quinctius to this day.[2]

This is one of the pleasures of being at Rome, that you are continually seeing the very place and spot of ground where some great thing or other was done, which one has so often admired before in reading their history. *This* is the place where Julius Caesar was stabbed by Brutus; at the foot of *that* statue he fell and gave his last groan;[3] *here* stood Manlius to defend the Capitol against the Gauls;[4] and *there* afterwards was he flung down *that* rock for endeavouring to make himself the tyrant of his country; through *that* and *that* and *that* arch always moved the triumphs to this hill; *there* did one famous soldier alone defend the bridge against a whole army of enemies;[5] and *here* did another plunge himself down the precipice, because the oracles had declared that if any one of the soldiers would voluntarily sacrifice his life there, he should save his country from ruin.[6]

All these places I have often seen with pleasure, but there's one thing that mortifies one—that they turn these old Roman things into modern popish ones.[7] Thus by the hole that the last gentleman flung himself into to save his country, they have now built a church to the Virgin Mary,[8] and call her over the door the *saviour* of mankind. In a round old temple just by was a statue of Romulus and Remus and their wolf, which the heathens used to carry their children to when despaired of by the physicians to beg Romulus to save them or take them to himself: 'tis now dedicated to some saint,[9] and the good women now, when their children are despaired of, play just the same trick.[10] There was another fine church dedicated formerly to *Juno the Royal*, and now to *Mary the Great*;[11] where the Roman ladies once a year used to prostrate themselves on the steps to beg children and good luck, the Christian ladies one day every year now do the same thing there. Just by is a church formerly dedicated to Diana, the patroness of all beasts, and now to St. Antony,[12] the patron saint of all cattle—on his day they bring horses, mules and asses from all parts to be blessed for about a shilling a head, or what the good farmer can afford to give.[13]

To a lover of antiquities this is a great fault to see these old things and customs turned into modern ones. The great amphitheatre is daubed over with pictures of saints in fifty places, and the Rotonda (the finest temple left of the ancients) which was dedicated to Jupiter and all the gods, is now dedicated to the Virgin and all the saints.[14] ⟨All our warm antiquarians in

England would go to loggerheads with them for this mixture of ancient and modern things together. For my part I am glad to see religion still go on in a better way, and to see that devotion has got the better of everything else among them. With services to my sister and all friends I am

Your most affectionate and dutiful

J: Spence.⟩

1. They arrived at Florence July 11.

2. Prata Quinctia, between the Tiber and the Ianiculum. The legend (Livy iii. 4.9–5.13) is a myth: the Prata Quinctia probably suggested the name of the hero.

3. 'This large statue of Pompey', explained Ficoroni at the Palazzo Spada, 'was probably the very same at the feet of which Caesar fell, for it was found on the very spot where the Senate was held on the fatal Ides of March' (*Obs.* No. 1383). The authenticity of the statue of Pompey has been discredited.

4. The attack occurred 387 B.C., but the story of Marcus Manlius, awakened by the cackling of the sacred geese, is another aetiological myth to explain the surname *Capitolinus* borne by a branch of the Manlii.

5. Horatius Cocles, during the siege of Porsenna, defended the wooden Sublician bridge. Another aetiological myth.

6. M. Curtius 'the hero of an aetiological myth invented to explain the name *Lacus Curtius*, a pit or pond in the Roman Forum, which by the time of Augustus had already dried up' (*Oxford Clas. Dict.* [1949], p. 246).

Spence remembered the stories from Livy, though already at this time the historicity 'of the first five hundred years of Rome' began to be doubted. In 1728 Bolingbroke told Spence of 'a set of stated paradoxical orations' held at the Académie des Sciences by Lévesque de Pouilly, purporting 'to show that the history of Rome for the four first centuries was all a mere fiction' (*Obs.* Nos. 884–5).

7. The following is an abstract of Conyers Middleton's thesis developed in his pamphlet entitled *A letter from Rome, Shewing an exact Conformity between Popery and Paganism: Or, The Religion of the Present Romans, derived from that of their Heathen Ancestors*, which appeared in 1729 and was well received in Anglican circles. (References are taken from the 4th edition, 1741.)

8. Santa Maria Liberatrice (or S. M. libera nos a poenis inferni), erected in 1550. In 1900 it was demolished to unearth the 6th-century basilica of S. M. Antiqua.

9. St. Theodorus. See Conyers Middleton, pp. 164–7.

10. 'But the priests now are perhaps more cunning than they were of old,' commented Ficoroni, 'for whenever they offer a child thus to the now saint of the place, they pray that "he would be so good as either to cure him or to take him to himself", so that the parents must always be obliged to them and their prayer can never be unsuccessful' (*Obs.* No. 1377).

11. S. Maria Maggiore. Spence made a slip here. The marble columns in the church come, according to tradition at least, from the temple of Juno Lucina. The ancient temple of Juno Regina was destroyed A.D. 425 during the construction of the church of S. Sabina (Ant. Nibby, *Roma nell'anno MDCCCXXXVIII*, pt. II Roma antica, pp. 670–3).

12. S. Antonio Abbate, in the immediate neighbourhood of S. Maria Maggiore.

13. Spence witnessed the ceremony on his third tour, and describes it at some length in *Letter* 142.

14. Conyers Middleton (pp. 161–2) adds: 'With this single alteration, it serves exactly for all the purposes of the *Popish,* as it did for the *Pagan worship,* for which it was built. For as in the *old Temple,* everyone might find *the God* of his country, and address himself to that *Deity,* whose religion he was most devoted to; so it is the same thing now; everyone chooses the Patron whom he likes best.'

*35

Source: Egerton 2234 ff. 62–63
Addressed: as in 29
Postmarked: AV 31 Ⓟ
Endorsed: descrip of viterbo,/Sienna; & Leghorne/
bisnes not to be seene
b. Road frō Rome to/Leghorn.

Florence,
August 23 ⟨12⟩, 1732

⟨Dear Mother,

I'm heartily glad to hear that [   ]¹ is paid off, and that that affair is
now entirely over. I'm afraid that you straitened yourself too much; if you
did, whenever Dick has anything for me, you may make it up to you again,
and then I shall be quite easy.⟩

In my last I sent you a little account of Rome—as to the particular
palaces, churches, fountains, pictures and statues, they are in such numbers
that they are only to be talked over when we meet ⟨round our coal fire⟩.²
At Rome there is what they call the 'mala aria', [wh]at we should call a
bad air at a particular part [of] the summer. They have great superstitions
about it, and are so exact as to name the very day that it comes in. The
country about Rome is almost a desert: scarce half of the ground is ever
cultivated, and there is sometimes not a house to be seen for five or six
miles together. This is one great occasion of the 'mala aria' which lies over
Rome in July and August, and in some parts for forty mile round it.³

We left Rome the 30th of June, and came all over a hillyish country to
*Viterbo.*⁴ ⟨I hope the map lies on your right hand.⟩ Just before Viterbo is a
very steep hill from which you have the view of a very fine lake:⁵ on its
right and on its left are two hills, all covered with woods, in the middle
lies the lake, as clear and as smooth as a looking-glass, all along beyond it
is a ridge of little hills rising one above another till they look blue, and are
lost in the clouds. The next day we passed another lake: much larger, and
with a great rocky island toward the middle of it⁶—and then got over a
ridge of hills which are the boundaries of the Great Duke of Tuscany's
dominions.⁷

The next great city is *Siena*, where we came on their great feast day and
saw a race after their fashion, without saddles and stirrups.⁸ The women of
Siena are extremely pretty, and their dress is still prettier. Their hair
brought up generally in three braids and twisted round at top like a coronet,

a little white hat, about as broad as my hand set on one side and a bunch of flowers on the other, is their general head-dress.

From Siena we went sixty mile by a very good and beautiful road to *Leghorn*. As Leghorn is a great port for trade, there are about three hundred English settled in the place, and there were then ten English ships in the harbour.[9] There are seldom so few, and they have sometimes above fifty at a time. The English consul[10] carried us to see a play ⌜*Invito di Pietra*⌝[11] there 'Twas an Italian *Don John*, but as they mix buffoonery with everything, when Don John sits down to supper he is attended by an harlequin who blunders about everything he is sent for and eats everything that comes to the table, without any compassion for his master. It was a scene longer than our *Don John*,[12] for he appears the last scene in hell, with a flame-coloured doublet on and three or four devils on each side of him, and would have made a very good speech there if he had [not] been so much interrupted by the devils' pulling him so often by the sleeve and spitting fire in his face so very plentifully.

In Leghorn you see immediately the benefits of trade and business: the town looks all alive, the people have an air of gaiety.[13] 'Tis a mighty place for pipes and fiddles, and the people are dancing somewhere or another all night long in the streets.[14] They say their Great Church was built by Inigo Jones,[15] and there are piazzas on each side of it not unlike those in Covent G[arden]. The mole too, out at sea, is said to have been built by the direction of an Englishman, a son of the great Earl of Leicester in Queen Elizabeth's time,[16] so that from the people, the place, the seaport and everything, we seemed at Leghorn to be half at least in England. ⟨I beg my humble service to my sister and all friends, and am ever

Your dutiful and affectionate

J. Spence.⟩

1. Two words obliterated, possibly 'Nanny Rhimes' (*Letter* 21).

2. For comments on some of these, collected during Spence's stay in Rome from Ficoroni, Foucquet, and Holdsworth, see *Obs.* Nos. 1365–1415a. Others are discussed in *Polymetis* and *Crito*.

3. As the causes of malaria were not understood, there were superstitious beliefs that sleeping outside Rome would be fatal.

4. 'Viterbo is particularly well paved, all with broad square stone, entire like a gentleman's court' (*Nbk.* 1 50ᵛ).

5. 'Lago di Vico: three beautiful views ... one on the flat, and two from the Montagna di Viterbo, but not one house in sight. On that

hill the stone they make use of to purify water' (ibid., 49ᵛ–50ᵛ).

6. 'The Lago di Bolsena ... at a distance' (ibid., 50ᵛ). Actually there are two islands in the lake.

7. 'On the highest point ... we passed by Radicofani, the first town of the Great Duke's. The barrenness and wild air of the country continues for some time, but grows handsome and cultivated twelve mile before you come to Siena' (ibid.).

8. The traditional *Corsa del Palio* is held on Visitation Day (July 2, also on Aug. 16): the seventeen *contrade* of the city are represented mounted on horses in mediaeval costumes, and a banner (*palio*) is raced for.

9. 'Twelve' says the *Notebook* (1 51ᵛ). Spence and Middlesex stayed four days at Leghorn, July 4–7.

10. Brinley Skinner, British consul at Leghorn 1724–33.

11. Inserted from *Notebook* 1 15ʳ.

12. Shadwell's *The Libertine* (1675), frequently performed between 1729–49 under the title *Don John; or The Libertine Destroy'd* (A. H. Scouten, *The London Stage 1660–1800*, pt. 3).

13. 'The merchants don't trouble the town with carriages, they live chiefly (or have their stock-houses) about New Venice, and so everything is carried by water' (*Nbk.* 1 51ᵛ).

14. Spence also saw an 'odd dance on the ramparts [with a] fellow that imitated the devil in it'. The English consul commented: 'Livorno sarà sempre Livorno' (ibid.).

15. 'The Dome and some of the arcades' (ibid., 51ʳ). Only the façade of the Duomo was designed by Inigo Jones during his second visit to Italy 1613–14.

16. Sir Robert Dudley (1573–1649), E. of Warwick, was one of the architects of the new mole in 1611 (G. Vivoli, *Annali di Livorno* [1846], IV, 122, 160).

Notebook 1
(54–56) 50ᵛ–51ᵛ

Siena [July 2–3] is seated beautifully on a hill, and the villas extend very thin on each side of it . . . ⟨about . . . are vineyards in the manner of our hop-gardens⟩. They call it seven miles round. There are many of their honorary square brick-towers, ugly enough and without inscriptions. The Cathedral has a tawdry look, especially from the lays of black and white. There's a pretty chapel in it, with two pictures by Marat and four statues by Bernini and his scholars. There's an apostle, too, against each pillar (in the great walk up the church) by the same school. Hospital handsome and airy [founded?] by the cobbler 'ultra crepidam' in the 9th century. Pius II's history painted in the library of the Cathedral; paintings in fresco that look at first like antiques; statue of three Graces. . . .

Leghorn [July 4] is about two mile round and the ramparts are a fine walk and with a fine view. The Great Street through the place to the port-gate very handsome, and the New Venice part of the town pretty. . . . The side of the port next the town is 720 paces, the line across 510, and the mole ditto. . . . There are thirty-five to forty thousand souls in the town, three hundred English. There were five thousand soldiers (with the Spanish) when we were there. . . . In the statue of the four slaves their affliction is admirably varied according to their age, the African seems to look as if he had nobody to tell his grief to. 'Tis ill placed, and the statue of the Duke is unworthy those of his slaves.

36

Source: Cocchi MSS in the collection of Count
Enrico Baldasseroni, Florence
Addressed: All Eccel^{mo}/Eccel^{mo} Dott^{re} Cocche/Padrono
mio Colendiss^{mo}

SPENCE TO DR. COCCHI   Florence,
                                              August 26, 1732

Dear Sir,

You will pardon my English familiarity when I call you so, and give me leave
to go on. I here send you the paper I spoke of last night.[1] Before you read
it 'tis proper that I give you the postulata on which this sort of translation
(or representation of the sense of an author) is founded. They are these:

1/ That the Eastern manner of expressing their thoughts is very different
from ours in the North.

2/ That the Eastern manner is more elevated and poetical, more full of
strong figures, metaphors, allegories and fables.[2]

3/ That to make an Eastern writer intelligible to the common people in the
North, you must do as you would do by any sublime poet: you must take
away the Eastern ornaments of speaking and give the plain sense.

4/ That by comparing passages, and drawing rules from thence, one might
come to some knowledge at least of the proportion between the Eastern
and Northern manners of speaking.

5/ That I have or ever shall be able to find out this proportion is a
postulatum that I have not the impudence to make.

If you have Villani's History by you, I beg you would be so good as to
lend it me for two or three days.[3] I am ever, Sir

                                        Your obliged humble servant

                                                        J. Spence

DR. ANTONIO COCCHI (1695–1758), physician,
minor littérateur, host to the English visiting
Florence. He had translated Xenophon of
Ephesus, and was something of a polyglot
scholar (his diaries are written alternatively in
English, Latin, Greek, Italian, French, German,
and Spanish).

1. The paper was evidently Spence's translation, perhaps from Hebrew, though this
accompanying letter gives no specific clue.

2. In 1730 Spence discussed with Lockier
'the proportion between the ways of speaking
used in the East, and those in such a northerly
country as our own'. Lockier pointed out that
'the disproportion between our ways of
speaking and those of the Orientals is much
wider ... than that between our plainness and
the Italian hyperbole' (*Obs.* No. 723).

3. Giovanni Villani's *Istorie Fiorentine* (1559),
reprinted in Muratori's *Rerum Italicarum
Scriptores* (vol. XIII, 1728).

37

Source: Egerton 2234 ff. 64–65
Addressed: To/Mrs Spence
Endorsed: a. ye descripshon of/ye vail & River/arno, &
the/tower of Hunger in pisa,/not maney miles
from florence
b. Pisa; & ye Vale of Arno.

Florence,
September 27 ⟨16⟩, 1732

⟨Dear Mother,

'Tis now six weeks since I have received any letter from Winchester, and I
long very much to hear how you all do there.⟩ Florence is so agreeable a
place that instead of one month we have already stayed above two here,
and may possibly stay yet longer.[1] The heats of the summer are now quite
passed, and, I thank heaven, without doing us any harm—and now we
have no more summers to pass in any of these hot countries.

I think my last left you at Leghorn. We came hence to Pisa,[2] through a
little paradise of evergreens and perpetual shrubs of myrtle, all in flower,
very much like our mayflower at its best. Pisa has on each side the river
Arno, which runs to it from this city. There's a castle there which is called
the Tower of Hunger, from an Earl and three of his sons being starved to
death in it.[3] The best poet the Italians ever had has left a description of
their manner of dying in a very natural way which for melancholy exceeds
even our 'Children in the Wood'. If I had time I'd make an English ballad
of it, and send it to you ⟨because I believe you can't so easily read the
Italian⟩.[4] There's another tower in Pisa which is remarkable merely for its
oddness. It stands all awry, and some imagine it was built so.[5] A little
beyond it is a church built about the same time, between five and six
hundred years ago, which is as handsome a building as the other is ridiculous.[6]

Most of the churches in Italy are refuges for rogues: before this, there
was eight or ten idle fellows lying on the grass, some of which we soon
learned were robbers, but the greater part murderers. They were some
playing at cards, and all seemed very much at their ease. I remember, in
going to see a nunnery at Rome, there was a woman sitting on the steps
who seemed particularly gay. As she was not ugly, one of the servants, who
was a wag, asked her whether she would go home with him, and she very
obligingly told him that she would have been very willing to have done so,
but that really she had killed her husband last night and was there at
present for a little security. Not the Pope himself, or the Emperor, can touch

the person that has got his foot upon sacred ground: so that if you kill anybody by a church door, you are safe.

Twenty miles before Florence we came into the vale of Arno, one of the most beautiful vales in the world. ⟨It runs on to Florence, and four or five mile beyond it.⟩ 'Tis all full of woods, cornfields, vineyards and country seats. 'Tis not near so broad as it is long, but the whole circumference of it every way is terminated with ground rising in unequal hills, which are cultivated on all sides as high as they can go. In the midst of it runs the Arno, which goes down to Leghorn, and furnishes them with easy carriage of goods and merchandise to or from the sea. All the roadside is thick of vines, the grapes hanging down from mulberry-trees and elms, and sometimes you see one tree of red and another of white grapes, continually for a long run together.

'Tis about a week ⟨now⟩ that they have begun the general vintage, and as the weather will now allow one to walk either on mornings or evenings, 'tis extremely agreeable to see how busy they are on every hand, gathering the grapes, treading them, and carrying away the juice. It was like to have been a bad year with them, but the rains, which came about a fortnight ago, have at the same time given them a rich crop and good cool weather to work in. ⟨One of the noblemen here has lent my lord a country house, so that we enjoy the season at present both in the town and country.

When we came to Florence we found Mr. Holdsworth in the same house where we lodged, and he stayed with us till within these five or six days.[7] He was very well and begs his service with mine to Nurse Page. In the same house we found and still have the company of a namesake of ours, one Capt. Spense who came hither for his health from Gibraltar, for the air of Florence is extremely good.[8] He is the only son of that Mr. Spense of Scotland, who was so cruelly tortured by King James in the Duke of Monmouth's time, his father being then secretary to the Earl of Argyle.[9] He outlived it, and King William gave him a place worth five or six hundred a year soon after the Revolution, which saved us all from any such barbarities for the future. I beg love and services to all friends and am ever

Your dutiful and affectionate

Jo: Spence.⟩

1. They stayed over nine months, till the end of April.

2. On July 7.

3. For the story of Count Ugolino's being starved in the Torre della Fame, with his sons and grandsons, see Dante's *Inferno* XXIII. In 1719 the elder Jonathan Richardson had given a version of it in blank verse (apparently the first translation of Dante into English), Gray in 1739 another. Reynolds's painting of this episode is at Knole.

4. 'The old ballad of *The Children in the Wood*' was praised by Addison in *Spectator* No. 85 as 'one of the darling songs of the common people'. Spence's ballad is not preserved, but a fragment of his poetic attempt at the next

canto appeared in 1746 in *The Museum*, I, 57, as 'The three First Stanza's of the 24th Canto of DANTE's *Inferna*, made into a SONG. In imitation of the Earl of *Surry*'s Stile'. It was reprinted in Nichols's *Select Collection* (1782), VIII, 24.

5. 'The leaning tower consists of six lessening stories of pillars all round, beside the base and the belfry: its variation is seven braces and a half' (*Nbk.* 1 52ʳ).

6. 'The Baptistery is round and something like an old temple. . . . 'Tis supported by twelve pillars, two round Corinthian and one square Gothic alternately. An inscription on one of them says 'twas built in 1153 [it was

actually commenced in 1063 by Buschetto], and sure 'tis a fine building, considering the time' (ibid.).

7. On Edward Holdsworth, see *Letter* 30.

8. Possibly John Spence, Master of the *John of Leith* in 1702–7 (James Grant, *The Old Scots Navy* [1914], pp. 252, 266, 284, 364). He was one of the English freemasons at Florence.

9. William Spence, as secretary to Archibald, 9th E. of Argyll, took part on May 2, 1685, in his expedition (three small ships) against the new monarch, James II. He was seized, however, by the Bp. of Orkney, sent to Edinburgh, and delivered to the government (Paul's *Scots Peerage*, I, 365).

Notebook 1
(56–61) 51ᵛ–54ʳ

Pisa [July 7]: The Dome is handsomer (less foolish) than at Siena—in it some pictures of Andrea del Sarto. The inside of the Dome was painted by Buffalmacco. The three gates at the west end are Scripture stories in compartments, brass alto relievo. In the Salutation piece the angel kneels to the Virgin. . . .

The Campo Santo is an oblong cloister, painted by some of the oldest masters and set out with rows of old bad sarcophagi. Cupid and Psyche on a Christian one, etc., the history of Job, six squares by Giotto, several by Buffalmacco, etc. Hell and Paradise, they say designed by Dante, probably taken partly from his poem. The hell is a very ridiculous and very comical one: the pulling for souls (little infants coming out of the mouth of the deceased, etc.), punishment of the Florentine vice, Solomon etc. On the vase before the Dome a bacchanal, old fat fellow with a boy. . . .

Lucca [July 8–9]: the ramparts very broad and a beautiful walk on them all round the town. The inward slope finely planted with trees, both for beauty and use. They reckon 22,000 souls in the city, including the regiment, which is about 1200 (?). They could raise an army of 30,000 on occasion. The country regiments are exercised thrice every month. They have arms for 22,000 in their Arsenal, but scarce any horse. 'Tis kept very well in order.

The chief governor is the gonfaloniero, changed every two months;[1] he can never stir out, except one of the three great holidays happen in his magistracy. One of these is the feast for liberty (di Libertà). The arms of the city are only a scutcheon with a scroll and *Libertas* on it. No one can be elected gonfalonier but once in six years[2] and nobody, of the thirty-six families capable of it, can be elected till he is forty (?) years old. There are nine 'antiani', (or ancients) who with the gonfalonier compose the chief magistracy. The magistrates are elected by ballot by the nobles, who are all regularly of the council at twenty-five years old. Three of these nobles every evening are obliged to walk the ramparts for so many hours, to see guard is kept and to look out themselves.

They have two judges: one for criminal, the other for civil affairs, and three others *conjunctim*, in whom lies the dernier resort for both. They can't imprison a citizen privately (as in Venice), and must give him a public trial. All the five judges are obliged by the constitution to be foreigners, that they may not have any attachment to families or separate interests, and are to continue but three years that they may not contract any; each is obliged to bring a certificate that he has acted well as judge in some other city, to be secure as they can of his knowledge and integrity.

The families in the country have partitions of land, as among the old Romans: they have three harvests a year (I suppose they mean of corn, wine and olives) but the clear gain of the first (?) is to be paid by the farmer to a sort of landlord or to the state. The greatest length of their territories is thirty-five mile and the greatest breadth sixteen. They lie chiefly in a vale between mountains, and a little part of it reaches down to the seaside. They have no barns (as is common abroad) and I think don't even put up their corn in stacks: when we saw it, its sheaves stood along in one row in each farmer's partition.

The plebeians have no share in the government: all their security is in the original laws. So that 'tis as absolutely an aristocracy as that of Venice, but not so absolute a one. The dress of the ancients is handsome and grave, they have something like a laticlave of cloth of gold over the shoulder—the gonfaloniero's is richer and his hat is all wrought over with gold. All the nobles have a particular dress:—'tis black and, when dressed in form, a very pretty one. They are under the protection of the Emperor.

Pistoia [July 10] is thin of people and has little remarkable in it ⟨the rope-dancing we saw there⟩, but the road immediately from the gate of Pistoia to that of Florence lies all through the beautiful vale of Arno. Just in the middle of the way is Poggio a Caiano, one of the Great Duke's seats, from whence there is one of the richest prospects of a vale that can be in the world. An inscription in the hall says that this palace was beautified by Leo X and that hall itself is painted by some of the best hands: in the 'Feast of Scipio' is a naked figure particularly graceful (like Apollo Belvedere), 'tis too divine an air for a servant. They have other fine pictures there of Raphael, Perin del Vaga, Jul. Romano, Andrea del Sarto, Rubens, etc. (in the same room where is the little Saviour with the Virgin washing her linen).

---

1. 'Even the officers of the city regiment take their turns every two months of being commanding officer of it.' [Spence's note]

2. 'Six changes a year for six years makes thirty-six, so that each family may have the principal office in it once in every six years.' [Spence's note]

38

Source: Egerton 2234 ff. 66–67

Addressed: To/Henry Rolle Esqr./at Stevenston, near
            great Tor/rington, in Devonshire,/Inghilterra
            Angleterre

Postmarked: SE 18 ℗

Endorsed: b. To Col: Rolle. A [descript.?] of England;
            &c.
            red wafer

SPENCE TO HENRY ROLLE

Florence,
October 11, 1732

Dear Sir,

I wish you joy of having made your tour of Holland and Flanders, and being
now as I hope at your ease in Devonshire to think over what you have seen.
Travelling anywhere, I believe, is agreeable, but what makes it most so is
perhaps its having that effect which it so seldom fails of, its making one's
own country the more agreeable to one afterwards. For my own part, here
on the other side the Alps, though I love to stay in Italy, yet I long to
see England, and when once we get there shall I dare say give a full loose
to the love of my dear country with ten times the pleasure I ever did
before. And indeed, though Italy be the country for the sights, England is
the country to live in, for my money. I have come here from seeing Julius
Caesar and the Capitol, when I have wished in vain, after it, to sit down to
a good piece of mutton; and though the statues here in the Great Duke's
gallery[1] are something better than what we meet with at Hyde Park Corner,
the Florentine beef is not half so good as our English. Our situation, too, in
England obliges us to sail for other commodities, and when we are a'
sailing, one can go easily for the best things to their own homes. We could
never buy even so good Burgundy at Dijon as may commonly be bought in
London, and the Florence I have generally tasted in England is better than
what we drink now on the spot. So that a man may perhaps be happier
in England, not only with liberty and the things of our own growth, but
with all the best foreign productions in an higher degree than the foreigners
themselves. So far for panegyric, though I had much a design when I began
to have carried it on to the end of my paper, to demonstrate to you how
happy you are in being in an island—the most beautiful, the most delicious,
the most improved of any under the moon, but as in all probability you
must feel that much better than I can tell you, I shall save my pen and ink
for matters of greater importance.

Don Carlos parted from hence the sixth for Parma.[2] The Great Duke paid him a visit the night before,[3] though so unused to move out of his chamber, and got up the next morning before sunrise to see him set out. 'Tis said there were tears on both sides at parting. I lay the night before at a villa which one of the noblemen here had lent Lord Middlesex for the season, and so only heard the discharges of the cannon at his going away. We shall stay here I believe all the winter. Florence is indeed a most agreeable place to live in, the vale of Arno is one of the finest in the world, and the city itself for buildings, statues and pictures stands among the first in Italy.

The Duke's gallery has an immense treasure of antiquities, many in age prior to what one generally sees at Rome, for this is the soil of the old Tuscan religious antiquities. There's a figure now in the gallery which used to lie despised under a heap of rubbish till Sir Andrew Fontaine discovered its worth.[4] It is a figure of the chimera in brass with old Tuscan characters upon it, which are somewhat the more valuable for being unintelligible: the old gentleman who presides over these curiosities[5] thinks it to be toward three thousand years old. There are two of the best tripods now extant in a room pretty near it, about a hundred dozen of antique lamps, a collection of all the ancient chirurgic instruments, several crowns (radial, mural, etc.), one of the brass pins from the portico of the Rotonda, built as you know by Agrippa. One may guess at the grandeur of the beams in that work (which were brass too) when this, which was one of the nails only to fasten them together, weighs eight and forty pound. Urban the Eighth, of the family of the Barberini, spoiled the Rotonda of its brass works,[6] which occasioned that piece of wit from Pasquin:[7] 'Quod non fecer[unt] Barbari, facient Barberini'. That poor fellow [has] now been a mute for some time. Marforio was first taken and carried a prisoner into the Capitol,[8] and Pasquin would have had the same fate had not a marquis to whose family he belongs been bound for his good behaviour. The first time he speaks, his master is to forfeit a round number of crowns; so he has left off his talent of railing. If you favour me ever with a line, please to direct À Monsr Spence avec Milord Middlesex, à Florence, en Italie. I long to hear how you liked your tour, and am Sir

Your most obliged and obedient humble servant

J: Spence.

---

1. The Uffizi, built by Vasari (1560–74), during the reign of Cosimo de' Medici, the first Grand Duke of Tuscany.

2. The succession of Don Carlos (1716–88), the sixteen-year-old heir to the Spanish throne, to the dukedom of Parma was the most talked of political event in 1732. In October 1731 a mixed English and Spanish fleet had effected his landing at Leghorn.

3. Giancastone de' Medici (1671–1737), the last Grand Duke of the Medici family.

4. Sir Andrew Fountaine (1676–1753), 'one of the keenest *virtuosi* in Europe'. See *Letter* 40 n. 7. Though Pope ridicules him as Annius in the *Dunciad* (IV, 347–54), his expert advice was much sought by English collectors of antiquities. The Etruscan chimaera, 5th century B.C., now in the Museo Archeologico

at Florence, had been discovered at Arezzo in 1555.

5. Sebastian Bianchi (1662–1738), the learned custodian of the Grand Duke's collection of gems and medals, from whom Spence gathered a number of anecdotes (*Obs.* Nos. 1571–9).

6. Maffeo Barberini, as Pope Urban VIII (1623–44), strengthened the Castel Sant' Angelo with cannons made from the bronze of the Pantheon.

7. A statue representing Menelaus with the corpse of Patroclus (or Ajax with the corpse of Achilles) in front of the Palazzo Corsini at Rome. During the Renaissance hundreds of pamphlets (called *pasquinate*), directed against the Pope or the government, were affixed on its pedestal and the walls about. Pasquin became the symbol of anonymous Roman satire. The statue belonged to the Corsini family; today it stands in the Piazza di Pasquino. Its name, according to tradition, derived from a tailor (or a barber or an innkeeper) who lived nearby (R. and F. Silenzi, *Pasquino, Cinquecento pasquinate*, Milan, 1932).

8. Soon a custom was established of giving Pasquin other statues as interlocutors. Marforio, the gigantic river-statue at the foot of the Campidoglio, was the best known among these, before it was removed to the Capitoline Museum. Spence seems to have obtained this information from Ficoroni, who was then in Florence. See *Letter* 40 and *Obs.* No. 1399.

39

Source:	Egerton 2234 ff. 68–69
Addressed:	*as in* 29
Postmarked:	SE 18 ℗
Endorsed:	*b.* Meeting wth Mr Smith./(This better omitted?) *Not transcrib'd*

Florence,
October 12 ⟨1⟩, 1732

⟨Dear Mother,

I believe all my letters from hence have given you an account how agreeable a place this is; in short, my Lord likes it so well that 'tis resolved at last that we shall pass all the winter here. This will make no difference as to our return into England: the only question was whether we should winter in Italy or in France. 'Tis settled for Italy, and you may for the future direct your letters to me—avec Milord Middlesex, à Florence, en Italie.

I have long wished to alter my direction, because they were very tedious by the way of Venice, but could not do it sooner—we were so undetermined as to place. When you are so good as to use this direction, I shall have your letter in about nineteen days, and from Venice they were sometimes five weeks in coming. This is the more necessary too at present, because I have not received any letter from England all the last month; or rather, not these seven weeks. I long to hear from you, and beg to do it as often as you can.⟩

Don Carlos, whose name has been so much mentioned in England of late, went from this place the 6th instant for Parma.[1] I have had the honour of seeing him both at a set audience and at a rabbit hunting: he was very grave at one, and very lively at the other, and I doubt not will make as good a sovereign when he comes to be one, as most in Europe.

⟨We have had here the last week one of Mr. Wells's family by Winchester, the captain of a ship which put in at Leghorn.[2] He used to table here, and talks of passing his winter in Hampshire. We were one supper three Hampshire men together at table here: Mr. Holdsworth, this Mr. Wells, and myself—where we all agreed that there was no bacon in the world so good as that in our own country. Mr. Wells came to Leghorn from Africa where he had been actually present in the battle between the Spaniards and the Moors.[3] He is now gone from hence to Leghorn again in order to set sail for England directly as I take it.⟩

Five or six days ago, as we were chatting here in my room, the servant came in to tell me there was a gentleman wanted to speak with me. I went out immediately, and expected to see some Italian bookseller, or some Italian knight ⌜who are as thick here as hops at Farnham⌝,[4] when with a great deal of pleasure I found 'twas a most particular friend of mine from Oxford, one Mr. Smith, son to the late Bishop of Limerick in Ireland.[5] My surprise was the more agreeable because I had not heard a word of his being abroad. When he had been but five days at Paris, he heard that I was then at Lyons, and set out immediately in a sort of stage-coach that goes from Paris to Lyons—that is three hundred miles. The night he came to Lyons, he went to the house where we lodged, and inquired for me: they said I was gone out with Lord Middlesex, which was very true. The next morning he came again, and they told him I was just set out with Lord Middlesex for Geneva. You may guess how vexed he must be that they never told him the evening before that we were to leave the town the next day. He wrote after me to Turin, the letter miscarried, too. In short I had never heard a word of the matter till I saw him here at Florence. ⟨He came abroad chiefly for his health,[6] for at Oxford he was near a consumption: but [   ] has recovered himself quite at Montpellier. [I] believe he is likely enough to stay in Florence too for all the winter, so that we may make up sufficiently for our missing one another at Lyons. I don't know whether you was acquainted with this Mr. Smith's name; he was a friend that Bob Downes[7] sent me from Ireland to Oxford, and one of the best-tempered men in the world.[8] With love and services of all sorts, I am

Your most dutiful and affectionate

J. Spence.⟩

1. See *Letter* 38.
2. Capt. Wells has not been identified.
3. On June 29, 1732, Spanish troops landed at, and the next day captured, Oran, held by the Moors. On Sept. 29 the Moors counter-attacked without success. See *Gent. Mag.*, 1732, pp. 879, 1086.
4. Emended to 'of which title there is plenty in this place'.

5. Arthur Smyth (1706–71), 8th son of Thos. Smyth, Bp. of Limerick, who died in 1725. Arthur Smyth attended Trinity College, Dublin (B.A. 1727) before he moved to St. John's College, Oxford (M.A. 1727, D.D. 1740–1). Under the patronage of the M. of Hartington, later 4th D. of Devonshire, Smyth pursued a successful ecclesiastical career in Ireland. In 1766 he became Abp. of Dublin (Cotton, *Fasti Eccl. Hibernicae* [Dublin, 1848], II, 24–6). Two of Smyth's letters to Spence are printed in Singer's edition of Spence's *Anecdotes*, pp. 391–4.

6. A commemorative inscription on Smyth's monument in St. Patrick's (composed by his and Spence's common friend Robert Lowth) reads in part: 'Gentes Europae humanitate maximè excultas / primò valetudinis causa peragravit: / simulque adfectas corporis vires recepit: / integrum animi robur firmavit' (Cotton, p. 26).

7. Robert Downes (1705–63), son of Henry Downes, Bp. of Derry, was educated at Merton College, Oxford, and at this time served as Rector of Kilcronahan. In 1744 he became Bp. of Ferns and in 1753 Bp. of Raphoe.

8. Lowth's obituary inscription describes him: 'Per omnem vitae et honorum decursum / sui similis et semper idem / mitis, facilis, humanus, candidus / moribus sanctissimis, / primaevâ integritate, / ipsâ simplicitate venerabilis.'

*40

Source: Egerton 2234 ff. 70–71
Addressed: To/Mrs Spence
Endorsed: a. Old Ficoroni: & petri-/fyd town.
b. Ficoroni's affair;/Dr Shaw, & Petrifyd Town.

Florence,
November 16 ⟨5⟩, 1732

⟨Dear Mother,

I had been without receiving any letter from you from the 7th of August to November the 9th; I had long begun to be uneasy about it, and was at last in a downright fright when, after sending three servants to the post-house, at last in comes one of them with a packet from Dick—in which, to my very great satisfaction, I found one from him, one from Mr. Rolle and five from you: which made me as chippant as a glass of sack and a kissing crust used to do at Kingsclere. Capt. Rolle has got a pretty little living by the interest of his cousin (he tells me),[1] which he can hold with New College. 'Tis in Devonshire, within three miles of the place where he was born, and there's a pretty little new-fashioned house upon it. He has been over there and seen his father and mother settled in the house which they like mightily, and 'twill be a great convenience not only for them but a variety too for himself the summers when he is in Devonshire, for 'tis but nine mile from his cousin's great house,[2] and he can amble over from one to the other mighty conveniently. His hurry about settling that affair is, to be sure, what has hindered him from writing to you since his return. I mentioned to you in my last that Capt. Wells of Hampshire[3] had been here, and that he was returned to Leghorn in order to set sail for England. When he came to Leghorn, he fell ill of the smallpox and had it pretty violently, but a merchant of Leghorn, a particular friend of his that is come hither, tells me he left him in a fine way of being recovered or rather quite got over it. We have had a great run of English here, and I find are likely to have more.⟩

There's an old gentleman that I was particularly acquainted with at Rome, who has been ever since we came from thence under a great deal of difficulty.[4] He is one of those people that we call antiquarians here. Their business is to go about Rome to show strangers the antiquities, palaces, pictures and statues that are there without number. They have generally old Roman rings and other pieces of antiquity to sell to the gentlemen they conduct about the town. This old Sir Clement Cotterel's[5] name is Signor Ficoroni. He is so old that he had been conductor to Mr. Addison when at Rome,[6] and was so to Lord Middlesex all the time we stayed there. A little after we left Rome, I received a letter thence that told me poor Ficoroni was confined to his house by an order from the Pope, that all his effects were sealed up, and a process issued out against him. The crime laid to his charge was [his] being concerned for forty years last past in selling the fine old playthings of Rome to the English. The occasion of this prosecution was said by the wicked to be something else. You must know this old lover of antiquities had heard of twelve fine pillars of a green marble (which is one of the finest sorts of all) which were found in Greece. He had managed so well by some merchants of his acquaintance, as to bargain for them less than £400, when they were really worth above £7000. They were come to one of the Pope's seaport towns, and there they were stopped. It was this prize, they say, was the occasion of all his trouble. His trial is now over: they have fined him in less than a £100, but I fear—though 'tis not spoken of—these green pillars are never to come into his hands.[7]

⟨We had here t'other day a brother of mine, a clergyman of the Church of England and my next-door neighbour at Oxford, for he is a Fellow of Queen's College there.[8] He has been chaplain a great while to our factory at Algiers, and is a great traveller in parts that we are not likely to see.⟩ He has been over several parts of Africa, and particularly in Egypt. He has seen the mummies there and taken the size of half a dozen of the pyramids, made a tour over the Red Sea, passed through the wilderness, and so went to Jerusalem. The world has been much amused about a town in Africa in which 'twas said all the people and everything in it were turned to stone.[9] I asked him about that story. He says he has never been there, because the journey is long, through the deserts, and dangerous, but the thing was so much talked of that the French consul[10] hired some poor people of the country to go thither and bring him what they could find. 'Tis true that the sands in the part named have the quality of turning things that are buried in them into stone, as some waters will do in England. The people that were sent brought away a branch of a palm tree that was perfect stone, and yet kept its natural colour and shape so well, that when you lay it by a true branch of palm you could not distinguish the difference without touching it. But for petrified men, they saw none.[11] Some country people that had travelled that way before, as they were digging, found a petrified man: 'twas showed about to the great surprise of all that saw it, till some Europeans at last heard of it, went to see it, and found immediately 'twas nothing but a statue. ⟨I hope to see you about June next, and am

Your dutiful and affectionate

J. Spence.⟩

1. At Monk Okehampton, Devon., near Meeth (Rolle's birthplace). 'His cousin' Henry Rolle was M.P. for Devonshire. (Spence probably calls young Rolle 'Capt.' because his cousin was a colonel.)

2. At Stevenstone.

3. Not identified.

4. Francesco Ficoroni (1664–1747), 'the Pope's antiquary' and virtuoso, 'fait depuis de longues années le métier de démonstrateur d'antiquités; il a une grande routine de connaissances: c'est le guide ordinaire des étrangers' (De Brosses, II, 254). Ficoroni who wrote a number of valuable treatises on Roman antiquities was a member of the Royal Society and the French Académie des Sciences. In spring 1732, he showed Spence and Lord Middlesex 'the vestiges and rarities of Rome'. Spence recorded his remarks in *Observations* (Nos. 1365–1401).

5. Sir Clement Cotterel (1685–1758), Master of the Ceremonies at Whitehall.

6. 'Mr. Addison did not go any depth in the study of medals. All the knowledge he had of that kind I believe he had from me, and I did not give him above twenty lessons upon that subject' (*Obs.* No. 816).

7. Ficoroni told young Richardson how he and Sir Andrew Fountaine joined wits to plunder an abbé who wanted to sell some medals; which proves that this was not the first 'crime' incident to his profession (*Richardsoniana* [1776], pp. 331–2).

8. Thomas Shaw (1694–1751), African traveller, Fellow of Queen's College 1727. He spent thirteen years as chaplain of the English factory at Algiers, and made a series of expeditions in the Middle East. He was now on his way back to England. In 1734 he was elected Fellow of the Royal Society.

9. The town 'Ras Sem, in the Kingdom of Barca' had been discussed as a curiosity in periodicals of the time, and in 1730 Thomson inserted a long passage on it into his poem. See A. D. McKillop, *The Background of Thomson's Seasons* (1942), pp. 154–8.

10. Perhaps 'Monsieur le Maire, Conseiller du Roy et Consul de la Nation françoise à Alger' in 1690 (*HMC*, Finch, III, 444) or Abbé Mathurin Rodolphe Lemaire, chargé d'aff. in England 1736, Denmark 1739–53, Germany 1754–7 (*Repertorium der dipl. Vertreter aller Länder* [Zurich, 1950], II, 103, 107, 110).

11. In 1738 Dr. Shaw confirmed this statement in his *Travels & Observations relating to several parts of Barbary and the Levant*: 'There is nothing at this Place besides such Remains of the Deluge as are common at other Places: all other Stories being vain and idle, as I was fully instructed not only by M. *Le Maire*, who, when Consul at *Tripoly*, sent several Persons to make discoveries, but also by two grave sensible Persons, who had been upon the Spot' (p. 383).

*41

Source:	Egerton 2234 ff. 72–73
Addressed:	*as in 29*
Postmarked:	DE [ ]O ℗
Endorsed:	*a.* came to winton yᵉ 24 of decᵇʳ /The Cassines; & yᵉ Tale of a Tub
	b. Seasons in Italy. Acct/of yᵉ Casini; & Tale of/a Tub.

Florence,
December 13 ⟨2⟩, 1732

⟨Dear Mother,

I have received all your letters safe, and indeed I believe there has not a single one of yours miscarried since I have been abroad.⟩ We here have had so temperate an air till the last week in November, that I used to sit and write with my chamber windows open, to enjoy the fresh air and the sun. But I find that we are to have our share of winter too, for 'tis now sufficiently cold for one to shut all the windows and doors, and keep a good fire into the bargain.

The seasons here are not distinguished by a gentle going off from one into the other as they are in England. After the winter, you fall almost all at once into the heats, and after the summer heats are quite conquered, winter steps in all in a day. One of the old Roman poets (but I need not talk at such a distance, for I'm sure you know Horace very well) says that their summer enters in a hurry, turns the spring out of doors, and treads on her heels as she is going out;[1] and I have seen a picture of the four seasons at Rome, done by one of their great painters, in which the spring and summer are kissing one another to show that they come as it were at the same time, and the winter and autumn are hand in hand.[2] The latter are really not so much huddled together as the former, for they may happen to have six weeks of autumn in Italy, but I believe they seldom have three weeks of spring. Indeed the autumn is the pleasantest part of the year here: everything begins to bud afresh in it—and 'tis rather a false spring that is killed before it comes to maturity by the succeeding colds.

A little way out of the gate that we live next to (and Florence I can assure you is worth no less than ten gates) is a place made for the pleasure of the Great Duke and his good subjects.[3] You go to it through a range of vast Scotch fir-trees: on your left hand is a long run of groves and pretty artificial islands full of arbours, and on the right lie the vineyards and cornfields interspersed, which is the manner all about Florence (as in Lombardy). This leads into a large beautiful meadow. The walk of firs is continued on, all the length of it; the groves and wood, with a variety of a thousand different walks on the left, beyond which, all along, runs the river Arno. These woods are at last brought rounding to join the fir-walk, and so terminate the meadow. This meadow all our autumn was almost as fresh a green as we have in England (a very uncommon thing here), and was all sprinkled with wild crocuses as thick as the stars in heaven. Many of the trees in the woody part wanted to show another crop of leaves, and the wild vines that are very frequent in it hung over your head from tree to tree with their glistening black bunches of grapes, that were left there for the happiness of the birds that inhabit those woods very plentifully. In short, all the autumn this place was the most like a paradise of anything I ever met with—but I have not seen it these three weeks, and I believe it now begins to look as rough as the rest of the world.[4]

⟨However, we have still a great deal of benefit from the Cassini—so they call this delicious place. In the entrance to it is a country house, which is the Great Duke's dairy: they make his butter there, and we have from it fresh and fresh every morning—a blessing which I assure you is very valuable and very uncommon out of England. Just by, they make some of his wine. Mr. S[myth] and I went in one day to see them at it. The grapes were left in so many tubs on very high stands: whether they had squeezed them, or whether they had squeezed themselves by their own weight, the juice was all fermenting so strong that it played up like a little fountain through the funnels. I had climbed up a ladder that stood by the side of one, to gape upon it, when all at once the ladder slips from under me, and in the hurry I got hold of the brims and hung there. Had the tub yielded upon me, I should at least have spoiled my best holiday clothes, or perhaps have gone out of the world almost in the way of the Earl of Clarence, if 'twas he that was drowned in malmsey:[5] but being somewhat light and the tub very large and heavy, it stood firm, and so did no manner of damage to

Your humble servant

J. Spence.⟩

1. *Carmina* IV. vii. 9–10: 'Frigora mitescunt. Zephyris, ver proterit aestas interitura. . . .'

2. Perhaps Albani's well-known painting on the ceiling of the Verospi palace (Thieme-Becker, *Künstlerlexicon*, I, 174).

3. The Cascine. *Promenades en chaise* in the park were in great vogue among travellers.

4. Spence considered the Cascine as 'very much like our new manner of gardening' (Spence Papers). See also *Hertford Corresp.* II, 42–3.

5. See Shakespeare's *Richard III*, I. iv.

Notebook 1

Florence—The senate is still called the Ducenti, though the number (if full) is but forty-eight, and at present there are only twenty-three. They are all named by the Great Duke from whatever order of citizens he pleases, and are all of equal authority. The chief of them is the representative or 'locotenente' of the Duke, and orders them to do what he pleases. They do not absolutely say 'Tel est mon plaisir', but 'tis the same in effect. The cases [senators?] wherever they act from themselves are chiefly as judges of civil cases. The senate meets on business only when the Duke pleases, and that has been but once these thirty years—to confirm Don Carlos's rights. There are of this body sometimes three, sometimes five, who (without pay) assist the civil magistrates in their sessions every Tuesday and Friday (they having generally passed through the civil offices before they are senators). 'Tis true, the senate meets every year on St. John the Baptist's day, but that is only to go and pay homage to the Great Duke. The Council of Eight is now no more. It consisted formerly of five senators and three plebeians, chosen all by ballot, and changed every two months. (This, in the whole round of the year, made up the number of forty-eight, which occasioned the same regular number's being settled for the senators at present.) The gonfalonier was of the eight, and the other seven were of the 'priori'.

The Great Duke's family revenue is about 150,000 crowns per annum. The rest comes from taxes and imposts, and amounts not quite to two millions of crowns in all. There is an easy land-tax (the rate of about 70 crowns in 3000) not sixpence in the pound. The thing most heavy is the imposts. Tuscany is strangely overrun with clergy: their lands are not to be taxed: so the Great Dukes have laid the weight on the fruits of the land more than on the lands themselves. The wine is taxed in general (two quadrines in particular for every flask that comes into Florence), the corn not, but the flour is. Whatever comes by sea to Leghorn pays nothing ⟨very little: about 3s. 4d. per cent⟩, that by land or the Arno does. Whatever comes thence to Florence pays at Pisa, etc. The Great Duke is rather out of pocket by Siena, though so fine a country. Formerly they used to get 200,000 crowns *per annum* by it, but at present, since the Florentines have industriously dispeopled it, the case is altered.

The archbishop of Florence has nothing to do with the administration. He is no cardinal, and they don't choose that he should be so. (There have been cardinal archbishops formerly who on public occasions have disputed the upper hand with the Great Duke.) On a vacancy, he sends three names to the Pope, who names the first of them: otherwise the Great Duke could hinder his taking possession.

The standing forces of the Great Duke are between four and five thousand, the militia fifty thousand at least, exercised every Sunday (?). They have no pay but several privileges.

Florence by the map is about six mile round and its breadth across the Arno 2 1/3 mile, across the other way two miles. They talk of 70,000 souls in it.

42

Source:	Egerton 2234 ff. 74–75
Addressed:	To/The Rev^d. Mr Rolle,/Fellow of New College/in Oxford/*per Francia en Angleterre*
Postmarked:	FE 1
Endorsed:	*b.* To Cap. Rolle—1733./Use of antiques toward expl^g/ye Classics. *red wafer*

SPENCE TO EDWARD ROLLE

[Florence,
January 1733][1]

Dear Cap,

Our last couple of letters had probably the same fate with what you mention of the pair before, for they are dated within five days of each other. I hope 'tis a sure omen that we are to meet ourselves on the continent, for I should be overjoyed to find Mr. Rolle and you at Paris. I am very much obliged to you for the description of your country house:[2] but when I looked into Horace, as you direct me, I could not find anything there to equal the very pretty fable at the end of yours.[3] When I come into England I already resolve to take a trip into Devonshire to step over your court, and pay my duty to your good mother.

In my last I talked to you more particularly of the thrice honourable post in the University—I hope that is by this time come to hand.[4] As to the last lecture, I must beg the favour of you to let it fall upon your hands; for if I should be able to get among you by the fifth of June 'twill be impossible for me to make a lecture soon enough, and you must imagine me too little acquainted with Latin and too much enamoured of stones and old brass, to set about one in this country of medals and statues. My madness that way is gone so far that were I to have another lease of the Poetry Lecture,[5] I verily believe I could easily fill up the other five year in comparing the mutual light that the statues of the ancients, and their poetical descriptions of them, give to one another.[6] You would then see that Lysippus often would explain a passage in Virgil with a stroke or two of his chisel better than a dozen commentators with all their lamps together, and that a medal is sometimes, modestly speaking, somewhat more certain than a conjecture. To fill up, I'll give you an instance of each: in two passages of your friend Virgil, which I have the rather chosen because they always seemed unnatural to me, not to say a little bordering on nonsense.

Don't you remember the appearance of the Po in his catalogue of rivers?

Saxosumque sonans Hypanis, Mysusque Caïcus:
Et gemina auratus taurino cornua vultu
Eridanus

(*Georg.* iv [370–2])

'Tis only considering that the good citizens of Rome had seen statues of the Po many of them more frequently than they had seen the Po itself.—The statues of rivers have often horns; there are several such still at Rome. *Elatis cornibus Amnes.* Val. Flac. Arg. I i.v, 106—Those rivers had horns, which fell by several channels into the sea; Fundere *non uno* tantum quem flumina *cornu* Accipimus; septem exit aquis, septem *ostia* pandit. Ib. 8, 187, of the Danube.—There's now in one of the palaces near Rome a figure of the Po, lying down, with the head of a bull (*taurino vultu*) and as good a pair of horns as any alderman in London need wear.—These horns were often gilded with gold in honour to the deity of the river: Sic et *cornibus aureis* receptis, Et Romanus eas utraque ripa.[7] Mart. 1. 10. Ep. [7] of the Rhine.[8] All this put together makes the passage very clear, and far from unnatural in those days and among those people for whom it was written.

The other passage is in the end of the eighth *Aeneid*:

—Patriumque aperitur vertice sidus. ([l. 681] of Augustus)

One of the medals of Augustus, and a very common one, has a star just over his forehead. Ille Deum gens, *Stelligerum* attollens *apicem*, Trojanus Jülo Caesar avo. Sil. Ital. lib. 13. [lines 862–4]. This star was the Julian star, in memory of the comet which appeared for seven days while Augustus was celebrating the games in honour of Julius.[9] Hâc de causâ *simulacro ejus* in vertice additur *Stella.* Suet. In Caes. cap. 88.—Hence 'tis plain that there were statues of Julius and Augustus with the star, and as probably pictures too, which would very well explain the line before in Virgil: Geminas cui tempora flammas Laeta vomunt—the star in a picture serving to fling a light over his forehead, as the glory does in those of our modern saints.—However, their pictures you know are almost all lost, and so we must stick to our sure proof, my good old friend the medal above mentioned. In it Augustus has the Julian star over his forehead, the rays (which afterwards all the emperors wore) round his head, and Jupiter's thunder before him: all these particulars are mentioned in one verse of Lucan's who, like a true virulent republican as he was, is pleased to be very angry at it: Bella pares Superis facient Civilia Divos; *Fulminibus* manes, *radiisque* ornabit, et *astris*.[10]— I won't trouble you with any more instances, though I believe I have already got erudition enough here to furnish out a very good brass-and-stone-comments on near a thousand passages in the ancient Latin poets, though I have not yet consulted above half of them, reckoning from Ennius to Claudian. The two above mentioned may be already explained so for what I know, for all my travelling classics are without notes, for the ease of being carried and, generally speaking, for the ease of understanding them the better.

Vive, vale, siquid novisti rectius istis,
Candidus imperti, si non, his utere mecum.[11]

And now I have filled my letter half with Latin, and displayed my erudition sufficiently and very much to the repose and satisfaction of my spirits, I heartily wish you as well, and about ten times as learned as

Your affectionate humble servant

J: Spence.

To close all I shall seal this letter with an intaglio found in the mausoleum of Augustus, at present in Musaeo Spenceaeano.[12]

---

1. The letter is undated. From its place in the Egerton MS it appears to have been written sometime in January 1733.

2. At Monk Okehampton, see *Letter* 40 n. 1.

3. In 1740 Spence (or Mr. T.) compiled an account of the Sabine villa from the numerous mentions of it in Horace's poems (*Obs.* II, pp. 672–8).

4. The letter is missing.

5. Spence was re-elected to his post for the remaining five years of the ten-year tenure shortly before his return to England (Wright, p. 35).

6. This letter contains the germ of the ideas which Spence later developed at length in *Polymetis*.

7. Spence incorporated this remark into the fourteenth dialogue of *Polymetis*, pp. 230–2. C. G. Heyne mentions it in his edition of Virgil: 'Apud Martialem X 7 *cornibus aureis*

receptis Rhenus appellatur, unde Spencius locum nostri poetae illustrabat' (Leipzig, 1788, I, 519).

8. In the letter Spence mistakenly refers to 'Ep. 6' instead of '7'.

9. In *Polymetis* (pp. 86–7), referring to this passage ('which I have formerly thought fitter for the affectation of an Italian epic poem, than for the propriety which generally reigns thro' the Aeneid') Spence explains 'sidus' not as the Julian star, but as 'the divine irradiation' which Suetonius attributed to Augustus, who seems to have prided himself on his good eyes.

10. *De bello civili* VII. 457–8.

11. Horace *Epist.* I. vi. 66–7.

12. The intaglio, first used on this letter, shows a dancing male figure. Spence thought a fitting 'Inscription for a cabinet of medals and gems' would be '*Senectutis crepundia* (playthings, for one's latter infancy)'. *Obs.* No. 1175.

*_43_

Source:	Egerton 2234 ff. 76–77
Addressed:	_as in 29_
Postmarked:	FE 9
Endorsed:	_a._ come to winton/feb ye 12:/an ac^t of the earthquake/at naples:
	_b._ Earthquake at Naples.

Florence,
January 31 ⟨20⟩, 1733

⟨Dear Mother,

I was too late to write to you last post, and am not very early this, however I hope I shall have time enough to fill up my letter. I have received an answer from Captain Rolle to one of mine, in which I desired him not to forget to write to you. I'll give you his own words to show you what a dutiful son he is to you, as followeth: 'I have long since and often acquitted myself of the duty I owe to Mrs. Spence. 'Twas my first concern after I came back from the country hither to Oxford. I take her complaint of me to you as an exceeding kind thing, and I believe we are upon as good terms with each other and as thoroughly acquainted as it is possible for two people that never once saw one another to be.' You see your son Ned is as good a boy as any of the rest.⟩

Dr. Shaw, a great traveller into Egypt and the Holy Land, whom I mentioned to you before about the stone-town in Africa,[1] is come hither again from Rome and Naples. He was in the latter at the time of the great earthquake that has done so much damage there.[2] It came before it was quite light: only light enough to add to their terror, by letting them see how the walls opened and shut in a thousand places about them. After all, there was but three people killed, though there are several thousands of houses very much damaged. Naples is the land of earthquakes: and so, the most agreeable place in the world is one of the most dangerous to live in. All the earth under it, and on each side of it has been turned into vaults by fire which, upon this shock, blazed very furiously out of Mount Vesuvius. ⟨I should not much care to have been upon the top of it at that time.⟩ I believe there were near thirty English gentlemen and ladies in Naples (for 'tis all the fashion at present for our ladies to travel), who all immediately hurried away together and got a' ship-board, which is one of the safest places one can be in upon such an occasion. They stayed there a night and two days, though the shock was not of above a minute and a half. At last they thought they might venture on shore, and they had not been all well got into their houses before the second shock came. This it seems is the usual method with earthquakes: but the second generally is not near so violent as the first.[3] We have lost one of the prettiest gentlemen we had there, Lord Benning, a Scotch nobleman and a mighty genteel man.[4] We were at the assembly at his house almost every evening when we were at Naples. He was there for a decayed constitution: the goodness of the air kept him alive for some time, but it could not cure him. He died not long after the earthquake, which, they say, always leaves a corruption in the air when violent.

⟨We have here a young gentleman that is mighty well acquainted with Mrs. Kelly and the Miss Keebles.[5] 'Tis pretty Mr. Dingley[6]—I believe he is in love with one or two of them at least, by the earnestness with which he desires his humble service to them. I beg my humble service to all that good family and all friends, and am ever

Your most affectionate and dutiful

Jos: Spence.

You desire a history of our weather here: the last week in November began our cold, and lasted severely enough for three weeks on in December. Then we had exceeding good till the 14th of January—wet weather—then the north winds from the mountains, which dry the streets in half an hour; they came yesterday and continue still, 'tis hoped they will be succeeded by fine weather and the opening of an early spring. No almanack maker could have given you a better account.⟩

1. See *Letter* 40.

2. The earthquake occurred on Nov. 29, 1732.

3. For an account, see *Mercure historique & politique* for January 1733 (vol. 94, pp. 34–5), which states that the second shock occurred on Dec. 1.

4. Charles Lord Binning (1697–1732), eldest son of Thomas, 6th E. of Haddington, 1718 Knight Marischall of Scotland. He had considerable taste for literature. In 1731 phthisical diathesis obliged him to go abroad; he spent the last sixteen months of his life at Naples, where he died on Jan. 13, 1732 (N.S.). Richardson's portrait of him appears in Walpole's *Royal and Noble Authors*, V, 142.

5. Not identified.

6. Robert Dingley (1709–81) of Lamb Abbey, Chiselhurst; London merchant, amateur architect and collector of works of art; one of the original members of the Soc. of Dilettanti (1736); founder of the Magdalen Hospital, 1758.

*44
Source:	Egerton 2234 ff. 78–79
Addressed:	To/Mrs Spence at/Mr Morecrofts in/ Colebrook Street/Winton/Hants.
Postmarked:	27 FE
Endorsed:	*a.* florence/come/to winton March ye first/ye carnival there *b.* Florence,/Acc^t of ye Carnival there. *red wafer*

Florence,
February 14 ⟨3⟩, 1733

⟨Dear Mother,

I'm very sorry my Tale of a Tub should have given you any concern, for as my good friend Mr. Smith was by I verily believe that at the worst it would only have spoilt me a suit of clothes.[1] However, I thank God I came off very well and continue at this writing in very good health.⟩

We are now in the liveliest part of our carnival, for it is always in most vigour towards its end, and we have now but five or six days of it to come. There's one particular here which we could not have at Venice: the different manner of setting themselves out in their coaches. The vehicle used on this occasion would be like our coaches with their tops off, and the back, before and behind, coming up no higher than your shoulders. In one of these you will sometimes see a Turk and a Christian lady forward, and an Empress and chimney-sweeper backward. Everybody has some disguise or other: the coachman is generally dressed as a harlequin and the footmen as pierrots. The general rendezvous is a place as big as St. James's Square: the coaches go round in a ring, all in masquerade, and the fools on foot have all the middle railed in to walk at their ease and see as great fools as themselves go round in the coaches. The inside is always well crowded. I have had a Pharisee there tread upon my toes, and, upon recovering myself, with some confusion, have run my head full into the face of a Roman emperor. The very coach horses are in a sort of masquerade: for I have seen for instance a coach and six horses with their hair dressed out in a particular manner all with ribbons and bells, and a marquis dressed in a harlequin's habit riding postillion. They go a regular trot, and as their bells sound all at the same time, make a very pretty sort of music. Today we had a stage built up, and some of the first noblemen (very probably) acting the parts of a mountebank and his attendants, all in fools' coats.

One of the great diversions upon the place is fishing. I have seen this at Venice, when two gentlemen have walked together with fishing rods baited with sugared almonds, and two or three score of little boys nibbling at them. Sometimes they got the bait very dexterously, and sometimes the hook got a piece of their lips: but a boy that's well exercised will play the fish very successfully. Here they have had the same sport, more in form. One day a fellow was got with all his baits and implements on a little stage raised on purpose: a heap of sausages of a yard or two high lay by him, which his servant fried off in a pan of oil with great expedition. As fast as one bait was snapped off he supplied his master with new ones, hot out of the pan. The gentleman had so many bites that all that monstrous heap of sausages was vanished in less than an hour. It would have surprised you to see the number of hungry faces and open mouths in the circle round him, in the height of his sport. The nearest would often bite whilst the bait was so hot that they were forced to quit it again ⟨when 'twas half down their throats⟩, to the great baulking of their appetites and distortion of their features.

The Italians are generally reckoned men of spirit and of a character rather serious than light: but when the season requires foolery, there are no people in the world that give in to it so much. I have often inquired what may be the reason of this, but could never yet get one that was satisfactory.[2] At the same time 'tis very odd to see numbers of people every day, of five or six and twenty years old only, going about the streets with a vast pair of spectacles upon their noses to be thought older and wiser than they are, and these very people at other times playing the fool together in the silliest and most childish manner that can be imagined. ⟨I'm growing too grave for carnival time, and therefore shall leave off with being

Your most dutiful and affectionate

J: Spence

This morning I am packing up a box of books to send by sea to London; so that, you see, I begin to think in earnest of returning to you, though I have been astray now upward of two years.⟩

---

1. See *Letter* 41.

2. 'Why are the Italians, that are a solid and grave people,' Spence asked Dr. Cocchi, 'the most fond of drolleries on their stage, and greater dealers in burlesque than any other nation?'—'Salvini used to think it was because when people have a mind to divert themselves they generally choose what is most different from their ordinary temper and practice, as most likely to divert them. That may be the reason, but I should not be apt to acquiesce in it.'—Lord Middlesex suggested: 'Perhaps he thought that their gravity was a cheat and ridicule their natural bent.'—But Spence was not satisfied: 'On the other side, 'tis evident that most of their drolleries are very low and violent. There is the same difference between fine drollery and theirs as there is between true and false wit. This would rather incline one to think that they are really grave, and only affect gaiety, because they pursue it so boisterously and so injudiciously' (*Obs.* No. 1493).

The following four letters to Henry Rolle were written after Spence's return to England. As they deal, however, with antiques in the Grand Duke's gallery (the present Uffizi), they have been incorporated into this section. Spence here evidently imitates the virtuoso style of Sebastian Bianchi (1662–1738), the learned Keeper of the Grand Duke's collection of gems and medals, some of whose remarks Spence recorded in his Observations *(Nos. 1571–9). Some of the statues mentioned below are discussed in greater detail in Spence's* Polymetis; *for a scholarly discussion of them, see G. A. Mansuelli,* Galleria degli Uffizi—Le sculture *(Rome, 1958–61), 2 vols.*

45

Source: Egerton 2234 ff. 292–3
Endorsed: To Col: Rolle. 1734?/1ˢᵗ, of yᵉ Flor: Gallery

SPENCE TO HENRY ROLLE

[New College, Oxford]
1734?,

Dear Sir,

My whole life since I have touched upon English ground has been a second sort of travelling . . . but now I am set down in my good old chamber at New College and have my pen, ink and paper about me, you must not expect to come off so easily, for a man of much leisure and a good deal of impertinence (which I think is and ever will be my case) has a certain aptitude and inclination to write long letters: as for example now—In this idle, leaning, sidelong posture 'tis ten to one but I write you on to the bottom of the third page, without the least compassion to your eyesight or once thinking that you may in all probability have business of greater importance on your hands.

Well, this Italy is certainly one of the most delightful places in the world! What a fund of entertainment does one single collection there sometimes afford one! For instance that in the Great Duke's gallery which, though we stayed nine months in Florence and visited above a hundred several times, was so far from being exhausted that I sincerely assure you I could very willingly go and see it a hundred times more. If you please, we'll take a walk round it directly.

You see that lady sitting on the low chair, in so very easy a posture?

That, Sir, is Agrippina,[1] and has perhaps the neatest pair of shoes on of any statue in Christendom.—The bust there, on your right hand, is Julius Caesar's: you may see by it that he was (as some historians report of him) of a weakly constitution.[2]—That large naked figure represents a victor in some of the ancient games, as appears from the fine goblet in his hand which he eyes so carefully and the palm-tree by his side.[3]—This bust, with no ill-natured face, is Nero, and as like his medals as he can stare: the Medusa's head on his breast-plate is very good work and very well hits a passage in Virgil (*Aen.* viii 438).[4]—Galba there, just by, has Janus' heads on his breast-plate: the faces both of the same age, as they are in all the antiques I have seen of him, and not one with a great beard and the other beardless after the Oxford Almanac fashion.[5]

This handsome figure is a vestal: her right arm naked to the elbow she holds, you see, over the sacred fire. She is all covered, except her other hand and her face: you find here all the manner of their habit, veils, etc.—That bust, with the neat bob wig on, is Otho: not only the face, but the wig too, exactly like one of his medals.[6]—This naked figure which holds his finger and thumb together as if there was a pinch of snuff between them, is an incognito, and so our antiquarians here call him a Genius[7]—but that statue of black marble you may easily know by his helmet, sword and shield to be designed at least at present for a Mars.[8] He has fierceness enough in his countenance and what I have always imagined the Romans meant by the word 'torvus', though I never knew how to English that word to my mind in my life.

This noble beautiful bust is the famous favourite of Hadrian, Antinous: 'tis evidently of Greek workmanship, and excellent even among the Greek pieces of work. You see very remarkably in it what Valerius Flaccus says of Meleager: 'spatiosaque pectoris ossa'.[9] I don't say I suspect this, but 'twould not be the first time perhaps that a Meleager has been called an Antinous.—That statue we passed before is a bacchanal, and that other, the famous Bacchus with which Michelangelo is said to have imposed on his contemporaries.[10]

On farther, where we were going before, is a noble naked figure: you see how graceful 'tis, how fine a face and how beautifully his hair falls in rings over each shoulder before: that plainly shows him to be Apollo; you must not mind the torch in one of his hands and his pointing to heaven[11] with the other, both those arms are modern, and only meant to degrade him from a god to the character of Prometheus. In the very good Greek statues you may see a plain difference between a human body and a divine: this is rather of the latter sort, and besides this face is beardless, which agrees with the 'imberbis Apollo' very well, and very ill with Prometheus who, as you may see in Montfaucon, etc., has always a very considerable beard.

That bust of Antoninus Pius is perhaps the finest of that emperor that is extant,[12] though they are in very great number.—The next statue is that of a censor, of a low, bad taste.[13]—You see there the first couple we have met yet: they are not man and wife, and so 'tis no absurdity in the statuary to have made them so kind and loving together: 'tis Mars, you see, and Venus. The good goddess is flattering him to go on some expedition to help her son Aeneas, or what you please, and the kind god seems consenting enough.[14] She is all naked, you see, only a bracelet on her arm, which the antiquarians here say is her famous cestus. I always took *that* to be a girdle, but I don't remember any passage that proves that it was so.

We have now done with one side, and if you are not tired too much now, I will take you on farther in our next walk. In the meantime I am, Sir,

Your humble servant

J. Spence

1. 'Statue of a Sitting Lady', 1st century A.D., resembling that of Agrippina at Naples (Mansuelli II, No. 53). In Egerton 2235 f. 114ʳ Spence gives 'The Proportions of Agrippina's Chair in the Florentine Gallery'. See *App.* 16.

2. It is 'as like Mr. Pope as any bust [that] has been made on purpose for him' (*Obs.* No. 1464). It is a 2d-century bronze replica of an original dating from ca. 40–30 B.C. (Mansuelli II, No. 32).

3. No. 131 in the 1835 catalogue (Mansuelli II, p. 286), now in the Bargello.

4. 'In pectore divae / Gorgona, desecto vertentem lumina coelo'. Pseudo-antique copy (Mansuelli II, No. 178).

5. 'In all the antient figures I have seen of Janus, the faces are both alike; and both old: which makes it the more unaccountable to me, whence some persons of the best taste, not only among us, but even in Italy itself, are got into the mode of giving Janus two different faces; one old and the other young' (*Polymetis*, p. 197). Mansuelli lists a bust of Galba (II, No. 67), but it has no 'Janus' heads on his breast-plate'.

Perhaps the Galba Spence saw was a different bust.

6. The likeness of this pseudo-antique is actually derived from medals (Mansuelli II, No. 179).

7. The Genius appears 'to be nothing but a particular bent and temper of each person, made into a deity' (*Polymetis*, pp. 153–4).

8. 'Ares Borghese', replica from Nero's time of an original ca. 400 B.C. (Mansuelli I, No. 20).

9. *Argonautica* IV. 244. For the 2d-century bust, see Mansuelli II, No. 98.

10. Created ca. 1497–8; now in the Bargello.

11. From where comes the fire with which to light the torch. It used to be called also 'Apollo caelispex' (Mansuelli I, No. 122).

12. See Mansuelli II, No. 106.

13. No. 59 in the 1769 catalogue (Mansuelli II, p. 221).

14. The two figures were no doubt originally independent; Mars' head and Venus' right arm are later restorations (Mansuelli I, No. 160). For an engraving, see *Polymetis*, pl. VIII, fig. 1.

46

Source: Egerton 2234 ff. 294–5
Endorsed: *b.* To Col: Rolle, 1734?/2ᵈ; of yᵉ Florentine-
             Gallery

SPENCE TO HENRY ROLLE

[n.d.]

Dear Sir,

Though you have complimented me enough in your letter to make one
almost afraid of receiving another, I must walk you on in the gallery in
spite of my teeth, and I believe shall walk you on till we have got through
that noble collection. But I must beg a truce of compliment for the future,
because it serves only to feed a certain human passion and consequently
draws so much off from the divine enthusiasm of antiquity, which ought to
take up the whole soul of every true adept.

Our first morning, I think, we left off at Mars and Venus, so that now
we are to turn the corner if you please and look upon that Somnus you see
there, of black marble. 'Tis a figure that deserves your attention. That mild
happy air all over him, the colour of the stone, the largeness of his wings,
the poppy in his right hand, and the horn full of poppy-juice in his left, are
every one of them particulars that are to be met with in the classics. I mean
the old poets, which are really a written school of statuary.[1] There is
something of the good Egyptian manner in this figure, especially in the
mouth, and if the 'Heros Aventinus' in the Capitol be really (as it is said
to be) Egyptian, I should much suspect this figure to be so too.

Those pillars on your right hand I should suspect to have belonged to
some temple, built possibly ex voto for some victory.[2] You see they are all
worked into arms of different sorts on every side and would be of good use
in explaining the ancient military instruments, etc. You see there's a little
statue now placed upon each of them: that with the urn held down against
her left side was a fountain-statue, of which there are great numbers still
remaining, though but little observed by the generality.

The distinguishing character of the ancients in the best ages was
simplicity. 'Twas what ever made the best poets and the best statuaries.
This is very particularly to be observed in the fountain-statues of the
ancients. Of hundreds that I may have seen, I can't recollect three in which
the design was not plain and proper. They don't fling water out of

dolphins' tails and men's eyes as the moderns have since contrived to do. 'Tis generally some water-god leaning on his urn, or a nymph standing (as that before us) and pouring the water out of one, or a satyr that is drunk, with the utris (in which they carried their wine) untied, or a Silenus sleeping, with one under his shoulder running out (as that fine one in the Tribuna).

This head between the two pillars, that has an air horrid enough to frighten one, is a Pan, and probably represented under his character of giving 'panic fears', a character which is given him anciently, as may be seen in short in Ovid and very particularly in Valerius Flaccus. His eyes, you may see, have been painted with red or minium, whether anciently or latterly I cannot say, but that too was an ancient custom! (Virg. *Ecl*. x 27).[3]

This old orator in brass is an old Tuscan figure, and Tuscany you know was beforehand with Rome, both in religion and arts. You that are so great an antiquarian may find out the meaning of the three lines in Tuscan characters on the hem of his garment, but for my part I shall be contented with observing the manner of their statuary which, you see, is not bad: the particularity of his sandals and the ties which go up half his leg, and the large ring with as large a gem on it on his left hand.

This next figure that we need stop at is old Tuscan too.[4] 'Tis the Chimaera that was killed by Bellerophon: the head leonine, the hinderparts of the dragon kind, and the head and neck of a goat rising from the middle of its back! This latter, you see, has received its mortal wound, and is dead before its companions. It was from this caprine head that the poets made the chimaera breathe flames and fire. As the statuary could not express that, it was probably no ill contrivance in him to represent that as already killed, to save his art the shame that he could not otherwise have so easily got over. This figure had been used almost as scurvily by the moderns as the chimaera was by Bellerophon; it had been a long while neglected and lay among some rubbish in the old palace over the way,[5] till our Sir Andrew Fontaine took notice of it and took care to inform the Great Duke of its value, for 'tis considerable certainly for its antiquity and the thing it represents, though the workmanship be mediocre.

This beautiful little Ganymede and Eagle was two hundred year ago nothing but the trunk of a young body, but an exceeding fine one and evidently of the high Greek taste. 'Twas Cellini who made a Ganymede of him and added the limbs, the eagle, etc., and indeed the little bird he holds in his right hand is a thought quite out of the taste and manner of the ancients.[6]

The figure distinguished there by so fine a pedestal was thought by Bembo to be a Bacchus, and is called so by the present antiquarians at Florence. The 'fine modern stories' round the pedestal allude to the same god. But there is no one thing in the figure itself which argues it to be a Bacchus, and his hair makes it more probable that it is not one. If you rub off any of this thin dark crust that time has petrified upon it, you discover everywhere the ancient gilding more strong and vivid under it than I ever saw in any statue.

That colossal head just by the end window, with that noble and passionate air, is called the head of Alexander the Great:[7] whatever he is concerned about (whether for more worlds to conquer or for having killed Clitus, or for what you will) there is a strong concern in the face, very nobly expressed.

Nay, if you begin to be tired, I have done. 'Tis so with most of you travellers who come to our gallery: for one indefatigable fellow that comes to see it in earnest we have a hundred that only walk through it for an airing. However, Sir, when you think fit to come here again, I shall be ready to attend you, and am / Your Excellency's / most obedient slave

Sebastiano Bianchi

1. 'The poets speak often of his wings; and mention their being black: that colour is the most proper for this god, as his empire is chiefly by night: and it is for the same reason I suppose, that the statuaries so often chose to make his figures of ebony, basalt, or any dark-coloured marble. Such is the fine statue of this god in the Great Duke's Gallery (*Polymetis*, pp. 263–4).

2. Apparently to the 'armilustrium', erected on the Aventinum at Rome after A.D. 112 (Mansuelli I, Nos. 2–3).

3. Mr. T. disagrees: the painting of eyes with red 'is not of any authority, because it has been done by somebody probably since it was set up there. Bianchi tried it, and the red came off upon his fingers' (*Obs.* No. 1465a). Perhaps

Mansuelli I, No. 128.

4. Both the chimaera and the 'Arringatore' (ca. 80 B.C.) are now in the Museo Archeologico at Florence.

5. ''Twas found in the Year 1548 near *Arezzo*, in the time of *Cosimo* I, and used to be always in his own Chamber, as I was told by *Bianchi*' (J. Richardson, *An account of Some of the Statues . . . in Italy* [1722], p. 46).

6. This late Hellenistic statue is heavily restored, but there is no evidence that the modern parts were done by Cellini, whose replica of Ganymede is now in the Bargello (Mansuelli I, No. 111).

7. Recent collations with the great altar at Pergamum have shown it to be the head of a dying giant (Mansuelli I, No. 62).

47

Source:	Egerton 2234 ff. 296–7
Addressed:	To/Henry Rolle Esqr/Stevenston, near/ Great-Torrington,/Devon.
Postmarked:	OXFORD By the/Cross-Post.
Endorsed:	To Col: Rolle, 1734./3d, of the Flor: Gal:

SPENCE TO HENRY ROLLE

[Oxford, 1734]

If you really are not tired, we may go on to this other side of the gallery without resting ourselves in that window.

That first figure of a man hanging against the tree by his hands tied across, is Marsyas. You see, his feet are stretched quite to a straight line and, for all that, his toes want something still of touching the ground. In such a posture 'tis no wonder that his face has that horrid sort of pain in it. The 'fronte obducta' in Juvenal (*Sat.* ix 2) is the most remarkable thing [in] his face. Horace mentions a different attitude of him, as not bearing to look on Apollo (out of envy and hatred), and Ovid gives yet another figure of him, when quite stript: for Marsyas, you know, was the St. Bartholomew of the ancient statuaries and painters.[1]

This bust is of Commodus, when young.[2] If you observed the bust of the young Aurelius before, you must remember that this is exactly like it, an observation which perhaps may serve a little to vindicate Faustina's character, especially if you consider too that the famous Annius Verus there is like his brother Commodus, though the likeness of the two brothers appears strongest where they are set face to face in the same medal.

This sober, serene-faced god is Aesculapius, in whom you see the dress of the ancient physicians. His right shoulder naked and a bundle of herbs in his left hand: the former of which shows that they were chirurgeons, and the other looks as if they were their own apothecaries too.[3]

The Phrygian general a little lower is a piece of curiosity, though most of him is modern, the trunk with his left shoulder and the right thigh is visibly all that is ancient, the head and Phrygian bonnet is copied from an antique in the antechamber to the gallery. They set him down for a Phrygian I suppose from the rest of his dress, which is very singular, and make him a general from the dress on his right shoulder. However, the (modern) Phrygian bonnet he wears is perhaps the best argument now of his being a Phrygian, and that sort of bonnet, too, by the by, was common to most of the people of the East.[4] A dealer in antiquities must never mind such things as those: a good faith is all, and the being credulous is the best half of the way towards being learned.

That bust of Caracalla is strong and worth one's attention, even after that at the Farnese Palace at Rome, of which this is probably a copy taken in or about Caracalla's time. The strength of expression in this and the softness in that of his empress Plautilla, over the way, shows that there were excellent hands even to his time: there's nothing after that comes near them in any degree among [the] busts I have seen, and I think the same [is] in a good measure to be observed in the gems.[5]

I have gone less way with you this morning than I expected; if you please, we will make it up in our next walk. I am ever, Sir,

Very much your humble servant

J. Spence

1. Mansuelli I, No. 57. For an engraving, see *Polymetis*, p. 301.

2. Mansuelli II, No. 128. The busts of Annius Verus, Commodus, and young Marcus Aurelius are Nos. 120, 128, and 129, respectively.

3. 2d century A.D. (Mansuelli I, No. 133). Spence repeats this in *Polymetis*, pp. 132–3, though Aesculapius 'in his left ... holds his stick, with the serpent twisted round it' instead

of 'a bundle of herbs'.

4. This statue of Attis was restored in 1712 by Francesco Franchi to represent a barbarian; also called Midas or Phrygian king (Mansuelli I, No. 148).

5. Baron von Stosch mentioned to Spence the 'busts of Caracalla and Plautilla, one so soft and the other so strong', as late examples of good taste in sculpture (*Obs.* No. 1555). See Mansuelli II, Nos. 140–1.

48

Source: Egerton 2234 ff. 298–9

Endorsed: To Col: Rolle,/4ᵗʰ, on the Flor: Gallery.

SPENCE TO HENRY ROLLE

New College,
November 23, 1734 [O.S.]

Dear Sir,

If you care for a fourth walk in our gallery, as Mr. Rolle says you do, I am always your humble servant. Let me see! We finished the last time I think with that fine bust of Caracalla. The next statue of the bathing Venus[1] is so complaisant as to have nothing on her except the bracelet on her left arm, and that indeed she should never be without if our Italian antiquaries are in the right, who will have it to be her cestus.

This lady with the serpent from her right hand and a patera, you know, is the goddess of health:[2] 'tis no improper emblem for her, one of the greatest medicines among the ancients being taken from those poisonous animals, and indeed the sign of a modern apothecary's shop in Italy is generally a great bundle of vipers, on the same account.

His thunder shows that god to be Jupiter, but, you see, 'tis held down by his side and his face is serene:[3] among several other distinctions of their Jupiters, the ancients had that of the 'Jupiter Placidus' and the 'Terribilis Jupiter.' 'Vultu, quo coelum tempestatesque serenat' in Virgil [*Aen.* I. 255] refers to the former, and Horace's 'Neque per nostrum patimur scelus Iracunda Iovem ponere fulmina' [*Carm.* I. iii. 40] may refer to the latter. If so, this will help us to a stronger sense of the epithet 'iracundum' when used with 'fulmen' than we had been used to have, opposed to the 'placidum fulmen' when 'tis peaceable and held only quietly in his hand as a sign of his authority.

You see next three statues in order after one another, which by their disposition and taking in one over the way, make up a sort of history piece, only the faces (it must be owned) are not in character in that light.[4]

That over the way, holding out the apple, is Paris, and these three the three goddesses between whom he was to adjudge the prize of beauty.— The Juno is dressed just like a Roman matron (her usual dress in the statues that remain of her, whence partly she is called 'matrona Juno' in the Latin poets).—The Venus is in the same posture with the famous Venus of Medici, and therefore improper to be placed here: for that hides its breast with one of its hands, whereas on this occasion she may be supposed to have shewed it to the best advantage, and a Greek poet who has written on this subject assures us that this was the very method by which she got the prize adjudged to her.—The Minerva here is far from handsome, though among the ancients she was often of so great a (manly) beauty that her face and Alexander the Great's is scarce to be distinguished on some medals.

The *fond* of this end of the gallery, you see, is nobly filled with Bandinelli's copy of the famous figure of the Laocoön at the Vatican, which very statue (in all probability) Pliny the Naturalist says was absolutely the finest in old Rome in his time, and therefore we need not wonder at its being the finest in the world at present. As this terminates these three sides of the gallery, we may leave the other for the next opportunity, and so I am, Sir,

Your most obedient

J. Spence

1. Perhaps that which Bianchi (p. 97) describes as 'tutta nuda, come la descrivono e Filosofi, e Mitologi ... *pingebatur Venus pulcherrima Puella nuda*'. See Mansuelli I, Nos. 54, 65; II, No. vii and pp. 275–6.

2. The Greek Hygeia holds the serpent and patera in her left hand (Mansuelli I, No. 21).

3. Originally a statue of Asklepios, it was restored as Jupiter in the 2d century A.D. The head and the right hand with the fulmen are later additions (Mansuelli I, No. 44).

4. Three of the statues in this group were destroyed during the fire of August 12, 1762; only the statue of Juno, 5th century B.C., has been preserved. See Mansuelli I, No. 17, and for contemporary engravings of the destroyed pieces, App. 1, 2, 5.

*49

Source:	Egerton 2234 ff. 80–81
Addressed:	*as in 50*
Postmarked:	AP 4 ℗
Endorsed:	*a.* from florence/still/came to winton/aprill ye 30: 1733
	b. Dr. Tomlinson's danger at Vesuvio

Florence,
March 28 ⟨17⟩, 1733

⟨Dear Mother,

I am very sorry that you were so long without receiving any letter from me, for though I am got into a pretty large correspondence of letters to new acquaintance at Rome and Naples, whatever business I otherwise had I always used to take care to write to you fast enough for you never to be a month at farthest without one, and generally much faster. We are still here, and the Great Duke's collection of ancient statues, medals, and jewels with beautiful figures cut in them, would be an entertainment for one's whole life. Not that we intend to live always here, I can assure you: as soon as ever the roads are right good we are actually to set out for France, and had not the winter continued longer than ordinary, we should have set out before this time. But as ill luck would have it, the hills all round us are still covered with snow, and there has some fresh snow fallen on the mountains even within these three days. When the spring is fairly settled in, we shall set out and make all the expedition we can for Paris, where I shall reckon myself half at home again, for 'tis not above five days' journey thence to Winchester and Mr. Morecroft's fireside.⟩

About a fortnight ago Dr. Tomlinson (a London physician who attended Sir R. Grosvenor who died lately at Naples) came hither from that city.[1] Though 'twas at a time that Vesuvius had been pretty angry, he was resolved to run the hazard rather than not see the wonders of that mountain. When he was got quite up to the top and was viewing the havoc that the late eruptions had made, all in one instant the smoke redoubled, it grew as black as night, and the fire flashed out from a thousand places up to the clouds. His guides immediately deserted him and ran down the hill without him: beside the danger of the fire and his not knowing the way down, the air was so full of sulphur that it was ready every moment to take away his breath. However, there was no possibility of staying on the top without being burnt to ashes in a few moments; so he was forced to get down whichever way he could, and half with crawling and half with tumbling and rolling he found himself at last at the bottom where were his two guides that were just then lamenting him as a lost man. The doctor does not talk of it as I do, who ever thought Vesuvius one of the finest sights I ever saw in my life, but is constantly wondering how anybody can be fool enough to go up it.—Had I been there at such a dangerous time, I suppose I should have had just the same opinion of it as he has.

⟨Though I like Italy more and more every day, I assure you I begin to long very heartily to be in England. I used to tell you that I should certainly come the beginning of June, but our time is deferred for a month or two longer, which will, however, make no great odds. For I hope fully to be with you the end of August, or the beginning of September, and a good deal of the time between will be taken up in moving from one place to another, and in our convenient chaises time never flies away so fast as then. The time between this and that of our meeting is not near so long as several of the times I have left you at Winchester to go to Oxford have usually been. I hope my sister and all friends are in good stout health, and shall be glad to hear as much in my next. Mr. Dingley is departed—not this life, but this place for Rome—and was gone before I received your last which was five days ago. My friend and namesake Captain Spence is there too at present, but we never want English company here—there is such a perpetual flux and reflux of our good countrymen.[2] About a fortnight ago Sir Hugh Smithson came here,[3] who left school, entered at Oxford, passed through all his university education, travelled through France, and came hither—all since I have been abroad. There is beside here at present Lord Harcourt,[4] and there are others whom we expect every day. When once we set out our faces for travelling, and the better weather comes on, we shall soon be with you in England. In the meantime you may depend upon hearing from me constantly; [   ] I have no greater pleasure than receiving your answers. I am ever

Your affectionate and dutiful

Jo: Spence⟩

1. Probably John Tomlinson (1663–1745) of Leeds, M.D., matric. at Jesus Coll., Cambridge, Nov. 7, 1688 (Venn). Sir Thomas Grosvenor (1693–1733) was M.P. for Chester 1727; suc. to the baronetcy July 12, 1732; died of consumption at Naples Jan. 31; buried May 28 O.S. at Eccleston.

2. Spence recorded no less than forty English travellers he met at Florence. See *App.* 1.

3. Sir Hugh Smithson (1715–86), Bt., matric. at Christ Church Oct. 15, 1730; F.R.S. 1736; M.P. for Middlesex 1740–50; E. of Northumberland 1750, when he assumed the name Percy in lieu of Smithson; cr. E. Percy and D. of Northumberland 1766. One of the original members of the Soc. of Dilettanti.

4. Simon Harcourt (1714–77), 2d Visc. Harcourt, another original member of the Soc. of Dilettanti 1736; raised to earldom 1749, F.R.S. 1753, Viceroy of Ireland 1772–7.

*50

Source:	Egerton 2234 ff. 82–83
Addressed:	To/Mʳ Spence/att the African House/in Leaden-Hall-Street/London/per Francia—*en Angleterre*
Postmarked:	AP [23?]
Endorsed:	*a.* the acᵗ: of the strong/man of Kent. onley/ came to winton/june: 11: 1733 *b.* Of the strong Man of Kent.

Florence,
April 21 ⟨10⟩, 1733

⟨Dear Mother,⟩

The continuing of the bad weather beyond what has been known in these parts has kept us here much longer than we expected: the snow yet lies on the mountains on each side of us. When that is quite gone away, as it must soon now, we shall move onward for England.

We have here a curiosity of English growth that I remember to have heard talked of ever since I was a child ⟨in leading strings⟩. 'Tis the Strong Man of Kent who has lived here in the Great Duke's pay above these twenty years.[1] He has showed often before the whole court, and used to make nothing of fixing himself so that four horses could not stir him out of the posture he had set himself in.[2] He used to let them pull and tug and sweat till they were satisfied, and then by giving a jerk to the rope by which he held them, would turn them up all four together upon their backsides and leave them there sprawling on the ground: after which he was ready to do the same to four of the largest oxen they could find, if the Duke and the mob were for more sport. He has bent a bar of iron above half as thick as my handwrist with hitting of it against his arm, and makes nothing of squeezing a man to death. We have been often diverted with hearing him tell over the adventures of his life, which he does with a great deal of honesty and vigour.

Soon after he was entered into the Duke's service there came a black to court, of a vast bulk, and famous for his strength. Our English Samson (for so they all call him here) was insulted by him. He would not believe the accounts he had heard of him, and offered to let him squeeze him in his arms as much as he pleased. Samson was so kind as to take him at his word, and at the third crush, he says, he heard his bones crackle in his body a little. The black cried out that he had enough to satisfy him, went off into the next room, threw up a good deal of blood, and died in less than a fortnight after.[3]

When Samson first came over, he had a fit of melancholy upon leaving his dear country: what increased it very much was his want of the language of the people he was amongst, which is really a distress not to be conceived but by those who have felt it. In these dark days he used often to take long walks out by himself, and one day, after straggling a good way from the town, sat down very gloomy under a fig-tree on a little hill, took out an English grammar for the Italian tongue and began reading it very attentively. 'Twas toward autumn and the tree was quite loaded with ripe figs, but he was so busy and the fruit is so common in every field here that he did not mind them. However, the farmer who saw a man under his fig-tree and did not think he came for nothing, came toward him with a pitchfork in his hand. Samson read on and did not mind him ⟨very much⟩ till he was got three quarters up the hill. He then thought 'twas high time to look about him for his defence, for the Tuscans are famous for knocking people on the head on the least occasion. He had nothing but a little English sword by his side, which would have been of no service to him against a pitchfork. So he got up briskly, laid hold of a high branch of the tree, and set his foot against the trunk to pull off the limb for his defence. As his enemy was near him, he made such an effort with all his strength that the whole tree came up by the roots.[4] So he caught it up by the bottom and ran to meet his adversary with all the boughs and figs rattling before him. This got him the victory without striking a blow. The farmer was so astonished to see a tree twice as big as his body pulled up at a stroke and pushed toward him, took to his heels as fast as he could, ran directly to his house, locked the door after him, and in seven or eight minutes he and all the family were at the windows setting out holy candles lighted, which is the usual method here to preserve them from any evil spirit. I could tell you a hundred more stories of Samson, but they are too long for a letter, and the history of the tree is run farther than I expected it would.

Samson has got a mother in Kent, that he has not seen these thirty years; they are both very fond of one another, and he talks of returning very soon to England to see her and lay his bones in his dear native country. He has a brother too in Kent who has showed feats of strength all over England, and a sister who[m] he always cries up for a mighty pretty girl.[5] She ought to be so, for by his account she is near six foot high, and the poor thing, he says, could carry a sack of wheat across the room well enough when he left her, though she was weakly in comparison with him and his two brothers.[6] ⟨I hope it will be in a few months that both he and I shall have the pleasure of seeing our mothers: though I am not quite so strong as he is, I believe you will be as glad to see me as his mother can be to see him, for all his broad shoulders. I told you in my last that I thought we might not come into England till September; I have now reason to think that it will be sooner—

for our stay here probably will only cut off so much of our stay in France.[7]
I hope brothers and sister and all friends are well, and am

Your affectionate and dutiful

J. Spence.⟩

1. William Joy or Joyce (1675–1734), b. at St. Lawrence in the isle of Thanet, a ship-carpenter by trade, made his *début* as 'the English Samson' at the Duke's Theatre in Dorset Gardens in 1699. His prodigious strength, in spite of his spare build, became proverbial until Fielding's day (*Joseph Andrews*, III, vi), yet there is no trace of him after 1701, beyond the statement that he 'afterwards followed the infamous Practice of Smugling, and was drowned 1734' (John Lewis, *The History and Antiquities . . . of the Isle of Tenet*, 2d edn. [1736], p. 189). Spence's letter contains hitherto unrecorded information about his later career.

2. This, according to a 1699 broadsheet, appears to have been one of his well-known exploits: 'a Rope of incredible thickness was . . . fast'ned about his middle, and the other end to an extraordinary strong Horse . . . Whip't in order to pull him out of the place, but notwithstanding all his strength Mr. *Joyce* stood immovable as an Oak Tree' (*English Sampson, His Strength Prov'd Before the King* [1699], B.M. press-mark 551. d. 18).

3. He had performed a similar feat in the 1690's:

A Carr-man once fell out with him,
A sower fellow fierce and Grim,
And as they went from words to blows,

Our Sampson *did his Corps inclose*
within his Arms, and hugg'd him so,
that straight his blood began to flow
Into his face, aloud he cry'd
For mercy, or he must have dy'd.

The Kentish Sampson; Or, A Brief Account of the Strong man William Joyce, *his wonderful Exploits set forth in Three Parts*, Nov. 14, 1699, p. 5 (B.M. press-mark 11644. g. 3). The verses contain information about Joyce's early life, his service in the navy, and 'How he served Sixteen *Frenchmen* when he was a Prisoner in the *French* Territories'.

4. On Nov. 14, 1699, 'the said Mr. *Joyce* pull'd up a Tree of near a yard and half Circumference by the Roots at *Hamstead* . . . in the open Viw of some Hundreds of People, it being medostly computed to Weigh near 2,000 weight' (*English Sampson*).

5. 'Not above nine and fifty years old', (Spence's note), a year older than her brother William.

6. Not identified.

7. They probably left Florence a week or two later, stopping at Bologna, and continuing via Modena (May 9) to Parma, which they reached on May 10. For a list of paintings at Modena and Parma, see *App.* 15.

Notebook 1
(63–73) 55ʳ–60ʳ

The fine theatre at *Parma* [May 10–11] is slightly built, but looks very grand. The stage is 51 f. (?) long and 46 broad; the open parterre 43 f. long. Then seats a great way up, like those in the Roman amphitheatres, and afterwards two rounds of columns and a gallery at top. 'Twas built by Ranuccio in 1518 (inscription there) and is scarce ever used but for *sposalizie* and such grand occasions.

Piacenza [May 12] lies like Oxford in a line with spires, etc. in the midst of a large open circle, in the same sort of fine manured country as Parma. The *maraviglia* of Piacenza (the two equestral statues of Al. Farnese and his son Ranuccio) very bad ones. An excellent Madonna of Raphael (a pretty large piece) in the church of St. Sisto. The dome of the Cathedral Church painted by Guercin, the Carraccis and Lanfranc. We missed the fresco painting of Pordenone at the Madonna di Campagna.

In the road on, as soon as you come to the state of Genoa, you are in the hilly part the moment you are out of Novi, and go all the way on to Genoa through the lesser Alps. You see hills lessening and growing more beautiful quite from Bologna to Tortona. There you see, from behind them, the range of rougher and higher hills continued on to Genoa, and then on till they join the greater Alps.

From Bologna to beyond Piacenza 'tis all the same Lombard style of cultivation, as from Florence to Bologna 'tis all Apennine and hilly—except where it breaks out into a fine vale, as that at Florence and the other of Mugello. ⟨The beautiful romantic view when you first see the fortress of the Genoese; the fine descent for a whole post, the last but one, as the [road runs] all along the bed of the river.⟩

Genoa [May 13]. The beauty of the town greater than that of Naples, of the port much less: for though it makes a noble half moon it wants the fine outlets of land that is in the other. Here 'tis only . . . a long run of barren Alpine hills. 130,000 people in the town, beside the suburbs, which are so very considerable. There is only one English merchant there, but fourteen or fifteen of our French refugees with their families.

The palaces in Genoa are extremely fine and beautiful, especially all the Strada Nuova and several in the Strada Balbi. The palace of Girolamo Durazzo in the latter is the largest in Genoa. Facing the door in the garden is a large statue of Aesculapius and Hygeia (both with serpents) on the same pedestal. A very good picture of Seneca bleeding to death by L. Giordano (and two other as large in the same room by the same hand). A large supper piece of Magdalen washing our Saviour's feet, an excellent piece of Paul Veronese's, a good bust of Vitellius. 'Twas the daughter of that family we saw who was just married and stood for forty-eight cicisbeos in her wedding articles, though it came at last only to four, and those to be named first.

The Cicisbee gallery round the pit. Walk by their ladies' chairs, etc. In the Palace Balbi, Andromeda and Perseus [by] Guercin, two priests and Madonna (id.), a fine lady, fam. piece by Vandyck. General Spinola very good and Vandyck himself (dit.), a San Francesco [by] Perin del Vaga. A little Venus and Cupid [by] Han. Carracci. All the roof of the gallery by Parmigianino.—The Balbi had another fine palace, which they gave to the *Jesuits* only to have mass stay for them on occasion, etc. 'Tis now *their* great school.

At the church of S. Maria Carignana (a little after the manner of St. Peter's) four large marble statues, particularly a St. Sebastian. The martyrdom of St. Biaggio by Carlo Marat, a piece of Procaccini's and another of Guercin. (The high bridge there with an arch 400 f. high.)

The Annunziata: middle roof etc. by Bolognini (Wise Men, Palm Entrance, Agony in the Garden, Ascension, Visit to the Virgin—with the John the Baptist, Moses and a whole cavalcade of saints quite from heaven to her chamber, and the Virgin's Ascension). Fine large Last Supper of Guercin, Saviour disputing with the doctors dressed all like Turks, and Presentation in the Temple; sides of the high altar. Terrible martyrdoms first altar to the left. Ep[itaph] in this church: 'Hieronymo Chiavara Lucae F. Ducali dignitate defuncto: quem ut laudes modestia, ut reprehendas veritas non permittit. Fratres, Filiique unanimes posuere. A.D. 1594.'

In the Doge's palace statues to Andrea Doria for recovering their liberty, and to Jo. Andrea Doria Patriae Libertatis Conservatori. Over the Arsenal door, what they call the rostrum, found in cleansing the port. The arms for the women (pressed on the breasts butting out under: Filippo Faerno on one of them) and Boniface VIII's letter in praise of them, dated 1301. Old cannon tube of brass, thick round of leather and round of wood, 7000 Corsican fasces. Great Council-Hall[1] painted by Franceschini, Senate House or Little Council by Solimena. One of his three large pieces [is] Columbus in his New World. St. Ambrosius high altar piece [by] Rubens, the Madonna like Titian's wife, face and colouring etc. not so light and glaring as his usual manner; S. Stephano, high altar piece, stoning of Stephen [by] Giulio Romano (?). Odd fountain in a palace in the Strada Nuova of a giant pulled down by the hair by a Cupid, another Cupid above looking down on him holds a great wreathed shell to pour the water out.

Savona [May 20] a little town thirty miles on, pretty gardens. At the church of S. Domenico pretty altar with fifteen oval histories in *basso relievo*, the two first the 'Salutation' and 'Visit of the Virgin', the two last her 'Assumption' and 'Coronation'. The inscription in the sixteenth oval is: 'Quindecim Humanae Reparationis Mysteria.' Chiabrera is buried in his family vault at the convent of S. Giacomo, out of the town.

Noli [May 21] ten miles; not under the Genoese, but governed by two consuls of their own. By *San Remo* (50 miles) the little square castles against incursions of the Turks.—*Monaco*. The road made by the late Prince of Monaco (three millions of florins in debt, almost two pauls each).—*Nice* (30 miles) to *Antibes* [May 22]. Rather a fortress than a town. The moment you turn to Nice the country is green and beautiful, and you have no more of those high brown mountains.—[May] 25th drove in rain to *Lavandu* (70 miles), the 26th forced to make *Hyères*. The delicious view thence: plain covered with orange-trees, bounded to the right with gentle woody hills . . . the sea before like a lake, terminated with one of the Iles de Hyères to the left and several others, that seem as one, to the right, that lie in a line before you: they open handsomely to the south about the middle of the sea and leave a less opening south-east.

Toulon [May 27]: a port for men of war and stores for them. A fine cable-room built on arches below, with two rows of columns within, two-story high, 200 brasses long above, exclusive of the offices at each end. Above they make the little ropes and below they tar them and twist them together. Several good cannon and mortars and a good number of bomb-shells. The man said there were fifteen men of war in the port. We were aboard *Le Solide*, a second-rate of 500 men and 60 guns. They use small arms and even pistols for the marines and sailors for boarding or being boarded. They talked of 1500 men for their admiral in one of their latter expeditions. The man who showed us the port remembered the making of everything that is there: 'twas all done by Louis XIV, and under his bust (against the Caryatides' House on the quay) the date is 1659. The quay (in a straight line to the port, only carried out farther opposite to the entrance) is 750 paces with the water, and a little more at each end. The houses lie in a straight line along the quay; within is a street parallel to them and the quay, and through both are twelve openings into the town. Behind it all great rocky hill, the shore, little green hills on to each of the castles. The town, a very indifferent one.

Marseilles [May 28]. The new town, several noble streets, and the country about a long run full of *bastides*. The port has a fort close to the sea on each side and above, on the left, is a fortress built by Louis XIV (after he had drove over their walls and when they asked him how he liked their *bastides*). The side of the port, where the Change, to the Maison de la Santé is 1440 paces long, that opposite to the entrance into the port 268. They have 16 or 17 galleys at present and two new ones upon the stock, conveniences for making ten at a time, and in wartime have forty. The place where Caesar made his attack: the angle that answers a little hill with a windmill on it (*Cole* from *Monsieur Olivier*). The number of slaves about 8000, 130 lately released, twelve every four days (one of the many we met with on the road, sitting, appeared the true picture of a slave). Twelve mile to the other side of the *rade* and six to the first of the three islands: between the two largest they perform the first quarantine, which is repeated from the death of anyone on board successively thirty days after on the farthest side of the port. 70,000 people died in the last plague and not above 90,000 now in the town. They are now opening the place where the deceased were buried. Good *cours* in the town.

Aix [June 1]. The pretty *cours* in the town between two double rows of trees and with three fountains. The country to it had a pretty look in general when half-way to Marseilles, but indifferent if you consider any piece of it. ⟨The wild plains, like the beach of the sea, and the vast flocks of sheep they were driving to the mountains for the summer: the last of five thousand. . . . Dog just like a lion: spiked collars.⟩ The King has forbid them to talk of the affair of Cadière and Gérard, and there have been eight or ten banished for doing so: some of them cavaliers and some cons. of parliament.

Arles [June 2]. ⟨A little out of the town we passed one branch of the Rhône just after its dividing in two. How wild it is above the division.⟩ The amphitheatre 243 f. diameter almost each way, 55 high—three stories, rounds at top, like the theatres at Oxford. Grand entrance to it, 35 paces. Houses built in it, some remains of a theatre. Old obelisk 72 f. high. Pretty Town House, with a copy of the Venus of Arles, and a body with a large serpent all twisted round it, which they call an Aesculapius. The signs of the zodiac in relievo between the folds of the serpent: there are nine, from Aries down to Arcitenens ⟨not of a bad taste, especially the Gemini, one of which leans on a harp⟩. In the Champs Elysiens are a multitude of sarcophagi, some heathen and some Christian. The Archbishop's Palace (and himself and his canary-bird).

Nîmes [June 3]. The amphitheatre much more complete than that of Arles, though the bottom has a little town built in it. Two stories, with pillars, entire almost all round except where the two little towers. Two places with large holes between each two pillars for masts to support the vellum. ⟨The two half-bulls and old Priapus on it.⟩ The temple of Diana half left, the five niches on the side at top, just like Michelangelo's windows. The old tower (the largest of seven) very large still, though much lost at top and bottom. The Maison Carée [is] a cleaner and ⟨for elegance⟩ more beautiful remain than any we saw in Italy. 'Tis 120 f. long, 60 f. high and 60 f. broad—a double cube, all surrounded with fluted Corinthian columns, six in the front and eleven the sides, thirty in all. The inside is spoiled by making a modern church of it, though that's the way of making it sacred and preserving the outside. The earth was cleared away, and the whole refitted by Louis XIV.

Montpellier [June 4] by Louis XIV's fine Languedoc road; stones every ten or twelve yards: what we saw of Languedoc south exceeding better country than Provence. From the Place of the Cheval de Bronze (on a fine marble pedestal) we saw the Pyreneans. [On] the gate to it four rounds of relievos: Holland conquered, the Empire reduced (the King as a Hercules, treading on a man with an eagle by him, his club stuck with flower-de-luces), heresy destroyed, and the two seas joined. The esplanade, the great walk. Not a large town, but well peopled (24,000).

Pont St. Esprit [June 6] (the bridge there 1000 paces). In going thither the Pont du Gard, a vast work but necessarily irregular enough: each of the great arches single [is] beautiful, the whole not so, especially from the ending arches and the whole row of little ones at top (6, 11 and 34, as I told them, there might have been more than 34 on the farther side). It joins two rocks and carried water over the river Gard in its highest channel. The middle one a man or a mule may go over, and the river runs through the largest arch below. Those below answer the middle arches exactly, the largest of which is 39 paces. The channel for the water is about three feet wide and near five feet high, covered all over with single flat stones. The rock in the ascent, marble.

From Pont St. Esprit you come all on the east side of the Rhône and see it often and the long ridge of rude mountains on the other bank of it all along. The Côte Notée hill is on that side of the Rhône, a little before Vienne, a most execrable town for narrow streets and ugly houses. The hills soften about twelve miles before Lyons and are full of villas and country-houses.

1. 'Twenty-seven senators, Little Council of 200, Great of 600. The ages: twenty to be of the Great, twenty-five of the Little, forty [for a] senator and fifty for Doge. The number of senators uncertain; if they choose one that was not a senator Doge, he is senator ever after.' [Spence's note]

*51

Source: Egerton 2234 f. 84
Endorsed: *a.* paris: the/first Letter from thence
            b. Paris, Great 2 days Journey, in/going thither.

〈Hôtel de Luynes〉,[1] Paris,
June 15 〈4〉, 1733

〈Dear Mother,〉

This is just to let you know that we are so near you that we could almost shake hands across the water. We came hither last night, and in that day and the day before had run 246 mile in our chaises:[2] by which you may guess we were pretty desirous to get to Paris and so near to you. There is nothing yet that surprises me so much here as the silence about us, in comparison of London. We are in the Faubourg St. Germain, one of the best parts of the town, and they say one of the most active, and yet I am retired now to a window that looks into a good handsome garden, without either noise, heat, or dust—and yet the summer is the chief time for company at Paris. Indeed, heat there may be and I not feel it, for, coming out of Italy and Provence, the warmths here were so cold to us that we were forced to wear our greatcoats in the chaises, and for all that, were often shivering as if 'twas winter. This was a great blessing to us, for the only insufferable thing to me on the road is heat, and we expected enough of it because the summer (which has been backward this year both in France and Italy) they said was just come in when we got to Montpellier. ⟨We are all perfectly well, and with services to Belle and all friends, I am ever

Your dutiful and affectionate

J. Spence

My brother knows how to direct to me here.⟩

---

1. Built 1650 by the Dsse. de Chevreuse, and until her marriage known as the Hôtel de Chevreuse. It was situated in what is at present Boulevard Saint-Germain.

2. The average travelling speed was sixty miles a day.

---

*52

Source: Egerton 2234 f. 85

Paris,
July 2 ⟨June 21⟩, 1733

⟨Dear Mother,

Your straggling, wandering prodigal son is at last coming home in earnest: we ought to be in London the 20th of this month N.S., that is the 9th of July with you.[1] I think my best gown and cassock is with you. I beg you would send it up to Dick in all haste, with a tolerable proportion of bands, and (if I have any such thing with you) a black suit of clothes, but I much question whether I'm worth any; and if you have none, I can take care to get some when I come, let the worst come to the worst. I desire my service to Belle and all friends and hope I shall find you all in very good health.⟩

Paris is a very agreeable place—and more full of nobility, [su]ch as they are, than London, but there's a great deal of difference between a marquis in England and a marquis in France. Here to be in possession of such a mansion-house or such a particular farm very often makes all the family lords, when with us the head of that family would be only a tolerable lord of a manor.[2] I have often seen the pretty Duchess of Bourbon, who is one of the three sisters I have talked to you of in a former.[3] Though she's as pretty as an angel, she's forced to paint here, for there's no being in fashion without it.[4] The actresses on the stage, and the ladies of the first quality in particular, lay on the red so unmercifully that in the side-boxes they look like a bed of old overblown peonies,[5] and as we are now in the month of July, it really makes one sweat to walk through them in the public gardens, in some one or other of which all the company is every evening.

I have not missed a night since we have been at Paris of being either at the Opera or the play. These diversions begin early, and after they are done we go regularly to the public walks. Their plays are good, and not ill acted very often, but their operas are things that I would not advise anybody to go to who has not lost his hearing or has not a mind to lose it. Beside the actors, there are generally six or seven women ranged on each side of the stage, to make the chorus and stun all good Christians that come to hear them. They really place the perfection of music in bawling,[6] and the ladies (who in all the countries that I have yet travelled through are particularly fond of hearing themselves either speak or sing) are so very vigorous here in lifting up their voices to an agreeable squall, that t'other night when it thundered [while] we were at the opera, it was really a sort of refreshment between whiles when they were low enough to let us hear it. However, tomorrow we must go through the persecution of hearing them again, because the Queen and King Stanislaus are to be there, whom we have not yet seen.[7] The court is out of town, and this is only an afternoon's visit they make to Paris, for the King of France never lies a night in his capital city.

⟨The letter I had to deliver here I will bring safe with me to Winchester.[8] Mr. Rolle I have not seen nor heard of in these parts, and know not whether he is in England or France. I believe I shall not stay above a fortnight or three weeks at London, for I shall come to you as soon as I can and in the meantime am

Your dutiful and affectionate

J: Spence.⟩

1. His return on 'July 9th 1733' O.S. is confirmed in Rolle's manuscript Life of Spence.

2. The same was true in Italy: 'A Florentine will call a good tolerable house, for instance, a PALLACE; and a little snug flower garden a

PARADISE' (Spence, *Life of Signor Magliabecchi*, p. 14).

3. For Caroline of Hesse-Rheinfels, see *Letters* 21, 30.

4. 'The Two prettiest Women I have ever

seen are the Duchess of B[ourbon], in *France*, and Mrs. *A****, in *England*; and the very Reason why I should give the Preference to the latter of the Two is, that the former is obliged, by the Fashion of the Country where she lives, to heighten the Color of the Roses which Nature had scattered over her Cheeks, into one great Mass of Vermillion' (*Crito*, pp. 50–1).

5. In fact, 'Were a Frenchman, on his first Coming over to England to see a Sett of our greatest Beauties all in a Row, he might, probably, think them like a Bed of Lilies,' notes Spence, adducing as a witness the Comte de Grammont, who said that 'the *English* Ladies were particularly handsome; but that it was a great Pity that they were all so pale' (ibid.).

6. The English, uncompromising partisans of Italian music, had no taste for the 'rondeur . . . de notre musique française' (De Brosses, II, 343).

7. Maria Leszczynska (1703–68), m. Louis XV in 1725. Her father, Stanislas I Leszczynski (1677–1766), was K. of Poland 1704–9.

8. Perhaps the 'nun letter' to Miss Belson. See *Letters* 4, 6.

*The
second tour*

*53

Source:	Egerton 2234 ff. 86–87
Addressed:	To/Mr Spence,/at the African-House,/in Leaden-Hall-Street/London *readdressed by Richard Spence:* To/Mrs Spence/In Colebrook Street/Winton/Hants.
Postmarked:	MA 10
Numbered:	No 2 2d B. 22 Letrs
Endorsed:	*a.* at his first Landing/in holland *b.* Landing in Holland.

Helvoetsluys,
May 18 ⟨7⟩, 1737
Saturday, between 5 and 6 in the morning

⟨Dear Mother or Dear Brother, for this must serve for both,⟩

We are just got to land in this dear country of Holland, after a long voyage, but not at all disagreeable to me. We set out from Harwich Wednesday night at eleven o'clock.[1] Neither Mr. Trevor nor myself were seasick all the way, though in the midst of a mob of people ⌈upon the high vomit⌉.[2] Our room is now full of as great a mob, half yawning and recovering themselves. There's so much noise that there's no writing any more:[3] you shall hear from me more fully from the Hague, where we hope to be by dinner-time. ⟨I am as well as ever I was in my life, and entirely

Your dutiful and affectionate

J. Spence⟩[4]

JOHN MORLEY TREVOR (1717–43) of Trevallyn, co. Denbigh, and Glynde, Sussex, matric. at Christ Church Apr. 2, 1734; M.P. for Lewes 1738–43; Commissioner of the Admiralty 1743. He was a relation of the Pelhams, his father having married Lucy Montagu, 1st cousin of Thomas Pelham, D. of Newcastle, and of Henry Pelham.

1. May 15 (May 4 O.S.). Actually, as the following letter shows, they had set out two days earlier.

2. Emended to 'that were very much so'.

3. The letter shows signs of having been splashed with water.

4. A postscript by Richard, dated 'London, May 10th, 1737' O.S., informs Mrs. Spence 'of the opportunity of forwarding to you what has given us here great pleasure and will give you the same, to see that honest Joss is got so safe and sound on terra firma'.

*54

Source: Egerton 2234 ff. 88–89

Addressed: To/Mʳˢ Spence/in Colebrook-Street,/in Winchester,/England

Endorsed: *a.* the first Letter from yᵉ hague/yᵉ descrip-/shon of helversluce: verrey pretey
b. Description of Helvoetsluys
red wafer ★

The Hague,
May 21 ⟨10⟩, 1737
⟨P.S. I have dated this the tenth because it will not
set out till Tuesday night: but to say the truth
'tis Sunday now I am writing it.—'Tis now Tuesday
noon, and I am already as much at home here
as if I was in England.⟩

⟨Dear Mother,⟩

I wrote a line or two for you yesterday from Helvoetsluys, the moment
after we were got to shore. I had not time in it to beg your pardon for my
roguery in telling you we were to set out this day from London, when I
really hoped we should be got to our journey's end, as I thank God we are,
and all of us ⌜stout and lusty⌝.[1] We set out from London Monday morning
before six; everything conspired to enliven our journey: for that day was
kept as the first of May,[2] and all through the town and Whitechapel we
saw the milkmaids with their garlands and practising their feet to dance in
the evening. At Chelmsford, where we dined, was a fair, and at Harwich
another for the Tuesday and Wednesday.[3]

    Wednesday night, about eleven o'clock, we were called upon to go aboard
the *Prince of Orange* packet-boat, and a good ship she is. 'Twas so calm a
sea and so fine a moonlight evening that I could not stir from the deck till
about four, when I went to bed for three or four hours, and out again.
Thursday was as fine a day for the sea as ever was, and Friday no bad one:
so that I was not sorry that the winds were against us, for to one who loves
the sea as much as I do, two or three weeks (instead of two or three days)
on the water would have been no undesirable thing. I was extremely well
all the while and ate every two hours whilst waking, and should have
dreamt of eating as often I believe in my sleep if I had not slept too soundly
to dream at all. Saturday morning we made the coast of Holland with a very
brisk gale, and landed in the midst of Helvoet about five o'clock.[4] I had the
pleasure of seeing the sun set very finely on the sea twice in this little
voyage, for both our evenings ⟨especially the first⟩ were very fair and serene.

Helvoet is a very little town, and looked to us like a town in miniature. The houses are very small and very neat: everything in little and so pretty that it looked like a street when you view it through the little end of a perspective glass. A Frenchman on board said 'twas a 'ville d'harlequin'—a harlequin town, for the bricks used in their houses are so small, and often interchangeably of two different colours, that they looked like patchwork or a board to play at draughts upon.

We went from Helvoet to Maeselandsluys in a long cart that they call here a *bolder waggon*, but, to make up for it, we were carried from thence to the Hague in a *phaeton*, which is not unlike a triumphal chariot. We had no difficulty on the road (which I apprehended a little before we got hither, where we have taken a servant that can speak English and Dutch) because Mr. Trevor, our Minister here,[5] was so good as to send one of the King's messengers to meet us at our landing and to conduct us to this place—so that between our triumphal car and our messenger we came in here in some sort of state.

The other towns we passed through, though larger than Helvoet, agree with it in the littleness and neatness of their buildings.[6] Nothing can be cleaner than their streets. The pavement exactly even and, without any stretch of a traveller, fitter to eat upon than many tables I have seen in France.[7] The country about has all a neat look too. Too uniform, for 'tis all on a flat on each side of you, but kept in mighty good order. The road is generally set with a regular row of trees on each side, and runs along by a canal, and on each side of it you frequently see gentlemen's houses and farmers' houses with walks of trees about them, and little gardens that are kept in the utmost exactness, so that you can scarce see a leaf under the trees or a weed in the parterre and flower-beds.

One could not help observing, as we came through the towns, that of the women who were busy about anything, at least nine in ten were engaged in work of cleanness. Scarce any knitting or spinning, but everybody rubbing the pavement before their door, dusting their houses and rinsing their kettles and skillets. I know a certain lady that loves dusting clothes very well, who would make an admired inhabitant of either of the towns we passed through, and who would be charmed with the neatness that reigns here.[8]

You have heard perhaps that storks are a republican sort of bird, that they love commonwealths, and will never live in a monarchy. Though 'tis a great mistake as to the latter, 'tis as certain that they love this republic very well, for there are great numbers of them here. We saw several of them on our road—twelve together in one spot[9]—and the people are so obliging to them that they set up an open wooden box on the tops of their churches, in which the storks build a great nest and sit very comfortably in it, with their long necks out for the diversion of travellers and strangers. This struck us at least at first sight: but in a few days we shall probably be better acquainted with them, for they say all Holland is alike, and we shall see more of them I suppose everywhere.

⟨I say nothing of the Hague yet, because I am very little acquainted with it. We shall stay here probably two or three months, and only go out one day to see one city, and another some other: for they lie here in a little compass. Capt. Rolle is by this time at Paris I hope.—I dined with him at London the Saturday before we came away, and he was to set out the next day.[10] I wish you all health and happiness, and am (with services to all friends)

Your loving cousin

J. Spence.

Please to direct to Mr. Spence, in the Keysershof, at [The] Hag[u]e, Holland.⟩

1. Emended to 'very well'.

2. Monday, May 2 (O.S.), was kept a holiday, because St. Philip and St. James's Day fell on a Sunday.

3. 'The road from London to Harwich, one of the best in England: made in King William's time for his convenience, as he passed that way so frequently. Grows less and worse after you have passed Colchester. The old castle there, and the pretty church (like a summerhouse) on the road after . . . the walk on the cliff [at Harwich] and the two lighthouses that direct by coinciding' (*Nbk.* 2 61ʳ).

4. Among the Spence Papers is a copy of verses entitled 'A Sabath Night's Prayer for the King, made at Helvoetsluys January 1736/7 after Our Wonderful deliverance from the great storm', by Thomas Brand.

5. Robert Hampden-Trevor (1706–83), Visc. Hampden and 4th Baron Trevor, cousin of John Morley Trevor. After graduating from Queens' College (1732) he acted as secretary to the British legation at The Hague under Horatio Walpole; envoy extraordinary 1739, British minister at The Hague 1741.

6. 'We saw Grotius' house to the left near Maeslandsluys: and Ryswick within a mile of the Hague' (*Nbk.* 2 61ʳ).

7. Originally 'in England'.

8. Mrs. Spence herself, who marked this letter 'verrey pretey'.

9. 'In the island of Rosenberg: [we] mistook those on the churches at first for stone-figures on them' (*Nbk.* 2 61ʳ).

10. By June 20 he was back in Oxford (*Letter* 57).

*55

Source: Egerton 2234 ff. 90–91

Addressed: To/Mrs Spence/in Colebrook-Street,/in Winchester,/Hants.

Postmarked: 28 MA

Endorsed: *b.* How ill they keep the/Sabbath in Holland.

Hague,
June 3 ⟨May 25⟩, 1737

⟨Dear Mother,

Last Saturday I received a letter from my good friend Mr. Smith[1] and had the pleasure of finding two of yours in it. They were both meant for me at London where Mr. Smith promised to receive them and send them to me, which he did without much trouble, as he lived almost next door to Mr. Jonquiere's.[2] I wrote to you as soon as ever I got afoot on the continent, from Helvoet the 18th of our May here, and again the next day from this place. I hope they both came safe to you, and suppose I have not received any answer possibly because you doubted how to send. You may put your letters always directly into the post at Winchester I imagine, and they will easily tell you whether you are to pay anything at putting them in and what. I have sent you before how to direct to me, but I will give you a new one on the other side, for my letter may have missed you, and as we are soon to be in France I think I had as good use you to French already. Write it just thus: À Monsieur / Monsieur Spence / Gentilhomme Anglois, / à Keysers-Hof, / à la Haye / Holland. If 'twas not a pleasure to me always to write to you I should think myself very much obliged to this direction for taking up half a side, but the truth is, when I sit down to write to you I could chat on all day long.⟩

Our chief business here has been visiting and going out to see the gardens, which are very frequent all round the Hague and add a great deal to the beauty of the country. At first when we came here 'twas very cold, but this week has made up for it by being extremely hot. I was measured for a summer suit of clothes this morning, and tomorrow perhaps shall be forced to wrap myself up in a greatcoat, in my winter ones. The weather here is exceedingly uncertain, and they may say what they will of England on this head, the people I meet here, who are acquainted with both, assure me that 'tis more fickle here than with you.

We set out tomorrow by water to see Leyden, and shall creep on to Utrecht, Amsterdam, North Holland, and so home by Leyden again. We were yesterday to dine at a very pretty village three miles from this place by the side of the Great Canal where, though it was Sunday, the boats went about in business almost as busily as they do on other days (and nineteen parts in twenty of the industry of this people lies on the water) not to mention that a man was mowing the meadow that belonged to the house where we dined, and that the public houses all along as we returned were full of music, dancing, and people playing at cards. You see, these Presbyterians are not over-rigid observers of the Sabbath, and indeed I think they outdo even the Papists in this particular. ⟨I am, with all services to all friends,

Your most affectionate

J. Spence⟩

1. On Arthur Smyth, see *Letter* 39.
2. Spence's 'Old Landlord Jonquiere in Suffolk Street', London (Wright, p. 217).

---

*56

Source:	Egerton 2234 ff. 92–93
Addressed:	*as in* 54
Endorsed:	*b.* The two fat Children,/& Clockwork man at Leyden.

Hague,
June 11, 1737

⟨Dear Mother,⟩

We came in last night about ten from our tour of Leyden, Utrecht, Amsterdam and North Holland,[1] when I had the satisfaction of meeting your first letter as soon as ever I came in ⟨with another from good Mr. Duck⟩.[2] Though I had a great deal of pleasure in the journey, or voyage, we had been taking (for we went above half of it by the canals) your letter far exceeded it all together. There's something in receiving the first letter that I can't express to you: all yours are a pleasure to me, but that has something more in it.

We went first to Leyden, where we saw the famous Dr. Boerhave, and heard him give a lecture.[3] I had heard he was an ugly mean-looking man,[4] but I can't think so. Nothing indeed can be plainer than his dress, but the dress with me has nothing to do with the man. His look is good-natured and open, and though he is within a year of seventy, there's a freshness and clearness in his face that makes him appear almost a young man. There's a great simplicity generally in his prescriptions; the things he orders are plain and easy, and he's a great enemy to loading people with powders and vials. I suppose he has followed the same method for himself, and by that means has preserved this youthfulness of his complexion to the last.[5]

I think we are eternally to have the luck of coming to towns on their fair day. 'Twas the great fair of Leyden when we got there. England is not the only place where people love to gape at fools and monsters. There was a place in the town as long as ⌜your Mall at Winchester⌝,[6] with booths continued the whole length of it for different sights of some kind or another. We went into two of them, because they were things that were then much talked of at the Hague and all over Holland. The first contained two Dutch boys who are shown for their corpulency remarkable even in this country. The eldest of them was three years old and two months, and weighed 150 pounds[7] (Dutch, which is near equal to 170 English). His thigh was much bigger about, I believe, than my body, his face all over-flooded with fat, and when he moved toward you 'twas more like the motion of a porpoise in the water than walking on land. The physicians say he may live to about five year old, and I fear 'tis his parents who show him that are guilty of his death whenever he dies, for they must have used some art to blow him up and to fatten him to that monstrous pitch. His brother is not a year old, and weighs but fourscore pound, the child's as yet but a starveling, but in two or three years more, with the same management, he may come to be as great a sight as his elder brother.

The other sight we were at was two pieces of clockwork. I never was surprised to see a man [and] a woman in clockwork[8] walk about a room, but these seem to understand you, and do whatever you desire them. They are placed fair on an open table. The showman stands as far from them as you are that see them. You are to say whether the lady shall pour out a glass of red wine or white, or both together, and immediately she does whichever of the three you desire, and this nine or ten times running without the man's ever going near her after you have given your orders. The clockwork man strikes a bell as often as you bid him, and no oftener, in the same manner. You'll say I'm very well employed to have time enough to give this long account of two Bartholomew babies, but really at first sight it is at least as odd as it may seem foolish to you.[9] ⟨However, I have done, and am with all services

Your dutiful and affectionate

J. Spence.⟩

1. Starting from The Hague June 4, they went to Leyden 'by water', and visited Utrecht (5), Amsterdam (6), Monnikendam, Purmerend, Alkmaar, Hoorn (7), and Edam, before returning through Monnikendam (8) and Haarlem to The Hague on June 9 (*Nbk. 2* 61ʳ).

2. Stephen Duck, the Thresher-Poet, championed by Spence. See *Letters* 8, 12.

3. Herman Boerhaave (1668–1738), the great physician and professor of medicine at Leyden. Spence heard him lecture 'in his own house' on 'colours that shew such and such diseases' (*Nbk.* 2 61ʳ).

4. 'È brutto, gambe grosse,' wrote Cocchi in 1726, 'non vuol pratticare fuori di Leida; è di vita semplice, aria contadinesca' (A. Corsini, *Antonio Cocchi* [Milan, 1928], p. 106). Spence may have heard of Boerhaave on his first tour from Dr. Cocchi.

5. 'His manner, both of writing and speaking, very clear and plain: his clear, plain, open look *viridisque senectus*' (*Nbk.* 2 61ʳ).

6. Emended to 'the Mall'.

7. Spence actually wrote '350 pounds Dutch', a mistake corrected in the following letter.

8. 'Mustapha and Rosetta' (*Nbk.* 2 61ʳ).

9. They also went up a 'mount whence you see Descartes' house', so the sight of mechanical toys was perhaps not quite inappropriate (ibid.).

Notebook 2

Egerton 2235 ff. (i–iv) 61ʳ–62ᵛ

In going to *Utrecht* we passed by a very pretty fortification, the castle of Montford, and through Waarden, which is very prettily fortified too with a double ditch. At Utrecht the part of the Great Church which remains shows it to have been a very magnificent building for the country and age when it was built.

We went down the canal of Utrecht which is very thick set with villas and villages, and afterwards down the Amstel to *Amsterdam*. Amsterdam is evidently built on a greater scale than the other cities in Holland. The buildings in general are neither good nor pretty, but it has an old, great and venerable look, especially in the three celebrated streets (the Prinsen-Gracht, the Heeren-Gracht, and the Keizers-Gracht). The best houses are in the Heeren-Gracht, and eight of their twelve burgomasters live there all together. The *marché* at the entrance, the Mall, and the great bridge on the Amstel (whence that noble view) are all of the character above-mentioned.

Though the Stathouse is far from perfect, it has something great and striking when you look up toward the cupola in the front: downward the seven openings are very little and unequal to the building. There are four rows of 21 windows (the second and fourth attic) in front, not reckoning the prison and what one may call the garret windows. There are two rows of pillars, the lowest composite with irregular things (little dolphins, etc.) in the midst of the capitals, and those above Corinthian with ditto: round the cupola there are Corinthians again.

The Great Hall is grand and perhaps too fine—you see nothing but painting and marble in it. There are Corinthians on Corinthians in that too. On the floor are two ter[restrial] plans of about 20 f. diameter, and one of the heavens in the midst: the stars according to their magnitudes and their names inlaid in brass. The hall is 54 of my paces by 30, and the goings off at each end 34 by 11.— There are some pictures that are pretty good and the statues and basso-relievos have some of them more of taste than I expected (the Apollo, Diana, Mercury, falling Icarus, and mighty pretty little reliefs over two or three of the chimney-pieces). Some of the brass-work is mighty neat, especially that below where the three reliefs are of Brutus' judgement, Solomon's, and Seleucus' eye putting out. Some of the figures at the end of the hall are truly Flemish and very bad (especially the Justice with Death on her right hand and the Torture and wooden-leg person on the left).

In one of the side-rooms we saw about thirty couples of Papists married by the Protestant magistrate, and below we saw the neat picsons, where K[ing?] Theodore had lately lain, instruments for giving the question.

We could only walk by the Arsenal and the India House (as we were there on Whit Sunday) but had better luck at both the Jewish synagogues.—The chief gentlemen have coaches, but most go in sleighs, which are coaches let down on their backsides and dragged along by one horse, directed by a coachman on foot. They have but two hackney-coaches in the town. They are so rare because the whole town is built on piles, and I think they say the Stathouse alone on nine thousand.

The city is about seven (?) mile round and has 400,000 souls in it (*Mons. Tronchin*). 26,000 houses, known by the taxation books ($\times 7 = 182,000$). About five mile round, two to the sea (*Mr. Melling*). It lies to the sea, the branch of Zuyder Zee that goes by there, in a long shallow segment of a circle, and is defended to the land with regular fortifications.

We went hence for North Holland, passed a bad country to *Monnikendam* and no good one to *Purmerend*. From thence we entered directly into the Beemster, a very pretty and well-cultivated spot, thick-inhabited and planted all in regular squares of about a mile each, like a chess-board. How pretty a spot of ground for what was formerly a lake! Here were the first flocks of sheep that looked anything like flocks which we saw in Holland.

Alkmaar is a very neat and very pretty town. I was surprised to find the Roman style in North Holland. On the Stathouse is the inscription: 'Opus hoc / Vetustate collapsum / Ex S.C. Restaurari curarunt Coss' (the date under it, 1694) and on another public building: 'S.P.Q.A. Restituit Virtus ablatae jura bilancis'. This city has a voice in the Provincial States of Holland.

The country to *Hoorn* is bad enough, where it does not border on the Beemster, and towards Hoorn the peasants' and farmers' houses run on oddly in sort of circles and regular lines, which I suppose is occasioned by their following the course of the canals and building nowhere else. The last mile or two to Hoorn we went over the raised way, or dyke, which is a work rather worthy of the Roman empire than such a little province as Holland (how evident here that the sea is much higher than the land). There's room I believe for four coaches to pass abreast: it goes down perpendicular to the sea and sloping to the canal. To the sea 'tis laced with sea-weed for several foot in (which perhaps breaks the force of the sea, as the woolsacks of old broke the blow of the battering ram) and flanked below with high piles and great stones. In these piles we saw the mischievousness of those worms that alarmed Holland a few years ago. Most of them were quite rotten, some perfectly hollowed (like trunks of trees for canoes) and in several places they had quite taken them away for ten or twelve yards together and flung in more stones—which is a method they now talk of pursuing in general there. The pieces eat like the honeycomb are not frequent there: the holes generally serpentise up from the bottom to the top in a gentle waving line. Just by the gate of Alkmaar they have made a new fence in the old way farther out to sea, which they seem to be carrying out farther from the town to the right, and on the left they won't suffer one to pass to see how it is.

⟨The girls dressed up on Whitsun Eve that Lord Paisley heard singing something like a paean: 'O Bacche, O Bacche, O Pan'.⟩

In passing to *Edam*, we had the dyke all along to our left, lines of scattering houses generally under it (the sea higher than the rooms they live in) and others going off by the sides of the canals. We went from Amsterdam by *Haarlem* to the Hague. The country to Haarlem bad; from thence mostly dunes, but well planted and inhabited, with an irregular pretty air enough.

All subsequent excerpts from *Notebook* 2 are taken from Egerton 2235.

57

Source:	Egerton 2234 ff. 94–95
Addressed:	*as in* 54
Postmarked:	16 IV
Endorsed:	*b.* The Fat Boy; 170 p^d, Engl:/This, not to be Copied (Omit this.)

Hague,
June 20, 1737

⟨Dear Mother,

Our weather here is rather cold again than warm, so that though my summer suit has been made some time, I have had no occasion for wearing it yet. Now I am doubly armed, I shall turn coats as fast as the weather changes.

I believe we shall set out next week for Flanders by slow easy journeys in a post-chaise. We think of passing the summer at some town in France, to learn the language; somewhere on the banks of the river Loire, as a very agreeable country for the summer, and I believe it will be either at Blois or Angers. We go from hence to Dort, Breda, Antwerp ⟨Anvers often in the maps⟩, Dendermond, Ghent, Bruges, Ostend, Ypres, Lille, Tournay, Valenciennes, Bouchain, Cambray, Paris, Orleans, Blois where the river (for I suppose you have got your map before you) will lead your eye down to Tours and Angers. That river is the Loire, and reckoned one of the pleasantest part of France. We shall winter I believe at Paris, and not go for fair Italy till the spring. French is so necessary everywhere that Mr. Trevor is resolved to make himself master of it before we go on, and I think he is much in the right of it. The next letter you write, and all the following till I come on English ground again, you will please to direct with all my foreign titles of honour as follows: à Monsieur / Monsieur Spence / Recommandé à Monsr. Alexandre[1] / Banquier, à / Paris. Mr. Smith has not met with so good success as I could have wished: I hope he will do better when he comes to try his friends in Ireland, for he has several and good ones there. I wish you were a magistrate, to put that and all things else, in good order.

174

I am overjoyed to hear that my plantation goes on so well,[2] and when I return I shall be very glad to conduct you to it for a month or so every other summer if you like it, and then I'll come and see you every other summer at Winchester, which will secure our meeting once a year, you know, and I'll never play truant again to go a' gadding into foreign parts as I have done, but will take up and be a very sober good man. I am very much obliged to you for the account of Job's great rejoicing at getting home to his country,[3] and have a great mind to imitate it the first [time I] get upon Giles' Hill, had not I su[ch great] aversion to letting off of pistols [in front][4] of horses.

Though a long letter from [you is always] a very great cordial to me, I be[g you not] to strain your eyes about it n[ow, for what] would tire them at twice may not hurt them [at] four sittings—and what if you wrote on larger paper and in a larger hand than usual?[5] Mr. Rolle is got to Oxford by this time;[6] I have wrote to him thither and told him how to direct to me. In my last to you I mentioned a true fat Dutch boy that we saw at Leyden, but I injured the poor child, and am sorry for it. I said he weighed but hundred and fifty pounds; he weighs so much Dutch, and that's equal to near a hundred and seventy English. I beg all services to all friends, and am their and your

Very humble servant

J. Spence.⟩

---

1. Alexandre Alexander (*fl.* 1727–51) is listed in the *Almanach Royal* (1739), p. 349, among the 'banquiers pour les traités et remises de place en place'. From 1729 until 1741 Alexander's address was Rue Saint-Appolline. Horace Walpole had also his letters directed to him (*H. W. Corresp.* XIII, 184).

2. His 'Lizard garden' at Birchanger in Essex, which Spence cultivated since 1728 (Wright, pp. 35–7).

3. 'Job the Black' or 'Job Ben Solomon' had been the subject of two long letters from Spence at Oxford to his mother (Nov. 6, 1735, Feb. 21, 1736). Job, an African prince, was transported in 1732 as a slave to America and, after many hardships, brought by General Oglethorpe to London, where he resided for a time with Spence's brother Richard at the African House. He learned English, was presented at Court, and in 1734 departed for Africa. Richard, who received letters from Job about his difficulties in getting back to his kingdom, wrote on May 21, 1737, to Mrs. Spence: 'The last accounts we have from Job's country inform us that there was a difference between the present king and one that had been deposed. . . . We are under some concern about it. But hope that the side Job is of will get the better and that I shall have that good news to send you the first time' (Spence Papers). Mrs. Spence no doubt transmitted this last bit of news to her other son. See Wylie Sypher, 'The African Prince in London', *JHI* II (1941), 237–9, which lists three printed contemporary accounts of the affair.

4. Part of the letter is torn off here.

5. Mrs. Spence wrote in a small 17th-century hand.

6. His visit to Paris (*Letter* 54) must have been a short one.

*58

Source:	Egerton 2234 ff. 96–97
Addressed:	as in 54
Postmarked:	21 IV
Endorsed:	*a.* a descripshon of the hague &/ye princ of orangis house
	b. Some acc^t of ye Hague;/Shevelin; & ye House in ye Wood.

Hague,
June 24, 1737

⟨Dear Mother,⟩

Now we are going from Holland and leaving the Hague, 'tis some mortification to me to tell you what an extreme pretty place it is.[1] I don't say the houses are so well built as those of the Italians, or adorned with so fine paintings and statues, that the streets are as regular as those of Turin, or the extent of it so large as that of London. 'Tis no grand town,[2] but 'tis one of the prettiest ⟨I think⟩ I have ever seen, and the places round it are a great addition to the prettiness of it.

I write now in the top part of the town (at the Keysers-Hof), and yet every time I look toward the window I look into a wood. 'Tis a square before us with a noble piece of water all over it, except the raised walks before our house and down one side of it, which latter is all planted with good old venerable trees. Most of the streets have rows of trees on each side, or a canal in the middle, and many have both. Out of every gate you go by a canal with rows of trees on each side, but we have two outlets that are better than the rest. One is through a regular walk of a mile and a half long, planted thick and paved all with brick just covered with sand, with a deep green on each side—though if you were to diverge for thirty yards on either side of you, you would be in the most detestable ground in the world. But this is hid to you, unless you creep out of your way on purpose to see it.

The walk joins to a little village[3] and terminates on the sea-shore, so that when you as much expected to step into the clouds the next step, you are all at once surprised with a view of the sea, and that nothing but sea, both before you and to your right hand and your left. I was there this morning, and our coach stopped with us within three yards of the waves that came in roaring and tumbling for as far as we could see all in one foam, for 'twas a rough morning. On each side of this walk, if you creep through the wilderness, work on either side from so neat and green and regular a thing, you are all at once in a desert of sand: white and wild and waved about in little inequalities. They call them here the downs (or dunes), but it looks

176

as if it was not yet created, or at least as the earth might when it was yet without form and void.

Another place that I have taken many a walk in is what they call The Wood.[4] 'Tis these dunes again with all their natural inequalities, but cultivated, clothed in green, and planted all thick with trees. 'Tis cut into a great many wild alleys, and is the great place for walking for all the town here on Sundays and holidays. It put me in mind of the Nightingale Wood near Kingsclere,[5] though I never heard in all my life put together so many nightingales as I did in this wood the first month of our being here. At the end of it is the Prince of Orange's house in which are all his ancestors in tapestry.[6] All the rooms almost below are furnished with the great men that have belonged to that family, and King William in particular appears thrice in one room.[7]

You would hardly believe how many country villas there are round the Hague, each of which appears like a house in a wood, from the garden and plantation about it. We have been to see five or six of the best of them at times, but for their gardens, I have not yet seen any one to my taste.[8] They are extremely regular: the walks are cut out in little sippets; grass in the middle scarce broad enough for three people to walk abreast in, and a dry walk on each side, about the same breadth each; and then a hedge of hornbeam on each side cut up as smooth as a die. They have no gravel, but they have found a pretty way of supplying the want of it, the dry walks being all covered with sea-shells. Straight walks that fall off on each side, exactly answer one another. The main walk generally leads you to a fish-pond in a semicircle of sloping banks, that are often laid out in slips of figures (like a pattern to work upon) and filled up, such a part with white shells and such an one with brown or perhaps some minerals, and the whole looking like carpets growing to the banks. Quite at the end of this is a summerhouse that looks all down the main walk to the dwellinghouse, and this is generally speaking a fine Dutch garden. I have often thought the Nightingale Wood here is the best garden I have seen in Holland, because 'tis natural.[9] The rest are all art, and appearing art, which is almost as bad as a face grossly painted. ⟨They are even too neat too, it's possible, but as you and I might not agree on that head, I'll leave off whilst 'tis well, and am ever

Your dutiful and affectionate

J. Spence.

Humble services to Belle and all friends.⟩

1. In his *Notebook* (2 62ᵛ) Spence recorded 'One of the inscriptions in the Schivelin road: Haya gentil tu sei gemma del mondo, / Nel tuo sen lieto ogn'un vive giocondo.'

2. 'Though the Hague itself is all a *rus in urbe*', 'or village, if one must call it so', it is 'the seat of public business and politeness for the seven provinces' (ibid.).

3. 'Schivelin', the present sea-side resort of Scheveningen. 'On the left hand is Mr. Bentinck's villa and gardens—above 1100 acres' (ibid.).

4. The Haagsche Bosch.

5. About seventeen miles north of Winchester.

6. The Huis ten Bosch (House in the Wood), a richly decorated 17th-century royal villa.

7. The Orange Hall.

8. Spence played an important role in promoting 'the new taste' in English garden designs. 'It was he and Pope, and another or two of his friends,' wrote Spence's friend Elizabeth Cartwright, 'who introduced the present taste in gardening, and rescued them from the imprisonment of high walls and clipt hedges' (Wright, p. 117).

9. Cf. Spence's comment in 1740: 'Though I have seen Versailles often, I should be apt to think that the woods of Chantilly may be called the best garden in *France*: they are cut into openings that are more regular than some of our best gardens in England, though they have more of nature unspoilt than any garden in France' (*Nbk.* 3 73ʳ). See also *Obs.* No. 1071.

Notebook 2

⟨*iv–vi*⟩ 62ᵛ–63ᵛ

The Hague is a beautiful town, or village, if one must call it so, and is the seat of public business and politeness for the seven provinces. There is little remarkable in it in particular. We saw the room for the States and the furious picture of war in it. The chief places lie all together, for the Voorhout comes round to the Vijverberg, and a step or two carries you thence into a plain where [is] Rozelli's coffee-house (as his burying place in going to Loosduinen).

Between the plain and the Vijverberg is the *palais*, where [there are] the apartments of the Prince of Orange and foreign ambassadors at first coming, which seems to be the truest building in the Hague [with its] Great Hall, rooms for the States to sit in, and the guards. . . .

The chief pleasure . . . is going into its environs. . . . In the road to Delft is Taxara's gardens, with some statues which they call good and a great variety of foreign birds. Hownslow Dyke is farther to the right beyond Ryswick. The most like an old palace of any we saw, formerly in the Prince of Orange's family, [is] now the King of Prussia's. There are several pictures there, particularly 'The Fortune Teller' of Rembrandt's.

On the wood side of the Hague is the pretty way to Voorburg: Leidschendam with the pretty little church and the view of the marshes where they have cut turf: Sticker's gardens with the star-wood at the end and the tame carp. Swart sows bounded so wildly by the dunes and the gardens of Mad[ame?]. Duinenpoort (Lord George B[entinck]) to which we went by so pretty a by-road as we traversed so vast a flowery mead from Lionstans to Leidschendam. . . .

In going from the Hague we passed Delft, so famous heretofore for its earthenware, which is now much fallen. The house where the Prince of Orange was murdered (1584), his tomb in the Great Church, with some of the best figures in Holland at the four corners and the Fame behind. Admiral Trump's in another (New?) Church.

And so to Rotterdam ⟨which is decayed too in its trade, from Amsterdam's drawing too much to it. The Boom quay, and the view from it, one of the prettiest lines you can see—the greatest beauty of Rotterdam. 80,000 souls there, one tenth English [according to] Edwards⟩. There we passed the Maas and afterwards the Hollands-Diep, where the present Prince of Orange's father was drowned, to Moerdijk.

---

*59

Source:	Egerton 2234 ff. 98–99
Addressed:	*as in* 54
Postmarked:	IV 29
Endorsed:	*a.* a descripshon of antwerp, yᵉ fine/pictures it abounds with/chefeley: & a descripshon/of yᵉ prince of oring/& his dominions there
	b. Of the Prince of Orange; &/the Blacksmith-Painter, at Antwerp.

Brussels,
July 5, 1737

⟨Dear Mother,

I think the longer I live the better I grow, for here am I going to write a letter to you in the midst of a journey on the road—which I don't remember ever to have done in my travels before.⟩ We left the Hague on the 28th; got to Rotterdam to a very good dinner; crossed the Rhine that evening; went on to Breda, and rejoiced all the people there by bringing them the first news of the Princess of Orange's being declared to be breeding again.[1]

That town belongs to the Prince of Orange, and he has twenty-seven villages belonging to him about it. With all this he is not so rich as one could wish, though he is richer than he is generally said to be in England. His estate is about £12,000 a year, and his income every way (taken all together) is £24 or 25,000 a year. He is much beloved by the common people all over his own country, but the great men, and particularly the great men in the province of Holland, are too much afraid of him to love him. They know his personal character and they know his power in three or four of the provinces. They have maintained their liberties for a great while and in a particular manner, and 'tis no wonder if they should be afraid to lose them, or any part of them, which they think would be the immediate consequence of his being made Stadholder.[2] They would be less apprehensive of a Prince of Orange that had less merit and spirit than they are of the present, for he has enough of both to rouse them and keep them on their guard. You won't wonder that I talk to you so much like a politician when I have told you that our acquaintance at the Hague lay chiefly among ambassadors and ministers of state.[3] ⟨I find myself sensibly grown the wiser for it, and think His Majesty would do a very good thing in putting me into some considerable post of that kind.⟩

After we left Breda,[4] we soon left the Dutch dominions, and got into those of the Emperor, in Flanders. Antwerp was the first considerable town we stayed at there, for three or four days, to see the pictures it abounds in.[5] That city was the great school for the Flemish painters: Rubens (and I think Vandyck) [were] born there.[6] There's a great number of pieces of both their hands, and 'twas there that love made a famous painter of a common blacksmith.

His name is Quintin; he made horse-shoes and hobnails, when he happened to fall in love with the daughter of a famous painter in that city.[7] The father would not hear of such a match; he had told him a thousand times that his trade was the most contemptible of any, but that as he was a very honest fellow he would have given him his daughter had he been a painter. Quintin was in despair; he quitted the place where he found himself so miserable and so despised; he roamed about in a melancholy way, till at last he flung himself into service—and as it happened into that of a painter. When he had spare time and his master was out of the way, he used to be always playing with the pencils and endeavouring to draw his mistress's face. This trifling by degrees had some effect that led him to set to it more in earnest, and at last he grew an excellent painter, returned to Antwerp, and carried his mistress. In Italy I have seen hers and his own picture drawn by him very well, and his name and works are to this day very much celebrated in Antwerp.[8]

⟨From thence we came to Brussels,[9] where we met with Lord George Bentinck,[10] and had like to have met with the Duchess of Dorset.[11] I was but an hour too late for it in my visit this morning, for they t[old me] she was but a little before set out for Namur. We go soon for Paris where (or whence) your letters will always find me by the directions I have sent formerly. I am perfectly well, and with services to all friends

Your most dutiful and affectionate

J. Spence.⟩

1. Princess Anne, the eldest daughter of George II, had married William, the Prince of Orange (1711–51), in 1734. On Thursday, June 9 O.S., 'It was notify'd at Court that the Princess of *Orange* was with child' (*Gent. Mag.*, 1737, p. 377).

2. The country had been without a Stadholder since the death of William III in 1702. During the revolution of 1747 the Prince of Orange was made Stadholder, despite strong opposition, especially from the Province of Holland.

3. In his *Notebook* (2 62ᵛ) Spence gives a list of 'foreign ambassadors' at The Hague; it has been omitted here because a much more comprehensive list appears in the anonymous *Description of Holland: or, the Present State of the United Provinces* (1743), pp. 135–66.

4. 'At Breda we saw [the Prince of Orange's] gardens, with the army, etc. in box, the abominable statues, and the delightful fortification view from the terrace. Tomb in the Great Church with statues more toward a true taste than any we had seen since our setting out (of

Comte Engelbert de Nassau and his wife, d. 1435; death is too strong, according to the Flemish style, in both their faces). The corner figures are Julius Caesar, Regulus, Philip and Hannibal. The two first are much better than the other, and they say done by Michelangelo, which is apparently false—from Regulus' holding a Gothic spiked club and from their habits' (*Nbk.* 2 63ᵛ).

5. In his *Notebook* (2 64ʳ–65ᵛ) Spence made an extensive list of the paintings he saw at Antwerp. See *App.* 6.

6. Rubens was born in Siegen, Westphalia.

7. Quentin Metsys or Massys (ca. 1465–1529). The story of a love-struck smith's apprentice is a legend developed in the 17th century (Jean de Bosschère, *Quinten Metsys*, Brussels, 1907). Spence shared the 18th-century interest in 'untutored genius', as his various accounts of Stephen Duck, Blacklock, Magliabecchi, Thomas Chubb, etc. show.

8. It is now established that the portraits in the Uffizi gallery are not by Metsys but by Van Cleves (Bosschère, p. 105). Metsys's only known self-portrait disappeared late in the 18th century.

9. July 4–5.

10. George Bentinck (1715–59), son of the 1st and brother of the 2d D. of Portland; M.P. for Droitwich (1742–7), Grampound (1747–54), Malmesbury (1754–9).

11. Elizabeth Colyer (1687–1768), mother of Lord Middlesex, whom Spence accompanied on the first tour. She had been Maid of Honour to Queen Anne, First Lady of the Bedchamber to Queen Caroline, but left the Court in 1731.

Notebook 2
(*vi–x*) 63ᵛ, 66ʳ–67ᵛ

The road by the riverside for two leagues before you come to *Brussels* [July 4–5] particularly delightful: that [is] their promenade; the park within the town too is pretty enough, the town itself has very little beauty in it. . . . There is not much to be seen at Brussels. The hangings in the Town House are good: in the first room is the history of *St. Louis* in four pieces, designed by Le Brun and wrought by Vandenberg; in the second is the province submitting itself to the Emperor, the demission of Charles V, and the 'Laetus introitus Philippi Boni', all designed by Jaenssen and wrought by Leyniers. We saw the tapestry work at Leyniers', not near equal to the former, and he said of the trade now 'qu'il n'a jamais été si faible'. The helmet and shield of Charles V in the Arsenal they say were taken by his army at Rome, and so was the Fabricius shield, cut with a diamond. They have confused the story: 'tis a battle-piece, with an elephant in it fighting and the enemy attacking him with torches. The inscription is, 'Fabricium frustra, Rex Pyrrhe, proboscide terres; Bellua namque licet saeva sit, igne perit'.

At *Ghent* [July 6] we saw a very good picture relating to Saint-Amand, by Vandyck. It used to be the high altar piece in the Great Church, but is now in a chapel just behind it. There's a great convent of Beguines there, and I think our guide said there were nine hundred belonging to it. Abroad their habit is black, but at home white: and in the church it looked as if the whole congregation had been just snowed upon.

Menin is small, but a very strong and beautiful fortification.

Lille [July 7–9] did not answer the character we had heard of it. The Rue Royale is a regular and handsome street, and is pierced regularly by several other streets, but the town in general can scarce be called a very handsome one. The esplanade (where the *cours* is) is no beauty, the citadel is the most considerable thing to see at Lille. 'Tis about a mile and a half round, consists of five bastions, four *courtines*, and four *sorties* in them. There was a regiment (600 men) in it and six in the town, so that in all the public places the gentlemen are almost all officers. There's a cavalier in the citadel that absolutely commands the town and makes them good subjects to whatever master they have (as at Tournay, etc. etc.). In the last siege Prince Eugene was lodged in the Abbaye de Lou with the Imperialists a league from the town, and the Duke of Marlborough with the English at the Abbaye de Maquette, at half a league ditto. On that side everything was laid level for a great way into the town, and 'twas on that side that the great breach was made: it still retains some of the marks of ruin and war about it.

At St. Catherine's is her beheading, by Rubens. At the Recolets, Saviour on the cross, St. John, Holy Virgin and Mary Magdalen by Vandyck. At the Hôpital de Comtesse two or three pictures by Arnauld d'Anvers, not bad. At l'Église de l'Ange Gardien the 'Fall of the Angels' by Rubens. Ib. (?) the devil whipping Job with serpents and his wife advising him, etc. At l'Abbaye de la Béate is an exact (?) copy of the Holy House at Loreto, her image, etc., and they say that on great festivals there are the copies of all the ornaments of it too. It looked naked when we saw it.

The citadel at *Tournay* [July 10] has the advantage of being on a hill, whereas that of Lille is on a flat. It has one of the strongest and grandest airs that ever I observed in a fortification. As to the first, it put me in mind of what I felt in seeing the citadel at Namur, and the officer that showed it us said that these of Tournay were the strongest fortifications in Flanders (and Namur owes more to its situation than Tournay, so that this should be the strongest work of art they have). We were all round the mines under the citadel as well as over the ramparts above and made pretty near the same walk underground that we had in the air. The long walks they call 'galeries', the rounds under each bastion 'chambres': they have a good sizeable baking-room to dress their victuals (for in a siege they quite live in these caverns) and a very spacious and airy long room for the sick and wounded. The miners now are ten, in wartime a hundred. The powder for blowing up is lodged in a close chamber where no air can penetrate: a pipe runs to it from thirty to a hundred foot long, and so 'tis sprung with danger to the engineer. The office of a miner is a terrible trade: they have a great pay, continued even in peace when they do nothing, but the labour and danger makes up for it in war. Even then the miners here have a vast advantage, for the counterminers are in a *terra incognita*, and these know every inch and winding of it. We were not in the out-mines which, they say, run for six miles into the country.

There's a very rich abbey at Tournay (St. Martin's) of [the] Benedictines: the church is a very handsome new building, a rich silver crucifix and the brasswork round the choir looks very light and pretty at a distance. There's a picture of a person possessed that is not bad, and two paysages of an odd particular manner. The library is a beautiful one and has a beautiful prospect in it (the stork's nest on a chimney, as in Holland).

At the little town of *St. Amand* [July 11] is the famous abbey of the same name. When you enter the church, you have something of the same feeling that one has in King's Chapel at Cambridge, though it wants vastly of the beauty of the latter, and the wide galleries of the side (which they talk so much of as an upper church) perhaps take away from the beauty it might have had. I could make nothing of the story told in statues in the front.

Cambray [July 11] is a very mean poor city. The Cathedral is loaded with statues in the inside (of which there are two or three not bad) and the spire is all pierced with little openings in a manner as uncommon as 'tis ridiculous. To one side of the choir is affixed the monument of the great Archbishop of Cambray [Fénelon] and under his bust, which is a good one and they say very like, is a long inscription in his honour. It calls him 'Homerus alter' and says as to his doctrine (for which he was censured) 'De casto amore ita disseruit, ut Vaticano obsequens oraculo, simul et sponso et sponsae placuerit'.

Roi [July 12] looks like the ghost of a fortified place and has some odd views about it.—*Pont St. Maxence* stands at the foot of a very beautiful semicircle of hills which are a step up to a higher range of country, where you pass through that noble road, with the Duke of Bourbon's woods on each side of it to *Senlis* [July 13], and thence to Paris même.

---

*60

Source: Egerton 2234 ff. 100–1
Addressed: as in 54
Postmarked: 23 IV
Endorsed: a. [Blois]
            b. Flatness of Holland; & Fertility of/
            Flanders.

Paris,
July 19 ⟨8⟩, 1737

⟨Dear Mother,⟩

I wrote to you on the road hither to let you know how we came on, and now I can let you know that we got safe ⟨and sound⟩ hither six days ago[1] ⟨and have been since to see the places most considerable round this good city.[2] We shall go in two or three days to settle about two days' journey from hence at Blois, one of the prettiest places in France as I hear and as I hope to find it, for we shall stay there all this summer on the banks of the river Loire.⟩

In coming hither we passed through Flanders, all a very rich and fertile tract of land, and they were at harvest work of some kind or another all the way as we came along. I don't see any ground that lies fallow among them. 'Tis covered with corn everywhere, unless where they are ploughing up ground to sow again, and wherever there is corn 'tis of an extraordinary height and uncommon goodness. They are very convenient neighbours for Holland, for they have scarce any corn there, and are almost altogether supplied with it from other countries. The province of Holland is scarce anything else but one great meadow interlaced with canals ⟨as the meads about Winchester, only with larger ones, and more regularly⟩. 'Tis so really one flat that I don't remember once to have seen a rising in the road before one in going from one end to the other of Holland, unless it were to go up a bridge over some of the canals, or to mount on the mounds they have made to keep the sea from running over the country. When we were going toward Breda we first perceived any inequality in the ground, after which the earth was rather in long waves than roughened with anything that could be called a hill.[3] There begins to be something more like it in and about Brussels, but the first chain of hills we saw (and 'twas a delightful sight after being so long used to flats) was at Pont St. Maxence, not forty mile from hence, where we rose up a pretty steep piece of a hill that seemed as a Welsh mountain to us Hollanders, from whence we came along through the woods of the Duke of Bourbon,[4] one of the most pleasant and most magnificent roads that you can anywhere pass.

Yesterday and the day before we were at Versailles where we saw the King go to chapel, and were good Catholics enough to attend him there all the service.[5] They say here that he is extremely altered of late, and he should be so by his pictures (for I never saw His Majesty in person before), but he has still beauty enough to be called a handsome man.[6] 'Twas generally said when I was here before that he was as like Lord Middlesex as ever two men were like one another. I believe it may have in a great measure been true, but a great deal of the likeness is now gone off. The King is so perpetually engaged in hunting that he has acquired a dark brown look which has altered him greatly. He is a very devout prince, at least as to the forms, for he was saying his prayers all the service through, and the moment he came out the horns sounded for hunting, and away he went in no very cool day, I'll assure you.

The gardens of Versailles were formerly reckoned extremely beautiful.[7] We could not see the Queen in them, because she had laid in of another princess (I think 'tis her seventh) but two or three days before we were there.[8] We saw the Dauphin at dinner; he is much mended since I saw him first, for he is now a handsome boy and grows every day more and more like what his father was at his age. ⟨ I had much more to say, but company is just come. I have received a letter of yours here, and yours may always be directed as the last was. With all services to all friends, I am ever

Your dutiful and affectionate

J. Spence.⟩[9]

---

1. They left Cambrai July 11, and via Péronne, Roy (12), Senlis (13), reached Paris July 14, and stayed till July 22.
   2. See *Notebook* following this letter.
   3. 'This, with what I have seen on the continent before, would make one imagine that there is a sort of gradual declension of the hilli-

ness of the country from Mt. Cenis quite to the north of Holland' (*Nbk.* 2 66^r).
   4. In the neighbourhood of 'his seat of Chantilly' (ibid., 67^v). Spence preferred the woods at Chantilly to Versailles.
   5. 'Paris was so excessively hot' that they did not enjoy it, but 'stole for a day or two to

Versailles and Marly, which were pleasant enough to make up for it sufficiently'. (See n. 9.)

6. 'It seems he is not near so handsome as he was, but the Dauphin is much handsomer and will probably, at fifteen, be just what his father was,' wrote Spence to his brother (see n. 9). Louis XV (1710–74) was only twenty-seven; the Dauphin (1729–65), eight years old.

7. Spence originally wrote 'are very beautiful'.

8. 'Madame Louise' was born July 15. Maria

Leszczynska had presented the King with five daughters in succession.

9. There follows in Egerton 2234 ff. 102–3 a letter from Spence's brother Richard to Mrs. Spence, dated London, Aug. 6, 1737 O.S.: 'I have a letter from my brother Jos., dated 31 July N.S. from the banks of the Loire . . . which came to my hands the 27th O.S.' As this letter duplicates Spence's earlier account of Holland, it has been omitted.

Notebook 2

(*x–xvii*) 67^v–71^r

Though I have been twice at Paris, I have not yet seen it as one ought: the first time our long stay in Italy had made me indifferent for almost everything in France, and the second was a week of so much heat that one could enjoy nothing. . . .

In the *Louvre* is the Academy for painting. In it prize pictures and prize sculptures, copies of the Hercules Farnese, Venus of Medici, Luttatori, Arrotino, Venus de belles fesses, Laocoön, Apollo Belvedere, Antinous, fighting Gladiator, etc. etc. One room of painters' portraits by themselves. No women are exposed in the great round—about a hundred that study there now.

The *Gardens of the Tuileries* . . . the terrace to the river is, perhaps, the best thing in it. There are statues both in the parterre and round the basin. In the former [one can see] Boreas and Orithya (?) by Fiamingo (? *Ant.*)[1] Ceres and Saturn, Lucrece and Cellatinus, Aeneas and Anchises etc.; in the other, four large river-gods: the Seine, the Loire, the Nile and the Tiber, copied from those at Rome.—Toward the *cours* are two equestrial statues brought thither in 1719 (*Ant.*) from Marly; Mercury and Fame: 'tis the first time I ever saw Mercury on horseback—Coysevox is to answer for it if 'tis improper.

At the *Observatoire* . . . armillary globes according to the three systems placed in line. You see them at once, [and] the difference hits strongly. The Copernican appears extremely the least embarrassed, and that of Ptolemy the most.

The *Luxembourg Palace* is reckoned one of the best in France. 'Twas built by Jacques de Brosses in 1615 for Mary de Medici and in several things somewhat resembles the palace of the Great Duke at Florence. There are three ranges of columns (Tuscan, Doric, and Ionic). The gallery in it is known to have one of the largest and completest works of Rubens in it. There are twenty pieces which furnish all the sides of it, all said to have been finished in two years (Wright): he was assisted by his scholars, and one may plainly discover whole figures by Vandyck in particular. In all of them the colouring is as excellent as the designing in general is bad. There's a head of Mary de Medici's horse, which is a masterpiece in painting and so is the face of the Queen after her delivery (the redness of her eyelids, the remains of her fatigue and the pleasing regard of her face admirably expressed). The flowing Virtues are to be known only by their badges stuck all over their oars. The Gardens of Luxembourg are in a fresher air and are rather less artificial than the Tuileries.

There is no collection of pictures in France, nor perhaps on this side the Alps any ways equal to that at the *Palais Royal*. There are said to be about 500 valuable pieces in it (*Ant.*), and the late Regent of France laid out above four millions of livres (above £163,000 English) in less than twenty years in getting them together (*Ant.*).[2]—A great part of them were from the Queen of Sweden's collection, though bought last from D. Livio Odeschalchi's. Antonini has made a list of this (not yet published). He says (p. 76) there are 29 or 30 Titians, about 15 Raphaels, 19 or 20 P. Veroneses, 16 Giulio Romanos, 18 Guidos, 28 of Hannibal Carracci (I suppose he means of the Carraccis) and 13 or 14 Correggios (the delightful Cupid).[3]

The young John the Baptist is a capital one of Raphael's and like that in the Florentine Gallery. There is a light Madonna of his too, with a flying thin veil, that was much esteemed by the Regent. His others run chiefly on Madonnas too.—Among Giulio's are the large cartons of the loves (?) of the gods and seven or eight long slips of battle and triumph pieces.—'The Seven Sacraments' of Poussin cost the Regent 5,000 guineas, and 'The Resurrection of Lazarus', designed by Michelangelo and painted by Piombino, above 1,600 (*Ant.*).—Two pictures by Paul Veronese: one of Virtue with Hercules, rough, and the other of two Vices leading away a spruce young man.

'The Family of Charles I' is reckoned a masterpiece of Vandyck's. There are several others by Vandyck, and I believe more by Rubens, [and] four or five Leonardo da Vincis.—There's a good Democritus and Heraclitus, both by Spagnolet (Democritus has been just measuring the globe of the earth, lays his hand upon it, and laughs).—One or two very good Tintorets; history-piece of Abigail by Guercin; a very good old man, etc. by Hans Holbein. The collection is as excellent almost for what is omitted as for what is got. I think there are but two Bassans in the whole and very little of Michelangelo Caravaggio.—There's one picture (by Vasari) observable for the persons represented in it, six of the earliest and best Tuscan poets: Dante, Petrarch, Boccaccio, Guido Cavalcanti, Cino da Pistoia, and Guitton d'Arezzo.

The roof and the sides of the gallery are (the Elements and Virgil stories) by Coypel.[4] They are in a bad neighbourhood ('ils ont des mauvais voisins,' as the person who showed it said), and though they might do very well in any other palace in Paris, they look but very poor and unaffecting after the company one has been in before you come to the gallery. The roof is better than the side-pictures. He took to drinking *eau de vie* before he began the latter (before he used to drink nothing but water). Several Coypels, this the best.—There are two very strong bold paintings of a man and bull and [or] a man and lion by Giorgione (?). One must have forgot several other very good ones (e.g. Alexander drinking the poison, [by] Le Sueur) in so excellent a collection as this is.

Hôtel Bourbon. Picture of Lewis XIV by Lebrun, different from any other picture of his. Aet. 24 or 25. Not unlike the little Lewis XIII in the Luxembourg and somewhat like the best pictures of the D. of Monmouth.—Lucian's picture of the Centaur and lion coming toward his wife and young ones.—Summer apartments towards the garden and river: winter, backwards: and so both furnished without altering.—Squares on the glass-doors to the garden etc., above 4 f. by 2½, each *quarre* 260 livres.

The best collection of statues at Paris is that of *Cardinal Polignac's*. . . . The glory of the collection is the story of Achilles' discovery of Ulysses. 'Tis in detached figures, disposed all round three sides of a chamber. Ulysses in the habit of a merchant (as they call it) is in the middle row; the regard of his face is very good but has not at all the air of being ancient. The good old lady stands in the same line with her purse out to pay him. Achilles is on your left hand near and Deidamia on your right, farther off. (The servant who showed it to us in 1739 said Achilles' head was refitted in Italy; that an artist who was to clean them began with all the heads and cleaned them with aqua fortis, the Cardinal was very angry and would not let him go on.) Achilles' sex is showed in a preposterous manner (for this story, though not uncommon in antiques) by the folding of the drapery, and the hand of Deidamia that is held up and appears so neatly through her vest is as fine as the other may be improper (both certainly ancient). [The servant told us] that they were found at Marius' villa at Frescati. —'When Cardinal Polignac was at Rome, hearing that a person building a house between Frescati and Grotta Ferrata was [engaged?] in laying the foundation by some very considerable ruins, he went to take a view of them and, surveying its position, concluded it to have been Marius' Villa. He set some men to work upon it, who had not gone far before they found an inscription in Marius' fifth consulship. In the process of the work they came to a stately saloon where, among other decorations, were ten marble statues of excellent workmanship, representing the defection of Achilles at the Court of Lycomedes' (*Biogr. Gall.*, II 298). Q. whether all the trinkets, the insignia and the heads are not modern, and if so whether the story itself may not be doubtful? The figures where they are ancient are of a good taste and age, and are well refitted.

In the first room below: busts of Julius, Caracalla, Antony, Silenus, Plato, Antony, Agrippa, pretty little Diadumenianus, two Greeks and gladiator with pain in his face and his eye wounded; the colours of the bruise very well represented by a natural flaw in the marble, a mezzo-relievo of Alexander (?), a statuette of Venus in the attitude of the Medicean Venus, a sarcophagus, Bacchus and Ariadne attended by fauns (very good).

In the second: busts of Seneca, Homer, [Hermes?], bacchanal, Adrian, Scipio Africanus (?) [   ] and beard ditto, pretty Cupid with hair dressed as the Cupid with Psyche in the Florentine Gallery, head oracle [with a] hole through to the mouth, holes through to the eyes, la belle Crispina, lady with long ringlets of hair and beautiful face, faun.— A little Venus from the bath, pretty statuette of Bacchus; a sarcophagus: three Graces in the midst, [the] two outmost hold something like zones; a Venus with different Cupids toward each end, scarce good enough for an authority.

Hall, etc: an emperor on horseback, alto-relievo; excellent head of Vespasian, black-coloured drapery; large statues of Hygeia, Aesculapius with great serpent and an empress; an excellent Egyptian statue of Isis in basalt.—Fine head of sleeping Cleopatra in passage room.

The chamber within: Ulysses, veste talari—head, arms and box modern; Achilles—head, arms, shield and spear ditto, very floating robe, sex very visible through the drapery; he regards Ulysses with pleasure, Ulysses him as discovering; Lycamede's wife—head, arm, hand and purse modern; in (the Scyriades) the daughters' every hand with a trinket in it ditto; Minerva, holding the little Pyrrhus in the skirt of her aegis oddly lifted up—a great deal of that part of the child and skirt modern: how much undistinguishable from [dirt?] like mortar on it, perhaps all the child; a little Cupid holding 'Dibs like those of Sors'; a statuette of Paris.

The chamber within that: Marsyas, hands tied down to two short stumps of a tree, fistula in one of them, face not in pain! A particular alto-relievo of Vulcan (face like Jupiter) sitting. A very good faun, holds up a shield with the hollow towards him and he is going to insert one of the straps. Another is preparing a helmet and a young idle faun playing the fool with him. Another with an Orea at his feet, the coat of mail above. 'Tis good work but [now comes] Vulcan or anybody [   ].

Above: ⟨there are some pictures and some very fine tables, especially one that looks like emeralds and amethysts in the mine.⟩ A head of Pallas, basalt; a little Pan in brass, with his fistula; Sors with head of Crispina, two dice (or dibs) in her hand. She is sitting in the posture of playing on the ground (which, with two dibs on it, is modern but authorized by those in her left hand). Beside its rarity, 'tis one of the prettiest statues in the collection.

In these rooms several pictures. Dead Saviour held up by the arms by two boys with beautiful heads [by] Michelangelo. Charming dying Cleopatra, flesh like HM, the mouth a little open, eyes ditto, both very fine [by] Correggio. Several pieces by Guercin, Guido and Dominiquin, etc.

The Comte de Toulouse's is a handsome palace (by Mansart) but we saw it at a disadvantage, only in its light summer furniture. The gallery is 120 f. by 20. The ceiling is painted (Apollo and the Seasons) by Perrier, and the sides adorned with pictures which they call of good masters. Camillus by Poussin, Coriolanus and the Romans by Guercin. Romulus and Remus, Caesar divorcing Pompeia, and the Sibyl piece by P. da Cortona, Helen by Guido (Q. whether it is not original of this which is at Rome: they look in general like copies and generally not very good ones neither. All of the same make and size.) Shutting of Temple of Janus by Carlo Marat, and others by Valentin and [Paul] Veronese.

We saw a painters' *collection, Mr. Paris's* which was going for England—with several Vandycks and Rubens's in it, and a St. Sebastian of Raphael's which I would rather have than all the kings and admirals and all the gallery of the Comte de Toulouse together.

Notre Dame gives you the best view of all the town (*Ant.*): it appears altogether as much like a circle as any town I ever saw. (From the Observatoire Paris has a semicircular appearance and looks more extended than from Notre Dame.) In the church you see the vast St. Christopher in stone and a row of pictures that are not bad on each side: St. Peter in prison and the angel, etc. They are well fitted to the squares of building as at Val de Grâce.

Val de Grâce—The church is handsome, front, body and dome. The altar is supported by six wreathed composite pillars, their bottom part channelled, two thirds not (of different marble and with gilded foliage). Group of the Virgin, St. Joseph, and little Jesus, by Anguier, very well. The dome at Val de Grâce is painted by Mignard, ill-coloured, but the God the Father is a great figure. 'Tis the glory of the blessed in heaven. There's a drawing of [the dome] by Corneille in the Academy of Painting.

In the church of the *Carmelites* the two sides are taken up with uniform large pictures. The left side, the Pharisee Supper, and another by Le Brun, two of [   ] and two of de la Hire's; the opposite six by Champagne. In the side-chapel where Cardinal Bernouilli lies, a Magdalen by Le Brun worth them all and a weak Guido (?) by the altar into the bargain. Her face like the famous Magdalen's at Venice by Titian. The Magdalen looks towards heaven, and the attitude of her hand, regards her looking glass as if she was saying 'See there the cause of my ruin!' The Magdalen's face in the Pharisees Supper (by Le Brun too) has the same features with Alexander's wife's in his famous tent-piece.

Bernardins Anglois—Here lies James II and his daughter. There's a grille round and they would not suffer us to see the inscription, which is covered. The woman who showed it said their bodies were kept above ground in order to be carried into England whenever his son, etc.

St. Sulpice is unfinished. Is not the half-dome at the end run in too far for its width?

In the *Church of the Sorbonne* is the excellent tomb of Cardinal Richelieu (d. 1642) by Girardon. His figure is in a handsome attitude and very well placed in regard to the dying Saviour at the altar, which is a figure of Girardon's too (Anguier's (?) *Ant.*). The allegorical figures (Religion standing at his head and Science mourning at his feet) are very good work, but ill-distinguished (each by a book!). The two genteel doctors dispensing the first time and the three eating the second.

As Richelieu built the former, Cardinal Mazarin founded the *College of the four Nations* (Italy, Germany, Flanders and Rousillon). The semicircle to the river is handsome. Mazarin is buried in the church (d. 1661 aet. 5[9])—the tomb by Coysevox indifferent though so much talked of. The altar-piece is by [Paul] Veronese and the rounds by Jouvenet.

The pictures not bad in the *Church of the Chartreux*, though not so good as Le Sueur's 'History of St. Bruno' (in 22 pieces) on the cloisters.

The *Hôtel des Invalides* (with a dome high enough in proportion to the arches) is extremely large (square of 17 arpens with five or seven (?) courts within, that in the middle as big as all the rest together).

The great court is porticoed all round, above as well as below. The dome is a well-finished thing in all its parts: its seven altars are visible from the centre at bottom: next the outdoor two round chapels, then two half-ovals quite open, then two chapels as before, and [   ] then in between them the high altar. The great dome and the four round chapels are painted at top. In each of these are three large statues, one of which appears through an arch in each when you stand at the centre. In the open half-ovals you have large gilt altars, the Virgin col Bambino and two angels worshipping on one side the foundress of some order (bas-relief of ditto fainting and angel with a dart) and two angels worshipping (or amazed?) on the other. The higher altar is open, with wreathed Corinthian pillars gilt (over on high God the Father and Son are painted holding a crown of stars, dove under, and in a compartment under that angels lifting the Virgin into heaven). You come to it strangely from the house, but it strikes well as soon as one can see it right, and on the whole is one of the noblest disposed things on this side the Alps.

The dome is handsome but cut off from the church by the largeness of the high altar (why not such an one as at St. Sulpice?). The dome is a hundred yards high (*Ant.*).

The *Place de Vendôme* (or of Louis le Grand's?) looks uniform and handsome: 'tis said to be 150 yards by 140 (Louis XIV's statue).—The *Place Royale* is 144 yards square (Louis XIII's statue).—The *Place de [la] Victoire* is semicircular: the subtendent 80 yards. Six streets fall into it. In the midst is the statue of Louis XIV with a Victory crowning him—four slaves at the bottom and bas-reliefs of his victories on the pedestal.

The *Pont Neuf* has a very good view from it. 'Tis said to be 340 yards by 24. 'Twas finished in 1604. The figure of Henri IV by Dupré, the horse by Jean de

Bologna. Reservoir of water for the Louvre, etc., against which [is] the fountain de la Samaritaine, our Saviour by Bertrand, the woman by Frémin, tolerably good.

The *Pont Royal* built by Louis XIV, 140 yards by 17—but five arches and the two outward ones of them irregular and hurt the eye.

The *Porte of St. Denys*, as those of St. Antoine and St. Bernard, was built by Blondel. St. Denys like a triumphal arch and St. Antoine actually for one (for Henri II originally, before improved by Blondel). The Porte of St. Denys is 72 f. high, dit. broad, and 24 f. the great opening. There is a less opening on each side. The bas-reliefs are the taking of Maastricht without and the passage of the Rhine within. They were begun by Girardon but finished by Anguier.

The measures and the names of the artists here are taken from Antonini, who says Paris is near six leagues round and that it contains 900,000 souls.

If Antonini's catalogue be true, certainly we saw but a small share of the pictures at *Versailles*. He talks of the Lord knows how many Raphaels, etc. The fine gallery (and perhaps 'tis too fine) is all gilding and painting and looking-glass. The view from the windows to the canal is worth a million of such tawdries as the room affords one within. 'Tis painted by Le Brun with the victories and achievements of Louis XIV. Length seventy yards by ten.

1. Spence in this account often acknowledges his debt for many details to Annibale Antonini's *Mémorial de Paris et de ses environs à l'usage des voyageurs*, nouv. ed. (Paris, 1734).

2. 'The person who showed it us in 1739 said the pictures cost twenty-five millions of livres, and particularly the St. Joseph, little Jesus and Virgin 15,000 *l.*, the little St. John, Jesus and Virgin 30,000 *l.*, and the St. John in the Wilderness 50,000 *l.* The sign by Correggio 12,000 *l.*, a Muleteer, etc. He told the story differently about his being obliged to a muleteer on the road and making an *albergiste* of him. It has been doubled in, by the upper corners.' [Spence's note]

3. See Spence's *Obs.* Nos. 1335–8, for further comments on the pictures in the Palais Royal.

4. See *Obs.* No. 1336.

---

*61

Source: Egerton 2234 ff. 104–5
Addressed: as in 54
Postmarked: AV 8
Endorsed: *b.* Pretty Situation of Blois;/& violent Thunder Storm there.

Blois,
August 9, 1737

⟨Dear Mother,⟩

I have been longer without writing to you than usual, as being come to a new residence where we shall settle down and rest for the summer: as I believe we shall winter at Angers about 130 miles further down the river Loire.[1] I should have writ to you sooner, however, had not I sent a letter to my brother which I don't doubt he has given you some account [of].[2]

I now write to you from the banks of the Loire, with the river running just by my window, and the prospect of one of the King's forests and of a fine country just beyond it. The end of the view is like yours at Winchester towards Southampton, and indeed there are a great many things here that put me in mind of Winchester and almost make me think myself at home. When I walk out, I have this Southampton-view before me, and when I return the thing that strikes one the most from the town is the King's House standing on an eminence, begun but left imperfect,[3] and carried on about as far as our King's House at Winchester. 'Twas in this house that the Duke of Guise was stabbed when the King had convened the Parliament to Blois.[4] The town is built on two hills and runs down the sides of them to the river. 'Tis no fine one, but the situation and the country all about it is very delightful and very well inhabited.

On the top of one of these hills, just without the walls, is a grove with walks which they call *Angleterre*, or England, so that I can take a walk into my own country at a quarter of an hour's warning. This town has been long famous for speaking the French language in its greatest purity: that has always drawn a number of our countrymen hither,[5] and as they took very much to the walk above the town, it has its name from them. I continue, I thank heaven, in very good health, and this is reckoned one of the best airs in France. It has been troubled a vast deal of late, for we have had very frequent and very great thunderstorms, but 'tis now all settled and serene again, and the air is the better for the exercise that has been given it.

A merchant of Lyons, that passed by here some days ago, told us a story that I have scarce faith enough to believe. He said he was on the road from Nantes, when the air grew all dark of a sudden. As he apprehended a thunderstorm he made the best of his way, and in coming along met a countryman driving a cart that was drawn by oxen. He spoke to the man to make [all] the haste he could, but the poor oxen were slow and could not rid the ground so fast as was to be wished. The storm began soon after: the merchant got to an inn, and stayed there the rest of the day. In the evening he heard that the oxen were killed about half a mile from the inn by the hail which, he said, fell in pieces bigger than his fist (which was no small one), but the man had escaped by getting under the cart in the greatest fury of the storm. It has done an infinite damage to the vineyards about the country, which is full of them, quite from Orleans hither and so on down the sides of the Loire. They talk of hailstones falling that weighed twenty-seven pound.[6] If this be false 'tis the Frenchmen that must go to old Nick for it, for I don't aver it myself. ⟨I hope you are very well, and long to hear from you. I am with all services to all friends

Your dutiful and affectionate

J: Spence.⟩

1. Passing through Estampes and Orléans, they reached Blois July 24, and stayed till November.

2. Dated July 31 N.S. See *Letter* 60 n. 9.

3. One of the finest châteaux of the Loire, the 13th-century 'King's House' at Blois was badly out of repair and abandoned early in the 18th century. There is a 'Jesuits' church just by, with some pretty relievos at each of the side-altars, the high altar at the Bourmoien's, and a good relievo of a woman like Mary Magdalen,

subscribed "Meditatio" (by Lerambert, anno 1660) in the chapel of the Courtin (or de Nanteuil) family in the Cathedral' (*Nbk.* 2 72ʳ).

4. Henry I, D. of Guise, was stabbed on Dec. 23, 1588, at the instigation of King Henry III.

5. Spence's French master, Abbé Philippeaux, told him about Addison's taciturn habits and lack of amours during his stay at Blois (*Obs.* No. 815).

6. Or did Spence mistake 'bien sept livres' for 'vingt-sept'?

---

*62

Source: Egerton 2234 ff. 106–7

Addressed: as in 54

Postmarked: AV 17

Endorsed: *a.* a descrip-/shon of paris, & a chaine of/yᵉ Royall seats belonging/to ye frensh King
b. A Word or two of Paris &/the Run of yᵉ Kings Villa's.

Blois,
August 21, 1737
⟨—I find by your last that you understand our style exactly, for we are just eleven days always faster than you.⟩

⟨Dear Mother,

If you were in some concern for me, I began to be in more for you, for I had not heard from you for above a month. You may imagine how agreeable your letter was. I find by that and others I have received here that they are a fortnight generally a coming. Mine was above a fortnight in getting to you, and yours a fortnight a coming, so that just makes up the time, and I believe we must agree for the future not to be in any fright if we should not hear from one another so soon as we could wish. Not that I shall ever delay writing, unless I have a vast deal of business on my hands, and indeed I received yours but last night and, you see, am answering already.⟩

I think I have never yet given you any account of Paris. 'Tis the largest city in Europe after London, which is twice as big, or one third bigger at least.[1] Paris lies more compact and makes almost a regular circle. The Seine is the river that runs through it, a dirty, contemptible river in comparison with the Thames, and instead of the multitude of merchant ships and other vessels that cover our Thames from the Bridge quite to Greenwich, they have nothing but a sort of barges which come loaded . . . with wood for firing, all piled up on each side of the river all along before the King's Palace, which is the last building towards the country on that side of the town.[2] Beyond it is the garden of the Tuileries, the Great Mall of Paris, where you see all the politer people every evening.[3] Beyond this is the Ring and the Elysian Fields (the name of which is much finer than the thing), and beyond them and the walks are woods that belong to the King, and reach almost to his best country-seats.

I have been often pleased with the chain of our royal seats about Kew and Richmond. First the Princess Amelia's House and the Prince's, then the Queen's at Kew, the garden of which unite with Richmond gardens and so lead you on to Richmond House all in their own territories, as these are continued on afterwards to the Duke's House on Richmond Green. This is very pretty, but 'tis nothing to the suite of the King of France's houses and gardens.

His palace of the Louvre joins that of the Tuileries, this opens into the garden of the same name, as that opens on the Ring and [a] long avenue for the coaches to roll in; this runs quite to the Park of Boulogne. That park reaches quite (or near) to St. Cloud and the King's House of Meudon, placed on the side of a range of hills, and with a lovely prospect. The Park of Meudon reaches to that of Versailles, as the Gardens of Versailles are united with the Park of Trianon, and that again with the Gardens of Marly, just beyond which is the Palace of St. Germains. These are all palaces or seats on the same range of hills, belonging to the King and where he chiefly resides:[4] for he seldom comes to Paris and scarce ever lies a night there. By this suite, or chain, of gardens and parks he may go perhaps one line of thirty mile almost entirely on his own ground, and that all to seats made and designed for pleasure, whereas our line of Kew and Richmond is not above two or three mile—and even that used to seem to me a fine acquisition to our royal family.

What I have told you now of this ring of seats is only a general map of them; in my next I may probably describe some of them in particular. ⟨I rejoice more to hear that your hospital thrives at Winchester than at any King's getting so many fine things together for himself.[5] The papers here tell us that the King has given £300 to it,[6] and if it be true I think he has laid out that money better than any that has been laid out on his gardens at Richmond. I hope you all continue well, and am with all services to all friends

Your dutiful and affectionate

J. Spence.⟩

1. In 1725 M. de Lisle argued 'that *Paris* is one *twentieth* Part greater than *London*'. Peter Daval in 1728 claimed that, by a more correct method of computation, '*London* will be one fourteenth greater than *Paris*' (*Phil. Transactions*, abr. edn., No. 402, pp. 432–6).

2. 'We did not see the inside ... as to the outside, neither the Tuileries nor the old Louvre have any great beauty, and the new Louvre (which would have been much more beautiful) is only begun: "pendent opera interrupta, minaeque murorum ingentes" [*Aen.* iv. 88]' (*Nbk.* 2 67ᵛ).

3. 'The Gardens of the Tuileries are far from well disposed, if our taste in England at present is a good one. It begins with parterre, goes on with grove-works ... that are uniform and insipid, and ends in a great basin with statues towards the corso' (ibid.).

4. 'What an addition, if the Duke of Bourbon were a traitor!' (ibid., 70ʳ).

5. The hospital at Winchester, one of the earliest in England, was 'in full work' by 1737 (G. W. Kitchin, *Winchester* [1893], p. 211).

6. Two months later *The Gentleman's Magazine* reported: '*By the Accounts of the County Hospital* at Winchester, *beginning* Oct. 18, 1736 *and ending* at Michmas 1737, The Subscriptions and Benefactions amounted to 1015 *l.* besides 200 *l.* given by His Majesty' (Oct. 31, p. 636).

---

*63

Source: Egerton 2234 ff. 108–9
Addressed: as in 54
Postmarked: AV 31
Endorsed: *a.* a descripshon of versailles,
          b. Gardens of Versailles

Blois,
September 4, 1737

⟨Dear Mother,⟩

I have just had the pleasure of receiving a letter from you, and I seldom put off the answering of them for a day. In my last (of our 21ˢᵗ of August) I have talked to you about the range of houses and gardens belonging to the King of France, not far out of Paris, and which are agreeable enough even to make a king happy, if kings ever could be so.

Versailles, you know, is the most celebrated of his palaces, but even there I like the gardens better than the palace which has been built at several times, and has an old face to a new back.[1] It stands on a sort of a hill, and the rising to it gives it something of a magnificent air, though the front is broke into little pieces that agree but ill with one another.[2] On the other side you are on an elevated ground again in the garden. This rising is laid out in flower beds, statues and fountains. There are two vistas from it, one to the right (with fountains in the line of the descent, and a very large one which they are now fitting up at the bottom),[3] and the other in the middle, which is the grand vista. I don't know the reason why they have not another to the right.

The grand vista is really a grand one. It runs down the slope to a long grass plot with groves and a row of statues on each side; quite at the bottom they are making a vast fountain, with a round of grove-work edged again with rows of statues, and opening on a canal which runs on for 1600 yards and is sixty-four yards broad; beyond this appears a distant view of the country which carries the eye on for a great length. The vista is as broad as the canal, though it does not look wide from the great stretch of the view all together. On the sides of the vista are walks into the grove-work, which lead you into several rounds and openings with fountains and statues in them. The whole garden is much over-furnished with both of these.

The best statues are in one of these fountains which they call the Baths of Apollo.[4] The heathens, you know, ⟨who were a very strange sort of people⟩ imagined the sun was guided by an Intelligence who for his ease sat in a chariot drawn by four horses, and so conducted the sun about with him, half round the world each day. For so great a journey he could not be seated too tranquilly. The figures in this bath is this Intelligence just alighted from his journey in the evening, the nymphs giving his horses water, etc. The figures, and especially the horses, are exceedingly well done, and the story has something to do with a fountain, which is not always the case at Versailles.

In another [part] is a fountain of the noblest design and greatest thought of any I saw there. 'Tis one of the giants that rebelled against heaven, flung under a burning mountain.[5] There is a rising of rough stones and vast cinders, like those of Mount Vesuvius, in the midst of the basin: the giant under this mountain is struggling to deliver himself from the pressure of it. He has already got his head out and one of his arms, and in another place you see a vast spradling leg that belongs to him. His face is full of pain and ill nature, and when the fountain plays he breathes a vast spout of water out of his mouth half way up to heaven (in the style of a traveller) as to revenge himself against the powers that have flung him there (in the style of a poet): but seriously (in my own proper style), 'tis a very great thought and very greatly executed.[6]

[To] go from the greatest things to the least [of] this kind: there is another range of this grove-work, with a ⌈thousand⌉ little openings in it, in each of which there's one of Aesop's fables for the subject of the fountain in it. There's all the birds spouting water at the owl, and many other such little devices. In short, 'tis all the pictures almost in Ogilby, expressed in little figures in lead.[7]

Out of these gardens you go into the park of Trianon, but as I have walked you enough at present, I'll keep that for another opportunity. ⟨I am very glad of the Princess's being a mother;[8] I should be glad in your next to know who has been sped this year to New College, and in whose places, and how all that sort of news goes on. I am with all services to Belle and all friends

Yours and her most affectionate

J. Spence.⟩

1. The small château was built for Louis XIII and later enlarged. Construction of the main edifice began in 1661; the great north and south wings were added by Mansart in the 1680's.

2. 'There's something handsome in the garden-front, even with all its disproportions. The excessive jutting out of the body of building in the middle, and that monstrous length of the sides to so moderate a height . . .' (*Nbk.* 2 70ᵛ).

3. Probably that of Neptune, which was being refitted with new groups of statues and fountains, and displayed in its new form for the first time Aug. 14, 1741 (L. Dussieux, *Le Château de Versailles* [1885], II, 237).

4. Designed by Lebrun, executed by Tuby, 1668–70.

5. Enceladus, in gilded lead, by Marsy, 1675–6.

6. Among the 'infinity of statues' at Versailles, 'the copies of Bacchus, Apollo, Antinous and Silenus, in the middle line, are of the best (in brass, by Keller); so are the copies of the Whetter, dying Gladiator in marble, and the Winter by Girardon' (*Nbk.* 2 70ᵛ–71ʳ).

7. John Ogilby (1600–76) published a number of works extravagantly 'adorned with sculptures'. 'Latona and several of the fountains are bad, and the Aesop's fables ridiculous—though it should be considered that to see a fountain when it does not play is like seeing a picture without its colours on' (ibid., 71ʳ).

8. On July 31 O.S. Princess Augusta, wife of the Prince of Wales, was delivered of a daughter (*Gent. Mag.*, 1737, p. 512). Richard Spence wrote to his mother from London on Aug. 6 that 'wonderful rejoicings have been made for the birth of a little princess' (*Letter* 60 n. 9).

---

*64

Source.	Egerton 2234 ff. 110–11
Addressed:	*as in* 54
Endorsed:	*a.* an/acᵗ: of Trianon, verey pretey
	b. Accᵗ of Trianon.

Blois,
September 14, 1737

⟨Dear Mother,

I'm overjoyed to hear Colebrook Street is growing so fine, and don't know what I had to do to go a' rambling for Rome when we have such fine cities and such fine streets in Hampshire. By your account of it I don't know whether it may not be your fate before I come back to live in a new house, but if such a thing should happen, I beg you'd take care not to go into any new building to lodge there till 'tis perfectly dried and undangerous— which is a piece of advice I think myself in gratitude bound to give you for your many advices to me to air my nightcaps and stockings thoroughly all the while I am in foreign parts.—Your letter came to me but last night as I was playing at backgammon with one Mr. Montague, a nephew of the famous Mr. Montague, acquaintance of Mr. Pryor and afterwards Earl of Halifax,[1] who always asks very kindly after you, and was overjoyed to hear you were so well. I could chat on, but 'tis time for us to take another walk in the King of France's gardens—if you are at leisure and the bells don't ring at St. Maurice.⟩

You may wander out of Versailles gardens into the way to Trianon[2] without knowing it. 'Tis like a sweet pretty byway to a farmhouse: the grandeur and ornaments[3] of the other are lost insensibly in a charming retired walk through little fields, meadows, and lanes to the left, and on your right is the park of Trianon, which is so full of partridges and pheasants that 'tis difficult to turn your eye any way without seeing some. At last you come to the house, which is a little, beautiful, magnificent retirement, like the enchanted palaces in Spenser's *Fairy Queen* or in the romances which possibly you read in your youth.[4] Most of the house is concealed, as if the King had affected a littleness for the place which he designed for forgetting the noise and bustle of a court in. In the front you see nothing but two wings joined by a colonnade at the bottom to its own little garden. The pillars and the building is all of a most beautiful red and white marble, and all of the finest and neatest sort of work you can imagine. 'Tis this makes it look like a little enchanted palace, raised by magic in the midst of this retirement—for 'tis finer than Versailles, though 'tis less than many a gentleman's country-house in England.

You see through the walk of pillars all along the middle into the garden, and when you step into it you have more house to the right, little flower-beds before you, groves cut into walks a little farther, and, facing the retired part of the house, a view to a great irregular body of water covered with wild ducks and edged with woods that are irregular enough to look natural, and regular enough to be just where they ought to be.

'Twas to this house that Louis XIV used to retire often with the Marquise de Maintenon, widow you know, of the famous Scarron, and mistress (or more probably wife afterwards) of that great monarch.[5] I am far enough from being grown a Frenchman, and hope when I return to meet with the old sincere Hampshire compliment 'of my being just as I was when I went away'; yet I am convinced every day more and more that 'tis our prejudices that make us not look on Louis XIV as a very great man. He had a thousand great qualities, and his fault was that of Caesar and Alexander—ambition. 'Tis true his ambition cost millions of lives, and so did theirs. I would not have been so great a man as Louis to have been so great a murderer as he was, but still he was what the world does and always will call a Great Man. 'Twas to this delicious spot that he retired from the crowd of his attendants and the fatigue of his councils,[6] and he retired with a lady who, if she was not young and handsome, had at least as much wit as any woman in the world, and he himself had as much good sense as almost any man in it, and what was more, loved her to excess though she was his wife. ⟨I suppose you'll all be in a clamour upon me after such a sentence as this last, and therefore am

Your most obedient humble servant

J. Spence.⟩

1. Charles Montagu (post 1695–1759) of Papplewick, Notts., M.P. for Westminster 1722–7, St. Germans 1734–41, Camelford 1741–7, Northampton 1754–9 (Namier and Brooke, *The Commons 1754–1790* [1964], III, 152). He was son of Sir James Montagu (1666–1723) and nephew of Charles Montagu (1661–1715), 3d E. of Halifax, Prior's collaborator in *The Hind and the Panther Transvers'd* (1687).

2. Built 1687–8 by Mansart, to replace the earlier 'Trianon de Porcelaine'.

3. 'There are but few statues, but the Laocoön quite behind the house (in marble, by Tuby) is worth dozens of some of those in the Gardens of Versailles' (*Nbk.* 2 71ʳ).

4. Mrs. Spence admired *The Faerie Queene*. 'After my reading a canto in Spenser' to her 'she said that I had been showing her a collection of pictures' (*Obs.* No. 419).

5. Louis XIV's marriage with Françoise d'Aubigné, Marquise de Maintenon (1635–1719), though never openly disclosed, was concluded in secret in January 1684. Paul Scarron, the author of *Le Roman comique*, whom she had married (1652) at sixteen, died in 1660.

6. 'This King neglects and unfurnishes it' (*Nbk.* 2 71ʳ). Louis XV had 'given Trianon to the Queen; it will cost the poor woman twenty thousand pounds to put it in repair' (*H. W. Corresp.* XVII, 126–7).

*65

Source:	Egerton 2234 ff. 112–13
Addressed:	*as in 54*
Postmarked:	SE 26
Endorsed:	*a.* the continans of the gardings
	b. Accᵗ of Marli & Sᵗ Ger:

Blois,
September 26, 1737

⟨Dear Mother,

Last night I had the longest letter from you that I have received since my being this time on the continent. I ought in return to send you one of a sheet, but as this happens to be a busy morning with me, I hope you will excuse me if I don't write quite so much as I ought. I am glad your election is over without me, for I don't love to wear velvet sleeves, and look upon that as upon most dignities which are perhaps always attended with more trouble than honour.[1] You have asked a thing of me which you might command as well as everything else that is in my power, but how far it may ever be in my power to serve poor Master Ball I can't say.[2] Were I more of a courtier I should say it shall certainly be done, and think no more of it. As I am very little of one, I must say that I am absolutely engaged to do whatever I can for young Bale,[3] and that if I can any way be of service to my little Kingsclere friend without injuring my interest for the other, I should not only be ready but glad to do it—but, to say the truth, what will be the interest of a Fellow on the other side the Alps even for my first engagement?>

I have been extremely tantalized here: I passed Brussels and missed of the Duchess of Dorset[4] by an hour or two; her Grace and all the family (except Lord Middlesex) are now at Paris, and I within a day or two's journey of them, and yet can't well have the pleasure of seeing them, for we shall stay here and hereabouts all the winter. All the fountains at Versailles played last Sunday sennight to compliment the Duke of Dorset and his family,[5] and 'tis a compliment that costs the King of France £300, by which you may guess a little at the number of fountains there—to cause such an expense for once playing only. The Duke was introduced to the King who spoke a great deal to him, which is almost the first time he has done so to any stranger.[6] He dined afterwards with the cardinal,[7] and was extremely well received all round.

But as we are got to Versailles, why should not we go on with our walk there? We were got to Trianon, you know, before. From that you walk to the gardens of Marly, and go down the great walk to the house[8] with grove-works and walks on each side of you. The house is not large, but an agreeable retirement. 'Tis an exact square. Behind it are fountains and a fine cascade, and before it is one of the most beautiful views I ever saw. The garden, or rather the grove-work of it, opens on purpose to show it to you: not wide at first, but goes on enlarging like the scenes from the bottom of a stage, and ends not in a very wide but a most delightful mixture of wood, fields, and hills. Near the house, and in the narrower part of it, are tufts of trees and little groves, and between them, at equal distances, there are six pavilions (or little pretty houses) on each side. These were for the chief persons that attended the court whenever Louis XIV went there, and I never yet saw any habitations so prettily disposed. 'Tis a court in a little paradise, and has all the charms of a retirement with all the convenience of good company.

From hence you go to St. Germains, which has little remarkable,[9] except its great terrace, from which you see a vast extensive view, and in particular all the places we have walked through, on the side of the hill on your right hand—where I shall leave you to contemplate them as long as you please. That black thing below the hill is the machine of Marly that carries such quantities of water up the ascent,[10] and that white long run of arches atop is the aquaeduct that conveys it to Versailles. ⟨I am, with all services to all friends

Your dutiful and affectionate

J. Spence.⟩

1. The ceremonial 'election week' at Winchester College was held between July 7 and Oct. 1. The electing body of six included two supervisors, or 'posers', who wore the full-dress velvet-sleeved gowns of Masters of Arts (H. C. Adams, *Wykehamica* [1878], pp. 49–55). Spence was one of the posers.

2. Thomas Ball (bapt. June 8, 1722) of Kingsclere had been elected Winchester scholar the previous year. Spence was probably asked to use his influence to get him to New College, where he matriculated Mar. 18, 1740/1, B.A. 1744. He later became schoolmaster at Oakham (Kirby, p. 240).

3. Joseph Challoner Bale (bapt. May 28, 1724) had become Winchester scholar that summer; in 1742 he followed the usual way to New College; B.C.L., Fellow 1743–9, later Rector of West Lydford (Kirby, p. 241).

4. Mother of Lord Middlesex. See *Letter* 59 n. 11. Her daughter Caroline accompanied both parents.

5. On Sept. 16, 1737, the Duc de Luynes noted: 'Hier les eaux jouioient ici à l'ordinaire, où il y avoit plusieurs Anglois et Angloises, parmi lesquels il paroissoit qu'il avoit une personne considérable. Le Roi nous dit à son souper que c'étoit Mme la duchesse Dorset, femme du vice-roi d'Irlande, et sa fille' (*Mémoires* [1860], I, 355).

6. They were 'presented to their Majesties, the Dauphin, and to Mesdames de *France*; his Grace the Duke of Dorset ... was introduced by the Chevalier de Sainctot, Master of the Ceremonies' (*Daily Advertiser*, Sept. 13, 1737 O.S.).

7. André Hercule de Fleury (1653–1743), the unofficial 'Prime Minister' of France.

8. Built by Mansart 1679–84. Spence found 'nothing very considerable within it' (*Nbk.* 2 71ʳ). It was destroyed during the Revolution.

9. 'St. Germains is a very bad old palace, and I did not mind anything there but the gallery that goes round the house and the terrace. ... There is but one church in the whole town, and the curé has above 800 *l.* a year, eight times as much as some bishops in France. The town is large, there's a great many Scotch and Irish there, and 'tis sometimes called "la petite Angleterre" ' (ibid., 71ʳ⁻ᵛ).

10. Constructed 1681–7 by De Ville, it consisted of a building situated on the Seine, with 221 pumps and dozens of rattling pulleys to convey water 'to the height of 120 yards up the hill, whence 'tis carried by an aqueduct (like the ancient ones) of 1000 yards long to the reservoir of Versailles' (ibid., and L. Dussieux, *Le Châteaux de Versailles* [1885], II, 410–12).

Notebook 2
(*xviii*) 71ᵛ

As the kings of France enjoy this fine range of parks, gardens, and houses in their lifetime, they are generally fixed afterwards at *St. Denis*. The tombs of the first kings there is a compliment paid to them long after their deaths. They look about the style of Louis XII's figure: death is represented horridly in their faces, as in some of the better Flemish tombs. The last king has always a funeral altar by the side of the great altar in mourning, with lamps burning, etc. The best tombs are Francis I with bas-reliefs, Le tombeau de Valois in which among others: Henry II and Mary de Medici's, made by her order by Phili[bert] Delorme, and Marshal Turennes, with Pallas and Liberality on each side, designed by Le Brun and executed by Tuby. The college of Benedictines (which joins the church) is a fine one, though not near so large yet as it is to be.

There's a pretty view before you come to *Estampes*, of rock and wood interspersed, which puts one a little in mind of Fontainebleau. The town is very long and very narrow. *Orleans* is no pretty city and the people are said not to be amiable. ' 'Tis a great mart for trade, the people are a money-getting people, and consequently not so free and polite as some other towns farther down the Loire' (*Abbé Boileau*). The Cathedral they say was built by the English and has something that strikes one in the old Gothic way. The *boiserie* in the choir is good. 'Tis the history of our Saviour and was done at Paris. (Jacques Petau buried here.) The country round it is taken up chiefly in vineyards, and so quite on to Blois.

66

Source:	Egerton 2234 ff. 114–15
Addressed:	*as in* 54
Postmarked:	OC 7
Endorsed:	*b.* Of my little Garden in Essex./Not to be transcrib'd.

Blois,
October 11, 1737

⟨Dear Mother,

Yesterday I received an honest large letter from you, and was very glad to find by it that young Barton[1] is at last safe landed at New College, where I have long wished him for his own sake: for by all accounts we have not had a boy come from thence of finer parts for some years. I'm surprised to hear Baile[2] will not be in there till Whitsuntide, and am sorry for it only on account of Dr. Kelley's son who I fear then may be in some danger of not getting in at all.[3]

Two or three days before I received yours I had a letter from good Mr. Holdsworth, the father of all us travellers—I mean for knowledge more than for age,[4] and with yours I had a letter from good Mr. Duck who has obliged me very much with the trouble he has taken to disperse my books about, and to pelt poor people that were easy in their great chairs with a thing that they would not give a farthing whether they ever read or not.[5] I ordered only one for you and my sister, because my allowance of books ran short, and because you had often told me one would do as well as two. I hope to come and see whether you keep it safe by you this time two year at farthest.

By that time my little garden at Birchanger (which I should be glad at any time to hear any news of, if at any time the fame of its growth and beauty reaches your ears) will begin to make some show, and my thoughts now, as one pleases oneself now and then with thoughts at some distance, is to come and see you at Winchester every other summer for three or four months, and the other alternate summers to invite you to Birch to eat some of my non-pareils, if you and my sister care to take such a great journey for a pippin. Though the place is not very magnificent, I can promise you it has quite another air than it had: for instead of walking into an orchard adorned with nothing but hog-sties and little-houses, you'll go into a garden that will be a little fop, strutting and pretending to be bigger than he is, where at least we shall be private and at our ease, and unseen ourselves when we have a mind to it, though from the little green square at the end of it we may stand like three statues on one pedestal and look out on a prospect that is no inconsiderable one for Hertfordshire.[6] By that word you may see the pride of my heart, for to say the truth, I don't care to be thought in Essex there and take all the advantage I can of my [fine?] neighbourhood to a better county.

I am reduced in this to French paper, and as 'tis of a larger size than the English, I have wrote larger and wider for the benefit of your eyes.[7] I wish you had some of the same (though not near so good otherwise as the English) because it would be still a greater benefit to them for you to write in a larger hand to me. The truth is that this is a whole sheet French, and what if you were to write on a whole English sheet? I leave it to your consideration, and am with all services

Your most affectionate and dutiful

J. Spence.⟩

1. Phillip Barton (bapt. Dec. 1, 1715) of Churchill, Worcs., Winchester scholar 1728, matric. at New College Sept. 1, 1737; later, Rector of Buriton and Petersfield. Canon of Exeter. He bequeathed to New College a collection of coins and £100 (H. Rashdal and R. S. Rait, *New College* [1901], p. 241).

2. No doubt young Bale, see *Letter* 65 n. 3.

3. John Kelley (bapt. May 13, 1726), son of George Kelley of Winchester, had become Winchester scholar that summer. He matriculated at Christ Church Feb. 26, 1742/3; Regius Professor of Medicine 1759–72 (Kirby, p. 241).

4. On Holdsworth, see *Letter* 30. Born in 1684, he was sixteen years Spence's senior.

5. It is not clear which of Spence's books Stephen Duck was 'pelting poor people with'. In 1737 came out the second edition of Spence's *Essay on Pope's Odyssey*; his edition of *Gorboduc* and Duck's *Poems on Several Occasions*, to which was prefixed Spence's *Authentick Account of Stephen Duck*, were published in 1736.

6. Birchanger is in Essex, just on the border of Hertfordshire.

7. This and the two following letters are written on 'French paper' in a very large hand.

67

Source: Egerton 2234 ff. 116–17
Addressed: as in 54
Postmarked: OC 25
Endorsed: b. Of my Mothers Health./Not to be
               transcrib'd.

Blois,
October 25, 1737

⟨Dear Mother,

I am extremely sorry to hear you have been so ill, and hope you got over
it soon, for those fits are too violent for one of your age to endure long.
What frightens me more is that they seem to come regularly every spring
and fall, for your last was about Lady Day, and this exactly at Michaelmas.
I hope in God you have got over this, and if you have, and they are apt to
come so regularly, would not it be best to take some physic to prevent them
before each spring and fall? I am no physician, but I remember how you
cured me of my long ague. I am a little afraid that you have relapsed into
your sour sort of wine of which I wish there was not a drop in the world,
because 'tis good for nothing but to raise a civil war in one's guts. If you
have, I beg you'd consult Dr. Rolle of New College,[1] who could advise you
to what sort of wine is best in your case. Nourish yourself up as much as
you can, for I do nothing but pamper this wicked body of mine that I may
come to you again sound and well.

Indeed I am in perfect health and in the way (please God) to continue so,
for nothing is more healthful than fresh air and frequent changing it. You
may do the same in some degree, and in little, by a month or two's visit to
Whitchurch[2] or elsewhere at a pleasant season, and when you are quite
stout. Variety is the great art of making life agreeable, and the mind's being
diverted is one of the greatest cordials for the body. Take care of yourself
to make us all happy, for you have been so long used to have more regard
for us than for yourself that I know that's the properest argument to use to
you, and I must return the civility once for all and assure you that I am
more concerned for you than I should be for myself. I hope to hear from you
soon, and am ever my sister's and your

most affectionate

J. Spence.⟩

1. No doubt Spence's friend Edward Rolle.
2. A market town, twelve miles N.E. of Winchester.

68

Source:	Egerton 2234 ff. 118–19
Addressed:	*as in 54*
Postmarked:	OC 31
Endorsed:	*a.* yᵉ first
	b. Q of Sʳ H Neville married to ⟨a daughter· of⟩ TE of D./Not to be Transcrib'd

Blois,
November 3, 1737

⟨Dear Mother,

I am much obliged to you for all your letters, but was more so for your last, because it took me out of a great deal of concern. I don't know how to express enough the obligation I have to Dr. Kelley for taking so much care of you.[1] I hope you may hold out a great while without having occasion for him again, but when you have, 'tis a great comfort to have so good a physician who is so well acquainted with your constitution and is so earnestly concerned for your health, so near you. I am very much obliged to Dr. Cheyney for his kind offer to you; he mentioned the same to me before we set out, and I find he does not forget his absent friends.[2] If you have occasion for any pagodas,[3] you will be so good as to send to Mr. Rolle who can furnish you with some of the best I know of, and I believe his shop is well stocked at present.

We are still at Blois where I enjoy so good health, and thrive so well that people in talking refer to me as an example: such an one, say they, is in good case as you are, and such an one has a double chin as you have, Sir. The truth is that if I go on at this rate of ease and laziness I may really grow to a bulk that would become a doctor's scarf very well, if I was puffed up with pride within as I may be with flesh without. In short I grow more and more orthodox every day, and want scarce anything but a rosy complexion of being fit to make a very good divine.

There's a gentleman here (and he is a man of quality in this place) who is translating a book wrote formerly by a Wickhamist in James the First's time.[4] He has been consulting me about some things in it, and I must consult you about it. 'Tis dedicated to a Neville. Pray do you know anything of a Henry Neville,[5] who was living in 1606 and was then married to Mary,[6] daughter of Thomas, Earl of Dorset, and had then at least two children by her, a son called Thomas (then a boy)[7] and a daughter by the name of Cicely?[8] I beg you would answer it in your next, because he is to publish his book in a month or two, and 'twould be of service to him if I could give him an answer before that time. I am, with all services,

Your most dutiful and affectionate

J. Spence.⟩

1. George Kelley, apparently a physician or apothecary at Winchester. His son John (see *Letter* 66 n. 3) became Regius Professor of Medicine at Oxford.

2. On Thomas Cheyney, see *Letter* 12 n. 8.

3. Humorous for 'guineas' (from a golden coin, formerly current in the East Indies).

4. A 'Wickhamist' was a Fellow of Winchester College—from its founder, William de Wyke-ham (1324–1404). I have not identified the author, nor his French translator.

5. Henry Neville (ca. 1580–1641), 9th Lord Bergavenny, M.A. Oxford July 9, 1599, first summoned to Parliament Feb. 12, 1623/4, and last to the 'Long Parliament' Nov. 2, 1640.

Mrs. Spence was related to the Neville family (Wright, pp. 3–4).

6. The last of three daughters of Thomas Sackville (1536–1608), 1st E. of Dorset, the author of *Gorboduc*. She married Henry Neville before 1601, and died before 1613.

7. Probably Sir Thomas Neville, d. 1628.

8. Cecily married Fitzwilliam Coningsby of Hampton Court, co. Hereford. She was cousin of the Countess of Pembroke, who mentions her in her diary (*The Diary of the Lady Anne Clifford*, ed. V. Sackville-West [1923], p. 29; H. J. Swallow, *The House of Nevill* [1885], p. 238; *G.E.C.* I, 37).

*69

Source:	Egerton 2234 ff. 120–1
Addressed:	*as in* 54
Postmarked:	NO 24
Franked:	de tours port paye jusqua Paris
Endorsed:	*b.* Walks & Prospects/about Blois.

Tours,
November 26, 1737

⟨Dear Mother,

After four months' stay there, we have at last left Blois, and got to Tours by a very easy day's journey.[1] You will see it in your map, fifty miles nearer the sea, and consequently here so much nearer England. If we go on much farther in the same manner we shall be almost able to shake hands together, which I hope we shall do in effect in a little less than two year now. Just before we left Blois I received your letter, and was extremely glad to receive in it a confirmation of your being stout and sturdy. I hope now you will take a new lease, and pray let it be for ninety-nine year at least.⟩

When we left Blois, the country had its winter suit on and looked very brown and rusty, but in summer I scarce ever saw a more agreeable place or better furnished with what I am so fond of, a variety of pleasant walks. I don't know whether I have yet given you an account of it, but I believe I have not, and so shall give you the following in full.

The river of the Loire comes to the town between the north and the east,[2] and runs on from it toward the sea between the west and the south ⟨so that I was out in my geography just now, for we are farther from England though nearer the sea—but that's a small fault between friends⟩. The river runs generally between two rising grounds that run on in a line (sometimes nearer and sometimes farther from the water) not only there, but quite down to the sea. This makes a view at Blois that is about two or three mile broad, and from twenty to thirty mile long.[3]

The southern line is a plain to the river, full of gardens, vineyards, and cornfields, interspersed and bounded by one of the risings I was speaking of, the slope of which is all covered entirely with a sort of underwood, as the top of it is with old high trees which make part of a forest eighteen or twenty mile round.

The western side, opposite to this, is a slope of vineyards quite down to the highroad and the Loire, on the top of which is a natural terrace to the town one way, and to another large forest, a mile and a half from the town the other. All the way you have the vineyards sloping down to the highroad, then the Loire with its vessels upon it going for Paris or the sea; beyond that, the vale I was speaking of, shut in with its woody terrace to the forest; at the end of this view, toward us now, is the view not unlike that you have at Winchester toward Southampton.

On the other side of the town is a plain of about a mile in from the water, mixed of meadow-grounds, little streams, and plantations of willows and osiers, which is bounded by the northern line, on the slope of which you see an odd mixture of rocks and shrubs, with a few poor hanging vineyards here and there betwixt them: and from the top of this (which is another natural terrace, but ruder than the former) you have a view of the meadows, river, and eastern line, which is a wider opening, spreading on towards Orleans, and so full of houses and villages and woodlands intermixed that it looks at a distance all like one great town in a wood.

You may guess, where there is four lines so different from one another, what a variety of walks such an inquirer that way as I am could find out, and there is not one of them where I have not thought of you.—We are now but two days old at Tours: before I leave it I shall be able to give you as full an account as I have of Blois, for I have been already two long walks to see the prospects round it, and I believe here, as at Blois, they are better than the town itself. ⟨With all services to all friends, I am your most dutiful and affectionate

J. Spence.⟩

1. They arrived in Tours Nov. 23. 'You go from Blois to Tours chiefly on the levee that runs quite from Briare to Nantes—'tis a considerable work, not only for its length ('tis said to be generally 50 f. broad at bottom, 24 at top, and 20 f. high—and the French foot is more than ours). Going to Tours you see the sides of the côteaux inhabited: the rock is of a soft stone and hollowed in. Rochecorbon in particular seems to be a town of this kind, and is perhaps the metropolis of all the caves in the world' (*Nbk.* 2 72ʳ).

2. 'They have at last got a bridge to their town,' notes Spence, who considered 'the city very indifferent', 'and now they should get a town to their bridge. The latter is really a great beauty, and would be still better perhaps without its obelisk' (ibid., 71ᵛ). On the bridge at Blois, see *Obs.* No. 1339.

3. 'The two best views of the country are from the Bishop's terrace, just by the Cathedral, and the Butte, a little raised hill near the château' (*Nbk.* 2 72ʳ).

---

*70

Source: Egerton 2234 ff. 122–3
Addressed: as in 54
Postmarked: DE 2
Franked: de tours port paye jusqu a paris
Endorsed: b. The very best step in Travelling, is/when we set foot on English/Ground again.

Tours,
December 3, 1737

⟨Dear Mother,

I hope you are now quite confirmed in your health, and that it may continue strong and tight for many years. As to the pagodas,[1] I hope Belle will look upon them as no loss, for while I have any I shall have some at her service, and by a calculation I have lately made I am like to be worth near a thousand of them when we come home.[2] After all, I can't blame the Chinese for worshipping pagodas: they are very necessary things, and there's no living well without them. My going abroad this time so soon was wholly owing to the respect I owe to them, and if I am an idolater, there are a great many such in Christendom as well as in the East Indies. In short, let the parsons say what they will, there's no living without pagodas.⟩

Tours (where I told you in my last we arrived by an easy day's journey the 23ʳᵈ of November) seems to be a very agreeable place. All the towns on the banks of the Loire are said to be so, but the country about Tours in particular is called the 'Garden of France'. We came here with the design of staying only a month, but if we find it as agreeable as it promises to be, we may stay much longer. In the spring we are (wherever we pass the winter, whether almost wholly here or equally divided between this town and Angers, two easy days' journey from hence) to pass through Rochelle, Bordeaux, Montpellier, Marseilles, Avignon and Lyons to Geneva, where probably we shall summer, and go about the end of October for Italy. 'Tis Italy that is my great favourite, and though I am easy and pleased here, I shall not be perfectly happy till I get into the country of the old Romans; or rather I shall not be perfectly happy till I have finished all, and can come and see you and my friends at ⟨old⟩ Winchester.

I own that we are delighted when we are abroad, but the greatest and truest satisfaction is when we come home again. I don't know whether you remember what the Prince of Yollocomia said to me and my dear friend Bob Down[es] several years ago at Oxford.[3] He was spotted all [like] a tortoise-shell snuff-box and shown about as a sight. He said that he wanted nothing, that he ate and drank well, that he was diverted continually with seeing new places: still, says he, there is something wanting; 'For de fader and de moder be alvais in de mind'. He spoke it with some commotion, and with a very sincere air. I remember it as well as if it had been but yesterday, and as he spoke it, he put his finger to his forehead and patted his forehead all the while he was saying the last sentence—which is a very true one, and very worthy of his Highness of Yollocomia.

⟨I would beg you if you have any occasion to write freely to Mr. Rolle, who will always be ready to serve you. A couple of years will soon run over, and then I hope to be near you myself; in the meantime he will be as myself. I desire you once for all to take care of your health and promise you to take care of mine. Whereunto I here set my hand (and shall by and by set my seal)

Your dutiful and affectionate son

Joseph Spence.⟩

1. See *Letter* 68 n. 3.
2. No doubt counting in his stipend at Oxford and income from his prebend. One thousand pounds seems too large a remuneration for a travelling companion.
3. The Prince was possibly identical with 'Job the Black' (*Letter* 57 n. 3). On Bob Downes see *Letter* 39 n. 7.

*71   *Source:*   Egerton 2234 ff. 124–6
          Addressed: *as in 54*
          Postmarked: DE [21?]
          Franked: tours port paye jusqu a paris
          Endorsed: *a.* the first/act of Mr shelvocs travills pretty
                      b. Capt: Shelvoc's Adventures. *1, 2, 3

Tours,

December 22, 1737

⟨—I wish you joy of more light, for this is exactly our
shortest day: sun rising 56 minutes after seven,
and setting four after four: which I mention to you as
knowing you to be a very famous astronomer.⟩

⟨Dear Mother,

I am sorry the poor gentlemen of the Cathedral are so unhealthy, but am
obliged to you for the particular account you give me of it. It came very à
propos, for I was just going to write a long letter to the family you mention
to put them in mind of a prebend in general, and what you tell me will give
me an occasion of mentioning that too in particular.[1] I keep up as constant
a correspondence here with the family, as if Lord M[iddlesex] was in
England: and after you and Mr. Rolle there is nobody that I write to or
hear from oftener. It's very certain that I must be an unaccountable fellow:
for to tell you the truth, I should really be sorry to be called into England
before I have had my months out at Rome, even for a prebend of
Winchester. The best of it is, there's very little danger of my being called
home on any such errand.⟩[2]

A little before we left Blois, a very pretty young gentleman came to the
house where we were, son of the great Coke of Norfolk, now Lord Lovel.[3]
He had a gentleman with him, of a weather-beaten aspect, a rough air, and a
rougher voice.[4] As Mr. Coke was acquainted with Mr. Trevor, he stopped
with us for three or four days. The first evening when we were got into a
good chat round the fire, as all people talk most of their own way of living,
we were deep on the subject of travelling. 'I am never seasick,' says I. 'And
I have some reason not to be so,' says Mr. Shelvocke, the rough gentleman
I was speaking of.—'Have you been much used to the sea then, Sir?'—'Yes,'
says Mr. Coke with his usual good-natured smile, 'You see there a second
Sir Francis Drake. That sunburnt face of his has been all round the globe.'—
'For God-sake, Sir,' says I, 'favour us with an account of your voyage:
there's nothing that can be so delightful, and I long to hear of the mermaids

209

and flying fish that you have seen.'—He answered nothing for a good while, looked very thoughtful, and when I began to despair, hemmed two or three times (for the poor man had a very great cold), and then began.

I suffered so much, gentlemen, and escaped with my life often so strangely, that when I look back now upon the things that happened to me, it seems to be all a dream. There's a Providence that rules all things. My father, who was a captain of a ship, had a commission in our last war with Spain to go into the Western Ocean ⟨or, in other words, we set out as a sort of lawful pirates⟩.[5] I was his lieutenant.[6] We set sail from Plymouth in the good ship *Speedwell*, of twenty-four guns and a hundred men,[7] about the middle of February 1719 together with Captain Clipperton (who had been put over my father's head) in a larger ship, called the *Success*.

In less than a week we were separated from our companion by a storm, and pursued our voyage alone. We passed the straits of Le Maire in September of the same year, and burned the town of Paita,[8] in five degrees of south latitude, in March 1720. We had picked up several vessels in our course, and had been often troubled with mutinous behaviour from several of our crew, before we had also called at the island of Juan Fernandez, in the thirty-third degree of south latitude ⟨and ninety leagues distant from the coast of Chile⟩ which had been appointed as a place of rendezvous with the *Success* on our setting out, but could learn no tidings of it. After the affair of Paita, and fighting for some time with the Spanish admiral in the harbour there, we returned in a bad condition (having no boat and but one anchor) toward Juan Fernandez again. To add to our misfortunes, we sprung a leak in our passage for that island, and to complete them, when we approached it (on the 25th of May) our ship was driven by a hard gale of wind on the rocks that face the coast.[9] She did not break all to pieces, though 'twas a rude shock she had. We had time to make a raft and to convey over some of the most necessary of our things to the island. We carried over a quantity of gunpowder, arms, and bread, etc. In these expeditions there was but one man of the whole company lost:[10] he had loaded himself too much, fell off by accident from the raft, and we saw his brains dashed out against a rock.

The island ⟨itself⟩ was uninhabited, and had a dismal and desolate appearance to us on our getting ashore.[11] We looked wildly about us, and seemed to pity one another. ⟨We were about a hundred in number.⟩ The first thing we did was to make a hut for the captain, of boughs and sailcloth, some which we had saved, and afterwards for ourselves. We dried fish, but our bread was soon out: and then we had nothing but dried fish to eat. We used to make large fires in the evenings and sat round them in circles.

After we had been there about a fortnight, the captain called a council.

He said that as we were on the island of Juan Fernandez, we must be ninety leagues from the coast of Chile, and out of the common course of any of our own ships. 'What shall we do, gentlemen,' added he: 'd'ye think of dying here, or endeavouring to escape? We have some iron with us, such a one can make tools, and then if we put all hands to work, we may make a vessel large enough perhaps to carry us to the continent.' Though the difficulty of such work in our circumstances was apparent, we all agreed to it, and for some days the whole company applied to the work.

Certainly man was [not] born for society, but for quarrelling. Though the only consolation we had was conversing together, a few days took that consolation from us. One Morphew, an Irishman (that was a very stout fellow, but as seditious as he was brave) was often whispering the sailors that the captain had set them about an impossible work; that they were not only to fight with the bad season but to be harassed with labour, and that a useless one; that the captain's commission was good at sea but good for nothing at land; and that he or any one of them ought to have as much authority there as Captain Shelvocke himself. 'This from murmurs at first grew to be the common talk of most of the crew, and at last appeared in a public mutiny. They almost all quitted the work when 'twas very little advanced, and we were not only cut off from our hopes of an escape, but were hourly plagued, and often in danger of our lives from their insolence. ⟨There's no more room; I shall send you the rest in my next. With all services I am ever

Your dutiful and affectionate

J. Spence.⟩

1. Early in 1737 the Duke of Dorset, father of Lord Middlesex, offered Spence the deanery of Clogher in Ireland, adding 'that he might depend upon him for any Future favour, even tho he should not accept of this' (Wright, pp. 55–6). The prospect of going to Ireland evidently did not appeal to Spence.

2. This is an amusing instance of dramatic irony. On Dec. 19 O.S., Horatio Walpole wrote to Robert Trevor at The Hague, soliciting the return of his cousin and Spence's companion to England. The request put a premature end to this tour. See *Letter* 73.

3. Edward Coke (1719–53), son of Thomas Coke of Holkham, Norfolk (1697–1759), Baron Lovel of Minstrel Lovel, 1744 Visc. Coke of Holkham and E. of Leicester. Edward Coke was M.P. for Norfolk 1741–7, for Harwich 1747–53.

4. George Shelvocke (1702–60), son of George Shelvocke (1675–1742), captain of the *Speedwell*, with whom he made a voyage round the world in 1719–22. The elder Shelvocke published *A Voyage Round The World* in 1726;

his son, a revised edition in 1757. W. G. Perrin's preface to his edition of the original *Voyage*, published for 'The Seafarer's Library' in 1928, gives biographical and other informative details.

Spence's account is full of inaccuracies, some of which were due to young Shelvocke, others no doubt to Spence himself, who at a later date, made an attempt to correct the errors by consulting the printed *Voyage*. Spence's two original letters are heavily edited and often very difficult to read. In most cases, however, the text can be supplied from the fair copy.

5. The commission was obtained on Jan. 1, 1719, and the semi-piratical enterprise ('lawful' because war with Spain had been formally declared on Dec. 17) was sponsored by a small company of merchants. For detailed proposals of what was to be looted and where, see Perrin, pp. xi–xiv.

6. In the MS list of the crew, preserved at the Admiralty, young Shelvocke is listed as 'Nothing'. His principal duty was to listen to

all that was said on board and report it to his father (Perrin, pp. xviii, xx).

7. 22 guns, 106 men (200 tons). Perrin, p. x.

8. On the coast of Peru (*Voyage*, chap. vi).

9. The passage from 'We set sail ...' originally read: 'We made a good voyage for several weeks, till at last a storm drove us; for some days we did not well know whether we saw any island before us in a sea we were unacquainted with and was drove by the weather on a sandbank. 'Twas near the island.'

10. John Hannah (Perrin, pp. xxii, 116). The following part of the narrative, as recorded by Spence, forms chapter vii of Shelvocke's *Voyage*.

11. The sentence originally read: 'When we were got on the island we had reason to think it was uninhabited: and by the observations we made afterwards, it was the island of Juan Fernandez, where none but he (or such miserable wretches as had been cast away like him), had ever lived.'

---

*72

Source:	Egerton 2234 ff. 127–8
Addressed:	*as in* 54
Postmarked:	OC 29 [*the postmark is quite clear; the date is perhaps due to mechanical error*]
Franked:	tours port paye jusqu a paris
Numbered:	B.
Endorsed:	*a.* yᵉ second actᵗ of capⁿ shelvocs voyages
	b. Continuation of Shelvoc's Advˢ:/4, 5, 6

Tours,
January 1, 1738

⟨All the people in town are running about, kissing one another in the streets, and wishing a Happy New Year. I wish you all the same with all my heart and blood.⟩

⟨Dear Mother,⟩

In my last I left my friend I saw at Blois on the desert island of Juan Fernandez, the work of making a vessel to carry them off at a stop, and almost all the crew engaged in a mutiny against him and his father. Mr. Shelvocke told us the particulars with a great air of sincerity, and you may imagine we listened to him with a great deal of attention. He thus went on:

Though the captain was a very prudent man and long used to command, though he had the arts of flattering a crew, and courage to oppose himself to them when proper, even all his skill was absolutely necessary on this occasion: we were often in danger of being rifled by them, and almost as often of losing our lives. When things were at the worst, the captain took me aside one day: 'You see the danger we are in,' says he, 'if they kill me, 'tis possible they may spare you. You know every creek in this island: here's the King's commission which names you in my place if I die;[1] take your time and hide it as safely as you can.'[2]

I was forced to do this by night. I had long used to walk out and think by myself. I loved reading, too, and had a Milton with me, which I got all without book in my walks. The island, which is about five or six mile round, is odd, and in the inward parts of it very agreeable, if one was there for pleasure. 'Tis full of hills and inequalities, woody, and with the greatest number of odd streams about it that ever I saw in such a compass of ground. My father had reason to say that I knew every spot of it. I stole out one night by one of my old walks, digged a hole in the ground, and lodged the commission in it, at the foot of a tree where I had often sat and read Milton in my solitary hours. I afterwards hid other things of value in several places after the same manner, and in particular above £1500 in money, for we were threatened perpetually with assaults from our mutineers.

This way of living always in fears and apprehensions continued all the winter. We, however, revived the thoughts of building a vessel, and I and the ship-carpenter,[3] and what few hands we could get to assist us, worked at it with more labour and assiduity than can be described. The rebels were continually ridiculing our attempt, and we ourselves often looked upon it as impossible to be brought to bear. A constant application conquers difficulties that at first seem invincible. Every day added to our work, and at last we began to see our labours likely to succeed. In short, we finished our vessel such an one as 'twas, and a longboat to attend her. Most of the mutineers came over to our party and were willing to venture with us in her on the ocean. We were forced to receive them, for we wanted hands to manage her, and were obliged to divide the enemy as much as we could. Others said she would be lost the first rough sea and resolved rather to stay on the island than venture out in her.[4]

She was indeed but a very indifferent vessel, but we had nothing to choose and resolved to trust to Providence. We got a large stock of fish dried in the sun; we made oil out of the seals[5] which we caught in great abundance: this was to boil our fish in. It was of a gross, disagreeable taste, and had long been very disgusting to us: but we were forced to make use of it. We had met with but little flesh since we had been in the island: and as for bread, we had almost forgot the taste of it. When all was ready, we entered into our vessel, about fifty of us, with arms, and set sail.[6] Our ship did pretty well. We intended for the continent of America, and had some time very good weather. In some days it turned against us and carried us away vehemently to the south. We suffered long and much by this bad weather, and began to be in despair, for our fresh water began to fail us: the captain apprehended we could not be very far from land, but there was no certainty of it, and the wind did not serve for the point where he imagined it lay. He said that if anybody would venture to go out in the longboat that way, he was in great hopes of some good event. I offered to go, and four or five our best rowers went with me.[7]

We were out several hours without discovering anything but the wide ocean all round us, and were quite dispirited. The night came upon us, when to our inexpressible joy, we thought that we saw candles: we made towards their light, and some time after heard the barking of dogs. Never was there any one sound which I ever heard in my whole life with so much pleasure as that. We rowed by the light of the stars and moon, and at last came to a village on the shore of an island. There were some boats lying before it, and a sailorly sort of people on the beach. They were surprised to see us when we landed, and looked quite frightened at us: we could not imagine why, for [we] did not consider at first what a terrible figure people must make who had not shaved nor shifted for half a year. The next morning, early, we got in our provision of fresh water, wine, flesh, and bread, and set out to carry the joyful news to our ship.[8] She was carried so far aside by the wind that we did not reach her till two days after, and were in the utmost terror till we saw her sails. We brought them a most necessary recruit, and the assurance of our being near the continent.

After this we engage some of the enemy's ships, in vain: but at last take one [of 2]oo tons and go on so fortunately,[9] that we at last saw ourselves mas[ters of an] excellent ship and a large crew. I was going to say a [good one, but] that was not true: for when our prosperity returned, [there broke out] new mutinies that put us into more dangers than all our engagements with the public enemy. After, scouring all those seas, we came round toward Japan and the East Indies. When our ship was once got to China, I thought myself at home: where at last we actually arrived safe, after four years of voyaging. What I am most thankful to heaven for is that in all this time and all these sufferings I never was one day out of order. I had my health then better than I have now, for the devilish cough tears me almost to pieces. Here his cough seized him, and he finished.

⟨These gentlemen-pirates made such havoc in those seas among the French and Spanish vessels that, after the Peace of Utrecht,[10] there were great complaints made against them to our ministry.[11] They were obliged to give in an account upon oath of their behaviour, and the sum of their depositions was published in a book called *A Voyage of Captain Shelvock round the World*,[12] printed in 1726.[13] If you have a mind to inform yourself further in the affair, that book may give you an account of it.

I beg you'd send to Mr. Rolle whenever you have occasion. I have received a letter from Mr. Duck, which looked as if things then were not likely to go well with him. I hope 'tis changed for the better. I sent him a long letter of consolation as he desired me, and as I am an excellent preacher I don't doubt 'twill have a good effect on him. With all services to all friends, I am ever

Your dutiful and affectionate

J. Spence.⟩

1. This is probably young Shelvocke's gratuitous invention. He was only eighteen, and is put down on the crew list as 'Nothing'.

2. The following lines offer new details. The *Voyage* (p. 122) reads simply: 'In the midst of these troublesome confusions I ordered my son to secure my commission in some dry place of the woods or rocks, if such could be found.' (Inability to produce the commission laid an officer open to being treated as a common pirate.)

3. Robert Davenport (Perrin, p. xviii).

4. The names of the men, ten in all, are given in Perrin's preface, p. xxii.

5. Originally 'sea-turtles'.

6. Oct. 5, 1720, after four and a half months' stay on the island. 'As she went off I named her the *Recovery*' (*Voyage*, p. 134).

7. The *Voyage* (p. 149) says that 'Mr. Randall, second lieutenant ... commanded in this enterprize.' Young Shelvocke's account is here inaccurate: his father saw the island of Iquique, but believing it was uninhabited, sent the boat to explore it.

8. Or more plainly, 'Being ashore, they went to the lieutenant's house, and finding it locked broke it open, and rummaged the whole village ... the few Indians they found seemed to be as glad of this opportunity of pillaging the Spaniards as we were' (*Voyage*, p. 149).

9. 'She was a good ship of about two hundred tons, called *Jesus Maria* ... laden with pitch, tar, copper and plank, but nothing else. The captain offered sixteen thousand dollars for her ransom, but I could not give ear to it ...' (*Voyage*, pp. 154–5). As the Peace of Madrid had been signed in June 1721, this—as well as the looting of two other Spanish ships—were acts of piracy, by which Shelvocke gained over £7000 (Perrin, p. xviii).

10. Spence's slip for Peace of Madrid.

11. Complaint by the Spanish ambassador that the *Sacra Familia* was seized after peace had been declared seems to have met with no redress. On his return to London, Aug. 1, 1722, Shelvocke was confined in the Wood Street compter and about to be tried by the Admiralty Court for piracy. However, he escaped from the King's Bench prison, and for three or four years thought it prudent to hide himself (Perrin, pp. xvii–xix).

12. 'About the year 1724 or 1725, when things quieted down somewhat, Shelvocke presented to the Admiralty a manuscript account of his voyage, which is still in the Admiralty Library. ... In 1726 he caused to be published *A Voyage Round the World* in which he had re-written and expanded the narrative referred to above' (Perrin, p. xix).

13. Spence wrote '1725'.

73

Source:	Egerton 2234 ff. 129–30
Addressed:	*as in* 54
Postmarked:	IA 17
Franked:	tours port paye j. a paris
Numbered:	B.
Endorsed:	*b.* Why returning to England/not to be Transcribed

Tours,
January 17, 1738

⟨Dear Mother,

I am just come home from a long walk of a fine frosty morning, and had the pleasure to observe that the trees have all little pods ⟨as indeed they have always at this time of year⟩ with leaves in them already turning greenish against the spring. This put me in mind of my garden at Birchanger, and set my head a' rambling as well as myself. What, says I, if we were to make a little step this spring into England—to see my mother, and how my things go on at Birchanger? 'Tis but a step, the business only of one week to a lazy man to get from this place to England. How pretty 'twould be to stay a month at Winchester and walk in Mrs. Morecroft's garden, and talk over old stories with my good old mother? To see my sister, and teach her the French way of playing at piquet? In short, to see all one's English friends and take a view of my dear parish in Essex?

You may think I am got a little wild this morning, but the thing is not quite so wild as you may imagine. 'Tis not impossible but I may actually pay you a visit this spring. The case is thus. A borough near an estate of Mr. Trevor's has lost its representative:[1] Mr. Trevor was apprehensive that he might be called home to stand for it, wrote a letter to let his friends know that 'twould break in upon all his designs too much for him to desire it, and hoped to hear no more of it. The day before yesterday he received a letter which presses him very much to return, and adds that 'tis very much the desire of the Duke of Newcastle and Sir R. Walpole that he should appear for it.[2] In short, they make it so much an affair, and Mr. Trevor has such particular attachments to the former as well as so much respect for the latter that I think we are in a very fair way of returning to good old England this spring; and if we do, while poor Mr. Trevor is soliciting his voters,[3] I shall have time enough to come and chat away a month with you at Winchester. You may guess what a pleasure that will be to me; and as for the journey, 'tis no pain: for 'tis only going four or five hundred mile north, instead of going a thousand south in the spring.[4] We travellers are citizens of the world: a journey is our profession, and generally speaking it does not signify toward which point of the compass it lies: but when it leads towards you and England, I must needs say 'tis always the most agreeable of any of them to me.

Your dutiful and affectionate

J. Spence.

Humble services to my cousin Belle, who will be as glad as you of this news; and to all friends that it may be agreeable to at all.⟩[5]

1. Thomas Pelham of Stanmore, M.P. for Lewes, died before Dec. 19 O.S. (not Dec. 21 as stated in *Gent. Mag.*).

2. On Dec. 19, 1737 O.S., Horatio Walpole wrote to Robert Trevor in The Hague: 'I am now to acquaint you at the request of the Duke of Newcastle and Mr. Pelham, that Mr. Pelham, who was commonly called Turk Pelham, and served for Lewes is dead, and that it is actually resolved to nominate your cousin Trevor to succeed him, in which it is hoped there will be no great difficulty, and you are desired, and I must add the credit of Sir R. Walpole and my own with you on this occasion, to procure his return into England against the meeting of Parliament' (*HMC*, 14th Rep., App. ix, pp. 9–10, 238).

3. *The Gentleman's Magazine* for Feb. 1738, p.

108, lists under 'Members elected': '*Lewes*, John Trevor, Esq.'.

4. 'Writing from New College, Dec. 3, 1738, Spence tried to interest Massingberd, then in Paris, in purchasing Trevor's Italian chaise, which had been left at Calais' (Wright, p. 216).

5. Spence and Trevor returned to England a month later. On Feb. 7 O.S., Andrew Stone wrote to the D. of Newcastle: 'Mr. Trevor is safely landed in England: He is expected every Hour in Town ... he is just come to Town, and will set out for Lewes as soon as he has had time to see his Friends' (Add. MSS 33065 f. 256ʳ⁻ᵛ). Spence's only extant letter to Trevor is preserved among the Spence Papers. It is dated 'Oct. 5, 1738', and written in a parody of 'Essex-Stile'.

The third tour

*74

Source: Egerton 2234 ff. 131–2

Addressed: To/Mrs Spence/in Colebrook-Street/
Winchester./Hants.

Numbered: N°. 3 45 C.

Endorsed: *a.* just gon/with Lord Lincoln.
b. Safe arrived at Calais.

Calais,
September 14 ⟨3⟩, 1739

⟨Dear Mother,⟩

This is to assure you that your humble servant and most dutiful son arrived safe at Calais between eight and nine o'clock this morning.[1] We had a most delightful passage, and without any manner of inconvenience ⟨to my sweet person⟩. I imagine you may receive a letter I left at London the very same post with this to inform you that I should set out for France in a few days: probably this will be the more agreeable to you of the two. We go tomorrow for Paris ⟨where we shall stay some time to rest ourselves. With all services to all friends, I am ever

Your dutiful and affectionate

J. Spence⟩

HENRY FIENNES CLINTON (1720–94) suc. on the death of his elder br. George as 9th E. of Lincoln. His father, the 7th Earl, died in 1728; his mother, Lady Lucy, in 1736. Her brothers Thomas Pelham-Holles, D. of Newcastle, and Henry Pelham took care of Henry's education: Eton 1729–35; admitted Clare Hall, Cambridge, Sept. 6, 1737. After his return from the Grand Tour, Lord Lt. of Cambridgeshire (1742), Lord of the Bedchamber (1743), Master of the Jewel Office (1744), Cofferer of the Household (1746), F.R.S. (1747). In 1744 m. his cousin Catherine Pelham; in 1768 became 2d D. of Newcastle-under-Lyme.

1. The first mention of this tour occurs in Lord Lincoln's letter from Cambridge ('Clare Hall, April 17, 1739') to his uncle, the D. of Newcastle: 'In regard to my travelling this summer, I still entirely and with pleasure submit myself to whatever your Grace shall think rightest for me. I own it is what very much suits my inclinations, and I hope I shall never behave myself, wherever I am, so as to repent of your sending me abroad' (Add. MSS 33065 f. 130^r). By July 31 the tour was quite settled: 'I am going once more to take a tour, with Lord Lincoln,' wrote Spence to Massingberd from London. 'We are going to go directly to Italy' (*N & Q*, vol. 188 [1945], p. 253). They 'set out from London September 1/12; landed at Calais 14; Bo[u]logne, ditto'.

Notebook 3
Egerton 2235 ff. (xxi–xxii) 73ʳ⁻ᵛ

Abbeville [Sept. 15] is the most celebrated of any town in France for their cloth, and indeed they seem to make some as fine, and as good, as any in England. This manufacture was established here in Louis XIV's time by Monsieur de Louvois who got over some workmen from Holland 'dans le plus chaud de la guerre' (Queen Anne's or King William's?). The building where they work, with gardens and courts, takes up fourteen acres. They had 3500 persons employed when we were there. They pay some by the day (from 10 to 30, 35, and jusqu'à 40 sous a day) according to the workmen, and others by the piece (36 livres to two, for a piece of twenty-five ells).

They say the church at *Amiens* [Sept. 16] is 335 f. high: the same person told us so who showed us the inscription in Saxon characters for a Hebrew inscription. The building is of the ornamented Gothic.

Though I have seen Versailles often, I should be apt to think that the woods of *Chantilly* [Sept. 17] may be called *the best garden* in France: they are cut into openings that are more regular than some of our best gardens in England, though they have more of nature unspoilt than any garden in France. The house is not to be mentioned in comparison of the outhouses, for the Duke's horses and dogs are lodged much more magnificently than their master. The Queen's apartment is adorned (over the doors etc.) with pictures for the fables of Aesop, there are some pretty light French closets that would be very pleasant to drink tea in, and in the picture-gallery you have the victories of the Prince of Condé, and two Fames in one of them, blowing his praises in the air and tearing the names of those exploits which he was then supposed to be ashamed of: *Quantum paenituit*, etc.—The stable is the noblest room I have seen in France: 'tis about 590 f. by 40, as near as I can guess by my paces (131 paces to the oval and 135 from the oval: 17 from manger to manger, 20 from side to side, 36 from the middle door to the watering fountain). Its proportions strike one very well, and it carries a truly great air with it. (Does not the management of the oval in the middle prevent its appearing too long?)

All subsequent excerpts from *Notebook 3* are taken from Egerton 2235.

Source:	Egerton 2234 ff. 133–4
Addressed:	*as in 74*
Postmarked:	18 SE
Franked:	Free/Andrew Stone
Numbered:	(2)
Endorsed:	*a.* yᵉ first/Letter: when he travild with/Lord Lincoln
	b. Well, at Paris.

*75

Paris,
September 23 ⟨12⟩, 1739[1]

⟨Dear Mother,⟩

You received my letter from Calais, I believe, the post after my letter from London. We had a fine voyage thither, and everything has answered ever since. We got by easy journeys to Paris, where we shall stay some time to rest ourselves and see sights.[2] Lord L⟨incoln⟩ I find so sensible, so agreeable, and so obliging, that I thought several times whilst we were upon the road that I was beginning a second voyage with Lord M⟨iddlesex⟩.[3] The only difference is that he is not of so strong a make, so that we go on by little day's journeys, which you won't be sorry to hear. I am already as much at home at Paris as if I were at my old friend Mr. Jonquiere's in Suffolk Street. We dined yesterday at our ambassador's my Lord Waldegrave's, where not only my Lord, which one might expect, but myself too, were particularly well received.[4] I hope you are very well: I never was better in my life, or better pleased with anything than my present voyage. ⟨I hope it will go on as it has begun, and then it will be one of the blessings of my life that I undertook it. I am, with all services to all friends, ever

Your dutiful and affectionate

J. Spence⟩

1. The letter was written from Lyons (see *Letter* 76) where Spence stayed Sept. 31–Oct. 3, and antedated.

2. They stayed a week (Sept. 18–25) and visited, among other sights, the late Regent's collection. Spence met his friend Edward Rolle in Paris.

3. 'He has the universal character of an ex-tremely good natured man,' Spence told Massingberd on July 31, 'which bids fair for making our jaunt the more pleasant' (Wright, p. 58).

4. James, 1st Earl Waldegrave (1685–1741), British ambassador to France 1730–40. He left Oct. 31, 1740, for England.

Notebook 3

The woods of *Fontainebleau* [Sept. 25] have the largest oaks I have seen in France, though not equal to our old British oaks. They are so ill looked after that a French nobleman, who should beg leave of the King to cut down the useless trees there, might put several thousands of louis d'or in his pocket, and not cut down any one tree that the wood would not be the better for losing. There are several that are fallen with age, like the trees at Juan Fernandez Island.

The landscape very pretty as you come to *Sens* (40 mile beyond Paris) and from Sens to Villeneuve-le-Roy you have an oval of nine mile diameter that is as pleasing. Here you begin to have higher ground and the hills grow larger and larger all the way till you come to the environs of *Dijon* [Sept. 28–29]. The last hill before that place is the first of the Alpine kind: you have another such a step a little before you come to *Lyons* [Sept. 31–Oct. 3] and three or four before you come to Chambéry. (To make a line of the swellings of the ground from Holland to Paris, and from Paris to the Alps.)

Lord B[olingbroke] was at the convent of Sens when we passed it.[1] 'Tis a convent of Benedictines (and very rich ones) for people that have forsworn the good things of this world. There are but five of them, and they are masters of thirty-five parishes.

The two famous tombs at the Chartreux by Dijon are very well worth seeing. One is of Philip the Hardy, in 1404, and the other of Jean Sans Peur, in 1419. They have each little figures all round them, which are better than the principal figures. There's a head like William of Wickham in the former, and one very like the famous Vespasian at the Great Duke's in the latter. The hands are not so well as the heads in these little figures; the body, drapery and design are very well and indeed extraordinary good for the time they were done in. They were done in Flanders.

I have already said that there is (what one may call) a detached step of the Alps before you come to Dijon and another before you come to Lyons. From *Pont Beauvoisin* [Oct. 5] the continued hills begin. There's a large one before you come to *Échelles*. . . . 'Tis all hilly and romantic from thence to *Chambéry*. Chambéry lets you into a sort of valley all encompassed with mountains; you go a good way from thence without mounting considerably. At last you have a high hill, then the mountain (Basque's Mountain) covered with pines where the road runs through a wood of them—which I don't doubt is often in the clouds—another high one (the Chapel Mountain) with a few scattered pines, but chiefly bare and strewed with large flaky pieces of rock. The next rising is towards *Laneburg* [Oct. 9] and Mount Cenis.

1. No doubt to visit one of his wife's daughters, who was abbess of the convent of Notre Dame at Sens. Lady Bolingbroke spent part of her time at this convent, and Bolingbroke was allowed to occupy a pavillion in a garden belonging to it, where he could pursue his studies.

*76

Source: Egerton 2234 ff. 135–6
Addressed: as in 74
Numbered: (3.) deleted: Nº 3/43
Endorsed: a. an acct: of/ye alps being mended from/
paris to turin
b. Wt a great Lyer I am. &c.

Turin,
October 13 ⟨2⟩, 1739

⟨Dear Mother,⟩

All travellers are a little noted for being liars, but of all liars I think your
son Joseph has of late been the greatest. First he sends you word that he
shall set out in seven or eight days by a letter that came to you when he
had been four or five days in France,[1] and in the next place he sends you
word that he likes Paris very well, when he was actually at Lyons. Truth
will out, and now is the time for it. We set out from London the 1st of
September, and arrived here at Turin the last of the same month, old style.
I told you this second untruth to conceal our passage of the Alps till we were
got safe over them, and I promise you, upon the word of a clergyman, that
I will never do so again.

And indeed there is no need of it, for the Alps are not now the formidable
things they were when first I was acquainted with them. On the war in
Italy, in the year 1734, the King of France and the King of Sardinia were
joined against the Emperor;[2] so the French troops came here as friends, and
the King had the ways levelled and widened where there was any occasion
for it, that they might come over his mountains with the more ease. About
two years ago the King married the Duke of Lorraine's sister,[3] and as her
Majesty was obliged to come the same way, in some of the places where the
precipices looked most frightful, he ordered walls to be built, high enough
to take off from the horror of the view or to save a chaise from falling down
the dangerous side.[4] So I have observed it is generally: the earth is
growing better, though men are growing worse.

We are very safe, and shall, I believe, be very pleasurably here. I wonder
why you are so alarmed in our native country.[5] What is it you apprehend at
home? Things I don't doubt will be very easy there, and if there should ever
be a storm, it would blow over our heads at Birchanger ⟨and though
Winchester is a more genteel place, it might indeed take off Trinity Tower, but
'twould scarce do any damage in Colebrook Street⟩.[6] Thanks be to heaven,
we are too inconsiderable to have anything to apprehend from it! Here at

Turin we are all still and safe ⟨both great and small⟩, and as to health, I never was better in my life.

⟨As you have a number of franks, I'll get you to write Dick word now and then how I do and how we go on: for as Lord Lincoln abominates writing of letters, I have the honour of being his Lordship's secretary as well as governor, and that costs me two or three letters every week to the secretary's office;[7] so that Dick will be so good as to excuse me if I look upon the letters that I write to you as wrote to him too.⟩

In eight or ten days we shall be quite settled and quite at home here: and with my books and papers about me, I shall think myself at my room in New College or in the garden chamber, and I shall want nothing but you to be sitting by me, to help me while I am composing my most notable book.[8] The court is not in town here: 'tis at present in mourning for a brother of the Duchess of Bourbon's and of the late Queen of Sardinia's, who was killed in the battle against the Turks.[9] They will be out of mourning in two or three days after their return hither, and I don't intend to go to court till then ⟨because I have taken an utter aversion to black. On my return I shall have enough of that, both in Queen's Street and at Birchanger. I am with all services to all friends, ever

Your most dutiful and affectionate

J. Spence⟩

1. Not preserved.

2. During the war of the Polish succession (1733–5), Charles Emmanuel III, seeing the opportunity of making territorial gains in Italy at the expense of Austria, allied himself with France.

3. Elizabeth (1711–July 3, 1741), dau. of Leopold-Joseph, D. of Lorraine (for her brother see *Letter* 106 n. 2). The marriage, the King's third, took place on Mar. 9, 1737; his 2d wife, Polyxena von Hesse-Rheinfels, died in January 1735. As the King's 2d son, Emmanuel-Philibert, also died, Charles Emmanuel, left only with one heir, married again to protect his succession.

4. 'There's a large [road] before you come to Échelles, which has a little wall that runs all along the precipice. . . . After Échelles you go through the hollow way made by Victor's father, which the inscription calls "a work unattempted by the Romans" ' (*Nbk.* 3 74ᵛ).

Horace Walpole, who followed this route a month after Spence, copied out the inscription in full (*Corresp.* XIII, 190).

5. War against Spain was declared on Oct. 23 O.S.

6. Mrs. Spence lived in Colebrook Street. On Trinity Tower, see *Letter* 25.

7. Andrew Stone (1703–73), private secretary to the D. of Newcastle and to his brother, Henry Pelham, with both of whom he had great influence. For a specimen of the reports which Spence was regularly sending to his office, see *Letter* 121.

8. *Polymetis.*

9. William, Prince of Hesse-Rheinfels (1700–39), Major-General of the imperial forces, was killed in the battle of Krozka on Aug. 22, 1739 (*Gent. Mag.*, 1739, p. 441). On Caroline, the ⟨pretty Duchess of Bourbon⟩, see *Letter* 21.

77

Source: Add. MSS 33065 f. 340^{r-v}

Endorsed: R[*eceived*] 13th.

LINCOLN TO NEWCASTLE

Turin,
October 13⟨2⟩, 1739

My Lord,

I am afraid your Grace (and with good reason) was not fully satisfied with the excuse Mr. Spence made for my not writing from Paris, as I know I ought to have done, when you was so kind as to express some sort of pleasure in hearing from me. But as I have so often experienced your readiness in forgiving me my faults, I will only say with Tully, *habes confidentem rem,*[1] and without filling up my letter with apologies let you know that we passed the Alps (which by looking at I should have thought unpassable), and arrived here the 30th of September O.S. in perfect health. I will say nothing of Turin to your Grace in this letter, but reserve that for the next, only that Mr. Villettes is exceeding obliging[2] and that we go together next Sunday alla Veneria,[3] where the Court is at present.

I should do great injustice to Mr. Spence and debar myself of a great pleasure if I did not acquaint your Grace how perfectly happy I am with him, and must very freely own that it won't be his fault if I don't turn out what I know you wish me to be. I can't finish my letter without telling your Grace how excessive kind and obliging my Lord Waldegrave was to me when at Paris; he complained of our being in such a hurry and thought it would have been our surest way to have stayed our time there in going rather than depend on the uncertainty of our being able to come back that way. I beg my duty in the kindest manner to her Grace[4] and my uncle Pelham,[5] and design writing them both when I am settled in the Academy. . . .

THOMAS PELHAM-HOLLES (1693–1768), D. of Newcastle, Secretary of State 1724–48. Lincoln's mother, Lady Lucy, was his sister. After her death in 1736 he assumed responsibility for the young Earl.

1. Perhaps adapted from 'cum habeam rem non dubiam' (*Pro. A. Cluent.* 64).

2. Arthur Villettes (ca. 1702–76), appointed Secretary at the Court of Turin July 6, 1734, Resident May 15, 1741, till July 29, 1749. Minister at Zurich 1750–62 (F. Hausmann, *Repertorium der diplomatischer Vertreter aller Länder* [Zurich, 1950], II, 163, 166).

3. The royal palace, not far from Turin, designed ca. 1670 by Castellamonte, and after the devastations of the siege of 1706, rebuilt by Juvarra and Alfieri.

4. Henrietta (d. 1776), dau. of Francis, 2d E. of Godolphin, granddaughter of the D. of Marlborough, married Thomas Pelham-Holles in 1717.

5. Hon. Henry Pelham (1695–1754), younger brother of the D. of Newcastle and of Lincoln's mother; from 1743 until his death 1st Lord of the Treasury.

78

Source: Egerton 2234 ff. 137–8
Addressed: as in 74
Postmarked: 2[ ] OC
Franked: Free/Andrew Stone
Numbered: (4.)
Endorsed: *a.* yᵉ actᵗ: of there/company at the Academey there.
b. List of the People in yᵉ Academy./to be omᵈ.

Turin,
October 24 ⟨13⟩, 1739

⟨Dear Mother,

I have received a second letter from you, which gave me a great deal of pleasure in letting me know that you were so well. I am quite so, and very much your humble servant.

We live here in the Academy, where my Lord learns to ride, fence and dance.[1] 'Tis to me quite a college life: for we are very regular in our hours of dining and supping, eat at a table with the governors and the principal scholars, who are a Sardinian marquis, a Polish earl, a young nobleman from Switzerland, an Irish gentleman, and ourselves from England, so that you see we are made up of all nations and, like old Noah in his ark, can show a specimen of almost every beast. I say that only in jest, for they are a very agreeable and very polite set of people.

We begin now to be settled after our month of perpetual motion, and to be quite at home here. The weather, for most part of our journey and almost continually since we have been here, has been rainy, so that I have not been able to talk [of] my walks as usual. This morning is a fine one, and I did not miss the advantage of wandering out in it. But I must stay a little longer before I pretend to give you an account of this place. I beg my most hearty services to all friends. I have wrote to Captain Rolle to be a good son to you in my absence, and if you have any occasion for anything from Oxford, you may write to him just as if I was there myself. He stays on in England, and his friend Sir Bouchier is ⟨I believe⟩ by this time in Italy, by way of Genoa, which your map will show you [to] be not far from us, but he takes I [think] a different route.[2] I am ever

Your dutiful and affectionate

J. Spence⟩

1. The *Academia Reale*, 'École militaire ...
pour l'éducation de la jeune Noblesse', founded
by the Duchess of Nemours, was constructed
in 1677 according to designs by Castellamonte.
The Academy 'qui, dans son commencement
n'était qu'une maison où l'on apprenait
l'exercice de l'équitation, la danse et les talens
d'agrément convenables à un gentilhomme ...
fut rétablie en 1713, après le traité d'Utrecht,
et fut érigée en Académie militaire par les
Rois Victor Amédée II et Charles Emmanuel
III. Toute personne du haut pairage s'empressait
d'y placer ses enfans' (Modeste Paroletti,
Turin et ses curiosités [Turin, 1819], pp. 240-2).

2. Sir Bourchier Wrey (1714-84), 5th Bt.
His mother was daughter of John Rolle of
Stevenstone. He attended Winchester College
and New College, Oxford, with Edward Rolle.
On July 31 Spence wrote to Massingberd:
'Captain Rolle had some thought of attending
Sir Bourchier Wrey ..., but Sir B. only goes
to the south of France' (*N & Q*, vol. 188
[1945], p. 253). On his return Sir Bourchier
became a member of the Soc. of Dilettanti.

---

*79

Source: Egerton 2234 ff. 139-40
Addressed: To,/Mrs Spence
Numbered: (5.)
Endorsed: a. the descripshon of turin/& the fine prospects round it
b. The Prettiness of Turin &/the pretty Walks ab^t it.

Turin,
November 7, 1739

⟨Dear Mother,

I have had no letter from you these seventeen days; however, like a good
dutiful son, here am I set down to write to you again—though 'tis pretty
hard to keep up a dialogue by oneself.—Let me see. Ay,⟩ I think we always
have the luck of settling in places where I, that am so great a lover of
walking, have a great variety of pretty walks. It would be difficult to name
any place equal to Turin in that particular.

When one has been six or seven days creeping up and down hills (or in a
loftier style, passing the Alps), one comes through the straits of Suse into
the beginning of a plain which winds on, and widens into the great vale of
Lombardy. The beginning of this plain is very narrow and confined, but has
a fine opening for nine or ten mile, before you come to Turin: the most
regular and prettiest city perhaps in Europe.[1]

It owes a great deal of its prettiness to the war in Queen Anne's time.[2]
The Duke of Savoy, you know, in the latter end of that war left the interest
of France and sided with the allies. Old Lewis was enraged at him: he sent
his armies this way, who took almost everything from the Duke, besieged
this city which was his capital, and reduced it to the last extremity.[3] When
they were just at their last gasp, Prince Eugene came with an army to their
relief, joined the Duke's forces, and obtained a complete victory over the
enemy.[4] The French retired, and when Prince Eugene came into the city,

227

the powder they shot off in the cannons to welcome him was the last powder they had. The enemies had used the town without mercy; their bombs and cannonadings had destroyed the greatest part of it. This was rebuilt: and as they had so much to new-build together, the streets are laid out as regularly as a line, all the openings answer one another, and the houses are generally pretty uniform and near of the same height.[5]

In walking through most parts of the town, you see vistas quite through it several ways to the ramparts, which are green and with rows of trees upon them. On your side of the town is the plain and a long half moon of high rough mountains.[6] On the other side of the town is a long line of unequal pretty hills, covered here and there with little woods and besprinkled with white houses. When one walks on the ramparts, this has a very particular effect: when you are walking south-east you have a fine summer view before you, and when you turn to go north-west you see the vast line of Alps, all covered with snow, and in the very depth of the winter.

The southern hills have a hundred delightful walks in them. At their bottom runs the Po, which derives its source from the winter side and begins from a mountain called Il Viso, which rises like a sugar-loaf, with its sharp point (often) above the clouds, higher than any of them and very visible on a clear day, though forty or fifty mile from this place. The walks in the plain between these ranges of winter and summer hills would be naturally very pretty, and are made prettier by the number of rows of mulberry and other trees planted by the roadsides and carried on often in double walks, quite from the town, to several of the King's country houses.

If the weather threatens to be bad, the Academy in which we live joins the King's gardens, which we have backdoors that open into, like some of the houses in St. James's Park. If it actually rains or snows, we have just before our great gate a street of half a mile long, with porticos the whole length on each side from the King's palace to the gate that leads to the Po.[7] ⟨After all this, had not I reason to say that I never was in a place so well furnished with walks? And as I have now just chatted through all my paper, I have as much reason to be this moment

Your most humble servant

J. Spence⟩

1. De Brosses, who visited Turin at this time, calls it 'la plus jolie ville de l'Italie; et à ce que je crois, de l'Europe, par l'alignement de ses rues, la régularité de ses bâtiments' (II, 574–5). See also *Letter* 21.

2. The war of the Spanish succession (1701–14). The Duke of Savoy then was Victor Amadeus II.

3. For further details of the siege, see *Nbk.* 3 74[r]–79[r].

4. François - Eugène de Savoie - Carignan (1663–1736) joined the Austrian army when his mother was exiled by Louis XIV. The breaking of the siege of Turin in 1706 was one of his most brilliant exploits.

5. 'They have long had a scheme of making them all so, which will yet cost the people, encouraged somewhat by the King, above a million sterling before 'tis completed. They are carrying on this scheme briskly at present in the Street della Dora Grossa, and anyone who builds in any of the irregular streets is obliged to build by the line that is to be' (*Nbk.* 3 75ʳ).

6. 'The Alpes Maritimae to Monviso, then the Graiae to Mt. Cenis or the opening at the Val de Suse, then the Cottiae to the little St. Bernard, and after that a run of mountains (the Penninae to Mt. Simplon and the Lago Maggiore, then the Rhaeticae to Verona, then the Juliae to Venice) more and more indistinct as far as the eye can carry you' (ibid., 79ᵛ).

7. 'They call the Strada del Po their best street, but the Strada Novella looks better. 'Tis of a great length, falls in with two great places and terminates one way in the Porta Nuova and the other in the King's Palace; so that when you stand in the middle you see into the King's gardens and out of town' (ibid., 1 30ʳ).

80

Source: Add. MSS 33065 ff. 342–3
Endorsed: Novʳ 14

LINCOLN TO NEWCASTLE

Turin,
November 25 ⟨14⟩, 1739

I don't know what expressions of thankfulness to make to my dear Uncle, for his very affectionate letter,[1] . . . but you will excuse me in taking the liberty of telling you that you have been guilty of the very same—I won't say greater—fault which you accused Mr. Spence of, that is in not being particular in regard to health, whereas . . . [we] read in the papers that you had been so ill as to keep house.—As I think by this time I can pretty well guess how I like an academical life, I will keep my promise I made to your Grace in my last and give you an account how I pass my time here.

As for Turin itself, I think it is the prettiest town I ever saw, both as to situation and the excessive beauty and regularity of the streets, and what is a great addition to it is the number of delightful walks that surround it on all sides. The view we have from the ramparts is the prettiest and the most extraordinary I ever saw in my life, for on one side you see the Alps, rugged and all covered with snow, and on the other the most beautiful hills sprinkled with little country seats, vineyards, fine clumps of wood, and the Po running at the bottom of them.

As for the Academy, it is a tolerable good building. I can't say that our apartments are very grand, for they consist only in one room, an alcove where my bed stands, and a little closet within that, and Mr. Spence has the very same close by me. But the other advantages we receive here make ample amends for our not being so well lodged as one could desire. All the masters are extremely good and take a great deal of pains. We begin riding at 8 o'clock in the morning, dance at 10, fence at 11, all dine together at half an hour after 12, the governor and sub-governor with us, who are both men of quality and have been particularly obliging to me, and I can assure your Grace I shall take care and behave in such a manner as to preserve the good opinion they at present have of me. My Italian master comes in the afternoon, who I take a great deal of pains with and don't despair in a little while of writing to her Grace[2] in Italian.

As taking my exercises only would not answer the end your Grace sent me abroad for, Mr. Villettes[3] has been so good as to introduce [me] to all the assemblies which we have here every night and all the best company at Turin, and indeed I have received great civilities both from the gentlemen and ladies, and am very much obliged to Monsieur Osorio[4] for his goodness in recommending me in so obliging a manner to most of the considerable men here. The King[5] in particular has been extremely civil to me: I had the honour last week of dining and hunting with his Majesty; we had a chase of five hours and a half, and I gained much honour in stopping the hounds as they were running the wrong deer . . . [I am] your Grace's most affectionate and dutiful nephew

Lincoln

P.S.
I have just had a letter from Read,[6] whom your Grace has often heard me mention under the name of Bug, who designs at the next election which is in January to offer himself as a candidate for a fellowship of Queens'. He desires me to use my interest with your Grace for a recommendatory letter to Dr. Sedgwick.[7] If this is an improper request I beg pardon

—quodsi

Depositum laudas ob amici jussa pudorem
Scribe tui gregis hunc, et fortem crede bonumque.[8]

---

1. Not preserved.
2. The Duchess of Newcastle (see *Letter 77*).
3. See *Letter 77*.
4. The Chevalier d'Osorio Alarcon (ca. 1697–1763), Sardinian minister at London, 1730–43.
5. Charles Emmanuel III (1701–73).
6. Probably Henry Read (b. 1716) of Shilling Okeford, Dorset. He had been with Lincoln at

Eton 1729–35 and Cambridge 1736–9. B.A. 1740, M.A. 1743 at Queens' College, Fellow 1744–55.
7. The D. of Newcastle was High Steward of the University of Cambridge 1737–48. William Sedgwick was President of Queens' College 1731–60.
8. Horace *Epist.* I. ix. 12.

*81

Source: Extra-illustrated copy of *Anecdotes*, ed. Singer, 1820, Huntington Library (RB 131213). Printed by Singer, pp. 397–400

Numbered: (6)

Turin,
December 2, 1739

⟨Dear Mother,⟩

Soon after I came to this place, as I was walking one evening under the porticos of the Street of the Po, I saw an inscription over a great gate, which, as I am a very curious traveller, you may be sure I did not miss reading. I found by it that the house belonged to a set of strollers and that the inscription was a bill of the play they were to act that evening. You may imagine how surprised I was to find it conceived in the following words: 'Here under the porticos of the charitable hospital for such as have the venereal disease, will be represented this evening *The Damned Soul*: with proper decorations.'[1] As this seemed to be one of the greatest curiosities I could possibly meet with in my travels, I immediately paid my threepence, was shewed in with great civility, and took my seat among a number of people who seemed to expect the tragedy of the night with great seriousness.

At length the curtain drew up and discovered the damned soul, all alone, with a melancholy aspect. She was (for what reason I don't know) drest like a fine lady, in a gown of flame-coloured satin. She held a white handkerchief in her hand, which she applied often to her eyes, and in this attitude, with a lamentable voice, began a prayer (to the holy and ever blessed Trinity) to enable her to speak her part well: afterwards she addressed herself to all the good Christians in the room, begged them to attend carefully to what she had to say, and heartily wished they would be the better for it. She then gave an account of her life, and, by her own confession, appeared to have been a very naughty ⌈jade⌉[2] in her time.

This was the first scene. At the second a back-curtain was drawn, and and gave us a sight of our Saviour and the Blessed Virgin—amidst the clouds. The poor soul addressed herself to our Saviour first, who rattled her extremely, and was indeed all the while very severe. All she desired was to be sent to purgatory instead of going to hell, and she at last begged very hard to be sent into the fire of the former for as many years as there are drops of water in the sea. As no favour was shown her on that side, she turned to the Virgin and begged her to intercede for her. The Virgin was a very decent woman, and answered her gravely but steadily 'that she had angered her Son so much that she could do nothing for her', and on this they both went away together.

The third scene consisted of three little angels and the damned soul. She had no better luck with them, nor with St. John the Baptist and all the saints in the fourth: so in the fifth she was left to two devils, seemingly to do what they would with her. One of these devils was very ill-natured and fierce to her, the other was of the droll kind, and for a devil I can't say but what he was good-natured enough, though he delighted in vexing the poor lady rather too much.

In the sixth scene matters began to mend a little. St. John the Baptist (who had been with our Saviour I believe behind the scenes) told her if she would continue her entreaties, there was yet some hopes for her.[3] She on this again besought our Saviour and the Virgin to have compassion on her: the Virgin was melted with her tears and desired her Son to have pity on her; on which it was granted that she should go into the fire only for sixteen or seventeen hundred thousand years—and she was very thankful for the mildness of the sentence.

The seventh (and last) scene was a contest between the two infernal devils above-mentioned and her guardian angel. They came in again, one grinning and the other open-mouthed to devour her. The angel told them ⟨that they had taken the wrong sow by the ear, that she was no meat for them, and⟩ that they should get about their business. He, with some difficulty, at last drove them off the stage and handed off the good lady, in assuring her that all would be very well after some hundreds of thousands of years with her.

All this while, in spite of the excellence of the actors, the greatest part of the entertainment to me was the countenances of the people in the pit and boxes. When the devils were like to carry her off, everybody was in the utmost consternation, and when St. John spoke so obligingly to her, they were ready to cry out for joy. When the Virgin appeared on the stage, everybody looked respectful, and on several words spoke by the actors they pulled off their hats and crossed themselves. What can you think of a people where their very farces are religious and where they are so religiously received?[4] May you be the better for reading of it, as I was for seeing it!

There was but one thing that offended me. All the actors, except the devils, were women, and the person who represented the most venerable character in the whole play, just after the representation, came into the pit and fell a kissing a barber of her acquaintance before she had changed her dress. She did me the honour to speak to me too, but I would have nothing to say to her.

It was from such a play as this (called Adam and Eve) that Milton, when he was in Italy, is said to have taken the first hint for his divine poem of *Paradise Lost*.[5] What small beginnings are there sometimes to the greatest things! ⟨I am ever (with all services to all friends)

Your dutiful and affectionate

J. Spence⟩

1. The original of this *sacra rappresentazione*, with Spence's marginal annotations, is preserved in the British Museum (1070. b. 27): *Opera nuova del pianto, Che fa la misera Anima dannata, da Dio condannata all' Inferno per i suoi mali portamenti—In Ottava Rima.—Composta da un divoto Servo di Dio, e di nuovo aggiuntovi un nobilissimo contrasto, che fu l'Angiolo, ed il Demonio.—In Torino. Per Gio. Battista Fontana, Con licenza de' Superiori*. On the back of the cover Spence jotted down the terms in which the performance was advertised: 'Si fa la Representazione [*sic*] del Anima Dannata, sotto i Portici del Ven: Spedale della Carità.'

2. Emended to 'woman'. In the printed text (pp. 2–4) the following allegorical characters express her naughtiness: Superbia, Avarizia, Lussuria, Ira, Gola, Invidia, and Accidia.

3. Here the printed text differs from Spence's account and annotations, for 'I Santi' utterly condemn the Soul: 'Vattene, e va all' Inferno scelerata/A stare in quel luogo condannata'. After this the Soul is '*tirata all' Inferno . . . I Demonij* gettano l'Anima nel fuoco, e spariscono'. The remaining pages (pp. 9–12) show the Soul denouncing the world.

4. Gray and Horace Walpole saw it during their stay at Turin (Nov. 7–18). Walpole called the play 'a sort of an heroic tragedy' (*Corresp*. XIII, 191), Gray 'an execrable Italian Comedy, and a Puppet-Show' (*Corresp*. I, 127).

5. Voltaire in his *Essai sur la poésie épique* (1727) first pointed out the connection between Milton's poem and Andreini's *Adamo* (publ. 1613), suggesting that Milton had seen a performance of *Adamo* during his visit to Italy in 1638–9.

---

*82

Source:	Egerton 2234 ff. 141–2
Addressed:	*as in 74*
Postmarked.	[ ] 6 DE.
Franked:	Free/Andrew Stone
Numbered:	(7.)
Endorsed:	*a.* a descripshon/of yᵉ fine bilding where they Lodg/& yᵉ warlike temper there top qua-/litey are bread up in &c.
	b. Accᵗ of yᵉ Academy; and Characters of yᵉ Governʳˢ.
	red wafer

Turin,

December 16 ⟨5⟩, 1739

⟨P.S. I heartily wish you a merry Christmas and the like to all friends —and a happy New Year.⟩

⟨Dear Mother,⟩

As my last letter was on domestic affairs,[1] I don't see why this should not be on foreign. I intend to give you an account in it of the place we are lodged in, and of the various company in it that sit down to dinner every day very comfortably together, though we are collected together from all the different parts of Europe, and belong some of us to houses perhaps five or six thousand miles apart.

The temper of this nation at present seems to be warlike:[2] they have a military air, and there's scarce a gentleman in the country that does not know how to manage his arms and ride a war-horse. The situation of Piedmont (on the frontiers of Italy, and between the chief contending powers) makes this necessary, and the King does everything in his power to encourage this humour in them. Among other things he has built a large square palace[3] (which is joined by a long gallery to the royal palace at Turin) where there are schools for fencing, etc., a long room to learn to ride in,[4] and large stables full of very fine managed horses. Two sides of the square are built with handsome large porticos before them, portico above portico, for three story high. The second and third story consists of apartments for the young noblemen of the country, or any strangers that come here: and 'tis in the second that your son Joseph, being a very military man, is at present lodged. The portico on our side is 220 foot long, for I am just come in from pacing it. A third side of the square is the King's library and the archives where the writings of state are kept,[5] and the fourth is a theatre (not yet finished, but covered in) for operas, which are the reigning diversion all over Italy.[6]

Each apartment in our row opposite to the theatre (which is the best) consists of three rooms deep: to the portico, a room to receive company; within that, the bedchamber; and last of all, a study. My great door opens to the north, and my study windows look to the south; on the left into the King's gardens, and on the right to the fine line of hills sprinkled with gentlemen's houses that I have mentioned to you in a former letter. Lord Lincoln's rooms run along with mine, and we have a communication door from his great room into mine, so that we are, as you may imagine, very good neighbours.

In this palace (which is considerably better than my house at Birchanger) we live very agreeably. There are two or three hundred in it, but I shall give you an account only of those who are of our table: for we dine in a parlour by ourselves and are entirely separated in all things from the rest.

First then there is the chief governor, who is an earl of this country: very good-natured and obliging, but awkward in his person and ungraceful (at least) in his speech. He is too apt to make minced meat of his language, and has a great talent at breaking a sentence in two. But he has a good heart, and is a very worthy man.

Next to him is a knight, an old soldier, rough and honest. He is like old port wine, which is the better, you know, for being a little rough.

The third is a great acquaintance of mine, and has been so good as to accompany me in several of my walks. He is the great favourite of the English, and ought to be so, for he is as like the best pictures of King William, as two of the best pictures of that King are like one another. He is an officer, too, a very gentlemanlike man, and extremely obliging. It does one's heart good to see him. ⟨The continuation of this, in my next. I am with all services

Your dutiful and affectionate

J. Spence.⟩

1. Missing. As Spence was writing home every Wednesday (see *Letter* 84), it was probably dated Dec. 9.

2. See further on this *Nbk.* 3 74ʳ–79ʳ and *Obs.* Nos. 1588, 1598–1602.

3. The Military Academy (*Letter* 78 n. 1) where Spence and Lincoln resided.

4. 'Le *Manège* ... bâti par le Roi Charles Emmanuel III sur les desseins de *Juvarra*. ... C'est un grand emplacement sablé, et couvert

d'une voûte, qui a une portée extraordinaire' (Paroletti, p. 241).

5. Spence no doubt met Dom Villa, the royal archivist, there. He supplied Spence with much information on Turin.

6. The Teatro Regio, once counted among the finest in Italy, was being reconstructed after a fire (Paroletti, pp. 261–3). Opera performances started in January.

---

*83

Source:	Egerton 2234 ff. 143–4
Addressed:	*as in* 74
Postmarked:	27 DE
Franked:	Free/Andrew Stone
Numbered:	(8.)
Endorsed:	*a.* an accᵗ. of/yᵉ companey in his apartment *b.* Characters of the/Young Nobility at yᵉ Acad:/Chopski & Narsinski/& their Governor; [ ]/words./Lanskaronski. *red wafer*

Turin,

December 23 ⟨12⟩, 1739

⟨Dear Mother,

I gave you an account in my last of the place we live in, and of the governors of this ark of Noah, into which they have collected beasts from all quarters of the world. I am now to tell you who are the good company in it that dine in the cabin that I belong to.⟩

Next me (to use Cardinal Wolsey's style)[1] is seated my good Lord Lincoln, and then a wild Irishman. The next in the circle is a young, plump, rosy-cheeked marquis: his title is Marquis of Leghorn. You know I have a great knack in finding out the likeness of some beast in the features sometimes of a very honest man.[2] One day I happened to whisper that this marquis was like a sucking-pig, and I believe he will carry that name to his grave. He is attended by a sensible-looking, well-behaved Roman abbé.

Then sits a thin-jawed, black marquis from Sardinia; they call him 'the Sarde' which, as it is a very common name for a horse here, and as his features have a very near resemblance to that animal, we always talk of him together under that character. If he comes brisk into a room 'tis 'See how the marquis prances!' and if he sneezes, we say he neighs. By the help of a bad countenance, he has passed himself so absolutely upon me for a horse, that I don't care to slide between him and the wall at any time for fear he should kick up behind—though the creature is very gentle and good natured, especially over his provender.

The next is a gentleman from Poland,[3] whose house is on the farthest borders of that country, within a dozen mile of the Turks. He's of a square make and meek disposition, extremely devout and very obliging; untalkative, tolerably read, and a great dealer in reliques. His governor comes from Prussia,[4] and if eating and drinking were acts of religion, would be more religious than his master. He has a tongue that runs very glib, after meals; but all dinner time the man has something else to do than to talk. 'Twould do you good to see how feelingly he eyes a fat capon, and with what perseverance he continues drawing at a bumper. He has a most lasting breath, and after dinner his belly, what with eating and what with drinking, is as hard as a rock. It rounds out in a semicircle before him, and would look stately, were he not of so short and squat figure; somewhat (if I may use such a simile to an ancient lady) resembling that most necessary utensil, commonly called a chamberpot.

Within a yard and a half of his chair (for the juttings out of his make won't let anybody come nearer to it) sits a modest simpering doctor of the university here, and after him a jolly, laughable, gentlemanlike earl of this country. Did you ever read Bishop Burnet's *Travels*? He says when he was in Switzerland, the chief man in that country was one Mr. d'Erlack, and he gives him a very fine character.[5] The present heir of this family is the next man at our table.[6] A young gentleman of about seventeen, a sensible, genteel, pretty person, and extremely well behaved; he is a captain in this King's service, though he has so much sweetness in [his] look and temper, and does his exercises as well [as any]body in the Academy.

Then follows a perfect German earl that talks so fast, and stares so about him, and is so full of tittering and uncertainty in his carriage, that one would think he had not been in the world above two or three hours; and indeed, to say the truth, he is but just come from college. His governor is a tall raw-boned man from Bohemia: with a green coat as old at least as himself (for he is not above sixty-seven years old), and a hat that may possibly have been a twin-brother of his coat, and born with it somewhere about the plague year or the fire of London. He and the horse from Sardinia seem to have the most humour of any of the company. As to an account of myself, I shall leave that to some more able historian to give it you, and am (with all services)

Your dutiful and affectionate

J. Spence.

1. Cf. Wolsey's address to his train in 1521, on landing at Calais as English Ambassador to France: 'I assume and take upon mee to bee esteemed in all honour and degrees of service as unto his highnes is meet and due, and that by mee nothing bee neglected that to his State is due and appertinent' (George Cavendish, *The Negotiations of Thomas Woolsey* ..., 1641, p. 39).

2. Among the Spence Papers is a select list: 'Bob Lowth, a guinea-pig—Mrs. Gauntlet, a hornet—Miss Pew, a goose ... Waller, a swine ... Mouse Rolle ... Lady Townshend, skinned cormorant—Whiting, Dr. Codfish,' etc.

3. His name appears as 'Lanskaronski' on the address page. Spence jotted down one of his sayings: 'Czas plynie jak woda na mlynie' (*Obs.* No. 1606). In 1750 Lowth wrote to Spence from Italy: 'Mr. Landskarounski is now in the Saxon service; I think he made a campaign or two in the beginning of the war in that of the King of Sardinia' (*App.* 14.)

4. Probably a different man from the governor of two other Polish gentlemen, Chopski and Narsinski, whose names Spence jotted down on the address page.

5. Sigmund Erlach (1614–99), 'a very extraordinary Man; he has a great authority in his *Canton*, not only as he is *Advoyer*, but by the particular esteem which is payed him. For he is thought the wisest and worthiest Man of the *State*. ... He is a Man of great Sobriety and Gravity, very reserved, and behaves himself like a *Minister of State* in a *Monarchy*, than a *Magistrate* in a *Popular Government*' (*Some Letters, containing an Account of ... Switzerland, Italy, Some Parts of Germany, &c. in the Years 1685 and 1686*, 1689 edn., pp. 25–9).

6. Louis-Auguste Erlach (d. 1748), Baron Erlach, Capt. in the Swiss Guard at Paris in 1742 (*Dict. hist. et biogr. de la Suisse* [1926], III, 6). In 1750 Lowth reported to Spence: 'Mr. D'Erlach died somewhere in Lombardy, six or seven years ago, of the smallpox' (*App.* 14).

84

Source:	Egerton 2234 ff. 145–6
Addressed:	[*in A. Stone's hand:*] Mrs Spence [*postscript:*] This Letter was receiv'd from Mr Spence at/ Turin, without any Direction: But It is/ concluded, It is to Mrs Spence at Winchester.
Numbered:	(9.)
Endorsed:	*a.* home affaiers *b.* Of the loss of the/2 Master Pelhams./not to be Copied. *red wafer*

Turin,
December 30, 1739

⟨Dear Mother,

This is the fifth Wednesday that I have sent a letter constantly for Winchester, and now I am got into the way of it, I hope to keep on the same custom all the time we stay at Turin. When we are moving, I can't promise for being so exact a correspondent: once a fortnight will be very fair then, and next winter, when we are to be settled at Rome, I may take to writing my weekly papers to you again.

I take all this immense trouble, to wheedle as many letters as I can out of you, for say what you please, they are very well wrote: and 'tis not the first time that I have said behind your back that you have a particular good manner of writing letters, and I'll say it again though the Pope and all the seventy-two cardinals were in the room. When I read your letters, I always think I am talking with you: and do you think that a small pleasure to a son who loves his mother as I do you? There's one thing that would always supply you with something to say, and that is if you would but consider 'that anything that happens to any one English person is worth sending to an Englishman on this side of the Alps'. As for instance: Miss Liss had a new pair of stockings last week. Why, I should be glad to hear at this distance whether they are blue or red. Mrs. Pescod has had another daughter, and she was christened by Mr. Ferne, and they were very merry at the christening, and Mrs. Betty Brewer drank two quarts of mulled white wine at it.[1] The school just by us flourishes again pretty well, and young Bale is to get to New College,[2] which I am very glad of, and hope you will be a good friend to him when you come back to England again, and help him on in his learning, which is the best thing in the world for a young man. Every word of this, or of things like this, would be welcome to me here, and if you have news but for half a letter, you may fill up the other half (as you do a travelling trunk when you have not clothes enough for it) with stay and waste paper.

We had last post a very ill piece of news from England which troubled Lord Lincoln extremely, and me too though a stranger (in a manner) to the family. The Duchess of Newcastle has had no children:[3] the Duke has but one brother,[4] and he had a little family, which were the hopes of both. He had two sons: the eldest about twelve. Five or six weeks ago they were both taken ill and died within a day of one another.[5] The whole family, as you may imagine, are inconsolable. The only hopes are that Lady Catherine Pelham may yet have another son (for she lay in a few months ago of a daughter), otherwise the estate I think goes into the hands of a stranger.[6] The two that are lost were cousins-german of Lord Lincoln. This is the only news we have had [since] the Lord knows when, and it brought a great deal of grief with it. I hope to have more comfortable always from you, and am with all services to all friends, ever

Your dutiful and affectionate

J. Spence.⟩

1. 'Mrs. Pescod' was probably wife of William Pescod of St. Michael, Winchester; Fellow of New College 1721–8, barrister, Steward to the College and Chapter, and Recorder of Winchester (Kirby, p. 224). Both she and her husband subscribed to Spence's *Polymetis*. 'Mr. Ferne' has not been identified. 'Mrs. Betty Brewer' was perhaps wife or relation of Nathaniel Brewer of Trowbridge, Winchester scholar 1682–6 (Kirby, p. 205).

2. Joseph Challoner Bale (see *Letter* 65). He did not get to New College, but matriculated at Balliol Oct. 12, 1742. In 1747, however, he received B.A. at New College.

3. See *Letter* 77.

4. Henry Pelham, Lincoln's uncle. See *Letter* 77.

5. The two sons Thomas (b. 1729) and Henry (b. 1736) died Nov. 27 and 28 'of soar Throats' (*Gent. Mag.*, 1739, p. 606).

6. It was saved by Lord Lincoln's prudent marriage in 1744 with his cousin Catherine, eldest daughter of Henry Pelham. 'On 17 Nov. 1768 he succeeded, as 2d D. of Newcastle-under-Lyne under a special Patent, dated 13 Nov. 1756, by which Thomas Pelham, D. of Newcastle-on-Tyne, was created D. of Newcastle-under-Lyne, with remainder to his nephew, the E. of Lincoln, when he resigned the prime-ministership' (*DNB*).

---

*85

Source:	Egerton 2234 ff. 147–8
Addressed:	*as in 74*
Postmarked:	10 [ ]
Franked:	Free/Andrew Stone
Numbered:	(10.)
Endorsed:	*a.* an acc^t of/there 'treros' wch are like our/ shaises but a great deal pretier
	b. Acc^t of y^e (Kg^s) Traineaux.
	red wafer

Turin,
January 5, 1740

⟨Dear Mother,

I shall write soon to Mr. Aldworth again,[1] who is within a hundred mile of us, diverting himself at Geneva, and all the English that are there, for he is said to be one of the merriest devils in the world, and everbody I meet with that has seen him is delighted with him.[2] 'Tis not impossible, I hope, but we may meet him somewhere in our tour; and if we do, the first time I see him I'll engage him to come and see you on his return in Queen's Street.⟩

I have hitherto diverted myself with laying in things for my book which 'when 'tis in print, will be well worth your reading'.[3] At present we begin to think of other diversions, for the carnival came in some days ago and lasts till the second of March. The court was expected in town last Saturday, but as the smallpox is much here, we are disappointed: and so I have not seen any of the royal family as yet, and don't know when I shall.[4] However, the opera began with the carnival, and I am such a lover of music that I have missed but one night yet, and that was I believe to write my last letter to you.[5]

This morning (your Christmas Day) is the first snow that I have seen fall here, though I have seen a ridge of mountains of twenty mile long, all covered with snow, twice or thrice a day for these eight weeks. I was very glad of its coming hither at last, for this is a mighty place for going out in a sort of sledges which they call 'trainoes'[6] here; and in two or three days (perhaps) we may have the street of the Po full of them, from one end to another. I have been already to see the King's trainoes, which are very fine things, and must make a very good show when in motion. They are low, and more like boats than chaises. They rise pointed behind and have a seat there for one, behind which comes out a little board to stand on, not a foot above the ground. A lady sits in each, her cavalier stands behind her and holds the reins, though the horse is before, and generally guided by a running footman. The trainoe rises broader before, and is generally formed in the figure of some bird or beast. Among the King's I saw a tiger, a swan, a lion, and an ostrich. When you see the trainoe in front, you see the swan's breast, neck, and head: its wings go off sloping down and make the sides of the boat, and the other part does not appear to you. So that if it was flying toward you upon the snow, it would look like a swan scudding along a clear stream. The other beasts and birds are adapted to the shape of the trainoe as well as they can, in the same manner: one like a bear coming down the snowy hills of Greenland, and another perhaps like a sea-horse striking away the white waves with his finny feet. These are all covered with quilting or painting, representing the proper colours of the several animals. They have a flag floating in the air before them, and the horses are set off with the finest harness and rubans of different colours, and are almost all over hung with little silver bells, which they delight in much, and which makes them curvet and toss their heads often: the first trainoes are full of trumpeters and kettledrums etc., and all together, it must be charming. I long to see them on their march—or rather their flight, and am

⟨Your obedient and affectionate

J. Spence.⟩

1. Richard Neville Aldworth (1717–93), matric. Merton Coll., Oxford, 1736, but left for the continent without taking a degree; between 1739 and 1744 passed every winter at Geneva. M.P. for Reading 1747–54, Undersecretary of State 1748.

2. In 1740–2 Aldworth with John Hervey, the E. of Bristol, William Wyndham, and Benjamin Stillingfleet founded a semi-literary circle at Geneva, whose members performed theatricals. 'Our success in this attempt', he writes, 'was enormous. Our countrymen flocked from all parts to see us, and flattered us by declaring that we excelled the London actors' (W. Coxe, *Literary Life . . . of Benjamin Stillingfleet* [1811], I, 75–80).

3. *Polymetis*. Gray had seen part of 'Mr. Spence's pretty Book' 'in Manuscript' at Turin or Florence (*Corresp*. I, 265, 268).

4. During Gray's and Walpole's visit (Nov. 7–18) the royal family were 'at a country palace, called La Venerie' (Gray, *Corresp*. I, 128). They returned between January 20 and 27.

5. 'L'Opéra de Turin a très bonne réputation; on dit qu'il est toujours fort bien composé' (De Brosses, II, 584).

6. 'Le français et l'italien sont presque en usage ici également' (ibid., 578).

*86

Source: Egerton 2234 ff. 149–50
Addressed: as in 74
Numbered: (11.)
Endorsed: a. home affairs/yᵉ first side:
             b. Hopes of seeing Traineaux/soon; &c.
             Chit-chat.

Turin,
January 13 ⟨2⟩, 1740
⟨P.S. I have received three of your letters
regularly in less than these three weeks,
and am extremely obliged to you for them.⟩

⟨Dear Mother,

Who was it that was saying Mr. Rolle had forgot his good mother at
Winchester? I never thought that he could, and I find by your last that he
has not. As to what he mentions in it, I would not have you be in the least
scrupulous on any occasion to do what he says. He's an honest man, and
much in the right in most things he says, and in this entirely of my mind.
You have enough perhaps without it, but I would have you be quite at
your ease, and to live without any solicitude as to that affair. 'Tis not
enough just to bring the year about and make both ends meet together. I
would have you bring it about comfortably and pleasurably, and not to be
in a moment's concern about double taxes, when you can supply them so
easily from elsewhere. What signifies whether 'tis from the first or the
second heap, if you are as welcome to the second as the first?⟩

I sent you in my last a long account of the trainoes here; I am in great
hopes to see them in motion soon, for the snow has been two inches deep on
the ground ever since I wrote last. It has been inclined to snow every day
since, and it has snowed all this morning very well, so that there will be
enough for those carriages to fly upon, I hope very soon. The King and
court are expected here this day, and so in a few days I may be enabled to
give you an account of this odd sort of cavalcade, which as yet I have never
seen in my life.

You need be in no pain for me for companions in my walks, for I have I
think infected all the Academy: they all begin to find that 'tis better to
stir than to get half asleep, and more than half cold, by the fireside. We
were no less than four on my walk yesterday after dinner: Mr. d'Erlack, the
Polish gentleman, a very honest priest here (that I am teaching to read
English),[1] and myself. ⟨My walking friends will rather increase here, and

241

when we leave this place we shall be three or four months taken up in shifting from one city of Italy to another, when travelling does instead of walking. After that we shall be five or six months at Rome, where I can't fail of finding companions for as many walks as I please; and after that, we shall be setting out for England, where I hope to walk every day with you about St. James's or Hyde Park in the winter, and about my Birchanger garden in the summer.⟩

You think very rightly that Rome is a finer place than Turin: Rome is beyond comparison more noble, and Turin is more pretty. The walks are much more charming here than there, especially among the southern hills, which I am got acquainted with for two or three mile each way, and with most of the white villas and the little groves about them, for they are groves and gardens, and not woods and forests as you have in Hampshire. With all these delights about me, I long much more to be at Rome. That's the great storehouse of pictures, statues, noble buildings and the noblest remains of antiquity. The statues there in particular are at present my great delight, as they are my present subject, and when I come back to you, you will scarce ever see me sitting, standing, or walking, but I shall be in the posture of some one or other of my marble friends at Rome. I should be an excellent neighbour to the good people at Hyde Park Corner,[2] who might copy from me the attitudes and airs of most of the celebrated figures in this country: and I believe I shall hire myself out, and get a little money by it on my return. In the meantime, I am

⟨Your dutiful and affectionate

J. Spence.⟩

1. Probably Dom Villa, archivist at the Royal Academy, 'a very worthy, sensible, and agreeable man', who supplied Spence with a few anecdotes (*Obs.* Nos. 1586–91). For 'Mr. d'Erlack' and 'the Polish gentleman', see *Letter* 83.

2. Hyde Park Corner was a headquarters for statuaries. 'The Bushnells, the great contractors for the statues and carvings ... had their establishment here. ... Thomson's Countess of Hertford in 1740 speaks of the statues at their country seat as "Hyde Park Statues"' (Wheatley and Cunningham, *London Past and Present* [1891], II, 255).

*87

Source:	Egerton 2234 ff. 151–2
Addressed:	*as in 74*
Numbered:	(12.)
Endorsed:	*a.* Lord/Sandwich. his travilling to/ constantinople, from naples/then to ye Holey Land, egypt,/troye Greece & then/back to Leghorn, & turin
	b. L Sandwich exp^d. Genl Acc^t of ye Tour he made.

Turin,
January 20, 1740

⟨Dear Mother,⟩

We have still snow, and snow enough on the ground for the trainoes, and yet I am afraid we shall miss the sight of them. The King has not had the smallpox (I wish to heaven he had been inoculated ten years ago!),[1] and as that distemper has been much about the town, and is not yet quite gone, the physicians advise him against making any public course of trainoes, as they call it here, for that would call all persons into the street or to their windows, and so might endanger his royal person. 'Tis not the first time I have wished most physicians where they will almost all go sooner or later. I have seen a single trainoe here and there, but for a general cavalcade (which is the fine show) I believe there is now no hopes of it: and so I must be content, till I take a journey into Lapland or Nova Zembla.

We have a great number of English here for the place and for the season, who are all as much disappointed as myself.[2] Here's a son of Lord Gage's[3] and a brother of Lord Darnly's[4] and eight or ten more, and we expect Lord Sandwich every day. Lord Sandwich[5] is one that I had an offer of travelling with, but as I was not in a travelling humour I excused myself as civilly as I could.[6] 'Twas well I did, for if I had went with him, what frights from time to time must you have been in? I don't mean anything rude against his Lordship, for he is a very agreeable, sensible, worthy man. But the spirit of travelling grew so strong upon him that he was not contented with Italy, and when at Naples (which you know is the end of my travels) he hired a ship and went with my old friend Mr. Frulick, who is his governor,[7] to Constantinople. He returned thence to Italy, but his eagerness of seeing distant realms would not let him rest there. He hired another ship, went to the Holy Land, travelled all over that and Egypt, where they were when the war broke out between us and Spain.[8] By good luck at Alexandria they met with an English man-o'-war, with which they set out for Italy, and arrived safe off Leghorn the 23rd of last month.[9] As they come from the East, which is generally infested with the plague, they are obliged to perform quarantine in an island near Leghorn, and as soon as that is over they are to set out for this place, to stay here some time. Their company must be agreeable enough to us that have never, and probably never shall, see the places they have been at, for besides what I have mentioned, they have been at Troy and all over Greece.

I send you no account of the court yet, but stay till I have seen a little more of it. I was there last Sunday morning for the first time. It seems to answer its character of being one of the politest courts in Europe ⟨and you know I am a good judge. With all services to all friends, I am ever

Your dutiful and affectionate

J. Spence.⟩

1. The practice of inoculation against small-pox was fairly recent (see Voltaire's *Lettres philosophiques* ix, and R. Halsband, 'New Light on Lady Mary Wortley Montagu's Contribution to Inoculation', *Journ. of the Hist. of Med.* [1953], VIII, 390–405).

2. See *Appendix* I for Spence's list of the English he met at Turin.

3. William Hall Gage (1718–91), the eldest son of 1st Visc. Gage; educ. at Westminster 1728–35; member of the Soc. of Dilettanti 1740/1; Equerry to Pr. of Wales 1742–57; Paymaster of the Pensions 1755–63; F.R.S.; suc. as 2d Visc. 1754.

4. John Bligh (1719–81), E. of Darnley 1747; M.P. for Athboy 1739–47, Maidstone 1741–7; one of Pulteney's opposition Whigs; member of Soc. of Dilettanti 1742. His elder brother Edward (1715–47), F.R.S., was Grand-Master of Freemasons 1737–8.

5. John Montagu (1718–92), 4th E. of Sandwich; educ. at Eton 1728–32, admitted as a nobleman at Cambridge (Trin. Coll.) Apr. 12, 1735, but did not graduate; F.R.S.; member of the Soc. of Dilettanti 1740. First Lord of the Admiralty 1749–51.

6. The offer was probably made in the spring of 1738, after Spence's unexpectedly early return from the second tour.

7. Apparently James John Frölich. He is listed as 'Mr. Frolik' among the freemasons at Florence whom Dr. Cocchi met Aug. 4, 1732 (Cocchi's manuscript *Effemeridi* under that date, Library of the Medical Faculty at Carregi, Florence). In the collection of epitaphs among the Spence Papers there is one 'On Mr. Frölich' by Lord Middlesex:

> *Here lies James John Frölich:*
> *Pray God he don't snoar*
> *As dead as a Drum*
> *Or a Nail in a door:*
> *He long strugled with Hip,*
> *& made a damn'd rout;*
> *But Hip got the better,*
> *& made him Hop out.*

8. Oct. 23, 1739 O.S.

9. Spence is probably wrong. *The London Gazette* for July 31–Aug. 4, 1739, reported that the E. of Sandwich, sailing with Lord Pomfret aboard *H.M.S. Dolphin* from Genoa, arrived at Leghorn at the beginning of July 1739. De Brosses saw him at Florence before Oct. 4, 1739 (I, 339).

*88

Source: Egerton 2234 ff. 153-4
Addressed: as in 74
Numbered: (13.)
Endorsed: a. yᵉ acᵗ of Sʳ John Royden
              b. of Sʳ J Royden; &c.

Turin,
January 27, 1740

⟨Dear Mother,⟩

You inquired two or three letters ago after Sir John R⟨oyden.[1] I forget
whether I have said anything in answer to it: if I have, there is no great
harm in repeating it, for as our letters are always only another method of
chatting together, we may at any time be allowed to say the same things
over and over again, as often as we please: as I have known some admired
talkers do without injuring their reputation, and even with great applause.⟩
I have never had the happiness to meet with that gentleman in my travels,[2]
but I have heard of him both from France and Italy.[3] Sir John, by what I am
told, must be of a very amorous complexion. 'Tis said (how true, heaven
knows) that he was in love over head and ears in Ireland, and that they sent
him to travel to wean him from that passion. This did it so thoroughly that
at Montauban (a very pleasant town in the south of France) he offered a
gentleman, if he would give him five guineas, to enter into articles that he
would pay him five hundred if ever he married his Irish mistress. And what
d'ye think it was that made him so positive in this affair? He was fallen
over head and ears in love with a young lady at Montauban. He is now in
Italy, and is I believe prodigiously in love in every town he makes any stay
at. I should imagine there is less danger in such a combustible gentleman
than in one of slower passions. These sieve-hearts have a hole always to let
in an amour, but then they have a hundred to let it out.[4]

⟨So much for Sir John (with my compliments to the good lady that
inquired after him), and now for myself. Though I pass in the world
(heaven knows how unjustly) under the character of a poet,[5] yet am I in
reality a very considerate man. Is not it being very considerate to think of
housekeeping and provisions for us in Queen's Street—a year and a half
before we shall come to eat them? And yet this is what I have done. My
Lord (who asks often after you and is always glad to hear of your health)
has promised me to give me a buck every year, because you love venison
and are (as I have done you the justice to tell him) an excellent pasty-

maker. This is to be done (if such a thing can be done in England) without paying keeper's fees etc. When we are established in our housekeeping, I hope to get the same promise from Lord M⟨iddlesex⟩, that we may abound in pasties and pasty-making every season. So that you have nothing to do but to get your roller ready and tuck up your sleeves to your shoulders, against I come to stand by you and see you salt it and pepper it as no mortal has done since the time of good King William but yourself. Rolle is very honest, as I have told you in a former: and our English here (which I told you in my last were very numerous) are increased by the arrival of Mr. Berty and Mr. Briscowe.[6] My Lord gave a dinner to them yesterday, and we were fourteen at table, though three or four missed us. With services to all friends, I am ever

Your dutiful and affectionate

J. Spence.⟩

1. John Rawdon (1720–93), 1st Bt. and 1761 1st E. of Moira; educ. at Trinity College, Dublin; member of the Soc. of Dilettanti 1741; F.R.S. 1744.

2. The happiness came in May, when Sir John visited Turin; see *Letter* 108.

3. He was 'something of a poltroon and a common butt'; according to one story 'he guessed that the Sublime Port was the Port of Leghorn' (*G.E.C.* IX, 29–30). When he was created Baron Rawdon of Moira in 1750, Lady Mary wrote: 'I dare swear he purchas'd his Title for the same reason he us'd to purchase Pictures in Italy; not because he wanted to buy, but because some body or other wanted to sell' (*Complete Letters*, II, 458).

4. This amorous propensity is corroborated by Sir John's three marriages. On Nov. 10, 1741 O.S., he married Helena, the youngest daughter of the 1st E. of Egmont, with whom he fell in love as soon as he returned from his travels (*HMC Egmont Diary*, III, 227–316). Lady Mary commented on Sir John's first two wives: 'I fancy they have broke their Hearts by being chain'd to such a companion' (*Complete Letters*, II, 458).

5. i.e., man of letters.

6. Norreys Bertie (1718–66) of Springfield, Essex; M.A. 1738 at Magdalen College; 1743–54 M.P. Oxon. Lady Mary met him at Venice in October 1739 (ibid., II, 156). 'Mr. Briscowe' was probably Mr. William Bristow (d. 1758), Commissioner of Revenue in Ireland; member of the Soc. of Dilettanti 1740; M.P.; F.R.S.

89

Source: Egerton 2234 ff. 155–6
Addressed: as in 74
Numbered: (14.)
Endorsed: a. a descrip/shon of yᵉ frost & extreamli/
pretey: in a Remarkable/hard winter; &
colder/there, by a great deale/then in england
b. Of seeing the Cold.

Turin,
February 2, 1740

⟨Dear Mother,⟩

Neither you in England, or I in Italy, have any particular reason to complain
of the cold or to boast of the heat. The cold of this winter is a general thing,
and is spread (perhaps more equally than is generally imagined) all over
Europe. As to Turin at least, I can answer for its being very severe here,
and this is the fifth or sixth day of its being so very severe. The water in
my basin this morning was froze the fifth of an inch in the middle, and three
quarters of an inch on the sides. I had some difficulty to break it with my
cane to get at some water to wash my head with. For these four or five
mornings the Po has run along all smoking like a furnace, but this morning
when I passed the bridge, I saw great cakes of ice floating down it, like
those the winter before the last at Tours: and if the frost continues, I
suppose 'twill be all frozen over in a few days, as we hear the Thames has
been for some time.[1] All this is common, but what I am going to tell you
will smell a little of the traveller, till I have explained it

'Tis common to *feel* the cold; but within these four or five mornings, and
this very morning among the rest, I have actually *seen the cold with my eyes.*
However it feels, I can assure you 'tis a very pretty sight. You have seen on
a cold market morning the farmers jog in to town, with their beards and
hair all powdered with hoar-frost. This hoar-frost was before all fluttering in
the air, too fine and thin for the eye, but when several pieces of it are fallen
upon one another on a fuzz-bush, or a farmer's beard, they grow
considerable enough to be visible. If they were thicker in the air, they would
be visible to us, and we should see millions of millions of little silver
spangles dancing about every way in different directions, as every different
breath of wind or as their own fancy led them (for whether they are mere
matter, or so many little airy sprites, I am not philosopher enough to
determine). But these, whether sprites or ingredients only for little icicles on
a farmer's chin, did I see this morning, and have seen several mornings, just
after I had passed the bridge of the Po and was going up the hill to the

Queen's villa. They are a very charming sight, and are (in miniature) like the little shining flies I have seen in a garden near Rome, of which I think I formerly sent you a description, or like the shining part[icle]s dancing in a sunbeam, after Betty has swept the room and put [   ] a window-shutter with a round hole in it. Whether it be that these little airy dancers on a frosty morning are more numerous here—as we lie in a sort of basin at the foot of the Alps, the great reservoir of frost and snow—or whether they are more sociable and join hands oftener together ⟨than in England⟩ in their airy dance, whence it happens I know not, but here they appear to the eye, and in England I don't remember ever to have discerned them. My paper won't let me say any more of my new acquaintance, and so I am

⟨Your dutiful and affectionate

J. Spence⟩

1. On Jan. 31 the *Gent. Mag.* (1740, p. 35) reported: 'This Month the Frost, which began the 26th of last, grew more severe than has been known since the memorable Winter 1715–16. ... The *Thames* floated with Rocks and Shoals of Ice. ... All Navigation being obstructed, Coals rose to *3l. 10 s. per Chaldron.* ... The Streets of *London* were so clog'd with Snow and Ice, that Hackney Coaches wait with 3 or 4 Horses.... The Rivers *Severn, Tyne,* the *Avon* by *Bristol,* the Rivers of *Forth, Tay* etc. in *Scotland,* and the *Liffy* by *Dublin,* were all frozen up like the *Thames:* And by all Advices from *Holland, France, Germany,* etc. the Cold was extreme.'

---

*90

Source:	Egerton 2234 ff. 157–8
Addressed:	*as in 74*
Numbered:	(15.)
Endorsed:	*a.* a further/act of ye frost & Lord sandwich
	b. Farther acct of the Frost/& Ld Sandwich.

Turin,
February 10, 1740

⟨Dear Mother,⟩

I sent you an account in my last of my *seeing the cold,* which you look upon perhaps to be as foolish or as groundless as Sir John Mandeville's account of his words being frozen in the cold country he was in.[1] However that be, I once more assure you that I saw it again today, and that in the most perfect and most beautiful manner I have seen it at all: and indeed the cold of today is almost as strong as that of last Wednesday, and the sun was brighter today than it was then.

I mentioned in a former that Lord Sandwich was expected here from

Egypt. He came this morning, drank tea here this afternoon, and I am to dine with him tomorrow. I shall stick as close to him as I can to get as much out of him as possible, for instead of five or six weeks which we expected, he stays here only two or three days. He has some affairs that require very much his presence in England, and will be there in a fortnight. We other travellers are quite eclipsed when one talks of Lord Sandwich. A man that has been all over Greece, at Constantinople, Troy, the pyramids of Egypt, and the deserts of Arabia, talks and looks with a greater air than we little people can do that have only crawled about France and Italy.

'Tis now that the Alps are really formidable, and yet he is going to pass them, and talks of them only as if he was going over a molehill. The snows are very deep there, and 'twas but last week that some people who were bringing over some clothes from Paris for the Queen found them so: six mules and one of the mulemen being lost in the snows, and their very bones won't be heard of any more till the thaw. When that comes, 'tis still more dangerous to pass these mountains. For the vast heaps of snow that hang sometimes over your head are then apt to fall, and on the treading of the horses and rattling of a chaise, they sometimes break off all at once; and sometimes so far in, that they come down in quantities enough to bury a little army under them. The French at that season are used to blow horns and shoot off guns a little before they are to pass under any of these impending rocks of snow, and if they continue firm, they then venture to pass under them. I hope Lord Sandwich may pass them before there is a thaw, but in case such a thing should happen, I shall tell him of this method of the French and, ten to one, he will laugh at me and say: 'Ay, that's just what we did when we passed Mount Taurus in Asia and the mountains of Atlas in Africa.' I wish he was in the mountains of the moon, for I don't like these people that overshine one so much. I had rather by half be in Hampshire, where I should see nobody that has been so far as myself, and where I can tell lies with safety and make people stare as much as I please. If I was to say there that I had *seen cold* or *ate half a pound of sunshine*, they'd say, ''Tis very strange, but Mr. Spence is a man of a very good character': they should not have imagined that cold was visible or sunshine eatable, 'but the world's wide, and they may have strange things in one country that are not in another'. Upon which footing I shall leave the doctrine I have advanced in this and my last letter, and am ⟨as ever

Your dutiful and affectionate

Jo: Spence.⟩

---

1. See Rabelais's *Gargantua and Pantagruel*, bk. IV, ch. 55 ('Comment en haulte mer Pantagruel ouyt diverses parolles degelees'), which Ad- dison in *Tatler* No. 254 (Nov. 23, 1710) mis- takenly attributed to 'our renowned Country- man' Sir John Mandeville.

91

Source: Add. MSS 33065 ff. 350–1
Endorsed: Copy to L. Lincoln/Feb^ry 4. 1739/40

NEWCASTLE TO LINCOLN

Newcastle House,
February 4, 1739 [O.S.]

My dear Lord,

I am extremely concerned that none of your friends and relations have had
a letter from you in so long a time—especially considering the very great
loss and misfortune that your poor uncle and I have had,[1] for which however
I am sensible from your great good nature, as well as love for us, you have
had a very true concern, as indeed Mr. Spence has assured me. These great
losses cannot but make . . . those that remain dearer to each other; and
therefore I must own to you my concern and fear for you daily increases. I
had some account that you had a breaking out in your face, and that you
had been tampering with a physician at Turin in order to remove it, who,
it seems, happening to be a very honest man, would not try any tricks. But
as that may not always be the case, I must beg you not to run the risk of
your health in order to remove a pimple out of your face. I desired Mr.
Stone[2] to give Mr. Spence a hint of what I had heard, and I hope by his
constantly sending me word that you are well that you are perfectly so;
otherwise I should be very much concerned to think that I could not depend
absolutely upon the accounts I have about your health. I am glad to find by
all Mr. Spence's letters that your behaviour is so agreeable to him. He knows
very well what it should be, and I dare say would not flatter me with
saying it was what it was not.

I was in hopes to have heard from you some account of the place, how
you went on in your exercises and studies, and what sort of diversions you
had. I suppose early in the summer that you will be moving further into
Italy. I should be glad you would send me word where you propose to spend
the summer, that you might have the thoughts of your friends here upon it
before you leave Turin.

There is one great misfortune which young men of quality are too apt to
fall into, I mean gaming. I never observed any tendency towards it in you,
so I hope my caution is altogether unnecessary; but as I know many

have fallen into that error, and even of late. And as I have seen the fatal consequences of it, I could not avoid mentioning it, if it was only to have the pleasure of hearing from yourself that there was no room for any apprehension of that kind. Play naturally leads those that are addicted to it into the worst company and into all sorts of vices, and if a young man gives himself a loose to it in his travels, he scarce leaves it afterwards, and often inconveniences his fortune for his whole life.[3] You know, my dear, the many encumbrances there are upon your estate, the payment of your sister's fortune, and perhaps some demand (and that a very heavy one) from the public; and if you should have the misfortune to add to this by any losses at play, it would not only distress you extremely, but make the Parliament less disposed to favour you in your public accounts.[4] I write this very seriously, and am persuaded it will have its due weight with you. I have no suspicion of any occasion to give you any advice with relation to your morals. I have always observed as good principles in you as ever I knew in any young man, and it has been the greatest satisfaction to me; principles of good nature, of honour and honesty, which I hope are inseparable from you: a love to your country and your friends and relations, with a due sense of religion, will carry you through the world with credit and reputation, and in setting out in that manner you will lay a foundation for a character which will be an advantage to you through the course of your life.

I thank God, my brother and Lady Catherine, and the poor children that are left, are well.[5] I suppose you know poor Miss Pelham was very dangerously ill and Lady Catherine also, of the same distemper; but I thank God they are now quite well.[6] . . . As to public affairs, we go on briskly with our preparations against Spain: where they will fall is not yet certain, however I hope they will be sufficient to make that court repent their behaviour towards us. I beg you would make my compliments to the Marquis d'Ormea[7] and all the ministers for their civilities to you, and I beg you would particularly thank both Mr. Villettes and Mr. Spence for their goodness and attention to you. Your aunt sends her kindest love, though you have been so bad a correspondent. I beg, my dear, we may hear oftener from you. Nothing can be a greater pleasure than to hear you are well, to My dearest Lord / Yours most sincerely and affectionately

Holles Newcastle

1. The loss of Henry Pelham's two sons; see *Letter* 84.

2. The Duke's secretary, to whom Spence addressed his reports on young Lincoln. See *Letter* 76.

3. Lincoln seems to have exhibited some inclination for gambling during his stay at Turin. Spence composed, for his edification, a 'moral history' on the evil consequences of gambling. See *Letter* 118 n. 1.

4. For an account of Lord Lincoln's estate at this time see the *Calendar of Treasury Books and Papers* for 1739–41 (pp. 115, 539, 561) and the Newcastle MSS at the Nottingham University Library.

5. Lincoln's aunt, Lady Catherine Manners, eldest dau. of John, D. of Rutland, had married Henry Pelham in 1726. Of their surviving children Catherine (1727–60) married in 1744 young Lincoln, her cousin. Frances (1728–1804) and the youngest, Mary (b. 1739), never married. Grace (1735–77) married in 1752 the Hon. Lewis Monson-Watson.

6. Only two days after this letter was written,

Lucy, the 5th daughter, died at the age of twelve (Dorothy having died an infant). 'The same distemper' of which the two boys died, probably diphtheria, became subsequently known as 'the Pelham fever'.

7. Carlo Vicenzo Ferrero di Roasio (1680–1745), Marquis d'Ormea; Minister of Interior at Turin 1730, for Foreign Affairs 1732. 'Le marquis d'Ormea,' wrote De Brosses at about this time, 'premier ministre, possède lui seul et en entier la confiance du Roi. Il passe pour très capable, et l'on dit que c'est bien lui qui contribue le plus au grand rôle que son maître joue en Europe' (II, 581).

*92

Source: Egerton 2234 ff. 159–60
Numbered: (16.)

Turin,
February 17, 1740

⟨Dear Mother,⟩

This last week has been a very agreeable week to me: I have enjoyed a good deal of Lord Sandwich's company in it. They came to Turin on Tuesday morning, and stayed here till Friday morning. We concluded we should have them with us for four or five weeks, but his Lordship had such pressing business in England that he was forced to go on, and to set out for Mount Cenis, deep as it is in snow, the very coldest day we have had this winter.

By what good luck, or by what impertinence of my own, I won't determine, but by the one or the other I had much the largest share of his Lordship's company of anybody here: and am rather better acquainted with him than I was even with Stephen Duck, the three first days he was at Winchester.[1]

As my good Lord may be the subject of two or three of my letters to you, 'tis fit I should let you know in the first place who he is. He is the great-grandson of the witty Earl of Rochester,[2] whom you must have remembered in Charles the Second's time, and whose works are read with so much pleasure by several of the young ladies at Winchester and all over England. He was bred up at Eton[3] with Lord Lincoln, and had the character there of being the finest scholar in that great school. He set out for his travels about four years ago, and observed the remains of the Roman arts and magnificence here in no common manner.[4] The love of the arts is a passion that grows strangely in every mind that ever received it, and much more so when it meets with fine sense. He was not therefore satisfied with the beauties he had met with here, but in the year —37 bought a ship, prepared everything for his voyage and his observations, and set sail from Naples for Sicily.[5] The compass of two or three letters won't let me mention half the things he has told me of, but I shall tell you the most considerable of them as well as I can remember them.

Much the noblest city in Sicily, and one of the noblest indeed in the whole world in the time of the old Greeks, was Syracuse; ⟨perhaps they had as good wine anciently, as they have now, and⟩ the whole soil there is nothing but antiquities. These are most of them only the ruins of fine things, but there is one there which is as entire as it was at first.

Dionysius the Tyrant reigned here. His cruelties have made his name a proverb. Of the multitudes of poor wretches, which he flung into prison for little or no faults, he used almost always to know what almost every one said of him in their confinement. This, no doubt, was a great mystery in his time, but the case now is clear. He flung them into a dark prison, where there was not the least glimmering of light: this was cut so artfully in a rock, that every the least whisper they made to one another, and every little complaint that they muttered between their teeth, was carried up to a chamber above, where he had always some creatures upon the watch, who gave him a very exact account of all that was said. This prison is still entire, and the watch-chamber over it. 'Tis formed in the shape of an ear, and is at this day called Dionysius's Ear.[6] 'Tis a monstrous large ear, for the entrance into it is seventy foot high, the breadth above twenty, and the depth in above two hundred. The hollow of the rock that includes this vast space is all cut and channelled like the foldings of an human ear. When Lord Sandwich was placed properly, and a piece of paper dropped to the ground, he could hear when it fell upon the ground distinctly; a letter tore gently in two made a great noise to him; and a pistol (which Mr. Frolick let off in the ear)[7] sounded like a vast and long-continued clap of thunder. I don't doubt but Dionysius was sometimes in the listening room himself, and heard perhaps at fifty yards distance perhaps curses (that were only whispered against him) more loudly than any boatswain in our fleet could swear, though he was to hollo one of his strongest oaths in one of his highest passions directly at your ear.

You see, I had reason to say that Lord Sandwich's expedition would furnish me out two or three letters, for in this we are got no farther than Sicily, and we have almost half the world to go over. However, I'll let you take a little breath here, and am ⟨ever

Your dutiful and affectionate

J. Spence.⟩

1. Spence first met Duck Sept. 10–11 and 15–18, 1730, at Winchester. 'I have pass'd the greatest part of Six Days with him, and had him Four Evenings entirely to my self' (*Account of Stephen Duck*, p. 5). See Wright, p. 47.

2. Rochester's 2d daughter, Elizabeth (1674–1757), who is said to have inherited her father's wit, married Edward Montagu (1670–1729), 3d E. of Sandwich, whom the protagonist of Spence's next few letters, John Montagu (1718–92), succeeded as the 4th Earl at the age of eleven.

3. 1728–32; admitted as nobleman at Trinity College, Cambridge, Apr. 12, 1735, but did not take a degree.

4. A voluminous account of the travels appeared in 1799, seven years after the Earl's death, under the title *A Voyage Performed by the late Earl of Sandwich Round the Mediterranean in the Years 1738 and 1739*. Although the book claims to have been 'written by Himself', it is suspected to have been in part written by Lord Sandwich's chaplain, John Cooke, whose 'Memoirs of the Noble Author's Life' are prefixed to the work.

5. Sandwich's *Voyage* (p. 3) begins: 'On the twelfth day of July N.S. I embarked from Leghorn on board the Anne galley, an English ship of about three hundred tons and sixteen cannon.' The title of the book makes it clear that the year was 1738. There are some discrepancies between Spence's narrative and the *Voyage*, for which Spence may not be entirely responsible.

6. See *Voyage*, pp. 22–3.

7. On Spence's 'good friend' and the Earl's tutor 'James John Frölich' see *Letter* 87. He arrived with Lord Sandwich in Turin, and his name appears next to the Earl's on Spence's *List* and several times in Spence's letters. Oddly enough he is not mentioned in Cooke's prefatory 'Memoirs', which state (p. iii) that 'Mr. Ponsonby, late Earl of Besborough, Mr. Nelthorpe, and Mr. Mackye, accompanied his lordship on this agreeable tour; with a painter [Liotard]. . . .' Not a word of 'Mr. Frölich'. Many drawings made on the tour by Jean-Étienne Liotard (1702–89) are preserved in the Louvre and the Bibliothèque Nationale at Paris.

---

*93

Source:	Egerton 2234 ff. 161–2
Addressed:	*as in 74*
Postmarked:	28 FE
Franked:	Free/Andrew Stone
Numbered:	(17.)
Endorsed:	*a.* an ac^t/of malta, & chios: both Greek/ eyelands: & famous for the/pretiest ladeys in the world.
	b. Of the Isle of Malta:/and ye pretty Ladies of/Chios.

Turin,
February 24, 1740

⟨Dear Mother,⟩

After Lord Sandwich had enjoyed for some time the finest remains of antiquity at Syracuse, and some other parts of Sicily, they set sail for the island of Malta,[1] so famous for the knights who are bound (by their oath of knighthood) to combat the Turks wherever they meet with them.

I have been acquainted with several Knights of Malta, particularly in my first tour in France,[2] who have all complained that they suffer much in their eyesight by the whiteness of the rock their town is built upon. The houses and the streets are all white, and the rock rises white all round them: so that they have nothing of that green there which nature has flung almost all over the world to refresh and relieve the eye. Lord Sandwich tells me that, to make up for this when they get out of their white cage, all the rest of their little island is extremely pretty and all dressed, like a forester, in green.

They went from this island to that of Chios,[3] famous for the pretty ladies that live in it. Greece, as well as England, has been ever remarkable for charming women. I have seen faces of Greek women in marble that I have been half in love with: and as to their modern faces, when I was at Venice the woman with the most delightful face there was a Greek.[4] ⌜The dear devil⌝[5] was too pretty to be honest, but that was no harm you know at Venice. The ladies of Chios, which is a Greek island, perhaps exceed the rest of their countrywomen in beauty, and they have a freedom of behaviour with it that exceeds even any of our European ladies.[6] When Lord Sandwich walked through their city, all the world was at their doors to see the strangers, and some of the prettiest women among them stopped him several times as he was going along to observe his ruffles, the fineness of his linen and the dress of his hair. They would look long and kindly in his face, with a little growing smile upon their own, then hold up their hands as pleased and admiring, and say something, perhaps of the fineness of his complexion, to the women that stood next to them. This is not meant as any particular compliment to his Lordship, for the men in the East are generally more sunburnt than we are.

My Lord afterwards, at dinner at the English Consul's, was talking of what had happened to him, and might possibly say (in the style of a sailor) 'that he should be very glad to marry two or three of them for the fortnight or so he was to stay in their island'. How seriously this was said, I know not, nor am I acquainted enough with his Lordship's temper to know whether he has been much used to these sudden marriages or not: perhaps he has been married a hundred times oftener than I shall ever be, who hope at least never to marry once, but there's a great deal of difference between a great Lord, descended from such a grandfather and a poor country-parson, the son of a worthy clergyman.[7] If I go on with my digression I shall forget that we are at the consul's table, at Chios. To return therefore: the consul told his Lordship 'that he was very much mistaken in the ladies of that island, that they always took such freedoms with the strangers that were well dressed, who came thither, but that all this freedom was only the mode of the island, and that if he should propose a fortnight's wedding to any one of them 'twas a hundred to one that he would be really and seriously refused by them'. This must no doubt have very much baulked a young gentleman who possibly had not been much used to refusals, and in effect I find by what he said that he left the island very soon after, extremely surprised at the uncommon incivility of a people who at first seemed the readiest to invite him to stay among them. ⟨I am ever,

Your dutiful and affectionate

J. Spence

P.S. The cold continues here very severe, and the earth is still eight to ten inches deep in snow. In spite of which (about noon especially) 'tis extreme fine walking. I have all this winter taken the precaution after my walks which you mention, and have not been so well, nor in so good spirits, any winter these fifteen year as the present.⟩

1. According to the *Voyage* (pp. 490–518) they visited Malta on their return from Egypt, on the way to Lisbon. From Sicily they sailed for Greece. The itinerary as given by Spence often conflicts with that of the printed account.

2. In *Letter* 6 Spence mentions one he had met at Dijon.

3. The *Voyage* (pp. 309–20) says they visited Chios on their way from Smyrna to Rhodes.

4. Commenting on the 'beautés et ... proportions du corps' of the Venus of Medici at Florence, De Brosses (1, 339) notes: 'Mylord Sandwich ... qui revenait de Grèce, me dit que toutes les femmes qu'il y avait vues, et qui passaient pour belles, avaient de cet air-là.'

5. Emended to 'she'.

6. The *Voyage* (pp. 319–20) elaborates at great length on this topic.

7. Joseph Spence (1661?–1715?), Rector of Winnall, near Winchester 1687–1701, later Curate of Crewkerne in Somerset (Wright, pp. 2–3).

---

*94

Source:	Egerton 2234 ff. 163–4
Addressed:	*as in 74*
Postmarked:	4 MA
Franked:	Free/Andrew Stone
Numbered:	(18.)
Endorsed:	*b.* Ld Sandwich gon to Lyons./in 4 days, & 3 hours. *red wafer*

[Turin,]
March 2, 1740

⟨Dear Mother,⟩

I have been obliged to write a long letter to Mr. Stone, and a longer to Lord Sandwich this morning,[1] so that I have only time to ask you how you all do. Lord Sandwich got from hence to Lyons, in all that bad weather, in four days and three hours, and hoped to get from Lyons to London in twelve days more. So that his name will be probably in the public papers before this time. I shall go on with his travels into the East in my next, and am ⟨in the meantime,

Your dutiful and affectionate

J. Spence.

Snow still all round us.⟩

1. Neither of these letters appears to have been preserved.

---

*95

Source:	Egerton 2234 ff. 165–6
Addressed:	*as in 74*
Postmarked:	13 MR
Franked:	Free/Andrew Stone
Numbered:	(19.)
Endorsed:	*a.* a descripshon of a grotto: at/paros: an Island famous/for the finest white marble/in the world: yᵉ passage in/to yᵉ Groto is yᵉ frightfullest in the/world: & a 150 yards under/ground, to get down to it *b.* The Grotto of Antiparos. *red wafer*

Turin,

March 9, 1740

⟨—I am overjoyed that you are got so well through so much cold, and beg you to take care of yourself on the thaw.⟩

⟨Dear Mother,⟩

Though I was so long before I mentioned Sir John R⟨oyden⟩ (who I fear is pretty much of a rake) yet you see I had not forgot him:[1] neither have I forgot the young prince you have so often asked after,[2] but shall give you an account of him, all in good time. To say the truth, I have not yet seen him. He was till lately at a palace in the country, and ever since he has been here, the court has been in deep mourning for the Duke of Bourbon.[3] As I have no black clothes here but a suit of black velvet, which is only second mourning, I must wait till they sink their mourning before I can see him: for he never stirs out, the measles having succeeded the smallpox here, and being still very much about the town.

To go on therefore with Lord Sandwich's voyage. From the island of Chios they passed several others (for the Archipelago is all thick-sown with islands), and among the rest the famous island of Paros, from whence they had formerly those stores of the finest white marble in the world for their buildings and statues.[4] They told us that this island, as they passed it, looked to them just as the little rising grounds about Turin, all covered with snow. There are such vast remains of the old houses fallen all in white heaps, beside the quarries which faced the sea, and are of a shining white, like snow when the sun glitters upon it.

From Paros they went to a little island just by it, called Antiparos, and landed to pay a visit to the grotto there, which nature has adorned the most artificially perhaps of any grotto in the world.[5] Indeed, it ought to be very beautiful, for 'tis very difficult to get at it. There is a cavern, with a great opening in the ground in it, which goes down nobody knows how far. You are let down into this with ropes, and at distances there are two or three landing places to rest you. 'Tis not only the danger of the cords breaking, or slipping, and letting a man fall down ⌐perhaps to hell¬, but the stones are loose, and as you are swinging down a good deal of the rock is apt to tumble after you, and nobody knows whether the next stone that comes may kill him or only break his head. To hear the manner of their getting along in all sort of postures, and all sort of dangers, would make one wonder how ever anybody could have resolution enough to go through them.

When they were 150 yards deep under ground, they came to the entrance of the great grotto: forty yards high and fifty long. All this grot is ornamented with wainscot and fretwork like the whitest marble. The water that has dropped continually there has by degrees petrified and made thousands of beautiful figures about it: you have bunches of grapes in one place and festoons in another, several sorts of fruits and flowers, and particularly a vast number of cauliflowers, more naturally represented than any statuary could make them. In other places you have columns and pillars, and several little pyramids reversed from the ceiling.

Monsieur de Nointel was perhaps the first person that ventured into this enchanted cave for many hundreds of years.[6] He was ambassador from the King of France to Constantinople in 1673. The people of the country at that time perhaps looked upon it as the habitation of evil spirits. He went down with all his train, and received the sacrament there on Christmas night on a little thick grove of marble trees, which is still called the altar.[7] The grot must have made a glorious appearance at that time, for he had it illuminated with a hundred torches and four hundred lamps. If you want a fuller description of the place, 'tis to be found in Tournefort's *Travels*, vol. i, let. 5.[8] He was down in it too, and what he says of the beautiful natural ornaments of the place was most seriously confirmed to me by Lord Sandwich. What wonders should we meet with if we could travel as conveniently under the earth, as we can on its surface! ⟨I am ever

Your dutiful and affectionate

J. Spence.

Please turn over.

I am much obliged to you for your frequent and kind letters. I received two together (one of them full of news) today, which makes ten since the first of our January. Most humble services to all friends. I long to be eating the pasty with you and Lord Lincoln.⟩

1. On Sir John, see *Letter* 88.

2. The D. of Savoy, now fourteen years old. See *Letters* 21, 111.

3. Louis-Henri, D. of Bourbon, died Jan. 27 at Chantilly. His wife Caroline of Hesse-Rheinfels (see *Letter* 30) was sister of the King's 2d wife, Polyxena, who had died in 1735. De Brosses, who was in Turin at this time, describes the formal mourning at court in detail and comments: 'Je me figure qu'une étiquette si divertissante ne fait pas moins bâiller le souverain que les courtisans' (II, 578).

4. 'The Turks are so blind to their own advantage, as not to suffer the exportation of this valuable commodity, out of religious fear lest the Christians should employ it in making statues, which is looked upon as a great abomination' (*Voyage*, p. 105).

5. Spence's following account agrees remarkably with that given in the *Voyage*, pp. 106–7.

6. Charles-François Ollier, Marquis de Nointel (d. 1685), French consul at Constantinople 1670–80, gathered a rare collection of antique curiosities during his travels in the East Mediterranean.

7. 'On the altar is the following inscription in memory of the presence of Christ at the celebration of the mass':

HIC IPSE ADFVIT CHRISTVS

DIE NATALI EIVS

MEDIA NOCTE CELEBRATA

ANNO MDCLXIII

(*Voyage*, p. 107)

8. *Relation d'un voyage du Levant* (Paris, 1717), I, 185–94, where two engravings of the grotto are given. Joseph Pitton de Tournefort (1656–1708), celebrated botanist, had been commissioned by Louis XIV to make a tour of the Mediterranean in 1700–2. His work appeared posthumously; English transl. 1718, 2d edn. 1741.

96

Source: Add. MSS 33065 ff. 352–3

LINCOLN TO NEWCASTLE

Turin,
March 9, 1740

My Lord,

I am extremely glad to find by your Grace's most obliging letter[1] that you do me so much justice as to think my silence on the late most melancholy affair[2] does not proceed from want of nature, as it certainly must do if I was not touched in the most sensible manner at so great and cruel a loss; indeed my Lord the greatness of my grief has been the real cause of neglect of duty, for in the condition I was in what could I say either to my Uncle Pelham or your Grace, either by condoling with you or endeavouring to mitigate your sorrows, when I was sure you both but too well knew the greatness of your misfortune; and good God how can I express what I suffered myself when I considered the dreadful way all that I have dear in the world must inevitably be in. We have just received Mr. Stone's most dismal letter.[3] I hope the melancholy contents of it will be an excuse for my not answering, as I fully designed, that part of your Grace's letter that regards our leaving Turin. Mr. Spence has promised to do it for me. Indeed I am little fit for writing or anything else at present.

As your Grace seemed to be under some apprehension in regard to gaming, I think I should be very little deserving the concern you are so good as to express if I was not to assure you that you may be perfectly easy on that head: for since I have discovered some little inclination I had for it, Mr. Spence has shown himself so thoroughly my friend by dissuading me against it, and has so fully convinced me of the folly of it and the fatal consequences that generally attend it, that I had seriously determined never to play again before I had the pleasure of receiving your Grace's letter, which I am sure I hope and believe you can't doubt will be a stronger motive for keeping my resolution.

Pray my duty to the D[uchess] of N[ewcastle] who I am extremely happy to hear is perfectly recovered, and most heartily pray may continue in perfect health. I design writing to her very soon. Pray, my Lord, with my duty to my Uncle Pelham say everything that love, pity, gratitude can suggest. I can assure you you can't express what, or how much, I suffer for him. I design writing to him, but don't know how to set about it. I am mighty glad to find poor Lady Catherine is so well; pray my duty to her and hearty service to Mrs. Spence.[4] I am / Your Grace's / most affectionate / and dutiful nephew

Lincoln

P.S. Pray my Lord let Mr. Stone write, for I want prodigiously to know how you all do; I am very well myself and design taking Mr. Hulse's powders immediately.[5]

---

1. *Letter* 91.
2. The death of his two cousins; see *Letter* 84.
3. Perhaps announcing the additional death of Lucy (*Letter* 91 n. 6).
4. On Elizabeth Spence, see *Letter* 109 n. 6.
5. Lincoln was not of a strong make, and his uncle, great believer in the art of Sir Edward Hulse (1682–1759), the royal physician, continually persecuted him with this medicine. On Apr. 17, 1739, Lincoln wrote from Cambridge: 'I cannot take Dr. Hulse's prescription above 2 or 3 days. ... I hope your Grace will not blame me for deferring it till my return' (Add. MSS 33065 f. 330r-v).

Source:	Egerton 2234 ff. 167–8
Addressed:	*as in* 74
Postmarked:	[ ]O MR
Franked:	Free/Andrew Stone
Numbered:	(20.)
Endorsed:	*a.* home affaires: but an acount/when he comes home &c.
	b. Of the Picture I bought/& w[n] we may return./Not to be Copied.
	red wafer

97

[Turin,
March 16, 1740][1]

⟨Dear Mother,⟩

I shall mark down the third of March as a fortunate day to me in all my almanacs, for it was on that day I made a purchase of a picture for six pounds, which may possibly turn out to be worth six hundred. If you remember, when I was last at Winchester, I came back from Lord Lymington's full of raptures about a picture I saw there of Raphael's.[2] This I have got is of the same kind, and I would not swear 'tis not the fellow of it. Mine is almost eight foot long and above six foot high. It hangs up now just by me, and gives me more and more pleasure every time I look upon it: which is the certainest sign of a right good picture. Though to say the truth neither Lord Lymington's, nor mine, are pictures, but what they call designs. That is, the first thought of the painter, done with a pencil (in black and white) from which their coloured pieces are exactly copied by them. When you come to see it, you may not like it at first, but in three or four weeks you'll be charmed with it. They are like those friends who have something displeasing about them in one's first acquaintance, and who grow more agreeable the more one knows of them. Under this character I hope you will give it a place in your house in Queen's Street, if I can but get it safe to London with me. I shall take all the care imaginable to do so, and to say the truth, shall be almost as glad to see it safe there as myself.[3]

⟨Now I am talking of my return, I shall tell you very honestly that 'tis at present very doubtful whether we shall come home in the spring or the autumn of next year; longer than that autumn we can't stay, because my Lord must be at home for the Parliament, and possibly he must be at home in that spring, because he will then be of age.[4] By the way, he loves you extremely; and there are others here, that you know nothing of, that have talked of coming to see you when they return into England, till I tell them that you live at Winchester, when they thought you had lived at *London*; so that you must fix *there* hereafter on all accounts, or you may lose a great deal of good acquaintance, for I promise you never to introduce anybody to you that does not deserve it. But to return: my Lord takes so well to his exercises here, that 'tis possible we may stay on here till the autumn (in which I can manage it so as to see all the great cities of Italy at our ease); we may pass next winter at Rome, set out early in the spring of '41 for France, be at Paris by the end of April, and stay there the summer, or else come directly and pay you a visit—either at Winchester or London, which you think fit.

I'm sorry to find by your last of the 16th of your February (which I received yesterday)[5] that the colds continue so violent with you. Just about that day they began to lessen here, and ever since we have had frosts every night and great thaws every day. This has gradually lessened our deep snow so much, that the earth begins to appear again in several places (as it did, after the deluge, to Noah and his good family), and in a fortnight more, I suppose, all will be dry land.[6]

As to my ever travelling to Egypt or anywhere out of England again, by the instigation of Lord Sandwich or any other person whatsoever, I hereby give you my word and honour that I will never do it during your lifetime without your *express orders* to do so, which was almost the case, you know, in this present ramble: for which I am very much obliged to you, for it is hitherto, and is likely to continue, a very agreeable one to me. I have not been ill any one day all this winter, though I don't know that I have had my great-coat on once, and have not missed going out six days in the whole time. With all services to all friends, I am ever

Your dutiful and affectionate

J. Spence.⟩

---

1. Date supplied from Spence's endorsement.

2. John Wallop (1690–1762), Baron Wallop and Visc. Lymington 1720; 1743 cr. E. of Portsmouth. He evidently was an amateur collector of paintings (*HMC*, 8th Rep., App., p. 63).

3. One is tempted to assume that this *cartoon* of Raphael for which Spence paid £5 17s. (*App.* 12) was a fabrication, produced for credulous tourist collectors of *virtù*. This particular one was perhaps of a painting of the same subject by Garofalo in the Galleria Sabauda at Turin. On May 23, 1752, Spence wrote to Lord Lincoln from Byfleet: 'I forgot to ask, whether you should care for the drawing from Raphael's Doctors for any room in your new house: if you should, it is extremely at your service, but if not, I may possibly find use for it here at Byfleet' (Nottingham University Library).

4. Lincoln was born Apr. 16, 1720.

5. i.e., in sixteen days.

6. 'On a ici une manière très commode de déblayer la neige des rues en très peu de temps,' observes De Brosses. 'Il y a dans le quartier le plus haut de la ville, laquelle est à peu près plate, un ruisseau qui donne de l'eau, dont on a amassé un lac, qu'on grossit en jetant de la neige dedans. Quand il est assez gros, on le distribue par toute la ville, selon les différentes pentes, tout le long des rues. . . . Ce torrent va se jeter dans le Pô, et en deux heures, il nettoie toutes les rues' (II, 583).

*98

Source:	Egerton 2234 ff. 169–70
Addressed:	*as in 74*
Endorsed:	*b.* Ld Sandwich's Character/of the Turks. *red wafer*

Turin,
March 23, 1740

⟨Dear Mother,⟩

We left Lord Sandwich, I think, in the grotto of Antiparos. I speak nothing to you of the old inscriptions there, because they are in Greek.[1] They sailed thence farther east, and passed along the shore 'Where corn grows, and Troy town stood'.[2] The destruction of that city is one of the earliest pieces of history that we have handed down to us. In Julius Caesar's time there were scarce any marks left of it. When Augustus came to the crown, as his family came from old Troy, he built a new city there, and the ruins of this appeared very considerable to them as they passed by: for there was some reason (they did not distinctly tell me what) that hindered their landing there.[3]

After this, they passed the Dardanelles (where Leander used to swim over every night to see his mistress) ⟨till his love was cooled at the bottom of that sea⟩, and came to Constantinople. They tell wonders there of the seraglio, which they say is three miles round, and of the prospect from the port which is generally allowed to be the noblest in the whole world.

Everybody that I have talked with, who have been at Constantinople, agree that the Turks in that capital of their vast empire are the politest, worthiest, and justest men in the world.[4] Lord Sandwich very much confirms this character of them. When he was to call in upon any of the Greek islands which are subject to them, he entered at first with fear: he had heard the people were a sort of savages, and thought he was in danger every step he made. He found it quite otherwise: but it was at Constantinople that he saw the politeness and worth of the Turks in its perfection.

Their empire is so wide, that one can't expect it to be all under an equally good regulation; and in Egypt (which belongs to them too) a traveller, he owns, is in danger without a good guard. That is at present the sink to which the rascals of that state generally resort, and may be in as bad a condition as any one of our colonies (which is obliged to us for the greatest share of our felons, which we are so kind as to send them) in America. But

263

one must not judge of the English in general by the English that are in Jamaica, nor of the Turks in general from the Turks in Egypt.

In general, no people are so just in their dealings, and they are so much given to charity that they extend it even to dogs and birds. If I don't mistake, they have hospitals for poor old superannuated animals, and 'tis not unusual to see a good charitable Turk cheapening a goldfinch or a linnet in their markets, only to give them their liberty. They pay his price, and then gravely open the cage and let him fly into the air, to enjoy the liberty and the pleasure which nature designed for the poor creature.

Their manners are grave and easy, a mixture of which, you know, I have always looked upon as the best breeding in all the countries I have seen. With this, they carry a dignity in their persons and their long robes, which one may distinguish even in some of the lower people of the East, whenever they come among us. An abbot of Mount Athos, or a pretended prince of Mount Lebanon, has more majesty in his gait and air than any real king I ever saw in Europe. ⟨I am, with all services to all friends,

Your dutiful and affectionate

J. Spence.⟩

1. Lord Sandwich's *Voyage* is illustrated with several inscriptions, but none appears in his account of Antiparos or Paros. Perhaps Spence made a slip here for Delos, where Sandwich stopped on his way to Paros, and where his painter Liotard copied several (reproduced on pp. 99–100).

2. *Aen.* iii. 10–11: 'Litora ... Et campos ubi Troja fuit'. According to the *Voyage* (pp. 290–2) they passed Troy on their return from Constantinople.

3. The reason was that the native inhabitants were 'resolved not to part with [the ruins] upon any consideration whatever; having a superstitious tradition among them, that upon the removal of another stone ... the village [would be] immediately attacked with a violent plague', and according to Lord Sandwich, 'to go there only with intention to copy it would be a very useless trouble' (*Voyage*, p. 291).

4. The manners and customs of the Turks are dealt with at great length in Lord Sandwich's *Voyage*, pp. 137–69.

99

Source: Egerton 2234 ff. 171–2
Addressed: as in 74
Endorsed: a. home affaires all out
              b. Promise of never Travel/ling again./Not to
              be Copied
              red wafer

Turin,
March 30, 1740

⟨Dear Mother,

You may be wholly out of any concern about my coming ever abroad again.
At least the scheme of life I have in my head is quite opposite to any such
thought. The large work I have on my hands will take up near four year
after I come home, before it is all published, and after that I have some other
little things which I think at present of publishing, and which in the
leisurely way I shall go about it, merely for my amusement, will take up six
year more.[1]

I leave you to judge whether I, that was not at all eager to travel at
forty, shall be much inclined to it after fifty, when I shall be used too
to a retired, settled way of living for ten years together, and shall have all
the plantations growing up about me which I have already laid out in my
head. I mention this particular, because I have found by the little experience
I have had, that nothing is so apt to attract one, and tie one down to a spot
of ground, as a plantation. You may remember how Paul Penton[2] used to go
to his nursery every day, near Kingsclere, and when I was abroad with Mr.
Trevor, I believe there was scarce a day that I did not visit Birchanger in
my imagination.[3] At present I am more busy and more diverted, and yet I
often think of it. But I shall have, I hope, a much greater tie to England
than any I have mentioned: I mean your ladyship. When we are once fixed
in a way of living together, I shall look upon it as my duty as well as my
inclination to stay with you in old England, and shall not think of stirring
a step out of our island, unless you should turn traveller—and then perhaps
out of complaisance I might take a little trip into Asia, or to the pyramids
of Egypt, purely to attend you thither.

The scheme I mentioned to you is the sincere design I have some time
had, and as it has long been growing gradually upon me, is of itself very
likely to last; but, with the other consideration joined to it, is I think as
strong as any human resolution can be. And indeed after forty, 'tis high
time to think of a settlement and to get a steady certain income somewhere or

another. When at home, I shall always be busy about something or another, to prevent my old age being uneasy to me. I guess you are already a' laughing to hear a son of yours talk of being an old man, but that will begin to be a very serious truth, perhaps in a few years more. Whenever it happens, I don't expect it as a very disagreeable thing: a good easy chair, good company, and the being able to look back upon one's life without anything to frighten one in it, make that season at least not so terrible; and I don't see why one may not enter upon it as agreeably as one goes into a bed after one's tired with the labour of the day.[4] For fear of falling too deep into a fit of morality, I will be this moment

Your most humble servant

J. Spence.

Lord Lincoln called in just now, and desires his humble service to you. I beg all compliments to all friends, especially those in Colebrook Street. I am overjoyed to find the thaw has not done you any great hurt.⟩

1. *Polymetis* was not published till 1747. On the slowness with which the book progressed in its last stage, see Wright, pp. 86–7.

2. No doubt a relation of Henry Penton (b. 1666), Fellow of New College 1683–1709, and subscriber to *Polymetis*.

3. See *Letters* 57, 66.

4. Spence shared Pope's affection for Cicero's *De Senectute*: 'On my saying that old Cato in Cicero's delightful treatise on old age mentioned planting as the greatest pleasure for it, Dr. Young observed that he thought he could mention a greater: the looking back on a life well spent' (*Obs.* No. 862).

---

*100

Source: Egerton 2234 ff. 173–4

Addressed: as in 74

Endorsed: a. a descrip/shon of egypt, & yᵉ over/flowing of the nile &/verey pretey:
b. Of Egypt; & the Overflow/of the Nile.
red wafer

Turin,
April 6, 1740

⟨Dear Mother,⟩

You know that in Egypt it scarce ever rains. Their great river of the Nile supplies this defect. In the beginning of the autumn he begins to swell, then rises o'er his banks, and at last covers all the country with his waters. As the harvest of the next year depends wholly on what quantity of water they have in this overflow, they have a pillar of marble at Grand Cairo by

the riverside, with exact measures upon it. This is carefully watched by
proper officers, appointed by the state, and in September there are criers
who declare in the great square every day how far the river is risen on this
pillar. If they have under eighteen foot at last, there is scarce enough for the
country; and if 'tis twenty-four, 'tis too much.[1] ⟨These criers have their
instructions, and sometimes call it twenty when 'tis really [more] perhaps,
not to strike a damp into the people: who would be in a general
consternation if he was to pronounce the worst—twenty-six.⟩

That part of Egypt is all a large plain: the inhabitants, as they are sure
of an overflow every year, have made the ground unequal, and raised little
hills of about forty foot high, where the people of fashion have their villas,
and the lower sort their farm-houses or country villages. As these spots only
appear above water, many of them very prettily cultivated and set off with
little groves and gardens, and all with the finest verdure that can be
imagined on their slopes as they stand so in the water, I have often heard
that there is not a sweeter sight in the world than this little deluge in
Egypt.

Lord Sandwich came thither just at this pleasing time to see it, and says
he can't express how charming a sight it was.[2] Everybody that can afford
it keeps boats at their country houses: these boats are many of them very
gay and painted, and some with silk-streamers. They make their visits and
take their journeys in them, and often make parties in the evenings to meet
so many together or to go out with music: and sometimes the whole surface
perhaps, as far as you can see, looks like a feasting or a multitude of
floating concerts of music. 'Twas in this sort of diversion that Mark Antony
passed so much of his time with the bewitching Cleopatra, and if you have
a mind to see them together in their boat, you may find a lovely description
of them in Mr. Dryden's play on those two unfortunate lovers.[3]

This overflow of the Nile does not only serve to water the land, but to
bring down one of the finest and richest soils with it that ever was seen.
When the water goes away, they sprinkle their corn upon it and rake it
over, and with this easy agriculture have the noblest harvests in the world.
There's no such thing as a plow in all this part of Egypt, and they are
excepted out of the curse of gaining their bread with the sweat of their
brows. What a blessing is this overflow to them, and what an instance of
Providence to make the most fertile spot on the globe, by an annual supply
of earth and water in a place which (without it) would be as barren as any
of the deserts of Africa.

You see by this account that the land in Egypt must be considerably
raised in a number of years by so many coats of earth upon one another.
One could measure this almost as well as the rise of the water. In the plain
by Grand Cairo, there's a monstrous great statue of a sphinx,[4] which was

formed out of a rock there above two thousand years ago. At present, nothing but the head of it appears above the earth: this only is above twenty foot high, so that there must be about forty underground at present by the rising of the earth in that time. I don't exactly remember the measures, but they both are in Dr. Shaw's and Dr. Pocock's travels.[5] ⟨I am, with all services

Your dutiful and affectionate

J. Spence.⟩

1. Spence later supplied a note: '18 pikes, an indifferent Nile; 20 is middling; 22 good Nile. 24 is an inundation, and of bad consequence; but it scarce ever comes so high. 'Tis generally at its highest about the middle of September. Dr. Pocock [*The Description of the East*, 1743–5], vol. I, pp. 200 and 201.' Sandwich's *Voyage* gives 13, 14, 15, 16 cubits, from Pliny (*Nat. Hist.* V. ix).
2. The account in the *Voyage* (pp. 391–410)

is less picturesque.
3. The barge passage, modelled on Shakespeare's, occurs in Act III of *All for Love* (1677). In neither, however, are the two lovers seen 'together in their boat'.
4. Of Gizah, see *Voyage*, p. 458.
5. Dr. Shaw in his *Travels* (see *Letter* 40) gives no figures; Spence later copied those given by Pocock (I, 46).

101

Source:	Egerton 2234 ff. 175–6
Addressed:	*as in 74*
Postmarked:	15 AP
Franked:	Free/Andrew Stone
Endorsed:	*a.* a descrip/shon of yᵉ Bigest piramid/in egypt *b.* Accᵗ of the largest of/the Pyramids. *red wafer*

Turin,
April 13, 1740

⟨Dear Mother,⟩

'Tis near Grand Cairo that travellers meet with this monstrous sphinx and with some of the most considerable pyramids in Egypt.[1] The greatest is as big as a little city; there was a whole army employed in building it: ⟨they used to feed their workmen in those days⟩ and the single article of onions and lentils for them came to several hundred thousands of pounds. If there were none but travellers that gave us this monstrous account of them, one should know how to take it: but all that I have mentioned is recorded in an historian so old and venerable that he has been often called the father of history.[2]

The outside of this pyramid is formed all like an ascent of steps, each less than the former, and ending at last in a point to one that views it from the bottom, though 'tis ⟨perhaps a good handsome⟩ 13 f. square when you come up to it. The door to go into the pyramid is not on the ground, as might have been expected, but a good way up, in the middle of one side of it. As Lord Sandwich and Mr. Frolick were mounting to this door, they sat down sometimes to take breath and look about them: which happened very unluckily for a poor eagle that was taking his rounds in the air. He ⟨had a mind perhaps to one of their noses, and⟩ skimmed along in the air so near them that Mr. Frolick, who had a long gun, whipped it up, and shot him through the body: he fell directly, and had the honour to die like the king of the birds, on the noblest of all the pyramids.

After you have entered the door, you have a long narrow passage to creep through, which Lord Sandwich, who is but slim, says was difficult even to him, and he is quite at a loss to conceive how Dr. Shaw, who is so very plump and round, could possibly get through it. After this you go by several descents and risings to a large room in the middle, where is the tomb of the king who built the pyramid, as Lord Sandwich supposes, or the long chest in which the freemasons in the heathen religion kept their great secrets, as Dr. Shaw imagines.[3] This monstrous palace, the inside of the pyramid, is inhabited by no living creatures but bats, which dart about in great numbers in it, and perhaps by poisonous and odious insects at bottom. ⟨So that if you and I ever go into this pyramid, we will have two pair of stilts to walk upon, to prevent the serpents winding up our legs whilst we are seeing this horrible curiosity.

Perhaps there are as many frogs too as the king of Egypt had at his table in the plague time, according to the representation of his Egyptian Majesty in that very ingenious work, Bloome's Bible.[4] Of late I have had frequent occasions of revenging myself on those animals, for all the times they have frightened me either in pictures or in their proper persons. We have ever now and then a ragout of them, and I eat them out of spite. They do very well thus at a table: for they are more tender, and have a finer relish than any ragout of chicken I ever tasted; and when we are at Birchanger, if you approve of the dish as much as I do, we will never fail of a handsome dish of frogs on either of our birthdays, and on the great state holidays we may add a plate of stewed snails, as they dress them here in perfection. If you care for it, I'll get you the receipt from the King's cook here, and when I come home will enter it in your receipt-book—if there's ever a half page in that vast folio that is not already written upon. I beg all services to all friends, and am ever

Your dutiful and affectionate

J. Spence.⟩

1. Described in the *Voyage*, pp. 457–66.

2. Herodotus (II, 125) mentions 'writings on the pyramids in Egyptian characters showing how much was spent'.

3. In his *Travels and Observations*, 1738 (I, 416–20), Dr. Thomas Shaw suggested that 'the second and third *Pyramids* were not intended as sepulchres.' 'This hypothesis', says Sandwich, 'appears to me extremely absurd and ridiculous' (*Voyage*, p. 461).

4. *The History of the Old and New Testament, Extracted out of Sacred Scripture and Writings of the Fathers ... Translated from the Sieur de Royaumont* [Nicholas Fontaine, 1625–1709] *By several Hands*. Second Edition, Corrected 1699. The book, brought out by Richard Blome (d. 1705), was 'Illustrated with Two hundred thirty-four SCULPTURES'. The picture mentioned by Spence (opposite p. 48) was meant to illustrate the second of 'The Nine *Plagues* of Egypt' (i.e., of 'Frogs, which covered the Face of all *Egypt*, and filled the very *Houses* and *Bed-chambers* of *King* and *People*').

*102

Source:	Egerton 2234 ff. 177–8
Addressed:	*as in* 74
Postmarked:	29 AP
Franked:	Free/Andrew Stone
Endorsed:	*a.* an act of ye frightfull crucked Ladys in egypt, *b.* Of certain Beauties, in ye/inner part of Egypt. *red wafer*

Turin,
April 27, 1740

⟨Dear Mother,

If Lord Sandwich has been so extraordinary good as to divert you for a little while, that was out of his particular good nature, and a thing that one must not expect to continue always. In effect, if I can furnish out this one letter more from what he has said to me, 'twill be as much as ever I can do.⟩

We left his Lordship, I think, in Egypt. You know, I believe, the way they have there of hatching chickens by fire. There's a great room made on purpose for this. The fire is in the middle, and there are little shelves, one above another, disposed at proper distances all round it. The eggs are placed in lines on these shelves, and they turn them sometimes, as we do an apple when 'tis roasting. When 'tis ready, the shell cracks, and the poor creatures get their little beaks out, and sometimes break through their prison themselves: if not, the supervisors help it out of its crust and set it a going in this miserable world—which is full of misfortunes, even for chicken. This is so common in Egypt, that there is not any country-town hardly that has not its chicken-hatcher. 'Tis as regular a trade there as a baker is with us, and 'twould astonish you to hear the number of them that there is in Grand Cairo.

That, you know, is one of the largest cities in the world; but Lord Sandwich says that neither that nor Constantinople is so big as London. Indeed our capital is vastly too large for our little dominions, and I have often of late thought that England is like a rickety child, that has a head too big for its body. 'Tis the distemper of our island to have its metropolis so large, and so out of all proportion, that it starves its limbs, which ought to share equally in the nourishment that is carried in such vast quantities to that overgrown part. I am no politician, but I can see that when a mouse has a head bigger than an elephant's it must be a monster, and that all does not go as it should do.

But to return to my good Lord: he went much farther into Egypt than Dr. Shaw, and came at last to a people in the hilly country whose name I have forgot, who are very brutish, and who have ideas very different from the rest of the world. No woman is reckoned handsome there that is not hump-backed,[1] and the ladies who have the misfortune to be straight (by the great negligence of those who had the care of their education) take care themselves to get as round-shouldered at least as they can by frequent stooping, and wear things under their gowns to make them appear as if they were crooked. If any lover was to be cheated into marrying one of them, and should find that she had only an artificial hump, you can't imagine what a noise the poor man would make. The people of quality (as they are most painted in England) are most humped in this part of Egypt, and to see them at one of their greatest assemblies, you would think that they had all got so many young pyramids peeping over their heads. ⟨Had Frank Riley[2] lived to have heard of this, she would have made a new collection of people to be transported to Egypt, where no doubt several honest women that are despised with us for their vast prominencies behind might make their fortunes and would be sought after by the chief lords of that land. With all services to all friends, I am ever

Your dutiful and affectionate

J: Spence.⟩

---

1. Spence gave this anecdote a slight twist ('scarred faces' instead of 'humps') in his *Crito*, p. 49. See also *Letter* 20 n. 2.
2. Not identified.

103

Source:	Egerton 2234 ff. 179–80
Addressed:	*as in 74*
Postmarked:	6 MA
Franked:	Free/Andrew Stone
Endorsed:	*a.* merriest, & short
	b. A short Dialogue-Letter./not to be Copy^d
	red wafer

Turin,
May 3, 1740

⟨Dear Mother,

As people generally say they are too busy to write, I must own at present
I am too idle to write, or indeed I might say that I am too idle and too
busy at the same time to do anything.—Why, the child's bewitched, I
think, or talking of riddles!—What I say is really true, for I am, and have
been these five days, wholly engaged in reading a long Italian romance,
which though you might like in your younger days, you must look
upon as a most frivolous employment in the age of discretion that you are
arrived at.—Indeed, my dear, you had better read *The Whole Duty of Man*.[1]
—The *Whole Duty of Man*! Why, there is not such a book in all these popish
countries: and so, with your leave, I'll go on with my story[2] and am, in
great haste,

Your most dutiful and affectionate

J. Spence.⟩

1. A popular devotional almanac by Richard
Allestree (1619–81). The full title runs: *The
Whole Duty of Man, Laid down In a Plain and
Familiar Way for the use of All, but especially the*
MEANEST READER. *Divided into XVII Chapters.
One whereof being Read every Lord's Day, the
Whole may be Read over Thrice in a Year. Necessary
for all* FAMILIES. First published in 1658, it
went through twenty-three editions before
1700, and was often reprinted in the 18th
century.

2. 'Reading of novels and Eastern fables, etc.
[is] like drinking drams. Wine tastes like water
after the latter, and the daily occurrences of
life seem quite tasteless and insipid after being
deeply engaged in the former' (*Obs.* No. 1179).

*104

Source: Egerton 2234 ff. 181–2
Addressed: as in 74
Endorsed: a. a let[er?]/more of Lord Sandwich
b. The fair Circasians.
red wafer

Turin,
May 11, 1740

⟨Dear Mother,⟩

If I am right in my reckoning, I have already sent you no less than seven
letters on Lord Sandwich's travels; my stock is now at an end, unless I was
to give you an account of all the old heathen temples and the other pieces
of antiquity which he saw at Athens.[1] But though those are things which I
should be more fond of seeing than anything he met with in all his travels,
they would be very undiverting in a letter, and so I shall leave them as he
found them, falling into ruins, that will grow every year more and more
and more venerable to all true antiquarians.

What you fear about the Grand Signior is but too true: his seraglio is
half stocked with Grecian women, and I don't doubt but there are many
ladies of Chios among the number. However, he has a country from which
he gets beauties that are more famous even than the pretty islanders of
Chios, and that is Circassia. We have a book, I remember, in England which
is entitled *The Fair Circassian*,[2] and the Circassians are indeed allowed to be
the prettiest women in the world. Should not you be glad to see some of
their breed in England? Why, the thing is not absolutely impossible: for
Lord Sandwich has been so wicked, I am told, as to bring over two fair
Circassians with him—I suppose not merely to show what pretty women
are born in that country, like patterns of a new silk from a mercer's shop;
and by that time we have been some time settled in Queen's Street, if my
acquaintance with his Lordship should happen to continue after my return,
I may be able to show you there perhaps a little half-Circassian, born in
England, who, if she has the wit of Lord Rochester, with the beauty of her
ancestors by the mother's side, will be the prettiest thing to prate with
that ever was seen.

'Tis a strange thing methinks that these noblemen can't go abroad without
bringing home women with them.[3] As if we had not women enough in our
island! or, to speak more civilly, as if our women were not as pretty as any
in the world. I'm sure I think so, for whenever I return to England from

273

any other country that I have been in, our women at first always look to me as if they were quite of another species than those I have been used to see abroad: England at first always seems to me to be a paradise, separated from the rest of the world, and inhabited by angels.[4] And now I have made them the compliment which I think they deserve (and which I am sure they would deserve, if they did not dress in that devilish ugly way that they do), I think 'tis high time to be their, and your

Most humble servant

⟨J. Spence.⟩

1. See *Voyage*, pp. 48–66, illustrated with several engravings.

2. 'A dramatic Performance' in eight cantos by Samuel Croxall (d. 1752) which aimed to copy the oriental warmth of the Song of Solomon. It first appeared in 1720 and, in spite of severe censure by James Craig (in his *Spiritual Life*, 1727), ran into a dozen editions.

3. Lord Middlesex, who was at this time pursuing the Muscovita, a 'dowdy' in Paris (*Hertford Corresp.* II, 137–9, 146), was to bring home to London an Italian opera singer on whom he lavished fortunes 'for secret services' (*H. W. Corresp.* XVII, 191). But I have found no corroboration of the Circassian gossip. In March next year Lord Sandwich married Dorothy Fane.

4. Or at least 73% angels. In *Crito* (p. 44) Spence set up a hundred points calculation-table, on the model of De Piles, for the gauging of female charms: 'If I was to state the Account, as to some particular Ladies, who have been generally allowed to be very great Beauties, I should assign to Lady L. B★★★, Eight for Color, Four for Shape, Twenty-five for Expression, and Ten for Grace; in all, Forty-seven; not quite half-way in the complete Sum of Excellence:—To Mrs. A★★★, Eight for Color, Seventeen for Shape, Fifteen for Expression, and Twenty for Grace; in all, Sixty Degrees of Excellence:—And to Mrs. B★★★, Eight for Color, Ten for Shape, Twenty-five for Expression, and Thirty for Grace; in all, Seventy-three. And that is the highest Sum, that I could in Conscience allow to any Woman that I have ever yet seen.'

Notebook 3

(xxiv–xxxiii) 74ʳ–79ʳ

Turin was (after Hannibal's time) very flourishing and large. In the beginning of the 5th century it was destroyed and soon after rebuilt, but upon a very little scale. Its form was square, and one may still trace the walls. (One angle was very near the subtendent of the Bastion Verde and run on in a line with the Palace and through the College of the Nobles to the farther side of the Strada Teresa; the second wall went straight along with the farther side of that street a little way into the citadel; the third from thence to the Madonna della Consolà; and the fourth from the Consolà to the angle by the Bastion Verde.) One may see by this how much it has been increased of late years. 'Twas let out towards the Porta del Po by Charles Emmanuel II, towards the Porta Nuova by Charles Emmanuel I, and towards the Porta Susina by the late King. With all this, Turin is at present scarce three mile round. . . . The town is well peopled, for there are 70,000 souls in it. . . .

The Strada del Po is the best built street in the town, all uniform and with porticos; the Strada Nuova the most striking from the houses being all stuccoed, from its falling in so with the Place of St. Charles and its being terminated with the Porta Nuova at one end and the King's Palace at the other.

The general fault of the town is that you have some houses covered with stucco and some not, and as in the latter they always leave the scaffold holes open (in order to stucco whenever they may have a mind to it) this has an extreme ill effect almost all over the town, and as much in the King's Palace as anywhere.

The city is at present of an oval figure, the longest line of it from the Porta del Po to the Porta Susina. Half of it is defended by the river Po and the river Dora, the other half by the citadel, very advanced outworks and perpetual minery. The delay of the French and the art of Victor was what saved the town in the last siege in 1706.

The French took a view of the town, as intending a siege the year before: they thought they could take it when they pleased, and as the season was far advanced, drew off their troops for the present. On this notice those very works [fortified outposts] were added, which took up the French all the first part of the siege, as Victor's decoying La Feuillade and so many of his troops into a wild-goose chase after him, ran out the siege to so great a length that Prince Eugene had time to come and beat them when they were at last all got together again in their entrenchments.[1] . . .

The spirit that is the most general in Turin at present is that of war. Their situation has almost always obliged them to be on their guard, and the late reign, which was so long and so military, has made them as it were a nation of soldiers. As they are the only military people in Italy, what might they not do there if the Greater Powers out of Italy were to let them alone? As so many of the states in Italy are either in the possession or under the protection of the Greater Powers, they must watch their occasions when those Greater Powers are embroiled and join with one to gain ground on the other.

The beaux arts are in a very low state at Turin at present—unless the art of war, the art of love, the art of gaming and the art of chit-chat may be reckoned among the beaux arts. These, indeed, are all very well studied and in a very flourishing condition. The other arts are very little regarded and less under stood. . . . There is scarce any prince (even on our wrong side of the Alps) who has a worse painter, a worse statuary or a worse architect than his Majesty of Sardinia is furnished with at present.

In former times 'tis said they had some taste for the *virtù* here. Charles Emmanuel I and his son Cardinal Maurice were pretty warm in making a collection of statues, busts, medals and pictures. His grandson, Charles Emmanuel II, began a gallery for them which might have been one of the most considerable in Italy ('twas to have been near a thousand feet long—the design of it is in the Theatre de Piedmont). The late King was perpetually engaged in affairs of so much greater consequence to his family and his country that the taste for these sort of things was quite lost among them, and so it continues to this day.

Most of the antiques that had been got together were flung as rubbish into a ground room of the palace, which the gentleman who told me of it called *le cimetière des statues*, and the part of the gallery which was built for them is turned into archives and offices for the Secretaries of State.

There are, however, several things of this kind left which are worth a stranger's looking upon that is going into Italy, though there is but very few that would be supportable to one that is going out. In the King's Palace, for instance, there are twelve old statues on the great staircase, of which five or six are tolerable ones. On your left hand a pretty-shaped Venus (that would be prettier if her fesses were not daubed over with plaster), a tolerable Bacchus, a good gladiator; on the other side a tolerable Venus (plastered as the former), a tolerable gladiator, a Mercury—perhaps tolerable, and a Bacchus with the fine *cothurni* (the body and legs ancient and very good). In going out of the King's Palace there is a little landing by the back stairs with a tolerable Minerva (as in a little chapel) and four statues in the portico, two of which may be called good—at least at Turin. One of these is a Season (?) with her head veiled, a hare in her right hand, and two birds in her left. The other is one of the most particular and one of the most puzzling figures I have ever seen. The face has the Greek air and its hair is collected over the forehead in two rounds, not unlike an Apollo's. There's a list appears under the hair of the forehead and then is lost in the hair of each side; a particular sort of *velum* behind the head with two *taeniae* on each side falling down a pretty way on the shoulders and breast; a sort of *paludamentum* fastened with a round gem about the middle of the breast, a *cingulum* appearing from under the *paludamentum* and going down to the left side; a vest with large folds succinct circularly an inch or more above the navel; then a *multilium* following closely the shape of the belly and limbs quite down to the feet, making a hard line of plaits between the legs and showing very plainly the sex; from under this there is an odd sort of ribbed stuff that comes half-way over the feet, as the soles appear under them. One foot is a little advanced before the other, the left (?) arm is held back, and the right arm (which is modern) might well have agreed with the same attitude. What it represented is very difficult to say, and 'tis as difficult to fix what nation it is of. If one was to see only the head, one should declare it Grecian; if one was to see only the breast and shoulders, it might pass for Roman; and if one was to see only from the navel downward, one should take it to be Egyptian. In a word 'tis all over a riddle and mystery.

At the Duke of Savoy's there are about sixty busts in the Great Hall, among which is a fine Greek head of Bacchus (?) with a diadem, Trajan with an eagle, holding the thunder and a slave under a trophy on his lorica (from some triumphal arch?), Sabina (?), Vitellius, Seneca, (head of spotted marble, looking up sideways with a lively air), Faustina, Vespasian, Greek head of Antinous, head crowned with laurel and *velum*, Vestal Virgin (veiled and particular coiffure under it, *manibus supinis*), Faustina (?) with two heads *sopraposte* on her shoulder. Germ[anicus?] and Nero.

At the statuaries in the Royal Academy are the débris that were found some time ago in the *cimetière des statues*, among which are the following that are either good, tolerable, or particular: busts of Janus (both faces very young and *sans barbe*), two of Seneca, Socrates (not that inscribed with his name), Polypheme (eye and eyebrow in his forehead, eyebrows and cavities below), bad. Alexander (dying?), two of Minerva and eight or ten other busts that may be tolerable. Statues: pretty little Bacchus playing with a tiger; woman about a foot and a half high, resting on a column; little Cupid sleeping, with lion's skin over his head and club in his hand; remains of a very odd female figure with a sort of night-robe over the shoulders, holding up several little children in her lap and disc[losin]g the *membrum virile* under it; satyr and Apollo, scarce inferior to the Lodovisian; young man, hair curled like Antinous'; Diana (body touchstone,

276

legs, arms and head added of black marble, *veste succincta*, one breast uncovered);
Atys (?) with the Phrygian bonnet, face as dying; little faun with grapes.[2]

At the university are several ancient inscriptions and relievos which were
ranged there (about 1728) by the Marquis Maffei of Verona, all round the court.
If you begin by the left-hand side you have four heads of soldiers as on a march,
altissimo relievo tolerably good; man sitting on a bull, holding him by the horn
with his left hand, and another with his right, the bull's roaring as in pain or
conquered (?); two slips of relievos: arms etc. of different sorts and one channelled,
which were found with a great many of the inscriptions there when the King
gave Monsieur Boursier leave to take down some of Stilicho's wall near the
Porta di Milano, with three other slips of arms and a [   ] of channelled
marble. They all perhaps composed the frieze to some temple of Mars, but have
met with very different usage: the former being ranged with great care in the
university and the latter placed upon the back side of a public sink in the Place-
Château (in 1725, inscr.). Sarcophagus of four bacchanals dancing, first with
torch in each hand and serpent about each arm, second with thyrsus in one hand
and head or mask in the other, third holding up fruit, and fourth with a sword,
going to kill a young fawn: tolerably good. (All the relievos here were copied
for Mr. Frederick.) Pillar and urn and man stopping four horses, imperfect work,
tolerably good. Young wild boar dead, ditto. Masks of Silenus, Muse (?) and
faun, good. Four bacchanal women tearing Orpheus to pieces (his fiddle which
lies by him is like a modern fiddle, very bad work),[3] Orpheus' face much better
than the rest. Achilles riding on Chiron (?) and Thetis (?) by. Priest and faun
sacrificing a pig (to Sylvanus?), middling. Sarcophagus, four B[achae] dancing,
bad. Little slip of fauns and nymphs, tolerably good. Two river-gods with fins
like wings, bad. Jupiter sitting with scepter, Venus flattering and complaining,
Juno (with scepter) disdainful and out of humour, tolerably good. Bacchanal
kneeling on an altar, head flung back and holding up a fig (like the palladium?)
before a Terminal Jupiter (?), very good. Two bacchanals with fawn cut in two,
tolerably good. Cupid with large curled wings and little wings to his feet,
'weighing nothing in unequal scales', tolerable.

The taste in building at Turin has never been good: it might have been better
had not Filippo been called to Madrid (where he drank a dish of chocolate too
much).[4] The best thing at Turin is the staircase in the Duke's palace by Don
Filippo, though they seem to talk of the chapel at St. John's and St. Lorenzo's
Church as the finest works they have: these were built by Guarini, *l'ennemi juré
de la ligne droite*, and that celebrated dome is all a collection of angles (something
like a pineapple on the outside and like nothing in the world on the inside). The
Superga and the gallery, chapel, orangery and baths at the Venerie (that is, all
the best things in that palace) are by Filippo too. There's a good Somnus (or
Cupid) and some busts at the Venerie, and an Egyptian sphinx and some other
old(?) statues on the staircase of the Valentin.

At S. Filippo Neri's (the only Roman building at Turin in the right good
taste, begun by Filippo) are three large pictures by Solimena, Trevisani and
Carlo Marat, and on a wet day one may go into the cloisters of S. Francis di
Paolo to see the fresco paintings there, which are not bad.

The King's Palace is bad enough on the outside, but finely (and perhaps too
finely) furnished within. There are several good pictures in it, the chief are the
four *tondi* or elements by Albani, Charles I by Vandyck, his children ditto, two
large Paul Veroneses and two of Bassan, 'The Prodigal Son' of Guercin, etc. As

the King has a great taste for public actions and partly for public buildings, 'tis a pity he has not a better architect.

From the citadel of Turin one may have leave to see the mines.

1. For the siege, the military and political situation of Turin in 1740, see *Obs.* Nos. 1595–1602. Spence's informants were Count Richa, the royal physician, and Dom Villa, the royal archivist.

2. For a description of the famous 'Tabula Isiaca', see *Obs.* No. 1590.

3. Spence drew a sketch of the fiddle in the margin.

4. Filippo Juvarra (1676–1736), the famous architect, went to Madrid in 1735 to construct a new royal palace, and died there Jan. 31, 1736.

---

*105

Source:	Egerton 2234 ff. 183–4
Addressed:	*as in 74*
Postmarked:	20 MA
Franked:	Free/Andrew Stone
Endorsed:	*a.* a carictor/of the king of serdinaya
	b. The King of Sardinia's Character
	red wafer

[Turin,
May 18, 1740][1]

⟨Dear Mother,⟩

'Tis now a great while that I have been indebted to you a letter on the royal family here: my Lord Sandwich's travels came in the way, and have deferred it hitherto. At present, as I have nothing else to do, I may very well sit down to pay my debts.

I don't know whether you have ever found out that I have something of my old Uncle Neville in me, and am consequently not apt to be overfond of kings.[2] The King of Sardinia would go a great way towards reconciling one toward that high species of animals.[3] He has not (by some uncommon piece of good fortune) forgot that he is a man. He is good-natured, and sensible enough. In his father's reign he was called young into the council, to use him to affairs of state and the art of government. It was observed of him there, that he was always silent and observing, unless the King asked his opinion on any case that was debating there, and then he always gave it readily, in a few words, and generally very much to the purpose. He came to the throne earlier than he might have done, without his own seeking, and when the scepter was once put into his hands he held it firmly and steadily. The late King not only made a kingdom of his family domains, but left it to his present Majesty almost doubled as to its extent, and above doubled as to its income. He was a lover of war and intrigues of state, of a very martial temper, and yet more cunning than martial. This, with a long reign and his knowing how to make advantage of the incidents between other princes extremely well, enabled him to aggrandize his country to so great a degree. Beside what he added to it, he had a longing eye on the Milanese ⟨or the state of Milan⟩, and used to say 'that state was like an artichoke; that one must not think of eating it all at once, but pull it leaf by leaf': and he himself had pulled two or three leaves of it with success.[4]

His son does not push into wars so often, or so busily, as his father did. He chooses rather to give comfort to his people, and satisfies himself with keeping up a strong military spirit among them, against any necessary occasions. The King found himself obliged to enter into the last war in Italy on the French side, and behaved particularly well in the battle of Guastalla (which was fought the summer after I left Italy with Lord Middlesex),[5] and at the end of the war got three leaves more from the Milanese. However, I like his character best in peace. The people are happy under him, and are (what the English I suppose never can be) sensible of the happiness they enjoy. They talk thankfully of it, and delight themselves with the blessing of having a good king; which I own seemed a little strange to me, as I came hither directly from the grumblings which one hears in every corner of our island. I thought the rest of the world had been as ungrateful as the Britons: but I beg the rest of the world's pardon, and begin now to think that we are the only people in it that have got that odd trick of winking hard at noon, and then vexing ourselves because 'tis so dark all about us.[6]

There was an accident here (which you may call trifling perhaps) just after we came, that gave me a very good impression of the King's goodness. He is a keen sportsman, and as he was in the heat of the chase, one of the lower huntsmen had a fall, and lay for dead. The King was near enough to see this accident; he immediately quitted the sport, galloped up to him, got off his horse, and was quarter of an hour taking care of him, till he was quite come to himself again. He was in short as tender and officious about him, and as ready as any common man could have been, and absolutely saved the poor fellow's life. The first time I heard this at our table (where there were eighteen or twenty people at dinner), it struck me so much that I could not help the tears getting into my eyes, and indeed they were ready to have run down my cheeks for joy, which (I have some reason to think) was afterwards told to his Majesty. For though I am a very low man, they generally look upon me here as a grave, thinking foreigner, not given to flattery, that reads and meditates much, of few words, and of great solidity. You see how much they are mistaken in their opinion of me, but 'tis easy to impose upon strangers by a grave outside and an affectation of deep scholarship.[7] But however I may cheat others, I am very sincerely

Your ⟨dutiful and affectionate

J. Spence.⟩

1. Date from Spence's endorsement.

2. Col. Henry Neville (1620–94) of Billing-bear, Spence's great-great-uncle, M.P. for Reading, and a political theorist admired by Hobbes and Harrington. His best-known work was *Plato Redivivus, or a Dialogue Concerning Government* (1681).

3. Charles Emmanuel III (1701–73) succeeded to the throne after the abdication of his father Victor Amadeus II in 1730.

4. The Novarese, the Tortonese, and the Langhe. As for Charles Emmanuel III, 'le duché de Milan est le véritable objet de sa concupiscence ... de toutes les puissances d'Italie, les Italiens ne craignent que lui; il est à leur gorge à ce qu'ils disent, et les suffoquera tôt ou tard. ... Le roi Victor, son père, disait que l'Italie était comme un artichaut qu'il fallait manger feuille à feuille. Son fils suivra tant qu'il pourra cette maxime' (De Brosses, II, 581–2).

5. Sept. 19, 1734, a bloody battle (12,000 dead) in which the Piedmontese under Charles Emmanuel and the French repulsed the Austrian Imperial forces under Königseck. For an account, see D. Carutti, *Storia del regno di Carlo Emmanuele III* (Turin, 1859), I, 98–103.

6. Spence had enlarged on this subject in a letter to Massingberd (Mar. 15, 1738/9): 'Our nation looks to me like a great fool that has got the hip: sits sullenly in the chimney-corner, by a good fire, cries pish to anybody that offers it a favour, and if they are quitting it, bawls out to 'em to come back and give it what it at first had refused. ... What can the wisest nurse do to satisfy such a peevish brat as this?' (Wright, p. 57).

7. In a panegyric made 'in ejusdem laude' during his stay in Italy, Spence is addressed as 'Vir doctus et Vatum elogiis dignissimus':

Fertilis Ingeniis est Pars haec optima Mundi;
Te nullum Ingenium cultius ipsa tulit ...

(Spence Papers)

---

*106

Source: Egerton 2234 ff. 185–6
Addressed: as in 74
Postmarked: 27 MA
Franked: Free/Andrew Stone
Endorsed: a. an act:/of ye ceremony on palm sunday
              b. Of ye Queen of Sardinia/& ye Ceremony on Palm Sunday.
              red wafer

Turin,
May 25, 1740

⟨Dear Mother,⟩

Though I could say a great many more good things of the King of Sardinia, I must now pay my compliments to the Queen.[1] She is a French woman, or at least of Lorraine, and sister to the present Great Duke of Tuscany.[2] The pretty Queen of Sardinia (of the Hesse-Rhinefield family) when I was here before, being dead, and indeed this is the third wife the King has ventured on already, though he is not quite so old as I am: which, by the way, perhaps shows his courage more than all the brave things he did at the battle of Guastalla. However, he has had good luck, or rather Providence has wrought miracles in his favour, for they were *all three* good women. The present Queen is very good-natured, rather tall, well-made, of a fine complexion, but not handsome. The under part of her face comes out a little too far, and that gives an ungraceful air, which would ruin the finest face in the world in my opinion.[3] She is lively and gay for a Queen, and on any public occasion seems to show a great deal of ease and good humour.

On Palm Sunday they have a ceremony here, which, I fancy, was formerly in use in England ⟨in the Roman Catholic times—but that you must know better than I, as you were born I think but a very little after the Reformation⟩.[4] On this day, here at least, the King washes thirteen charity boys' feet and serves their dinner to them, and the Queen does the same to thirteen charity girls. I saw the whole ceremony—as you know I always thrust myself in wherever there is a crowd, whether occasioned by kings or ballad singers. In the great hall of the palace were two long tables covered with an infinity of dishes, all of cold things, and all dressed out with flowers and greens to such a degree that you could scarce distinguish a pickled trout from a cold pasty, or an otter from a neat dish of snails. The King and all the court came from mass, in a sort of procession, through this room into the next, where the children were seated in two rows, very neat and (as it seemed by their looks) very much afraid. Here the ceremony of the washing was performed. Their majesties just touched their feet with a sponge, and then passed a towel over them, genteelly enough: but if their feet had not been very well washed before they came thither, they would have been but very little the better for their royal operation. After the washing, the staff-officers, the Knights of the Annunciation (which is the chief order here, like the Knights of the Garter with us) and the other chief courtiers went out, one by one, and returned each with a dish of flowers (with something eatable under them), which they handed to the King, and he to his almoner, who gave them to servants that carried them downstairs into a room where the poor children were to eat. For as to their dinner in sight, 'twas just like the dinner of poor Sancho Panza in his government.[5] The Queen in her turn, did the same, only she was served by all the chief ladies of the court, dressed in the Spanish fashion, with puffed sleeves to their gowns, and a vast deal of brown-looking Flanders-lace, which is more esteemed here than when it is washed very white. The Queen's part of the ceremony lasted half an hour, and you saw the pretty ladies going and coming all the while in a long line through the crowd, and as busy as a line of emmets in a sand-walk. The Queen (in all this tedious time for her to be stared at as the principal object) kept always a good-humoured gracious smile on her face, and shifted the dishes from her pretty waiter to her almoner with a great deal of grace.[6] However, my paper says I must now leave the ceremony, to be

Your ⟨dutiful and affectionate

J. Spence.⟩

1. Elizabeth-Thérèse (1711–41), dau. of Leopold-Joseph, D. of Lorraine, became the King's 3d wife on Mar. 9, 1737. See *Letter* 76 n. 3.

2. Francis I of Lorraine (1708–65), Grand Duke of Tuscany 1737–65, husband of Maria Theresa; later Emperor Francis I, 1745–65.

3. 'Sa lèvre d'Autriche se marque de plus en plus,' wrote De Brosses, 'et elle est encore plus couperosée que nous ne l'avons vue à Dijon: à cela près, sa figure n'est pas déplaisante, elle a surtout l'air noble et majestueux' (II, 577).

4. A slip for 'Restoration'. Mrs. Spence was born ca. 1670 (Wright, p. 4). The King's washing the feet of the poor was known as 'the Maundy ceremony'; James II in 1685 was the last to observe it. In 1731 the ceremony was performed by the Abp. of York; after 1736 it was discontinued (A. R. Wright, *British*

Calendar Customs [Cambridge, 1936], I, 61–5).

5. Where 'a Page put a lac'd Bib under *Sancho*'s Chin; and another . . . set a Dish of Fruit before him. But he had hardly put one Bit into his Mouth, before the Physician touch'd the Dish with his Wand, and then it was taken away. . . . *Sancho* was amaz'd at this sudden Removal, and looking about him on the Company, ask'd them why they shou'd tantalize People at that rate, feeding their Eyes and starving their Bellies. . . . Because, answer'd the Doctor, our great Master *Hippocrates*, the North-Star, and Luminary of Physick, says in one of his Aphorisms, Omnis saturatio mala' (*Don Quixote,* tr. P. Motteux, II, iii, chap. 47).

6. The court of Turin was 'reckoned one of the politest in Europe' (*Letter* 21) in part because it kept strict observance of formal ceremonies.

107

Source: Joseph Warton's transcript in his Notebook, Trinity College Library, Oxford

SPENCE TO CHRISTOPHER PITT

Turin,
May 25, 1740.

Dear Pitt,

(For I think we have long left off the word Postle,[1] as too old-fashioned and indeed not very creditable at this time of day) do you think that fame is so forgetful of you that I should not have heard of you and your two great quartos on this side the Alps without your taking the pains of writing to me?[2] That you may not distrust her when you come to write a folio, I assure you I heard of it as early as we hear of anything from England; the news first came fluttering here in the shape of a gazette,[3] and since I have had it in two or three letters. I hope it will sell briskly and am pretty sure you could not be in honester hands than Dodsley's, which is a very considerable point with an author that publishes at his own expense.

Now you talk of Dodsley, do you know whether Lord Sandwich does, or is likely to, make use of him? His Lordship was so good as to show me (in the little time he stayed here) what he had wrote on his travels, and surprised me very much, not because there was a great deal of learning and judgement shown in his remarks, for I was well enough acquainted with his character before, but because they were as well wrote at the first heat, and as correctly, as most people's things are at the third or fourth copying. I told his Lordship 'twould be a sin not to publish them, and mentioned Dodsley's name and character to him then, and wrote to him about it afterwards.

You gave me a great deal of pleasure in letting me know that you and the other friends you mention are well. Heaven keep you so till September twelvemonth when I hope to be among you, and when once I am in England again I believe I shall be there for life. Not but what I love travelling still and am like to love it (perhaps a little too much!) but 'twill be high time then to think of other matters, as a settlement for the time |of | one's stay in this world and the affairs of one's poor soul (as the phrase in England is) for the next. These are two very material points in both of which I have been rather too negligent hitherto, and which I hope to make some amends for on my return. A fool at forty is a fool indeed—and I am somewhat past forty, but o' my conscience as deep in my follies as ever! When I should be getting a good fat living I am wandering about Italy, and when I should be saying my prayers am thinking of some fine statue. At this very instant all my desires are at Rome, as if the Pope would make a cardinal of me or as if his pretensions of helping one in the road to heaven were really well grounded. Happy, thrice happy, are the plump rosy country-rectors in England, who know nothing of these vanities and spend all their time in drink and devotion! Well, I will mend one time or another, that's flat. And in the meantime (which may be a vast while for what I know) whatever happens to one, or wherever I am, I shall be

Most assuredly / and affectionately yours

J Spence

My Lord was very glad to hear Mr. Read is well, and has long expected a letter from him.[4]

1. In his early letters, Spence used to address Pitt as 'Dear Postle'.

2. Pitt completed his translation of the *Aeneid* on June 2, 1738; in April 1740 it was published by Dodsley in two handsome quarto volumes, with a dedication to the Prince of Wales.

3. *The Gentleman's Magazine* (X, 208) lists in its 'Register *of* Books *in* April, 1740': '57. A new Translation of the Aeneid of *Virgil*. By Mr *Pitt*. 2 Vols. 4to. price 1 *l*. 1 *s*. *Dodsley*.'

4. See *Letter* 80 n. 6.

*108

Source:	Egerton 2234 ff. 187–8
Addressed:	*as in 74*
Postmarked:	3 IV
Franked:	Free/Andrew Stone
Endorsed:	*a.* a good ac^t/of S^r john Royden, & there pro-/cessions, bare foot, for Raine: *b.* Of Sr J^n Royden & y^e/Processions for Rain. *red wafer*

Turin,
June 1, 1740

⟨Dear Mother,⟩

Sir John R⟨oyden⟩ has been here some days, and sets out this afternoon for France.[1] One cannot know a vast deal of a man in a week's travelling-acquaintance, but by what I have seen of him, I should take him to be a good-natured good sort of a man. We have here in the Academy a countryman of his,[2] who lived in the same house with him all the winter at Rome. He tells me that he is good-natured, loves company and expense: that he did not mind that he was particularly amorous, only that it was once talked of that he would marry an English lady at Siena, but, as far as I can find, that matter is off. This English lady, by what I hear of her, is enough to make anybody in love with her. 'Tis Lady Sophia Fermor,[3] daughter of the Earl of Pomfret, who was a celebrated beauty in England, and must be a double beauty here. ⟨I have not yet seen her, and so am as yet—thanks be to heaven—in perfect good health, and with a heart that I think has not one flaw in it.⟩ With Sir John R⟨oyden⟩ is his brother,[4] a young sea-officer, that never was heard to swear an oath or to say an indecent thing: the truth is, he seems to be a very sensible young man, and too modest for an Irishman. Sure, my Lady laid in of him in England.

I have made it a general observation (by our comparing notes together) that the large turns of the weather are pretty much alike, in our island and on the continent. We had a long and hard frost, and so had you: it was followed by fine weather here, and the same in England.

The beginning of May, all this place was full of processions for rain; you could not cross the streets of an evening without meeting a number of barefoot people, some with lighted holy candles, others with death's-heads or ropes about their necks, several dragging heavy chains at their feet, several sinking under vast heavy crosses, some with crowns of thorns—all in shrouds, and many half covered with blood and slashing themselves (with bundles of whipcord) at every step they made. On Sunday sennight I met a procession of this kind in my morning walk, in which there were forty-eight of these slashers only from one country town.[5] They all come hither to 'the Virgin of Consolation' who has done a world of miracles, and is perhaps the statue that is at present the most worshipped of any in all Piedmont.[6] The Virgin was so good as to give them some rain that very afternoon, and they were all easily wet to their skins before they got home. We have had rain ever since, three days and three nights of the time without ceasing. It rains at this instant, and if it continues but a very little longer, we expect all the processions over again, for dry weather.

⟨As we have had so much rain here, I hope you have had your share too in England, before this time: if not, I would advise you to have a procession as soon as possible. Crowns of thorns you may have out of every hedge, and death's-heads out of every charnel-house: but if they should be scarce, I know some faces in Winchester that would serve full as well for the purpose. The difficulty will be to get the slashers. My subject is ready to make me melancholy, and crying is not the water we want. As it is, I am already much disposed to be, very seriously

Your most humble servant

J. Spence

All services to all friends⟩

---

1. See *Letter* 88.

2. No doubt the 'wild Irishman' (*Letter* 83) who sat next to Spence at dinner.

3. The beautiful elder daughter (1721–45) of Lady Pomfret. The Pomfrets stayed at Siena from July to December 1739.

4. Arthur Rawdon of Rathmullyan (1723–66), later Sheriff of the county of Meath (*Peerage of Ireland* [1789], III, 108).

5. Conyers Middleton compared this with the practice of heathen '*fanatical Priests* of *Bellona . . . Isis*', etc. who 'used to slash and cut themselves of old, in order to please the *Goddess*, by the *sacrifice of their own blood* which *mad piece of discipline* we find frequently mentioned, and as oft ridiculed by the *antient writers*' (*A Letter from Rome*, 1741 edn., pp. 190–1). See also Gray's *Corresp.* I, 147.

6. The image of the Madonna della Consolata, worshipped in the chapel of Our Lady of Consolation, was transferred in 1704 to a chapel designed by Juvarra. The Consolata was built 1679 by G. Guarini.

109

Source: Add. MSS 33065 ff. 365–6
Endorsed: R[eceived] 4. (by Crew.)

LINCOLN TO NEWCASTLE

Turin,
June 3, 1740

My Lord,

I should have sooner returned your Grace my thanks for your most obliging letter[1] if I had not waited the messenger's return from Florence, as I desired Mr. Spence to acquaint your Grace with. You may easily guess what pleasure I had of seeing my old friend Crew at Turin,[2] who gave me such fresh accounts of your Grace and my friends being perfectly well. I can but say I was a little surprised, and I must own uneasy, at his not having a letter for me. But yours, which I received the post after, made me [so] entirely happy that were I to write you a dozen, I could not repay the debt I owe you for the last, which I cannot be sufficiently grateful for.

I can't help taking notice to your Grace that Mr. Villettes was extremely cast down after the coming of the messenger, that he had often mentioned his hopes of having a secretary allowed him, but that now he seemed to despair of it. I sincerely have often observed that after a fatiguing post day he is so low-spirited and tired that he usually [doesn't] recover [till] three or four days after. I am very certain your Grace, whose good nature I am so thoroughly acquainted with, can't be surprised at my being sorry to see him in this way or most heartily wishing to see him easy after the particular obligations I have to him.

I rejoice with your Grace at our success against Spain, and am in daily expectation of having some more good news.[3] I am sorry my Lord Halifax has showed so much warmth the last sessions,[4] I should wish my Lord Sandwich was of another way of thinking,[5] for his great abilities must necessarily make him of great consequence whichever way he turns. Since your Grace does not dislike our staying on here, we don't design moving till August, and then go on by small journeys further into Italy. I desire my duty to the D[uchess] of Newcastle who, I am very glad to hear, is so well. I have been in great hopes of a letter and won't give up the thing yet.

Pray my duty to my Uncle Pelham and Lady Katherine, who I hope are well. I am / my Lord, / your Grace's most affectionate / and dutiful nephew

Lincoln

P.S. I beg my compliments to Mrs. Spence, Jemmy, and all who are so good as to remember me.[6]

---

1. Missing.

2. Probably Samuel Crew, serving in 1722–45 as 'one of his Majesty's messengers'. He arrived at Florence on May 22 (*H. W. Corresp.* XVII, 6 n. 9), so he must have passed through Turin about the middle of May. Crew was in close touch with Andrew Stone and the D. of Newcastle.

3. The news of Admiral Vernon's victory over the Spaniards at Porto Bello (Nov. 22, 1739) reached London Mar. 13 O.S., and English spirits were naturally high. There were (unfounded) rumours at this time that Admiral Haddock intercepted Spanish troops destined for Majorca (Gray, *Corresp.* I, 155).

4. George Dunk Montagu (1716–71), 2d E. of Halifax, joined the Prince of Wales and the opposition Whigs. For his speech made in the House of Lords on Feb. 28, in which he 'showed so much warmth', see Cobbett's *Parliamentary History of England* (1812), IX, 450–5. On his assumed name 'Dunk', see *Letter* 125 n. 5.

5. Immediately after his return to England, Lord Sandwich plunged into politics, joining the opposition Whigs under the D. of Bedford and Carteret.

6. Elizabeth Spence, according to John Wright, was related to Spence. 'She died in 1768, after being friend and companion to the Duchess of Newcastle for more than forty-five years' (*Letters of Horace Walpole*, ed. Bentley [1840], III, 40 n.). She had a family and a sister at Bath (Add. MSS 33066 f. 13ʳ). 'Jemmy' has not been identified.

---

*110

Source: Egerton 2234 ff. 189–90
Addressed: as in 74
Postmarked: 10 IV
Franked: Free/Andrew Stone
Endorsed: *a.* an actᵗ/of yᵉ marage of yᵉ prince of Carignon/to yᵉ princess of Hesse—sister/to the pretoy queen of sardinia
b. Of the Princess of Ca-/rignan; & her Marriage-/Ceremony
red wafer

Turin,
June 8, 1740

⟨Dear Mother,⟩

Sir John R⟨oyden⟩ last week interrupted my account of the great people here: if you please, we will now go on with it. The pretty Queen of Sardinia[1] left behind her three little daughters, one son and a sister,[2] who loved her so extremely, that she left her own country to be always near her on this side of the Alps. I have told you formerly in a letter that there were three sisters of the Hesse-Rhinefield family,[3] who, though they had very

287

small fortunes, were married very greatly in the world: one to a very rich German prince, another to the Duke of Bourbon,[4] and the third to the King of Sardinia. I did not then know anything of this fourth.[5] How often have I went since to court only to look upon her face at a distance through the crowd! She is very pretty, though not so fine a face near as the Duchess of Bourbon's: but the character of her face is all sweetness and good nature, and there's a little modest and a little slyish cast with it that is ⌜irresistible⌝.[6]

When the Queen her sister died, she went to the King, all in tears, and begged his leave to return into her own country. The King was extremely moved with what she said (for she had dropped something, from the anguish she was under for so great a loss, of her now having no friends here), and assured her 'she should always find as true and as affectionate a friend in him as she had lost in her sister'. He entreated her to stay here, that they might talk together of their common loss and comfort each other, or at least indulge their melancholy together. He promised her 'that all her interests should be his care, and that he would think of a settlement for her that should not be unworthy her merit and her beauty'. If any young lady was to read this, she would think that all this tenderness must mean something else at the bottom: but the King of Sardinia is a good man, and no modern gentleman. She has stayed here ever since, beloved and esteemed by everybody, and the King, beside a continued course of goodness, has not forgot the last part of his promise to her.

The first prince of the blood here, is the Prince of Carignan (of the family of the famous Prince Eugene) who is young,[7] of a pretty personage, and good-natured. The first time I saw him was on horseback, in which case he looks particularly graceful: he is not so genteel afoot. This prince has for some time been in love with the Princess of Hesse that I have been talking of so much, and if it had not been the fashion (here, as well as everywhere else) for young ladies not to own what they feel within them, I believe one might fairly have said that she was as much in love with him. The King saw this amour early, and encouraged it. Last month they were married,[8] and the King was so good as to increase her family fortune of only three thousand pound to thirty thousand, and was her father, to give her to the prince she loved.

And how could you be such a creature as not to be at the ceremony?—Not at it! Why, d'ye think there can be any ceremony at Turin without my being there? Yes, I was there, and in as good a place as anyone in the whole company.

The Archbishop of Turin officiated, in robes all cloth-of-gold or embroidery. The Prince and Princess knelt on the steps of the altar. The King and Queen stood behind them, and almost as near as their Majesties was (by mistake I believe of my conductor) your most humble servant. I never in my life saw so thick a crowd as there was in the church below: but the King and I, and two or three more, stood quite at our ease. Everybody's face had joy upon it. The King (though rather a grave man than a merry) looked particularly pleased, and there were several smiles passed between him and the Queen.

But the person that was most evidently merry was the pretty Princess of Hesse. She really tittered through the whole ceremony, and I was literally afraid that she would laugh some of the diamonds out of her hair, which was stuck as full of them as it could well hold. When she rose from her knees to go away, her face was all vermilioned with laughing, which made her look handsomer than ever, for, if anything, her usual complexion is rather too pale. But let her be ever so pale, if she had had a fever for a month and looked as white as the mountains do behind us, let her but smile and show that dimple in her right cheek, and who is the mortal that can find any the least fault about her?[9] ⟨I am somewhat, you see, in love, but much more

Your dutiful and affectionate

J. Spence.⟩

1. Polyxena of Hesse-Rheinfels, 2d wife of Charles Emmanuel III, died Jan. 13, 1735.

2. Her daughters were Eleanora (1728–81), Maria-Felicità (1730–1801), and Marie-Louise (1729–67). Her son was the D. of Savoy (b. June 26, 1726), later (1776–96) K. Victor Amadeus III (her 2d son, Emmanuel-Philibert, had died in infancy). Her sister was Christina-Henrietta (1717–78), the youngest of the Hesse-Rheinfels sisters. Pompeo Litta, Celebri famiglie italiane (Milan, 1838).

3. See Letter 21. Actually there were five sisters, but Sophia, the eldest, died in infancy (La Chenaye-Desbois Badier, Dict. de la noblesse [Paris, 1861], X, 606–7).

4. Eleonora-Philippina (b. 1712) had married Johann Christian, Prince of Sulzbach, who died in 1733; on Caroline, Dss. of Bourbon, see Letter 21 n. 7.

5. Christina-Henrietta, see note 2.

6. Emended to 'extremely pleasing'.

7. Louis-Victor-Joseph of Savoy (1721–78) was only nineteen at the time. Christina-Henrietta was twenty-three.

8. On May 4.

9. Ten years later 'a good deal of her beauty' was gone. See App. 14.

*111

Source: Egerton 2234 ff. 191–2
Addressed: as in 74
Postmarked: 17 IV
Franked: Free/Andrew Stone
Endorsed: a. a descripshon/of the young duke of savoy
b. Of the Young Prince of/Piemont; & yᵉ Princesses.
red wafer

Turin,
June 15, 1740

⟨Dear Mother,⟩

Your great favourite, the young Duke of Savoy (eldest son of the pretty Queen of Sardinia) knelt behind his father all the while mass was saying before the Princess of Hesse's wedding, and looked like a little angel between his beauty and his devotion.[1] He has something of the Neville family in his face, and I fancy you might make it out to yourself, between the beauty of Mr. Grey Neville and the round face and good-natured look of Mr. Harry Grey, when they were boys.[2] His face is round, and himself short of his age. I have seen boys taller at ten, and he is fourteen. He has good nature and good sense in his look, without which the finest features are either dead or displeasing:[3] and a remarkable cloud over his eyes, which is very uncommon, I think, in good-natured faces. It would have done you good to have seen him that evening at the ball at court. The occasion gave him more gaiety than usual, though he is usually pretty gay, and you could not have helped observing that everybody's eyes were fixed upon him, and that they seemed to say in their hearts, 'Hereafter that delightful prince is to be our king, and to increase the happiness that we enjoy under his father.'

The three little princesses,[4] his sisters, I have seen often—but only in their coach, as they go out to take the air every evening. They seem to be pretty too, but I have not so distinct an idea of their faces, because I have seen them always with their little heads all together, and only in passing by them.

The present Queen made a prince last year,[5] and is every day ready to make another, or a princess. The great guns are all ready: if 'tis a prince, we shall hear a hundred and fifty[6] of them roaring off all together, but if 'tis a daughter, there will not be one let off. I am amazed at their making such a vast difference between the sexes, and placing the honour all on the wrong side. Is there anything so soft or so delightful as what they contemn so much? A celebrated French author calls the women 'the prettiest half of creation', but I don't know what title the Italian authors would give them. They were made to soften man, and to make life agreeable. When there is no news stirring, and nothing material has happened for the day, women can talk as well about nothing as about something, and can divert you with the least trifles. Their tongues are always active, and run the better for having no weight upon them: whereas men are like old rusty kitchen-jacks that never run unless a load of business be hung on upon them.

Who was it that turned out the Tarquins, and saved the liberties of the Roman state? A woman. Who was it that produced all the succeeding heroes, the Scipios, the Catos, and the Caesars? A woman. Who was it that ate the first apple that ever was eaten, and set all the world a going? A woman.—Dear, charming, heavenly delightful woman![7]—And yet these insensible rascals here are to let off hundred and fifty cannons if a man be born into the world, and no so much as a single pop-gun if 'tis a woman. I'm in so great a passion, that I can talk no more of it: and so am ⟨in much haste

> Your dutiful and affectionate
>
> J. Spence⟩

1. See *Letter* 110 n. 2. On his first tour (*Letter* 21) Spence described him as 'a beautiful child'.

2. Mrs. Spence came from the Neville family and was naturally interested in the Nevilles. 'Mr. Grey Neville' was Richard Aldworth (see *Letter* 85). On Henry Grey, see *Letter* 131 n. 5.

3. 'Per certa bontà di natura e prontezza d'ingego molto felicemente di lui si augurava' (P. Carutti, *Storia del regno di Carlo Emmanuele III* [Turin, 1859], I, 128–9).

4. See *Letter* 110 n. 2.

5. Carlo Francesco, the D. of Aosta, b. Dec. 1, 1738. He died in 1745 (Litta).

6. Spence originally wrote '250', but later corrected it here as well as in the following letter.

7. Spence is paraphrasing a passage from Otway's *The Orphan*, Act III:

Who was't betray'd the Capitol? A woman.
Who lost Mark Antony the World? A woman.
Who was the Cause of a long ten years War,
And laid at last Old Troy in Ashes? Woman.
Destructive, damnable, deceitful Woman.

*112

Source:	Egerton 2234 ff. 193–4
Addressed:	*as in 74*
Postmarked:	24 [ ]
Franked:	Free/Andrew Stone
Endorsed:	*a.* an act:/of ye Lodges of ye mysticks, or like/ye free masons: *b.* Ansr to a Query abt ye/Inscription at Athens, to the/Unknown God. *red wafer*

Turin,
June 22, 1740
⟨P.S. This morning at two o'clock the Queen was delivered of a daughter: so the hundred and fifty cannons were all silent.[1] I called them two hundred and fifty in my former by mistake.⟩

⟨Dear Mother,⟩

I was very glad of such a subject as Lord Sandwich's travels to divert you a little, and was as pleased to find that you asked (from time to time) for farther accounts of him. I shall wish to meet with such another wanderer for your sake, and if anybody comes in my way that has been at Prester John's[2] or the Great Mogul's, I shall not fail to pump everything I can out of him, that you may grow as well acquainted with Abyssinia and India as you are with Egypt and Athens.

As for the inscription you ask after at Athens,[3] I believe there is nothing left of it:[4] but I doubt not there are some in Greece of the same nature, for I know there are some even in Italy. You must know that among the heathens there were several companies of people, something like our freemasons at present. They kept several secrets, with an inviolable secrecy, for several hundreds of years (I think there were no women among them). These secrets were chiefly of a religious nature, and 'tis said that in these societies they laughed at idols and gave up all the heathen deities as false ones. 'Twas a great maxim in all these lodges that there were three great gods that governed the whole universe, and that these three were of one and the same mind. They called them the great, the powerful, and the unknown gods, and sometimes 'the unknown god'. The ancients had many inscriptions to him, and that mentioned by St. Paul (Acts, 17) was no doubt one of them. The chief lodge in the whole world of these 'mystics' (for *so* they called themselves) was in an island called Samothracia: it was propagated from thence to Troy and Asia on one side, and into Greece and Italy on the other. The first Tarquin (not that villainous tyrant) was of a

292

Grecian family (the son of a nobleman of Corinth), and brought the secret to Rome a few years after it was founded.[5] It continued long and spread much in Italy, and that is the reason that we meet with inscriptions of the same nature here. If you had consulted all the members of the Upper and the Lower Houses of Convocation,[6] I question whether any of them could have answered you so fully:[7] but I have had a particular reason, long ago, for looking into this case, and beside (as my Lord Ball[8] used to say) 'I have travelled for it.'[9]

⟨I am very much obliged to my friends, for ever thinking of me, and to you for thinking of me so much. I believe I am pretty near even both with them and you: for I think of them often, and of you whenever I have any leisure to think. I don't doubt but what I talk of you sometimes, when I am walking by myself (for talking is only thinking aloud, as thinking is a sort of talking to oneself). When I do talk to myself, you are generally the subject. Sometimes I am very busy with you in fitting up the parlour at Birchanger and planting the little garden between that and the church. Sometimes I am laying out our best room in Queen's Street, and then taking a walk with you for Hyde Park by Buckingham House. Sometimes I am writing and you are sitting by me, reading the psalms of the day and dropping your spectacles upon the book: for who can keep their eyes always open? Sometimes you are at work, with your spectacles fixed more resolutely, and I am sitting by you and asking how much that muslin cost a yard. All this is very easy where there is a strong degree of friendship, and, if you will, something of a poetical imagination: which, heaven help me, has been now and then laid to my charge. Witness when you told honest Stephen Duck that I had a knack of enlarging stories a little and setting them off with a small matter of invention. Beside all this, I talk of you very often with my Lord Lincoln, and sometimes with some other friends: for, I assure you, you are very well known at Turin. With all services to all friends, I am ever

Your most dutiful and most affectionate

J. Spence.⟩

1. Victoria Marghareta (1740–2). The cannons were heard no doubt a year later, almost to a day: on June 21, 1741, the Duke of Chiablese was born; the Queen herself, however, died a few days later (July 3, 1741).

2. Abyssinia, kingdom of the fabulous Prester John in Mandeville's *Travels*.

3. Mrs. Spence asked about the altar mentioned by St. Paul (Acts 17) with the inscription, TO THE UNKNOWN GOD.

4. 'There is no evidence of the existence of any such inscription in the singular number ... Pausanias bears witness to the existence of altars "to unknown gods" ' (*The Interpreter's Bible* [New York, 1954], IX, 234–5).

5. Tarquinius Priscus (616–579 B.C.) was according to tradition the 5th king of Rome. He was probably a historical figure, though the stories of his Greek descent appear to be late inventions.

6. The synodical convocation of the Church of England.

7. Spence may be hinting here at secret information derived from masonic sources.

8. Perhaps Sir Peter Ball (d. 1680), Bt., of Mamhead, Devon., or his son Thomas (1672–1749), though the latter did not assume the title.

9. Among the Spence Papers is a manuscript essay by Spence on the Samothracian mysteries, which deals with the cult of the three deities (Jupiter, Juno, Minerva) 'often join'd together' by the ancients. In discussing the origin of the *dii magni* and their spread from Samothracia, Spence refers to Herodotus (29, 2) whose account seems to be echoed here. The idea, no doubt influenced by Cudworth's, Ramsay's, and early 18th-century semi-deistic views of the Trinity, was shared by some freemason theorists.

113

Source: Egerton 2234 ff. 195–6

Addressed: as in 74

Endorsed: *a*. not a reading/letter. onley: there moveing to genoa
b. Of the Weather; & our Route on/Not to be transcrib'd.
red wafer

Turin,
July 6, 1740

⟨Dear Mother,

I expected to hear that you had had a dry fit after the hard weather, and I expect in a little time to hear you complaining of having had too much rain. This, at least, was the course of the weather here, and we are too near neighbours (for what's seven or eight hundred mile between friends?) to have any great difference in the general course of the weather, though your situation in an island may give you a cloudy day or two when we perhaps have a fine clear sky over our heads. By the same rule, I reckon it begins to grow warm with you now: we had cold weather, and were forced to have fires a good way into May,[1] as you have to June. The warm weather has been come in here these three weeks, and I hope you will have your share of it, though a little after us, for the sun always takes care first of his next neighbours.

I have been got some time into my old custom of going to bed in the afternoons, which is a very pleasing and very refreshing fashion on this side the Alps. I tried it once on the other, one of the hottest days we had at Oxford, but it would not do: and I was forced, after some tumbling, to be content to get up with a headache for my pains—whereas here one has a difficulty to keep one's eyes open whilst one's pulling off one's stockings; then you are asleep as soon as ever you're in bed; and after lying there about two hours, you get up, and have quite a second morning: 'twould do you good to hear how sweetly I sing all the while I am washing my head after it.

Mr. Holdsworth stayed here four or five days,[2] and is gone to Milan, where I hope to see him again six or seven weeks hence, for we are to leave this place as soon as ever the heats will give us leave, and I hope they will not last so long as usual in this country, because the winter was so severe and of such continuance. When we go from hence, we shall set our faces toward Genoa (prithee, Betty, get the map as fast as ever you can); thence to Milan; thence to Verona, Padua and Venice, thence to Bologna and Florence; thence to Leghorn; and so, by Siena, to Rome: which is the centre of all my wishes out of England. We are to stay at Rome all the winter, and Mr. Holdsworth is to do the same: so that there will be two as honest Hampshire men there as ever sat down to a dish of beans and bacon. And now you talk of beans I am vastly concerned that you have such a scarcity of them: as for peas, they have been old here these two months, and we had a dish so long ago as Christmas Day, but (not to do more honour to Turin than it deserves) it must be owned that they came from Genoa: at which place, and at Naples, they have them generally all the winter long.

Though I like this place so very well, I shall be glad when we begin to move, because it will put me in mind of coming home, and my going five hundred mile farther in this country is now nothing to me. As this autumn we shall be tending toward Rome, next spring we shall be tending toward old England: where I hope to find you and all friends, and my little garden at Birchanger, all in good health. That little garden may be all covered with one great weed, for anything that you say of it: I should be very glad to hear that 'tis pert and flourishing. I am with all services to all friends,

Your dutiful and affectionate

J. Spence.⟩

1. On May 17 Lady Mary wrote to Lady Pomfret: 'You are still in ice and snow at Florence, and we are very little better at Venice, where we remain in the state of warming beds and sitting by fire-sides' (*Complete Letters*, II, 187).

2. Edward Holdsworth, the travelling tutor and Virgilian scholar whom Spence had met on the first tour (*Letter* 30 n, 6) and was to meet again at Rome.

114

Source: Egerton 2234 ff. 197–8
Addressed: as in 74
Postmarked: 29 IV
Franked: Free/Andrew Stone
Endorsed: b. Of the Weather, &c./Not to be Trᵈ.
             red wafer

Turin,
July 27, 1740[1]

⟨Dear Mother,

I don't know how it has been with you, but for us on this side the Alps, we have had the heats come in above a month which, though not violent to that degree they are usually in Italy, have been warm enough of conscience. Ever since they came in, I have taken to my old foreign custom of going to bed every afternoon. This does not agree with some English, but as for me, I take to it as naturally as if I had been born in the middle of Florence or Rome. I don't know a more refreshing thing where it meets with a proper constitution. It gives one new spirits, and I rise every afternoon about four to a second morning, and after washing my head and face, fall as naturally to singing 'Johnny Armstrong' or the 'Fair Maid of Islington', as I do in the first. These are tunes that are fitted to my voice (which, you know, is a pretty good one) and the harmony I make resounds in the chambers on each side of me to the great edification of my neighbours.

We have had a good deal of thunder this summer in these parts, four or five times in particular this last week, and this has cooled the air to such a degree, that I came in this morning from a walk of two hours without being the least hot. I don't know whether I have not formerly told you that a thunderstorm is one of the most delightful things in the world in a hot country. When you have been long scorched, and are quite languishing with heat, the heavens are clouded over of a sudden (which scarce ever happens here in summer without thunder), and the showers which follow it cool everything about one and give one quite a new turn of spirits. This is so agreeable in here, that one of the best Italian poets that ever was has a long simile, in which he says that 'the favour of his mistress is as lovely and refreshing to him as a thunderstorm':[2] to understand which, 'tis necessary to have passed the Alps. Had that poet lived in England, probably he would have said the favour of his mistress was as comfortable to him as a good kitchen-fire. Such is the difference of countries, and such of course must be the difference of compliments.

But to return to our late thunderstorms: they have made the air so cool that I was yesterday to pay a visit to our chaise, to see that it was in order, for I am in great hopes that we may be moving now in two or three weeks. I want to be setting out, for that's doing something, and looks at least like being nearer coming home. As much as I long to see Rome, I long more to be with you, and to be settling our little affairs, in order to live together in a comfortable ma[nner] the rest of our time that we have to be in this wicked world. Whether that is to be long or short I think does not signify a great deal; but one would make the time, whatever it is, as agreeable as one can. Thank heaven we are likely at present (even in the very worst view, of three or four that I could reckon up to you) to have enough to live comfortably, and to do some little good round about one, and that I always reckon among one of the highest diversions both for you and me. I am ever, with all services,

Your dutiful and affectionate

J. Spence.

Cap. Rolle is very well, and I am just going to scold him violently. Lord Lincoln is very much yours.⟩

1. One or two letters, probably dated July 13 and 20, in which Spence recounted 'the history of Florio', missing. See *Letter* 118 n. 1.
2. Or, as the passing of a thunderstorm. See

Petrarch's sonnets xli–xlii: 'Quando dal proprio sito si rimove', 'Ma poi che'l dolce riso umile e piano.'

---

*115

Source:	Egerton 2234 ff. 199–200
Addressed:	as in 114
Postmarked:	5 AV
Franked:	Free/Andrew Stone
Endorsed:	*a.* an act of the/nightingales & quails
	b. Of ye Nightingales &/Number of Quails there.
	red wafer

Turin,

August 3, 1740

⟨Dear Mother,⟩

Among all the excellences of Turin I forget whether I have yet told you that 'tis the country of nightingales: they are in great numbers here, and I have heard more of their singing in this last spring and summer, from my own closet and in the King's Gardens (which, you know, are just by it) than I have everywhere else in my whole life all put together. In the spring they sung all day long, and even in the summer they are making a little concert in the mornings, or whenever the air is cool and the heavens clouded.

There is one in particular, which comes every year, they tell me, to the same place (a little grove in the King's Gardens, directly opposite to my window), and which is remarkable over all the rest for the fullness and the variety of his notes. There can't come a little cloud over the heavens but he immediately flings you out a piece of music. The last thunderstorm we had, he struck up just after the greatest clap began, and kept gurgling and rolling his notes along all the while it lasted—and was so clear that I could hear his music very distinctly all the time, in spite of the deepness of the thorough-bass from above.

There is another sort of birds which I love to see, almost as much as I love to hear the former, from their genteel make and look: what I mean are quails, which we have here in vast numbers. And as 'tis now our second hay-harvest, I hear them almost every evening in the meadows, flirting out their little note (which has a certain cheerfulness, though it has no music in it) on each side of me. They say that they come over the sea, in vast droves, when it grows too hot for them in Africa; and at their first coming they are so tired and panting with heat and with their journey that 'tis very easy to catch them, almost by handfuls.

Sometimes the little creatures are tired before they reach the shore, and if they can meet with a ship, huddle round the mast and shrouds of it. If there's no ship near, when they are quite spent, they must fall into the sea, and this happens so frequently that it has given occasion to the sailors in the Mediterranean Sea to think that they come over to Europe from Africa by swimming as well as flying. I wish with all my heart they could swim, it would save a great many of their lives: but the poor creatures are not made for it. The coast of Africa is about as far from us as Paris, but our shores are in some places much nearer, and there are two islands (Corsica and Sardinia) which lie like halfway houses and are excellent resting-places for them. The caravans of quails that have good guides and take these islands right may come over perhaps without losing any of their company; but if they go to the left, they have nothing but Minorca, and on the right Sicily—rather at too great a distance to save them.

The evening is coming on, I see the people mowing from my window in the meadows: I must go and see some of my new African acquaintance, and so am

⟨Your most obedient

Joseph Spence.⟩

116

Source: Egerton 2234 ff. 201–2
Addressed: as in 74
Postmarked: 12 AV
Franked: Free/Andrew Stone
Endorsed: *a.* an act/of Mr greville & Mr ellis:
b. Of Mr Ellis, & his Villa./Not to be Transcrib'd.
red wafer

Turin,
August 10, 1740

⟨Dear Mother,

We have two sets of English here that have taken little country houses just out of town, and one of them I am just come from visiting, so that I have made an inroad into my time and shall not be able to go much above this side in all human probability. I lay there but two nights, and when I came home this morning, my nightingale fell a-singing immediately to welcome me to my closet again, as loud and as finely as if I had been gone a month.

At the villa I have been at is Mr. Greville, who was bred up at Dr. Burton's,[1] and one Mr. Ellis, the son of an Irish bishop.[2] 'Tis very particular in his family that his father was a Protestant bishop, one of his uncles a Popish bishop in Italy,[3] another had a post in King William's court,[4] and another in James the Second's[5]—all at the same time. His father was the richest bishop in the King's dominions, and has left him between four and five thousand pound a year, and he is likely to make a good use of it: for he is very sober, very sensible, and of a very good taste. I left his house with some regret, though I was to come to my dear closet, and that is a great compliment to any house at present.

The violence of our summer is past and 'tis probable I shall never sweat extremely ever again in Italy, for we shall have left this country before the next great heats come on.—They sometimes play me the same trick (of sending me two of your letters together), and I am got not to mind it. I hope you will do the same. Beside, when I am upon the road, I can hardly be so constant in sending of letters, though I shall endeavour to write at the rate of once a week as near as I can, even when we are moving from one place to another. Some of them may miss you, for I hear the posts are ill regulated at present in several places. I am in perfect health, and very much

Your humble servant

J. Spence.⟩

1. Francis Greville (1719–73), Baron Brooke of Beauchamp Court, educ. at Winchester 1728–33 (together with Ellis and Sir Bourchier Wrey). Recorder of Warwick 1741 till his death; in 1746 cr. E. Brooke of Warwick Castle. On Dr. Burton see *Letter* 15 n. 7.

2. Wellbore Ellis (1713–1802), of 'the ancient family of Kiddal Hall in Yorkshire', politician. B.A. Christ Church June 5, 1736; member of the Soc. of Dilettanti 1741; at the general election of May 1741 contested the borough of Crickdale; later opponent of Pitt. His father was Wellbore Ellis (1651?–1734),

Bp. of Meath Mar. 13, 1731, until his death Jan. 1, 1734.

3. Philip Ellis (1652–1726), converted to Roman Catholicism, chaplain to James II, went to Rome after 1688, where he became a friend of Cardinal Howard; 1708–26 Bp. of Segni.

4. John Ellis (1643?–1738), Undersecretary of State to William III. His letters were edited in 1829 by the Hon. Agar-Ellis.

5. William Ellis (1642?–1732) followed James II into exile after the Revolution and became his secretary.

117

Source: Extra-illustrated copy of *Anecdotes*, ed. Singer, 1820, Huntington Library (RB 131213). Printed by Singer, pp. 400–3

Endorsed: ★

Turin,
August 17, 1740

⟨Dear Mother,⟩

I have been a little journey out of town since I wrote my last. My Lord Lincoln took a ride out with the Prince of Carignan to a nobleman's about 24 miles off, to be at a ball: the next day I heard he had sprained his foot and was in a great deal of pain.[1] So I took a chaise immediately and carried a very famous old surgeon with me,[2] recommended by our Minister here, to see whether there was any greater harm than was imagined, and I hope my Lord is now in a way of being well soon.

My old surgeon I found to be the oddest figure, and one of the oddest men that ever I met with in my life. He is a mountaineer, born amidst the Alps, and as learned as the people generally are among wild mountains.[3] He is a short man, fat and clumsy, with a great pair of Dutch trousers to his backside, and with a face that does not at all yield for breadth or swarthiness to the place above-mentioned. His face was overrun with beard, for he said he was obliged to go to mass and so had not time to be shaved. In his face (or his upper breech, whichever you please to call it) were a pair of little merry eyes, deep in his head, but yet with a droll gay air in them, and the two little caves that go down to them are wrinkled all the way up to his forehead and his temples. Whenever he laughs (which is very often) all these wrinkles are in motion together and make one of the most diverting sights that can be imagined.

When we were a little seated together and jolted into our proper places by the chaise, 'Is it a long time, Maître Claude (says I) that you have been in this sort of business?' 'Yes,' says he, 'I have been in it for several generations.' Upon this I thought myself with the Travelling Jew and blessed heaven for bringing me acquainted with a man that I had so long wished to meet with.[4] 'For several generations, Maître Claude? I don't understand you.' 'Why, Sir,' says he, 'our family has always been barber-surgeons from father to son, without any interruption for these twenty-eight generations; my son, who is a promising youth and is scarce fifty yet, is the twenty-ninth. I am but seventy-five, and I have had this plaguy gout these twelve years. Will you be so good as to let me replace my foot again, for that last jolt has quite put me out of order.' 'And how old was your father, Master Claude, when he died?' 'Ah, poor man, he died at a hundred and three— but 'twas by a fall from his horse, in going to visit a patient. He was hurried out of the world: Rest his soul!'—'At this rate, the first surgeon in your family might have been the surgeon to Noah and the good people in the ark.' This set all his wrinkles in motion. 'Oh no,' says he, 'we are not of so great an antiquity as that comes to, at least our accounts don't reach up so far—'

'Have you a history then of the twenty-seven surgeons, your predecessors?' 'Have I!' says he, 'yes, that I have, and I would rather lose my legs than lose it. But that does not go so far as I could wish: the furthest thing back of a remarkable thing that I find by it is that the fifth surgeon of our family shaved Hannibal, the night he lay at Laneburg in his passage over the Alps: I wish he had cut his throat! for he did a deal of mischief here at Turin.' 'And did he shave ever a one of his elephants, Master Claude?' 'Not that I know of,' says he, 'but our day-book says that this same Hannibal had to do with the devil, that he put life into castles and made the castles walk over the mountains with him against the Romans, and he says, in a note [on] the side, that he heard afterwards that these castles fought like mad things, and that any one of them that had not killed his hundred of Romans was very little regarded in the army.'

He then took out a prayer-book and prayed aloud, as he had done at every cross or old statue we had passed by the road-side.[5] 'I don't see ever a Virgin Mary, why are you praying, Master Claude?' 'I'm saying a devotion to pray poor Hannibal's soul out of purgatory,' says he; 'he was a great thief and murderer, and may very probably be there still, but he paid my ancestors well and so I am bound to pray for him. You see that house there —'twas built by a Savoyard: he put his collar-bone out and I set it. Lord have mercy upon poor Hannibal! Will you have another pinch of snuff? This snuff-box was given me by the Maréchal de Créqui—'[6] 'You have travelled then?' 'Ay, Sir, nobody is regarded in our country unless they have rolled over the world. I lived twenty year in France and Germany, I was barber-surgeon to the Maréchal, and was with him when he received his death's wound'—'And is it true that the ball that killed him was directed *to the Maréchal* [*de*] *Créqui?*' 'No, Sir,' says he, 'that I can assure you, for 'twas these fingers took it out of his body.' Just as he said this we came to our journey's end, as I am at the end of my letter.

⟨Your most affectionate humble servant

J. Spence.⟩

1. For a full account of the incident, see *Letter* 120.

2. 'Master Claude', recommended by Arthur Villettes, the British Resident at Turin.

3. ' 'Tis not learning that does any good. A man may read post-books for ever without knowing a road. One must have travelled them to know anything of them. I practise, and let the others read, in God's name,' says M. Claude (Spence's note).

4. See next letter.

5. 'In passing along the road,' observed Conyers Middleton, 'it is common to see travellers on their knees before these *rustic altars* . . . huge *wooden crosses*, dressed out with flowers, and hung round with trifling offerings of the country people; which always put me in mind of the *superstitious veneration*, which the *Heathens* used to pay to some old *trunks of trees* or posts, set up in the highways, which they held *sacred*' (*A Letter from Rome*, 1741 edn., pp. 182–3).

6. Charles I de Blanchefort (b. ca. 1567), Marquis de Créquy, was killed by a cannon-ball during the siege of Brema, on Mar. 17, 1638. Spence was testing Master Claude's assertion that he was 'but seventy-five'.

118

Source: Extra-illustrated copy of *Anecdotes*, ed. Singer, 1820, Huntington Library (RB 131213). Printed by Singer, pp. 403–5.

Addressed: as in 74

Postmarked: 26 AV

Franked: Free/Andrew Stone

Endorsed: *a.* an ac^t of/a sett of philosophers call'd Adepts/superiour to whatever appear'd/among either ye Greeks, or Romans/& Gustavus adolphus, king of the swedes
b. Andre's Acct of him-/self; & a Story of Gustavus.

Turin,
August 25, 1740

⟨Dear Mother,⟩

If the history of Florio[1] was too melancholy for you (as I fear it was) I am now going to give you an account of some people that may be too mysterious for you: such as some persons will scarce believe ever were, or ever will be, in the world: however, one of them I have very lately met with, and I must give you an account of him whilst 'tis fresh in my memory.

Have you ever heard of the people called Adepts?[2] They are a set of philosophers, superior to whatever appeared among the Greeks and Romans. The three great points they drive at is to be free from poverty, distempers, and death—and if you will believe them, they have found out one secret that is capable of freeing them from all three.[3] There are never more than twelve of these men in the whole world at a time, and we have the happiness of having one of the twelve at this time at Turin. I am very well acquainted with him, and have often talked with him of their secrets, as far as he is allowed to talk to a common mortal of them.[4]

His name is Andrey: a Frenchman, of a genteel air, but with a certain gravity in his face that I never saw in any Frenchman before. The first time I was in company with him, as I found he had been a great traveller, I asked him whether he had ever been in England and how he liked the country? He said that he had, and that he liked it more than any country he had ever been in. 'The last time I was in England,' added he, 'there were eleven philosophers there.' I told him I hoped there might be more than eleven in England. He smiled a little and said, 'Sir, I don't talk of common philosophers, I talk of Adepts,[5] and of them I saw in England what I never saw anywhere else: there was eleven at table, I made the twelfth; and when we came to compare our ages all together they made somewhat upward of four thousand years.'

I wondered to hear a grave man talk so strangely, and asked him, as seriously as I could, how old he might be himself. He said that he was not quite two hundred, but that he was one of the youngest at the table.[6] He said that the secret of carrying on their lives as long as they pleased was known to all of them, and that some of them perhaps might remove out of this world, but that he did not think any one of them would die: for if they did not like this globe, they had nothing to do but to go into another, whenever they pleased. How soon that might be he did not know, but St. John and the Travelling Jew, he said, had stayed in it above seventeen hundred years, and some of his friends perhaps might stay as long. He said the Great Elixir, of which he had some in his pocket, made him look no older than forty, that he was afraid of no distemper, for that would cure him immediately, nor of want, because 'twould make him as much gold as he pleased. He said many other things as strange and as surprising as what I have told you.

I was talking of him and his gold-making to our Minister here,[7] who upon it told me a very odd story which he had from Maréchal Rhebender, general of the King of Sardinia's forces at present.[8] The general (who comes from those parts) says that when Gustavus Adolphus was going to make war with the Emperor, he found himself at a loss for money sufficient for so great an undertaking. He was very melancholy upon it and everything was at a stand: when, one morning, a very old man came to his court and told the Gentleman of the Bedchamber in waiting that he wanted to speak to the King. The gentleman desired his name; he refused to tell it but said he must speak to the King, and that it was on business of the utmost importance to his Majesty's affairs.

Gustavus, who was incapable of fear, ordered him to be admitted. When they were alone, the old man told him that he knew what straits he was in for money, and that he was come to furnish him with as much as he should want. He then desired him to send for a crucible full of mercury, he took out a white powder, and put in only about the quantity of a pinch of snuff. He then desired him to set by the crucible till the next morning, gave him a large bundle of the white powder, and departed. When Gustavus called for the crucible the next morning 'twas all full of one solid piece of gold. He coined this into ducats, and on the coin, in memory of the fact, was struck the chymical marks for mercury and sulphur. Rhebender had several of them thus marked and gave one of them to our Minister who told me the story.[9] ⟨I am with all services

Your dutiful and affectionate

J. Spence⟩

1. A gruesomely moral tale about a young rake who started with gambling, sank deep into vice, and came to a melancholy end. Spence had originally composed it 'for the use of a young nobleman'—obviously Lord Lincoln, who seems to have exhibited an inclination to gambling (see Letters 91, 96). Later he no doubt transcribed it for the diversion of Mrs. Spence in one or two letters. See Letter 114 n. 1. It was printed in the first number of Dodsley's The Museum, I, 7–10 (Saturday, March 29, 1746) as 'FLORIO: A Moral History', by 'our worthy Correspondent who signs himself MORALIS', and reprinted in Spence's Moralities (1753).

2. Alchemists who have professed to have discovered the Philosopher's Stone.

3. The Adept's aim was 'de se débarasser quand il voudra de la chair corruptible sans passer par la mort . . . délivré des contingences et des accidents de l'expérience terrestre' and to attain Knowledge, Power and Immortality. See N. Lenglet du Fresnoy, Histoire de la philosophie hermétique (Paris, 1742), 3 vols., which lists several hundred works on the subject, and for its relation to freemasonry, O. Wirth, Le symbolisme hermétique dans ses rapports avec l'alchimie et la franc-maçonnerie, 2d edn. (Paris, 1931).

4. In the Turin archives was a curiosity called 'Tabula Isiaca' (a Roman forgery of an Egyptian work, see Obs. No. 1590). Spence jotted down, for his amusement no doubt,

Monsieur André's hermetic explications of its hieroglyphics: 'Les Soldats qui vont égorger les Innocens—stills, receivers etc., all chimical. The Table of Emrod or Hermes Trismegistus. A composition: all the materials in it that are necessary for making the Philosopher's Stone; 'tis composed of all the Seven Metals.—Most of the figures [are explained] in Abraham le Juif's (le vieux) account of the Apocalypse, where he shews that all the great secrets of chemistry are contained in that book' (Nbk. 3 78r).

5. Originally 'Rosicruscians'.

6. Lenglet du Fresnoy (III, 105) lists Arthepius' de vita Proroganda, commenting on the author: 'aitque se anno 1025 aetatis suae scripsisse librum suum'. Hermann Kopp (Die Alchemie [Heidelberg, 1886], pp. 100–3) mentions two other Struldbrugian adepts: one Trauttmansdorf (1462–1609) and one Federico Gualdo, who claimed to have lived 400 years before he died 1724 at Venice. On the latter, see two pamphlets published in 1700 at Augsburg: 'Communication einer vortrefflichen Chymischen Medicin, Krafft welcher nebst Gott und guter Diät der berühmte Edelmann Fridericus Gualdus sein Leben auf 400 zu diesen unseren Zeiten conserviert . . .', and 'Der entlarvte Gualdus, sive Frid. Gualdus ex se ipso mendacii et imposture convictus, das ist, ausführlicher Beweis, dass dasjenige, was von einem 400 Jährigen Venetianischen Edelmann

und seiner Medicin vorgeben wird, mehr für eine Fabel als wahrhafte Geschichte zu halten'. Such impostures on men's credulity were common (see e.g., Robert Samber's translation of Harouet de Longeville's *Long Livers: a curious history of such persons of both sexes who have liv'd several ages ... as also how to prepare the Universal Medicine*. By Eugenius Philalethes, F.R.S. 1722), and were perhaps another 'source' for Swift's satire on the Struldbrugs.

7. Arthur Villettes, see *Letter* 77 n. 2.

8. Bernard Otho Freiherr von Rehbinder (1662–1743), general of artillery (1708) and commander-in-chief under Victor Amadeus II and Charles Emmanuel III (*Le Campagne di Guerra in Piemonte, 1703–1708* [Turin, 1909], VIII, 153–65).

9. The story first appeared in *Iovrnal des voyages de Monsieur de Monconys* (Lyon, 1666), II, 381. Lenglet du Fresnoy, who gives this version (II, 44–6), cites Oluf Borch's *Dissertatio de Ortu et progressu Chemiae* (1668) as further evidence: '*Borrichius* assure qu'il avoit vû un de ces ducats entre les mains de M. Elie de Brachenhofer Echevin de Strasbourg; & je puis certifier la même chose en ayant vû un pareil entre les mains de M. Dufay Capitaine aux gardes, & père de M. Dufay de l'Académie Royale des sciences.' He adds: 'D'un côté étoit le Portrait de Gustave & de l'autre on y avoit marqué les Signes de Mercure & de Venus, pour désigner la matière, dont avoit été formé le métail qu'on y employoit.'

119

Source: Egerton 2234 ff. 203–4
Addressed: as in 74
Postmarked: 2 SE
Franked: Free/Andrew Stone
Endorsed: *a.* not a/Reading Letter
b. Content./Not to be Transcrib'd
red wafer

Turin,
August 31 ⟨20⟩, 1740

⟨Dear Mother,

Though you talk very well of contentment and of the happiness of a low state of life, 'tis some time that I have suspected you a little of an ambitious turn in your mind—why else should you always be teasing your poor son to be a queen or a bishop? To speak more seriously, I don't think there is anything lost to me by my being out of England at present: your wardenship will never go a begging,[1] and ours, if I were on the spot, I should have no manner of chance for; and if any fellowship at Winchester should be vacant on this occasion, I believe I should have as little for that. However true all this be (and I believe 'tis all as true as the Gospel of St. Luke), 'tis full as true that I don't at all desire wardenships, or indeed any high dignity in the world, and that not out of wisdom but a love of ease. I am for happiness in my own way and according to my notions of it; I might as well have it in living with you in our cottage at Birchanger (and better) than in any palace the King has. As my affairs stand at present, 'tis likely that we shall have enough to live quite at our ease: when I desire more than that, may I lose what I have!

My Lord's sprain of his leg has kept us here longer than we intended. I hope, however, we shall set out in ten or twelve days for Milan, where we have yet some chance of meeting my two dear friends, Mr. Holdsworth and Mr. Smith.[2] I write six letters this post, and as you are a good old lady, I'm sure you will therefore excuse me if I am directly

Your most humble servant,

J. Spence.⟩

1. After the death of Henry Bigg in 1740, the wardenship of Winchester College was vacant. On Aug. 18, 1741 (O.S.), John Coxed was elected as the new Warden (Kirby, p. 2).
2. Arthur Smyth, whom Spence had met on the first tour. See *Letter* 39.

120

Source: Add. MSS 33065 ff. 374–6

LINCOLN TO NEWCASTLE

Turin,
September 2, 1740

My Lord,

If I had not received your Grace's most obliging letter, I should not have been able to leave Turin so soon as we intended. Mr. Spence has already informed you of the occasion of it, but I must beg leave to give you a more satisfactory account of my adventure, which I am afraid you will think don't redound too much to my honour.

About three weeks ago[1] the Prince of Carignan[2] and your humble servant, hearing of a party of pleasure at the Marquis de Riverols,[3] one of the chief noblemen of the country, about twenty miles off, took post in order to surprise them, which we accordingly executed, though not without being wet to the skin, for it proved but a bad day. However, we arrived very well in every respect but our not having a dry thread about us, which was nothing to his Highness, who could change clothes immediately, but not at all comfortable to me, who was not in the same case, having nothing but my wet rags about me. I am very certain when your Grace comes to this part of my letter you will say 'this is so like him, never to think of anything but follow his own way,' but I desire you won't find me guilty before you know the whole state of the case, which is this.

There were but five post horses . . . for the Prince, his *écuyer* who always attends him, his page, myself, and the postillion. 'Twas for this reason I was obliged to hire a horse for my servant who, you can't be surprised, did not keep up with us who rid post. However, to make the best of a bad matter I could, and remembering what your Grace has so often told me, that is not to mind what figure one makes when one's health is in danger, I accepted the Count de la Trinité's offer, which was to equip me with some of his clothes; he said he thought indeed they would be a little of the largest, but . . . much better than my wet ones. They were indeed a little of the largest, for you must know this Count de la Trinité is much bigger than Glazier and a considerable deal taller.[4] However, I surrendered myself very submissively to the Count's valet de chambre, who stript me of all my wet clothes and dressed me from top to toe in his master's. When he came to the breeches I could not help thinking of my friend the Speaker,[5] whose breeches, if you remember, I once had the pleasure of wearing. You may be sure I cut a very ridiculous figure in this whimsical dress, with coat, waistcoat, breeches, shoes and stockings six times too big for me, and my hair, which had been sufficiently soaked by the rain, hanging down like a pound of candles; and I believe you will easily imagine it not a little mortifying for me, dining with so much company, accoutred after this manner—for you may be sure many jokes passed on my score at dinner. . . . However, I was resolved to go through with it, for otherwise your Grace knows my health would have been in danger. After dinner my servant arrived and I had the pleasure and satisfaction of appearing once more in my own clothes—but alas! this proved but a misfortune: for I am very sure if he had never come, I should not have been for jumping in the above-mentioned dress.

I say jumping, my Lord, for that was the occasion of my disaster, which happened as follows. As we were a walking in the garden after dinner, whilst they were a preparing everything for the ball, the Prince proposed jumping with me for the diversion of the company. Upon that, you may be sure I was not a man to refuse a challenge. So accordingly we immediately stript and went to it. The Prince has presently enough of it, and the victory was entirely on my side—for though in England I should be reckoned but a very bad jumper, yet, I can assure you, amongst Piedmontois I made a very considerable figure.

Happy should I have been if I had contented myself with the applause I had just acquired; but, greedy of glory, I needs must take up another champion who offered to enter the lists with me. But alas! my success with him was very different than that with the Prince; for having a mind to exert myself more than usual, my honour fell in the dust—*ibi omnis effusus labor!*[6] [I] was carried off the field of battle, whilst my victorious antagonist, exulting over me, reaped [?] from me the immortal honour I had so very lately gained. This, however, I could have borne with (though not without much envy), but my leg soon informed me I had something else to think of, for in my fall I sprained it most violently, which obliged my staying there three days, and then was conveyed in a chaise to Turin and have been confined to my room ever since.

I have had all the proper care imaginable. Mr. Spence came to me the next day with a surgeon, by whose means, and my own patience in my confinement, my leg is entirely well in every respect but a stiffness in the nerves and muscles for want of use; for which reason they make me walk a good deal about my room, and in about ten or twelve days the surgeon assures me I may set out for my journey without any manner of danger, the great heats being sufficiently over.

This, my Lord, is really the truth of the whole affair, which I thought much better giving you an exact account of than to make any manner of mystery about it. It will but too easily appear to your Grace by this letter that you have the same giddy unthinking nephew you had when he left England, but this I can most faithfully assure you, that the older he grows the greater sense he has of the many respected obligations he owes to your Grace, and does, if possible more than ever, feel the sincerest love and gratitude to his dearest uncle.

I must own, my Lord, I was a little surprised at one part of your Grace's letter, you may easily guess at which I mean. All that I can say is this, that upon no consideration in the world I could think of marrying anyone I had the least aversion to, not even if she had six times the fortune your Grace mentions; but . . . I am . . . thoroughly persuaded that your Grace out of your love to me would not press the affair any further, if that should be the case. On the other hand, if it should be other, I would readily submit to whatever your Grace thinks proper for me. I have racked my brains to find out this pretty young lady with a certain fortune of upwards of ninety thousand pounds,[7] however, my Lord, I hope there will be no hurry in the affair, for I must own I am not as yet steady enough to enter in the holy state of wedlock. I beg my duty to my uncle Pelham who, I am exceeding happy, is so well. I must own it vexes me my not hear[ing] one word from him in answer to my letters. I writ to the D[uchess] of Newcastle last post, who I conclude is still in Yorkshire, but wherever she is, desire my kindest remembrance. I am, my Lord, your Grace's most affectionate and dutiful nephew

Lincoln

P.S. We are here in great hopes of Admiral Norris's expedition.[8] . . .

1. Between Aug. 10 and 17.

2. The newly married Louis-Victor-Joseph (*Letter* 110).

3. Domenico Rivarola (1687–1748), Corsican patriot, since 1737 self-exiled in Turin, where Charles Emmanuel authorized him in 1744 to raise and command a Corsican regiment (F. Guelfucci, 'Le Comte Dominique Rivarola', *La Ruche historique, littéraire et agricole* [1873], pp. 129–40).

4. 'Count de la Trinité' has not been identified. 'Glazier' was possibly Thomas Glasier (d. Jan. 16, 1756), 'proctor in Doctors commons' (*Gent. Mag.*, XXVI, 43).

5. Arthur Onslow (1691–1768), Speaker in the House of Commons 1728–61.

6. *Georgics* iv. 491–2.

7. She was Ann Dunk (see *Letter* 125 for a fuller note), and the Pelhams seem to have pressed on the match to get Lincoln out of financial difficulties.

8. Sir John Norris (1670?–1749), Admiral of the Channel fleet, sailed out in July with a squadron of twenty-four men of war from St. Helen's to engage the Spaniards. 'We are in great expectation of some important victory obtained by the squadron under Sir John Norris,' wrote Horace Walpole July 31 from Florence (*Corresp.* XIII, 226). The fleet, however, was forced three times to return (*Gent. Mag.*, 1740, pp. 356, 467).

121

Source: Add. MSS 33065 f. 377[r-v]

Endorsed: Turin. Sept 7 1740/M[r] Spence/R[eceived] 7th

SPENCE TO STONE

Turin,
September 7, 1740

Dear Sir,

Lord Lincoln wrote a full history of his sprain to my Lord Duke last week, and the occasion of it, which I left to his Lordship to mention himself, and which he has done I think as a very faithful historian. His Lordship went out of the Academy yesterday for the first time, made two or three visits, and walked up and down two or three pair of stairs; he was a little tired at night, but is not at all the worse for it this morning. Indeed he has walked on plain ground visibly better and better every day for a good while, and I hope will mend faster now he begins to go into the air than when he was stived up so much in his chamber. Mr. Villettes has much recommended my Lord's going to some baths in this country, near Asti, and I have often desired my Lord to try them at least. But as his Lordship seems much disinclined to them, and as both our surgeon and our physician have hitherto said there is no manner of occasion for them,[1] it would be very difficult to persuade my Lord to go thither. However, we shall soon see how it goes on, I hope that will be as well as it has done hitherto, and that will determine whether it is desirable to go to any baths, as well as when we are to leave this place, which is yet uncertain. Mr. Villettes loves my Lord so well that I believe verily he would be glad if we were to stay here all the winter. 'Tis uncertain yet when it will be proper for us to be moving: you may be sure we won't stir till it is proper, and I hope that will be in eight or ten days. I am ever, dear Sir,

Your most obedient humble servant,

Joseph Spence

On Andrew Stone, see *Letter* 76. The letter is of interest as a specimen of a travelling governor's report. It is the only one of Spence's weekly reports known to be extant.

1. Dr. Carlo Richa, chief physician to Charles Emmanuel III. A copy of his Latin letter (marked by Spence 'Dr. Richa's Advice'), dated 'Taurini, 4 Idus Septembr. 1740', concerning the beneficent influence of the waters at Acqui, is preserved in Egerton 2235 f. 95r-v. It is signed: 'Carolus Richa/ Serenissimorum Principium / a Sabaudia Archiater.' The surgeon was no doubt 'Master Claude' (*Letter* 117).

122

Source: Egerton 2234 ff. 205–6
Addressed: as in 74
Postmarked: 11 SE
Franked: Free/Andrew Stone
Endorsed: a. yᵉ carictor of/good Lady Lincoln
b. Impatient to be going/Not to be Transcrib'd.
red wafer

Turin,
September 7, 1740

⟨Dear Mother,

I find by my good Lord Lincoln that sprains in the leg are more considerable things than I used to think them. This is the first day of his going out, and 'tis just a month now since he first had it. Never did sprain happen more unluckily: we should by this time have seen Genoa and been at Milan with my dear friends Mr. Holdsworth and Mr. Smith,[1] and instead of that, here am I still in my study at Turin: and what is worse, likely to stay here till Holdsworth is gone on for Rome and Smith for Germany. The people here, at every turn, when anything does not go on as they would have it, cry out 'Pazienza!' and shrug up their shoulders: I have nothing to do but to say the same, and indeed 'patience' is the best thing in the world on this or any like occasion. As soon as we can go on with safety, we shall, and I hope it will be in eight or ten days. Lord Lincoln has suffered a good deal of pain in the beginning, though 'tis now pretty well over, and you ought to pity him, at least a little, because he has a great deal of friendship for you.

Lord Lincoln had one of the best mothers in the world himself,[2] and that makes him the more inclined to value other people's mothers that are good. Lady Lincoln, when she lost her husband, was left with a numerous little family that had no very strong constitutions. Her life, from that time, was wholly taken up in being a nurse to her children, and in doing good round about her, for she was extremely charitable. She went over with two or three of her children to the south of France, and lived at Montpellier with them for several years. The people of that neighbourhood talk of her as the best woman that ever was: but all her piety and all her charities could not save her children. When she died, about three year ago, she left only one son and one daughter behind her. Lady Lucy is well in England,[3] and I hope in God to bring Lord Lincoln well there too, in a year's time, where we are already whetting up our appetites to eat one of the best puddings you can possibly make, and if 'tis the season a piece of venison. I long to know who is Warden of New College more than ever I should long to be Warden there: you will be so good as to give me all your news, of all sorts, and I shall give you an account of our voyage as we go on. I wish we were now just going to step into our chaises, and the servants clacking their little short whips. Heaven bless you, till we clack them home again, and may it do the same to your

Most humble servant

J. Spence.〉

1. Holdsworth had left Turin for Milan at the beginning of July, and Spence had hopes of joining him there before the end of August (*Letter* 113). On Arthur Smyth, see *Letter* 39 n. 5.

2. Lady Lucy (1692–1736), dau. of Thomas, 1st Baron Pelham, m. May 16, 1717, Henry Clinton, E. of Lincoln. After her death (July 20, 1736) her brother, Thomas Pelham-Holles, D. of Newcastle, took care of young Lincoln and his sister Lucy. On the 'numerous little family', see *Letter* 169.

3. Lincoln's sister, Lady Lucy Clinton (1721–63), stayed at Claremont.

123

Source:	Egerton 2234 ff. 207–8
Addressed:	*as in 74*
Postmarked:	16 SE
Franked:	Free/Andrew Stone
Numbered:	C.
Endorsed:	*a.* the Last Letter from turin/september yᵉ 18: 1740:
	b. Turin; Sep: 18, 1740./Going to Aqui./Not to be Transcrib'd

[Turin,
September 14?, 1740][1]

⟨Dear Mother,

My Lord Lincoln's leg is much better; we set out from Turin tomorrow morning for Milan: but go out of our way to go to a place called Acqui (near Alessandria) where there are baths that are very good to prevent any ill consequences that might follow such a strain. We shall go thence to Milan, and so (through Placentia, Parma, Modena, Bologna, Florence, Leghorn and Siena) to Rome, where we hope to be about the end of November before the winter begins in this country. I am in very good health, and have continued so ever since I left you: I hope, as the saying is, you are the same. I have some chance of meeting Mr. Smith a Thursday night at Alessandria.[2] He is at Milan, and is to go thence for Genoa. I have wrote him word that I shall be there a Thursday night, and as his road lies through the same place, I may possibly catch him after all. I am with all services, dear mother,

Your dutiful and affectionate

J. Spence⟩

1. Date supplied from *Notebook* 3 79ᵛ: 'Set out from Turin Septʳ: 15, 1740.' The endorsed address page gives the date 'Turin, Sept. 18', evidently a mistake, for on Sept. 17 they were already at Acqui.

2. Sept. 16. He met Arthur Smyth together with Lord Hartington (*App.* 1).

Notebook 3
(34) 79ᵛ

Alessandria [Sept. 16] lies between the Tanaro and Bormida. They are hard at work about the citadel, which is a regular hexagon (?) and will be very strong. The town itself is weak and mean enough, all in a flat and a very bad air.

Acqui [Sept. 17–27] 'Aquae Statyliae' of the ancients is got more down the hill to the NW (or is much lessened to the NE) as one may guess from the aquaeduct that crossed the Bormida, and of which the remains are yet consider-able enough. There are some medicinal waters in the town, almost boiling hot, and some near it, on the other side of the river, which are very hot at their first source and less and less so at others. . . . The old Roman road at Acqui is said to go on to Final and Ventimiglia, and so into the south of France, and (they say) comes to them from Placentia (Via Aemilia?).

124

Source:	Egerton 2234 ff. 211–12
Addressed:	*as in 74*
Postmarked:	25 SE
Franked:	Free/Tho[s]. Ramsden
Numbered:	D. N[o] 4./39
Endorsed:	*a.* sep[t]: 29: 1740: from y[e] Baths/near aqui, & alessandria/in Italey. an ac[t] of/S[r] Bouchier Wreys coming/back to england, & M[r]. Smith/to Ireland,
	b. Aqui: Sep: 29 [*mistake for* 20], 1740./Have met wth S[r] B[r] Wrey, &c./Not to be Copied *red wafer*

The Baths, near Acqui,
September 20, 1740

⟨Dear Mother,

We have been here four or five days;[1] the waters have a very good effect on my Lord's leg, and the doctor hopes they will soon absolutely cure him. We shall then go on, which I long to do. I had the pleasure of meeting Mr. Smith and Lord Hartington[2] (who came a little out of their way to Genoa) at Alessandria, and stayed a day and a half with him. He is going on; I hope in some time to be able to call him my Lord of some good see in Ireland, or at least dean of some very good deanery there.[3] Holdsworth set out from Milan yesterday, as I learn from my friend Sir Bouchier Wrey who came from that place hither to pay me a visit,[4] and who is now sitting by me: he goes this afternoon for Turin, and hopes to be in England in three or four weeks, where Capt. Rolle will be much rejoiced to see him. You would do a very charitable thing in sending Capt. Rolle word of it, for 'tis one of the best friends he has in the world. I hope to catch Holdsworth again at Florence, where Sir Bouchier tells me we shall meet with Lady Walpole, Lady Mary Montagu, Lady Pomfret and her two charming daughters Lady Sophia and Lady Charlotte.[5] Heaven defend the heart of

Your most obedient humble servant

J. Spence.⟩

1. They arrived on Sept. 17 and stayed till Sept. 27.

2. William Cavendish (1720–64), styled M. of Hartington, 4th D. of Devonshire; member of the Soc. of Dilettanti 1740/1; Chief Governor of Ireland 1755–6, First Lord of the Treasury and Prime Minister 1756–7. He was patron of Spence's friend Arthur Smyth (see *Letter* 39) who now accompanied him as a travelling tutor. They were in Rome May 14, ready to 'set out for Venice' (*H. W. Corresp.* XVII, 23). By Sept. 14 they reached Milan (see *Letter* 123) and were now returning to England via Genoa.

3. Smyth became successively Dean of Raphoe 1743–4, of Derry 1744, Bp. of Clonfert 1752, of Down 1753, of Meath 1765, and Abp. of Dublin 1766–71. 'Hoc praecipue patrono ... ad summos in Ecclesia honores gradatim ascendit' (Cotton, *Fasti Eccl. Hibernicae* [Dublin, 1848], II, 24–6).

4. On Sir Bourchier, see *Letter* 78. After his return from Italy he became member of the Soc. of Dilettanti (1742). Horace Walpole called him 'a very foolish knight' (*Corresp.* XIX, 224).

5. Margaret Rolle (1709–81) was Baroness Walpole, later Countess of Orford. In 1724 she had married Robert Walpole, eldest son of the Prime Minister (whom he succeeded 1745 as 2d E. of Orford). She eloped in 1734 with Samuel Sturgis and was now living in Florence. Lady Mary Wortley Montagu (1689–1762) arrived in Florence from Venice in August 1740, but left before Spence got to Florence. He met her later at Rome. See *Letters* 149 to 151. Henrietta Louisa Jeffreys (ca. 1700–61), the third of 'this triple alliance', had married (1720) Thomas Fermor, cr. 1721 1st E. of Pomfret. They were staying at Florence (Dec. 20, 1739–March 1741). Lady Sophia (1721–45) was the celebrated beauty with whom Lord Lincoln was to fall in love. Horace Walpole described her as 'very beautiful and graceful; much prejudiced in favour of her own person, but not to the prejudice of anyone that liked it' (*Corresp.* XXX, 6 n. 31). Lady Charlotte (1725–1813) was Lady Pomfret's 2d daughter. She was at fifteen 'the cleverest girl in the world', according to Horace Walpole (*Corresp.*, Toynbee edn., I, 76). In 1746 she married William Finch, son of the E. of Winchelsea, and later became governess of George III's children.

125

Source: Add. MSS 33065 ff. 383–4
Endorsed: L[d] Lincoln R[eceived] Oct [20?]/1740

LINCOLN TO NEWCASTLE

[Acqui,
September 1740][1]

My Lord,

... my leg grows daily better and better since the doctor's last account of it from Acqui, though the lameness and weakness is not entirely gone off. We arrived here last Thursday and design setting out for Bologna in two or three days. ... What Mr. Hume[2] mentions in his letter to me from your Grace of our returning home in a few months into England, I own surprised me a little, for your giving me more time at Turin (which I desired that I might make some real progress in my exercises) I thought implied a longer stay in Italy, and now this accident has made it still more necessary. By means of both together we are got so late into the season that we are obliged to go directly for Rome, without making any of the detours we intended in our former schemes. We hope, as it is, to be at Rome by the beginning of December; three or four months is as little as almost anybody stays there that makes the tour of Italy. We thought therefore of going from thence to see Naples in March and to Venice in April, to be there for the Ascension, which is reckoned one of the greatest sights in Italy.[3] As soon as ever that is over, we thought of setting out for the South of France, to see my old friends there,[4] from whence I can come home in the summer or stay till the autumn at Paris, whichever your Grace thinks proper. As our tour of Italy must be very imperfect without the time above-mentioned, I hope your Grace will be so good as to comply with it. . . .

I am better in health at present than ever I have been, and have by no means any thoughts of dying abroad, but hope when the above-mentioned time is past, your Grace will with some pleasure receive your humble servant Linki, who loves nothing in this world or aims at nothing so much as pleasing his dear uncle. If I am not very much mistaken, the last time I had the pleasure of seeing my uncle Pelham he did not reckon on my coming home till the autumn following, for he said that he thought that less than two years could hardly be sufficient to travel as I ought to do, and that if I came home before, I should find your Grace and himself entirely taken up with the thoughts of the next approaching election.

There is another affair of the greatest importance that Mr. Hume mentioned to me in his last letter, which at the same time he hinted your Grace expected to have my thoughts upon. I must own the person he names to me is much above anybody in my circumstances could possibly pretend to in regard to fortune, but sure in other respects there is much to be said.[5] When I reflect that my father, whose affairs in those times your Grace knows better than I can tell you,[6] did marry not only the most agreeable woman but of the greatest quality in England, and that I, . . . though by no means in an abounding fortune yet far superior to his at that time, should for the sake of some thousand pounds marry a person whose family I never so much as heard of, whose person I am very sure there is not much to brag of, and who has nothing to recommend herself but the greatness of her fortune—what are the consequences, my Lord, of all these sort of marriages? Why, nothing but a continual series of unhappiness. . . . What indeed can one possibly expect when she marries me for the sake of being called a Countess and I her for her fortune? I own my Lord I should blush to see such a Lady Lincoln, when I think of that we had the happiness of having not many years ago! Lord what a difference! And I am very certain if it had pleased God to have kept her alive, she, who always despised riches and show in comparison of real and essential happiness, would never have been for such a marriage as this.

But if your Grace thinks it absolutely necessary for me to marry, there is a near neighbour of mine who has not only fortune but quality too and all the qualifications one could desire. This my Lord I must own would be much more agreeable to me, if it could be brought about, though I think it impossible when I consider the number of young men she may pretend to, who so far exceed me both in fortune and merit. Your Grace may easily imagine I mean Miss Boyle.[7] But as this is an affair I build very little upon, I can assure you I am very certain of being able to live very happy and contentedly with the fortune I have at present. . . .

I should do Mr. Villettes great injustice if I did not myself let you know what a true friend he has been to me all the while I stayed at Turin, but more especially in my late accident. Indeed, my Lord, his whole behaviour to me has been such that one only finds in those who really love and esteem one. . . . I waited on the Marquis D'Ormea[8] a little before I left Turin, who was exceeding obliging to me: he desired his compliments to your Grace and gave me a letter of recommendation for Rome himself to the Princess Colonna Borghese,[9] who is not only of one of the greatest families there, but the most agreeable and politest lady at Rome. . . .

1. They stayed at Acqui Sept. 17–27; so the letter was written about Sept. 24.

2. Rev. John Hume (1703–82), Lincoln's tutor at Cambridge; his reports to the D. of Newcastle are among the Newcastle MSS in the British Museum (Add. MSS 33065). Later Bp. of Bristol 1756–8, of Oxford 1758–66, of Salisbury 1766–82.

3. Gray also planned to reach Venice by then 'to see the old Doge wed the Adriatic Whore' (Corresp. I, 182).

4. At Vigan, where he had been with his mother for health in 1733. Several of Lady Lincoln's letters from Vigan are among the Newcastle MSS deposited at Nottingham University Library.

5. This almost certainly was Ann Dunk (1726–53), dau. of William Richards (afterwards Dunk) of Tongues in Hawkshurst, Kent, whose dowry of £110,000 was at this time being bartered for a nobleman's title. The conditions were curious. By a will dated July 8, 1718, Sir Thomas Dunk, Sheriff of London 1709–10, left his estate to his illegitimate son William Richards, 'citizen and ironmonger', with remittance to his issue in full, on condition that all who so succeed take the name of Dunk (G.E.C. VI, 247–8). On Oct. 15, 1740 O.S., Lady Hertford wrote that 'a Miss Dunk' was to marry George Montagu, E. of Halifax

(1716–71), 'as soon as an act of parliament can pass for him and his posterity to take her name' (Hertford Corresp. II, 165). The marriage took place on July 7, 1741, the Earl signing himself thereupon 'Dunk Montagu'.

6. Henry Clinton (1648–1728), 7th E. of Lincoln, who apparently had 'only £500 per annum', was considered as one of 'the poor quality in England', and 'lived in an obscure manner for want of what to support him in his dignity' (G.E.C.).

7. Dorothy (1724–42), dau. of Pope's friend Richard Boyle, E. of Burlington, of the 'softest temper, vast beauty, birth and fortune' (£40,000), m. Oct. 10, 1741, George Fitzroy, E. of Euston (1715–47), who treated her with such revolting brutality that she died half a year after her marriage (Hertford Corresp. II, 162–5).

8. The Sardinian Prime Minister, see Letter 91 n. 7.

9. The Princess Agnese Colonna (1702–80), dau. of the Constable Colonna, m. in 1723 Camillo, the Prince Borghese (1693–1763). '[Sa] maison...est aussi le rendez-vous ordinaire des Anglais, qui sont ici en grand nombre, la plupart fort riches. . . . La princesse est aimable, enjouée, spirituelle, galante et d'une figure agréable' (De Brosses, II, 201).

Source:	Egerton 2234 ff. 209-10
Addressed:	*as in 74*
Postmarked:	2 OC
Franked:	Free/Andrew Stone
Endorsed:	*a.* aqua: a Bath, among yᵉ apennines/a descripshon of/a thunder storm there, terable/fine; *b.* Fine Thunder-Storm. *red wafer*

Acqui,
September 27, 1740

⟨Dear Mother,⟩

We have now lived ten days in the midst of the Apennine mountains, and
last night had a thunderstorm which continued (almost without any silences
between) for four or five hours. The echoing of the thunder from rock to
rock, together with the falls and hollow murmurs of the water on every side
of us, made up one of the noblest concerts that ever I heard. You know I
am a lover of thunder everywhere, but your thunder in England is but poor
music in comparison of a good noble thunderstorm among the Alps and
Apennines. ⟨The waters have done so well with my Lord,[1] that we are to go
on upon our journey tomorrow,[2] and in two or three days shall be at Milan:
from which place I hope to write to you again. I am, with all services to all
friends, ever

Your dutiful and affectionate

J. Spence.⟩

1. Spence commemorated the cure in a pretty
votive epigram addressed to the healing waters
of the river Bormida:
Nympha loci! calidam vertens de montibus urnam,
  Bormida juxta flumina sancta patris;
Accipe blanda preces Britonum cultumque rogantis
  Linconiae ut serves spemque decusque domus:
Sic semper jaceas humili tranquilla sub antro!
  Tutaque ab infidi mobilitate soli!
(*Nbk.* 3 79ᵛ)

The last two lines read 'first': 'Sic nunquam
desit lymphae medicina! Decorum / Sic semper
jaceas floribus apta caput!' On the 'mobilitas
soli' see the following letter.
2. On Sept. 28 they were in Alessandria on
their way to Milan, where they stayed Sept.
29–Oct. 4.

*127

Source: Egerton 2234 ff. 213–14
Addressed: *as in 74*
Postmarked: 11 OC
Franked: Free/Andrew Stone
Endorsed: *a.* an act of/the travilling Hill at Aqui, in/ Italie
b. Acct of the Sliding/-House, at Aqui
red wafer

Milan,
September 30, 1740
⟨P.S. I have received no less than four
letters from you, since I left Turin.⟩

⟨Dear Mother,⟩

You have heard of the hill in Gloucestershire or Herefordshire,[1] I forget
which, that travelled three days and three nights: there was half a hill in
our neighbourhood at Acqui that made almost as great a journey in half an
hour. I had heard of it at Turin, and at Acqui I lived upon it: for our house
was upon part of the travelling ground.

In the year 1686, after a very deep snow, and on a sudden thaw, a great
part of a good high mountain parted from the rock and slid down into the
vale. The crack of the earth in parting, its rushing on, and the crashing of
the trees which fell on the sides of it (where the earth that moved was
shallowest) were heard at Acqui (which is about half a mile from it) like the
letting off a number of cannons all together. The good people were then at
their afternoon-prayers (their vespers, as they call them), for it happened on
Good Friday, about two and twenty o'clock, which is the way of counting
in this country, and there in particular was about an hour before sunset.[2]

As soon as they came out of the church, the news was brought that such
a hill was travelled down into the plain, and that 'twas that part of the hill
where farmer such one's house stood. The farmer and all his family were a
part of the congregation, and you may be sure were some of the first to run
to see this terrible sight. They crossed the river Bormida as fast as they
could, and you may imagine the farmer's surprise when he was got on the
other side of the river to find his house was come down above two hundred
paces to meet him, and stood as well almost in the vale by the riverside as
it used to half way up the hill.

When they had the courage to enter it (which was not till two or three
days after for, though they saw it standing, they were afraid the beams
must be displaced, and expected it to fall every minute at first) they found

318

everything in good order: and in particular, as the farmer has told me several times, there were two calves in the stall which were not at all hurt, and which they found alive, though they stayed so long before they ventured to go to them. There was a small niche too in the wall in which there stood a little Virgin Mary of earthenware, not larger nor so handsome as a common jointed-baby. The figure was not moved out of its place, and there was a little basket of eggs by it, which were not broke.

The house stood on the middle, and consequently on the most solid part of the earth that travelled down, and, if what they say be true, it must have travelled very equally and leisurely. The chief harm that was done, was the bed of the hot-baths being overlaid and lost for some time: at last the waters worked themselves a way lower down than before and on a level with the plain,[3] and the next year the Duke of Mantua[4] built a house there for those who should come to use the baths, over the door of which there is an inscription that mentions this accident. This house we lived in.

The thing is strange, but I give it you from the spot. I don't know whether you will believe it, but I have no manner of doubt of it myself, for I viewed the place every day whilst I was there, and 'twas evident there had been such an accident: and for the particulars, I had them from the Bishop of Acqui,[5] the people that live in the house, and indeed all the neighbourhood. ⟨I am with all services,

Your most dutiful and affectionate

J. Spence.⟩

1. The latter. John Colet recorded in his manuscript *Collection of severall very remarkable Stories*, p. 32: 'Marche hill in Heresfordshire in the year 1571 removed for three dayes together about 400 yards from its place carrying with it about 26 acres of ground, it went with a great noise overwhelming kinaston chappell, and trees that stood in its way' (Osborn Collection at Yale).

2. About 5 P.M., an hour and a half before sunset, which on Easter Friday (Apr. 13 N.S.) was at 6:36 P.M. (Lodovico Quadri, *Tavole Gnomoniche* [Bologna, 1743], p. 132). According to the Italian planetary time, the twenty-four hour day began at the Ave Maria, half an hour after sunset, and was announced by the ringing of church bells. As the time of sunset varied from day to day, clocks had to be moved so many minutes ahead or back, depending on the season of the year. The planetary time was abolished in Italy in December 1749 (*Daily Advertiser*, Jan. 1, 1750). I owe this note to George L. Lam.

3. In his *Notebook* (3 79^v) Spence drew a diagram of the displacement.

4. Ferdinando Carlo Gonzaga, D. of Mantua and Monteferrato 1663–1708.

5. Giovanni Battista Rovero (1684–1766), Bp. of Acqui 1727. In 1744 he became Abp. of Turin, Cardinal 1756 (F. Savio, *Gli antichi vescovi d'Italia* . . . [Turin, 1899], p. 16).

Notebook 3

(35–36) 80r–v

The Certosa by Pavia built by John Gal. Visconti, Duke of Milan, the same who built the hospital and began the Great Church. The church there pretty light Gothic. The pretty close road from Pavia to Milan.

Milan[1] [Sept. 29–Oct. 4]. In the Ambrosian Library 35,000 printed books and 15,000 manuscripts, including the catenae: eight or ten sometimes in one volume. 'Sc[hool] of Athens' 80,000 crowns.

The hospital is very rich: 150,000 scudi a year. They take in infants to five or six year old. Three brought in that night and 25,000 in the last five years. The coalman left 150,000 livres Mil[anese], or £5,000 English.

At Count Porta's the very great *deceptio visu* by Castellino da Monza. The building humours it at top, but is an absolute flat—the story there: the Reception of the Prodigal Son.

In the treasury at the Dome a mitre of S. Carlo like bad embroidery in feathers; a rock imitated in rock crystal (how much like ice melted a little and froze again together). The two great pillars at the entrance of the church. The fine beginning of the façade—five doors in it finished, and ruins over it.

At Settala's gallery a carpet of feathers, long robe for a man and a *mantile* for a woman, of ditto, from the Indies. Emeralds as in the mine, clock that goes for six months, perpetual motions and motions from loadstone(?); little cart on glass.—Sixteen pillars, old Roman, of the Corinthian order just by the Colonna Infame and the Porta di Pavia.

Piacenza [Oct. 5]. Dome by Pordenone at Madonna di Campagna.

Parma [Oct. 6]. The great theatre was built (by the inscription over the stage) in 1607. The length from the fond of the stage to the bottom of the parterre is 165 braccias (about two English feet each) and the greatest breadth 122 dit. One sees conveyances for water, and there have been naumachias in it. The mark of the height of the water about my mouth. They now talk of *balli di cavalli* in it; the last time seven year ago.—The cupola at the dome (Ascension of the Virgin by Correggio, vile colours) almost quite spoilt. Cupola at St. John's (Ascension of our Saviour, by ditto) great air, larger figures and better preserved. Two pieces at a side-altar (ibid. by ditto): Dead Saviour and Martyrdom of two saints. The conversion of Mary Magdalen (at a private house, till the church of S. Antonio is finished) is the best picture we saw of Correggio's at Parma: St. Jerome holds a Bible and the Virgin argues out of it to convince Magdalen. There's a very good angel in it, the Bambino's face not graceful (? copy of some friend's child, for 'tis very natural).

Modena [Oct. 7]. See separate paper.[2] The dusty rivers from Plaisance to Modena, and some from Modena to Bologna.

1. See also First Tour, *Nbk.* I 30v–31v
and *Letter* 23.

2. *App.* 15.

*_128_

Source:	Egerton 2234 ff. 215-16
Addressed:	as in 74
Endorsed:	a. an act/of ye new pope, who was born there/& arch bishop there; & a man/of fine carictore;
	b. Two or three Stories of the/New Pope (Ben: 14th.)
	red wafer

Bologna,
October 12, 1740

⟨Dear Mother,⟩

'Tis a great pleasure to me, if my letters can give any to you; indeed my whole design in sending you so many, and so long ones, is to send you a sort of _Tatlers_ that may chat to you in my absence, and make the time run off a little the faster, till I come back. All people that talk much must talk sometimes very ill,[1] so I make no manner of excuse for them: and when they are duller than ordinary, you may look upon them as a sort of Irish hummers, which are meant (very honestly) to talk you to sleep. ⟨I don't love to talk of myself, or of anything I do, so I have done with them: which is more than you are like to do, till I come home again.⟩

We are now at Bologna,[2] where we came the very day before their rejoicings for the advancement of the new Pope.[3] He was born in this town, and was Archbishop of it before he arrived to the high dignity in which he is at present invested.[4] He is by all accounts a very good, worthy man.[5] When the magistrates here sent to him for his leave to make such and such rejoicings for his promotion, he sent them word that he was very much obliged to them, but that he thought it would be much better to give the money they designed for that use to the poor. The magistrates, on receiving this answer, computed what expense would be necessary, gave the sum to the poor, and afterwards had the rejoicings too. which looked much the better for having the blessings and prayers of so many poor people mixed with them.

The Pope is by all accounts of him a learned man, a man that knows the world, of a great spirit, of very good sense, and no bigot. I must tell you two or three stories of him, that show his character a little more strongly. When the late Pope[6] was at Genoa, there came a report to Rome that he had done a great miracle there. Lambertini (the present Pope) who was then at Rome, was told it as a great matter, in all its finest colours, but instead of falling into raptures upon it, his answer was that 'if it was true, it was very strange to him that a man should do miracles at Genoa, that had never done anything but follies and rascalities at Rome.'

321

'Tis true he used to treat the late Pope a little cavalierly now and then. Lambertini, as Archbishop of Bologna, had a deputy under him (which they here call their 'vicar') who was an excellent man for business. The Pope had heard his character, and wanted to have him in his service. He wrote on some occasion to Lambertini, and toward the end of his letter just dropped that he should be obliged to him if he would send him his vicar, and that he would be of great use to him on such an affair, then in agitation. Lambertini answered his letter very respectfully, but said not one word about his vicar. The Pope used the same method two or three times after, and was always served in the same manner: all the other articles answered very fully, but not one word about sending his vicar. The Pope, tired out, writes to Cardinal Spinola,[7] his legate here (for Bologna is a city in the Pope's government), tells him how he had been used, and says he must and will have the man sent him. Spinola on this paid a visit to Lambertini, expostulated with him, and desired to know what answer he should return from him to the Pope. Lambertini, at first, was for using his old way, and desired him to say nothing at all about it in his answer. Spinola said that was impossible, that some answer from him he must have: 'Well then,' says he, 'if the Pope must have an answer, be so good as to give him this: that I neither can, nor will part with him, and that my reason is this: that the Archbishop of Bologna is much better served by his Vicar at Bologna than Christ is by his Vicar at Rome.' Spinola laboured much for some other answer, but Lambertini stuck to this, and this was actually sent.[8] ⟨I am ever, with all services to all friends,

Your most dutiful and affectionate

J. Spence.⟩

1. 'No one will ever do for conversation,' Lockier told Spence in 1730, 'who thinks of saying fine things. To please, one must say many things indifferent and many very bad' (*Obs.* No. 741).

2. They left Milan Oct. 4 (Piacenza 5, Parma 6, Modena 7) and stopped at Bologna for ten days, Oct. 8–18.

3. Prospero Lorenzo Lambertini (1675–1758) was elected on Aug. 17 as Benedict XIV. See De Brosses's letters LIV–LV for a vivid account of the election.

4. He was translated to the archdiocese of Bologna in May 1731 (L. von Pastor, *History of the Popes*, XXXV, 29).

5. De Brosses gives him the following character: 'Bolonais, archevêque de Bologne, bonhomme, uni, facile, aimable et sans morgue, chose rare en ceux de son espèce; goguenard et licencieux dans ses discours; exemplaire et vertueux dans ses actions; plus d'agrément dans l'esprit que d'étendue dans le génie; savant surtout dans le droit canon; passe pour pencher vers le jansénisme; estimé et aimé dans son corps, quoique sans morgue, ce qui est très singulier' (II, 492).

6. Lorenzo Corsini (1652–1740), Pope Clement XII 1730–40.

7. Giorgio Spinola (1667–1739), Nuncio at Vienna 1713–20, Cardinal 1719, Papal Secretary 1721, Legate to Bologna 1727.

8. The anecdote of Lambertini's flippant answer to Clement XII occurs, in a somewhat mitigated version, in Louis Antoine Caraccioli's *La Vie du Pape Benoît XIV* (Paris, 1783), p. 19, which abounds in anecdotes about the witty 'new Pope'.

*129

Source: Egerton 2234 ff. 217–18
Addressed: as in 74
Endorsed: *a.* an act of ye young Ladys ill/yousage, in ye
convent/unknown to ye present/pope, till his
return back/to Roome,
b. Another Pope-Story; of/the Young Lady
& ye Jesuits.
red wafer

Bologna,
October 18, 1740

⟨Dear Mother,

You need not make excuses to me for wishing me a good wardenship;[1] on
the contrary, I ought to thank you very much and think myself much
obliged to you, and to oblige you would not only consent to be a Warden,
but Pope of Rome—if you desired it, and the cardinals would be so good as
to elect me.⟩

I told you in my last two or three things relating to the present Pope—a
few months ago Cardinal Lambertini, but now Benedict the Fourteenth.
But I forgot to tell you that he is a Pope that has some chance of pleasing
the Protestants, because he hates the monks in general, and particularly the
Jesuits.[2] The occasion of his dislike to the latter was this, as I have been
told the story by a great many very good Catholics.

There was a young lady, an orphan, whose parents had been Lambertini's
particular acquaintance. When they died, they left this only daughter in
mean circumstances, and Lambertini was so good as to breed her up and pay
for her education. 'Tis the fashion for almost all the young ladies of
condition here to be bred up in convents. Lambertini therefore, when he
was to leave Rome to go to his archbishopric, placed her in a convent in
the former, advanced a handsome sum to the Lady Abbess, and desired
them to take particular care of her education. The Lady Abbess promised
no care should be wanting, and the cardinal went to Bologna.

'Twas the misfortune of many a young lady, and of this in particular, that
this convent was under the influence of three or four Jesuits, of holy faces
and very debauched hearts. After our poor orphan had been there some days,
they made their addresses to her, and were so pressing that she found
herself obliged to write to the cardinal that she should be ruined if she
stayed there. She got a trusty friend to carry her letter to the cardinal's
house in Rome; he was already set out for the country, but one of his
servants promised to send it to him: instead of which (on a rumour that the
cardinal was coming back to Rome on some particular business) the servant

323

thought it might be as well to lay it on his writing-desk. The rumour was false; the cardinal did not come, and the letter was forgot.

About two months after, when he did come, he found this letter in his closet. On reading it, he sent immediately to the convent for the lady to be sent to him, but was answered that she had had a violent fever which carried her off, and that she was buried in their chapel the Wednesday before. On this the cardinal sent proper officers to open the grave and see her body, on the suspicions he had too reasonably entertained on reading her letter. This was done, and when the coffin was opened, they found her body hacked to pieces in the most barbarous manner.[3] The cardinal, by that letter, knew where to lay the blame, but was wise enough to stifle his resentment for the present. Now he is Pope, he may possibly punish them as they deserve, ⟨and 'tis thought he will. Possibly whilst I am at Rome I may hear their trial. If I do, you shall have the end of this tragedy, for in all good tragedies, you know, not only the innocent suffer, but the wicked are to be hanged.[4] We set out for Florence tomorrow.[5] I am ever

Your most dutiful and affectionate

J.S.⟩

1. Mrs. Spence was answering *Letter* 119.

2. Not in general, though he disliked a few, among them Le Fevre, the confessor of Philip V of Spain, who was spreading rumours that Benedict XIV was preparing an anti-Jesuit bull. The rumours had wide circulation as late as 1745 (Pastor, *History of the Popes*, XXXV, 63–6, 307–11).

3. This gory tale has an air of having been made up for Protestant consumption, though it derived probably from an actual incident, for Caraccioli also relates it, in a somewhat softened version. (*La Vie du Pape Benoît XIV*, pp. 24–6).

4. Later, as he prepared the letters for a fair transcript, Spence revised the last paragraph to read: 'and there are some who think he has courage enough to do it: but he has full as much prudence, and I should rather think that will keep him from irritating a body of men who have long since owned to all the world that they think it just and religious to put any prince out of the way by any means they can, who is so capitally an enemy to the Church as to be an enemy to their order.'

5. They left Bologna Oct. 18 (Fiorenzuola 19, Ponte 20) and arrived at Florence Oct. 21.

'*The court of Rome has more or less power in all the states of Italy. 'Tis their interest that the people should be kept in ignorance. Knowledge is therefore more or less discouraged in all the states of Italy, and if any person shows a particular eagerness for it, they either drive him away, or at least oblige him to hold his tongue.* ⌐*There's no impunity for sense in this country.*⌐ *When one considers how far this is carried in most parts of Italy, one would rather wonder that there should be so much knowledge left than that it should be so much fallen among them*' (*Lady Walpole, October–November 1740, Obs. No. 1562*).

*_130_

Source: Egerton 2234 ff. 219–20
Addressed: as in 74
Endorsed: _a._ his first/Letter from thence, & yᵉ actᵗ: of
his/jurney theather, over yᵉ apennine/
mountains
_b._ Partᵗ Accᵗ of travelling thro'/the Clouds;
in pasᵍ the Apennines
red wafer

Florence,

October 21, 1740

⟨P.S. My Lord Lincoln is much obliged to you:
I tried what you mentioned, and find it all well.⟩

⟨Dear Mother,

When I came to Florence, I looked upon it as I should on Winchester
(bating that you were not here) as an old friend and acquaintance. I am
here at my old home, and among old friends; beside which we have a
number of English here, most of whom we either knew in England or saw
at least in their passage through Turin: which, since the war,[1] has been the
great and almost the only passage into Italy.⟩

The passage of the mountains between Bologna and this place is certainly
the most troublesome pass of all the Apennines; but though I had some
pains in it, 'twas fully made up in the pleasure I had of experiencing what
it is to travel among the clouds, more strongly than I ever did before, either
on the Apennines or the Alps.

When we set out 'twas a tolerable clear day in the vale of Lombardy, but
the hills were capped with clouds. Our first post was on pretty even
ground,[2] our second all mounting, and when we were got about half way
of it, we entered into the clouds. The first entering into them felt to me
just like the coming on of the great eclipse when I was boy at Winchester
school,[3] and the poor rooks were so disturbed and in so great a doubt
whether it was night coming on or not: for the dark came on so fast then,
too, that one could feel it advance, and the air was chilled as suddenly. When
we were thoroughly in the clouds 'twas just the same as a thick mist, and
had the same effect on the trees, which in some places had gathered so
much moisture from the clouds that, when the wind shook them, I mistook
it two or three times for a shower coming on, but upon looking out found
it was only the droppings of the leaves.

The clouds, which seem to us to be one great canopy over our heads,
are certainly of a very different make: you have sometimes a great layer of
cloud, then a serene open space, and then a layer of clouds again, and so on;

325

for when we got about half an hour higher, all was clear round us, and a fine sunshine gilded everything about the road. We had then a canopy of clouds over us, were in clear daylight ourselves, and saw the clouds lying under us in the great hollows between mountain and mountain, all white, and not unlike the froth that covers the whole surface of a tub where Betty has laid some of your linen a'soak.

Thus we went on, with more changes than I can tell you, sometimes in the dusk and sometimes in fair daylight, till about two hours before night. We were then on the top of a hill when, on a sudden, a thick mist scudded along before us, and in a little time grew so strong that we could not distinguish anything fifty yards (nor I believe half fifty yards) before the chaise. I concluded this would be a lasting thing, and was very sorry for it because we had a very ugly hill to go down, and was in danger of being benighted. After descending about an hour, we found this was only a cloud too; the air below was all serene, and the night, when it came on, was to us in the valley a clear starlight night.

The next day we had much the same sights: the same sort of mist on the highest hill of the Apennines, and the same clearness and starlight night in the valleys. A little of this will not be easily accounted for, and a little will be attributed to the spirit of travellers, but as I take it upon me to send you a full and true account of everything I see in these my peregrinations ⟨John Bunyan would have said, in this my pilgrimage⟩ I shall not fear any of those aspersions which malicious and ill-minded people are so apt to fling out against us poor travellers. ⟨With all services to all friends, I am ever

Your most dutiful and affectionate

J. Spence.⟩

1. England had been at war with Spain since Oct. 23, 1739.

2. ' 'Twas at Pianoro, the first posthouse from Bologna that there were those fine remains of the Deluge: the great square stone all covered with very little shells in the Chemin du Torrent, but fallen from the side of the hill' (*Nbk.* 3 80ᵛ. See also *Obs.* No. 1460).

3. The eclipse of the sun of Apr. 22, 1715: 'what light (or the mixture of light and darkness) remained, was of a bluish cast, like burning brandy in the dark, and like it, it made people's faces look ghastly' (*Gent. Mag.*, 1748, p. 404). Spence was to enter Winchester College that summer (Kirby, p. 225).

*131

Source:	Egerton 2234 ff. 221–2
Addressed:	*as in* 74
Postmarked:	8 NO
Franked:	free/Thos. Ramsden
Endorsed:	*a.* an act/of ye light yt apeares at pietra mala
	b. Of the Light that ap-/pears at Pietra-Mala.
	red wafer

Florence,
October 29, 1740

⟨Dear Mother,⟩

I gave you an account in my last of our travelling through the clouds from Bologna to this place: but I did not mention to you a thing that is much more unaccountable to me than anything I saw in the clouds. I had often heard of it indeed, but though I had passed this road, I had never seen it before. The thing they said (and which I always looked upon half as a lie) was that there was a fire which appeared always by night, at a little distance from a place called Pietra Mala.[1] That it was a fire in the air, but a very little above the ground, and that it had burnt there, but without doing any harm, time out of mind. The first time I went this road was in the middle of the day, so that it did not appear at a distance. In passing now we were benighted, by a princess being on the road and taking up all the post-horses before us. It began to be dark when we were at Pietra Mala, and we were to go to Fiorenzuola, the next town, for lodgings. As soon as we were got out of Pietra Mala, I asked our postillion about the fire. He said that there were three in three different places, that one of them had not burnt lately, but that the other two had: and the largest and most famous of them we should see as soon as we were got half a mile farther. I believe I asked the poor man every twenty yards of this half mile whether we could see the fire yet? And if he had not been a good-natured fellow, he would certainly have cursed me very heartily, in very bad Italian, for being so impertinent.

At last we came to the place whence we could see it, very distinctly, though through some trees; which made it look only like a great candle: and as I had then some doubts still about it, I thought it might have been only some candle or lamp in one of the houses of the village. But when we got on farther, and were clear of the row of trees, it appeared in all its lustre. 'Twas an even yellow light, like the body of the sun, and appeared at that distance to be about three foot long and one foot broad; the postillion told us that 'tis really about ten foot, and broader in proportion.[2]

He said he had been often on the spot, and lately with some English gentlemen, whose names he did not know. That the ground where it appears, and whence it comes, is of a reddish colour, and that that is the colour of the soil in general about it. That there is no cavity in the ground, nor anything burnt away, though the oldest man in the parish always remembered the fire there as long as they could remember anything, and so did their fathers and their grandfathers. That there was sulphur in the ground and 'oleo de' sassi' (which in English may be called 'flint-oil'). The most learned man and the great physician in this place[3] has told me since I came here, that the curious have searched and found there was a great deal of petroleum in the soil, which is much the same with the other oleo de' sassi. My dear friend Mr. Holdsworth (whom I have met with at last in this place) tells me that it does not burn always, though it does generally, and that some friends of his went to see it once, and that the people in the neighbourhood said it was not on fire: and on their being very sorry they said, 'Oh, we can light it for you!' Upon which one of them immediately ran for a candle, and upon drawing it along through the air over the place, the air there appeared all in flames and burnt on as it does at its best. ⟨There's a great deal in it that is still unaccountable to me: by [the] time I come home I hope to be able to give you a better account of the matter.[4]

The newspapers here had told me the ill news of Mr. Grey;[5] I hope your last is the truest. We are here in a crowd of English. I was this morning with Lady Walpole (with whom I am a sort of a favourite, as being a very great philosopher),[6] and this afternoon with Lady Pomfret and her two fair daughters[7]—with whom I should be very glad to be a favourite, as very little of a philosopher. However, my Lord is gone with them to an assembly, and I came home, as a good boy, to write to you and the secretary's office. I am ever

Your most obedient

J. Spence.⟩

---

1. See also Spence's *Obs.* No. 1462.

2. De Brosses thought it looked like 'une espèce de phosphore; mais c'est terriblement exagérer que de dire, comme Misson, qu'ils jettent une flamme haute et claire comme un feu de fagots' (I, 312).

3. Dr. Antonio Cocchi.

4. 'At Fiorenzuola', Spence copied down the following verses: 'Adspicite O Cives, quam sit volatile tempus; / Volvitur & semper non redditura rota' (*Nbk.* 3 80ᵛ).

5. 'Henry Grey Esq. of Billingbear, Bucks, Member for *Reading*', died Sept. 9 O.S. 'of a mortify'd Leg. He left no Issue, but a very good Character behind him, being a common Parent

to his Relations, and just and generous to all Men' (*Gent. Mag.*, 1740, p. 469).

6. Spence recorded some of her sayings in his *Observations* (Nos. 1556–68). Her remark that 'the chief aim of any young nobleman on his travels should be to make a man of sense his friend' obviously refers to himself and Lord Lincoln.

7. On her daughters see *Letter* 124. 'Lady Sophia is still, nay she must be, the beauty she was: Lady Charlotte is much improved, and ... speaks the purest Tuscan, like any Florentine' (*H. W. Corresp.*, Toynbee edn., I, 76).

Notebook 3
(36–37) 80ᵛ–81ʳ

At Pratolino there are pretty grots and waterworks. The pictures in the House are not worth seeing, but the 'Genius of the Apennines' by John di Bologna is very much so. The length of his foot is about nine foot English; 'tis not easy to know where his heel (which is confounded with the rock) ends, but 'tis 9 f. 9 in. or 9 f. long, almost twelve times as much as mine, so that the whole height should be about 60 f. A pede Herculem. His face is painted (and mean enough), the hand that comes down before is ill contrived for viewing the figure (I suppose 'tis meant to say: 'These hills are mine'), but in the side view, and especially on his left hand, it shows a *grand* idea. The icicles (of the same style) were in great abundance about him. There are several now, almost on every part of him, but some are quite fallen and others broke. Six people might dine at their ease with their attendance (three servants) in the grotto in his back, which might have been vastly larger if a good deal of solid had not been necessary to support so great a weight and half as large again. The fountain from him is frivolous. How much nobler would it have been if there had been a vast rock under him and several streams rolling down rude rough channels, as they do really in the Apennines![1]

1. Compare Spence's account of this landscape gardening tour de force by Giovanni Bologna (1524–1608) in the gardens of the Medici Villa with Pope's idea of how Dino-crates might have transformed Mount Athos into a vast statue of Alexander the Great (*Obs.* No. 618).

132

Source: Egerton 2234 ff. 223–4
Addressed: as in 74
Postmarked: 15 NO
Franked: ffree/Andrew Stone
Endorsed: *a*. not a/Reading letter
b L.ᵈ L.ˢ Goodness; &c./Not to be copied.
red wafer

Florence,
November 7, 1740

⟨Dear Mother,

I have had the pleasure of receiving no less than nine letters from you since I left the good town of Turin, and you should have received near as many from me, if the post has been honest and done its duty. Lord Lincoln (who talks often of you, and who at least among his many ways of obliging me, has that of talking fondly of you) is I thank God pretty well, though he made a shift to strain his leg a little again, before we had been an hour in this place. I had immediately the best surgeon in the town to it,[1] who said there was no great harm done, and that rest would be the best cure. As he said, so we found it to be; and my Lord is now able to go every day to the famous gallery here,[2] though there are above a hundred steps to go up, before we come to the beauties in it. Indeed they deserve going up ten times as high. Mr. Smith, you know, I met with at Alessandria, and Mr. Holdsworth I caught in this place.[3] The latter goes on Wednesday next for Rome, whither we shall be tending too, in about a fortnight's time. We have got Mr. Walpole here again, and dine with him almost every day.[4] He stays here the winter, and I don't envy him, because we are to stay at Rome.[5]

I received three of your letters which speak of poor Mr. Grey;[6] I was afraid the news would turn out as it does in your last, because Mr. Walpole had received a letter before to the same purpose. If one was to choose for our own sakes, I had rather it had been Mrs. than Mr. of that name; and for his, one does not know how to choose: for, to say the truth, one does not know whether 'tis better for any one man one could name to be in or out of this world. The last I heard of Mr. Aldworth was, that he was at Geneva, and I hear here that his inclinations (if his uncle should fail) were to come to Rome.[7] As much as I should be glad to see him there, I had rather hear of his being gone to England, where his presence is more necessary.[8] Pleasure is a very pretty thing, but it should never interfere with great business: and he may probably have much to do in your part of the world. If you can learn anything with any certainty of him, I should be very glad to hear of it. Rolle is an honest fellow, but he would be honester if he would write to you often: what has he to do but to write to his two mothers as often as he can? A lazy, lath-gutted fellow, with a weasel face! He's thin, and made for business: he should write as fast as a greyhound runs. I always thought he'd come to little or nothing, and so he's like to do if he grows much thinner. I am ever, with services to all friends,

Your most dutiful and affectionate

J. Spence.⟩

1. Dr. Antonio Cocchi.

2. Spence accompanied him to the Uffizi together with Lady Sophia, who criticized the waist of the Venus de' Medici 'as not fine and taper enough' (*Polymetis*, pp. 66–7).

3. As he had hoped to (see *Letter* 124).

4. Horace Walpole and Gray arrived at Florence early in July. It was here or during their visit at Turin (Nov. 7–18) that Gray saw Spence's manuscript of *Polymetis* (Gray's *Corresp.* I, 268).

5. On Nov. 11 Lady Mary wrote from Rome:

'I am told Lord Lincoln has taken a large house, and intends to keep a table, &c.' (*Complete Letters*, II, 210).

6. The lately deceased Hon. Henry Grey Neville.

7. Richard Aldworth was nephew of Henry Grey Neville, whose sister Catherine Neville (Richard's mother) married Richard Aldworth of Stanlake. On young Aldworth's stay in Geneva, see *Letter* 85.

8. He was evidently one of his uncle's heirs. See *Letter* 144 n. 4.

133

Source:	Egerton 2234 ff. 225–6
Addressed:	as in 74
Endorsed:	b. In great Haste./to be omitted
	red wafer

Siena,
November 30, 1740

〈Dear Mother,

We are got to Siena, in our way to Rome; so that I am within three days'
journey of the place I have so much and so long wished to be at.[1] When I
am there I shall have time and leisure to write to you more fully: at present
I have neither. But whether busy or idle, whether very active or half
asleep, am always equally

Your dutiful and affectionate

Jos: Spence.〉

1. They left Florence Nov. 24, visited Pisa (25), Leghorn (26–28),
and stopped in Siena Nov. 30 to Dec. 1.

---

*134

Source:	Egerton 2234 ff. 227–8
Addressed:	as in 74
Endorsed:	a. maxentius/the tierent, drounded in yᵉ
	tiber, &/several of his officers, fell with/him,
	b. The Waters how much out/in our Journey.
	red wafer

Rome,
December 8, 1740

〈Dear Mother,〉

We are got at last to the place that I have so long wished to be in,[1] after a
journey that was bad enough, by being so deep in the year, and made a
great deal worse by the rains which have fallen most part of the forty days

last past.[2] We were stopped upon the highest mountain of the Apennines this way for a whole day, upon a torrent of water being at the foot of it. When that was run away, we got on; and they assured us we should have no more trouble from waters all the way to Rome.

However, they were much mistaken, for when we were got within three mile of this place, we found that the Tiber was overflown, and was got all over the road we were obliged to pass immediately before the bridge where Constantine drove Maxentius, and whence the latter fell with several of his officers and were lost in the Tiber.[3] We sent our servants over first, and then our postillions on horseback, to see whether the road was fordable: and as they returned their answer that it was, we passed boldly over it, and as soon as we were got on the bridge, who should we see there but the Pretender's second son[4] with his governor Lord Dunbar (as they call him)[5] and others of his attendants, who had stayed for some time to be witnesses of our courage: which we should be more ready, no doubt, to make use of against him and his than against the waves of the Tiber. We passed afterwards half a mile, I believe, in water in the suburbs, though not often deep and never dangerous; and this day we could not pass through some streets in the town for water to St. Peter's and the Rotonda there was no getting into on the same account. There has not been such an inundation here for several years.

Our house is on an eminence,[6] in a very good air, safe from the rising of the river, if he should be inclined to rise more: and what I value most of all, next door but one to Mr. Pitt[7] and Holdsworth, whom I can visit at any time in my night-gown and slippers. We are about twenty English here, almost all together in the Spanish Square, or Piazza di Spagna. ⟨I write this in haste, for we came hither the fifth, and are scarce quite settled yet. I am, with all services to all friends,

Your most dutiful and affectionate

Jos: Spence.⟩

1. They arrived at Rome Dec. 5, through Radicofani (2–3) and Viterbo (4), and stayed until May 15, 1741.

2. 'Florence has been a perfect Deluge,' wrote Sophia Fermor to Mrs. Wallop, 'and there is no getting out of one's doors; people, children and cattle drowned, ground-floors, cellars, etc. entirely under water' (Finch MSS, Leicestershire Record Office. See also *H.W. Corresp.* XIII, 237, and *Hertford Corresp.* II, 187–8).

3. *The Craftsman* reported on Jan. 10, 1741: 'Our advices from Rome of the 16th of last month inform us, that the Tyber has over-

flowed its Banks. . . . The Government took care to send Provisions in Boats to such as were blocked up by the Waters in their Houses . . . at Florence and in the Neighbourhood, the Damage done by the overflowing of the Arno amounts to about 2,000,000 of Roman crowns.' Ficoroni informed Spence that 'the top of the column by which they measure the risings of the Tiber at Rome is twenty-two feet higher than the street . . . and yet the water has risen so high as to hide the very top of the column' (*Obs.* No. 1400). The bridge was Ponte Milvio, where M. Aurelius Maxentius perished in battle A.D. 312.

4. Henry Benedict (1725–1807), cr. Cardinal of York 1747. The 1st son was Charles Edward (1720–88), the Young Pretender.

5. The Hon. James Murray (ca. 1690–1770), 2d son of the 5th Visc. Stormont, cr. E. of Dunbar 1721. 'I meet him frequently in public places,' wrote Horace Walpole, 'and like him. He is very sensible, very agreeable and well-bred' (*Corresp.* XIII, 218).

6. In the Piazza di Spagna, the favourite residential section of the English at Rome.

7. George Pitt (1721–1803) of Stratfield-Say, Hants, had graduated from Magdalen College, Oxford, in 1739. Member of the Soc. of Dilettanti 1741; M.P. for Shaftesbury 1742–7, Dorset 1747–74; cr. Baron Rivers 1776. Lady Pomfret called him 'another very agreeable young man' (*Hertford Corresp.* II, 160), the other being Lord Lincoln.

Horace Walpole, with whom Lord Lincoln and Spence renewed acquaintance at Florence, wrote on Dec. 27 to Lincoln: 'I was really uneasy till I heard by Mr. Spence, that you had escaped all those torrents. We had calculated your being on the road, just as we were swimming in the Arno.' He adds: 'I must beg you to say a great deal for me to Mr. Spence, as Mr. Mann writes to him tonight, I would not give him the trouble of a second letter. Will you give him this epigram for me; 'tis spick and span new out of Mr. Pope's shop—

To Sir R. W.

Walpole, be wise, let each man play his part,
You mould the state, let others judge of art;
What though by either Andrew often bit,
You scarcely know a Jervas from a Tit;
Blush not, great Sir, you cannot know it less,
Than we (God help us) if it's war or peace.

(*Corresp.* XXX, 3–5)

135

Source: Cocchi MSS in the collection of Count Enrico Baldasseroni, Florence

Addressed: Al Illmo Sign^r Sign^r Prōn Col^mo Il Sign^r Dottore Cocchi,/*Firenza*
red *wafer*

SPENCE TO DR. COCCHI

Rome,
December 17, 1740

Dear Sir,

I have been very much concerned, with the rest of your friends here on the news of your suffering so much by the late inundation at Florence.[1] A library like yours, and papers like yours, did not merit so hard fortune. I hope the damage is not so great as has been represented, and should be extremely glad to hear from you better news than we have yet heard of it.

When I was at Florence, I went two or three times to see the labours of Hercules on an old marble at the Niccolini palace, but could never get the sight of it.[2] If they are the twelve,[3] and are good work, I should be extremely obliged to you if you would get them drawn for me by the best hand you have in Florence, on a large half-sheet of paper of a fit size for a folio book. If they are not good work, I should be at least obliged to you for the names and order of the labours which it represents.[4]

When I had the pleasure of conversing with you, I once mentioned that I feared my Lord Lincoln was fallen in love at Florence. I wanted to talk with you farther on that head, but never could get an opportunity of doing it. 'Twas with Lady Sophy that I imagined he was in love, and I find it to be but too true. I have some reason at present to think that he carries on a correspondence with a friend at Florence on that subject, and suspect a little that it may be with the abbé Buondelmonte.[5] As you are so well acquainted with him, I should be extremely obliged to you if you would try in conversation adroitly to find out whether he is in letters with my Lord, and any lights you could give me as to that affair would be the greatest obligation to me in the world. If I have any occasion of mentioning this to you in any letter hereafter, I will always call it the *Affair*, and you will know what I mean by that word. I beg my sincerest compliments to Mrs. Cocchi and to your little family, and am ever/Dear Sir

Your most obliged humble servant

J. Spence

1. See *Letter* 134 n. 2. Dr. Cocchi's house was on the Arno where, according to Lady Pomfret, the water 'came up to the first story, and was no where lower than two feet in depth' (*Hertford Corresp.* II, 187–8). The inundation damaged Dr. Cocchi's library.

2. On the twelve labours of Hercules, see *Polymetis*, pp. 115–25.

3. The Latin poets usually mingle Hercules' 'extraordinary and ordinary labours so much together, that it is impossible from them alone to know the one from the other, [but] one may learn what the twelve were, from several relievo's on the subject' (117–18).

4. The bas-reliefs from the sarcophagus in the Palazzo Niccolini do not appear in *Polymetis*.

5. Giuseppe Maria Buondelmonte (1713–57), a nobleman at Florence and a minor poet, whose prose version of Pope's *Rape of the Lock* Bonducci turned into Italian verse (1739). He was called *abate* from the ecclesiastic habit he wore.

*136

Source: Egerton 2234 ff. 229–30
Addressed: as in 74
Postmarked: illegible
Franked: Free/Andrew Stone
Endorsed: b. Little or nothing in it.
red wafer

Rome,
December 17, 1740

⟨Dear Mother,⟩

As for my letters ⟨which when they are in print will be well worth your reading⟩[1] I wish they could give you, and any friends you please, ten times as much diversion as you say they do. Laughing is a wholesome thing: and they'll do well enough to laugh at. A person that makes another laugh is a useful man in his generation. Who can say that Dicky Norris was not an honest man?[2] And I should think more likely to go to heaven than most of the monks and melancholy people I have met with. So much in praise of being ridiculous.

Now to talk a little more seriously (as there is a time for all things); I find myself at this great city just as I did the first time I was here. Though I have been here a fortnight, I have not yet recovered myself: 'tis all astonishment at the greatness of the things about one, and they are so very great, and in such numbers, that one does not know where to fix one's attention or what to look at first.

One thing that I have wanted to see much, and which it has not been my fortune to see yet, is the Pope. However, in all probability, I shall see him often enough before we go away: for he is a hale strong man, not like the other Popes of late, goes out every day, and performs all the great ceremonies in person. The late Pope was so weakly when he was chose, and grew so much more so afterwards, that at last it grew very difficult to get a sight of him: and this had brought in a custom, unknown in my first being here, which was that the English gentlemen who came here on their travels generally made interest for an audience of his Holiness, which was allowed them without going through the ceremony of kissing his slipper. As this Pope is not commonly so invisible, the custom seems to be dropped again at present: they leave it to chance now, and I don't doubt but we shall see him somewhere or another before we are a fortnight older here. In particular, in the Christmas week he gives a dinner to all the cardinals in public, and then we may have a sight of them all together.

⟨When I have studied his person sufficiently, you shall have a character of it: at present I have nothing more to say, but that (if he is a handsome man) I wish you were married to him—and 'twould be no bad thing to be popess and queen of this fine city of Rome. I am ever

Your most dutiful and affectionate

J. Spence.

P.S. There's one passage in your letter which gives me some pain. 'Tis where you say, 'if that were the only trouble I have': I was in hopes you had no trouble, and want to know what you can have to trouble you. If you won't tell me, I'll come home as fast as I can, to lessen it if I can, or to share it with you if I cannot. As to what you mention with it of the K^s,[3] I hope they cannot give you any great trouble; or if they do, why should you have anything to say to them? However, I shall naturally see you, in a few months I may call it now, and then I shall know all in our chats by our Birchanger or Queen's Street fireside.⟩

---

1. Spence later revised his letters, had them transcribed in a fair copy (now in the Osborn Collection), and may have intended to publish them. See *Introd*. p. 23.
2. Not identified.
3. Probably the Kelleys (see *Letter* 66).

137

Source:	Egerton 2234 ff. 231–2
Addressed:	*as in* 74
Endorsed:	*a.* a full/descripshon of ye new pope
	b. Acc^t of the Popes Dress; in/a Consistory.
	red wafer

Rome,
December 22, 1740

⟨Dear Mother,⟩

I have, at last, had a very full opportunity of seeing the Pope. A few mornings ago there was a consistory: which is a council of the Pope and cardinals, in their robes (like our King in the House of Lords).[1] I went thither with my Lord, and found an easy admittance at the beginning of the council. As we were the only strangers there, we were very conveniently placed, and saw the cardinals drop in one by one, make their reverences to one another, and take their places. When the council was full, the Pope himself came in, and took his seat in a throne of state with a canopy over it.

He was dressed in white robes, not unlike a surplice, with close sleeves [and] with a shorter laced surplice over it. He had a sort of deep-red roquelaure[2] over that, lined with ermine, and over that a thing like a broad embroidered belt, which came round his neck over his shoulders, crossed upon his breast, and then fell down about half way to the ground. He had a deep-red cap on his head, and a little white satin one under it. And this was all his dress, except a very bad muff: which might possibly be ermine too, but at a distance looked more like a cat's skin.

The affair to be settled was the long dispute that has been between this court and the King of Portugal: the cardinals meet in this senate of theirs not to vote but to give their advice, and the Pope has the power to determine everything as he pleases after he has heard what they have to say: which, by the way, is the method in all absolute monarchies as well as in this. When the Pope was seated, the cardinals who had the chief interest in the affair, or who were best informed in it, drew toward his throne, and he heard (in private) what each of them had to say on it. After these private audiences were over, a public officer called out 'to clear the house', and we left them to debate the affair aloud and in general.

I took notice that the Pope in these private audiences looked like a man that was a master of business. He heard everybody calmly, and answered them with a great deal of ease in his behaviour. He was never in a hurry, nor ever seemed puzzled about what they said to him, or what he should say to them. This dumb show gave me the opportunity of having my eye upon him almost constantly for half an hour together, so that I could get a pretty distinct idea of his person.

He is rather short than tall, and of a thickish make: his face is no good one, but he has a strong, hearty look in it for a man that is not of a florid complexion. There is something droll in his face, and his eye has a particular sort of life and cunning in it: so that his look, of the two, rather diverted me more than it pleased me. He seems strong and able to live long enough to give his officer the lie, who always, when a Pope is made, is obliged to say to him: 'Sir, you have the keys of St. Peter, but you will never hold them so long as St. Peter did.' That apostle is supposed to have been Pope three and twenty years, and there has been no Pope (at least none for these three hundred years) who has sat in his chair so long.[3]

⟨This morning I met his Holiness in my walks, and shall see him officiate on Christmas Day. Apropos, I wish you and all friends a merry Christmas and a happy New Year: which will be much the happier to me, because I hope to see you in it. I am ever

Your most dutiful and affectionate

Jos: Spence.⟩

337

1. 'On the 19th the Pope held a private Consistory, in which he declared the Reconciliation with the Court of Portugal, and at which 12 Bishops of that kingdom were acknowledged' (*London Gazette*, Jan. 17–20, 1740/1, reporting for December). See also *Mercure historique*, Jan. 1741, pp. 28–9.

2. A cloak reaching to the knee, named after the D. of Roquelaure (1656–1738).

3. The dates of St. Peter's papacy are uncertain; Adrian I (772–95) had held the office for twenty-three years.

---

*138

Source:	Egerton 2234 ff. 233–4
Addressed:	*as in 74*
Franked:	Free/Andrew Stone
Endorsed:	*a.* a ferther/descripshon of yᵉ new pope/after he had seen him,
	b. The Pope at Mass.

Rome,
December 31, 1740

⟨Dear Mother,⟩

We have since seen the Pope at mass; he performs his part very well: but of the two, his religious look is not so good as his look of business.[1] 'Twas on St. Stephen's day. Just before the Nicene creed, a young English priest got up, and made a sort of sermon (or speech) in Latin, in praise of St. Stephen. It was a mixture of the English good sense and of the high flights of this country. Before his sermon he said an Ave Mary, as we do the Lord's Prayer: and after the sermon he made a present, in the Pope's name, of thirty years out of purgatory and thirty times forty days to every single person then at church. Every time he named the Pope's name he bowed very low, as we do at the name of our Saviour. Before the sermon he had the honour of kissing the Pope's toe, which is the first time I have been present at that ceremony. I did not carry off my thirty-three years of indulgence for nothing, for just as I was going out of the chapel-door, where the crowd was very great, I had my pocket picked, and so it cost me a handkerchief: which some vile heretics would think a very bad bargain.

⟨Three or four days ago I received four of your letters all together: I am sorry to find by them that you are in danger of so hard a winter: the letters, even from the south of France, say the same. You have reason for once to envy us here: for at Rome we have had extreme fine weather all this month, or at least ever since we have been settled here. So warm that I write generally without a fire, and that we often leave our windows open, without knowing anything of it from the air.

The uncertain state of Europe makes it doubtful as yet which way we shall come home. If we have a war with France, we must come through

Germany to Holland.[2] If Germany should be too confused, through Switzerland. For my part (and you know I am a very great politician) I have all along said that we should have no war with France, and I think so still. But be that as it will, there will always be a road open one way or other: and the apprehensions of a war (if it should be more likely in the spring) may possibly occasion our coming home so much the sooner rather than keep us longer from you.

I hope you continue stout and well: as for my part, I was never better. Since I came here, I have set again about my book, which was interrupted ever since our leaving Turin: and it goes on most currently. I verily believe I shall write enough abroad to tire all the good people of England when I come home again. But however, my book is to be a picture-book,[3] and so it may divert the little boys of seven or eight year hugely—and improve them vastly in their studies.[4]

You say nothing yet of my garden at Birchanger. I long to hear how it does, and that it flourishes finely against my coming to see it. What a pleasure will it be to me, to see you puddling in it and setting of beans to eat with the hocks of bacon that we shall carry out of Hampshire with us! I hope, however, you will take care and not work long enough to catch cold, for the air is but damp in England, and I don't know how to transfer the warmth of this climate to my parsonage house in Essex. With all services to all friends, I am ever

Your dutiful and affectionate

Jos: Spence.⟩

1. 'If you observe his Holiness at any long religious ceremony,' said Abbé Niccollui, 'especially if he is to officiate himself, you will see that he has a faint look and a tired eye: but see him in a conclave on business—you will find his look more enlivened and his eyes quick and piercing. He has always loved business, and has no relish for formal devotions' (Obs. No. 1446).

2. So Gray wrote on Oct. 9, 1740: 'If we remain friends with France, upon leaving this country we shall cross over to Venice, and so return through . . . Marseilles, and come back through Paris. If the contrary fall out, which seems not unlikely, we must make . . . our way to Venice; from thence pass through the Tirol into Germany, and come home by the Low-Countries' (Corresp. I, 178).

3. Polymetis is profusely illustrated with engravings, done by Louis Pierre Boitard.

4. In 1764 Nicholas Tindal published an abridged version for use in schools, which went through six editions before 1802 (Wright, p. 103).

139

Source:	Cocchi MSS in the collection of Count Enrico Baldasseroni, Florence
Addressed:	Al Illmo Sign^r Pad^o Colend^{mo}/il Sign^r Dottore Cocchi/à/*Firenza* *red wafer*

SPENCE TO DR. COCCHI

Rome,
December 31, 1740

Dear Sir,

I troubled you with a letter the 17th of this month and long very much for your answer to it. I believe I forgot to mention (both in yours and Mr. Mann's)[1] that my letters are directed to me here, 'recommandé à Monsieur Belloni, Banquier'.[2] 'Tis my fate to be always troubling you: I have received a letter from a friend in England since I came hither, with queries relating to a MS in the Lorenzo Library, and must be at a loss how to answer them without your assistance. I beg leave to send you the paper of queries inclosed.[3] I long much more to hear from you in answer to my former letter, than this: for the queries may very well wait your leisure and lay by till a time when you have nothing else to do. I beg my compliments and best wishes of the season to Mrs. Cocchi, Signora Beatrice, and Signor Raimondo,[4] as well as to yourself, and am ever / Dear Sir,

Your most humble servant

Jos. Spence

I should be much obliged to you, if you would mention our direction to Mr. Mann the first time you see him.

---

1. Horace Mann (1701–86) had been appointed in 1737 assistant to the Minister at the Court of Tuscany, and from 1740 until his death acted as British Minister at Florence. Spence had met him in 1732 at Naples, and in October 1740 at Florence. Dr. Cocchi was Mann's personal physician.

2. Girolamo Belloni (d. 1761), prominent banker, author of *Dissertazione sopra il commercio* (Rome, 1750) which gained him title of papal Marchese. He acted as forwarding agent for travellers' letters. For his 'Bill of Credit' made out for Spence, see *App.* 10.

3. Enclosed was the following slip written in a small hand I have not identified:
'The book I desire may be consulted is Plut: 1 Cod. 9. in the Library of St. Laurence in Florence. Vid. Le Long, Bibl. Sacra, edit. 1723, Vol. 1. p. 100.

Query:
1/ Does it contain more than the Gospels?
2/ Is the Doxology read, Math. 6.13?
3/ And the History of the Woman taken in Adultery? Joh. 8.
4/ What account is given of the date of the Version; or Copy; by Whom, When,

Where, Translated, Transcribed, Collated? (N.B. I believe an account of this is given at yᵉ end of St. John.)

5/ Is it on Paper or Vellum?

6/ If on Paper, of what kind is it; Silk, Cotton, etc?

7/ If it contains more than the Gospels, what are the Contents?

8/ Does it read Acc or Ptolemais Acts. 21.7? and what follows Church of—Acts 20.28?

9/ How many Catholick Epistles, 3 or 7?

10/ Three that bear record in Heaven, Joh: 5.7. Is that verse there? and in the following verse does it read These 3 are one or these 3 agree in one?

11/ How reads Rom: 9.5 of whom—Xᵗ—who is over all etc.

12/ How does it read, Tim: 3.16. God was manifest in the flesh? N.B. I should be glad to have that verse transcribed as it is in the Syriac.

13/ Are there any other Syr: or Gr: M.S.S. of the N.T. or its parts in that Library? what is their age? in what character wrote? Have yᵉ Greek M.S.S. yᵉ accents? on paper or vellum? how do they read the above mentioned Texts?'

4. Cocchi's children. Raimondo Cocchi (1735–65) later became antiquarian in the Grand Duke's gallery.

140

Source: Egerton 2234 ff. 235 6
Addressed: as in 74
Endorsed: a. a short/Letter:
b. Nothing/to be omitted
red wafer

Rome,
January 7, 1741

⟨Dear Mother,

I find myself so full of business (and so much employed, particularly with the antiquities of this good old city) that you will excuse me if my letters are sometimes not of so vast a length as they used to be. I mention this particularly at present, because I have this very morning only time to tell you, that I am mighty well, and entirely

Your humble servant,

Joseph Spence.⟩

141

Source: Egerton 2234 ff. 237–8
Addressed: as in 74
Endorsed: a. an ac^t/of ye shavilear &c:
b. The Opera, & the Pretender.
red wafer

Rome,
January 13, 1741

⟨Dear Mother,

I begged you in my last to excuse me if I wrote but short letters to you from this place, where there are certainly more sights to engage me than in all the rest of the world together. However, this evening I have got, I think, a spare hour, and so may possibly fill up my paper.⟩

'Tis now some time that our operas have begun here. They are the chief diversion of all the cities in Italy, and this is as largely furnished with them as any one. We have now two operas almost every night,[1] and three or four burlettas: which are mock operas, and meant only to play the fool with the more serious ones. The opera that we chiefly frequent is I may say, without any manner of partiality, the best; and by good luck 'tis very near us, in the very next street.[2] We are seated in the second row of boxes, and, whether by good or bad luck, in the very box under the Pretender's. He was there last night, with his second son (the eldest was gone out on a party of hunting) and some other blue and green garters, for red, you know, they have none.[3]

The custom of operas here is to visit from one box to another:[4] and though I never make any visit to my neighbour above stairs, I went over to my Lord Strafford,[5] who is opposite to us, to take a view of them. The Pretender looks sensibly olded since I was here last;[6] he read his opera-book with spectacles; his son sat by him in front, the Duc de St. Aignan behind,[7] and by him Dunbar. He has three boxes all flung together, and they were all filled with his company and attendants of one sort or another. They supped (as they often do here) in the box, and the dessert was ranged in the little passage behind ours, before it was sent up. Lord Strafford, who was so kind as to return my visit, came by it, and as they often sell little eatables and sweetmeats here about the opera house, as he came along he took it for one of the places of sale, and cheapened a jelly—at which the ranger of the dessert seemed very much offended: but he perceived 'twas a stranger, and there's scarce anything that a stranger may not do in this place, so he came off without a reprimand.

342

The chief singularity in the operas here is that all the parts are acted by men. The Romans are so nice as to think that 'tis indecent for a woman to appear upon the stage: half the dancers are boys dressed like women, and the queen and all the ladies of the play are eunuchs. You'd be surprised to see how much they all look like women, and how well they manage the fan: but this is not so great a wonder among the modern Romans, as it would have been among the ancient ones. They are now in general effeminated to the last degree: and that roughness and courage that formerly made them masters of all the world is sunk into such a softness and indolence, that I verily believe they could not now defend their own city against five hundred good old battered soldiers—unless the prayers of the priests should be sufficient to save themselves and the laity. However, their town has a vast many fine things in it, whatever the people are; and we don't come here to see troopers, but antiquities. ⟨With all services to all friends, I am ever

Your most dutiful and affectionate

J. Spence.⟩

1. 'A chaque théâtre', wrote De Brosses, 'on exécute deux opéras par hiver, quelquefois trois. . . . Ce sont chaque année des opéras nouveaux et de nouveaux chanteurs. On ne veut revoir, ni une pièce, ni un ballet, ni une décoration, ni un acteur, que l'on a déjà vu une autre année' (II, 338). His *Letter* L contains a vivid account of the theatres in mid-18th century Rome.

2. 'Le théâtre Alle Dame construit par le comte Alibert, gentilhomme français au service de la reine Christine, est le plus grand, et passe pour le plus beau; c'est là que se fait ordinairement la grande tragédie' (ibid., 335). Teatro Aliberti was a few steps from the Piazza di Spagna.

3. Jacobite kings conferred the Order of the Garter and the Order of the Thistle, but not the Order of the Bath.

4. 'Les dames tiennent, pour ainsi dire, la *conversazione* dans leur loges, où les spectateurs de leur connaissance vont faire de petites visites. . . . On braque sa lorgnette pour démêler qui sont les gens de sa connaissance, et l'on s'entre-visite si l'on veut. Le goût qu'ont ces gens-ci, pour le spectacle et la musique, paraît bien plus par leur assistance que par l'attention qu'ils y donnent. Passé les premières représentations, où le silence est assez modeste, même au parterre, il n'est pas du bon air d'écouter, sinon dans les endroits intéressants' (ibid., 337).

5. William Wentworth (1722–91), cr. 4th E. of Strafford 1739; member of the Soc. of Dilettanti 1741. Lady Mary, just back from Naples, may have attended the performance, for she writes on the same day as Spence: 'Lord Strafford behaves himselfe realy very modestly and genteely, and has lost the pertness he acquir'd in his mother's assembly' (*Complete Letters*, II, 220).

6. 'He is a thin ill-made man,' wrote Gray in July 1740, 'extremely tall and aukward, of a most unpromising countenance' (*Corresp.* I, 167). On Dunbar and the Pretender's 2d son, see *Letter* 134.

7. The French Ambassador, whom Spence saw at Dijon in 1731 (*Letter* 18) on his way to assume his post at Rome. 'Le duc de Saint-Aignan,' writes De Brosses, 'lorsqu'il va au spectacle, fait une galanterie fort bien imaginée. . . . Il envoie ses officiers servir des glaces et des raffraîchissements dans toutes les loges des dames' (II, 338).

*142   Source: Egerton 2234 ff. 239–40
          Addressed: as in 74
          Endorsed: a. an act/of ye cerimony on St antonys day,
                       wch is kept ye 17th of/january:
                       b. The Blessing of Horses/&c; on St Antony's
                       Day.
                       red wafer

Rome,
January 21, 1741

⟨Dear Mother,⟩

The seventeenth of this month was a ceremony which I have often heard of, but never saw before;[1] it continued all day long, and I was there no less than three several times, and last of them in a vast crowd ⟨to have my bellyful of it⟩.

There is a church on one of the hills in Rome,[2] which was formerly dedicated to Diana, the patroness of all beasts among the heathens; 'tis now dedicated to St. Antonio Abbate, the patron of beasts among the Catholics.[3] The 17th of January is his feast day, and on that day almost everyone that has a horse, mule, or ass in Rome, sends them to this church to be blessed. There is a convent belonging to the church, a court behind, two gates on each side of it, and a pretty large opening before. This you see full of the aforesaid animals, dressed out with ribbons, and some with garlands; they drive in at one of the gates, where stands a priest in his surplice and other ecclesiastical ornaments, with several tubs of holy water by him and an aspergitoire (or instrument to sprinkle it on man or beast)[4] in his hand.

The coaches, carts, and saddle horses that are next to this gate, go in (in a sort of procession), and as they pass the priest, they give him a piece of silver, a wax candle or a wax torch, who takes care to wet them according to their present. A coach and six with a vast torch has half enough to drown the coachman, if 'twas all well placed in his face; a muleteer has but a little sprinkling, and an ass-rider may come off quite dry. We drove in our coach, and had sixpenny worth of it. After you are in the great gate, you go on in a semicircle and come out at the other; and there was a line of animals, always going and coming, from sunrise to sunset.[5] This is the chief revenue of the convent, and they are said to make a thousand pound of what they receive this day: the chief of which income is in wax.[6] I have heard that the men bring their hounds, and the ladies their lap dogs, to partake of the blessing: what I can aver myself is that I saw a cartload of wood blessed there among other things, and 'twas so plentifully wetted that I believe it must have burnt the worse for it. All the times I saw it the same priest officiated; he was perhaps the strongest fellow in the convent, yet the last time I was there (about 23 o'clock)[7] he seemed very much fatigued with blessing, and almost quite spent.

⟨This St. Antony, who is so obliging to all sorts of beasts, is different from the famous St. Antony of Padua, and is always to be known, in his pictures, by a little pig which is running by his side:[8] whence in all probability we have our expression of a child's 'doddling about one like a tantony-pig'. They call this saint too here San Antonio di fuoco, or St. Antony of the fire: whence a distemper among us too (that he, I suppose, used to be prayed to for a cure) is called 'St. Antony's fire'.[9] You see I have given you some learning, as well as history, in this. I am ever, with all services to all friends,

Your most dutiful and affectionate

J. Spence.⟩

1. Spence had mentioned it on his first tour (*Letter* 34). He certainly read accounts of the ceremony in *Three letters Concerning the Present State of Italy ... Being a Supplement to Dr. Burnet's Letters*, 1688 (pp. 139–40), attributed to Dr. Hutton, and in Conyers Middleton's *A Letter from Rome* (1741 edn., pp. 137–43). See also *Gent. Mag.*, Oct. 1741, pp. 543–4, on the subject.

2. On the Esquiline, near S. Maria Maggiore.

3. The church was actually built on a private basilica of Junius Bassus (consul in the age of Constantine). Because of the mosaics of hunting scenes discovered there, the basilica was until the early 19th century considered to have been a temple dedicated to Diana.

4. 'A Broom in *Holy Water*', says Dr. Hutton.

5. 'The force of this hallowing is believed to be such, that if any should fail to bring his *Horses* thither, all the Neighbourhood would look on those that have no *Portion* in it, as accursed Animals, upon whom some unlucky *Accident* were hanging; which is so firmly believed, that none would hire a *Horse* or *Mulet* that had not been sprinkled' (ibid.).

6. i.e., 'great Wax-Lights, all stuck full of *Testons* (a piece of 20 Pence)' (ibid.).

7. Half an hour before sunset. See *Letter* 127 n. 2.

8. Also by a T-shaped cross. The pig, originally perhaps a symbol of evil, became associated in the 17th century with the blessing privilege of the Hospital Brothers of St. Antony.

9. St. Antony's fire was apparently an epidemic form of erysipelas against which the Saint's intercession was invoked.

Lady Mary Wortley Montagu returned to Rome from Naples on Jan. 12. The unusual welcome and admiring attention she received from the expectant young English lords at Rome was of a kind that miraculously restores confidence in the slightly battered charms which a woman at fifty-one begins to feel sensitive about. From the manner in which she recalled, twelve years later, 'the Winter I pass'd at Rome', one might assume that it was the last éclat of her expiring womanhood: 'There was an unusual concourse of English, many of them with great Estates, and their own masters. As they had no admittance to the Roman Ladies, nor understood the Language, they had no way of passing their Evenings but in my Apartment, where I had allwaies a full drawing room. Their Governors encourrag'd their assiduities as much as they could, finding I gave them Lessons of Oeconomy and good conduct, and my Authority was so great it was a common Threat amongst them—I'll tell Lady M[ary] what you say.—I was judge of all their disputes, and my Decisions allwaies submitted to. While I staid there was neither gameing, drinking, quarrelling, or keeping. The Abbé Grant . . . was so much amaz'd at this uncommon regularity, he would have made me beleive I was bound in conscience to pass my Life there for the good of my Countrymen' (Complete Letters, III, 32).

Lord Lincoln became her great favourite. The day after her arrival she wrote to her husband: 'Lord Lincoln appears to have Spirit and sense, and proffesses great abhorrence of all measures destructive to the Liberty of his Country.' On Jan. 20 she wrote to Lady Pomfret: 'I see all the English here every day, and amongst them Lord Lincoln, who is really, I think, very deserving, and appears to have both spirit and understanding' (ibid., II, 221–2).

143

Source: Add. MSS 33065 ff. 391–2

LINCOLN TO NEWCASTLE

Rome,
January 21, 1741

. . . Well! my Lord, we have at last Lady Mary Wortley at Rome,[1] who is as extraordinary as my imagination had fancied her (which by the by is not saying a little). I am so happy as to be mightily in my kinswoman's good graces, for you must know she claims a relation, which I own I did not in the least suspect. She takes a sure way to be well with me, for she flatters me so much as to tell me that I am extremely like your Grace, not only in person but in my ways, though I have not vanity enough to think this is true. You can't conceive how it pleased me, and the Lord knows what would happen if it was not for the nearness of blood.[2] / I am / your Grace's / most affectionate and dutiful nephew

Lincoln

1. They missed her at Florence, and again by a few days on their arrival in Rome, which she had left at the end of November for Naples.
2. 'Aye, my Lord,' she told Lincoln, 'we had both of us our love of reading from the same source . . . she seemed to be fond of speaking of their near relation 'from "Wise William" Pierrepont' (Obs. No. 760). 'Wise William' Pierrepont (1607–78) was great-grandfather of Lady Mary and great-great-grandfather of Lord Lincoln.

Lord Lincoln must have written to Horace Walpole a letter to the same effect, for on Jan. 31 the latter wrote to him from Florence: '... I did not doubt but Lady Mary would be glad of having you flesh of her flesh, but did not imagine she would try to bring it about by making you of her blood; of her poxed, foul, malicious, black blood! I have gone in a coach alone with her too, and felt as little inclination to her as if I had been her son. She is a better specific against lust than all the bawdy prohibitions of the Fathers. She comes up to one of Almanzor's rants in a play of Dryden—"The thought of me shall make you impotent!"'

Horace Walpole then continues: 'Is Mr. Spence enough at liberty among his antiquities to think of me? I deserve it a little, for I have a vast esteem for him. Do you hear, Mr. Spence, though I naturally love anyone that has so real an esteem for Lord Lincoln, yet I hope you won't put all my friendship to his account. When we meet in England, I hope we shall be vastly well together, without any other consideration. I design to visit the Virgil you tell me of [Spence had mentioned a gem in Baron von Stosch's famous collection], but for getting it, I have no hopes. If I could steal it roundly, I would without any scruple, but for procuring it from so thorough a rogue as Stosch without paying double its value, I despair' (Corresp. *XXX, 10–12*).

144

Source: Egerton 2234 ff. 241–2
Addressed: as in 74
Postmarked: 5 FE
Franked: Free/Andrew Stone
Endorsed: *a.* not/a reading letter
b. of Mr Aldworth./Not to be Transcrib'd.
red wafer

Rome,
January 28, 1741

⟨Dear Mother,

I began to be in great fears for you, not having received any letter of yours for a month; yesterday morning the man brought me in two together, and made me quite easy.

Your second, which gives so full an account of Mr. Grey's will,[1] gave me some pleasure and some pain. By what we had heard, I feared 'twas yet worse than it is; but by yours I find that if the grey mare would kick up her heels,[2] one might still pay a visit to Billingbear,[3] and see it in the hands that one would most wish. Whenever that time comes, young Mr. Neville (and I am extremely glad he is to have that name)[4] will be at the head of a handsome estate, clear of encumbrances, and by all accounts I don't hear of any young gentleman that better deserves one. But what is he to do, and

347

how to live, in the meantime? His father had run out his family estate, and died more in debt perhaps than he was worth: however, there happens to be a first cousin of Mr. Aldworth's now in Rome, and one Mr. Jackson,[5] who tells me that there is two hundred pound a year of his father's estate, which is not obliged to pay his debts. If so, he may have that to live upon for the present, and when the Billingbear estate comes in, he may pay off what debts remain of his father's. His own good qualities have made him several friends who, with his old family friends, if they would stir heartily, might possibly get him some place of the government, and the sooner they were in motion for it the better. I have some thoughts of writing to him on that subject, and should be as glad to hear that he had got something, as if I had got something myself. I hope indeed they are already in action: for his case is one that won't bear delays.

I sent a box of things from Florence to Leghorn.[6] It was arrived there, before me, but was forced to wait for a convoy. I believe it is by this time on board a ship which is under convoy, and will be soon jogging on for old England. I shall be extremely glad to follow it. We shall certainly leave Italy before the great heats come on; and after that we shall be in countries not much hotter than England, so that there is no great danger from change of climates, coming to England. We have now been some time in nothing but rain: the Tiber is again got over his banks, the couriers can hardly come along with their letters, and the inundations are universal. Keep yourself warm and well, stick to kitchen physic, and follow the advice of the almanac. I am extremely glad that young Mr. Wavil is to have St. Maurice, on his father's and his own account.[7] With all services to all friends, I am

Your most dutiful and affectionate

J. Sp:⟩

1. On the recently deceased Henry Grey Neville, see *Letter* 131.

2. Henry Grey's widow, Elizabeth (1691–1762), elder dau. of James Griffin, 2d Baron Griffin of Braybrook. On June 9, 1741, she was to marry again John Wallop (1690–1762), Visc. Lymington, later E. of Portsmouth.

3. The estate of the Neville family in Berkshire, near Wokingham. Mrs. Spence was related to the Nevilles.

4. His uncle had advised 'Mr. Richard Neville Aldworth, to take [the surname] of *Neville*' (J. Nichols, *Literary Anecdotes* [1814], VIII, 367) and in his will evidently stipulated that after Elizabeth's death his nephew should inherit his estate; which he did in 1762 (Burke, *Extinct and Dormant Baronetcies of England*, 1844, p. 228; G.E.C. X, 611).

5. George Jackson (ca. 1692–1764), Leghorn merchant, British consul at Genoa 1737–40.

6. No doubt some of the *virtù* he purchased in Italy, see *App.* 11 to 13. Lord Lincoln was sending a present of silk to his sister (*Treas. Bks. & Papers, 1739–41*, p. 554).

7. On Richard Wavell, see *Letter* 9. In 1739 he took his B.A. at Pembroke College, Oxford, and was to become shortly Rector of St. Maurice at Winchester.

*145

Source:	Egerton 2234 ff. 243–4
Addressed:	*as in* 74
Postmarked:	14 FE
Franked:	Free/Andrew Stone
Endorsed:	*a.* candlemas/day, why so call'd & cardi-/nal finis will:
	b. Candlemas-Day, & Card: Fini.
	red wafer

Rome,
February 4, 1741

⟨Dear Mother,⟩

Yesterday was Candlemas Day, and do you know why it is called by that name? There is certainly nothing equal to travelling for the improvement of the mind and the acquisition of knowledge. I might have lived in Hampshire till I was a hundred year old, and never should have known why we call the second of February *Candlemas*; but the very first February I am at Rome, I find immediately that the Pope that day celebrates high *mass*, and that all the persons of any distinction at it are admitted to kiss the Pope's foot, and have each a holy *candle* presented to them by him as soon as they have kissed it.

These holy candles are of great use: the devil can never come into a room where one of them is; they have an infallible power of driving away all evil spirits (I question whether a rogue would come in whilst one of them should be lighted up);[1] and they must be very good for the eyes for all students and scriveners, they being of white wax and each a pound [in] weight. I just went to see the Pope, but I did not stay out the ceremony, it being one of the finest mornings for walking that could be, and I being naturally not a great lover of any ceremony whatever. If I had stayed, I might perhaps have got a kiss and a candle, but I am not sorry for it, for the latter would but have increased our luggage—I having had a full resolution to bring it as a present to you, if I had got one.

There is one of the cardinals who I saw in the last ceremony I was at before, who is dying. His name is Cardinal Fini;[2] he is one that had not the best of characters formerly, but is now going to make amends for it by dying and making a very good will. He is extremely rich. He leaves ten years' wages to be paid directly to each of his servants, of which a cardinal has enough to make a little army, and all his money beside is to be divided among the poor of this city, who are so numerous that they would make a considerable army: not of fighting men indeed, for the Romans have quite

349

lost the military spirit which used to be so strong among them in days of
yore.

The spring is coming here; and indeed there have been appearances of it
ever since the first of January. For my part, I have scarce seen a bud or a
flower that has not put me in mind that the time is coming on when we
shall pursue our journey, and so be in the way of coming homewards to you.
⟨I long to see you, either at Winchester, Birchanger or London. When we
come, you may name your place, and I will give you the meeting with
great pleasure. With all services to all friends, I am ever

Your most dutiful and affectionate

J. Sp.⟩

1. According to Conyers Middleton they demonstrate again 'the folly and absurdity of a *heathenish custom*' (*A Letter from Rome*, 1741 edn., pp. 158, 187).

2. Cardinal Francesco Antonio Fini (1669–1743), protégé of Pope Benedict XIII, after whose death he was accused in 1730 of various transgressions. In 1741 he gave up all benefices into the hands of Pope Benedict XIV and retired to Naples, where he died in 1743 (Gaetano Moroni, *Diz. di erud. storico-ecclesiastica* [Venice, 1840–61], vol. 24).

146

Source: Cocchi MSS in the collection of Count
Enrico Baldasseroni, Florence

SPENCE TO DR. COCCHI

Rome,
February 11, 1741

Dear Sir,

I am extremely sorry for your loss, especially of your papers,[1] though you
talk so light of it. I have always known you to be a philosopher, and should
expect that you would bear much greater losses than this like one: but you
must give your friends leave, who are no philosophers, to be very much
concerned for it, as I assure you I am.

I heard by Mr. Allen of Messina[2] that you and all your good family were
very well, and received your kind compliments by him. I beg to return
mine to you and to all that belong to you, for I have a regard for everything
that does belong to you. May the Arno for the future always keep within
due bounds—if it be only in respect to you and yours.

I can guess a little I believe at 'the second' whom you hint at as concerned in a certain affair,[3] and am apt to think his name begins with the first syllable of the English word Ugly.[4] That affair has given me, as you may easily imagine, a great deal of concern, and will probably give me more, though I hope it will not have any bad consequence in the end.

I am much obliged to you for the great deal of trouble you have taken on my account. As to the sarcophagus, if 'tis bad work, I should be glad at least to hear what the labours are and in what order they are placed. The account of the MS will be very welcome to[o] at your leisure. I am ever, Dear Sir,

Your most obliged humble servant

Joseph Spence

1. During the December flood at Florence (see *Letter* 135).

2. No doubt Edward Allen, chargé d'affaires 1728–9, Secretary at the British Embassy in Turin 1729–34, consul at Naples ca. 1737–53. Spence met him at Naples in March 1741 (*App.* 1, *Obs.* No. 1435).

3. 'The *Affair*' between Lord Lincoln and Lady Sophia. See *Letter* 135.

4. Signor Giovanni Battista Uguccioni (1710–82), who had 'an employment in the office of records' at Florence. He was an admirer of Lady Sophia, and evidently Lord Lincoln's rival. 'I often receive and answer letters from poor Uguccioni,' wrote Sophia Fermor from Brussels on Sept. 19, 'who expresses great concern for our having left Italy' (Finch MSS, Leicestershire Record Office).

'The Affair' went on in the meantime, as Lord Lincoln continued to write in secret from Rome to Lady Sophia. On Jan. 3 Horace Walpole informed him: 'Lady Sophia bids me tell you, you remember her a long while, that you are a parlous man and she did not think it had been in you.' On Jan. 31 he promised to 'make all your compliments, general and particular' at Florence, and sent Lincoln a French sonnet on the 'belle Sophie':

> *Nous vous voyons, belle Sophie,*
> *Dans l'âge heureux où les plaisirs*
> *S'offrant en foule à vos désirs*
> *Doivent bannir de votre vie*
> *Et la tristesse et les soupirs . . .*

'If you have a mind to sing it, the three first stanzas go to the tune of the "Black Joke", and the two last to that of "Patient Grisel".' He concluded the first letter: 'Good night, my dear Lord! I hope Mr. Spence is as busy as a bee about gods and goddesses' (Corresp. XIII, 8–12).

*147

Source: Egerton 2234 ff. 245-6

Rome,
February 18, 1741

⟨Dear Mother,⟩

We are now entered upon the melancholy fasting time of Lent: I mean
melancholy for the Catholics, for 'tis as good as any other time of the year
for us heretics.[1] Tuesday the 15th was the last day of our carnival. It lasted
ten days, and on every one of them we had fine weather: not a drop of rain
fell in either of them. The carnival of Rome is reckoned the best in Italy,
after that of Venice.

When [you] enter Rome from England, [you] come into an open square,[2]
with three streets facing you: the middle one lies straight before you ⟨as
you may see in my great map of Rome, if you can place it together right⟩
and is a mile long.[3] 'Tis of a handsome breadth and delightfully paved. This
is the place where the coaches of the nobility make their tours on festivals:
they go up on one side and down the other, and so keep rounding it as our
coaches used to do formerly at the Ring in Hyde Park. They do the same
every afternoon in carnival time: but the difference is that 'tis then full of
people in masquerade, and that there's a horse-race down the middle of it
between two rows of coaches, every public afternoon.

One of the grandest things in these sights are the coaches of some of the
nobility, which are made some like open triumphal chariots, and others like
rich boats and gondolas on wheels. Everyone in these long boats is in
masquerade: on an eminence at the end sits a favourite lady, and the
gentleman himself, often dressed like a Punch or a harlequin, sits on the
coach-box and has that unaccountable diversion of driving his own horses.
There was one of this kind drove by the young Duke of Rospilliozi,[4] before
which marched eight or ten of his servants dressed as old Roman lictors,
with the fasces and axes in their hands: and there was a triumphal car raised
up five lines above one another (or five-story high) all full of Punchinellos,
except the coachman, a conjurer that sat in the midst of the highest row
but one, and a devil of quality who sat alone on the fifth and presided over
the whole company. These two were the most considerable things I saw.

352

The sides of the street are lined with seats and chairs for spectators, the windows, with a carpet out of each of them, are filled with other curious people, and all the street between the coaches is crowded with mob and gentlemen in masks. The great compliment, when you pass by any friend, is to pelt them with sugar-plums, and there's a basket full in every coach for that purpose.

'Tis inconceivable what a crowd there is all along the street when at a signal given the horses are brought out, the rope let down, and they holloed on to scamper as fast as they can up the street. 'Tis a miracle that there is not more mischief done, for the street is all crowded in each point of it just till the horses are coming upon it, and then the crowd fall back on each side, hollo, and let them pass. The horses have great feathers of different colours (to distinguish them) on their heads, and tinsel about them, and spurs to make them go on: What with the tinsel and galloping on the pavement, they make a furious rattle when they come by you—for there's generally six or eight horses that start, and there have been to eighteen or twenty. This they call seeing a race.[5]

Of all the mob dresses about one in the crowd there's none I love so well as the Punchinellos. Their vast humps behind and before are diverting enough, and, as they are in such numbers, they find out a thousand odd ways of dressing themselves. Among them all a female Punchinello was my favourite. She was in her dress in general just a fit wife for the male animal of the same name; but as 'twas holiday time, she was dressed out finer than ordinary. She had three great turkey's eggs hanging as pendants at each ear, a necklace of common eggs instead of a pearl necklace, and two pipkins before for breasts. The state with which she walked, and the holding up her head, cannot be expressed: and indeed who would not have been as proud, that was so fine as she was?[6] But alas! now the carnival is over!—and so is my letter. ⟨I am ever

Your most dutiful and affectionate

J. Spence.

P.S. Among the many dresses, there was one for a poet: his coat was made up all of laurel leaves and laid down the seams with real flowers. A very cheap and very poetical dress.⟩

---

1. 'In lent, and on other fast or meagre days, the protestants never fail of meeting with butcher's meat, &c at the inns and taverns, without being at the trouble to procure a licence for eating it' (J. G. Keysler, *Travels* [1730], 1757 edn., II, 39).

2. Piazza del Popolo.

3. The Corso.

4. Probably the grandson of Gianbattista Rospigliosi (1646-1722), general and Prince of the Holy Empire (Vittorio Spreti, *Enc. storico nobiliare* [Milan, 1932], V, 799).

5. Six lithographs of the horse races at Rome are reproduced in *Enc. Italiana* (1931), vol. IX, pls. xix–xxi. See also De Brosses, II, 292-3.

6. 'The ladies for the most part wore breeches ... shoes buckled to the toes, a laced coat, and a hat cocked *à la mode de Paris* ... affecting to stare, strut, and look big. ... A young handsome lady, I assure you, newly married, sent her compliments to me, desiring the use of a pair of my breeches: but my backside being unfortunately not so big as hers in circumference, they were returned back unused, and deprived of an extraordinary honour' (John Russell, *Letters from A Young Painter*, 2d edn. [1750], I, 44–5). Russell's account, dated Mar. 2, 1741, is contemporary with Spence's, who met the young English painter at Rome.

148

Source: Extra-illustrated copy of *Anecdotes*, ed. Singer, 1820, Huntington Library (RB 131213). Printed by Singer, pp. 405–6

HORACE WALPOLE TO SPENCE

Florence,
February 21, 1741

Sir,

Not having time last post, I begged Mr. Mann to thank you for the obliging paragraph for me in your letter to him. But as I desire a nearer correspondence with you than by third hands, I assure you in my own proper person, that I shall have great pleasure on our meeting in England to renew an acquaintance which I began with so much pleasure in Italy.[1] I will not reckon you among my modern friends, but in the first article of virtù: you have given me so many new lights into a science that I love so much, that I shall always be proud to own you as my master in the antique, and will never let any thing break in upon my reverence for you, but a warmth and freedom that will flow from my friendship, and which will not be contained within the circle of sacred awe.

As I shall always be attentive to give you any satisfaction that lies in my power, I take the first opportunity of sending you two little poems, both by a hand that I know you esteem the most: if you have not seen them, you will thank me for lines of Mr. Pope; if you have, why, I did not know it.

On the Grotto at Twickenham.[2]

Thou, who shalt stop where Thames' translucent wave
Shines a broad mirror thro' the shadowy cave,
Where ling'ring drops from mineral roofs distill,
And pointed crystals break the sparkling rill,

354

Unpolish'd gems no ray on pride bestow,
And latent metals innocently glow;
Approach! great Nature studiously behold,
And eye the mine without a wish for gold;
Thou seest that country's wealth, where only free
Earth to her entrails feels not slavery;
Enter! but awful this inspiring grot,
Here wisely pensive St. John sat and thought;
Here British sighs from dying Windham stole,
And the bright flame was shot thro' Marchmont's soul;
Let such, such only tread this sacred floor,
Who dare to love their country and be poor.

Epitaph for Himself.[3]

Under this marble or under this hill,
Under this turf or e'en what you will,
Whatever my heir or some friend in his stead,
Or any good Christian lays over my head,
Lies one who ne'er car'd and still cares not a pin
What they said or may say of the mortal within;
But who living and dying, resign'd still and free,
Trusts in God that as well as He was, He shall be.

I don't know whether Lord Lincoln has received any orders to return home:[4] I had a letter from one of my brothers last post, to tell me from Sir Robert that he would have me leave Italy as soon as possible, lest I should be shut up unawares by the arrival of the Spanish troops;[5] and that I might pass some time in France if I had a mind. I own I don't conceive how it is possible these troops should arrive without its being known some time before. And as to the Great Duke's dominions, one can always be out of them in ten hours or less. If Lord Lincoln has not received the same orders, I shall believe what I now think, that I am wanted for some other reason. I beg my kind love to my Lord, and that Mr. Spence will believe me

His sincere humble servant

Hor. Walpole.

1. Horace Walpole first met Spence as he passed with Gray through Turin, Nov. 7–18, 1739, and they met again at Florence in Oct. 1740.

2. Pope had enclosed the lines on his grotto in a letter to Bolingbroke, dated Sept. 3, 1740. They were first published in *The Gentleman's*

Magazine, Jan. 1741, p. 45 (see Pope's *Minor Poems*, Twickenham edn., pp. 382–7).

3. The epitaph first appeared on Jan. 10, 1741, in *The Public Register; or, Weekly Magazine* (ibid.). Horace Walpole, however, seems to have obtained this version from another source.

4. See *Letters* 153, 154. Lincoln received his uncles' advice six weeks later.

5. Rumours of intended Spanish invasion of Italy reached London at Christmas. *The Craftsman* (Saturday, Dec. 27 O.S.) printed a letter 'from Madrid', dated Dec. 5: 'It is certain that the Court has taken a firm Resolution to make good certain Claims upon Part of Italy; and it is given out on this Occasion that the King intends to claim the Duchy of Milan. . . . In the meantime we work so hard in all the ports of this Kingdom, that it is said we shall have a Squadron of twenty-two Men of War in readiness in six Weeks, to convoy the Infantry destined for the Expedition to Italy. The Horse will march through France.'

*149

Source:	Egerton 2334 ff. 247–8
Addressed:	*as in* 74
Postmarked:	[ ] MR
Franked:	Free/Andrew Stone
Endorsed:	*a.* a pertickeller/fine corrictor of/Lady Mary Wortley
	b. Character of Lᵞ Mᵞ.
	red wafer

Rome,
February 25, 1741

⟨Dear Mother,⟩

One of the greatest advantages in travelling, for a little man like me, is to make acquaintances with several persons of a higher rank than one could well get at in England, and to converse with them more on a foot, and with greater familiarity than one ever could have done, had one stayed always at home.

I have had an instance of this here at Rome. I always desired to be acquainted with Lady Mary Wortley,[1] and could never bring it about, though so often together in London; soon after we came here, her Ladyship came to this place, and in five days' time I was as well acquainted with her as a modest man could be.[2]

Lady Mary is one of the most extraordinary shining characters in the world; but she shines like a comet; she is all irregular, and always wandering. She is the most wise, most imprudent; loveliest, disagreeablest; best-natured, cruellest woman in the world.

As she was born with fine parts enough for twenty men, she took early to study, and her infancy was very learned. As she read extremely, somebody put it into her head that 'twas a great pity she should not understand Latin.[3] Her gouvernante, who was a very rigid one,[4] she thought would never allow this; so she got a dictionary and grammar with all the privacy in the world: and as she had the use of the library, she hid them in a private corner there, locked herself in every morning from ten to two, and every afternoon from four to eight, and set to the study of those two very dull

356

books. By this means, in two years' time, she stole the Latin language, and at fifteen understood it perhaps as well as most men. 'Twas Mr. Wortley (her husband afterwards) that first gave her this thought, and Mr. Congreve was of great use to her,[5] after it came to be known. She now understands at least seven languages: English, French, Italian, Spanish, German, Latin and the modern Greek.

She was married young,[6] and she says (with the liberty which much travelling is apt to give) that she never was in so great a hurry of thought, as the month before she was married: she scarce slept any one night that month. You know, she was one of the most celebrated beauties in England; she had a vast number of offers,[7] she was but fifteen or sixteen, and the thing that kept her awake was, who to fix upon. Most part of the month she was determined but as to two points; which were, to be married to somebody, and not to be married to the man her father (the Earl of Kingston)[8] advised her to. The last night of the month she determined: and in the morning left the man her father had fixed upon,[9] buying a wedding ring for her, and scuttled away and married Mr. Wortley.

Soon after their marriage, Mr. Wortley was named ambassador to Constantinople. Lady Mary, who had always delighted in romances and books of travels, was charmed with the thoughts of going into the East, though those embassies are generally an affair of twenty years,[10] and so 'twas a sort of dying to her friends and country: but 'twas travelling, 'twas going farther than most other people go, 'twas wandering, 'twas all whimsical and charming, and so she set out with all the pleasure imaginable.

'Tis said by the malicious world that at Constantinople she saw the inside of the seraglio, and that the Grand Signior had the politeness to fling a handkerchief at her there:[11] but I have nothing to do with scandalous history,[12] and would only tell you what she has told me herself. Women are treated in Turkey as something between beasts and men. The Turks don't believe that they have souls, or if they have souls, they believe that they are of a lower degree than ours are.[13] 'Twould be a profanation to a church to have such a beast as a woman enter into it. This abominable belief of the Turks embarrassed Lady Mary extremely. ⟨The rest in my next.

Your most dutiful and affectionate

J. Sp.⟩

---

1. She arrived in Rome on Jan. 12 and left Feb. 19. 'The English Travellers at Rome behave in general very discreetly,' she wrote Feb. 25 from Leghorn. 'I have reason to speak well of them since they were all exceeding obliging to me. It may sound a little vain to say it, but they realy paid a regular Court to me, as if I had been their Queen, and their Governors told me that the desire of my aprobation had a very great Influence on their conduct. ... I us'd to preach to them very freely, and they all thank'd ⟨me for⟩ it' (*Complete Letters*, II, 228–9). Spence, who had collected some of his best anecdotes from her

(*Obs.* Nos. 743–65), wrote this and the following two letters after her departure.

2. 'Lady Mary is at Rome at present,' wrote Sophia Fermor to Mrs. Wallop from Florence, 'she sups and dines with the English. She, I hear, diverts them very well, adapting her conversation and humour to their taste; when I see you I can tell you a thousand things of her that will make you laugh' (Finch MSS, Leicestershire Record Office).

3. 'When I was young I was a vast admirer of Ovid's *Metamorphoses* (she speaks of it now more temperately), and that was one of the chief reasons that set me upon the thoughts of stealing the Latin language' (*Obs.* No. 743).

4. Perhaps 'a Mrs. Dupont ... French governess' whose education, 'one of the worst', filled Lady Mary's head with superstitious tales and false notions (R. Halsband, *The Life of Lady Mary Wortley Montagu* [1956], pp. 3, 5).

5. 'I never knew anybody that had so much wit as Congreve,' she told Spence, 'perhaps his conversation was, like his plays, too full of it' (*Obs.* No. 744).

6. On Aug. 20, 1712, at the age of twenty-three, she secretly married Edward Wortley Montagu (1678–1761). *Life*, pp. 10–28.

7. Spence writes as Lady Mary, then fifty-two years old, saw her youth in retrospect, probably exaggerating the number of her suitors. Horace Walpole speaks of the 'quantities of Lady Mary's amours and infamies' as the gossipy world saw her (*Corresp.* XIV, 243–4).

8. Evelyn Pierrepont (ca. 1665–1725), M. of Dorchester 1706, D. of Kingston 1715.

9. Probably the Hon. Clotworthy Skeffington, later 4th Visc. Massereene (*Life*, pp. 23–5).

10. Her husband's embassy lasted less than two years. They left England early in 1716 and returned in August 1718.

11. 'Whenever the Grand Signor is desirous of variety, he has several girls in the seraglio be brought before him dressed in the most splendid and engaging manner ... takes a full view of the different objects of temptation; and when he has determined his choice, confirms it by throwing a handkerchief at the feet of her, whom he has destined to partake of his bed' (Lord Sandwich's *Voyage* [1799], p. 212). Lady Mary herself had denied the story in a letter to Lady Mar (Mar. 10, 1718): The Sultana '... assur'd me that the story of the Sultan's throwing a Handkercheif is altogether fabulous' (*Complete Letters*, I, 383).

12. That a 'scandalous history' was circulating abroad is clear from a spurious letter in which 'Lady Mary'—writing supposedly from Florence in the autumn of 1740—attributes this slander to 'the wicked wasp of Twickenham: his lies affect me now no more; they will be all as much despised as the story of the seraglio and the handkerchief, of which I am persuaded he was the only inventor' (*Works* [1861], II, 75).

13. In a letter to Conti (Feb. 1718) Lady Mary insists 'que c'est une chose certainement fausse, quoique communément crue parmi nous, que *Mahomet* exclut les femmes de toute participation à une vie future & bienheureuse. Il etoit trop galant homme & aimoit trop le beau Sexe, pour le traiter d'une maniere si barbare. Au contraire, il promet un très-beau Paradis aux femmes Turques. Il dit à la verité, que ce sera un Paradis separé de celuy de leurs Maris: mais je crois que la pluspart n'en seront pas moins contentes pour cela' (*Complete Letters*, I, 375–6).

In the fair copy of Spence's 'Travelling Letters', Letters 149, 150, and 151 are combined into a single continuous narrative. They should be read together with the remarkable series of anecdotes (Obs. Nos. 743–65) which Spence collected from Lady Mary during her winter stay at Rome.

*150

Source:	Egerton 2234 ff. 249–50
Addressed:	as in 74
Postmarked:	12 MR
Franked:	Free/Andrew Stone
Endorsed:	a. a ferther/act of Lady mary wortley/& the princess of/transilvania b. Ly My's Adventures/in ye Ch: of S Sophia & ye Baths. /to be writ on wth ye last as one Letter red wafer

Rome,
March 4, 1741

⟨To go on with my Lady Mary, whom we left at Constantinople.⟩ She had a vast curiosity to see the Great Church of St. Sophia; she had demanded a permission, and could not get it: but the curiosity of a lady is not so easily to be baulked.[1] There was then at Constantinople the Princess of Transylvania, a Christian (as much at least as herself), though of the Greek Church. They were equally desirous of seeing this fine sight, and consulted together what was to be done. They at last resolved to dress themselves up in men's clothes, and to run the risk of it together.

They got in without being suspected, and were forced to leave their men's slippers at the door, for the place is too sacred to be trod on by anything but naked feet. This embarrassed Lady Mary extremely. As she had been used to walk with high heels, she tottered, and was ready to tumble down every moment. In short, she was forced to return to the corner where she had left her slippers, and to steal them on again. The men wear long robes in Asia, and she had so long an one that she contrived to hide her feet so well with it, that they ventured on again into the church with them. The Princess went before her, and she walked slow, and with all the care and concealment she could, after her.

When they came into the finest part of the church, the Princess of Transylvania could not help bursting into tears. She was struck with seeing all those riches, which had belonged formerly to the Christians, in the hands of the infidels: and beside, it put her strongly in mind of the Greek emperors who formerly reigned in that city, till they were drove out by the Turks. She was herself descended from one of those emperors, and when she thought of that, the tears flowed down in spite of all her resolution. Lady Mary did all she could to stop her: 'Do you consider where you are?' says she to the Princess, as softly as she could, 'and what a discovery in this place would cost you? I indeed might escape under the character of Mr.

359

Wortley, as ambassador now here, but if you are discovered, you know what a cruel death must be the consequence. Methinks I see the flames already lighted. For God's sake, leave off blubbering! Why will you be your own destruction?' The Princess on so just advice restrained her grief, wiped her eyes in private, and went on as well as she could. After this they had no other particular danger. They took a view of all the beauties of the place, and returned home undiscovered, and in safety.[2]

Lady Mary did not converse only with Christian princesses at Constantinople: she visited the ladies of the country, and has a great esteem in general for the Turks.[3] The Turkish ladies, you know, are a sort of prisoners; they have very little liberty, and their chief place of their meeting and conversing together is at the women's baths.[4] Lady Mary went thither, and says she never saw finer shaped women than the Turkish ladies, though they never wear stays. Their make is more natural, and really more beautiful than that of the ladies with us. The first time she was at one of these baths, the ladies invited her to undress and to bathe with them: and on her not making any haste, one of the prettiest ran to her to undress her. You can't imagine her surprise upon lifting my Lady's gown and seeing her stays go all round her. She ran back quite frightened, and told her companions 'that the husbands in England were much worse than in the East, for that they tied up their wives in little boxes, of the shape of their bodies'. She carried them to see it; they all agreed that 'twas one of the greatest barbarities in the world, and pitied the poor women for being such slaves in Europe. ⟨ I am, dearest mother, with all services to all friends

Your most dutiful and affectionate

J. Spence.⟩

1. 'St. Sophia ... [is] very difficult to see,' she wrote from Constantinople to Lady Bristol. 'I was forc'd to send three times to the Caimaicam (the Governour of the Town), and he assembl'd the Chief Effendis or heads of the Law and inquir'd of the Mufti whether it was Lawfull to permit it. They pass'd some days in this Important Debate, but I insisting on my request, permission was granted' (Complete Letters, I, 398).

2. Prof. Halsband, who prints this account (pp. 82–3), comments: 'Perhaps her visit was actually as decorous as an ambassadress's; but in retrospect she preferred to convert it into an adventure in an oriental romance.'

3. 'The ladies at Constantinople used to be extremely surprised to see me go always with my bosom uncovered. ⟨She had frequent disputes with them on that subject.⟩ It was in vain that I said that everybody did so among us, and added everything I could in defence of it. They could never be reconciled to so immodest a custom, as they thought it, and one of them after I had been defending it to my utmost, said, "O my sultana, you can never defend the manners of your country, even with all your wit! But I see you are in pain for them, and shall therefore press it no farther" ' (Obs. No. 763).

4. See Lady Mary's letter of Apr. 1, 1717 (Complete Letters, I, 312–14), where she describes her visit. It was on the way to Constantinople, 'at Sophia, one of the most beautifull Towns in the Turkish Empire and famous for its Hot Baths'. Also Obs. Nos. 763–4.

*151

Source:	Egerton 2234 ff. 251–2
Addressed:	*as in* 74
Postmarked:	24 [ ]
Franked:	Free/Andrew Stone
Endorsed:	*a.* a fer-/ther ac^t of Lady Mary Wortley *b.* L^y M^y's Maxims, ab^t/Matrimony. *red wafer*

Rome,
March 11, 1741

⟨Dear Mother,⟩

Lady Mary ⟨for we have not yet done chatting of her Ladyship⟩ left
Constantinople with Mr. Wortley the very day after she had seen Santa
Sophia, and come for England through Italy and France.[1] Though they
were called away a great deal sooner than she expected, she brought off
with her a very great regard for the Turks and the Turkish customs. I have
seen a paper written by her Ladyship on a very odd subject: 'That it is
possible for two people to be happy in the state of matrimony'.[2] She does
not pretend to say that this has ever happened, but she thinks 'tis not quite
impossible that this may happen, one time or another, before the world is
at an end. In spite of this, she holds two maxims which she learned in the
East, and which she wishes were put in practice among us.

The first is that husbands should not have any portion with their wives.[3]
This would certainly have several good consequences attending it. Men
would not then marry for money, but for the real merit of the woman; and
women would endeavour to deserve as much as they could, when merit was
to be their only fortune. If husbands did not receive portions, they would
not be [obliged] to pay them neither for their daughters, nor elder brothers
for their sisters, nor would estates be clogged as they are at present with
jointures. This is what she says for it, and perhaps there may be a great
deal to be said against it: but her second maxim I think all the world must
be for. 'Tis as follows.

She would have an Act of Parliament made in England, that at the end
of every Parliament, when that is dissolved, it should be at the choice of
every married couple in England to dissolve their marriage too, and to
choose anew if they did not like their old choice.[4] Any couple that had a
mind to continue on together, might do so without any further ceremony,
and every couple that thought they could better themselves, should be at
liberty to part, without any ceremony likewise. The effect of this would be,
that a multitude of slaves would be set free with us every seventh year,

and possibly, after this act was passed, all the world would be for another, for annual parliaments—to the end that this general release of prisoners might return [   ] every year. This would make Great Britain truly free, and we might then boast, with all our other liberties, of what is as great as any of them: 'that with us only, of all the nations in Europe, a few words spoke by a man in a black coat did not oblige two people to live together all the days of their life, who may wish themselves apart perhaps in two or three days after they came together.' ⟨I am ever

Your most dutiful and affectionate

J: Sp:⟩

The original is dated from Rome, though Spence was then (Mar. 5-19) at Naples.

1. She left on July 6, 1718. In an undated letter that follows her description of St. Sophia, Lady Mary says she is 'prepareing to leave Constantinople' (*Complete Letters*, I, 405, 415).

2. Lady Mary allowed her works to circulate in manuscript. In *Polymetis* (p. 70) Spence quotes a couplet of hers as written by 'a lady of our own country' from 'the poems she has been so unkind as to keep in her closet'. (I owe this identification to Mr. Wilmarth Lewis. It was made by Horace Walpole in his copy of *Polymetis*, now in Mr. Lewis's possession.) Horace Walpole, too, read 'her works, which she lends out in manuscript', particularly her *Town Eclogues* which she 'allowed me to transcribe from a volume of her poems in MS

at Florence in 1740' (*Corresp.* XIII, 234, XIV, 38 n. 40).

The 'little treatise in prose' seems to have disappeared. Spence's letter and a shorter version in his *Observations*, No. 765, provide the only extant information on it.

3. Compare this with 'An Essay on the Mischief of Giving Fortunes with Women in Marriage' printed in Curll's *Miscellanea* II (1726, dated 1727) which Prof. Halsband has identified as Lady Mary's (pp. 121-2).

4. This, according to Prof. Halsband, 'seems incongruous if marriages without dowries result in perfect unions. Once, however, Lady Mary had recommended "a general act of divorcing all the people of England" as a way of saving the reputations of unfaithful wives' (*Life*, p. 122).

---

*152

Source: Egerton 2234 ff. 253-4

Rome,
March 25, 1741

⟨Dear Mother,

I have been very unlucky as to receiving letters, ever since I have been at this good city. I stayed at first a month without receiving one from you, and that gave me so much concern that I resolved not to be frightened again if they should be long a coming. At present I have been two months without hearing a word of you, and in spite of all my resolutions, I have some time been in as great fears for you as ever. I hope in God this will find you well, and that I shall soon have the comfort of seeing your handwriting.⟩

We are now come on a hundred and fifty mile of our way on our return to England, for we have been this last fortnight at Naples.[1] Mount Vesuvius, you know, is the utmost boundary of my travels: I did not go up it this time, but instead of that, went all along the foot of the mountain by the sea-shore, to observe the streams of fire that had flowed down from it into the sea.[2]

The last great eruption was in 1737. The firing off of the mountain continued for above thirty days,[3] in the midst of which, when it was in its greatest violence, the people of Naples heard a particular horrid sound in the middle of the night, which made them all cry out for mercy.[4] 'Twas four hours before they knew the cause of it. It then appeared that the boiling matter in the great cauldron of the mountain had burst a hole in the side of it towards the sea, and issued out from thence like a heavy-rolling river of fire.[5] The matter within was in such quantities that, for all this, it did not cease ever[y] now and then to boil over at top and to heave out some of it over the same brim, toward the sea too.[6] These two rivers of fire met, and rolled on together, or rather heaved itself along slowly by fits down a great channel made by the waters that tumble from the mountain after violent rains, to a town called Torre del Greco, eight mile from Naples, and half a mile from the sea. Toward the end of this town it met with a great cavity—or pit—above forty foot deep,[7] which it filled up, and then heaved on again (though with less force) over the high road.

Just beyond the high road is a convent of priests and a little chapel for the souls in purgatory.[8] It made directly towards them, but widening its course, and so still more weakened.[9] The space between the chapel and convent is 140 feet wide. All this space it has filled up, beside its spreading against the road-front of each of them. It entered in several of the lower rooms,[10] and as the priests afterwards cleared the matter away from those rooms and in a line all along that side of the house, one sees the height of this stream and the settling down of the different parts of it, when it came to cool, very distinctly. 'Tis about twenty foot high there. The top of it is unequal, wavy, rough and ragged, and consists chiefly of pieces like the cinders at a smith's forge: two or three foot below the surface 'tis now hardened all into a sort of metallic stone, of which I have several pieces, and which they sometimes cut out and use for buildings or paving the streets, for 'tis particularly hard.

Some of the stream that widened against the road-front heaved into the church belonging to the convent, at a side door, and as its force was cooling, hangs there suspended in the air, as if it had respected the high altar. They leave it still there as a miracle, visible for ever: and indeed (though there was no more in this than what might be naturally expected from such matter in such a motion) I never saw anything that looks so like a miracle in my life.[11] It will be a demonstration to all people who just look in upon it, but anyone who studies the whole stream with attention, and its usual manner toward the end of its course, would be able very easily to account for it. ⟨I am, with all services to all friends,

Your dutiful and affectionate

J. Sp.⟩

1. Mar. 5–19.

2. 'The shore under Mount Vesuvio, from Naples to Capo di Minerva, seems all more inhabited than any one line I have ever seen in Italy. In the first eight mile you have four towns: S. Giovanni, Portici, Resina, and La Torre del Greco, all on the foot of Mount Vesuvio' (*Nbk.* 1 48ᵛ–49ʳ).

3. From the beginning of May until June 4, 1737.

4. The eruption culminated on May 21, when the 'particular horrid sound' was heard. For a full account, see *Mercure historique & politique* (July 1, 1737), CIII, 16–20, and F. Serao, *Istoria dell'incendio del Vesuvio ... MDCCXXXVII* (Naples, 1740), 2d rev. edn., which Spence owned. 'How very considerable that of 1648 ... the water flew about ... as when you quench a red-hot piece of iron. The mountain made a noise 7 or 8 days before the eruption, which they say was heard to Caieta. And afterwards "Faceva tremar tutto il regno, risuonare tutto il mondo" ' (*Nbk.* 1 49ʳ).

5. 'As appears by the height to the left, when you view it from La Torre' (ibid.).

6. 'It probably poured down the greatest part of the low ground (though it is now covered again with ashes), spread wide and black over the next rising, and then took the Chemin des Torrents, where one sees the whole course of it (like a river, but black) for a mile or two' (ibid.).

7. '50 palms: made formerly by the torrents. This certainly broke the force of it and made it come with the less impetuosity' (ibid.).

8. 'Monastero del Carmone', 'Capella del Purgatorio' (ibid.).

9. 'And coming afterwards into a narrow way, with walls on each side, it stopped—a gunshot short of the sea. Two *bowshots* before the cavity it is 90 f. broad ... 60 f. between the Carmone and Capella; from corner to corner 140; at its end (three or four bowshots below the Carmone) about 26 f.' (ibid.).

10. 'Le souffre ... est entré dans la Sacristie de l'Eglise de la Tour des Grecs, desservie par les Carmes. Ces Religeux ont à peine eu le tems de sauver les vases sacrez, l'argenterie de l'Eglise, & une image miraculeuse de la Vierge' (*Mercure historique*, CIII, 16–19).

11. 'The Fryars', wrote Gray, who had seen it in 1739, 'left it whole riseing in a great rough mass at the door where it enter'd, as if the miraculous power of our Lady had forbid it to advance further: this is well-contrived, & carries some appearance with it' ('Notes of Travel' in D. C. Tovey's *Gray and his Friends* [1890], p. 252).

153

Source: Add. MSS 33065 ff. 397–99
Endorsed: Copy to Lord Lincoln/March 16. 1740/1

NEWCASTLE TO LINCOLN

Newcastle House,
March 16, 1740/41 [O.S.]

My dearest Lord,

I am quite ashamed of having so long delayed writing to you; I can have
no good excuse and so I will not pretend to make any, for it would be a
very bad one to justify myself by your example. But as I am sure it does
not proceed on either side from want of affection and concern, we may the
more easily forgive each other. I have the excuse of having been really
extremely taken up with public business, and particularly with our affairs
in Parliament, where we have met with as much and as unreasonable
opposition as ever I remember, but I thank God to as little purpose.[1] I am
sorry to say that our young men, who must want experience, take upon
themselves to judge and determine upon all public measures, and to censure
as freely and as decisively as their fathers or grandfathers could do if they
were now alive. I flatter myself, could you have been present to see it, you
would need no other inducement to dissuade you from following their
example. The situation of the nation is such as requires all the attention and
support that every honest man in his station can give it, and I hope and
believe by the blessing of God that success will attend His Majesty's
endeavours for the honour and interest of his kingdoms.

We have an account that Sir Chaloner Ogle was safely arrived with his
fleet at St. Christopher's, about seven days' sail only from Jamaica, and we
are in daily expectation of some good news from Admiral Vernon.[2]
Notwithstanding every thing has been done that could possibly be thought
on to carry on this necessary war against the Spaniards with vigour and
success, the spirit of opposition will never be at rest, and great industry has
been used to make the world believe that the war was either ignorantly or
knavishly carried on; but that has not prevailed, and I think people are so
convinced of the contrary that this session, which has hitherto been the
most successful of any we have of late had, will certainly end so, and there
is no doubt but we shall have a new Parliament, as good as this. You have
heard how honourably and by what great majorities in both houses Sir

Robert Walpole got the better of the personal attack that was made upon him. Having thus given you some account of our public affairs, I must now come to what I have very much at heart, I mean to what relates particularly to yourself. I am glad to hear from Mr. Spence that you are quite well. I hope you have no remains of the lameness in your leg: I should think it might not be amiss if you would take Sir Edward Hulse's medicine now, alterative physick being particularly good in this season of the year.[3]

The moment you showed dislike to the proposal of marriage I hinted to you we laid aside all thoughts of it here, and there has since been a proposal made (which I believe will take place) for the young lady and Lord Harrington's eldest son.[4] As to the other party you mentioned,[5] as you seem yourself not in haste, nothing has been done in it, and indeed poor Lord Shannon's death makes any consideration of that kind at present very improper.[6] But whatever your thoughts may be as to the time of your marriage or the object of it, I should hope you would seriously determine to come to England as soon as you conveniently can, and this is the opinion of your uncle Pelham and of all your friends. You will be of age next month,[7] and (as I take it) you may then cut off the entail of your estate and make such disposition of it in favour of your sister as you shall think proper, whereas at present it is settled upon Greenwich Hospital. No time therefore should be lost in doing that, which cannot be done whilst you are abroad. We have not been idle with regard to the great point which you so rightly have at heart, I mean the debt due to the Crown. Mr. Sharpe is taking the necessary steps towards settling it and everything will be in a method against you come over.[8] . . . These private reasons I hope you will think sufficient to hasten your return to England, but if you had none of them, the cloud which seems to threaten Italy makes it a very improper place to reside in at present. It is certain the Spaniards are going to send a great number of troops thither, which must necessarily create a war in all parts of Italy.[9] I hope you will not be so mad (pardon the expression) as to think of making a campaign, and lest you should, I must earnestly press you to return to England as soon as you can. Nobody can tell what may be the consequences of a general war in Italy, and how improper in every respect it may be for an English nobleman to be there at that time. I therefore hope I shall have the pleasure to hear from you immediately upon your receiving this letter that you are preparing to come home. I must leave it to you which way you will come back, whether through France or Germany.[10] . . .

Pray my compliments to Mr. Spence, and thank him for his constant care, attention, and correspondence. / I am, my dearest Lord, / most affectionately and sincerely yours

Holles Newcastle

1. On Feb. 14 the Patriots, led by Lord Carteret, made a vigorous attempt to remove Walpole from his office on the grounds of corruption and 'destructive Mis-management of national Affairs'. Their motion was defeated 59 to 108 votes (*Gent. Mag.*, Feb. 1741, p. 106; the March issue gives an account of the heated debates).

2. Reports had reached London that Sir Chaloner's fleet arrived Dec. 27 at St. Christopher's, ready to join Adm. Vernon (*Gent. Mag.*, March 1741, p. 165). Sir Chaloner Ogle (1681?–1750), Rear-Adm., commanded a fleet of 115 ships and 10,000 troops. As he sailed out to join the victor of Porto Bello, English hopes of a victory were high, though the venture at Cartagena turned into a bloody fiasco.

3. See *Letter* 96 n. 5.

4. William Stanhope (1719–79), son of the 1st B., later 2d E. of Harrington, m. 1746 Caroline Fitzroy, dau. of the D. of Grafton. Miss Dunk's 'hundred and ten thousand pounds', however, captivated my Lord Halifax (See *Letter* 125 n. 5).

5. Lady Dorothy Boyle (*Letter* 125 n. 7).

6. Richard Boyle, 2d Visc. Shannon, a distant cousin of Lady Dorothy, died Dec. 20, 1740 (*Gent. Mag.*, 1740, p. 622). Earlier in October 1740 'a marriage was agreed on (between the families) for [my Lord Euston] and Dorothy Boyle' (*Hertford Corresp.* II, 162–3).

7. Lord Lincoln was born Apr. 16, 1720.

8. John Sharpe (1700?–56) of East Barnet, Herts., head of a law firm and agent to the West Indies 1733, Solicitor to Treasury 1742–56, M.P. for Callington 1754–6 (Namier and Brooke, *The Commons 1754–1790* [1964], II, 428). On July 17, 1741, he wrote to the Duke's secretary Mr. Hume, enclosing 'a Power of Attorney for the Earle of Lincoln' (Add. MSS 33065 f. 430r).

9. Horace Walpole was advised to return (*Letter* 148) for the same reasons.

10. Earlier in Florence Lady Walpole had advised Spence: 'As you are to go through Germany, I should think 'tis very happy that you don't understand the German language, for by what I have seen of that people 'tis much better not to know what they say than to know it' (*Obs.* No. 1569).

154

Source: Newcastle MSS, deposited at Nottingham University

HENRY PELHAM TO LINCOLN

London,
March 23, 1740/1 O.S.

My dear Lord,

I am told that you were justly complaining of your friends here that they are not so good correspondents as they ought to be. I will not endeavour to vindicate myself by retaliation. It is a great pleasure to me to hear you are well from any hands, and much more so when from all I am assured how well you have conducted yourself abroad, and that wherever you had been you deservedly leave the best of characters behind you. Believe me, my dear Lord, no one can love you better than I do, and of consequence must rejoice at everything that leads to your welfare.

Mr. Stone[1] says you are gone for a little while to Naples and then return to Rome again. Where this letter will find you is uncertain, but I presume at the latter place. I hope the troubles of Europe won't intercept you, but as they seem to thicken, I imagine your friends here will receive some benefit from them, I mean that of seeing you in England sooner than they would otherwise do. Upon all accounts I think you should make us a visit at least this summer, though you left us again soon after. My brother has wrote to you more fully upon this subject[2] and I [have] given you such reasons as will convince you it is right for you to come over.

I won't trouble you more upon the subject, only hope you will believe whatever liberty I take proceeds from an unalterable affection for you, for now I think I have nothing left that I love so well.[3] I have inoculated two of your cousins.[4] They are, I thank God, very well, though Grace had it very full. I am afraid you will think us grown old and unfashionable people, but the sight of you will restore a little of the former happiness and pleasantry of our lives.

I am impatient till I hear you give an account of what you have seen, that you may convince us true-born Englishmen that we are but servile and low imitators of the ancients. Architecture, gardening, painting and the more useful and instructive [arts?] I conclude you are master of, and I can assure you when you [are] at Claremont you will think that place has been travelling into Italy as well as yourself. I have seen some of your old acquaintance, Lord Fitzwilliam, in particular,[5] but none of them had the good fortune to meet with you abroad.

We shall soon enter upon that great nine of month, a new election.[6] This [time] I think in our county there will not be near so much opposition as there was last time. . . .

This is all the trifling news I can send you, the best is that your friends are well, the Duchess of Newcastle quite recovered and Lady Katherine as well as she ever will be. Your sister I saw the other day in the Park in perfect good health. I don't see her so often as I wish to do, from the extraordinary behaviour of the family she lives with.[7] All desire their sincere love and affection, but none more warmly so than, my dearest Lord, your most affectionate Uncle and faithful servant

H. Pelham

HON. HENRY PELHAM (1695–1754), younger brother of the D. of Newcastle and of Lincoln's mother. Warm supporter of Sir Robert Walpole's policies; in 1743 became First Lord of the Treasury.

1. Private secretary to Henry Pelham and to the D. of Newcastle. See *Letters* 76, 121.

2. *Letter* 153 (Mar. 16 O.S.).

3. Because of the recent death of his own two sons and heirs (*Letter* 84 n. 5).

4. Two of Henry Pelham's four surviving daughters. See *Letter* 91 n. 5.

5. William, Baron Fitzwilliam of Lifford (1720–56), educ. at Eton 1732, M.P. for Peterborough 1741–2. In 1742 cr. Lord Fitzwilliam, Baron of Milton, and in 1746 Visc. Milton and E. Fitzwilliam of Norborough.

6. For the D. of Newcastle's comment on the new election, see *Letter* 159 n. 2.

7. Lady Lucy was staying in July 1741 with 'my Aunt Shelley' at Michelgrove, Sussex (Add. MSS 33065 f. 418ʳ). Lady Margaret (1700–58) was 2d wife of Sir John Shelley (1692–1771). She was sister of the D. of Newcastle and of Lady Lucy's late mother.

Lincoln and Spence returned to Rome from their excursion to Naples on Mar. 19. The Pomfrets arrived from Florence the day before, and Lord Lincoln naturally wished to make the most of Lady Sophia's company. On Mar. 23 Lady Pomfret wrote: 'Being invited by my lord Lincoln to dinner, we did not go any where this morning, for fear of not being back in time enough to dress. We had an extremely fine entertainment, of eleven dishes at a course, and a great variety of wines. Mr. Pitt, Mr. Dashwood, and Mr. Castleton, were invited to meet us. My lord Lincoln did the honours perfectly well: and we passed our time very agreeably till five in the afternoon' (Hertford Corresp. II, 307–8). On Apr. 1: we 'drank tea this evening with lord Lincoln, Mr. Harvey, Mr. Pitt, Mr. Dashwood, Mr. Naylor &c; some or all of whom, besides foreigners, come to us every evening during these latter days of Lent, when company do not meet in public' (ibid., III, 38).

155

Source: Add. MSS 33065 ff. 405–8

Addressed: For/his Grace yᵉ Duke of Newcastle/in Lincoln's Inn Fields/à/Londre
red wafer

LINCOLN TO NEWCASTLE

Rome,
April 8, 1741

My Lord,

I never could have thought it possible for Lord Lincoln to write to his dearest uncle with such fears and tremblings as he does at present.[1] The apprehensions of offending your Grace in the least point (whose repeated and numberless favours I shall for ever and ever acknowledge) makes me more unhappy than I can possibly express. . . . My duty to your Grace and the promise I have given Mr. Spence oblige me to write upon a subject which I own I should have been glad to have avoided, [were] it consistent with my duty to your Grace and the friendship and love I have and ever shall have for my dearest Mr. Spence.

I am sure, my Lord, I should be very ungrateful and very undeserving the infinite obligations I owe him if I did not let you know the truly friendly part he has professed for me throughout the whole affair; yes, my Lord, he has done everything your Grace could possibly expect, or even more than I am afraid I have deserved from his hands. He has in the most friendly manner imaginable pointed out to me my fault in encouraging a passion which, alas, I do but too well see myself the little prospect I have of ever being happy in, he has constantly repeated to me what I owe to myself, your Grace and all my friends, and in such a manner that, though I had not resolution enough to follow in everything his excellent advice, I could not but help approving and heartily wishing that I deserved the fondness and friendship he has with so much sincerity shown he had for me. But good God, my Lord, how hard it is in some cases to follow what one even knows is right oneself, and how very weak reason is when one's inclinations lead one to the so much more pleasing, though far more dangerous, way.

But now, my Lord, as I have endeavoured to do Mr. Spence the justice, which I should have been inexcusable if I had not done, give me leave to take up a little of your time in trying to do the same for myself, in putting off my journey to Venice a little longer.[2] It would be nonsense in me after Mr. Spence's letter[3] to Mr. Stone to pretend to disguise anything, and as I have constantly acted plainly and openly with your Grace, I shall do the very same in this affair.

Why then, my Lord, I own to you I love Lady Sophia more than words can express. True it is that I love her to the greatest degree imaginable, but I can most faithfully assure you nothing can ever be capable of making me forget what I owe to your Grace, or ever so much as to think of entering into the least engagement without your approbation and the rest of my friends', that I give you my honour of my Lord, and hope you won't do me the injustice as even to doubt of my being capable of breaking it. But, my Lord, since I have done so much (for I can assure you it is not little) I hope you won't be angry at my not leaving Rome quite so soon as we intended, when you may be so thoroughly easy and assured of my not doing the least thing that may displease you.

This, my Lord, I can't help owning myself is not the prudentest step, though far far the pleasantest, for in prudence to be sure Rome should be the last place where I should stay; nay even prudence would advise me to fly from Lady Sophia; but prudence at twenty-one is not to be expected. I can assure you, my Lord, I think I show more [prudence] than I ever could have thought I had, in commanding myself as much as I do. In short, my Lord, I am most sincerely to be pitied for the greater the sense I have of my Lady Sophia's merit, consequently the loss of her, if that should happen—

as I greatly fear [it] will—must make me the more miserable: for I do but too plainly see, my Lord, the many obstacles that must necessarily arise from such a proposal. I am but too well acquainted with the many encumbrances upon my estate and that marrying without a fortune would be reckoned very imprudent, for you know, my Lord, Lady Sophia has nothing what the world calls fortune, though more qualifications than one could ever expect to find in any one person. Never did I want to be rich before, nor ever did I despise riches in comparison of real merit so much as I do at present.

I think I have detained your Grace long enough with my misfortunes, but must entreat you to consider them and let me know your thoughts upon them. In the meantime pardon me if I indulge myself a little at present in staying on at Rome, when I give you my solemn word not to do the least thing without my dearest uncle's advice and approbation. I promise to do all that is in my power in endeavouring to get rid of a passion which I am afraid must end in my unhappiness. Give me but a little time, that is all I desire at present; the consequences your Grace may be very sure shall be such as you think most proper for me, for though love is a strong and dangerous passion, yet nothing in the world can possibly make me forget the duty and gratitude I have for my dearest uncles, and I declare I would rather give up any happiness of my own than to have it said that ever Lord Lincoln could . . . be ungrateful or ever gave the least uneasiness to your Grace, who has ever been to him more like a father than anything else.

So I must desire of you, my Lord, not to be uneasy at my staying a little longer at Rome. I promise you once more to endeavour as much as possible to conquer my passion, but at least, if I can't do that, I will certainly be guided entirely by my dearest uncles' advice. I beg my duty to the Duchess of Newcastle, my uncle Pelham, and Lady Katherine, and service to all friends. You can't conceive, my Lord, how unhappy I am in not hearing from your Grace or anybody else. Do, my Lord, give me that satisfaction. I am afraid poor Villettes has not as yet felt the effects of the obliging promises your Grace was so good as to make him.[4] I think I cannot do less than remind you of one who I am so much obliged to. I beg pardon, my Lord, for writing so long a letter, but [I] know you have goodness enough to excuse it, but I will detain your Grace no longer at present, only to assure you how truly and sincerely I am your Grace's

> most affectionate and dutiful nephew
>
> Lincoln

I must desire of your Grace to show the letter to nobody but my uncle Pelham, whose advice and counsel I shall always be glad to have. I take it as the greatest favour whenever he will give it me. . . .

1. In writing this confession, Lincoln was as yet unaware of his uncle's letter to him (153), which appears to have reached Rome on Apr. 18 (see *Letter* 157).

2. The Pomfrets were to leave for Venice in May, and Lord Lincoln wished to enjoy Lady Sophia's company at Rome.

3. Not extant, though one can assume it revealed Spence's concern about the turn 'the Affair' between 'Linki' and Lady Sophy was taking.

4. Lincoln had interceded several times on behalf of the chargé d'affaires at Turin (*Letters* 77, 80), apparently with some success: on May 15, 1741, Villettes was appointed British Minister at Turin.

During his excursion to Naples, Mar. 5–15, Spence was more fortunate in seeing the recent finds at Herculaneum than Horace Walpole, who had visited the excavations in June 1740. The newly discovered ancient paintings were 'kept in the King's apartment, whither all the curiosities are transplanted; and 'tis difficult to see them' (Corresp. XIII, 223). *Lady Mary was even more frustrated during her visit to Naples, a month before Spence met her. On Dec. 12 she wrote to her husband: 'The ground [is] falln in that the present passage to it is, as I am told by every body, extreme dangerous.' On Dec. 27: 'I did not write to you last post, hoping to have been able to have given you an account in this of every thing I had observ'd at Portice, but I have not yet obtain'd the King's License, which must be had before I can be admitted to see the Pictures and fragments of statues which have been found there, and has been hitherto delaid on various pretences, it being at present a very singular favor. They say that some English carry'd a Painter with them the last year to copy the Pictures, which renders it more difficult at present to get leave to see them. . . . I hope in a few days to get permission to go.' Then on Jan. 13 from Rome: 'I waited 8 days in hopes of permission to see the pictures and other Raritys taken from thence which are preserv'd in the King's Palace at Portice; but I found it was to no purpose, his Majesty keeping the Key in his own Cabinet, which he would not part with, thô the Prince di Zathia (who is one of his favourites) I beleive very sincerely try'd his Interest to obtain it for me. . . . The Court in General is more barbarous than any of the ancient Goths'* (Complete Letters, II, 215–16, 220).

*156

Source: Egerton 2234 ff. 255-6

Rome,
April 15, 1741

⟨Dear Mother,⟩

I gave you some account, a week or two ago, of the last eruption of Mount
Vesuvius; and now shall give you one of the effects of its first eruption on
record in the historians.

Mount Vesuvius was the most charming mountain perhaps in all Italy,
in the beginning of Titus's reign, who destroyed Jerusalem: at least 'tis
called the most charming of all those which appear round the Bay of Naples,
which is still the most pleasing view in all Italy, and I think the most pleasing
I have ever seen in my life. If they went to the top of it, indeed even then
they found scars of its old burnings—but when they happened, and how
far back, was not known: all the sides of it were clothed with vines, its
descent was easy and regular to the sea, and its sides sloped off for about
four mile each way, as prettily as ⌜Bridgeman's⌝[1] slopes do in a garden. Art
could not have shaped it better than nature had done.

In the second year of Titus,[2] this beauty all of a sudden presented you
with nothing but horrors: the combustible matter in its entrails took fire,
burst its sides, flung up a night of smoke at midday, and darted a thousand
lightnings through the gloom that environed it on all sides. Old Pliny, the
philosopher (whom you may have consulted in English about the nature of
plants and salves good for green wounds) was then admiral of one of the
Roman fleets which lay at anchor ten or twelve miles from the mountain,
and as he was a very inquisitive old man, he ordered a brigantine to be got
ready immediately, and went in it to see this terrible sight. He moved on
boldly toward the danger, and came to a town called Resina at the foot of
the mountain on the sea-shore, and intended to land there; but the ashes
fell in such quantities all over the town that he found it impracticable. He
went therefore farther to the right, to a friend's house. His curiosity,
however, cost him his life, for whilst he was at his friend's, he dropped
down all of a sudden, as 'tis supposed choked by the sulphur in the air, and

so did not live to give us an account of what he had seen and observed in his approaches to the mountain.

At the place where he was stopped by the fall of the ashes (and where there is another town now, still called Resina) they show the underground town, which you have heard me talk of.[3] 'Tis probably the old town buried under the modern, and 'tis buried very deep—in some places they say near eighty foot. The King of Naples has had people continually at work there for some years, and they have wrought narrow passages, perhaps quite through it. We walked a line of near a mile in it, and they say one might go six, if one was to take all the turns of it.[4] They have generally followed the line of a wall, wherever they met with one (and they met with them perpetually) sometimes the inside, and sometimes the out, just as it happened: so that the line goes zigzag. The insides are generally covered with stucco (a better kind of plaster) and painted red,[5] of which I have a great many pieces to show you. In several places they have found pictures on it, and some very good ones. The best are conveyed to a house of the King's in that neighbourhood,[6] in which they have already about 140 pieces of these old pictures, beside statues, columns, and other pieces of wrought marble; and they continually find something new, of one or other of these kinds. 'Tis all dark, and we walk all the way with torches, which makes it rather too hot than too cold, though you are so deep under the present surface of the earth. We mounted out of it by a staircase of sixty steps, and went thence to the King's house to see the curiosities that had been discovered in it. Among the pictures some were excellent, but the world will one day or other know more of them, because they design to publish prints of them.[7] ⟨With all services to all friends, I am ever

Your most dutiful and affectionate

J. Spence.

We are obliged to stay on at this place till the 30th to see the great ceremony of the Pope's taking possession of St. John Lateran, and then shall be going soon for Venice.⟩

1. Emended to 'beautiful'. Charles Bridgeman (*fl.* 1713–38), landscape gardener, influential in the development of the new English taste in gardening.

2. A.D. 79. Spence's account is based on two famous letters of Pliny the Younger to Tacitus (*Epist.* VI. 16, 20).

3. Herculaneum. In 1711 Prince d'Elboeuf made the first discoveries, but excavations on a large scale were not begun until Oct. 22, 1738. For other early descriptions of the newly opened up city, see Knapton's article in the *Philosophical Transactions* (1740), No. 458 Gray's Notebook (D. C. Tovey, *Gray and his Friends* [1890], pp. 252–7), De Brosses's *Letter* XXXIII, and for a historical survey, Michele Ruggiero, *Storia degli scavi di Ercolano* (Naples, 1885).

4. 'A hundred palms, under the surface Resina stands upon' (*Nbk.* 3 49[v]).

5. 'And sometimes with bad figures, for the best they carry away as they meet with them' (ibid.).

6. The former Casino d'Elboeuf at Portici. In his *Observations* (No. 1435) Spence recorded a story of how Charles IV of Naples requisitioned it for his own use from a Neapolitan nobleman.

7. The projected *Le Pitture antiche d'Ercolano* did not appear till 1757 at Naples, though in Dec. 1753, Spence reported in a letter to Dr. Mead, published in the *Philosophical Transactions*, XLVIII, ii, 486, that the volume was ready for publication in 1754 (Wright, p. 239). Camillo Paderni, a Neapolitan painter whom Spence met and who did some engravings for *Polymetis*, was in charge of the work (see *Obs.* No. 1433).

Notebook 3
(52–54) 49^v–50^v

At Resina is what they call the underground town. The passages that we went through (in 1741) seem[ed] to be all new made. ... 'Tis a dome-room (half of which is hollowed) that one of the largest [figures painted on the walls] was taken from. What we see of walls stands all erect, and I met with nothing like the remains of a torrent of fire in our way. Indeed, one sees it in haste and very imperfectly. Several pieces of beams overspread are as black as coal throughout (will not wood become so when buried for several centuries?). ... The marble pillars they have met with are carried away; we saw some of brick (particularly three in a line) covered with stucco.—The king has a pretty house and gardens at Portici ... 'tis here they keep most of the things found in the underground town, and particularly the old paintings.

There are six consular statues in the little theatre and several others about.— Horse and man (which seems as big as Aurelius) in bronze—they found a triumphal car, also bronze—Ercole col mitra ed occhi in vitro—a pretty one of a lady with a mitra just like it—little termini, as wide at bottom as at top (one with a woman's head above and feet below, another with a good Pan's head and middle parts in bronze on the marble).—Several inscriptions and two ... catalogues of names, which we had not time enough to consider as I could have wished. One of the finest and plainest inscriptions was: DOMITIAE CNF. DOMITIANI CAESARIS DD.—There's part of a fountain (buffet-fashion) in a bad mosaic and two squares with marine deities in each, the tails of sea (or olive) green.

The chief things are the old paintings: they say they have to the number of 140, some very good. There's a fine piece of Theseus for the pathetic: the Minotaur lies under his feet, and the children he has delivered are kissing his hands and embracing his legs.—Another of Chiron and young Achilles with a lyre, in which the face and attention of the latter is very beautiful; and another of Chiron and Achilles with two darts (or little javelins) in which the instructing face of the former is as remarkable.—Little Hercules with two serpents, sitting on the ground. Amphitryon sitting just by him, drawing his sword doubtfully as willing to kill the serpents and afraid to hurt his son: behind stands Alcmene, exclaiming as in the greatest distress and fright, and on the left hand is a nurse with young Iphicles. The little Hercules is not of an Herculean make any otherwise than that he looks like a child of a year old, whereas he had not been born an hour.—In another is Hercules, a very good figure, shooting Stymphalides, which are high in the air and under them on the ground sits a water deity.—Person sitting, with glory round the head (not unlike the Sol's head in

MSS Vat.), another standing, with the same sort of glory, and a person standing by the latter, crowned with laurel.—One of the best pieces, and the most pathetic of them all, has to the left a man sitting, with two fingers to his forehead, in a very thoughtful and pensive posture; a man, also sitting, by him, turned towards him and reading a little volume or scroll to him; two women (in what one may call the mid-ground) with great sorrow and distress on their faces; an old man beyond them, attentive and concerned; and an old woman (before to the right) attentive but without concern on her face. Behind (or in the background) appears a statue of Diana.

Of the second-rate pieces, there is one large square with Hercules and Victory on one side, and Bacchus and a faun on the other.—Jupiter, with a cupid resting over his right shoulder and as it were keeping down his arm and hand that grasps the angry sort of fulmen; then a half-rainbow across the picture and a little without it the eagle: the face that of Jupiter Pacatus.—A pretty little Bacchus playing with a tiger (like that in the statue at Turin) &c. —Among the lowest or worse preserved is a long slip of cupids, chasing—Cupid in car drawn by two swans—ditto, by two lions, &c.—and several others only of a single bacchante or Genius or some animal in each piece, etc. etc.[1]

---

1. See also *Appendix* 9 for 'A List of some of the antique Paintings and Statues found in the underground town (as 'tis called) at Resina near Portici'.

157

Source:	Egerton 2234 ff. 257–8
Addressed:	*as in* 74
Postmarked:	30 AP
Franked:	Free/Andrew Stone
Endorsed:	*a.* a/good, ⟨but not a reading⟩/Letter: & very/ frendley *b.* Packet of Letters come/at last; how welcome./Not to be Copied. *red wafer*

Rome,
April 22, 1741

⟨Dear Mother,

I am very much concerned to think you should have suffered so much on not receiving letters from me: I am and (I thank God) have been perfectly well ever since I came abroad, and have wrote to you constantly every week. But the posts are so uncertain to and from Rome that this has occasioned both of us a great deal of trouble: for I have had my share too, and was not eased of it till yesterday. I was from the 25th of January to the 18th of April without seeing your hand. For three or four weeks I kept myself up with blaming the posts, but after that I began to fear the worst, and every week added to my fears. I wrote to Paris and to his Majesty's ministers at Florence and Turin[1] to beg them to forward letters for me if there were any mislaid, and yesterday, as I was at dinner at Lord Pomfret's,[2] there came in a packet (from Turin) of above a dozen letters for my Lord and me. I opened my bundle, saw your hand, and was satisfied. There were no less than five together from you. We must both of us resolve not to be frightened if our letters should miss for the future, after so notorious instances of the negligence or roguery of the post.

After dinner, I stole away with Mr. Holdsworth for a walk in one of the gardens out of Rome (of which there are multitudes), and stole time enough to run over all my letters. We did not return home till the dusk of the evening, when I met Lord Lincoln on the square before our house, who had been waiting for me to tell me that in his packet he had received a letter from you. He loves you so well, that it made him cry to read it: and you can't imagine how kindly he spoke of you.[3] We have both of us suffered a good deal, but I hope for the last time:[4] for if your letters should fail again for a month or two, I will most certainly lay it upon the post.

'Tis now all very well again. An unexpected shower was never more reviving to a traveller that is fatigued and languishing with heat, than your letters were to me. You will say, I know, that your son Joseph is apt to be a little poetical in his expressions, but this is a real truth: and just such an effect I felt from receiving your letters. They revived me in a moment.

We shall leave this place about the middle of next month for Venice, and thence shall go on by easy journeys for France: I this very day am making up my last box of curiosities to send for Leghorn, in its way to England, and shall be very glad when we are following it. I reckon (for, for once, I will deal honestly with you) that we shall hardly get there till September or the beginning of October. If we cross the Alps again, 'tis not a work of several weeks as you seem to fear in one of your letters; for one goes slowly from Turin to Lyons in seven days, or seven days and a half: and when I am there I shall think (as old Captain Shelvocke said of China) that I am at home.[5] Settle beforehand whether I should come to you to Winchester, or whether you will come to me to London, for I shall do everything as you choose, and as will be most for your pleasure. With all services to all friends, I am ever

Your most affectionate and dutiful

J. Spence.⟩

1. Sir Horace Mann and Arthur Villettes. Both letters are missing.

2. These were almost daily affairs: 'Lord Lincoln, and Mr. Spence his governor, Mr. Pitt, and Mr. Holdsworth his governor ... dined at our lodgings to-day,' writes Lady Pomfret. On Apr. 23, the eve of his coming of age (see *Letter* 161 n. 1), they went 'to lord

Lincoln's; who had invited us all to the finest concert Rome could afford, and which was the best I ever heard. There were all kinds of ice, chocolate, &c; and the honours of the entertainment were perfectly well performed. As it was St. George's day, all the English wore red crosses; which, when together, made a considerable number and looked very pretty' (*Hertford Corresp.* III, 92).

3. Lincoln acknowledged the kindness in a letter (174) from Paris. Mrs. Spence marked

this 'a good Letter & very frendley'.

4. In an undated letter, written after his return, Spence complains to Lord Lincoln about 'a sort of gloom as I contracted in endeavouring to serve you in Italy, and I shall never forget the melancholy kind of pleasure I felt when you was so good as to ease me from it, in part, in our walk by the Monte Testaceo' (Newcastle MSS, Nottingham University Library).

5. See *Letter 72.*

158

Source: Egerton 2234 ff. 259–60

Addressed: *as in* 74

Endorsed: *a.* a descrip-/tion of yᵉ chinese flowers/the finest in the world
b. Of the Artificial Flow-/ers.
red wafer

Rome,
April 29, 1741

⟨Dear Mother,

When I wrote my last to you, I was like a man after a storm, who though recovered from the danger still feels some remains of the apprehension he had been under, and though he treads on the shore, still trembles to look at the sea that was like to have swallowed him. I have every day grown more serene and easy, and am now quite in a calm. As I don't doubt your fright had the same effect, I hope it went off as well.

Tomorrow is our great ceremony, which I suppose will furnish me with things to talk of all my next letter. When that is over, we shall be setting out in fourteen or fifteen days for Venice, and hope to be in two months at Paris: where we shall probably stay about two months more, and then for old England!⟩

I have a box of beauties come in this morning, among which there will probably be a present for you, if they get safe to England; for they are very tender and difficult of carriage. 'Tis a set of artificial flowers made of feathers, and so well made that I have often taken some of them up to smell to them and been really surprised not to find the sweetness of a rose or a jonquil, where there was everything else of those flowers. The art was brought hither so far as from China. Some of the missionaries that went thither were so pleased with them that they sent a box of them to Rome, to be presented to the Pope. When they came to the Jesuits' college here, everybody was mightily pleased with them, but they thought there was not enough for a present to his Holiness: so they privately employed a woman here (who was very clever at such sort of work) to imitate them; and she did it so well that you could not distinguish hers from the Chinese. Signora Vannimanni[1] (for that is her name) afterwards made others, and has got a great deal of money by it. I have been several times to see her at work; she is as ugly as they are pretty; but however ugly she is, she has sent me in this morning a box of the delightfullest things of the kind I ever saw in my life ⟨and I shall send them to be shipped off for old England in my Lord's great box two or three days hence. I am with all services to all friends, dear mother,

Your most affectionate and dutiful

J. Spence.⟩

---

1. 'So many of whose Works in this kind are continually brought home by our Gentlemen who travel' to Rome wrote Spence in 'A Letter from China' (Dodsley's *Fugitive Pieces* [1761], I, 66). Earlier in the year Sophia Fermor sent 'my Italian flowers' to Mrs. Wallop (Finch MSS, Leicestershire Record Office).

159

Source: Add. MSS 33065 ff. 409-11
Endorsed: R[eceived] May 6th.

LINCOLN TO NEWCASTLE

Rome,
April 29, 1741

My Lord,

I won't so much as pretend to describe the pleasure I felt in reading over your Grace's obliging letter,[1] for I own I was greatly uneasy at my being so long without hearing from you, and frightened myself (though thank God unnecessarily) with the fears and apprehensions that my absence had caused an alteration which I should reckon as the greatest of misfortunes. . . . [I] hope my Lord, you won't think me undeserving that attention and love you are so good as to express for me in so very kind a manner, if I don't entirely comply with your Grace's commands.

I must own, my Lord, the reasons your Grace gives me for my returning are very strong, but I own to you freely I can't have any thoughts of coming home before the winter, for ... if I don't stay till that time I can't possibly see, as I ought to do, the many places I have as yet to see, and what is still more, England at present can never be the place where I should choose to be, for I never could think or so much as pretend of having half so much of your Grace's and my uncle Pelham's conversation as I should so greatly desire, and be so uneasy at not having, when both of you must inevitably be so entirely taken up with election affairs.[2] I own my Lord I could not help smiling a little at the obliging apprehension your Grace expresses for me on account of the Spaniards. Our politicians here say they never can get into Italy without the English please to let them come,[3] but your Grace knows this much better I am sure than I can tell you, so will say no more of it, but most certainly I can never be in any danger. I am now in the Pope's state and shall soon be in the Venetian, and in case of a débarquement shall always have time enough to get out of Italy, which we design doing the shortest way we can, which is by Genoa to Nice, and so take the southern parts of France in our way to Paris, where we shall be the latter end of the summer, and, if politics don't interfere, hope your Grace will give me leave to stay there some time, for your Grace knows very well I have as yet seen nothing of Paris, but hurried as fast as we could from Dover to Turin. And when I am so near as Paris, it will be very easy to send a messenger over if you think it absolutely necessary for my affairs. ...

But now, my Lord, I have something to tell you that I hope will make ample amends for my not returning so soon as I should, and flatter myself will convince you that whenever I promise anything to your Grace, I do my utmost to fulfil [it], let it cost me ever so much. Your Grace leaves it to me to return either through France or Germany. My Lord Pomfret and his family come back through Germany; I choose France. My dearest, dearest uncle, how much is comprehended in those few words.[4] ... For our parts here, we all wait for tomorrow with the greatest impatience, for his Holiness, attended with all the sacred college, takes his possession with the greatest pomp and magnificence imaginable. ...

---

1. *Letter* 153, which arrived in Rome on Apr. 18.

2. Elections were held in May. On Apr. 27 O.S. Newcastle wrote to Lincoln: 'We are now going to our new elections. They will be over in a fortnight; we shall I believe have no opposition for the county. Mr. Sergison gives us trouble at Lewes, but we think ourselves very sure. I have in the several places where you are concerned given directions to your agents to do as I think you would if you was here' (part of *Letter* 161, omitted from the printed text).

3. Horace Walpole (*Letter* 148) also could not 'conceive how it is possible these troops should arrive without its being known some time before'.

4. The Pomfrets were to leave Rome on May 18. Lincoln, however, was to see them again at Bologna, Venice, and Padua, before their home-bound routes separated.

*160

Source: Egerton 2234 ff. 261–2

Rome,
May 6, 1741

⟨Dear Mother,⟩

Sunday last[1] was our great ceremony of the Pope's taking possession of his own proper church of St. John Lateran. It began just at one and twenty o'clock, which at this time of year is between three and four in the afternoon.[2]

'Twas opened by the Pope's light horse (or horse guards), each guard with plumes of red and white feathers (which nodded all over his head) alternately. The gentleman who was with me[3] pointed out among these Fisher, who escaped from England several years ago for the black action he committed in the Temple.[4] He came here, turned his religion, and serves the Pope. After them followed the foot guards. Then the officers of the palace, the trumpets, drums and kettledrums: then the officers of the guards dressed in armour, complete from head to foot, and very rich and shining like gold—like Earl Percy['s] and Douglas's of old in 'Chevy Chase'.[5] Then the Governor of Rome and Constable Colonna,[6] then came the prelates, and after them the bishops, all on horseback; then the cardinals, on mules; and last of all, the Pope, in a rich open litter. His coach of state followed him empty, and drawn by eight white horses with very rich caparisons. They went all in this order to the Capitol, where the senator made a speech to his Holiness: and then proceeded, along the way where the Roman triumphs used to pass of old, under two old triumphal arches (one of which was built for Titus after his destruction of Jerusalem, and a modern one,[7] raised by the King of Naples in honour to the Pope) for St. John Lateran.

After seeing them begin their march, my friend and I took a shorter way to that church, and got into an apartment which he had provided for me and situated most conveniently for seeing the sight.[8] In half an hour the procession began again to appear and went all along under our window. And after the ceremony was over in the church, we had a view of them for the third time, in the same place. When the Pope comes to the church-door, he knocks, and the priests from within ask 'who's there?' He says: 'Benedict the Fourteenth.' After staying a little, he repeats the same, but without their opening to him. When they ask 'who's there' for the third time, he answers 'The Bishop of St. John Lateran', and then they let him in. This methinks is very selfish of them to make the Great Universal Bishop only bishop of their church: but 'tis a very old custom, and they no doubt can show their rights for it.

When the Pope set out at first, he looked quite tired and apprehensive of the fatigue he was to go through, of being stared at for three hours by a hundred thousand people: but when he set out to go away, which was (by his order) by a more retired way and in some degree incog, he was mightily pleased, and the good old man smiled to see the confusion which the suddenness of his order had given to the procession and to the people. He ever loved a jest, and hates ceremony: so much that a person who has the honour of being very intimate with him[9] has assured me that he is already heartily tired of being Pope. Indeed, in the last thirty days there are fifteen at least in which he has been forced to bear being made a sight of. ⟨With all services to all friends, I am ever, dear mother,

Your dutiful and affectionate

J.S.⟩

1. Apr. 30. Cf. Spence's account with Lady Pomfret's (*Hertford Corresp.* III, 106–9).

2. Or rather between four and five; the sunset on Apr. 30 being at 7 P.M., the new day, according to Italian planetary time, began at 7.30 P.M. See *Letter* 127 n. 2.

3. Probably Signor Niccolini; see note 9.

4. 'On *Sunday* the last Day of *April* [1727], about Two o'Clock in the Afternoon, Mr. *Henry Fisher*, an Attorney at Law, was committed to *Newgate* by Sir *William Thompson*, Recorder of this City, upon a violent Suspicion of his murdering and robbing Mr. *Widdrington Darby*, Jun. on the 10th of *April*, at Night. . . . On Tuesday, the 15th Instant [May], the Grand-Jury at *Guildhall* found two Bills of Indictment against Mr. *Fisher*; one for the murder of Mr. *Darby*, and the other for *Burglary* and *Felony*, in entring the Office of Sir *George Cook*, and stealing the Goods of the said Mr. *Darby*: Upon which Indictments he was to have been try'd on *Thursday* the 17th. but the Night before he found Means to make his Escape out of *Newgate*, together with another Criminal' (Boyer, *The Political State of Great Britain*, XXIII [1727], pp. 530–2). On Dec. 16, 1727, *The British Journal* reported that he 'hath lately wrote a Letter to his Father, a Clothier in Somersetshire, importing that after a violent illness in the Dominions of the Duke of Tuscany, he had retired to Florence, where he had embraced the Romish Religion, and was become Servitor to a Monk, designing to trouble his Father no more, and to persevere all his Days in a religious Life.'

5. *Earl Douglas on a milk-white steed*
   Most like a baron bold,
   Rode foremost of the company
   Whose armour shone like gold.
'Chevy Chase' had been praised by Addison in *Spectators* Nos. 70, 74.

6. Fabrizio Colonna (1700–55), suc. his father as Great Constable of the Kingdom of Naples in 1714; brother of Princess Agnese Colonna (see *Letter* 125).

7. A festive arch erected by Don Carlos de Bourbon 'near the little Farnese Palace' (*Hertford Corresp.* III, 109).

8. The sentence originally ran: 'After seeing them begin their march, I had taken a shorter way to this place, and was got snug in a little ale-house, drinking and smoking like a country parson, ready against they should come again. After I had been there about half an hour. . . .'

9. Antonio Niccolini (1701–69) 'dont le frère a épousé la nièce du pape'. He was a man of letters, friend of Montesquieu, and an *abbé de convenance* (De Brosses, I, 317). He was a frequent visitor of the Pomfrets at Rome (*Hertford Corresp.* III, 125–6). In his *Observations*, Spence jotted down some of Niccolini's quips on Spanish religiosity (Nos. 1438–47).

161

Source: Add. MSS 33065 ff. 412–15 (The original
letter is in the Newcastle MSS deposited at
Nottingham University Library)

Endorsed: Copy to L^d. Lincoln/April 27th. 1741.

NEWCASTLE TO LINCOLN

Newcastle House,
April 27, 1741 [O.S.]

My dear Lord,

I cannot but take the first opportunity of congratulating you upon your
birthday, which was last Friday.[1] We did not fail to remember you and I am
persuaded you think no one can wish more happiness to another than I do
to you. You are now, my dear Lord, arrived at that age that enables you to
be serviceable to your country, and I have not the least doubt but you will
steadily pursue the true interest of it in the same manner that your
ancestors have done before you, in which you will have the example and
assistance of those whom I am persuaded you will be the most inclined to
regard.

As to your private conduct, nobody can pretend to have any other
influence over you than what will arise from the weight and force of the
advice they give and a sincere and disinterested concern for your welfare. I
wrote a very long letter to you the middle of last month,[2] and I can add
very little to what was in that letter: I own I am impatient for your answer,
since by your letter of the 8th of this month N.S.,[3] which I received last
Tuesday,[4] I fear we shall not have the pleasure of seeing you here so soon
as I think absolutely necessary for your affairs in all respect. I must return
you, my dear Lord, my most sincere thanks for your goodness and affection
for me. Give me leave to assure you, you shall never have any reason to
alter your opinion with regard to me; I shall always most tenderly love you,
and from that love give you my opinion in what I think essential to your
welfare and happiness.

I shall not at present enter into what you mention about your attachment
to the young lady you have met in Italy any further than to beg you would
not lay yourself under any kind of engagement till you see the state of your
affairs, hear the advice and opinion of your best friends, and then you may
determine for yourself. For, my dear Lord, should you under the influence
of youth and a passion contracted so early in your life engage yourself further

than perhaps hereafter you may find advisable, you may, by that one indiscreet step, have laid yourself under difficulties which you may not easily get out of: and for this reason I most earnestly desire you would come to England immediately, make yourself master of your estate by cutting off the entail, which you may by law do, settle it on your sister or make such disposition of it as you shall think proper, see how your affairs stand with regard to the Crown debt and what method can be found for settling that, hear the opinion of your best friends, see what proposals may be made to you for settling yourself in the world, and if after all this you shall then be of opinion you cannot be happy without this young lady, it will then be time enough to determine upon it. You will always have it in your power to please yourself, and however your friends may think any other proposals more for your advantage in your circumstances, I dare say no one will presume, I am sure I shall not, to press any thing that may be disagreeable to you . . . upon the subject. But if, from an apprehension that what is agreeable to you will not be approved by your friends in England, you should either determine to stay abroad (which is so inconvenient for your affairs) or engage yourself to this young lady so as you may not be at liberty afterwards to do what perhaps upon discourse with your friends you may yourself think right for you, then indeed, my dear, I shall think those who love you and who can have no interest but yours, will be a little unkindly treated by you. But that I don't in the least apprehend. You have been so good as to give me your word not to enter into the least engagement: that is all I desire of you at present, or till you yourself shall think proper to go further. Upon that word I entirely depend, and I know very well I may do so: trust yourself and depend upon yourself, you are always master to do what you like.

I have not had an opportunity of talking to my brother since I received your letter, which, however, I will do as soon as possible. But I know his thoughts, they agree entirely with mine, that it is absolutely necessary for you to come immediately to England.[5] That is all I ask besides the promise you have given me. Come my dear Lord . . . I will trouble you no more upon the subject. . . .

I have ordered the King's speeches and the addresses of both houses to be sent you, by which you will see how our foreign affairs stand.[6] We have no doubt but we shall have a good Parliament. Mrs. Spence and Mr. Stone and Carpenter desire their compliments.[7] I am, my dearest Lord, ever most affectionately yours

Holles Newcastle

1. Apr. 24 O.S. was the date of Lincoln's baptism, on which his birthday was celebrated. He was born on Apr. 16 (*G.E.C.*).

2. *Letter* 153.

3. *Letter* 155.

4. Apr. 21 O.S.

5. See *Letter* 154.

6. For the King's speech made on Apr. 8 O.S., see *Gent. Mag.*, 1741, pp. 216–17.

7. On 'Mrs. Spence' see *Letter* 109 n. 6. 'Carpenter' has not been identified. Possibly 'Jemmy' (*Letter* 109) or John Carpenter (b. 1698), a Cambridge graduate.

On Apr. 18, Horace Walpole wrote to Lord Lincoln from Florence: 'I hope Rome answers the expectation of one so capable of being pleased with antiquity and erudition as my Lady [*Pomfret*]. For Lady Sophy, 'tis impossible the antique world should delight her so much, as she must the modern. . . . 'Tis with infinite reluctance I leave Florence without the hope of returning—my dear Lord, you have had of these reluctances, have you not? [*Horace Walpole was leaving Signora Grifoni, his cicisbea at Florence*] if you have, pity me, me who at most can carry away but a picture to England.' *He sent* 'remembrance, especially of Mr. Spence, whom I would not forgive forgetting me.' *And on Apr. 29,* 'I go tomorrow to Modena, and thence to Reggio. . . . I pity you extremely for the separation you mention, but yours can be but for a short season: mine may be endless!' (*Corresp. XXX, 14–16*).

In the meantime at Rome Lady Pomfret began on May 9 her 'formal visits of taking leave'. *The day before* 'my lord Lincoln, Mr. Pitt, abbé Grant, my lord Pomfret, my daughters, and myself, set out in two coaches to see Albano.' *On May 11* 'Lord Lincoln, and Mr. Spence, his governor, Mr. Pitt, and Mr. Holdsworth, his governor, with the Abbé Grant, and Mr. Parker, dined at our lodgings.' *On May 12* 'about nine, we went, with Lord Lincoln, Mr. Pitt . . . in two coaches to Frescati'; *next day* 'we all dined at Lord Lincoln's.' *Sunday, May 14* 'In the evening lord Lincoln came to take leave of us, being to set out to-morrow for Reggio, where I am told there is a very fine opera' (*Hertford Corresp. III, 123 5, 143–6*). *The Pomfrets set out three days later* (*May 18*) *for Bologna, where Lincoln and Spence, who had taken the longer route along the Adriatic via Otricoli, Foligno* (*16*), *Loreto* (*17*), *Ancona,* (*18*), *Rimini* (*19*), *briefly rejoined them on May 20, to continue on to Reggio* (*May 21–27*), *which had long enjoyed a reputation for excellent opera festivals.* 'On y tient tous les ans une foire assez fameuse, pendant laquelle la Cour de Modène vient à Reggio se divertir. Il y a toujours en ce temps . . . un fort bon opéra' (*De Brosses, II, 560*).

*162

Source: Egerton 2234 ff. 265–6
Addressed: as in 74
Endorsed: a. an/ac^t of ye 4 fine italian/voyces at ye Opera there
b. Of the Opera there.
red wafer

Reggio,
May 22, 1741

⟨Dear Mother,⟩

This letter comes to you from a place from whence you never, I believe, received a letter before, unless my old uncle Harry Neville used to correspond with you from Italy.[1] We are got from Rome to Reggio, the second city in the state of the Duke of Modena, and are lodged just opposite to the door of the new theatre,[2] for 'twas the opera that tempted us to this place. We, last night, heard four of the best voices in Italy on the stage all together: Caristini, Salimbeni, Amorevoli, and the Tesi,[3] the latter of which is my great favourite, and I believe I wrote a letter to you giving an account of her, when in Italy with Lord Middlesex. She is one of the most agreeable women in the world without any one good feature in her face, and sings the most pleasingly with a very indifferent voice. All her perfections are owing to herself, for nature has done nothing for her, except giving her a great deal of good sense: and she is one of the best proofs I ever met with that this supplies the want of everything else. She is very genteel and, I believe, the best actress now in the world. With this, and the other three charming voices, you may imagine that we shall pass four or five days here very agreeably, and then we return to Bologna, and so go on for Venice. ⟨My Lord Lincoln is extremely well, and desires his hearty services to you. I was I think never better, and [am] always, with all services to all friends

Your most dutiful and affectionate

Joseph Spence.⟩

1. Henry Neville (*Letter* 105), political theorist and admirer of Machiavelli, whose works he published in 1675, had returned from his tour of the continent in 1645, twenty-five years before Mrs. Spence was born!
2. Teatro della Cittadella was built in the record time of ten months to replace the Teatro Vecchio which burnt down in March 1740. Designed by Antonio Cugini on the model of Maffei's new theatre at Verona (see *Letters* 23, 24) and decorated by Giovanni Paglia, it opened the *fiera* of Reggio on April 29, 1741,

with Luccarelli's adaptation of *Volgeso re de'*
parti (G. Croccioni, *I Teatri in Reggio nell' Emilia*
[Reggio, 1907], pp. 39–47).

3. Giovanni Carestini (ca. 1705–58?), called 'il
Cusanino', was first a soprano, then a contralto
(castrato). An excellent actor, he sang in
Prague, Munich, as well as in Italy. Felice
Salimbeni (1712–51), a soprano (contralto)
from Milan, sang in Italy, Vienna, Berlin,
Dresden. Angelo Amorevoli or Amerevoli
(1716–98), from Venice, tenor, sang in Vienna,
Dresden. At the end of 1741 Lord Middlesex
engaged him for his expensive experiments in
Italian opera at London (*H.W. Corresp.* XVII,
190–1). Vittoria Tesi (1700–75) was a contralto
less known for her good sense than for her
passion and vivaciousness. Between 1736 and
1741 she wrote a series of love-letters to a priest,
Enea Silvio Piccolomini, and in 1743 she married
a barber named Travestini to escape the
importunities of a certain nobleman.

163

Source: Egerton 2234 ff. 263–4

Addressed: as in 74

Endorsed: *a.* an ac^t of Mr Wallpoles/daingerous Illness./
not to be seen:
b. Mr Walpole's Illness./not to be Copy'd.
red wafer

Bologna,
May 29, 1741

⟨Dear Mother,

We are got on as far as Bologna[1] in our way to Venice, and have been, as I
told you in my last, a opera-hunting at Reggio. After we had been there a
day or two,[2] we heard that Mr. Walpole (who we thought was gone) was
still there, but that he was ill abed.[3] We went, you may be sure, immediately
to see him, and found him very ill with a quinsy, and swelled to such a
degree as I never saw anyone in my life. We went from him to the opera,
whence I got to bed at two, and between three and four was surprised with
a message that Mr. Walpole was extremely worse and desired to speak with
me immediately. I dressed as soon as I heard it, stepped into his coach,
which waited at the door, and found him scarce able to speak. I soon found
there, upon talking with his servants, that he had been all this while
without any physician, and had doctored himself. So I sent immediately for
the best physician the place could afford, and dispatched an express to
Florence to our minister there,[4] with orders to bring a physician from
thence, who is a very good one and my particular friend, Dr. Cocchi,[5] and
who (which was a very material thing in these parts) understands and talks
English like an Englishman.

In about twenty hours' time Mr. Walpole began to grow better, and we
left him with his Florentine doctor in a fair way of recovering soon. I was
with him perpetually till the doctor came, and if he had been worse, had

got leave of Lord Lincoln to stay behind for some days to take care of him: but I thank God all went well before my Lord went away, and so we took our leaves of him with pleasure,[6] and hope to see him next week at Venice, whither he is bound as well as we,[7] and then for England. You see what luck one has sometimes in going out of one's way: if Lord Lincoln had [not] wandered to Reggio, Mr. Walpole (who is one of the best-natured and most sensible young gentlemen that England affords) would in all probability have been now under the cold earth.

After seeing Venice, we shall come on as fast as we can for Paris. We have great luck in the weather. We have yet had no summer in Italy, and they are not likely to have any. 'Tis mere spring weather, refreshed every other day with little rains, and the day we came from Reggio, the 27th of May, 'twas rather too cold than too hot on the road. This is a particular blessing, for had the season been as usual we [should] have travelled only the mornings and evenings, whereas now we have the whole day as agreeable travelling as 'tis in the month of May in England. I am perfectly well, and with all services to all friends, am ever

Your most dutiful and affectionate

Joseph Spence.⟩

1. Th y arrived in Bologna late on May 27 for a week's stay. They left June 3.

2. About May 24.

3. Horace Walpole had arrived in Reggio with Gray about May 5. They originally planned to be in Venice by May 11 to see the great festival of Ascension, the espousal of Venice and the Adriatic (Gray, *Corresp.* I, 182). It was at Reggio that their famous quarrel occurred. Gray went on 'with Mr Francis Whithed and Mr John Chute' to Venice, leaving Walpole behind (*H. W. Corresp.* XIII, 9–10). Spence and Lincoln, unaware of the quarrel, naturally assumed that Walpole had left with Gray. This is the most complete account of Horace Walpole's dangerous illness, otherwise known only from Walpole's brief note: 'I fell ill at Reggio of a kind of quinsy, and was given over for fifteen hours, escaping with great difficulty' (ibid.).

4. Horace Mann. Spence later sent him another 'little bit of a letter', assuring him of Walpole's recovery. Mann received it on May 30 (ibid., XVII, 51). Neither of these is extant.

5. Antonio Cocchi (*Letter* 36) jotted down in his manuscript *Effemeridi* (Notebook for 7141): '26 Apr . . . set out very early and travelled all day . . . 27 Sat. . . . arrived in the morning at Reggio . . . 28–29 at Reggio . . . 30 Tuesday. I set out from Reggio and went to Bologna. I dined there with Mil^d Lincoln . . . 31 Wednesday . . . lighted at Mr. Mann's at Florence. The particulars of this journey in another book.' I have not found the 'other book' among Cocchi's MSS in the library of the Medical Faculty at Carregi, Florence, only a note: '90 Venesiani da Mr. Walpole p. La visita fattagli a Reggio.'

6. On Saturday, May 27.

7. Horace Walpole arrived in Venice on June 9 (*Hertford Corresp.* III, 221). His memory slipped when later he wrote in his short notes: 'I went to Venice with Henry Clinton, Earl of Lincoln and Mr Joseph Spence, Professor of Poetry' (*Corresp.* XIII, 10). 'Rejoined at' or 'went from Venice' would have been more accurate.

The Pomfrets had reached Bologna on May 25, two days before Lincoln and Spence. On May 31 a party of five coaches, 'lord Lincoln and my lord [Pomfret] in a fourth . . . set out to pay our devotions to the Virgin at the Monte de Guardia, or rather to see a fine colonnade of three miles in length, up a very steep hill that leads to it, from whence there is a delightful prospect of the distant city and the country about it' (Hertford Corresp. III, 182). After a week's stay, Spence and Lord Lincoln left Bologna (June 3) for Padua (4) and reached Venice by coach on May 5. The Pomfrets set out the day after, taking the slower journey by boat from Padua along the Brenta, vaunted for its picturesqueness. On May 6 Lady Pomfret wrote from Venice: 'The English here are lord Lincoln (who arrived the night before us, having set out in the morning before us from Bologna), lord Elcho, Mr. Dashwood and Mr. Naylor. . . . In the afternoon I had a visit from them all.' On June 8 'we went all together to see the arsenal' (ibid., 209, 212).

164

Source: Finch MSS, deposited at the Leicestershire Record Office

Addressed: Milord/Milord Lempster à l'Academie Roiale/à/Turin

SOPHIA FERMOR TO HER BROTHER

From aboard a boat upon the Brent
Monday, June 5, [1741] N.S.

Dear Lord Lempster,

This is the only opportunity I've had since the letter I sent you from Rome of writing to you. I had the pleasure of hearing and talking much of you with one Conte Cavalca, a well-bred man and a fine dancer.[1] I saw him at Bologna, where we spent eight days in the most agreeable manner imaginable. They've a very good opera and a public assembly every night in the year, which is called the Casino, but infinitely finer and more lively than that of Siena, which is the only Italian one I believe that you have seen.

Bologna, as to its inhabitants and their manner of life, is I think preferable to any place I've ever seen in Italy, excepting Genoa. In the short time we stayed I contracted an intimacy with two of the most agreeable and good-humoured ladies of the place, the Signora Teresa Gozadini and the Contessa Rossi,[2] who say that if ever you come that way they will be acquainted with you and show you what civility they can for the sake of your sisters. The Princess Amalia, sister to the Duke of Modena,[3] came to Bologna (in her way to the baths of Lucca) where she stayed two days. We waited upon her at her palace, where there was a vast crowd of people. She received us very graciously; salutes all ladies and makes them sit down with her. She seems very good-humoured and is much beloved. Her face is ugly, but her person very fine. The next night she came to the opera, where we went into her lodge to wish her good journey. She received there the compliments of all that were at the opera, men and ladies, and supped with a few she selected in a little room by her lodge.

When we arrived at Bologna, we found Uguccioni had been there two days, expecting us to come sooner.[4] He is now in this boat with us, the only company we have going to Venice, where we shall be (they tell us) in four hours. Mr. Walpole has been extreme ill at Reggio and sent an express from thence to Florence to fetch Doctor Cocchi, but the Princess of Modena told me that when she left Reggio he was quite out of danger, and he is to set out today from thence for Venice. Mr. Gray is already there, and Cecchino Suarez travels with Mr. Walpole.[5]

Yesterday, coming to Padua, we met Mr. Sturgis and Signor Cerotesi, a Florentine going to Bologna.[6] They got out of their chairs and told us they'd left Lord Lincoln, Lord Elcho[7] and Mr. Dashwood[8] that morning at Padua, but they designed all to return. [We] set out after dinner in a boat for Venice, which is hitherto the most pleasant way of travelling I ever knew. It is much the same thing as the *coche d'eau* that goes to Lyons, and puts me in my mind not only of the pleasure of having that agreeable company and hearing French songs sung so well as you sing them, but also of what we all suffered from the impertinence of the French lieutenant and his other companions, the reflection of which makes me thankful for the quiet I at present enjoy in Uguccioni's company, who thinks only of being helpful to us, and is so much so that without his assistance I couldn't have the pleasure of employing this time in assuring my dearest brother how glad I was to hear that the 24 ounces of blood you took away was for nothing worse than a fluxion in your eye, and that you are now perfectly recovered.

The shore on each side of us is so inexpressibly beautiful that the gardens, groves and villas that compose it deserve each their panegyric, and was I capable of writing such as they deserve I certainly should do it out of gratitude for the pleasure they afford me.

We have the company of Tisbe, Maschera, Devil and Cochetta all at once in the cabin. The two last are as pretty as nasty and as troublesome as one can imagine. They're darker than the mother and are the only two of the six puppies she had that have black noses; all the others have white ones and their ears ill cut.[9] Lord Lincoln is vastly fond of his, but had her ears cut again at Bologna by a famous woman, which, though it cost the dog great pain, was to very little purpose, for a Dutch mastiff with a white face must always be shocking, let the ears be as they will. However, I couldn't prevail upon my Lord to change it again for a blacker.

I can send you no news for our letters wait for us at Venice, and if there should be any in them when I come I will insert it in this letter. In order to leave room for news I must make haste to conclude this and tell you I'm sincerely concerned that I shan't see you before I leave Italy, and God knows how long the time will be before we meet. But in the meanwhile let me beg you, my dear Lord Lempster, to remember one that is with great truth your most affectionate sister—

S.F.[10]

GEORGE FERMOR (1722–85), styled Lord Lempster 1722–53, 2d E. of Pomfret 1753. A year younger than Lady Sophia, he was completing his education at the Royal Academy in Turin, which Lord Lincoln had attended the year before.

1. Not identified.

2. 'Signora Teresa Gozadini' was Teresa Margherita del Vernaccia (1712–59), a Florentine lady, m. senator Alessandro Gozzadini (1674–1746) of Bologna (Pompeo Litta, *Celebri famiglie italiane*, Milan, 1839). De Brosses (I, 275) calls her 'la chère petite dame, ma bonne amie, à laquelle [mon coeur] appartient . . . depuis si longtemps'. 'Contessa Rossi' was perhaps Alba Rasponi who m. in 1728 Antonio Rossi of Ravenna (Pompeo Litta).

3. Aurelia Giuseppina (1699–1778), sister of Francesco Maria d'Este (1698–1780), D. of Modena. Horace Walpole met her and her sister at Reggio: 'two . . . woefully ugly, old maids and rich. They might have been married often; but the old Duke', their late father, Rinaldo III d'Este (d. 1737), 'was whimsical and proud, and never would consent to any match for them, but left them much money . . . and so they mope old virgins' (*Corresp.* XIII, 242–3).

4. Lady Sophia's Florentine admirer (see *Letter* 146 n. 4). He 'intends going with us to Venice,' writes Lady Pomfret. 'I need not tell you that we were very glad to see a person from whom we have received so many civilities, and with whom we have lived so long in friendship' (*Hertford Corresp.* III, 168–239 passim).

5. Cavaliere Francesco Suares de la Concha (1720–77), known as 'Cecco' or 'Cecchino', accompanied Horace Walpole from Florence, but he apparently was not at Reggio when Horace Walpole was taken ill there.

6. Samuel Sturgis (ca. 1701–43) with whom Lady Walpole was living at Florence (*Letter* 124 n. 5). She had eloped with him in 1734. 'Signor Cerotesi' was probably Giuseppe Cerretesi (b. 1702), freemason and poet (*H. W. Corresp.* XVII, 459 n. 24).

7. David Wemyss (1721–87), styled Lord Elcho. He became an ardent Jacobite and was attainted for his part in the '45.

8. Sir Francis Dashwood (1708–81), later Baron Le Despenser, famous rake and one of the original members of the Soc. of Dilettanti. Spence had met him at Turin.

9. On Apr. 29, Lady Sophia wrote from Rome: 'Maschera's six puppies are very pretty creatures, and as they are now big enough to run about, we shall send them to their respective masters: my Lord Lincoln takes one, Mr. Pitt another, and Mr. Sturgis must have a little Taff; my sister has one she calls Devil, and I have one with the prettiest little black phiz I ever saw; the other is not yet disposed of' (Finch MSS).

10. In Venice packets of letters were awaiting the Pomfrets, and on 'June 9, N.S.' Lady Sophia filled up her letter with a long postscript, full of the latest news from England, here omitted.

*165

Source: Egerton 2234 ff. 267–8
Addressed: as in 74
Endorsed: b. The line of scatterd Houses/to yᵉ right,
            wⁿ you go to Venice
            red wafer

Venice,
June 9, 1741

⟨Dear Mother,⟩

We are now three days old at Venice which, though I had seen it before, struck me again (on our approaches toward it) as one of the strangest sights I had ever seen in my life. You know 'tis a whole city standing in the water, just like a man-of-war at anchor; but as the ground, which has been formerly I suppose flooded by the Adriatic Sea (both where the city is built and for a great way round it), lies but a little way under water and in many places and spots rises a little above it, they have taken advantage wherever the ground is higher than the water to build either single houses, or two or three together, or a little village, according as the ground that appeared was more or less spacious.

Ground, you may imagine, in their watery situation is the thing that they must most want; so they seldom lose an inch of it. Every spot above the high-water mark that is large enough for a house, has a house upon it: and this at a distance, to the right hand of Venice, looks like the scattering suburbs to a great city, and makes a line that appears as well inhabited as one of our roads for five or ten mile from London. But then these little villages on the line I mention (or if you will on this roadside), and even each of the single houses in it, are all encompassed with sea, and seem to float upon the water. This line, on my second coming, gave me more pleasure and struck me more than the city itself: the first time I was so surprised and so taken up with the city that I did not take notice of it so particularly as it deserved.

One may judge by this where the overflow of the sea I mention happened (for I don't know that any of the historians have marked it). To the left hand of Venice you have none of these scattered swimming habitations; they lie all to the right, stretch on far to the distant shore, and go out in some parts much wider than the city itself. So that in all probability a space of ground (part of which I now write upon, with the sea all round our house and the crabs and cockles sticking against the walls) of above twenty mile

long and ten mile broad, was formerly all a moorish country, then gained
by the sea, and now recovered from it in part by the industry and buildings
of the Venetians. ⟨We shall stay on this odd ground about a fortnight. I am
with all services

Your most dutiful and affectionate

J. Spence.⟩

166

Source: Egerton 2234 ff. 269–70
Addressed: as in 74
Endorsed: a. the/fine sett of desrt knives/& forks, yᵉ
handls made of/the noblest Rich marble/usd
by the old Romans
b. Of my Lapis Lazuli han-/dles for dessert
knives./not to be copied.
red wafer

Venice,
June 16, 1741

⟨Dear Mother,

I have been this morning purchasing some household goods for us: no less
than handles for a dozen dessert knives and forks. Among all the noble rich
marbles used by the old Romans (of which I have seen above a hundred
sorts) the most esteemed is what they call 'lapis lazuli'. 'Tis blue, streaked
with gold, and is so scarce at present that it sells for above its weight in
gold. They have of late years found out a way of imitating this at Venice,
and 'tis of this imitation that our knives and fork handles are made.[1] I have
been thinking all this morning how pretty they must look with your china
plates and the various fruits of my garden at Birchanger.

All Essex, to be sure, will be astonished at it, and it may afford some
talk to the good people in the Orcades of Scotland. Who knows but what
the double-sighted men and women in those parts have already seen them
in vision, and are now blessing the name of Joseph Spanco for bringing
such beauties into the island of Great Britain? They are no doubt already
scouring out their plaids and preparing to toss them over their left shoulders,
in order to come and see a dozen of such beauties as no common northern
eye was ever yet blessed with the sight of: and I am afraid we shall be
pestered with broad-talking visitors (some with packs upon their backs,
like prudent travellers to save the expense of the journey; some with their
wooden swords by their sides, by way of ornament and finery; some
scratching their ears for admiration, and others their hands for another

393

reason) to such a degree, that we shall perhaps wish our lapis lazuli again at Venice, or at the bottom of the Adriatic, rather than to be pestered so much (as we must expect to be) by so many wild English, sputtering out their admiration all together with coarse voices and in an unknown tongue. The very thoughts of it are so terrifying to me, that I am in some doubts whether I shall bring them along with me or leave them here, for our barns will never hold the numbers of Highlanders that will be footing it over the Tweed to see them. What would you advise me do? Well, I'll leave it to Providence, and bring them along with me. I am ever

Your serious humble servant

J.S.⟩

1. On June 14 Lady Pomfret wrote from Venice: 'We went in our gondola to Murano, another little city in the Lagunes. Here they make looking-glass; and here (what we call in England) Milan-stone is made, as well as the false lapis-lazuli, with the broken glass, filings of brass &c. thrown into a furnace' (*Hertford Corresp.* III, 228).

Most of the fortnight was spent with the Pomfrets. On Tuesday, June 13, writes Lady Pomfret, 'We found all the English at home . . . and they staid the evening with us.' On Thursday, 'In the evening . . . we went, with lord Lincoln, Mr. Naylor, and signor Uguccioni, to the place of St. Mark, to see the masks. . . .' On Saturday, June 17, 'The first thing I heard this morning was, that the doge died suddenly.' We were solicited 'to stay and see the coronation of a new doge, which they all say is full of diversions and magnificence,' but Saturday was the Pomfrets' day of departure; their boxes were all packed. 'Lord Lincoln took leave, as setting out to-night for Padua', on his way to Genoa and France. This was merely Lincoln's stratagem to see Lady Sophia once more, for landing in Padua Sunday at night, writes Lady Pomfret, 'we found my lord Lincoln and Mr. Naylor, who supped with us.' But the separation could no longer be postponed. On Tuesday, June 20, 'Betwixt eight and nine this morning we took our leave of lord Lincoln . . . and began our journey . . . to Vicenza' (Hertford Corresp. III, 228–32, 238–44).

Horace Walpole, in the meantime, was busy in Venice observing the events following the death of the Doge: 'We have been in confusion about the new election: no one would stand for it, no one would accept it. The Barnabotti, or poor nobles who live at St. Barnabas, have been distracted; they used to sell their votes, and here was no chapman. The Procurator Grimani, formerly ambassador to England, has been prevailed on to accept the dignity, with the addition of three thousand ducats a year; and the privilege of giving the long sleeve to his nephew or grandson, which formerly was confined to the Doge's son or brother. He will be chose on Saturday; there will be three feasts for him, and three for a new Procurator' (to Mann, June 29, 1741, Corresp. XVII, 75–6).

*167

Source: Egerton 2234 ff. 271–2
Addressed: as in 74
Endorsed: a. the act/of ye coronation of ye new Doge
b. The New Doge's procession/round ye
place of S. Mark, &c.
red wafer

Venice,
July 5, 1741

⟨Dear Mother,⟩

I told you in my last[1] that the death of the Doge had prevented our leaving
this place:[2] we have now seen the coronation of the new one,[3] and shall
soon be going on. He was crowned the first of this month, and carried all
round the Place of St. Mark, in a machine something like an old triumphal
chariot, on men's shoulders. There were between twenty and thirty of his
workmen in the Arsenal that performed this office. The machine would hold
five or six people very well: at present there was the Doge himself, two of
the chief senators, and the little boy who assisted at the balloting on his
election. You must have heard my good old uncle Harry Neville talk of
balloting, for 'twas a thing he understood perhaps better than any man in
England, and what he has wrote a great deal about[4] ⟨so that I shall not
explain it to you: and indeed there's another very good reason for my not
doing so, which is that I don't at all understand it⟩.

The whole place (which is very large) was so full of people, that about
six foot above the ground it looked all as if it were paved with heads.
Several of the Arsenal-men, each with a red baton, kept the whole line clear
where the triumphal chariot was to pass. The Doge had a sack of money
open by him, and all the way, as he passed along, tossed out handfuls of
crowns and half-crowns among the mob: which gave me much more
diversion than the sight of his Serenity. From the Church of St. Mark quite
down to the bottom of the place, and then all along to the door of the
palace, it was all one scramble: and I believe one may say with great
veracity that the Venetians are the best scramblers in the whole world.

Just by the entrance to the palace was the highest diversion: there is the
Broglio, the walk, at some times wholly appropriated to the Venetian nobles.
When he is over against that, 'tis said that he flings handfuls of gold (the
usual coin here is sequins, like our half-guineas), and many a good senator
is there with his hands and cap held up to catch what he can among the
crowd. There are others with odd bags at the end of long poles, which

395

they manage very dexterously to fish at the money whilst 'tis flying in the air. These bags are made somewhat like a hoop-petticoat, tied fast at top, and ⟨saving your presence⟩ turned upside down, the bottom with a hoop to it gaping in the air to catch all the money it can.

One fellow, in particular, was got on the top of one of the columns at the entrance to the palace, and as they had but little space to stand upon there, and might lose their balance in the eagerness of fishing, he had tied a girdle round the bottom of the upper pillar and fastened a basket to it, in which he stood and caught crowns and half-guineas, to the admiration of all the beholders. 'Tis said he got more than any five of all the other money-fishers, though there were many very expert ones employed that way. For three days the Doge flung about money and bread too in his palace, and I counted at one time above fifty of these hoop-petticoats, darting about in the air, in a space scarce so big as ⌜Mrs. Morecroft's garden⌝.[5] ⟨I am, with all services to all friends,

Your most dutiful and affectionate

J. Spence.⟩

1. Missing; probably dated June 23.

2. Luigi Pisani, Doge of Venice 1735–41, died on June 17.

3. Pietro Grimani (1677–1752), Venetian Ambassador in London 1710–13 and in Vienna 1715–20. 'He is rich and powerful,' writes Horace Walpole, 'for which reasons they wanted him Doge; he has five brothers and two nephews in the senate, who all lose their votes on his election' (*Corresp.* XVII, 75–6).

4. Henry Neville (see *Letters* 105, 162) as 'one of the chief persons of James Harrington's commonwealths men', frequented in 1659 'Miles's Coffee-house', where his 'smart ... discourses about government and ordering of a commonwealth' were attended by a crowd of 'disciples and virtuosi'. 'This gang had a balloting box, and balloted how things should be carried by way of *tentamens*; which being not used or known in England before [made] the room every evening ... very full. ... The greatest of the parliament men hated this design of rotation and balloting, as being against their power. ... Hen. Neville ... proposed it to the house, and made it out to the members thereof, that except they embraced that way of government they would be ruined' (A. Wood, *Athenae Oxonienses*, ed. Bliss, III, 1119–20).

5. Emended to 'a little garden (18 paces by 24)'.

168

Source: Egerton 2234 ff. 273–4
Addressed: as in 74
Endorsed: a. an act of/the fine concerts perform'd at/
            venice; by women only & the/finest of any:
            b. The Fine female Con-/certs at Venice.
            red wafer

Genoa,
July 24, 1741
⟨We had very favourable weather hither; and are all quite well⟩

⟨Dear Mother,⟩

We left Venice some time ago, and are got here to Genoa, where, as 'tis
just half way of our journey (reckoning from Naples to England), we shall
stay some time to refresh ourselves.[1]

Whilst we were at Venice, I was several times very finely entertained
with a thing which I should acquaint you with. It has long been my
opinion that the ladies (if they applied themselves to them) would excel the
men in the practice of the finer arts, such as poetry, painting,[2] and music.
We had a proof of this, in part, during our stay at Venice. I think the best
and exactest concert I ever heard in my life was performed there, all by
women. The Roman Catholic countries excel us in variety of public
charities: in some of these houses at Venice where they have a number of
young girls, they have had a very good thought. Those that have fine
voices are taught to sing, and those who show some genius for music have
masters for the particular instruments they are inclined to. These, every
holiday (which is near one third of the year in Italy) have concerts in the
church of their particular hospitals,[3] and there are no less than four of these
concerts every holiday at Venice: at the Hospitaletto, the Mendicanti, the
Pietà, and the Incurabili. The Pietà is the house for young innocents that
come into the world without any fault of their own: these are famous for
instrumental music,[4] and the Catharina there brings finer notes out of a
violin than perhaps any man in England ever could. The Incurabili is chiefly
for orphans: and the young women there excel in voices—not but what their
instrumental music too is some of the best in the world. The most famous
voices here are the Isabetta, the Emilia, the Teresa, and the Cecilia.[5] Teresa's
voice is weaker than the rest, but extremely sweet, various, and flexible;
Emilia's is stronger and very delicious: one word which she sings in
salutation to the Virgin is almost worth all the singing on our side the
Alps; but the chief of them all is the Isabetta: her voice surprises one every

397

time she sings. 'Tis as full and as rich as a man's, with all the fineness and softness of a woman's. She makes one tremble with pleasure to hear her.[6]

What a very pretty method have they found out of enlivening the manners of an hospital, of getting money to the society, and sometimes fortunes to themselves: as at this very time, Emilia (one of those whom I have just mentioned) is going to be married to a gentleman in Venice. He fell in love with her voice, and a good old lady, who had been a constant hearer and admirer of her, gives her a fortune of above a thousand pound (which is two or three times as much in Italy as it would be in England) to make her a proper match for him. Things of this kind happen ever[y] now and then: and if they did not, how delightful at least must it render their way of living to have so fine music so perpetually practised within their walls? The worst of it is that these nightingales are pent up in a cage of an organ loft, and are scarce to be seen through the grates of it.[7] ⟨I have no more room, and therefore am, with all services to all friends,

Your dutiful and affectionate

J: Spence.⟩

1. They left Venice, together with Horace Walpole, on July 12, and via Padua (13), Vicenza (14), Verona (15), Mantua (16), Cremona (17), Tortona (18), reached Genoa on July 19.

2. Spence may be thinking more particularly of Lady Mary, whom he met again at Genoa, and of Rosalba Carriera, the Venetian portrait painter.

3. The *conservatorios* were originally four 'hospitals' for foundlings and orphans. In the mid-17th century music became an essential element of the instruction, and in the 18th century they developed into the best musical *scuole* in Europe.

4. 'Celui des quatre hôpitaux où je vais le plus souvent, et où je m'amuse le mieux, c'est l'hôpital de la Piété; c'est aussi le premier pour la perfection des symphonies' (De Brosses, I, 238).

5. In March 1740 Lady Mary heard 'a Consort of voices & instruments at the Hospital of the Incurabili, where there are 2 Girls that in the Opinion of all people excel either Faustina or Cuzoni' (*Complete Letters*, II, 180).

6. 'La Zabetta, des Incurables, est surtout étonnante par l'étendue de sa voix, et les coups d'archet qu'elle a dans le gosier, comme si elle maniait le violon de Somis. C'est elle qui enlève tous les suffrages; ce serait vouloir se faire battre par la populace que d'égaler quelque autre à elle, mais ... je vous dirai à l'oreille que la Margarita, des *Mendicanti*, la vaut bien et me plaît davantage' (ibid.).

7. In 1754 Rousseau complained: 'Ce qui me désolait était ces maudites grilles qui ne laissaient passer que des sons et me cachaient les anges de beauté dont ils étaient dignes.' Perhaps it was just as well that Spence did not see them. When Rousseau at length received permission to visit the Mendicanti, 'M. le Blond me présenta l'une après l'autre ces chanteuses célèbres dont la voix et le nom étaient tout ce qui m'était connu. Venez Sophie ... elle était horrible. Venez, Cattina ... elle était borgne. Venez Bettina ... la petite vérole l'avait défigurée. Presque pas une n'était sans quelque notable défaut' (*Confessions*, II, vii).

On July 19 Horace Walpole wrote to Horace Mann, describing the journey from Venice to Genoa: 'You will laugh to hear how we shortened the tediousness of the last day; as

Lord Lincoln rode, Mr. Spence and I went together in the chaise; and employed ourselves
the whole day in counting the number of loaded mules etc. that we met on the road: they
amounted to eight hundred forty-seven. I once counted only on the Bouquet four
hundred and fifty, but that was earlier in the morning. We were so intent on this diversion,
that we were literally sorry whenever we came within sight of the post-house; would you
believe that possible?

'*Lord Lincoln, I told you, rode most of the way,* pour se dissiper: *he is quite melancholy,*
and one day that we went together, talked to me the whole time of Lady Sophia. He says
he is determined not to engage with her again on his return, unless he can settle his affairs
so as to marry her. He is resolved to try all ways to have her, for, says he, nobody can say
she wants anything but fortune: and added "till now I never wished for riches." I pity his
determination of marrying much more than his present pain' (Corresp. *XVII, 91*).

---

1 6 9

Source:	Egerton 2234 ff. 275–6
Addressed:	*as in 74*
Postmarked:	8 AV
Franked:	Free/Andrew Stone
Endorsed:	*a.* they landed at/St Antibes in france
	b. not to be copied.
	red wafer

Antibes,
July 31, 1741

⟨Dear Mother,

I reckon you have been for some time in a little sort of a fright, either about
our crossing the Alps, or passing the sea. You may now be quite at your
ease as to both, for we are well and safe in France, and have been here these
two days. We set out from Genoa the 28th at seven in the morning, and
landed here (at Antibes) the 29th, about three in the afternoon.[1] We had so
fair a wind that we came near a hundred mile the last day, and the whole
voyage was to me as agreeable as an airing in a pleasure-boat on the
Thames.[2] We have not suffered anything from heat as yet, either by sea or
land, and find the air very temperate here. In short is seems to have been
a summer made a purpose for us, to travel without any inconvenience in
July and August.

We set out in our chaises tomorrow morning for Fréjus, and so shall go
on by very easy journeys for Montpellier and Vigan. Vigan is the place
where Lady Lincoln lived with her children for a year or two,[3] in the
Cévennes, among the Protestants, and in one of the finest airs in the world,
in spite of which she lost her eldest son there,[4] but brought off my good

Lord stronger and better than she carried him—though I dare say they will be surprised to see how much stronger and better he is grown now.[5] We shall stay there a week or two to rest and refresh ourselves, and then go on for Paris. 'Tis said that the name of Lady Lincoln is blessed by all the good people in the Cévennes, among whom she did a world of good, as I don't doubt we shall have the pleasure of hearing and seeing when we come there. I shall write to you again, either from Montpellier or from Vigan; rather the latter, because 'twill be a place of rest for us. Lord Lincoln and Mr. Walpole are very well, and very much your humble servants, and I am ever, with all services to all friends,

Your most dutiful and affectionate

J: Spence.⟩

1. On July 29 Lady Mary wrote from Genoa: 'Lord Lincoln and Mr. Walpole (youngest Son to Sir R[obert]) left this place 2 days ago. They visited me during their short stay. They are gone to Marseilles and design passing some months in the South of France' (*Complete Letters*, II, 245).

2. 'In passing from Genoa to Antibes we saw the Spanish packetboat in the port of San Remo and Lord Lincoln passed two other Spanish vessels at Arassi. The Torbia appeared very plain, both before and after we had doubled the Cape of Monaco. We dined soon after in an arched cave just by Nice, and drank of the spring that runs out of it into the sea. The country about Antibes looked very pretty after the rocky views we had been used to' (*Nbk.* 3 81r).

3. Several of Lady Lincoln's letters, written from Vigan in 1733, are among the Newcastle MSS, deposited at the University of Nottingham.

4. George (Jan. 16, 1718-30), heir of the family. The youngest son, Thomas (b. 1723), died three years old, and of the five daughters four died in infancy: Margaret (b. 1722), Anne (1724), Grace (1726), and Caroline. Only Lucy, Lincoln's eldest sister (1721-63) survived (A. Collins, *Peerage of England* [1756], II, 166-7).

5. When they left England in 1739 Lincoln was 'not of so strong a make' (*Letter* 75). On his first appearance at court in November 1741 George II said: '*Lord Lincoln is the handsomest man in England*' (*H. W. Corresp.* XVII, 210).

Notebook 3
(37–39) 81r–82r

Between *Antibes* [July 29–31] and *Fréjus* we passed the mountains of L'Éstrelle; no town but a post-house, very prettily placed on the side of one of the hills (orange-trees in the garden and the cool air there) and with a hanging wood all above it. As I walked almost all the post to it [August 1], I had time to observe the pretty views among those hills and the roadside which is all just like a physic garden. (The brown and yellowish lizard of two feet long.) There seems to be a run of hills from these all along the seaside to Marseilles. 'Twas in going along the champain the next day that we saw the countrymen setting fire to the standing stubble on the wind side and the fire running on so swiftly along the field (as it is often described by the Latin poets). The day before: the fishers' dance at *Cannes*, the first post from Antibes.

Toulon [Aug. 2–3] is but an indifferent, noisy, disagreeable town—but has a good safe port, and even the *rade* looks all land-locked, with waving hills that seem to shut it in all round. There is a fort out on each side and the ships get out to sea by that on the left hand. The officer who showed us the store-houses told us that they had 25 men of war there and two new ones a building, but Capt. Hope and Ransford (who are so well acquainted with that port) assured us there was but 16 or 17.

In the last post to *Marseilles* [Aug. 4–5] you begin to see that neater pleasing air in the houses which reigns there, and at *Aix* [Aug. 6], and in all the country round about them. The *cours* at Aix is perhaps what makes it be called so pretty a town. 'Tis 1500 f. long and 125 f. broad (20 f. street, 20 f. sidewalks, 45 middle; 20 side and 20 street). Four streets fall into it on each side at right angles, opposite to each other, most of them *tirés à corde*. There are two fountains in the great walk which fall in with the line of the two middle streets on each side. At the lower end of the *cours* is a larger fountain and basin, and the trees are planted semicircularly there to humour it. The other trees in general are planted the two inward rows to answer one another, but not to answer the outward rows, which occasions a mixture of variety and uniformity together, and which (with the trees that are wanting here and there by accident) gives it a more wild and woody look than regular walks generally have. At the end you have a pretty view over the city-wall which rises there only as a parapet: the ground slopes from it, then rises gently in little hills covered with cornfields, which is followed by a long rising, quite to the horizon. ('Twas on the first hill—or rather rising— that we saw what appeared from the *cours* like a town of corn-ricks: near a hundred of them together, some less and some greater, and generally squared like houses, and the number of horses *treading out* the corn in the different areas between them: in some two, in some four, in some eight, and in some twelve going their rounds all together.) This is so common in the south of France that we did not see any one person *threshing* corn, till we came to *Béziers* (where, by the way, we had the best bread that we met with upon all the road).

Avignon [Aug. 7] is an ugly old-fashioned town in a very pretty country: the Rhône washes its walls on one side (for it seems to be a sort of square) with a fine long island in it that, as it were, divides it into two rivers on that side, and there are the remains of a bridge which went over both of them and the island quite from Avignon to the Castle of [Philip the Fair]. As to its vastness, it looks more like the remains of the Roman grandeur than the work of a little province, and the workmanship itself has a better air than one would expect. They say 'twas above a mile long, and I believe it could not want much of it. If so, it far exceeded the bridge at St. Esprit, the longest I have ever passed.

At *Nîmes* [Aug. 9] they were very busy about the baths that have been lately discovered there: the ground was all laid open and the foundations appear all very distinctly. There was a large square building in the middle: round this are all the old channels for the conveyance of the water, and round them thick walls with large niches in the inside of them. It seems to have been of a very good taste and probably of Hadrian's time. The *femme à quatre jambes* has a vast beard— perhaps a Jupiter? Whatever it is, 'tis very indifferent work.

170

Source: Egerton 2234 ff. 277–8
Addressed: as in 74
Postmarked: 18 AV
Franked: Free/Andrew Stone
Endorsed: b. Of yᵉ Shadowyness of Cap: Rolle/not to be Copied.
red wafer

Montpellier,
August 14, 1741

⟨Dear Mother,

I had received no letter from you for above eight weeks, but was in no manner of pain about it, because I had ordered them in general to this place. In our last day hither, I said in the chaise, that I should meet with six letters from you here,[1] and so I did—exactly that number from you, and one from Captain Rolle. The Captain mentions a thing in his letter which charms me extremely, and for which I shall think myself ever obliged to you. His accident of being robbed of all he had, and left stripped and tied in a wood, I learned by the English newspapers whilst we were at Rome:[2] but I did not know the kind offer you had made him, which is just the very thing I should have done myself had I been in England, had I had but fifty pound in the world and he in want of it. His letter is all full of gratitude and fondness for you, and the rascal calls you his mother, and pretends to rival me in your affections, for which I shall have a pull at his weasel-face the very first time I meet him. A thin leather-chopped whelp! He think of supplanting me, who am, at this present writing, rather plump than otherwise, and (thanks to heaven) in good liking. If I had him here, I could see the sun through him, and when I catch him in London I don't know whether I shan't make a lantern of him; 'tis nothing but putting a lighted candle down his throat, and the first linkboy I meet shall take him by the head and carry him about the streets to light me to the tavern o'nights: a little, thin, transparent insignificant thing! He think of supplanting me in your affections, or to compliment me only with the rights of an elder brother, as he has the insolent humility of saying in his letter! No, No, I don't desire any brotherhood with a shadow: let him get under an elm-tree when the sun shines, and he may there meet a fitter brother for him than I am. To be a brother to him is next door to being a brother to nothing: and so I think I have done with him, till he provokes me again. The rogues that robbed him would have taken away his body too perhaps, had not it been thinner and more wore out than his shirt: but I will have patience and leave him to be blowed away, with dry leaves and butterfly-wings, next autumn.[3]

We are now got over all the hottest part of our journey, and in three days shall be in a climate that is but very little warmer than England. We set out from hence tomorrow for Paris, by Narbonne, Toulouse, and Orleans. The French are so polite, and we (if you please) so prudent, that we don't meet with the least inconvenience in travelling through France, even in the present situation of affairs.[4] It has been always my opinion we should not have a war with them, and I am still in no apprehension of one, at least before the next spring. If there should be one sooner, they always give three months for the strangers that are in France to settle their affairs before they go away, and at Paris, we shall be within three days' journey of England. When we are at Paris, I shall consult about our way of going from Calais to Dover, and have the good luck to be with people that you may be sure will be taken care of: if it should be necessary I don't doubt but we could get a man of war ⟨or so⟩ to guard us;[5] but I apprehend it would be needless. I shall know when I get there. I am ever,

Your dutiful and affectionate

J. Spence.⟩

1. They reached Montpellier on Aug. 10 and stayed to 'rest' till Aug. 15.

2. 'On Friday last [Mar. 13] about two o'Clock in the Afternoon the Rev. Mr. Rolle, of New College in Oxford, in coming from that Place to London, was attack'd at the Bottom of Stokenchurch-Hill by a seeming Country Fellow in his own Hair, aged about 40, and mounted on a sorry brown Horse, who forced him into a Wood, and took from him ten Guineas in Money, a Watch, and a Pair of Silver Spurs' (*The London Evening Post*, March 17–19, 1741).

3. This was a favourite jest. 'The fellow's a good-natured fellow,' Spence wrote to Massingberd (July 31, 1739), 'only he's too lank and meagre. I wish he were fatter. I have

seen as proper men as him cut out of a cheese-paring after supper' (*N & Q*, vol. 188 [1945], p. 253).

4. Rumours of expected war with France were continuous. On May 10 Horace Walpole wrote from Reggio: 'I am going from hence to Venice, in a fright lest there be a war with France, and then I must drag myself through Germany' (*Corresp.* XIII, 243). See also *Letter* 173.

5. In October Lincoln wrote from Paris to the D. of Newcastle: 'I should think it is not at all necessary to send a convoy for me. . . . I will certainly be at Calais, the day you shall know time enough, if you still think it absolutely necessary for me to be convoyed into England' (*Letter* 178).

Notebook 3
(39–41) 82ʳ–83ʳ

One sees the Pyreneans very plain in going from *Montpellier* to *Narbonne* [Aug. 17] and coasts them afterwards through a more bleak and barren kind of country quite to *Carcassone*. 'Twas by Béziers that we saw the hill that vessels may go up, in what they call the Great Canal of Languedoc. 'Tis like a pair of stairs composed of sluices. There are eight sluices, or steps, to it, the perpendicular rising of each about ten foot. The canal in general is much narrower than I expected to find it, and the entrance to the highest of these sluices in particular is not twenty foot over, so that no vessel twenty foot wide can pass down the canal. I should question whether it answers its expense. Is it much used? I don't remember that we saw any one boat, going or coming, in any part we saw of the canal.

In the same post we walked through what they call the Montagne Percée. The greatest height of this hill, if it may be called a hill, cannot be I think above fifty foot from the level of the water. You go down fifty-six steps of about eight inches each (which is 37 f. 4 inch.) to the entrance, and the rising above the highest step is not considerable. Below, the work looks really noble and great. 'Tis of the breadth of the canal, with a raised paved walk on each side, in all perhaps forty feet, is turned all along in an arch, and the greatest part of it is all lined with smooth handsome stonework. The whole length of it is 470 f. (or 235 of my paces) of which 326 f. is handsomely arched with stone. (The odd insect we found in it.)

I have said already that the country from Narbonne to Carcassone is all bleak and Alpine. As soon as you get out of Carcassone it begins to mend, and improves all on till you come to *Montauban* [Aug. 20–21]. The view of all the country about Montauban is still and delightful. It gives a sort of serenity to the mind, like the view of the Bay of Naples, or the pleasingness of laudanum. The city of Montauban itself is placed on a rising that looks more like a great natural terrace than a hill: the river runs all along at the foot of this terrace, though it winds to it and from it, which has a very good effect: the little isles that appear in it, with the wood and willow plantations, and the fine champain country that spreads on all to the west, make a very pleasing prospect (either about sunrising, when you see it most distinctly, or at sunset, when you have the accident of gilded clouds or streaks of red to terminate it).

171

Source: Egerton 2234 ff. 279–80
Addressed: *as in* 74
Endorsed: *a.* in/the south of france
b. not to be Copied.
red wafer

Montauban,
August 21, 1741

⟨Dear Mother,

We are now got to Montauban,[1] over all the worst of our journey, in a temperate climate and absolutely the prettiest part I have seen of all France. We have stayed here a day or two,[2] and could very willingly stay longer, but business must be done, and tomorrow we set out for Paris, where we must take some time to rest and enjoy ourselves after so long rolling from one inn to another, which has been our case these three months: and then for old England, hoy! We are all very well, and I hope to be able to write the same to you eight or nine days hence, from the good town of Paris. In the meantime and ever I am

Your most dutiful and affectionate

Joseph Spence

The day we set out from Montpellier, we set out in a shower, which was the more welcome, because 'tis a received maxim in the South of France that the first rains in August lay the heats. We have found it to be very true, at least this August, to our very great pleasure and comfort. At present we are quite out of the hot part of the world, and 'tis as pleasant travelling as in May.⟩

1. From Montpellier by way of Pézénas (Aug. 16), Narbonne (17), Castelnaudary (18), and Toulouse (19). 2. Aug. 20 21.

Notebook 3

(41–42) 83ʳ⁻ᵛ

The country from Montauban to Brives is all hilly and barren, and I think the most inconvenient travelling for a chaise that ever I went. Beside the roughness and steepness of the road, the posts are very ill furnished with houses, and I was forced to walk a post and a half of those eternal Yorkshire posts afoot—not to mention how often we were forced to be assisted by oxen to be got up the hills.

At *Brives* one gets rid of these inconveniences and come[s] into a beautiful country, like the Birchanger part of Essex, only finer and with more enlarged views. They run much on chestnut woods and walnuts even all along the roadside.

Limoges [Aug. 26] is a very ugly town, very finely situated, on the side of an easy and noble rising ground. In Berry we first saw corn of several sorts standing and some wheat cut but not carried in. (In the State of Venice all was housed when we passed it, so that the harvest must have been two months earlier there than in this part of France.) 'Tis all on open and poor country, and looked still worse when we saw it, from the great drought of that summer.

At *Orleans* [Aug. 27–28] I took more notice of the statue of the Pucelle (on the great bridge over the Loire) than I ever had done formerly. In the midst is a statue of the Virgin Mary sitting with the dead Christ over her knees: on her right hand is the king [   ] in armour, kneeling, and on her left the Pucelle, ditto. The Pucelle looks at first as much like a man as the king does, and is only to be distinguished by her long hair which is collected in a knot and then falls in eight or nine waving lines all down her back. Both she and the king had dry garlands on their heads, which is one of the species of worship in fashion among the Catholics as it was formerly among the heathens.

172

Source: Egerton 2234 ff. 281–2
Addressed: as in 74
Endorsed: b. not to be copied

Paris,
September 1, 1741

⟨Dear Mother,

I can at last have the satisfaction of telling you that we are got safe and well to Paris, where we are already settled, and quite at home.[1] I went last night into the warm bath, a thing which makes one almost forget that we have made any journey at all. I am much delighted with the news of Miss Flora's being so well married,[2] and wish her elder sister had had the same good luck, for she will begin to be what they call an old maid, and won't grumble perhaps the less for being alone under that most intolerable of all misfortunes. My next letter to you will probably be longer; at present we are just going out to pay the visits we received yesterday. I am with all services to all friends ever

Your most affectionate and dutiful

Jos: Spence.⟩

1. They arrived on Aug. 29 from Orléans, where they had stopped for two days, and stayed with Horace Walpole 'at the Hôtel de Luxembourg, Rue des Petits Augustins; Lord Chesterfield was there at the same time' (*H. W.* *Corresp.* XIII, 11 n. 68) talking to Spence about vices of young people and boasting about 'putassiers': 'J'ai l'honneur d'en être [un], Monsieur' (*Obs.* Nos. 1043–5).

2. Not identified.

173

Source: Egerton 2234 ff. 283–4
Addressed: as in 74
Endorsed: *a.* home affaires/upon his being near comeing/
to england, & Lord Lincolns Letter inclosed
in this
b. This (& the next after; L^d L^s:) not to/be
copied.
red wafer

Paris,
September 9, 1741

⟨Dear Mother,

This is my second letter to you from the good city of Paris, where we are
all very well. 'Tis said that the Cardinal de Fleury has declared that if
anything should happen between England and France,[1] the gentlemen who
are here on a visit shall be considered always as friends, and the merchants
and people established here would have six months allowed them for
conveying away their effects and settling their affairs. The truth is that war
of late years is not quite so rude a thing as it was in days of yore, and has
admitted of some sort of politeness among all its roughnesses and horrors.
In our last war with France[2] there were several civil messages occasionally
sent from our generals to theirs, and kindnesses often offered, though not so
often accepted. When Turin was besieged,[3] the French general sent to the
Duke of Savoy to know where his quarters in the city were 'that they
might not direct any of their bombs to that part of the city': the Duke's
answer was 'that he was obliged to be everywhere'. This was a civility
unknown to former ages, though that siege was carried on with as much
fury, and as much damage in general, as any in that whole war.[4]

I wrote to you from Orleans,[5] to know your inclinations and orders about
our settling in England, and shall be very glad of them that I may set to
work as soon as we are at London. I should think four good rooms on a
first floor, with the use of kitchen, brewhouse, washhouse and cellaring
would do our business very well. We must be in a house where there is a
family all the summer, because of our going on then into Essex. One would
have it near the Park,[6] for the convenience of walking and air, and I fancy
our old place of Queen's Street (or somewhere thereabout) will still do best,
because of the houses being so much cheaper that way than on the Pall
Mall side. If you should be still for that part of the town, I shall look upon
the builders of the New Bridge[7] as our singular benefactors, for that will be
a great convenience to let us into the Surrey side of the country and the
diversion of seeing Vaux-Hall: which is a sight that they tell me is

improved,[8] and which was better (even before I came abroad this time) than any diversion I have met with on the continent. 'Tis a wonder nobody endeavours to imitate it in some of the great cities in Italy, and at Florence in particular, where during all the summer the people of any fashion lie abed the greatest part of the day, and walk about in the fresh air almost all the night.

I think you have not once mentioned to me my little garden at Birchanger. I suppose by this time my plantation has throve so much that it may be grown too mighty for it, and when one enters it one is got into a thicket and scarce able to stir. If it should be so, 'tis easy enough at any time to thin it, and there's nothing I should like better than to have a wild wood, and to have the pruning of it myself. I don't think it would be amiss if you design to favour it with a visit next spring,[9] that I should go down eight or ten days before you to get the gravel walks laid and everything else in order to receive you. However, we shall have time enough to talk of that this winter by our coal fire; and in expectation of the pleasure of seeing you in some weeks, talking over these matters for some months, and living pretty comfortably together for some scores of years (if it please heaven to make us such an unreasonable old couple), I am, with all services to all friends

Your most affectionate and dutiful

Jos: Spence

I send you enclosed a letter from Lord Lincoln, who would have wrote to you much sooner, had not he been willing to be in a place of safety first: and the first week we were so, you see he has wrote it, and so has been (not like most Lords) as good as his word.⟩

1. In August 1741 there were rumours that 'the *French* and *Spaniards* intend a Descent upon *Britain* with their Joint Forces' (*Gent. Mag.*, 1741, p. 446). André Hercule de Fleury (1653–1743) was the French 'Prime Minister' since 1726, though he never assumed the title.

2. 'Marlborough's war' (1701–13).

3. May 13–Sept. 8, 1706.

4. The incident occurred June 7, 1706, when the Count de Marignani 'maréchal des logis de la cavalerie française' sent by the French commander La Feuillade, asked to be informed 'où était dans la ville, le quartier du duc pour le préserver de la fureur ... et offrait en même temps, des passeports aux Princesses Souveraines pour se retirer de la place' (Solar de la Marguerite, *Journal historique du siège ... de Turin en 1706* [Amsterdam, 1708], p. 18. For other versions of the incident, see *Le Campagne di Guerra in Piemonte, 1703–1708* [Turin, 1907], VII, 247).

5. Missing (dated Aug. 27 or 28). Spence

wrote on this subject in April from Rome (*Letter* 157).

6. Between 1741 and 1748 a number of letters were addressed to Spence at Stratton Street, near Picadilly.

7. The first stone of the new Westminster Bridge was laid Jan. 29, 1738/9. Spence's joy, however, was premature, for it was not opened till Nov. 18, 1750 (Wheatley and Cunningham, *London Past and Present* [1891], III, 481).

8. The Vauxhall Gardens had been reopened June 7, 1732, under new management by Jonathan Tyers, who employed among others Hogarth and Roubilliac 'to enlarge the beauty and attractions of the ground' (ibid., 428).

9. The following summer Spence was to lose his 'little garden at Birchanger' for the more valuable living of Great Horwood in Buckinghamshire, presented to him by the Warden and Fellows of New College (Wright, p. 68).

174

Source: Egerton 2234 f. 285
Endorsed: *see* 173

LINCOLN TO MRS. SPENCE

Paris,
September 9, 1741[1]

Madam,

I must own all appearances are against me, and don't in the least doubt
but you have often pitied your poor son, for being two years with a person
so rude and ill-bred, who could be capable of letting so many months pass
without thanking you for your obliging letter.[2] But now, Madam, for my
own justification I must beg leave to take up a little of your time, and give
you my reasons for my not troubling you sooner with my letter.[3] Thought I
to myself, what signifies my writing to Mrs. Spence at present, when I know
by this time she is easy and satisfied, and has received dozens of letters from
that very son for whom she had expressed so much concern in not hearing
from. (You see, Madam, I begin well in concluding not to write to you, but
I beg leave, one word more.) I long argued to myself. I said we have a long
tedious journey to take, seas to traverse, full of Spanish vessels, the violent
and scorching heats of France and Italy to go through, and numberless
other dangers; for what purpose then should I at present write to Mrs.
Spence and tell her that her son is well and in perfect health, when she must
necessarily know the many accidents that may happen in so long and
dangerous a journey. But whenever we are at Paris, with what pleasure shall
I write to the fondest of all mothers, and let her know that she has now
nothing to apprehend from either land or sea, for these have brought to her
safe and sound so very near home the best of all sons, and the best of friends,
and that now in all human appearance there is no manner of likelihood of
your losing him. And give me leave to tell you that, except yourself, there
is nobody upon earth would have suffered so much if any misfortune had
happened as your humble servant. You see, Madam, my way of reasoning,
whether good or bad I must leave it to you to decide, but whether that
decision is in my favour or no, to make matters sure, I am fully resolved as

soon as ever you are in town, to wait upon you and make my excuses in person. Till when I am, Madam,

Your most obedient servant,

Lincoln

1. Lincoln's letter was enclosed in the previous one.
2. Probably written on the occasion of his twenty-first birthday. See *Letter* 157.

3. The true reason was, no doubt, that 'Lord Lincoln abominates writing of letters' (*Letter* 76).

175

Source: Add. MSS 33065 f. 457–8
Endorsed: R[eceived] 17th

LINCOLN TO NEWCASTLE

Paris,
September 14, 1741

My Lord,

I should have immediately on receiving your message from Mr. Thompson[1] been preparing things in order for setting out, had not it been for a reason which I think your Grace can't but approve of. I shall tell it you in as few words as possible, because 'tis a subject I don't care to talk much of. The result of my thoughts in relation to my Lady Sophy (and I have now had a good deal of time to think of it) is that it would be unhappy both for myself and her to carry that affair so far as I might otherwise have wished, and as that is the case, I would for her sake and my own avoid any occasions of meeting.

The reason I before wanted to stay longer out of England was not to be at the Birthday[2] where I could not have avoided it, and I was unwilling too to come to England about the same time they did, because that might increase a report which I hear is but too much about town already. Were I to set out in a few days, 'tis very probable I should meet Lord Pomfret at Calais, for by a letter he sent to a gentleman here a few days ago, he says he shall set out very soon for that place.[3] The coming into England so together might justify the town in such a report [as] might do hurt to her, and I can't say that I could by any means answer for myself. My staying here some time would every way have a contrary effect; I therefore hope your Grace will approve of it.

I can't imagine by what I hear in this place that if a war was to break out immediately it would be of any ill consequence to the English here. In the common course of things if they are like to run in a more violent channel than usual, and your Grace should think it proper, I could remove from hence to Holland; if there is no particular danger could stay here till I could come into England (with any decency) after the Birthday. I leave it to your Grace's better judgement what I should do, and am my Lord your Grace's

most affectionate and dutiful nephew

Lincoln

1. Rev. Anthony Thompson, British chargé d'affaires at Paris 1740–4, later Dean of Raphoe.
2. The royal birthday on Friday, Oct. 30, was an occasion for a formal ball. (George II was born Nov. 10, 1683 N.S.)
3. On their return to England through Germany the Pomfrets reached Brussels in August, but were detained there by a 'long depending business' of Lord Pomfret's (*Hertford Corresp.* III, 413). They arrived in London Oct. 9 O.S. (*Daily Advertiser*, Oct. 12 O.S.).

176

Source: Add. MSS 33065 f. 461–2
Endorsed: R[eceived] 4th

LINCOLN TO NEWCASTLE

[Paris,
October, 1741]

My Lord,

I must own to you I have been extremely uneasy at my not receiving an answer to the letter I sent to your Grace by Mr. Dashwood,[1] who tells me that he delivered it immediately on his coming to town to one of your Grace's servants. I am afraid that you take it amiss and are angry with me on my not complying with your orders. But, my dearest uncle, . . . be fully assured that was I only to follow my own pleasure, London would be the place in the world where I should wish to be. I only offered my reasons. . . . If your Grace thinks it would be wrong for me not to come over by the Birthday,[2] I will most certainly be there. . . .

411

I am mightily pleased with the thoughts of my sister's living with me, 'twas what I designed proposing to her. Since your Grace is so good as to give yourself the trouble of taking lodgings for me, I should choose it was somewhere in the New Buildings, for if I am not mistaken a house thereabouts of the same rent is twice as large as they are in Pall Mall or that part of the town.[3] I entirely agree with my friend Jemmy[4] (who I hope has not forgot an old friend) in loving space, especially if it is to be had for the same money. . . .

Lincoln

1. See *Letter* 164.
2. Oct. 30 O.S.
3. The D. of Newcastle must have made suitable arrangements, for the *Daily Advertiser* reports on Nov. 16 O.S.: 'The late Earl's house in St. James's Square is fitting up for his lordship [the E. of Lincoln] to live in.'
4. Not identified.

On Sept. 18 O.S. Horace Walpole, who had left for England, wrote to Lord Lincoln from London: 'I have been much asked about a dear Lord and a charming Lady! I always deny there being any thing in it; several say they are married. I will write you word next post if the Duke mentions it to me or Mr Pelham. But don't tell Mr. Sp[ence] I said anything of it. You may tell him, that I found four verses in the gazette on Rollin's death, which I will believe are his; if he does not prove the contrary—.' (There is no evidence to show that the verses on the late historian, 'said to be by an English gentleman now at Paris', are by Spence.)

On Oct. 13 O.S. Horace Walpole wrote again to Lincoln: 'Lord Pomfret and his family are arrived: Lady Sophia has been out of order with a fatigue and a cold, but is recovered, and looks as much handsomer than the bride, as she used to do than all other women. She asked extremely after a Lord at Paris; I was very sorry I could not tell her we were likely to see him before the Birthday. I have begged much that at least on that day she would let people see what it is to be well-dressed and nobly genteel, not gim and smart like a dairy-maid. She will dress her head French, but that charming shape is condemned to be bound up in an English manteau, till it looks like a wasp ready to break in the middle. . . . P.S. A thousand compliments to dear Mr. Spence' (Corresp. XXX, 23–31).

*177

Source: Egerton 2234 ff. 286–7
Addressed: *as in* 74
Postmarked: 8 OC
Franked: ffree/Thoˢ. Ramsden
Endorsed: *a.* yᵉ acᵗ of the/artificiall duck
red wafer

Paris,
October 14, 1741[1]

⟨Dear Mother,⟩

I was yesterday to see a sight here, which is so surprising that I must give you an account of it. You must know that there was an old philosopher lived in this gay city, about a hundred year ago, and was the most esteemed of any philosopher of his time in it: his name was Descartes. 'Tis observed, that there is nothing so foolish, but that some philosopher or another has maintained it. This Descartes, in particular, held that all animals were nothing but so many ingenious pieces of clockwork.[2] If his horse carried him on briskly, when he rode out to see any friend in the country, he would say that the poor thing had been well wound up; and when his dog ran to him and fawned about him upon his coming home, he would commend the machine for going so well and imitating the motions of gratitude as exactly as any human flatterer could do. He would not allow that his dog *tasted* anything, even whilst he was feeding him; or that a kite *saw*, though it twirled round in the air over his yard and soused down on one of his chicken. All this he has maintained, in the several books that were published by him in his lifetime, and which were then, and are still, very much read here.[3] In some of these he has said that he did not at all doubt but that a good artist might make an animal in clockwork, that should do everything that the same real animal can do.

A great artist here (who had read this in him) set himself some years ago to work, to try whether this could really be done.[4] The particular creature he chose for the experiment was a duck. He kept several about him, studied all their motions and all the make of their body: and at last made a duck in clockwork, which, if you were to judge only by the motions of it, you would think was really alive. It is now showed at half a crown a head (more than a real duck would sell for), and this was the sight we went to see.[5] If it were only an artificial duck that could walk and swim, that would not be so extraordinary: but this duck eats, drinks, digests ⟨and sh-ts⟩.[6] Its motions are extremely natural; you see it eager when they are going to give him his meat, he devours it with a good deal of appetite, drinks moderately after it, rejoices when he has done, then sets his plumes in order, is quiet for a little time, and then does what makes him quite easy.

There was in the same room a clockwork man that plays upon the tabor and pipe, and another that plays upon the flûte-traversière.[7] The latter in particular makes very fine music. One of them can play twelve different tunes, and the other sixteen. I know you will think me got into my travelling style, but as it happens (very luckily for me) the duck, the fluter, and the drummer are now actually packing up, and set out for London the 25th of this month: they are to lodge in the Haymarket;[8] and as Jonquiere's is just by that street,[9] I hope to have the pleasure of going with you to see them whilst we are in their neighbourhood. ⟨I beg all services to all friends, and am ever,

Your most dutiful and affectionate

Joseph Spence.

Your last gave me a great deal of pleasure, because I find by it that your race in the churchyard was no uncommon thing, and that you are able to run up and down stairs as well as upon a level.⟩

1. Three or four letters are probably missing.

2. In his *Discours de la méthode* (1637), sect. 5, and in some of his letters to Henry More.

3. Descartes's argument provoked a controversy on whether animals have souls or not, which continued for over a century. The 'bête-machine' theory found little favour in England. See L. Rosenfeld, *From Beast-machine to Man-machine* (New York, 1941).

4. Jacques de Vaucanson (1790–82), the celebrated maker of automata, had presented his first ingenious devices before the Académie des Sciences in 1738. In 1746 he became a member of the Academy and made important contributions to the invention of silk-weaving machines.

5. It was shown 'dans la Salle de Figures Automates', as appears on the title page of his work *Le Mécanisme du flûteur automate* (Paris, 1738).

6. 'The Matter digested in the Stomach', writes Vaucanson, 'is conducted by Pipes (as in an Animal by its Guts) quite to the *Anus*, where there is a Sphincter that lets it out.—I do not pretend to give this as a perfect *Digestion* . . . I only pretend to imitate the Mechanism of that Action in three Things, *viz. First*, to swallow the Corn; *secondly*, to macerate or dissolve it; *thirdly*, to make it come out sensibly changed from what it was' (pp. 21–2,

see n. 7).

7. The full title of Vaucanson's pamphlet reads: 'An Account Of the Mechanism Of an Automaton, Or Image playing on the *German-Flute*: As it was presented in a *Memoire*, to the Gentlemen of the Royal-Academy of Sciences at Paris By M. Vaucansson, *Inventor and Maker* of the said Machine. Together with / A Description of an artificial Duck, eating, drinking, macerating the Food, and voiding Excrements; pluming her Wings, picking her Feathers, and performing several Operations in Imitation of a living Duck: Contrived by the same Person As also / That of another Image, no less wonderful than the first, playing on the Tabor and Pipe; as he has given an Account of them since the *Memoire* was written. / *Translated out of the French Original, by* J. T. Desaguliers, L.L.D. F.R.S. *Chaplain to his Royal Highness the* Prince *of* Wales. / London . . . 1742.' An engraving by H. Gravelot of the three automata appears both in the French original and in the English translation.

8. 'At the *Long Room* at the *Opera House* . . . where these Mechanical Figures are to be seen at 1, 2, 5 and 7, *o'Clock* in the Afternoon' (title page).

9. In Suffolk Street.

178

Source: Add. MSS 33065 ff. 463–4

LINCOLN TO NEWCASTLE

Paris,
October 21, 1741

My Lord,

Millions of thanks to you for your kind letter.[1] I entirely agree with your Grace in thinking it right for me to come into England, both for my own private affairs and to be at the meeting of the Parliament.[2] You may assure yourself that I will be in England by the beginning of November; 'tis impossible for me at present to be certain the day we shall be at Calais; I leave it entirely to your Grace, but I should think it is not at all necessary to send a convoy for me. Dashwood writ word to Mr. Spence that the privateer was gone away,[3] and everybody here confirms the same. . . . The first week of November I will certainly be at Calais, the day you shall know time enough, if you still think it absolutely necessary for me to be convoyed into England. . . .

I hope your Grace will excuse me (I am sure you can't in reality be angry with me) for putting you in mind of the promise you was so good as to give Mr. Spence on his coming abroad with me. 'Tis impossible to tell you, my Lord, the numberless obligations I have to him; his behaviour to me has been such ever since we have been together that I shall always remember as long as I live. No father could ever show more fondness for his child or study more what was really for his honour and advantage than he has done for mine. When I have the pleasure of seeing your Grace I shall be able to give you so many instances of his friendship and attachment to me that will surprise you. I won't trouble you any more at present, but I can't help assuring you that any favour you bestow upon Mr. Spence I shall be much more obliged to you than if it was for myself.[4] . . . I am, / my Lord, / ever most affectionately and unalterably yours

Lincoln

P.S. I have not been presented to the King, but am satisfied when I have the happiness of meeting your Grace that I shall be able to give you such strong reasons for my not going to Court that you will think I judged right.[5]

1. Missing. Written in reply to Lincoln's *Letter* 176.

2. The new Parliament met on Dec. 1.

3. On Sept. 13 Lady Pomfret wrote from Brussels: 'There is now risen a new difficulty as to our return to England, for the Spanish privateers are so dispersed about, that no passage is secure. Lord Cornbury is confined at Cadiz on their account; and it is reported, that two young ladies, who had been for their education in a convent at Bruges, and were returning home from Ostend, are taken prisoners' (*Hertford Corresp.* III, 391).

4. Among the Spence Papers is a copy of a contract, dated Apr. 28, 1742, and witnessed by Horace Walpole and Thomas Ashton,

whereby Lincoln binds himself to 'a Grant of 100 G's a year' to be paid during Spence's lifetime 'or until the s^d Joseph Spence shall be possessed for the Term of his life or in some place or preferment of the clear yearly value of two hundred and ten pounds or upwards of the gift or procurement of the s^d Henry Earl of Lincoln' (Wright, p. 68).

5. 'A lady who came out of the country this summer to see the Court at Versailles, on her return said that "bating the amours and debaucheries that reign there, she never saw so dull a thing in her whole life." ("Outre la passion, je n'ai jamais vu de chose plus triste.")' *Obs.* No. 1360.

179

Source:	Egerton 2234 ff. 288–9
Addressed:	as in 74
Postmarked:	29 OC
Franked:	Free/Andrew Stone
Endorsed:	*a.* his thoughts/how to provide for gorg k—y/ abroad
	b. not to be Copied.
	red wafer

Paris,
November 4, 1741

⟨Dear Mother,

I received your letter of the 13 Oct. O.S. in a week after it was wrote, and read over the account of your dinner at Dr. Kelley's with great pleasure.[1] I join heartily with you in your compassion for his eldest son,[2] who seems to be a very honest lad (as the Scotch say of anybody fifty or sixty year old) and after reading your letter had a thought come into my head which may possibly be of service to him, but I would not have you hint it to him, or any of the family, till I see whether I can make anything of it or not. If it should ever have any effect, it might transplant him into another kingdom, if he should be inclined at all for such a change. There are two 'ifs', and Mr. Dryden has taught us long ago that

Two Ifs scarce make one Possibility.[3]

However, my thought (whether it may ever come to anything or not) is this. My old friend Bob Downes is at present Dean of Derry in Ireland,[4] and as such has, I hear, several preferments in his gift. My other great friend, Mr. Smith (who paid me that unlucky visit at Lyons when I was

416

with Lord Middlesex) is perhaps not unlikely to be bishop in the same country. Either of these, I should think, would grant me anything that I could reasonably ask of them; and if George designs for orders, as I think he did when I left you, I would certainly try to get something from one or other of them to surprise him with when he least thought of it: but this, and a thousand other good things, may be best talked over by our fireside, when we get together in the good city of London, where I long to be, and thank heaven the time is now drawing on apace. I beg all services to all friends, and am ever

Your most dutiful and affectionate

Jo: Spence.⟩

1. George Kelley, the apothecary. See *Letter* 68.

2. George, possibly the Rev. George Kelley of Orton-on-the-Hill, Leicestershire, whose death is mentioned in the *Gent. Mag.* for Feb. 1789 (p. 178). His younger brother John (*Letter* 66) became Regius Professor of Medicine at Oxford.

3. Lyndaraxa in the *Conquest of Granada*, Pt. I, Act II.

4. Robert Downes (*Letter* 39) had become Dean of Derry Aug. 4, 1740.

*180

Source:	Egerton 2234 ff. 290–1
Addressed:	*as in* 74
Endorsed:	*a.* a descripshon of/yᵉ fine gardnes abroad: paris *red wafer*

Paris,
November 11, 1741

⟨Dear Mother,⟩

The hotter countries I have been in, are not so well supplied with gardens, shady walks, and defences of that kind against the heats, as we are in England. In all Paris, I know of but two places where one can walk with any pleasure. One of these is the garden of the Luxembourg Palace, and the other the Tuileries, or garden of the King's Palace.[1] Our house is placed just in the midst between these two gardens, about a quarter of a mile from each: so that you may imagine that I have not missed being in each of them very often.

The great fault of the gardens in France (and wherever I have been out of England) is their not being natural enough. You come first into an open flower-garden, laid out in some very regular figure, and then go into the grove-work, in which the groves are planted all in straight lines, the grove

417

on one side always answering that on the other: like two twins, or rather like your face in a glass. This is the case in both the gardens I am speaking of, and yet there is something left, in spite of their bad taste, to give one pleasure in them.

The first part of the grove-work in the Luxembourg has some resemblance to our Serpentine walks, which are so infinitely better than straight ones, and as they have been pretty much neglected, have got an air that is more wild and natural than they were intended to be; and the Great Terrace in the Tuileries is certainly a noble walk, though a regular one. It goes all along by the riverside, there is nothing but the Great Road betwixt them (so that you see everything that comes to Paris, either by land or water, from that side of the country) and is terminated by a view of the Elysian Fields, the Ring, and the finest prospect one has anywhere from this city.

In these gardens, you have among the grove-work several openings, sometimes a little meadow, sometimes an oval of green or a great basin, which would be charming if they were not so regular. The greatest pleasure I used to take in these gardens was to see them well peopled. On saints' days and holy days these openings are all sprinkled with people: some sitting on the grass and chatting with their mistresses, others lolling and reading, and others stretched out and fast asleep (the effect I suppose of the former). I wonder there should be so much difference between our climates, that are so little distant, but this (as I observed this autumn) was entirely the mode till pretty far in October, and even till now you will meet every now and then with two or three people still reading on the ground in these grass-plats. There is a great oval in the Luxembourg, in particular, rising on each side, and which they call an amphitheatre, which I have seen five or six weeks ago as entirely filled with people sitting or lolling at their ease as a Roman amphitheatre would have been of old, when their shows were represented in them.

⟨You will think me an idle fellow to talk so long to you about gardens, when [we] are so near coming home; 'tis that perhaps [puts] me into so good humour, and makes me think [of] such agreeable subjects. However, both these gardens begin to grow dull now, and we shall leave them as soon as we can,[2] that I may come and tell you how much I am

Your dutiful and affectionate

Jos: Spence.⟩

1. 'You were observing the other day', said M. Le Grand to Spence, 'how sickly that row of trees in the Tuileries looked, from its being pent up so much between the terrace and the wall' (*Obs.* No. 1359). 'The gardens of the Luxembourg are in a fresher air than the Tuileries' (*Nbk.* 2 67ᵛ).

2. They left within a week and reached London before Nov. 14 O.S. when Lincoln 'was most graciously received' at Court (*H. W. Corresp.* XVII, 210 n. 14).

Appendix 1

LIST OF THE ENGLISH SPENCE MET ABROAD
(Egerton 2235 f. 94r ̄v)

FIRST TOUR, 1731

Namur

Genl. Collier

Dijon

Villars
Denny
Shuttleworth +
Sir. G. Colgrave +
Lady Colgrave

Lyons

D. of Kingston
Hickman
Cotton
Ld R. Montagu
Talbot
Thomson
Ld. Bellieu
Sir Wm. Stuart
Sr. Al. Murray

Geneva

Ld J. Sackville
Delmé
Hambleton
Lutterel
Meggot

Milan

Shirley

Verona

Noel
Clarke

Venice

Thomson
Sr. Rob. Merton
Winne

Dr. Hays
Count Nassau +
Philips
Elton
Ld. Radnor
Green
Swinny
Sr. Rob. Long
Sr. Rob. Brown
Lady Brown
Col Burgess +
Brown +

Naples, 1732

Ld. Benning +
Lady Benning
Lady Grisel
Man
Temple
Duglass
Allen

Rome

Sr. Jam. Grey
Alston +
Clark
Degg
Watkins
Grimston
Lyddal
Knapton
Herbert
Holdsworth
Edwin
Miss Edwin
Britton
Lady Bellieu
Lady Ann
Lady Fanny
Dr. Irwin

NOTE: The names marked with a cross probably indicate persons deceased by the time Spence was revising his travelling papers. Most persons are more closely identified in the Index.

Stevens
Parker

Leghorn

Skinner
Shuttleworth

Florence

Spens +
Dundass
Smith
Clark
Smith
Turnbull
Mitchel
Strowde
Thomson
Holbitch
Doddington
Morris
Bayly
Vincent
Sir Marm. Constable
Townley
Wells
Bagshaw
Howe
Mr. Archer
Mrs. Archer
Harris
Shaw
Deze
Hambleton
Lewis
Fielding
Swinton
Dingley
Gage
Lambert
Crawley
Tomlinson
Sir H. Smithson
Crowe
Ld Harcourt
Bowman
Mr. Coleman
Mrs. Coleman
Goddard
Lucas
Wright

Bologna, 1733

Sir T. Twisden
Brown
Jackson

Marseilles

Cole
Floyd
(Syling)
Mills
Fullerton
Lee

Paris

D of Leeds
Hay
Piaget
D of Portland
Achard
Ld. Graham
Ld. Jedburgh
Ld. Hume
Ld. Tullimore
Ld. Waldgrave
Ld. Churton
Waldgrave
Burnaby
Sr. Harry Liddal
Liddal
Warrender
Turner
Philips
Mr. Knight
Mrs. Knight
Gore
Honeywood
Bridgeman
Herbert

SECOND TOUR, 1737

Hague, etc.

Trevor
Man
Lord G. Bentinck
Bentinck
Mason
Alcock
Ld. Strange
Andrews
Gower +

Beckford +
Beckford
Beckford
Herring
Ld. [   ]

Paris

Ld. Barrington
Ld. Fitzwilliams
Ld. Barclay
Crawley
Tomlinson
Vezey
Coke
Shelvocke
Alexander
Sr. Br. Wray

Blois

Williams
Newport
Montague
Ld. Clanrickard
Palmer

Tours

Englis

THIRD TOUR, 1739

Calais

Ld. James Cavendish
Humphrey Parsons

Paris

Ld. W.
Ld. Shⁿ.
Thomson
Herb. Young
Hippolite
Rolle
Thomson

Lyons

Ld. Lemster

Turin

Villette
Allen
Twisdale
Selwyn
Sharral

Belgarde
Ld. Mansel
Clifton
Walpole
Gray
Blythe
Chetwynd
Perrault
Moor
Devnish +
Gage
Philips
Ld Sandwyche
Frolich
Colebroke
Knatchbull
Vernon
Cotton
Sr. J. Forrester
Ld. Deskford
Barty
Briscow
Curtis
Williams
Sr. J. Royden
Royden
Bates
Ld. Quarrington
Woods
Sr. R. Nudigate
Sr. H. Inglesfield
Ld. Elko
Mackenzie
Pitt
Holdsworth
Castleton
Dashwood
Greville
Ellis
Anstruther
Kennedy
Palmer
Dailley
Wood
Wolf

Route

Ld. Hartington ⎫
Smith   ⎬ Aless^a
Sr Bou^r. Wrey—Acqui

421

Sir Fr. Dashwood—Modena
More ⎱
Melvin ⎰ Bologna

(Florence)

Lady Walpole
Lady Pomfret
Lady Sophia
Lady Charlotte
Ld. Pomfret
Ld. Shrewsbury
Bulstrode
Man
Sturgess
Boughton +

(Leghorn)

How
Jackson
Goldesworthy

(Siena)

Whitehead
Chute

Rome

Ld. Strafford
Blathwayte
Naylor
Seignoret
Slingsby
Jackson
Russel
Tripland
Dalton
Pocock
Lady Mary
Sr. Edw. Smith
Parker
Grant
Belches
Stuart
Allen

Naples

Allen
Hammond
Cantillon
Hunter
Mrs. Allen etc.

Route

Sr. Eras. Philips—Reggio
Smith ⎱
Sr. W. Stuart ⎰ Venice
Mr. Birtles Cons. ⎱
Mr. Barbaud ⎰ Genoa
Merril
Capt. Cope ⎱
Lt. Ransford ⎬ Marseilles
Dr. Nicholson ⎰
Moore—Montpellier
Lady Brownlow ⎱
2·daughters ⎬ Vigan
& son ⎰

Paris

Knight
Alexander
Hume
(Ramsay) +
Mrs. Hayes & her niece
Miss Sackville
(Lady Pen Cholmondeley)
Mrs. Masham
Lady Lambert
(Ly. Shrewsbury etc)
Sir J. Lambert
Masham
Berringer
Ld. Stafford
(Ld. Bateman, Son & Br^r.)
Dundass
Hilman
Monro +
Kilby +
Walwin
Hayes
Tilson

Appendix 2

12 GUINEA CUT FROM LONDON TO ROME

(*Egerton 2235 f. 174^{r-v}*)

From London to Dieppe	1–11–6

    Guinea for your passage, half a guinea provisions.

You have a horse from Dieppe to Rouen at	0–6–0
From Rouen to Paris in the diligence, your place and expenses at I believe	1–1–0

This I am not sure of, having rode post. Some French with whom I came from England told me I could go in the *coche d'eau* from Rouen to Paris for less than 20 livres.

From Paris to Lyons: you (160 livres), your baggage (4s per pd), &c.	5–5–0

    In the *coche d'eau* you go for three pound three shillings. You are ten days in the *coche d'eau*, 6 days the diligence. From Lyons to Marseilles in a returned chaise (you will always find one) expenses and chaise — 1–11–6

fifteen livres a common price for a place—Another method of going to Marseilles is taking the *coche d'eau* to Avignon, 10 livres your passage. At Avignon you will always find a chaise for Marseilles. By that method you will have an opportunity of staying, if you please, some time at Avignon and saving something out of your guinea and half, and go it sooner. The *voiture* from Lyons won't stop anywhere but to lie and dine. From Marseilles to Leghorn or perhaps Città Vecchia, your place in the ship and provisions — 1–11–6

Returned chaise from Lyons to Rome ⎫ 14 louis d'ors for two persons; all expenses born ⎬	7–7–0
Chaise taken on purpose—20 louis d'ors	10–10 0

Appendix 3

TIPS FROM SMITH

(*Egerton 2235 ff. 169^{r}–70^{v}*)

Milan: At Monsieur Louis': lodging ten paols a day, eating ten paols a day, when you advertise that you don't eat at home to pay nothing. Coach eight Milanese livres a day; coachman and valet de place all over Italy, the former at one paol, the latter [at] three p. day. (N.B. all zechins, except Roman, are of equal value at Milan).

Bologna: Pelegrino. Each chamber a paol a day, eating on the same conditions as at Milan. Coach *twelve* paols a day, though I believe you may have one for *ten*. Breakfasts a paol a head. N.B. here the Venetian zechins are of more value than any other.

Florence: Collins. Each chamber a paol a day, eating ten paols a day, without any allowance when you eat abroad. Coach ten paols a day. N.B. Collins has left the house, and I fancy you will be as well entertained and much cheaper at the Aquila Nera—you are charged for fire two paols a day each chamber and each person pays half a paol for the fire in the dining room. All zechins (except Roman) of equal value here; so you may save your Venetian zechins for Naples and Venice, where they are of more value than any other.

Rome: Coach according to the demand for them, from thirty to thirty-six crowns a month. Lodgings from thirty to fifty, including kitchen-furniture and table-linen.

Monsieur Lambert, Lord Hart[ington]'s cook, the best; he is to be paid three paols a day, and expects some small dinner when you dine abroad. It is customary to put the coachman and valet de place in livery and to leave them to them when you go away. When you hire the coach by the month, a zechin a month is enough for the coachman. N.B. pay Mr. Parker what expense he has been at about sending Lord Hartington's box to Città Vecchia.

Naples: at the Tre Ore: Chambers and eating twelve carlins a day, both together. Coach 12 carlins.

Venice: D'Eury: Chambers according to their goodness. Dinner six livres each, supper four. Pay nothing when you eat abroad. Gondola two zechins and half a week, if not at the Ascension; then it will be three.

Generally upon the road you will be charged five paols a head. In some places they will charge the chambers besides which you need not pay; however, to prevent disputes, the best way is to let them know beforehand how much a head you will be served at, including chambers.

Posting in the Genoese and Milanese and Mantuan 15 paols a chaise and five each saddle horse; in the Parmesan and Modenese 8 a chaise and 4 a saddle-horse; in the Bolognese, Tuscan, Lucchese, Roman and Neapolitan 8 a chaise and 3 a saddle-horse; in the Venetian 15 livres a chaise and 5 a horse. From two paols and a half to three will be a good reward for the postillion. I am told that between Bologna and Florence they are very troublesome about making you pay for additional horses. In the rest of Italy let your whiskered servant look them in the face and tell them they are obliged to carry you to the end of the post for eight paols, and that absolutely you will pay no more, let them put as many horses as they will. But if the fellows are obstinate, it is better submitting than having a dispute before a governor. If you travel light, you will have a better pretence for refusing to pay for a third horse.

Never give anything to a *maestro di stalla*.

(Notizie: Smith)

Appendix 4

MEMOIR FOR THE PROVINCES OF FRANCE (FIRST TOUR)
(Mr. Bowman's: Blois-Vienne)
(*Egerton 2235 f. 185ʳ–6ᵛ*)

Vienne: See an old temple, now a church. Some old Roman buildings and a fine inscription by a gate within the town and a Roman funeral mon[umen]t without the town on right hand of the post-road.

Tain: See the hermitage and tauribolium found there.

Orange: See the triumphal arches of Caius Marius, the theatre under the hill, a piece of a mosaic pavement with the figure of a cat, and an old Roman gate behind the hill. N.B. near the theatre is the amphitheatre to the west.

Avignon: Take a view from the castle, pay our respects to Major Lawless who will show you what is curious. Thence go out to Vaucluse. Enquire of the Major what is become of poor Dr. Cantwell.

Aix: See the baths and two Roman *tours* by Fennhouse, and if possible the library that belonged to Mr. Peyrete. Lodge at the Mulet Blanc without the town. Mr. Capitaine la Haye is obliging.

Marseilles: See Mr. Olivier: who eats at the 13 Cantons, and desire him to make the walk of the old town which he did with me and explain to you our reasoning about Caesar's siege.

Toulon: See the harbour etc. and if you h[ave time] the orange groves of Hiè[res]
In going from Aix to Arles see the antiquity of St. Rémy.

Arles: At Arles observe the theatre, the amphitheatre, the tombs and aquaeduct without the town, the townhouse, Constantine's palace.

Nîmes: Take the man who shows the amphitheatre and he'll show you the Maison Carée, the temple of Diana, Tour Magne, etc. Go out to the Pont du Gard and passing half a league beyond the river, see more of the aquaeduct. If possible ask of that man to show you the conduit under ground in going or coming to Pont du Gard, which I wanted to have seen, and if you see it, only measure its wideness and height. Lodge Aux Arèncs.

Montpellier: If you have time go to Port Cette and see the mouth of the canal, and at Baluruc the remains of Forum Domitii. In our name see Président Le Bon and give us news of Dr. Cantwell.

Béziers: At Béziers see the sluices, and going thence pay half a post extraordinary and turn to right to see where the canal goes under a mountain.

[*Narbonne:*] See Latout's collection of manuscripts of [the] antiquities of the place.

Carcassone: In lower town only an old fountain.

Toulouse: Lodge at the Hôtel de Béarn. In our name ask for Mr. Grahame, known by the name of Chevalier Gram (see Président Colette's medals in my Lord's name). If you have time, see an old amphitheatre a mile out of town, going over the bridge through that part of the town and following the road near the river. Atop of an height it is a tuft or grove of wood. If you go down from hence by water to Bordeaux, pay 130 livres for boat.

Montauban: If you go to Montauban avoid the Tapis Vert and go to the Hôtel de Béarn; if room here for a boat, pay 80 livres to Bordeaux or at most 100 *l.*

Bordeaux: See in our names Présidents Montescue [i.e., Montesquieu] and Barbot and Mr. Ainsley, merchant; if for a very short time you may go to Bennet's and pay him 4 *l.* a day a head if his company be good, if not, six by yourselves. See the amphitheatre.

Poitiers: Go to the 3 piliers and see the aquaeduct by the Capucins out of town and the amphitheatre within town.

Chatellerault: If you have time see Richelieu, 7 leagues from Chatellerault, and if you go to Angers from Richelieu go by Loudun, Giron, Thouars and Doué, where a theatre cut in the rock.

425

Angers: And at Angers apply to Mr. Mercier our friend with young Mr. Churchill.

Tours: Thence come up by Tours and at Amboise, see Roman magazines below the town in the garden of a convent.

Blois: At Blois either the English or Phillipeaux the French master who will serve you.

Appendix 5

QUERIES [MADE BEFORE THE SECOND TOUR]
(Egerton 2235 f. 168ʳ)

—To inquire at the foot (of this side) of Mount Cenis, whether there is not a passage on the left there, on by the side of the river arc? or elsewhere?

—Caesar passed the Rubicon in going from Ravenna to Rimini: best therefore to take Ravenna in our way; from whence we may go by water to Venice. There are two streams, one from Cesena to the sea, called Pisatello, and the other running nearer by Rimini to the sea, still called (?) il Rubicone (the sands red: 'Puniceus *Rubicon*' in Lucan, Mr. Addison)

—Directions for travellers in France, of the government of the towns, etc. Which the best? One of 5 vols. oct.

—Of the two dangerous points one not dangerous at all; in the other how the gentleman with Mr. T behaved at N.

—As we stay so long at Rome, better to have a bill of credit in Italy, and best at Leghorn.

—May get a chaise at Paris as well as at Calais, from the intercourse of the two places: to write to a friend before at Paris about it. A balder waggon to Brussels and thence may hire a chaise to Paris? (May get further information for this at the Hague). Best way to go to Holland by Harwich, and thence in a packet boat to Helvoetsluys.

—Bills from banker here to one at the Hague. Bills there, on one at Paris; and there to serve us till fixed in Italy. To get the bill for Italy sent 3 or 4 months before you want it. By this means Mr. H[oldsworth] gave but 75 crowns for what would have cost him 110 without that precaution. What they call these bills?)

—To get Cluverius's Geography, in 4 vols, fol. whilst in Holland, and to leave his Italia with Consul Brown at Venice, just as we are going out of Italy, for the use of Mr. Holdsworth.

—Footman better than the valet de chambre, and why.

—Postillion may demand 5 sous, and 'twas usual to give him 5 more: but that depends on the then customs (12 most convent.) and is easily learnt from the comers and goers.

Valet: £12 wages ... 2 s. a day, board w. £48 10s. 0. *per annum*
Footman: £10 or 12 ... 1.6 a day (£37 7s. 6 *p.a.*)

—If you quit the chaise for a ride out of the way, to send the servant with your chaise and hire a man to go with you if necessary.

426

Appendix 6

Grand Carmes: little marble *chapel*, two reliefs of Quellinus (Antro: and Alva's army). The Saviour's head, full printed, on marble, nat[ura]l and not to be imitated. Refect: statue of the Virgin, words in wire from her mouth: Ecce hi sunt fratres. Cloister: not bad wind[ow?] painting 1613.

Académie des Peintres: Italian hand, Justice and another woman, inserted, made by Raphael, an Italian that studied here. Good old man by Martinus de Vos. Head of Quintinus, the blacksmith of Antwerp.

Dominicans: Mount Calvary with several statues and rockwork, terrible purgatory. Q. of the high altar-piece.

St. Vanburgius: high altar, Rubens's cross taking down with side-pieces by ditto. Very good.

Jesuits' Church: Front designed by Rubens (?), good, but too much ornamented; the inside the handsomest we saw (pillars, arcades, gallery, roof). High altar: St. Ignatius preaching devils out of the infidels, by Rubens. In a side chapel Assumption of the Virgin by Van Dyck, very good. Other of Van Dyck ibid.

Shooters' Hall: Venus stopping Mars, very good body but very bad posture, by Villabor[g]ius, scholar of Rubens. Things in it, as generally in the best pieces here, overdone: Mars too furious, etc.

Peeter Snyers: Several things exact. The twelve months of the year 1727, very exact things in them. Disposition of the signs generally well introduced as part of the action: Leo and Taurus flung on antiques very justly, Scorpius and the Indian with his bow improperly. December—the snow imitated in falling, excellent old man and cold old woman.

St. Michael's: the ref[ectory] all painted by Quillinus. In the church: Vavasour, Anglus—ex familia Haselwood—Deo et hominibus carus, mundi osor suique negligens.

Great Church (St. Mary's): Rubens's famous picture, taking the body down from the cross: leaf-pieces by ditto (leaves and all are excellently and perfectly finished. Nine persons in the grand one: the three women differently concerned; the mother dead, pale; that holding the foot [shows] steady concern, and the middle with a fear wildly moved and all over tears). Virgin and our Saviour's circumcision. Thirty-six altars in the church for the different trades. High altar: Assumption of the Virgin by Rubens. Saviour's body etc. with leaf-pieces, Herod at [dinner]. In the baptistry Saviour's head etc. and St. John's death by Quintinus Metsys (at the great door is an inscription relating to him and the verse: Connub. amor de mul. fecit apetᵐ). Dead Saviour against a column with leaf-pieces (Virgin and Bambino; St. John and the eagle) by Rubens—very good. Steeple there 542 feet high, 620 steps. Great bell 18,800.

St. Jacques: high altar—a handsome work in m[arble?] by Quillinus. In the semicircle of [car?]pets behind it one has a statue of our Saviour in m[arble?] with two execᵗˢ (hands tied) by Kerkes,[1] much more spirit and the story better told than in the statues of

---

1. Kerricks.

Quillinus. A picture by it of Abr. Janssens' Saviour coming with a victorious banner to the Virgin sitting, more like the plain Italian manner than the common Flemish. Several other statues and pictures, pretty good, in this church.—In another [semicircle?] lies Rubens (d. 1657 aet. 43): over the altar a picture of his in which he has introduced all his wives—the first not handsome, the second handsome with flaxen hair, the third handsomest, with darker hair. His daughter behind the second and time at the bottom. Statue of the Virgin over it in marble and iron sword stuck into her breast. Another with a very big-bellied Virgin and Eliz. grossly observing it, but a good painting—by Teniers. Woman lying, in marble, by Mic. Van Voort, 1701, admired there. Very high re[lief?] of cross taking down etc. by ditto—very good. A Resurrection by Jordaens, and two heads over, very well painted by Cornelius Vos.

Augustins: Our Saviour on the cross, by Van Dyck, very finished and fine air of the head, two or three feet. How often copied about the town. Two flower-pieces by Bosschaert.— Refectory: angel-piece by Jordaens. Pope with thunder in his right hand, flat wood. The shepherds with our Saviour, by Verbruggen. Windows painted 1675. The church itself pretty, two arcades, roof high in the midst. The high altar in mourning, masses said there, and so Rubens's St. Sebastian etc., not to be seen. Another by him: St. Apollonia's tongue tearing out as in the prints.

Mr. Clasen's: In one room only a piece of Bloemaert, Vedor and Angelique—very particular painting: the drapery puts one in mind of some of Guercin's. Three fine portraits by Van Dyck, that of himself exquisitely finished, like some of Leonardo da Vinci's paintings. 'La Continence de Scipio' by Van Dyck ('He was not so good for history as Rubens,' Mr. Clasen's observation). Six Don Quixote pieces done by Mr. Clasen's order by Heemskerk. [Flower?]pieces by Van Huysum. A little head—Rembrandt's, and an excellent head of St. Antony by Girardon.

Mr. Ferrari's: five portraits by Van Dyck, several hunting pieces as at Mr. Clasen's before. Landscape by Rubens and Breughel. [Vul]can arming a young person, by Villaborgius.

Mme Lunden: Most of the pictures in the country. A fine large hunting piece by Snyder, and Melchisedec's sacrifice by Rubens.

Recolets: high altar in mourning and so the Miracles of St. Francis by Rubens hid. A good dead body of our Saviour, etc., the Father said by Van Dyck, and a saint giving the host to a person possessed, by Ver Voort. Snyder buried here (d. 16[5]7).

Mme de Wiet's: Boar-hunting by Boel.—rough and a good deal of force in it. Holy family, a capital piece of Rubens's; the Virgin [with] darker hair his second (?) wife [said] the secretary who showed it. Boar-hunting by Snyer (?). Imitation (?) of about forty masters in one piece. John Baptist preaching, Luc. Jordaens's. Susanna and the Elders, a good Rubens. Two clear natural portraits by Parbus.[2] A family of three persons and two portraits, very good, by Van Dyck. Rubens's third wife and a Saviour on the cross, whence Van Dyck seems to have taken his famous one about the same size.

Flower-pieces by De Heem. Ditto by Mignon. [Two] shore-pieces by Voermans.[3] Our Saviour sleeping in the storm [by] Rubens, unfinished and very strong. Gallery all wainscoted with three rows of smaller pictures to the left and pyramid of the smallest sort at the end: by Voermans, Bourguignon,[4] Tanis[5] etc., etc. There are several paysages by Breughel, one with the figures in it by Van Dyck and another with the figures by

2. 'Parhasius', i.e., Anton Schoonjans.
3. Vorstermans.

4. Bourgonjon.
5. Teniers?

Gonzara ('whom we call le petit Van Dyck'—*the secretary*). Sleeping Venus, unfinished, by Van Dyck, etc. etc.

M. de Leyck's: Collection to be sold soon. Three old heads in one piece, very strong (Rubens's or Van Dyck's?). Portraits by Van Dyck, Rubens, etc. Little exact single pieces by [   ] ('Tis not imitation that pleases, hence . . .).

L'Abbaye des Bernardins sur le Schelde: a mitred abbey, 35 brothers, the abbot has 150,000 florins a year for his table, equipage, etc. and 64,000 for his purse; above £17,000 English. The whole society reckoned worth about a million of florins a year, beside what they get by commerce. The marble altar-piece by Quillinus very good—the story of it: the Assumption of the Virgin. The building something grand and magnificent. The wainscoting of the choir handsome and the confessionals (with four large figures à la mode d'Anvers) well contrived. A very high ascent to the altar: when you are up it a marble scroll on each side, in one this inscription:

Serenissimi Principes Henr: 1 & 2, Lotharingiae & Brabantiae Duces; Vir quoque nobilis, Aegidius de Berthout, Dominus de Baerlaer, Gert. Duffel, Waelhem, Hegem, Uremde, Keerbergen, Ecquerspoul, &c&c&c; hoc loci S Bernardi in vico Uremde, uno a Lirâ milliari fundarunt monasterium Anº 1235; quod huc ad Scaldim translatum Aº 1246, annoque 1560 Episcopatui Antverpiensi incorporatum; Anº 1584 ab Iconoclastis demolitum; per Innocentium 12 & Philippum 4 Hispaniorum regem, ad instantiam serenissimi Principis Leopoldi Guielmi Belgii Gubernatoris, ab eodem Episcopatu dismembratum, in abbatilem dignitatem 90 annis suppressam restituitur An: 1649.— Hujus autem Ecclesiae primum lapidem posuit Joannes 3 Lotharingiae Brabantiae ac Limborgi Dux Aº 1330 primaque missa celebrata Aº 1444, 13 Sept:—On the opposite scroll is a list of all their abbots. Series abm̄ RR ac ampliss: Durum ex gremis mo[rt]u[a]rii loci S. Bernardi ad Scaldim Abbatum. I.D. Hugo de Bierbeek, ob. 1243 . . . 33 D. Gerardus Rubens, ob. 1736. 34. Alexʳ Adriaensens (the present abbot).

Appendix 7

SPENCE'S NOTE TO A GENTLEMAN AT BLOIS
(*Egerton 2235 f. 175ᵛ*)

Nollem equidem tam bello tamque eleganti poemati edendo mores aliquid subjicere; at nollem magis ejus editionem ipse quodammodò promovere: quòd ex ignorantiâ meâ verear, ne in illo fortasse nonnulla occurrant quae possunt esse offendicula Ecclesiae gentis extraneae in quâ benignissimè semper cum summa humanitate acceptus sum.

Josephus Spencaeus

To ye Gentleman, at Blois?

NOTE: The occasion which prompted this draft of a reply is unknown. Perhaps Spence showed 'ye Gentleman' the Latin translation of Pope's first epistle of the *Essay on Man*, which

Spence had arranged with Dobson in 1736, a year before he visited Blois. See *Observations*, No. 309.

Appendix 8

A LIST OF THINGS TO BE PROCURED
FOR THE TOUR WITH LORD LINCOLN

(Spence Papers Ln[27])

3 pair of Pistols. (Powder, & Ball)   all but 1 pair of P[s] will do.

A Blunderbuss   Lewis

3 Saddles   Brumley [*illegible*] Street

3 pair of Jack-boots; & pumps, &c   = Better at Paris.

3 Hangers.

2 Pair of Sheets.

Large Trunk.

Portemateau.   } Lewis

An Ecritoire: paper, &c.

Maps of France, Italy, Germany, & the Low-Countries.   } Myself.

Travels of Misson, Add[n], & Burnet.   Pignerol, It: 1. Fr: 2.

Great Coats (Shoes & Stock[gs])

Riding-Britches

Livery Suit & [*crossed out*] 2 Wastecoats 1 Frock 4 Hat. & 3 Britches   Ward, Castle-Street

Knife & Fork

Tea & Sugar

        Shoes?

        Cam: bis. Coachman, & footm:
                Turin, Rome, Paris.

        Bill of Credit ✕ Bankers?

        Am: Any priv. Instr?

        Card: at R.

        Calais, Paris? Dijon, Lyons, Gen?, Turin.

        Embas[r] at Paris?

        Allowance.

Appendix 9

A LIST OF SOME OF THE
ANTIQUE PAINTINGS AND STATUES FOUND IN
THE UNDERGROUND TOWN (AS 'TIS CALLED)
AT RESINA NEAR PORTICI

(Egerton 2235 ff. 100ʳ–1ʳ)

Bacchus sitting, and Hercules, with a Genius behind him, standing by; a youth laughing behind Bacchus, and below a little boy sucking a doe. The figures of Hercules and Bacchus larger than life.

Theseus standing, with the Minotaur dead under his feet. Three or four youths caressing him, embracing his arms or feet.—The figures big as life.

Jupiter with thunder in his hand. A little Cupid behind taking hold of him by the shoulder. Half length.

A figure of a man sitting, with a writing in his left hand, held out towards another man who sits in a thoughtful posture, with his head inclined on his arm. A woman behind pointing up with her right hand; another on the left side of her, with a quiver behind her, and a third next to her. A man bending forward in a supplicating posture, with his finger at his mouth. Behind him stands an old man. The figures full-length and three quarters life.

Hercules strangling a serpent with each hand. Amphitryon with his hands on his sword hastily drawing it. His wife standing by.

Chiron teaching Achilles to play on the harp. The figures at full length, and about three parts as big as life. The expression admirable.

Another piece, its fellow, where Chiron is teaching Achilles to cast the javelin.

Figure of a woman (the head wanting) with a child in her arms, damaged.

Three figures finely coloured; two with rays round their heads, the third crowned with laurel. A small figure above crowned also with laurel, and a pastoral crook in his hand, leaning towards the other figures; half-length and half as big as life. This called the Judgement of Paris.

Paintings in small

Cupid in a chariot drawn by swans.—Ditto drawn by lions.—Ditto on the back of a stag, which he holds by the horns, the stag seeming to be falling down.—Ditto pulling a ram along by the horns.

Two fine heads. One holding something like a book.—Head of Hercules, with his club.—Two small Medusa's heads.—A little Bacchus playing with a tiger.—A small figure of Victory with laurel in her hand.—A duck, finely painted, as big as life.—Figure of a man holding a patera, white drapery, crimson ground.—A woman struggling with a satyr who is attempting to force her. Another woman more complaisant to a satyr. Figures of these two pieces half-life.

NOTE: This 'List', included among Spence's miscellaneous travel papers, is not in Spence's hand.

Several pieces representing architecture, in one lately found the colours remarkably fresh.

A man sitting, armed with a double halberd, exactly like the modern ones. Another man armed with a halberd of a different sort. Both pieces small.—Several pieces of chase. One particularly of a leopard pursuing a deer.—Other pieces representing household utensils etc. In one the figure of a candlestick of the same make with one of brass found in the same place.

Among the curiosities found and preserved in those two rooms where the antique paintings are kept, are some glass vials, shaped exactly like some of our modern ones. In one the liquor and cork still remaining.

Statues

Six brass ones, all considerably larger than life. First, naked with a long wand in his hand. Probably an emperor. Second, in the habit of a consul. Third, in a sacrifying habit. Fourth, resembling Cicero. Fifth and sixth, women, perhaps priestesses. Some of these figures have the eyes yet remaining, which are not of metal, but some composition representing the natural colours of eyes.

In the same room are eleven marble statues. One considerably bigger than life, in a military dress, supposed to be Vitellius.—Two Jupiters of the same proportion, and each without a head.—The other large figures are Roman ladies etc.

There are likewise some small figures, as a Silenus, and another of a woman, the drapery and workmanship of which are excellent.

In another little room are nine busts, found all together in the underground theatre. The two best, a Pallas and Jupiter Ammon, with goat's ears and large ram's horns.

In the theatre belonging to the King's Villa at Portici are six consular statues. In one of the apartments, two brass heads, and a bas relief representing a scene (seemingly) in some comedy. The actors masked.—In another room, a bas relief, a sacrifice etc.

The sculptor who has the charge of restoring these statues says that they found in the underground theatre in great quantities fragments of equestrian statues in bronze, the horses of which he imagines to have been as big as that of M. Aurelius.—One of these statues, he says, was thought to be Caligula, and of excellent workmanship.

Appendix 10

BELLONI'S BILL OF CREDIT
(*Egerton 2235 f. 97*)

Roma 13 Maggio 1741.

Vi sarà resa la presente dall' Illmo Sr Giuseppe Spence, Gouernatore di Sua Eccza il Sig:r Conte di Lincoln My Lord, e Pari d'Inghilterra; lo raccomando però alla uostr' amoreuolezza per tutto quello potesse occorrerli nel suo passaggio, e dimora cossì, poichè trattandosi del Seruigio di un tanto personaggio molto m'obligarete per ogni fauore, che gli compartirete, e richiedendoui denaro vi prego pagarli quella somma, che

potrà occorerli fosse anche di Doppie duemila di Spagna, contro lettere di Cambio per
Londra di detto Sig:^{r} Spence pagabili al mio ordine S.P. a 30 g^{ni} di data, e dirette a chi
vorrà, da trasmettermi, regolandone la ualuta, ed il uostro rimborso conforme u'auuiso
per la Posta, e resto a uostri Commandi con Caram^{te} Salutarui

Girolamo Belloni

Bologna SS^{tt} di Orazio, e Lodovico Dal Monte

NOTE: On Girolamo Belloni, see *Letter* 139 n. 2. Lady Mary Wortley Montagu wrote to her husband on Nov. 23, 1740: '. . . there is litterally no money in the whole Town, where they follow Mr. Law's System and live wholly upon Paper. Belloni, who is the greatest Banker not only of Rome but all Italy, furnish'd me with 50 sequins, which he solemnly swore was all the money he had in the House. They go to market with paper, pay the Lodgings with paper, and, in short, there is no Specie to be seen, which raises the prices of every thing to the utmost extravagance, no body knowing what to ask for their goods. It [is sa]id the Present Pope (who has a very good character) has declar'd he will endeavor a remedy, thô it is very difficult to find one' (*Complete Letters*, II, 212).

Appendix 11

FOR VIRTÙ—THIRD TOUR

(*Egerton 2235 f. 172^r*)

	Cr[owns]	Bai[ocs]
To my Lord	102	50
Map of Rome	2	10
Prints, Faen. etc.	13	0
Fic[oroni]: two gems	14	35
Enamelled snuff-box	36	90
Guido's Aurora	28	0
To my Lord	102	50
Artificial flowers	20	20
3 marble tables	100	0
Stones for cabinet	30	0
Neap[olitan] boxes	92	25
Cippitelli, in part	20	0
12 views	48	0
Perseus, and little Jupiter	61	50
Dalton's prints	65	80
Rossi, for prints	13	0
Florence—virtù	195	70
Lot and his Daughters	300	0
Ariadne	30	0
Medusa	35	0
Prints from Polidore	1	50
Dalton for cleaning	6	15
Mr. Grant	21	0
Mr. Parker	20	0
Sulphurs	51	50

Rosa Alba	176	0	
Canaletti's Views	12	80	
The two Bourgignons	81	0	
Boxes to Leghorn	20	0	

===

Appendix 12

EXPENSES—THIRD TOUR

(*Egerton 2235 f. 173*[r])

	£	s	d
Umicalia	0	6	0
Raphael	5	17	0
Mendicità sbandita	0	2	6
Burra's landscape	0	19	6
Map of Turin &c.	0	12	0
Museo Florentino 3 vols	10	10	0
Gemme Antiche	3	0	0
Colonna Antonina	1	5	0
Cupid and Psyche &c	1	2	0
Arcus Triumph[s]	1	2	6
Admiranda	1	10	9
Atlas and Globe	5	2	6
Books for Ellis and Palmer	3	7	6
Lin. Incombust. etc.	0	7	0
Inc. del Vesuvio	0	1	6
Giac: Frey	1	9	6
Binding of prints etc.	0	15	0
Artificial flowerets	6	1	6
Adonis of Marini &c	0	10	3
Caesar Borgia	0	3	0
Lapis Lazuli handles	1	0	0
Sulphurs	12	10	0
Rosalba	11	5	6
Views of Venice	0	10	0
Map of Paris &c	1	1	0
Two rings	3	3	0
Machiavel	0	8	6
Perelle's Lansc[s]	2	5	0
Medals	11	17	9
	87	16	9
Seals	4	11	0
First box from Leghorn car.	1	4	0
Duties for ditto	0	12	0

Appendix 13

FOR VIRTÙ

(Egerton 2235 f. 177ᵛ–8ʳ)

	Cr.	P.	B.[1]
Guido's Aurora	1	0	0
Guido's Bac. & Ariadne	1	0	0
Raphael's Hol Fam.	0	3	0
4 Tondi's of Domⁿᵒ	0	8	0
Harv. Vintage (ctc?)	0	4	0
Lot	0	1	5
Young Herc.	0	0	5
4 Card. Virtues on Colˢ	1	5	0
S. Romualdo	0	3	0
Dying S. Jerome	0	6	0
4 Drs: Sacri Interpreti	0	3	0
Petronilla	0	5	0
Marat's Madonna	0	2	0
Sacchi's dying Ann	0	3	0
Jos. and his Lady Cignani	0	2	5
Il Riposo in Egitto	0	2	0
Marat, Sacchi, Rafael	0	3	0
David?	0	1	5
Marat's Octagon, H. Fam.	0	2	0
Pan and Luna	0	1	5
Marat's dead Jesus	0	2	0
Rebecca at the [well?]	0	3	0
Marat 2 sheets			
Apollo and Daphne	1	0	0
Romulus and Remus	0	5	0
Janus	0	5	0
Blasius	0	4	0?
Chr. Baptism	0	4	0
Guido's Aurora (3)	5	0	0
—Bacchus & Ariadne (3)	5	0	0
Raphael's H: Fam: (2)	0	6	0
4 Tondi's of Dom. (2)	1	6	0
4 Card. Virtues dit. (2)	3	0	0
S. Romualdo (2)	0	6	0
Dying S. Jerome (2)	1	2	0
4 Drs (2)	0	6	0
Pan & Luna	0	3	0
Apollo & Daphne	2	0	0
	19	9	0

1. 10 baiocs = 1 paul
   10 pauls = 1 crown

Appendix 14

ROBERT LOWTH TO SPENCE

Turin, July 11, 1749

Dear Mr. Spence,

You know me so well that you will rather be surprised at hearing from me at all than wonder that 'tis so long first: besides I told you that I must have time to take a view of the place before I could give you an account of it and of your friends. I must thank you in the first place for introducing me to Mr. *Dom Villa,* who is a very worthy, sensible and agreeable man. He was very glad to hear from you and was extremely pleased with your book, which I gave him. He tells me he has not English enough to sit down to read it through, without a great deal more leisure than he has at present: but he has been very busy in looking it over and consulting particular places by the index and plates. He desires you would accept of his compliments and many thanks for your present.

From what I have said you begin to be in pain for your friend *Count Richa*: he died here three or four days before we came. He had been confined for some time, and as the beginning of his illness was attended with some very odd circumstances, I'll give you as good an account of it as I have been able to get.

Four or five months ago the Princess of Carignan happened to observe that some of the china that stood in one of the antechambers was missing and that it continued to decrease by degrees; she took notice of it, and enquiry was made about it among the servants: they could give no account of it; but one of them to clear himself and his comrades of suspicion was resolved to watch it and hid himself in the room for that purpose. He was much surprised to see Count Richa, the first time he came to visit the children as usual, as he returned through the room, go to the place where the china stood, choose out a piece or two of it, put it in his pocket and carry it off. The fellow did not care to risk his credit against the Count's by declaring immediately what he saw: he only said he knew who had the china, and if they would send him in all the messages to the houses about the town, he should soon be able to get very satisfactory intelligence of it. It was not long before he had an errand to Count Richa's, where he saw all the china that was missing openly displayed upon one of his tables. When the story was known, everybody looked upon it as a plain indication that the Count's head was disordered: however, the Prince of Carignan immediately forbid him his house. The Count hardly appeared abroad afterward: his illness soon took a different turn; his health decayed apace, and at last he died of a dropsy. . . .

From the extra-illustrated copy of *Anecdotes*, ed. Singer, 1820, Huntington Library (RB 131213). Printed by Singer, pp. 431–5.

Dear Jo,

. . . I read the description of your garden to Signor Domvilla; he found it to be the same in the main that you had talked over with him eight or ten years ago. I left him well at Turin about a month since. He gave me some information with regard to those friends you enquired after. *Mr. Landskarounski is now in the Saxon service; I think he made a campaign or two in the beginning of the war in that of the King of Sardinia. Mr. D'Erlach died somewhere in Lombardy six or seven years ago, of the smallpox.* I must not forget your old flame, the *Princess of Carignan.* She has lost I believe *a good deal of her beauty, being now pale and very thin; but will always retain her agreeableness. She lay in while we were at Turin, and has now about six children.*

A good part of this day and yesterday I spent in the company of your friend *Signor Camillo Paderni.* He is settled at Portici in the King's service, and is employed in making drawings of the antiquities found in Herculaneum, of which they are preparing to give the world a large account. He has been there upon this business above a year and a half. He has received your book from Mr. Nash, who was here lately. Signor Camillo is very well with the King, has access to him at all times, and frequent conversations with him. *He has presented your book* to his Majesty as an example proper to be followed for the beauty of the paper, impression, etc. in the work which they are now going to put to the press. . . .

They have lately been digging in another part of Herculaneum, but I don't find they have had any great success. Signor Camillo has been very obliging in accompanying us through the several sights of the place, and today has been with us to the top of *Vesuvius,* which he had not seen before. He desires his compliments to you. I should have told you before, as you desired particularly to be informed, that *he has long ago dropped his design of publishing* a collection of basso relievos. . . . *Pray sit down immediately, and write me a letter for Dr. Cocchi. . . .*

I had almost forgot to tell that I asked Signor Paderni what he *thought of the engravings in your book. He commended them much in general, spoke in high terms of many of the small pieces, but did not seem to think so well of the large figures. I asked him particularly of the two basso relievos. He thought one much better performed than the other.* You will know which, I have forgot.

Appendix 15

COLLECTION OF PAINTINGS AT MODENA AND PARMA
(Egerton 2235 ff. 17ʳ–18ʳ)

Modena[1] [May 9] on the route to Genoa—dark mean town. [   ] the Duke's palace by Avanzini (unfinished).

First room: Triumph of Ariadne in the same car with Bacchus, with a great number of figures, said to be of Benvenuto Garofalo or more generally of Raphael. Christ carrying

---

1. This paper on Modena and Parma was written on the first tour, but the section on Modena was supplemented and corrected by Spence when he revisited the gallery in 1741 (the parts in angle brackets) by which time some of the paintings had been rearranged.

the cross and another large one—Paul Veronese. A Madonna—Titian, and a St. Jerome of Rubens.

⟨Great bacchanal designed and painted by Benvenuto di Garofalo; Bacchus and Ariadne in the chariot, elephants by—; Give to Caesar [by] Pordenone; Constantine and his army on Ponte Molle (?) [by] Jul. Romano; St. Sebastian [by] Spagnolet, not so horrid as his usual manner (owing to the subject?).⟩

Second room: Purification (?) of the Virgin [by] Palma Vecchio. A San Sebastian [by] Spagnolet. Sacrifice of Isaac, a very good Andrea del Sarto. Three pieces: Battle, General passing a bridge, and Triumph [by] Giulio Romano, of the taste with his Dido history [at] Florence. Odd piece of Francia's. Little St. John bringing a lamb to Christ, Virgin, etc. [by] Titian.

⟨Parmigianino's Fortune on a globe—fine head, face and hair. Constantine's triumph and battle [by] Giulio Romano. Portata del Croce [by] P. Veronese. Ascension of the Virgin, d[   ]rs at bottom [by] Dosi di Ferrara—very good. The little *tondi* in the ceiling of this and the other four rooms by Tintoret, very well coloured for him.⟩

Third room: Our Saviour etc. and a Madonna etc., both by Guido—his dark manner. Apollo flaying Marsyas [by] Bassan. Fortune [?] standing on a globe [by] Parmigianino. Semiramis dressing a soldier who brought her word etc. [by] Guercin. Set of people at cards [by] Michelangelo Caravaggio.

⟨Paul Veronese and all his family making a vow to the Madonna (excellent little boy against the pillar). The sacrifice of Isaac [by] Andrea del Sarto, extremely good. Venus in concha and sea-gods [by] Geronimo da Carpo, very good.⟩

Fourth room: Excellent Magdalen's head [by] Agostino Carracci. Angel flying with a crown etc. [by] Annibal Car[racci]. Virgin, St. Joseph at work as carpenter etc. [by] Perugino—very good for him. Four pieces (the four elements?) by the three Carracci. Virgin and three or four other saints—Correggio, first manner; the roof by Albano and his school.

⟨Adoration of the Magi [by] Paul Veronese. Il Medico, portrait by Correggio. Giocattori di Caravaggio. Noli me tangere (?) [by] Guido—his dark manner.⟩

Fifth room: St. Anne (?), the Virgin, St. Joseph, little Jesus and St. John playing—one is pouring water on the other—a noble piece of Giulio Romano's. Mars (?), Venus (?) and Cupid [by] Benv. Garofalo. The Assunta by L. Carracci and a saint kissing the little Christ's foot, by Han. Carracci, both large figures and designed for a greater height. A very large piece by the three Carraccis conjointly.

⟨Marriage of Cana [by] Paul Veronese: scarce anywhere four better Paul Veroneses than in these four rooms. St. Francis kissing our Saviour's foot [by] Han. Carracci—Saviour's head thorned [by] ditto; great [style?]—Magdalen [by] ditto—Very great Hercules and Cerebus (like the torso for great designing) [by] Han. Carracci—Virgin and four saints [by] Correggio.⟩

Sixth room: Three large pieces by Correggio. [   ] the little Jesus in the Virgin's lap, particular for the light that comes from him and makes him and the Virgin's face all dazzling. Another very beautiful Madonna and fine Bambino in the clouds, and the third, Virgin with a particular beautiful face and turn of the head, speaking to an ecclesiastic.— The Marriage at Cana and the offering of the Wise Men, two very large pieces by Paul Veronese. A fine Virgin (his own wife) etc. and the woman taken in adultery, both Titian.

⟨Titian and his family, by himself. Virgin, S. Sebastian, S. Geminiano and S. Rocco [by] Correggio. Old Elizabeth etc. [by] Raphael. Woman in adultery, by Titian (with his

Venus face when that says the nasty creature etc.). Give to Caesar [by] Titian—the expression in the two faces. Madonna etc. [by] Correggio. St. Girolamo, the only Rubens in the collection. La Notte di Correggio—long tremble at first, less striking after—the Virgin's face not handsome, something soft and maternal, but his whole force was laid out for the light on it, a pale light—Signor Fr's grotesque idea of the good women at her lying in. Virgin and Bambino [by] Titian. The little Magdalen lying along [by] Correggio —long fine hair and flesh luminous, face a little shaded, book in her hands as exact as a Flemish painter. Good Samaritan [by] Caravaggio, one of his softest and best pieces.⟩

Antichamber: Portraits full length, and a little picture, with covers, set round with precious stones. 'Tis a Magdalen lying along and reading, an exquisite soft graceful piece of Correggio's: it shows his illustrated manner and looks better when shaded with the cover. Q. whether the little shiny Saviour in the famous Notte di Correggio would not do better without so strong a light from the window?

⟨The illuminated MSS Muratori [   ] is very pretty, with copies of old (?) cameos, etc.⟩

Parma [May 10–11]—In the gallery Judgement of Hercules, without lion's skin, though older than usual, [by] Han. Carracci. The famous copy of Raphael's Leo X. Little Christ and St. John, Virgin, Joseph [by] Raphael, Finding of Moses, small, [by] P. Veronese. Sleeping Venus with great number of cupids playing about [by] Han. Carracci, Lucretia stabbing herself, old woman [by] Novalloni. St. John, Jesus, Virgin and St. Anne (?) with a cat in the corner, called 'Madonna dello gatto' [by] Raphael. The same persons again [by] Raphael. Lucretia [by] Parmigianino. A Magdalen's head, the same design with the fine one at Venice, [by] Titian. Old man writing [by] Luca d'Ollanda. Paul III full length and a whole set of portraits, chiefly of the Farnese family, all by Titian. A woman's head [by] Giorgione. Four pieces, loves of the gods, by Bertoio, scholar of the Carraccis—very good. Last Judgement, coloured [by] Michelangelo Buonarotti. Venus and Cupid [by] Michelangelo Buonarotti, same design and the vast hips of the Venus of Bronzino's at a painter's at Florence. The Transfiguration of our Saviour, by Titian's master Giovanni Bellini.

The noble large cameo in agate bottom of a basin, all of one piece, of the apotheosis of Hadrian, who stands before Jupiter; fine illuminated types and antitypes by a Greek, done in 1546. Iulius Iovius Macedo.

Isis kneeling with a god in a case before her, her face handsome Egyptian, hands and feet bad Egyptian. Several strips of painting found negli orti Farnesiani in Nero's Golden House, very bad faces originally—so almost all round the room. A piece of painting from the Villa Hadriani: a woman ending in a fish (?), mixed foliage etc. (grotesque). She-goat, dark, very strong and good from Nero's Golden House. Little brass figures. Jupiter sitting holds his thunder to his side, severe. Less Jupiter, standing, holds up his thunder and is going to fling it, face in a passion. Figure of a man with sea-feet and fish-tail, wound about with two large serpents—head and face as Laocoön's. Saturn with a child sitting at his feet, another held up to his mouth in his left arm and scythe by his right side. It does not look ancient and the whole collection of figures is mixed up of modern, ancient and pretended ancient ones. Fine basso relievo of a drunken Silenus on his ass, held up by two fauns, etc., from Nero's Golden House. The antique called Silenus [is] a Bacchus—very good sistrum, three loose bars.

St. Sepolcro. Virgin with Bambino, Joseph ga[ther]ing a palm branch, going to Egypt [by] Correggio. Virgin, Jesus, several angels attending on him [by] Mazzola (?)—good.

S. Giovanni dei Benedittini. Altar-piece, Transfiguration of our Saviour [by] Mazzola, demi-dome over it; Christ crowning the Virgin [by] Cignani. Martyrdom of Santa Praxida [by] Correggio. A Descent from the Cross [by] Correggio.

Il Duomo. The great dome is painted by Correggio. 'Tis a round on an octagon, eight little round windows among the painting. The subject: the Assumption of the Virgin—a row of figures all round the bottom and a globe of figures from the centre. Among these the Virgin, though scarce to be distinguished at present, very much damaged all over and large patches together quite fallen off, particularly in the centre.

Appendix 16

LIST OF ITEMS IN EGERTON 2235 RELATING TO SPENCE'S TRAVELS ABROAD, NOT INCLUDED IN THIS EDITION OF HIS CORRESPONDENCE

95^{r-v}	'Dr. Richa's Advice'. Spence's copy of a Latin letter, dated 'Taurini, 4 Idus Septembr. 1740,' concerning the beneficent influence of the waters at Acqui for Lord Lincoln's injury. Signed 'Carolus Richa / Serenissimorum Principum / a Sabaudia Archiater'
96^{r-v}	'Dedication of the Roman Almanac for the Year 1741 'al Gloriosissimo San Nicolo di Bari'. In Italian, by Francesco Conti
98^{r}–99^{v}	Notes on antiquities near and about Rome (not in Spence's hand). Includes a drawing of 'one part of the covering of the Portico of the Pantheon'
102^{r-v}	Misc. notes taken in Lyons, chiefly inscriptions; also drafts of some anecdotes by Legris, Loinville, and Père Colonia.
103^{r}–4^{r}	'The Catalogue of Learned Men, &c. in the Great Duke's Gallery'
112^{r}–13^{r}	Extract from Vasari on 'Raphael's Doctors Disputing ab^t the Eucharist, & of other pieces of Raphael' (in French and in Italian)
114^{r}	'The Proportions of Agrippina's Chair in the Florentine Gallery'
115^{v}–16^{r}	List of 'Pieces by Raphael' (compiled from Vasari)
117^{r-v}	Jottings of various inscriptions for Spence's Collection of Allegorical Beings
119^{r}–20^{r}	'Observations on the D. of Devonshire's Gems'
121^{r}–2^{r}	Inscriptions at Florence and Bologna; public notice of indulgences to visitors of 'the Minims Ch: at Sens'
123^{r}	List of Roman emperors (their dates and representations)
124^{r}	Printed list 'delle Stampe di Giacomo Frey'—with 'those I have' marked with a cross, duplicates with '2'. 'Summe Total 15.65'; Spence paid for them and for the duplicates '9.70'
125^{r}–6^{r}	Misc. notes
127^{r}–36^{v}	Excerpts 'From Flav: Philostratus's Icones . . . For the List of Allegorical Beings'

index

187; Mark Antony, 187; Mars, 277 (*see also* Ares Borghese); Mars and Venus, 144, 145; Marsyas, 148, 187; Medusa, 143, 431, App. 11; Menelaus, 127 n.7; Mercury, 113, 172, 275; Minerva, 108, 150, 187, 276; Minotaur, 375, 431; Muse?, 277; Neptune, 99 n.8, 196 n.3; Nero, 78, 143, 276; Old Orator, *see* Arringatore; Orpheus, 277; Pallas, 188, 432; Pan, 146, 188, 375; Paris, 150, 187, 431; Patroclus, 127 n.7; Perseus, App. 11; Phrygian general, *see* Attis; Plato, 187; Plautilla, 148, 149 n.5; Po (river), 136; Polyphemus, 276; Pompey, 115; Priapus, 108, 158; Psyche, 123, 187; Pyrrhus, 187; Romulus and Remus, 115; Sabina?, 276; Saturn, 185, 439; Satyr, 106, 276, 431; Scipio Africanus, 187; Scyriades, 187; Season?, 276; Seleucus, 172; Seneca, 187, 276; Silenus, 146, 187, 196 n.6, 277, 432, 439; Socrates, 276; Somnus, 145, 277; Sylvanus, 277; Tabula Isiaca, 278 n.2, 304 n.4; Theseus, 375, 431; Thetis, 277; Trajan, 276; Ulysses, 186, 187; Venus, 83 n.8, 113, 144, 149, 150, 185, 187, 276, 277; Venus of Arles, 158; Venus of Medici, 15, 150, 185, 256 n.4, 330 n.2; Verus, Annius, 148; Vespasian, 187, 222, 276; Vestal, 143, 276; Victory, 376, 431; Vitellius, 156, 276, 432; Vulcan, 188; Winter, 196 n.6

Antonini, Annibale (1702-55), misc. writer: *Mémorial de Paris et ses environs . . .* (Paris, 1734), 185-90 *passim*

Antony, Mark (83-30 B.C.), 65 n.3, 267, 291 n.7

Antwerp, 174, 180; l'Abbaye des Bernardins, 429; paintings at, 180, 427-9

Anxur, 106 n.1

Aosta, Carlo Francesco, D. of (1738-45), 290

Apennines, the, 99 n.6, 156, 317, 329, 332; passing of, 101-2, 325-6

Apollo, 148

Aragon, Petrus Antonius (ca. 1670), 108 n.1

Arassi (?Grasses), 400 n.2

Archer, Thomas (1695-1768), cr. B. Archer 1747, President Soc. Dilettanti,

subscr. *Polymetis*, and wife: met at Florence, App. 1

Arezzo, 127 n.4, 147 n.5

Argyll, Archibald, 9th E. of (1629-85), 122

Ariosto, Lodovico (1474-1533), It. poet, 19, 67 n.7; his tomb, 99 n.6

Arles, App. 4; amphitheatre and Town House, 158; Bp. of, *see* Forbin-Janson, Jacques de

Arnauld. *See* Arnaut d'Anvers

Arnaut d'Anvers(?), Flemish painter: pictures at Lille, 182

Arno, 133, 134, 350; overflown, 333, 334 n.1; vale of, 122, 124, 126, 156

Arpino, Giuseppe Cesari (1568-1640), It. painter: 'Crucifixion' at S. Martino (Naples), 107; two pictures at Count d'Arese's gallery (Milan), 78

Arthepius, adept, 304 n.6

Ashton, Rev. Thomas (1716-75), divine, 416 n.4

Asti, 309

Athens, 273; inscription 'To the Unknown God', 292

Athos, 264, 329

Atkinson, Father, Scots Jesuit at Loreto, 99 nn.9, 14

Atlas, Mount, 249

Augusta, Princess of Saxe-Gotha (1719-72), wife of Frederick, Pr. of Wales: delivered of a daughter, 195

Augustus, Caius Julius Caesar Octavianus (63 B.C.-A.D. 14), 13, 49, 116 n.6; his birthplace?, 106; mausoleum, 137; medal of, with Julian star, 136; rebuilds Troy, 263; triumphal arch, 99, 100

Avanzini, Bartolomeo Luigi (end 16th cent.-1658), It. painter: paintings at Duke's Palace (Modena), 437

Avignon, 56 n.3, 207, App. 4; bridge at, 401; cost of transportation to Marseilles, App. 2

Bacon, Francis (1561-1626), philosopher: on beauty, 17

Bagshaw, Rev., subscr. *Polymetis*: met at Florence, App. 1

Baile. *See* Bale, Joseph Challoner

Bailley, Rachel (1696–1773), m. 1715 Charles Hamilton, styled B. Binning: met at Naples, App. 1

Bale, Joseph Challoner (b. 1724), Winchester scholar, 199, 201, 238

Ball, Sir Peter (d. 1680), *or* his son Thomas (1672–1749), 293

Ball, Thomas (b. 1722), Winchester scholar: S. asked to help him, 199

Ballotting, 87, 395

Baluruc, App. 4

Bandinelli, Baccio (1493–1560), Florentine sculptor: bas-relief at Santa Casa (Loreto), 100; copy of 'Laocoön' (Florence), 150

Bandini, Giovanni, di Benedetto da Castello (1540–99), Florentine sculptor: statue of Ferdinand I (Leghorn), 119

Barabbas, 42

Barbaud, Mr.: met at Genoa, App. 1

Barberini, Maffeo, Pope Urban VIII, 1623–44, 126

Barbot, Jean de (*fl.* 1719–52), President of the Academy of Sciences and Arts at Bordeaux, App. 4

Barclay, Lord. *See* Berkeley, Augustus

Barrington, Lord. *See* Wildman, William

Barton, Philip (b. 1696), L.L.D., 53–4 n.8, 67

Barton, Philip (b. 1715), Winchester scholar, 201

Barton, Stephen (b. 1701), Winchester scholar, 53, 54 n.8, 67

Barty. *See* Bertie, Norreys

Bassano family (ca. 1549–1621), Venetian painters: 'Apollo flaying Marsyas' (Modena), 438; pictures at Grimani's (Venice), 91; at the Palais Royal (Paris), 186; at the Royal Palace (Turin), 277

Bassi, Martino (1542–91), Milanese architect: mistaken by S. for G. Bologna, 78

Bassus, Junius (3d cent. A.D.), Roman consul: basilica of, 345 n.3

Bateman, William (1695?–1744), 1st Visc. Bateman, M.P.: met at Paris, App. 1

Bates, Mr.: met at Turin, App. 1

Bayly, Hon. or Rev., subscr. *Polymetis*: met at Florence, App. 1

Beauvillier(s), Paul-Hippolyte de (1684–1776), D. de Saint-Aignan: at Lyons, 67; at Rome with the Pretender, 342

Beckford, Mr.: met at The Hague, App. 1

Bedford, D. of. *See* Russel, John

Bedford, Lord Robert, Scottish freemason, 5

Beemster, the, 173

Beguines, 181

Belches, Mr.: met at Rome, App. 1

Belgarde, Mr.: met at Turin, App. 1

Belle. *See* Spence, Belle

Bellerophon, mythical slayer of the chimaera, 146

Bellew, Sir Edward (d. 1741): met at Lyons, 54; at Rome, App. 1

Bellew, Lady Eleanor (d. 1752?), née Moore, of Drogheda, m. Sir Edward ca. 1728: met at Rome, App. 1

Bellini, Giovanni (ca. 1430–1516), It. painter: 'Transfiguration' (Parma), 439

Bellona, 285 n.5

Belloni, Girolamo, marchese (d. 1761), banker at Rome, 340; bill of credit for S., App. 10

Belson, Frances, English nun in Paris: S. brings letters to her, 36, 37 n.7, 40, 161

Bembo, Pietro (1470–1547), cardinal, 67 n.7, 146

Benedict XIII, Pope. *See* Orsini, Francesco Piero

Benedict XIV, Pope. *See* Lambertini, Prospero Lorenzo

Benedictines: at Ferrara, 99 n.6; Reims, 32; St. Denis, 201; Sens, 222; Tournai, 182

Bennet, Mr., inn-keeper? at Bordeaux, App. 4

Benning, Lord and Lady. *See* Binning

Bentinck, Lord George (1715–59), M.P.: met at Brussels, 180; The Hague, 178, App. 1

Bentinck, William (1709–62), 2d D. of Portland: met at Paris, App. 1; The Hague, 178 n.3, App. 1

Bentivoglio, Guido (1577–1644), cardinal and historian: his language frenchified, 67 n.7

'Genius of the Apennines' (Pratolino), 329; horse (Paris), 189–90; mistaken by S. for M. Bassi, 78

Bolognese, 99 n.6, App. 3

Bolognini, Carlo (ca. 1662/78–1704), It. painter: mistaken by S. for Carlone, Gianbattista, 156

Bolsena, Lago di, 117

Bonazza, Giovanni (1654–1736), Venetian sculptor, 90

Bonazzo. See Bonazza, Giovanni

Bonducci, Abbé Andrea, It. translator: *Il Riccio rapito* (1739), 334 n.5

Boniface VIII, Pope 1294–1303, 157

Borch, Oluf (1626–90), Danish polygraph, 305 n.9

Bordeaux, 207, App. 4

Bordone, Paris (1500–71), Trevisan painter: 'The Ring Delivered' at albergo (Venice), 91

Bordoni Hasse, Faustina (1693–1781), It. soprano, 398 n.5; sings at Venice, 84

Borghese, Pr. Camillo (1693–1763), 316 n.9

Borgia, Cesare (1475–1507), It. statesman, App. 12

Bormida (river), 312, 313, 318; S.'s Latin verses on, 317 n.1

Borromeo. See St. Charles Borromeo

Bosschaert, Ambrosius (ante 1570–1645?), Flemish painter: two flower pieces at Augustins (Antwerp), 428

Botticelli, Sandro (1445–1510), It. painter, 15

Bouchain, 174

Boughton, Mr.: met at Florence, App. 1

Bouillon, Charles-Godefroi, D. de la Tour d'Auvergne (1706–72), 66

Boulogne, 219 n.1

Bourbon, Don Carlos de. See Carlos III

Bourbon, Dss. of. See Hesse-Rheinfels-Rothenburg, Caroline

Bourbon, Louis-Alexandre de (1678–1737), Cte de Toulouse: his gallery, 188

Bourbon, Louis-Henri, D. de (1692–1740), 74; his death mourned at Turin, 257; his mistress at Dijon, 36; neglects his wife, 102; stables more magnificent than château, 220; his woods near Chantilly, 183, 184, 194 n.4, 220

Bourchier, Sir. See Wrey, Sir Bourchier

Bourgonjon, Pieter le (*fl.* 1687), Flemish painter: picture(s) at Mme de Wiet's (Antwerp), 428

Bourguignon. See Bourgonjon, Pieter le

Boursier, M.: at Turin, 277

Bowman, Mr., travelling tutor of Lord Harcourt, member Soc. Dilettanti: his 'Memoir for the Provinces of France', App. 4; met at Florence, App. 1

Boyle, Lady Dorothy (1724–42), dau. of E. of Burlington, 316, 366

Boyle, Richard (ca. 1675–1740), 2d Visc. Shannon, 366; met at Paris, App. 1

Boyle, Richard (1695–1753), 3d E. of Burlington, 316 n.7

Brachenhofer Echevin, Elie, of Strasbourg, 305 n.9

Bradeniga: a martyr?, 90–1

Brand, Thomas (ca. 1717–70), of The Hoo, Kimpton, Herts., M.P., member Soc. Dilettanti, subscr. *Polymetis*, 168 n.4

Breda, 174, 179–80, 184

Brenta, 3, 84, 390

Brescia, 81 n.5

Breughel. See Brueghel, Pieter(?)

Brewer, Mrs. Betty, of Winchester, 238

Brewer, Nathaniel, Winchester scholar, 238

Briare, 207 n.1

Brideoake, Mr.: at Oxford, 60

Bridgeman, Charles (*fl.* 1713–38), landscape architect, 70, 373

Bridgeman, Mr.: met at Paris, App. 1

Briscowe, Mr. See Bristow, William

Bristol, Elizabeth, Css. of (1676–1741), 360 n.1

Bristow, William (d. 1758): met at Turin, 246, App. 1

Britton, Mr.: met at Rome, App. 1

Brives, 405

Bronzino, Angiolo Troti, called (1503–63), It. painter: 'Venus at the painter's' (Parma), 439

Brosse, Jacques de (1562–1626), French architect: Luxembourg Palace (1615), 185

Brosses, Charles de (1709–77), Président: *Lettres familières écrites d'Italie en 1739 et 1740* quoted, 81 n.4, 131 n.4, 162 n.6, 228 n.1, 240 nn.5, 6, 252 n.7, 256 n.4,

448

Carignani, D. of, banker at Naples, 113

Carlo, Francesco (1738–45), D. of Aosta, 290, 291 n.5

Carlone, Gianbattista (1594–1680), It. painter, mistaken by S. for Bolognini: roof of the Annunziata (Genoa), 156

Carlos III de Bourbon (1716–88), D. of Parma and Piacenza 1731–5, K. of Naples and Sicily 1735–59, later K. of Spain, 134, 381; his house at Portici, 372, 374, 375 and n.7; parted from Florence, 126, 127; patronizes excavations at Herculaneum, 372, 374; shown *Polymetis* by Paderni, App. 14

Carmelites: at Torre del Greco, 363–4

Caroline of Ansbach (1683–1737), Q. of England, 36 n.1, 181 n.11; her house at Kew, 193

Carpenter, ?John, 384

Carpi, Girolamo da (1501–56), It painter: 'Venus in a sea-shell' (Modena), 438

Carpo, Geronimo da. *See* Carpi, Girolamo da

Carracci, Agostino (1557–1602), It. painter: engraving of Tintoretto's 'Crucifixion', 91; 'Magdalen's head' (Modena), 438

Carracci, Annibale (1560–1609), It. painter
—paintings at Genoa: 'Venus and Cupid' at Balbi Palace, 156
—at Loreto: 'Meeting of the Virgin and Elizabeth', 100
 at Modena: 'Angel flying with a crown', 438; 'Hercules and Cerberus', 438; 'Magdalen', 438; 'St. Francis kissing Bambino's foot', 438; 'Saviour's head thorned', 438
—at Parma: 'Judgement of Hercules', 439; 'Sleeping Venus', 439

Carracci, Ludovico (1555–1619), Bolognese painter: 'The Assunta' (Modena), 438

Carracci brothers: dome of cathedral (Piacenza), 155; at Palais Royal (Paris), 186; various pieces (Modena), 438

Carriera, Rosalba (1675–1757), Venetian portraitist, 398 n.2; how much S. paid her, App. 11, App. 12; S.'s conversation with, 12, 16

Cartagena, 367 n.2

Carteret, John (1690–1763), 1st E. Granville, politician, 287 n.5, 367 n.1; marries Sophia Fermor, 9

Carthusians: at Antwerp, 427; Dijon, 40–1, 222; Ferrara, 99 n.6; Naples, 107

Cartwright, Elizabeth, S.'s friend, 178 n.8

Caserta, Pr. of, 106

Cassini. *See* Florence, Cascine gardens

Castellamonte, Amedeo (d. 1683), It. architect, 225 n.3, 227 n.1

Castelli, Giuseppe Antonio, styled Castellino da Monza (*fl.* ca. 1700): his *deceptio visu* (Milan), 320

Castellino da Monza. *See* Castelli, Giuseppe Antonio

Castelnaudary, 405 n.1

Castleton, Nathaniel (?d. 1782), subscr. *Polymetis*, 369; met at Turin, App. 1

Catharina, violinist at Venice, 397

Catherine of Braganza (1683–1705), Queen consort of Charles II, 98

Cato Marcus Porcius, the Censor (234–149 B.C.), Roman statesman, 18, 266 n.4, 291

Cavalca, Conte, 389

Cavalcanti, Guido (ca. 1255–1300), It. poet, 186

Cavendish, George (1500–61?), author of *The Negotiations of Thomas Woolsey* (1641), 237 n.1

Cavendish, Lord James (post 1698–1741), M.P. for Malton, Col., 34th Foot: met at Calais, App. 1

Cavendish, William (ca. 1720–64), styled Marquess of Hartington, later 4th D. of Devonshire, 129 n.5, 312 n.2, 313, App. 3; his cook, App. 3; met at Alessandria, 313, App. 1; 'observations' on his gems, App. 16

Cecil, Margaret (ca. 1696–1782), wife of Sir Robert Brown: met at Venice, App. 1

Cecilia, singer at Venice, 397

Cellini, Benvenuto (1500–71), Florentine sculptor: 'Ganymede'? at Grand Duke's gallery, 146

Cerretesi, Giuseppe (b. 1702), Florentine poet and freemason, 390

Cervantes (1547–1616), 281

Cesari, Giuseppe. *See* Arpino

Cesena, App. 5

6 leagues, 190; Pistoia, 'thin of people', 124; Rome, 13 miles, 'not a third inside fairly inhabited', 114; Rotterdam, 80,000, 179; Siena, 7 miles, 119; Turin, 70,000/3 miles, well peopled, 274

Hulse's powders, 8, *260*, 366; sprains his leg in a jumping contest, 300, 306–8, 310; goes to Acqui to take waters, 312, 313, 314, 317, App. 16; is examined by Dr. Cocchi, 330; returns home healthy and stronger, 10, 400

—letters: from H. Walpole, 333, 347, 351, 385, 412; from H. Pelham, 25, *Letter 154*; from D. of Newcastle, *Letters 91, 153, 161*; to D. of Newcastle, 25, *Letters 77, 80, 109, 120, 125, 143, 155, 159, 175, 176, 178*; to Mrs. S., *Letter 174*

—on return to England: hopes to settle in London with his sister, 412; marries Catherine Pelham, 9, 239 n.6; received graciously by George II, 418 n.2

Clinton, Lady Lucy (1692–1736), Lincoln's mother, sister of D. of Newcastle, 219 n., 225 n., 251; character of, 311, 315; in France with her children, 311, 316 n.4, 399–400

Clinton, Lady Lucy (1721–63), Lincoln's sister, 8, 311, 366, 384, 400 n.4; stays with her aunt Shelley, 368; to live with her brother in London, 412

Clinton, Margaret (b. 1722), 400 n.4

Clinton, Thomas (1723–6), 400 n.4

Clipperton, captain of the *Success*, 210

Clitus (4th cent. B.C.), Illyrian prince, 147

Clogher, 10

Cluver(ius), Philip (1580–1623), German scholar, App. 5

Cocchi, Dr. Antonio (1695–1758), physician at Florence, App. 14; asked by S. for help in 'the Affair', 334, 351; with drawing of sarcophagus, 14, 334, 351; with MSS, 340, 351; in translating *Crito* into Italian, 17; becomes freemason, 5, 6; on Boerhaave, 172 n.4; on Correggio, 16; on Eastern manner of writing, 120; on *improvvisatori*, 20; on Italian character, 141 n.2; on Italian literature, 12, 19, 21; his letter on ethics translated by S., 17; his library damaged by inundation, 333–4, 350; Lord Lincoln examined by, 330; on oleo de' sassi, 328; on Pope and Boileau, 22; S.'s letters to, 17 nn.70, 73, 25, 120, 333–4, 340, 350–1, *Letters 36, 135, 139,*

146; talks English like an Englishman, 387; translates S.'s treatise 'sul Rinascimento della Letterature'?, 17; travels to Reggio to treat H. Walpole, 387–8, 390

Cocchi, Beatrice, dau. of Dr. Cocchi, 340

Cocchi, Dr. Raimondo (1735–65), son of Dr. Cocchi, later antiquarian in Grand Duke's gallery, 340

Cocchi, Teresa (ca. 1711–post 1774), née Piombanti, wife of Dr. Cocchi, 334, 340

Cocles, Horatius, legendary Roman hero, 115

Coke, Edward (1719–53), B. Lovel of Minstrel Lovel, M.P.: met at Blois, 209; at Paris, App. 1

Coke, Thomas (1697–1759), of Norfolk, later E. of Leicester, 209

Colchester, 168 n.3

Cole, Mr.: met at Marseilles, 158, App. 9

Colebroke, Mr. *See* Colebrooke, Robert

Colebrooke, Robert (1718–84), of Chiltham Castle, Kent, M.P., diplomat, member Soc. Dilettanti, subscr. *Polymetis*: met at Turin, App. 1

Coleman. *See* Colman, Francis

Colet, John (1467?–1519), Dean of St. Paul's, 319 n.1

Colette, Président: at Toulouse, App. 4

Colgrave, Sir George: and wife at Dijon, 36, 40, App. 1

Col(l)eoni, Bartolomeo (1400–76), condottiere: equestrian statue of, 90

Collier, General: met at Namur, 30, App. 1

Collins, John, inn-keeper at Florence, 6, App. 3

Collyer, Thomas, S.'s grandfather, 29 n.

Colman, Francis (1690?–1733), British resident at Florence: on *improvvisatori*, 20; met at Florence, App. 1; opera enthusiast, 6

Colonia, Dominique de (1660–1741), learned Jesuit at Lyons, 66, 81, App. 16; on tauribolium, 61–2

Colonna, Princess Agnese (1702–80), 316

Colonna, Fabrizio (1700–55), Great Constable of the Kingdom of Naples, 381

Colvil. *See* Colville, John

Colville, John (1542?–1605), Scottish divine, R.C. convert, 80 n.2

Colyer, Elizabeth (1687–1768), Dss. of Dorset, mother of Lord Middlesex: at Paris, 199; S. missed her at Brussels, 180, 199

Condé, Louis, Pr. de (1621–86), 220

Congreve, William (1670–1729), dramatist: encouraged young Lady Mary, 357, 358 n.5

Constable, Sir Marmaduke (1656–1746), Bt.: met at Florence, App. 1

Constantine the Great (288?–337), Roman Emperor, 92 n.2, 332, 345 n.3, App. 4

Constantinople, 91, 92 n.2, 243, 249, 271; St. Sophia, 359–60; seraglio, 263, 273, 357

Contarini family, 91

Conti, Antonio (1677–49), Abbé and man of letters, 358 n.13

Conti, Francesco (*fl.* 1741), App. 16

Cook, Sir George, 382 n.4

Cooke, John (1738–1810), chaplain of Greenwich Hospital, 254 n.4

Cope, Capt. (?William, d. 1769): met at Marseilles, App. 1

Copernicus, Nicholas (1473–1543), astronomer, 185

Corfu, 86

Cornbury, Lord. *See* Hyde, Henry

Corneille de Lyon (*fl.* 1534–74), French painter: drawing of the dome of Val de Grâce, 188

Correggio, Antonio Allegri (ca. 1489/94–1534), It. painter
—paintings at Modena: 'Bambino in Virgin's lap', 438; 'Il Medico', portrait, 438; 'La Notte', 439; 'Little Magdalen, lying and reading', 439; 'Madonna, etc.', 439; 'Madonna and Bambino in clouds', 438; 'Virgin and four saints', 438; 'Virgin speaking to an ecclesiastic', 438
—at Paris: 'Cupid' at Palais Royal, 186; 'Dying Cleopatra' at Card. Polignac's, 188; 'Muleteer' at Palais Royal, 190 n.2
—at Parma: 'Ascension of Our Saviour' at St. John's, 320; 'Ascension of the Virgin' at the Duomo, 320, 440; 'Conversion of Mary Magdalen' at S. Antonio, 320; 'Descent from the Cross' at S. Giovanni dei Benedittini, 440; 'Holy Family going

to Egypt' at S. Sepolcro, 439; 'Martyrdom of St. Praxida' at S. Giovanni, 440
—praised by Cocchi, 16

Corsica, 298

Corsini, Lorenzo (1652–1740), Pope Clement XII, 350 n.2; English visitors did not have to kiss his slipper, 335; treated flippantly by Lambertini, 321–2

Cosimo. *See* Medici, Cosimo de'

Côte Notée hill, 159

Cotheret, M., director of hospital at Dijon, 34; S. stays at his home, 36; wife of, 38

Cotterel, Sir Clement (1685–1758), Master of Ceremonies, 130

Cotton, Sir John Hynde (1717?–95), 4th Bt., M.P., subscr. *Polymetis*: met at Turin, App. 1

Cotton (?Sir Robert, 1669–1749, of Gidding Huntingdon, succ. as 5th Bt. 1631, subscr. *Polymetis*): met at Lyons 1731, App. 1

Courtin family: at Blois, 192 n.3

Coustou, Nicolas (1658–1733), and Guillaume (1677–1746), French sculptors: river-statues at Lyons, 53

Cox, Michael (1697?–1779), Bp. of Ossory 1743–54, subscr. *Polymetis*, 29

Coxe, William (1747–1828), historian, 2

Coxed, John, Warden of Winchester College, 306 n.1, 311

Coypel, Antoine (1661–1722), French painter: at Palais Royal, took to drinking, 186

Coysevox, Antoine (1640–1720), French sculptor: 'Mercury' and 'Fame' (Tuileries), 185; tomb of Card. Mazarin, 189

Craig, James, minister of the Gospel, Edinburgh, author of *Spiritual Life* (1727), 274 n.2

Cramer, Gabriel (1704–52), Prof. of Mathematics and Philosophy at Geneva, 70, 71 n.1

Crashaw, Richard (1613–49), poet: his epitaph at Loreto, 99 n.9

Crawley, Mr.: met at Florence, 420

Cremona, 398 n.1

Créquy, Charles I de Blanchefort, Marquis de (ca. 1567–1638), French marshal, 301–2

Crescimbeni, Giovan Maria (1663–1728), literary historian: *Istoria della Volgar Poesia* (Venice, 1730), 18, 19

Crew, Samuel (*fl.* 1722–45), His Majesty's messenger, 286

Crowe, Edward, subscr. *Polymetis*: met at Florence, App. 1

Crowley, Ambrose (d. 1754), subscr. *Polymetis*: met at Florence and Paris, App. 1

Croxall, Samuel (ca. 1689–1752), D.D.: *The Fair Circassian* (1720), 273

Crudeli, Tommaso (1703–45), It. poet: on Accademia della Crusca, 19; freemason, 6

Cudworth, Ralph (1631–1718), Anglican divine, 294 n.9

Cugini, Antonio (1678–1765), It. architect, 386 n.2

Cumae, 107, 113

Curtis, John (1691–1789), merchant, subscr. *Polymetis*: met at Turin, App. 1

Curtius, Marcus, legendary Roman hero, 115

Cuzzoni, Francesca (1700–70), It. operatic singer, 398 n.5

Cyprus, 86

Dailley, Mr.: met at Turin, App. 1

Dalton (?Richard, ca. 1715–91, engraver and antiquarian): met at Rome, App. 1; his prints, App. 11

Dante Alighieri (1265–1321), It. poet, 19, 67 n.7, 121, 123, 146; S.'s translations from, 122–3 n.4

Danube, 136

Darby, Widdrington (d. 1727), 382 n.4

Dardanelles, 263

Dashwood, Sir Francis (1708–81), later B. Le Despenser, 369, 389, 390, 411, 415; member Soc. of Dilettanti, 7; met at Turin and Modena, App. 1

Dauphin, the. *See* Louis XV

Dauphiné, 49

Davenport, Robert, carpenter, 213

Degge, William (b. 1698), of Derby, Lt.-Col. of Dragoons, member Soc. Dilettanti 1736: met at Rome, App. 1

De Heem. *See* Heem, Jan Davidz, de

Delft, 178

Della Casa, Giovanni (1503–56), It. humanist, 67 n.7

Delmé, Peter (1710–70), M.P., member Soc. Dilettanti: met at Geneva, App. 1

Delorme, Philibert (ca. 1512–70), French architect, 200

Delos, 264 n.1

Dendermonde, 174

Denny, William (1709–90): met at Dijon and Lyons, 46, 53, App. 1

Desaguliers, John Theophilus (1683–1744), natural philosopher, 414 n.7

Descartes, René (1596–1650), philosopher: animals as machines, 413; his house at Leyden, 172 n.9

Desjardins, Martin van den Bogaert, styled (d. 1694), Dutch sculptor: statue of Louis XIV, 53

Deskford, Lord. *See* Ogilvy, James

D'Eury's, inn at Venice, App. 3

Devenish, Charles, subscr. *Polymetis*: met at Turin, App. 1

De Ville, Chevalier, architect: Machine de Marly, 200 n.10

Devnish, Mr. *See* Devenish, Charles

Devonshire, 51 n., 59, 62, 125, 129, 135

Devonshire, D. of. *See* Cavendish, William

Deze, Mr.: met at Florence, App. 1

Diana, temple of, 344

Dick. *See* Spence, Richard

Dieppe, App. 2

Dijon, 17, 31, 33, 34 n.1, 47, 53, 54, 57, 125, 222, App. 1; Carthusian monastery, 15 n.62, 40–1; College of Chartreux, 40–1; concerts, 36; Easter procession and *crécelles*, 42–3; heathen temple at, 44, 50–1, 61; hospital, 34; how long letters from England take, 33, 37, 39, 44; Jesuit library, 43–4; picture of, 66; principal buildings, 34; public walks, 34, 35; ramparts, 34; Sainte Chapelle, 34; university, 34; women, 36, 38

Dingley, Robert (1709–81), virtuoso: met at Florence, 139, 152, App. 1

Dinocrates (4th cent. B.C.), Greek architect, 329 n.1

Dionysius the Elder (430?–367 B.C.), tyrant of Syracuse, 253

Dobson, William (*fl.* 1734–50), classical scholar, App. 7

Doddington, George Bubb (1691?–1762), M.P., later B. of Melcombe Regis, patron of letters, member Soc. Dilettanti: met at Florence, App. 1

Dodsley, Robert (1703–64), publisher, 59 n.3, 282–3

Domenichino, *or* Domenico Zampieri (1581–1641), It. painter: at Card. Polignac's (Paris), 188; four *tondi* (reprod.), App. 13; print of?, App. 13; 'St. Jerome', celebrated painting, 16

Dominiquin. *See* Domenichino

Don Carlos. *See* Carlos III

Don Filippo. *See* Juvarra, Filippo

Dora, 275

Dordt (Dordrecht), 174

Doria, Andrea (1466–1560), It. admiral, 156

Doria, Gian Andrea (1607–40), Viceroy of Sardinia, 156

Dorset, D. of. *See* Sackville, Lionel Cranfield

Dorset, Dss. of. *See* Colyer, Elizabeth

Dorsetshire, 30, 48, 109

Dort. *See* Dordt

Dosso Dossi (ca. 1479/90–1542), It. painter: 'Ascension of the Virgin' (Modena), 438

Douai, App. 4

Doué. *See* Douai

Douglas, Charles (1698–1778), 3d D. of Queensberry, 85

Douglas, Earl, 381

Douglas, Henry (1722–56), styled E. of Drumlanrig, 85, 94 n.9

Douglas, Robert, of Morton (d. 1745), Col., M.P.: met at Venice, App. 1

Dover, 10, 29, 380, 403

Downes, Robert (1705–63), Bp. of Derry, 128, 208, 416

Drake, Sir Francis (ca. 1540–96), explorer, 209

Drumlanrig, E. of. *See* Douglas, Henry

Dryden, John (1631–1700), poet, 109 n.2, 267, 347, 416

Duck, Stephen (1705–56), the Thresher-Poet, 181 n.7, 252, 293; corresponds with S., 170, 201, 214; disperses S.'s books, 201; S.'s pamphlet on, 44–5 n.7, 53

Du Deffand, Marie-Anne de Vichy-Champrond (1696–1780), marquise, 12 n.47

Dudley, Robert (1532–88), E. of Leicester, 118

Dudley, Sir Robert (1573–1649), styled D. of Northumberland and E. of Warwick, 118

Dufay, M., Capt. in the Guards, 305 n.9

Duglass, Mr.: met at Naples, App. 1

Duinenpoort, 178

Dunbar, Lord. *See* Murray, Hon. James

Dundass, Robert (1713–87), P.M.: met at Florence and Paris, App. 1

Dunk, Ann (1726–53), rich heiress: match for Lord Lincoln, 308, 315, 366

Dunk, William Richards, of Tongues, 316 n.5

Dunke, Sir Thomas (d. 1718), Sheriff of London, 316 n.5

Dunkirk, 29, 30

Dunk Montagu, George (1716–71), 2d E. of Halifax, 286, 316 n.5, 367 n.4

Duns Scotus, John (ca. 1270–1308), theologian, 80 n.2

Dupont, Mme, French governess of Lady Mary, 358 n.4

Dupré, Guillaume (1574–1647), French sculptor: statue of Henri IV (Paris), 189

Durazzo, Girolamo: his palace at Genoa, dau. of the family married, 156

Durham, 10; S. granted prebend at, 10

Échelles, 222, 224 n.4

Edam, 172 n.1, 174

Edwards, Mr.: met at Holland, 179

Edwin, Charles (ca. 1699–1756), M.P., and wife: met at Rome, App. 1

Egeria, grotto of, 22

Egmont, E. of. *See* Perceval, John

Egypt, 130, 243, 249, 256 n.1, 263, 264; hatcheries and female hunchbacks, 270–1; pyramids, 265, 268–9; Sphinx, 268. *See also* Nile, the

Elboeuf, Pr. d'. *See* Emmanuel-Maurice de Lorraine

Elcho, Lord. *See* Wemyss, David

Eleanora (1728–81), dau. of Charles Emmanuel III, 289 n.2

Elizabeth-Thérèse of Lorraine (1711–41), Q. of Sardinia, 3d wife of Charles Emmanuel III, 223; delivered of a

456

daughter, 292; made a prince last year, 290; at marriage of Prince Carignan, 289; at Maundy ceremony, 281; not handsome, 280; dies, 293 n.1

Ellis, John (1643?-1738), politician, 299

Ellis, Philip (1652-1726), Bp. of Segni, 299

Ellis, Wellbore (1651?-1734), Bp. of Meath, 299

Ellis, Wellbore (1713-1802), politician, M.P., 299, App. 12; met at Turin, App. 1

Ellis, William (1642?-1732), secretary to James II, 299

Elton, Mr.: met at Venice, App. 1

Emilia, singer at Venice, 397-8

Emilian Way. *See* Via Emilia

Emmanuel-Maurice de Lorraine (1677-1763), Pr. d'Elboeuf: and Herculaneum, 374 nn.3, 6

Emmanuel-Philibert (1731-5), 2d son of Charles Emmanuel III, 224 n.3, 289 n.2

Emperor of the Holy Roman Empire. *See* Charles VI; Ferdinand II

Emrod, table of, 304 n.4

Engelbert, Cte de Nassau (d. 1435), 181 n.4

Englefield, Sir Henry (?F.R.S., d. 1778, *or* Bt., d. 1780): met at Turin, App. 1

Englis, Mr.: met at Tours, App. 1

Ennius, Quintus (239-169 B.C.), Latin poet, 14, 137

Erlach, Louis-Auguste (ca. 1722-48), B. Erlach, Capt. in the Swiss Guards, 236, 241, App. 14

Erlach, Sigmund (1614-99), Swiss advoyer, 236

Ernest-Leopold (1684-1731), Landgrave of Hesse-Rheinfels-Rothenburg, 74, 102

Erskine, John (1675-1732), 22d E. of Mar, Jacobite leader, 36 n.4

Essex, 216, 339, 405, 407

Estampes, 192 n.1, 201

Este, Amalia Aurelia Giuseppina d' (1699-1778), Princess of Modena, 389-90

Este, Francesco Maria d' (1698-1780), D. of Modena, 389

Este, Mary Beatrice Eleanor (1638-1718), 2d wife of James II, 98

Este, Rinaldo III, D. of (d. 1737), 391 n.3

Eton, 8, 252

Eugene, Pr. *See* Savoie-Carignan, François Eugène de

Euston, Lord. *See* Fitzroy, George

Fabricius, Roman consul 282 B.C., 30, 181

Faerno, Filippo: at Genoa, 157

Fane, Hon. Dorothy (1716-97), dau. of 1st Visc. Fane, 274 n.3

Fanny, Lady: met at Rome, App. 1

Fano, 99

Farnese, Alessandro (1545-92), and Ranuccio (1569-1622), Dukes of Parma: statues of, by F. Mochi, 155

Farnham, 128

Faustina. *See* Bordoni Hasse, Faustina

Faustina, wife of Marcus Aurelius (A.D. 125-75), 148

Feilding, Hon. Charles (d. 1746), Lt.-Col. in the Army, member Soc. Dilettanti 1736: met at Florence, App. 1

Félibien, André (1619-95), French historiographer, 87 n.1, 90

Fénelon, François de Salignac de la Mothe (1651-1715), French ecclesiastic and writer, 22; his monument at Cambrai, 183

Ferdinand II (1578-1637), Holy Roman Emperor from 1619, 303

Fermor, Lady Charlotte (1725-1813), 2d dau. of Lady Pomfret, 313, 328 n.7, 385; met at Florence, App. 1

Fermor, George (1722-85), styled Lord Lempster, later 2d E. of Pomfret: met at Paris, App. 1; at the Turin Academy, 389, 391 n.; Sophia Fermor's letter to, 389-91

Fermor, Lady Sophia (1721-45), dau. of Lady Pomfret, 313, 328, 351 n.4, 385, 389, 394, 399, 410, 412; her beauty, 9, 358 n.2, 412; courted by Sir John Rawdon, 284; by Uguccioni, 351; her dogs, 390-1; on flood in Florence, 332 n.2; French sonnet on her, 351; lacks nothing but fortune, 9, 370-1; on Lady Mary, 358 n.2; letter to her brother, 25, 389-91; Lord Lincoln's affair with, *see* Clinton, Henry Fiennes; met at Florence, 328, App. 1; on the river Brenta, 390; sends home artificial flowers, 379 n.1;

on Venus de' Medici, 330 n.2; verses on her marriage, 9

Fermor, Thomas (1698–1753), 1st E. of Pomfret, 244 n.9, 284, 314 n.5, 377, 385, 389, 410, 412; met at Florence, App. 1

Ferne, Mr.: at Winchester, 238

Ferrara, 97, 98

Ferrari, Mr., art dealer at Antwerp, App. 6

Ferrers, Lord. *See* Shirley, Hon. Sewallis

Fiammingo, François Duquesnoy, styled Il F. (1594–1643), painter and sculptor: 'Boreas and Orithya'? at Tuileries, 185; 'Susanna', celebrated statue, 16 n.66

Ficoroni, Francesco (1664–1747), antiquary and S.'s cicerone at Rome, 12, 13, 116 nn.3, 10, 118 n.2, 127 n.8; on Addison's knowledge of medals, 13 n.49; his character, 130, 131 n.4; on contemporary decline of arts, 16; on overflow of the Tiber, 332 n.3; prosecuted at Rome, 130; sells S. an intaglio, 137; two gems, App. 11; on superiority of Greek over Roman art, 15

Fielding, Henry (1707–54), novelist, 155 n.1, App. 16

Fielding, Mr. *See* Feilding, Hon. Charles

Filarete, Antonio Averlino (ca. 1400–post 1465), It. architect, 78 n.4

Filippo. *See* Juvarra, Filippo

Final, 313

Finch, Hon. William (1691–1766), M.P., son of E. of Winchelsea, 314 n.5

Fini, Francesco Antonio (1669–1743), cardinal: dying, 349–50

Fiorenzuola, 324 n.5, 327, 328 n.4

Fisher, Henry (*fl.* 1727–41), murderer and convert: at Rome, 381

Fisher, John (1459?–1535), Bp. of Rochester, theologian, 80 n.2

Fitzroy, Lady Caroline (1722–84), dau. of D. of Grafton, 367 n.4

Fitzroy, Charles (1683–1757), 2d D. of Grafton, 9

Fitzroy, George (1715–47), styled E. of Euston, 316 n.7

Fitzwilliam, William (1720–56), B. Fitzwilliam of Lifford, 3d E. Fitzwilliam, 368; met at Paris, App. 1

Flaccus, Valerius (1st cent. B.C.), Latin poet, 146; quoted, 136, 143

Flaminian Way. *See* Via Flaminia

Flanders, 183–4

Fleury, André Hercule de (1653–1743), cardinal and statesman, 199, 407

Flora, Miss: at Winchester, 406

Florence, 114, 122, 124, 138, 295, 296, 312, 324, 325, 327, 348, 387, App. 1; Bargello, 114 nn.3, 10, 147 n.6; carnival, 140; Cascine gardens, 132–3; no Vauxhall there, 408; city government and taxation, 134; cost of lodging, App. 3; Great Duke, *see* Medici, Giancastone de'; Great Duke's palace, 185; histories of, 18; *improvvisatori*, 20–1; inns, App. 3; inscriptions, App. 16; inundation, 332 n.2, 333, 334; Lorenzo Library, 340; masonic lodge, 5–6; Museo Archeologico, 126 n.4, 147 n.4; Niccolini Palace, 334; snow in late spring, 151, 153; S.'s letters dated from, 117, 120, 135, 354; S.'s stay at conducive to his interest in the antique, 13, 15

—Great Duke's gallery, 125; Agrippina's chair, App. 16; catalogue of the learned men at, App. 16; chimaera, 126, 146; *Museum Florentinum*, App. 12; Sansovino's Bacchus, 15; tour of the gallery, 24, 142–50; Venus de' Medici, 15, 256 n.4, 330 n.2 (*see also* Antiques); visited every day by S., 13, 142, 151, 330. *See also* Bianchi, Sebastian

Floyd, Mr.: met at Marseilles, App. 1

Foligno, 103 n.1, 385

Fondi, 106

Fontainebleau, 201; woods of, 222

Fontana, Domenico (1543–1607), It. architect: mistaken by S. for G. Alessi, 78

Forbin-Janson, Jacques de, Bp. of Arles 1711–41, 158

Forli, 99

Formiae, 107

Forrester, Sir John, 'literal son of Don Quixote' (*Obs.* 759): met at Turin, App. 1

Fortifications: Alessandria, 312; Amsterdam, 173; Antibes, 157; Calais, 29, 30; Corfu, 86; Dijon, 34; Geneva, 70; Genoa, 156; Leghorn, 119; Lille, 181–2; Lucca,

British minister at The Hague, 7, 167, 168 n.5, 211 n.2, 216 n.2; met at The Hague, App. 1

Hampshire, 64, 70, 80, 102, 112, 128, 196, 197, 242, 249, 295, 339, 349

Hannah, John, 210

Hannibal (247–183 B.C.), Carthaginian general, 181 n.4, 274, 301

Harcourt, Simon (1714–77), 2d Visc. Harcourt: met at Florence, 152, App. 1

Harpocrates, 6

Harrach, Alois-Thomas-Raymond, Count de (1669–1742), Viceroy of Naples, 108, 113

Harrington, James (1611–77), political theorist, 280 n.2, 396 n.4

Harrington, Lord. *See* Stanhope, William

Harris (?James, 1709–80, of Salisbury, Wilts., classical scholar, M.P., subscr. *Polymetis*, *or* Henry, d. 1764, Commissioner of Wine Licences, Treasurer of Soc. Dilettanti): met at Florence, App. 1

Hartington, Lord. *See* Cavendish, William

Harvey. *See* Hervey, Hon. George William

Harwich, 165, 166, 168 n.3, App. 5

Hay, William (1695–1755), M.P. for Seaforth, author of *Essay on Deformity*, subscr. *Polymetis*: met at Paris, App. 1

Hayes, Mr. and Mrs.: met at Paris, App. 1

Hays, Dr. (?Cherry, d. 1763, *or* William, d. 1777): met at Venice, App. 1; his well near Naples?, 112 n.7

Hearne, Thomas (1678–1735), antiquary: on S. at Oxford, 2

Heem, Jan Davidz, de (1606–84), Flemish painter: flower pieces at Mme de Wiet's (Antwerp), 428

Heemskerck, Egbert van (1645?–1744), Flemish painter: six Don Quixote pieces at Mr. Clasen's (Antwerp), 428

Helvoetsluys, 165, 166, 168 n.4, 169, App. 5; harlequin town, 167

Henri I (1550–88), D. de Guise, 191

Henri II (1519–59), K. of France, 190, 200

Henri III (1551–89), K. of France, 192 n.4

Henri IV (1553–1610), K. of France: statue of, 189

Henry V (1387–1422), K. of England, 49

Henry Benedict (1725–1807), later Car-

dinal of York, the Pretender's younger son: with his governor, 332; at the opera, 342

Henshaw, Mr.: his vault in Dover Castle, 29

Herbert (?Robert, 1693–1769, M.P. for Wilton, *or* his brother Sir Nicholas, ca. 1706–75, of Great Glenham, M.P., subscr. to *Polymetis*): met at Rome and Paris, App. 1

Herculaneum: buried during eruption of A.D. 79, 2, 373–4; recent excavations, 112 n.7, 372, 374; difficult of access, 372; list of new findings, 375–6, App. 9; Paderni makes drawings of the finds, 375 n.7, 437

Hercules, Edward (*fl.* 1754–67), copyist for S., 25; transcribed S.'s travel letters, 23, 24

Hermes Trismegistus, 304 n.4

Hero, 86 n.11, 263

Herodotus (ca. 480–ca. 425 B.C.), Greek historian, 268, 294 n.9

Herring, Mr.: met at The Hague, App. 1

Hertford, Lady. *See* Thynne, Frances

Hertford Correspondence quoted, 274, 316 nn.5, 7, 332 n.2, 333 n.7, 334 n.1, 369, 378 n.2, 382 nn.1, 7, 9, 388 n.7, 391 n.4, 394 and n.1, 411 n.3, 416 n.3

Hertfordshire, 202, 318

Hervey, Hon. George William (1721–75), later 2d E. of Bristol: at home, 369

Hervey, John (1665–1750), 1st E. of Bristol, 240 n.2

Hesse-Rheinfels-Rothenburg, Caroline (1714–41), Dss. of Bourbon, 74, 288; her brother, 224; neglected by her husband, 102; his death, 256; S. saw her in Paris, 161

Hesse-Rheinfels-Rothenburg, Christina-Henrietta (1717–78), m. Pr. of Carignan, 11, 288–9, 290, App. 14; in 1750 mother of six, lost her beauty, App. 14

Hesse-Rheinfels-Rothenburg, Eleonora-Philippina (b. 1712), 74, 288

Hesse-Rheinfels-Rothenburg, Ernest-Leopold, Landgrave of (1684–1731), 75, 102

Hesse-Rheinfels-Rothenburg, Polyxena (1706–35), 2d wife of K. Charles

Emmanuel III, 102, 224, 280, 288, 290; her beauty, 74–5; her children, 287, 290

Hesse-Rheinfels-Rothenburg, Sophia (d. infant), 289 n.3

Hesse-Rheinfels-Rothenburg, William, Pr. of (1700–39): died in battle, 224

Hetty, S.'s 'mistress' at Winchester, 52–3

Hickman, Nathan (1695–1746), D. of Kingston's governor: met at Lyons, 54 n.6, App. 1; 'portly, plump', 72

Hillman, Rev., subscr. *Polymetis*: met at Paris, App. 1

Hinksey(?), Mr.: at Lyons, 49

Hippolite, Mr.: met at Paris, App. 1

Hobbes, Thomas (1588–1679), philosopher, 2, 280 n.2

Hogarth, William (1697–1764), engraver and painter, 408 n.8

Holbein, Hans (1497–1543), German painter: 'Old Man' at Palais Royal (Paris), 186

Holbitch, Mr.: met at Florence, App. 1

Holdsworth, Edward (1684–1746), classical scholar, 99 n.9, 106 nn.5, 6, 112, 118 n.2, 377 n.2, 385; advises S. on bill of credit, App. 5; 'father of all us travellers', 200; at Florence, 122, 128, 313, 328, 330; geographical approach to Roman classics, 14, 112; how to save on the Grand Tour, App. 5; met at Milan, 306, 310; at Rome, 102, 332, 377, App. 1; at Turin, 295, App. 1; on Pietra Mala, 328, on Posillipo, 106 n.5; remarks on Virgil, 14 n.53, App. 16; robbed at Rome, 102; writes to S., 201

Hollands-Diep, 179

Homer, 183; *Odyssey*, 107

Honeywood, Mr.: met at Paris, App. 1

Hoorn, 172 n.1; dyke at, 173

Hope, Capt.: met at Toulon, 401, App. 1

Horace, Quintus Horatius Flaccus (65–8 B.C.), Latin poet, 13, 14 n.53, 135, 137 n.3, 148; account of his villa, 137 n.3; quoted, 107, 132, 137, 149, 230

Hospitals for foundlings: Dijon, 34; Geneva, 70; Lyons, 49–50; Milan, 77, 320; Pavia, 320; Siena, 119; Venice, 77, 397–8

Howard, Philip Thomas (1629–94), Cardinal of Norfolk, 300 n.3

Howe, James (d. 1760), Leghorn merchant: met at Florence (1732) and Leghorn (1740), App. 1

Hownslow Dyke, 178

Hulse, Sir Edward (1682–1759), Bt., physician, 8, 260, 366

Hume, Rev. John (1703–82), Lord Lincoln's tutor at Cambridge, D. of Newcastle's secretary, 8, 9, 314, 315, 367 n.8; met at Paris, App. 1

Hume, Lord. *See* Hume-Campbell, Hugh

Hume-Campbell, Hugh (1708–94), 3d E. of Marchmont, politician: met at Paris, 355, App. 1

Hunter, Mr.: met at Naples, App. 1

Hutton, Matthew (1693–1758), D.D., later Abp. of York and Canterbury, 345 nn.1, 4, 5, 6

Huysum, Jan van (1682–1749), *or* his father, Justus van (1659–1716), Dutch flower painters: flower pieces at Mr. Clasen's (Antwerp), 428

Hyde, Henry (1710–53), B. Hyde, styled Visc. Cornbury, 416 n.3

Hyères, 157, App. 4

Iaci, Don Stefano Reggio, Pr., 372

Imola, 99

Improvvisatori, 6, 19–21

Inglesfield. *See* Englefield, Sir Henry

Iquique, 215 n.7

Irwin, Dr.: met at Rome, App. 1

Isabetta (Zabetta), singer at Venice, 397–8

Isis, 285 n.5

Isis (river), 53

Jackson (?George, ca. 1692–1764, Leghorn merchant, British consul at Genoa 1737–40), 348; met at Bologna (1733), Leghorn (1740), and Rome (1741), App. 1

Jamaica, 264, 365

James II (1633–1701), K. of England 1685–88, 98, 122, 282 n.4, 299; buried at the Bernardins Anglois, 189; his dau. Louisa-Maria-Theresa, 189; his wife, *see* Este, Mary Beatrice Eleanor

James Francis Edward (Stuart) (1688–1766), the Old Pretender, 5–6, 37 n.4; at the opera, 12, 342, 'sensibly olded', 342

Janssens, Abraham (1574–1632), Flemish painter
—paintings at Antwerp: 'Saviour with victorious banner' at St. Jacques, 428
—at Brussels (Town House): 'Demission of Charles V', 181; 'Laetus introitus Philippi Boni', 181; 'Submission of the Province to the Emperor', 181

Jean de Boulogne. See Bologna, Giovanni da

Jean le Juste, Giovanni di Giusto Betti (1485–1545), sculptor of Louis XII's tomb, 200

Jeanne d'Arc (1412–31), French heroine: statue of, 405

Jean sans Peur (1371–1419), D. de Bourgogne: his tomb, 222

Jedburgh, Lord. See Kerr, William

Jeffreys, Hon. Henrietta Louisa (ca. 1700–61), Css. of Pomfret, mother of Sophia Fermor, 8, 9, 11, 21 n.94, 313, 346, 385, 394; met at Florence, 328, App. 1. See also *Hertford Correspondence*

Jemmy, Lincoln's friend, 287, 412

Jerusalem, 130, 373, 381

Jervas, Charles (ca. 1675–1739), Irish painter, 333

Job the Black, African prince, 175, 208

Johnson, Dr. Samuel (1709–84), lexicographer: on seeing Italy, 1

John William Frison (1687–1711), Pr. of Orange, Stathouder, 179

Joinville, 34 n.1

Jones, Inigo (1573–1652), architect, 118

Jonquiere, Mr., S.'s landlord in London, 169, 221, 414

Jordaens, Jacob (1593–1678), Flemish painter: 'angel piece' at Augustins (Antwerp), 428; 'Resurrection' at St. Jacques (Antwerp), 428

Jordaens, Luc. (*fl.* 1650), Flemish painter: 'John Baptist preaching' at Mme de Wiet's (Antwerp), 428

Josephus, Flavius (A.D. 37–94), historian, 81 n.3

Jouvenet, Jean (1644–1717), French painter, 189

Joy (*or* Joyce), William (1675–1734), Strong Man of Kent: account of his feats abroad, 12, 153–4; his family, 154

Juan Fernández, Island of, 210–13, 222

Juno, 294 n.5

Jupiter, 294 n.5

Juvarra, Filippo (1676–1736), It. architect: his work at Turin, 75 n.2, 225 n.3, 235 n.4, 277, 285 n.6

Juvenal (1st–2d cent. A.D.), Roman satirist, 14; quoted, 148

Keebles, Miss, of Winchester, 139

Keller, Jean-Balthasar (1638–1702), and Jean-Jacques, Swiss casters of statues: copies of Bacchus, etc. (Versailles), 196 n.6; Louis XIV (Lyons), 53

Kelley, George, S.'s neighbour at Winchester, 11, 201, 336; called 'Dr. Kelly', 204, 416; his wife, 36, 84, 139

Kelley, Rev. George (d. 1789), of Orton-on-the-Hill, 416

Kelley, John (b. 1726), Winchester scholar, later Regius Prof. of Medicine at Oxford, 201, 417 n.2

Kelley, Père, Jesuit priest at Lyons, 49

Kelly. See Kelley

Kennedy, Mr.: met at Turin, App. 1

Kerkes. See Kerricx, William

Kerr, William (ca. 1690–1767), Marquess of Lothian, Lord Jedburgh: met at Paris, App. 1

Kerricx, William (1652–1719), Flemish painter: 'Our Saviour, hands tied' at St. Jacques (Antwerp), 427

Kew, 193

Kilby, Mr.: met at Paris, App. 1

Kingsclere, Hants: S.'s birthplace, 129, 177, 265

Kingston, D. of. See Pierrepont, Evelyn

Knapton, George (1698–1778), painter, 374 n.3; met at Rome, App. 1

Knatchbull, Dr. (?prebend. Durham, d. 1760), subscr. *Polymetis*: met at Turin, App. 1

Knight, Robert (Paris banker, d. 1744, *or* M.P., later B. Luxborough and E. of Catherlough, 1702–72, member Soc. Dilettanti, subscr. *Polymetis*), and wife: met at Paris (1733, 1741), App. 1

Maese, the, 30, 178

Maeslandsluys, 167, 168 n.6

Maffei, Marquis Scipione (1675–1755), It. virtuoso: antiques at the university of Turin, 82, 277; his character, plays, and operas, 21, 80; shows S. collections of antiques, 83 n.2; on superiority of Greek over Roman art, 83 n.2; Teatro Filarmonico, 21, 80; on women, 21, 80

Magliabecchi, Antonio (1633–1714), Florentine librarian: S.'s life of, 181 n.7

Mahomet, 358 n.13

Maintenon, Françoise d'Aubigné, Marquise de (1635–1719), mistress of Louis XIV, 12, 197–8

Malamocco, 99 n.2

Malta, 254–5, 256 n.1; Knights of, 41, 254

Manchester, D. of. See Montagu, Robert

Mandeville, Sir John, 14th-cent. traveller, 248, 293 n.2

Manfredi, Eustachio (1674–1739), of Bologna, poet: 'the best poet we have now in Italy', 19

Manlius, Marcus Capitolinus, legendary Roman hero, 115

Mann, Sir Horace (1701–86), British minister at Florence: corresponds with S., 333, 340, 354, 377, 387; met at Naples (1732), The Hague (1737), Florence (1740), App. 1

Mansart, François (1598–1666), French architect: Cte de Toulouse's palace, 188; Marly, 199; Trianon, 197; Versailles, 196 n.1

Mansell, Lord Thomas (1719–44), B. Mansell of Morgan, member Soc. Dilettanti, subscr. *Polymetis*: met at Turin, App. 1

Mantegna, Andrea (1431–1506), It. painter: in Ambrosiana (Milan), 80 n.3; 'his manner stiff and dry', 16

Mantua, 398 n.1

Mantua, D. of. See Gonzaga, Ferdinando Carlo

Mantuan, 79, App. 3

Mar, E. of. See Erskine, John

Mar, Lady Frances Pierrepont, Css. of (d. 1761), Lady Mary's sister, 358 n.11

Marat. See Maratta, Carlo

Maratta, Carlo (1625–1713), It. painter: 'enfeebled the Colors', 16; 'Janus' at Cte de Toulouse's (Paris), 188; 'Martyrdom of S. Biaggio' at S. Maria Carignana (Genoa), 156; prints of 'Madonna', 'Octagon', Holy Family', 'Dead Jesus' bought by S., App. 13; 'St. John baptizing our Saviour' at S. Martino (Naples), 107; at S. Filippo Neri (Turin), 277; at Siena, 119

Marca di Ancona, 100

Marchmont, Lord. See Hume-Campbell, Hugh

Marforio: statue of, 127 n.8

Margarita, singer at Venice, 398 n.6

Maria-Felicità (1730–1801), dau. of Charles Emmanuel III, 289 n.2

Marie-Louise (1729–67), dau. of Charles Emmanuel III, 289 n.2

Marie de Medici (1573–1642), Q. of France, 185; picture of, 185; her tomb, 200

Marignani, Cte de, French general: at siege of Turin, 408 n.4

Marini (*or* Marino), Giambattista (1559–1625), It. poet: *Adone* bought by S., App. 12

Marius, Caius (156–86 B.C.), Roman general: triumphal arch, App. 4; his villa, 187

Marlborough, D. of. See Churchill, John

Marly, 185 and n.5; gardens, 193, 199; machine at, 199–200

Marne, 33

Marseilles, 65, 207, 339 n.2, 400 and n.1, 401, App. 1; bastides, released slaves, recent plague, 157–8; Caesar's siege of, 158, App. 4; cost of transportation to, App. 2

Marsy, Balthazar (1628–74), *or* Gaspard (ca. 1627–81), French sculptors: 'Enceladus' (Versailles), 195

Martial (ca. 40–ca. 104), Latin poet: quoted, 136

Mary, Lady. See Montagu, Mary Wortley

Masham, Henrietta (d. 1761), née Winnington, m. Samuel Masham 1736: met at Paris, App. 1

Masham, Samuel (1712–76), later 2d B. Masham: met at Paris, App. 1

More, Sir Thomas (1480–1535), author of *Utopia*, 80 n.2

More *or* Moor(e), Mr.: met at Turin, Bologna, and Montpellier, App. 1

Morea, 86

Morecroft, Mr. and Mrs., of Winchester: Mrs. S. lives at their house in Colebrook Street, 11, 29 n., 36, 85, 215, 396

Morice, Sir William (ca. 1707–50), 3d Bt., M.P. for Lancaster, subscr. *Polymetis*: met at Florence, App. 1

Morphew, Mr., seditious Irish sailor, 211

Morris, Mr. *See* Morice, Sir William

Morrison, Mr.: at Oxford, 60

Motteux, Pierre-Antoine (1663–1718), translator, 282 n.5

Montague. *See* Montagu

Mugello, 156

Munatius Plancus (*fl.* 54–22 B.C.), friend of Caesar, 106

Murano, 314 n.1

Muratori, Lodovico Antonio (1672–1750), It. literary historian, 18, 19, 120 n.3

Murray, Sir Alexander (1712–78), Jacobite: met at Lyons, App. 1

Murray, Hon. James (ca. 1690–1770), E. of Dunbar, 332

Namur, 32 n., 33, 35, 38, 180, App. 1; citadel at, 30, 31, 182

Nantes, 191, 207 n.1

Nanteuil (de), family, 192 n.3

Naples, 97, 104, 108, 109, 138, 151, 243, 295, 315, 345, 346 n.1, 350 n.2, 367, 369, App. 1; account of (mole, corso, paintings at S. Martino, palaces of Marquis Marino and Caraffa, catacombs, Teatro San Carlo [1737], population, German oppression, lack of justice), 24, 107–8, 113–14; compared with Genoa, 156; cost of lodging, App. 3; earthquake of 1733, 138–9; King of, *see* Carlos III of Bourbon *and* Charles VI; Viceroy of, *see* Harrach; view of, 104, 112

—neighbourhood of: Agnano, Lake, 105; Avernus, Lake, 105; Baiae, 113; Bauli, 113; Bay of Naples, 108, 110, 373, 404; Caieta, 364 n.4; Capella del Purgatorio,

364 n.8; Capo di Minerva, 364 n.2; Carmone, Monastero del, 363, 364 n.8; Casino d'Elboeuf (King's House), 372, 374; Chemin de Torrents, 364 n.6; Cumae, 107, 113; Grotto del Cane, 105; Dr. Hay's Well, 112 n.7; Herculaneum, *see separate entry*; Lago Morto, 113; Lucrine Lake, 112; Mergillina, Sannazaro's villa, 106 n.7, 108; Monte Nuovo, 112; Pausilippo *or* Posillipo, Grotto del, 104–5, 106 n.7, 107, 109; Portici, 364 n.2; Puzzuoli, 112, 113; Resina, 364 n.2, 373, 374, 375 (*see also* Herculaneum); San Giovanni, 364 n.2; Sibyl's Grotto, 105, 113; Solfatara, 112 and n.6; Tempio della Fortuna, 106 n.7; Torre del Greco, 363, 364 nn.2, 5; Vesuvius, *see separate entry*; Virgil's tomb, *see* Virgil

Nar, the, 101

Narbonne, 403, 405 n.1, App. 4

Narni, 101, 103

Narsinski, Mr.: at Turin Academy, 237

Nash, Mr., at Naples: brought *Polymetis* to Paderni, App. 14

Nassau, Count Maurice, member Soc. Dilettanti 1736, brother of Lord Grantham: met at Venice, App. 1

Natter, Lorenz (1705–63), engraver and medallist: his medal of Lord Middlesex, 5, 6

Naylor, James, subscr. *Polymetis*, 369, 389, 394; met at Rome, App. 1

Neapolitan (kingdom), App. 3

Nelthorpe, James (d. 1767), member Soc. Dilettanti 1740/1, 254 n.7

Nemours, Marie-Jeanne-Baptiste, Dss. of (1644–1744), wife of Charles Emmanuel II, D. of Savoy, 227 n.1

Nero (37–68), Roman Emperor, 92 n.2; baths of, 113; 'centum camerae', 113; Golden House, 439

Neville, Catherine, mother of R. Aldworth, 330 n.7

Neville, Cecily, 204

Neville, Henry (ca. 1580–1641), 9th Lord Bergavenny, 29 n., 204

Neville, Col. Henry (1620–94), political theorist, 278, 386; introduced ballotting to England, 395

Neville, Katherine, S.'s great-grandmother, 29 n.

Neville, Mary, 204

Neville, Richard. *See* Aldworth, Richard Neville

Neville, Thomas (d. 1628), 204

Newcastle, D. of. *See* Pelham-Holles, Thomas

Newcastle, Dss. of. *See* Godolphin, Lady Henrietta

Newport, Robert Jocelyn (ca. 1688–1756), B., Lord High Chancellor of Ireland, subscr. *Polymetis*: met at Blois, App. 1

Niccolini, Abbé Antonio (1701–69), man of letters, 12; on Benedict XIV, 339 n.1, 382; freemason, 6

Nice, 157, 380, 400 n.2

Nicholls, John (b. 1692), of Winchester, 80

Nicholls, Mrs., of Winchester, 80

Nicholson, Dr.: met at Marseilles, App. 1

Nicol, Charles Gunter, Knight of Bath, 93

Nieuport, 30

Nile, the: overflowing of, 266–7; statue of, 185

Nîmes: amphitheatre, Maison Carrée, 158, 401; inn at, App. 4

Noel, Hon. James (d. 1752), M.P. for Rutland, member Soc. Dilettanti, subscr. *Polymetis*: met at Verona, App. 1

Nointel, Charles-François Ollier, Marquis de (d. 1685), French consul at Constantinople, 258

Noli, 157

Norris, Dicky, of Winchester, 335

Norris, Sir John (1670?–1749), British admiral, 308

North, John, of Winchester, 52

Novalloni (?Nivellon), painter: 'Lucretia stabbing herself' (Parma), 439

Novarese, 279

Novarra, 78 n.1

Novi, 156

Nudigate, Sir Roger (1719–1806), Bt., antiquary: met at Turin, App. 1

Oatlands: Lord Lincoln's seat at, 10

Odeschalchi, D. Livio (1652–1713), D. of Bracciano, 186

Ogilby, John (1600–76), miscellaneous writer, 195

Ogilvy, James (ca. 1714–70), styled Lord Deskford 1730–64, later E. of Findlater, member Soc. Dilettanti, subscr. *Polymetis*: met at Turin, App. 1

Ogle, Sir Chaloner (1681?–1750), rear-admiral, 365

Oglethorpe, James Edward (1696–1785), general, 175 n.3

Olivier, M.: at Marseilles, 158, App. 4

Onslow, Arthur (1691–1768), Speaker in the House of Commons, 307

Oran, 128 n.3

Orange, App. 4

Orange, Pr. of. *See* John William Frison; William I the Silent; William IV

Orange, Princess of. *See* Anne, Princess

Orcades, 393

Orléans, 2, 174, 191, 403; not a polite city, 201; statue of Jeanne d'Arc, 405

Ormea, Carlo Vicenzo Ferrero di Roasio, Marquis d' (1680–1745), Minister for Foreign Affairs at Turin, 251, 316

Orsini, Francesco Piero (ca. 1649/50–1730), Abp. of Benevento 1686–1724, then Pope Benedict XIII, 350 n.2; conflict with Viceroy of Naples, 113

Osborn, Dr. James M.: his edition of *Observations*, 25; Spence Papers in his collection, viii; on S.'s 'First History of English Poetry', 18 n.76; on S.'s notes for projected Poetical Dictionary, 18 n.76

Osborne, Thomas (1713–89), 4th D. of Leeds, F.R.S., K.G., subscr. *Polymetis*: met at Paris, App. 1

Osorio Alarcon, Chevalier Giuseppe d' (ca. 1697–1763), Sardinian minister at London, 230

Ossory, Bp. of. *See* Cox, Michael

Ostend, 174, 416 n.3; ramparts, Town House, 30

Otho, Marcus Salvius (32–69), Roman Emperor, 143

Otricoli, 103, 385

Otway, Thomas (1652–85), dramatist, 291 n.7

Ovid (Publius Ovidus Naso) (43 B.C.–A.D. 17), Latin poet, 60, 146, 148, 358 n.3

Oxford, 1, 7, 45, 59, 60, 62, 93, 128, 130,
155, 158, 168 n.10, 266; New College,
31, 45, 51 n.4, 60, 88, 129, 142, 149,
195, 201, 224, 238; S.'s residence at, 2,
12, 21, 24, 33, 35, 37, 82, 112, 152, 294
Oxford Almanac, 143

Paderni, Camillo (*fl.* 1728–69), painter,
437; supervisor of excavations at Her-
culaneum, 375 n.7; shows *Polymetis* to
Carlos III, App. 14
Padua, 84, 90, 295, 380 n.4, 389, 390, 394,
398 n.1; 'ghost of a great city', 93;
'Lapis Vituperii', 93; lecture at university of, 93; St. Anthony's tomb, 94
n.8
Page, Nurse, of Winchester, 41, 102, 122
Paglia, Giovanni Antonio (d. 1765), It.
painter, 386 n.2
Paisley, Lord. *See* Hamilton, James
Paita, 210
Palladio, Andrea (1508–80), It. architect,
85 n.5, 90, 91
Palma Vecchio, Jacopo Palma (1480–
1528), Venetian painter: 'Purification(?)
of the Virgin' (Modena), 438; at Scuola
di S. Marco (Venice), 91
Palmer (?John *or* Peregrine, 1703–62, of
Fairfield, Som., M.P. for Oxford University, subscr. to *Polymetis*), App. 12;
met at Blois and Turin, App. 1
Paolo di Matteo da Siena, 14th-cent. It.
painter: at S. Martino (Naples), 107
Paris, 2, 36, 48 n.1, 67 n.7, 128, 151, 168,
174, 180–4 *passim*, 206, 219–25 *passim*,
249, 262, 298, 315, 339 n.2, 377–88
passim, 400–18 *passim*, App. 1; account of,
185–90; arrival at, 159, 219; art collections at Palais Royal, Hôtel de
Bourbon, Card. Polignac's, Cte de
Toulouse's, M. Paris's, 185–90; chaise,
App. 5; compared with London, 159,
192–3; cost of transportation to and
from, App. 2; map of, App. 12; painted
women and opera, 161; too hot to be
enjoyed, 7. *See also* Le Sage
—buildings and public places: Bernardins
Anglois, 189; Bois de Boulogne, 193;
Carmelites, 188; Chartreux, 189; Collège

des Quatre Nations, 189; Elysian Fields,
193, 418; Faubourg St. Germain, 159;
Faubourg St. Jaques, 22; Hôtel de
Bourbon, 186; Hôtel des Invalides, 189;
Hôtel de Luxembourg, 185; Hôtel de
Luynes, 159; Louvre, 108, 185, 190,
193, 194 n.2; Luxembourg gardens,
159, 185, 417–18; Notre Dame, 32,
188; Observatoire, 185, 188; Palais
Royal, 186, 193; Place Royale, 189;
Place Vendôme, 189; Place de la Vic-
toire, 189; Pont Neuf, 189; Pont Royal,
190; Porte St. Denis, 190; Ring, 193,
418; St. Sulpice, 189; Sorbonne, church
of, 189; Tuileries, 185, 193, 194 nn.2,
3, 417–18; Val de Grâce, 188
Paris, M., art dealer at Paris, 188
Parker, Mark (ca. 1698–1775), English
Catholic antiquarian and spy at Rome,
385, App. 3; met at Rome, 1732, 1741,
App. 1; S. pays him for virtù, App. 11
Parma, 127, 155 n.7, 312; paintings at,
App. 15; theatre, 155, 320
Parmesan(o), App. 3
Parmigianino, Francesco Mazzola, styled
(1503–40), It. painter: 'Fortune on a
globe' (Modena), 438; 'Lucretia'
(Parma), 439; roof in Balbi Palace
(Genoa), 156
Paros, 257–8
Parsons, Humphrey (ca. 1676–1741), M.P.,
Lord Mayor of London: met at Calais,
App. 1
Pasciò, Monsiù, inn-keeper at Florence, 6,
12
Pasquin: statue of, 126
Pausanias (2d cent. A.D.), Greek his-
torian, 293 n.4
Pausilippo. *See* Naples, neighbourhood of,
Grotto del Posillipo
Pavia, 320
Pelham, Lady Catherine (1701–80), née
Manners, wife of Henry Pelham, 238,
251, 260, 287, 368, 371
Pelham, Catherine (1727–60), dau. of
Henry Pelham, 251, 252; marries Lin-
coln, 9, 219 n., 239 n.6
Pelham, Dorothy (d. infant), dau. of
Henry Pelham, 252 n.6

Pelham, Frances (1728–1804), dau. of Henry Pelham, 252 n.5

Pelham, Grace (1737–77), dau. of Henry Pelham, 251, 252 n.5, 368

Pelham, Hon. Henry (1695–1754), First Lord of the Treasury, brother of D. of Newcastle, 216 n.2, 219 n., 225, 251, 287, 308, 315, 366, 371, 380, 384, 412; letter to Lincoln, 25, 367–8; loss of two sons, 9, 238, 250, 259–60; on May elections, 368

Pelham, Hon. Henry (1736–9), son of Henry Pelham, 9, 238

Pelham, Lucy (1728–40), dau. of Henry Pelham, 251, 252 n.6

Pelham, Mary (b. 1739), dau. of Henry Pelham, 251, 252 n.5

Pelham, Thomas (1729–39), son of Henry Pelham, 9, 238

Pelham, Thomas (d. 1737), of Stanmore, M.P. for Lewes, 7, 216

Pelham-Holles, Thomas (1693–1768), D. of Newcastle-upon-Tyne and New-castle-under-Lyme, Secretary of State, 165 n., 216, 219 n., 412; advises Lincoln to take Dr. Hulse's pills, 8, 366; asked to recommend Lincoln's friend, 230; congratulates L. on birthday, 383; on forthcoming elections, 380; ill, 229; letters from L., *Letters 77, 80, 109, 120, 125, 143, 155, 159, 175, 176, 178*; his letters to L., *Letters 91, 153, 161*; on L.'s character, 8–9; on opposition in Parlia-ment, 365; orders L. not to 'lay himself under any kind of engagement', 383; recommends L. to marry Ann Dunk, 308, 315; retracts, 366; takes care of L. after his parents' death, 8, 225 n.; urges L. to return, 366, 384; warns L. against gambling, 251

Pellegrino's, inn at Bologna, App. 3

Penton, Henry (d. 1769), M.P. for Win-chester, 59 n.4, 266 n.2

Penton, Paul, of Winchester, 265

Perceval, John (1683–1748), 1st E. of Egmont, 246 n.4

Percy, Earl, 381

Perelle family, 17th-cent. French painters: landscapes (?), bought by S., App. 12

Perfetti, Cavalier (1681–1747), of Siena, *improvvisatore*: met at Florence, 20

Perin del Vaga. *See* Vaga, Pierin del

Péronne, 184 n.1

Perrault, Mr.: met at Turin, App. 1

Perrier, François (1584–1656), French painter: 'Apollo and the Seasons' at Cte de Toulouse's (Paris), 188

Perugino, P. Vannucci, styled (ca. 1445/50–1523), It. painter: 'Virgin and St. Joseph as carpenter' (Modena), 438

Pesara. *See* Pesaro

Pesaro, 99

Pescod, William (*fl.* 1721–47), of St. Michael, Winchester, 11; his wife, 238

Petau, Jacques, 201

Petrarch, Francesco Petrarca (1304–74), It. poet, 19, 67 n.7, 186, 296

Pew, Miss, of Winchester, 237 n.2

Peyrette, M., at Aix: his library, App. 4

Pezénas, 405 n.1

Philip II (382–336 B.C.), K. of Macedonia, 181 n.4

Philip III le Bon (1396–1467), D. of Bur-gundy: picture of, at Brussels, 30, 181

Philip V (1683–1746), K. of Spain, 78

Philippe le Bel (1268–1314), K. of Navarre: his castle, 401

Philippe II le Hardi (1342–1404), D. de Bourgogne, 41 n.3, 222

Philippe III d'Orléans (1674–1723), Regent of France: his collection of paintings, 186

Philippeaux, Abbé (?Jean, 1680–1740), French master at Blois, 192 n.5; recom-mended by Bowman, App. 4

Philipps, Sir Erasmus (1699–1743), Bt., M.P. for Haverford, member Soc. Dilettanti, subscr. *Polymetis*: met at Reggio, App. 1

Philips, Dr., subscr. *Polymetis*: met at Venice (1731), Paris (1733), Turin (1739), App. 1

Piacenza, 155–6, 312, 313, 320

Piaget, Mr.: met at Paris, App. 1

Pianoro, 326 n.2

Piccolomini, Aeneas Sylvius (b. 1405), Pope Pius II 1458–64, 119

Piedmont, 70, 74, 234, 285

Portland, D. of. *See* Bentinck, William

Porto Bello: battle of (Nov. 22, 1739), 287 n.3, 367 n.2

Posillipo. *See* Naples, neighbourhood of

Postell, William: account of, App. 16

Pouilly, Louis-Jean Lévesque de (1691–1750), French erudite: early history of Rome 'mere fiction', 116 n.6

Poussin, Nicolas (1594–1665), French painter: 'Camillus' at Cte de Toulouse's (Paris), 188; 'Seven Sacraments' at Palais Royal (Paris), 186

Pozzo, Leopoldo (d. 1745), Venetian mosaicist, director of mosaic school at St. Mark: mezzolane at St. Mark, 89

Pratolino: 'Genius of the Apennines' at, 329

Prester John, 292

Pretender, Old. *See* James Francis Edward (Stuart)

Pretender, Young. *See* Charles Edward (Stuart)

Price, Mr.: at Oxford, 60

Prior, Matthew (1664–1721), poet and diplomat, 197

Procaccini, Giulio Cesare (1574–1625), It. painter: at S. Maria Carignana (Genoa), 156

Prometheus, 143

Provence, 158, 160

Prudentius (348–ca. 410), Latin poet, 62

Pryor. *See* Prior, Matthew

Ptolemy, Claudius, 2d-cent. astronomer, 185

Purmerend, 172 n.1, 173

Pyramids, 268–9

Pyrenees, 158, 403

Pyrrhus II (ca. 318–272 B.C.), K. of Epirus, 30, 181

Quarrington, Lord. *See* Lee, George Henry

Queensberry, D. of. *See* Douglas, Charles

Quellin (?Artus I, 1609–68), Flemish sculptor

—sculptures at Antwerp: 'Assumption of the Virgin' at l'Abbaye des Bernardins, 429; handsome work at St. Jacques, 427; refectory at St. Michael's, 427; Saviour's head? at Grand Carmes, 427; two reliefs at ibid., 427; Virgin, words in wire from her mouth? at ibid., 427

Quillinus. *See* Quellin

Quintinus. *See* Massys, Quentin

Rabelais, François (ca. 1494–1553), French writer, 249 n.1

Radicofani, 118 n.7, 332 n.1

Radnor, Lord. *See* Robartes, Henry

Rainsford, Thomas (d. 1754), Lt.-Col.: met at Marseilles, App. 1; at Toulon, 401

Ramsay, Chevalier Andrew Michael (1686?–1743), freemason, 12, 294 n.5; met at Paris, 22, App. 1; on Pope and Boileau, 22; recommends Italian writers, 18, 67 n.7; recommends S. to learned Jesuits, 45 n.1, 66; tutor of D. de Bouillon's nephew, 66; writes to S., 18, 66

Ramsden, Thomas (1709–91), Latin secretary to the D. of Newcastle, head. to *Letters 124, 131, 177*

Randall, Mr., second lieutenant, 215 n.7

Ransford, Lieutenant. *See* Rainsford, Thomas

Ranucci, Giacomo (d. 1549), Bolognese architect: theatre at Parma, 155

Ranuccio. *See* Ranucci, Giacomo

Raphael, Raffaelo Sanzio (1483–1520), It. painter

—general: admired, 15; compared with Correggio, 16; 'design from R.'s Doctors' bought by S., 16, 261, App. 12; Frey on 'Transfiguration', 14 n.55, 16; 'Holy Family', print of, bought by S., App. 13; 'St. Sebastian' at M. Paris's going to England, 188

—paintings at Antwerp: 'Justice and another woman'? at Acad. des Peintres, 427

—at Foligno: altar-piece, 103 n.1

—at Loreto: 'Virgin showing little Jesus to Joseph', 108

—at Milan: 'School of Athens' at Ambrosiana, 80 n.2, 320

—at Modena: 'Old Elizabeth, etc.', 438; 'Triumph of Ariadne' attributed to, 437

—at Paris (Palais Royal): 'Little St. John, Jesus and Virgin', 190 n.2; 'Madonna, with a flying veil', 186; 'St. John in the

Wilderness', 190 n.2; 'St. Joseph, little Jesus and Virgin', 190 n.2; 'Young St. John Baptist', 186; fifteen other paintings, 186
—at Parma: 'Leo X' copy, 439; 'Madonna dello gatto', 439
—at Piacenza: 'Madonna' at S. Sisto, 155
—at Poggio a Caiano, 124
—at Venice: 'Madonna' at S. Maria delle Virgini, 91
—at Versailles, 190

Ras Sem, 130–1

Ravenna, App. 5

Rawdon, Arthur (1723–66), of Rathmullyan, sea officer: met at Turin, 284, App. 1

Rawdon, Sir John (1720–93), Bt., 1st E. of Moira, 257, 287; his character, 245; met at Turin, 284

Read, Henry 'Bug' (b. 1716), Lincoln's friend at Cambridge, 230, 283

Recanati, Giovan Battista (1687–1734), nobleman of Venice: his collection of Provençal poets, 18 n.77

Red Sea, 130

Regent of France. See Philippe III d'Orléans

Reggio, 8, 385, 387, 388, 390, App. 1; opera at Teatro della Cittadella, 385, 386

Regulus, Roman general during First Punic War, 181 n.4

Rehbinder, Bernard Otho Freiherr von (1662–1743), general, 303–4

Reims, 32, 34 n.1

Reking. See Wrekin, the

Rembrandt van Ryn (1606–69), painter, 16; 'Fortune Teller' at Pr. of Orange's palace, 178; 'Little Head' at Mr. Clasen's (Antwerp), 428

Reni, Guido (1575–1642), Bolognese painter
—general: 'Aurora', print of, App. 11, 13; 'Bacchus and Ariadne', print of, App. 13; disguises nature, 15; Frey on, 14 n.55; introduced 'glaring Lights', 16
—paintings at Milan: 'St. Francis' at Count d'Arese's gallery, 78
—at Modena: 'Madonna', 438; 'Noli me tangere'?, 438; 'Our Saviour', 438

—at Naples: 'Natività', unfinished, at S. Martino, 107
—at Paris: at Card. Polignac's, 188; 'Helen' copy? at Cte de Toulouse's, 188; at Palais Royal, 186; weak picture at Carmelites, 188

Reynolds, Sir Joshua (1723–92), painter, 122 n.3

Rheims. See Reims

Rhimes, Nanny, of Winchester, 75, 118 n.1

Rhine, the, 79, 136, 179

Rhodes, 256

Rhône, the, 49, 52, 68, 158, 159, 401; statue of, 53

Ribera, Giuseppe or José, styled Lo Spagnoletto (1591–1652), painter: 'Dead Saviour, the prophets' at S. Martino (Naples), 107; 'Democritus' at Palais Royal (Paris), 186; 'Heraclitus' at ibid., 186; 'St. Sebastian' (Modena), 438

Richa, Dr. Carlo (d. ca. 1745), royal physician at Turin, 278 n.1, 309, App. 16; on beneficient influence of waters at Acqui, App. 16; developed kleptomania in last years, App. 14

Richardson, Jonathan, the Elder (1665–1745), painter, 139 n.4; his translation from Dante, 122 n.3

Richardson, Jonathan, the Younger (1694–1771), painter, 131 n.7; quoted, 147 n.5

Richelieu, App. 4

Richelieu, Armand-Jean du Plessis de (1585–1642), cardinal: his tomb, 189

Richmond, 193

Riley, Frank, of Winchester, 11, 271

Riley, Mr. and Mrs., of Blandford, 109

Rimini, 99, 385, App. 5

Rivarola, Domenico (1687–1748), Corsican patriot, 306

Rivoli castle: Victor Amadeus imprisoned at, 74

Robartes, Henry (ca. 1695–1741), 3d E. of Radnor: met at Venice, App. 1

Rochecorbon, 207 n.1

Rochelle, La, 207

Rochester: bridge at, 29, 58

Rochester, E. of. See Wilmot, John

Roi, 183, 184 n.1

Rolle, Edward (1703–91), S.'s friend, 13, 34, 45, 51, 149, 203, 208, 214, 246, 313; his appearance, 330, 402; called 'Captain' or 'Cap', 62, 129, 131 n.1, 135; on the continent, 168, 175; cousin of Henry Rolle, 50, 60 n.3; is another 'son' to Mrs. S., 138, 226, 402; letters to Mrs. S., 31–2, 88; met at Paris, 221 n.1, App. 1; his MS 'Life of S.', 10; receives living at Monk Okehampton, 32 n., 129, 132; robbed, 402; S.'s deputy at Oxford, 3, 32 n., 37, 39 n.1, 50; S. writes to him, 32 n., 33, 35, 38, 56, 88, 102, 135–7, 209, 226; to visit France, 60, 135, 161, 168; verses to S., 60 n.8; visited by his parents, 129; writes to Mrs. S., 138; but seldom, 241, 297, 330; writes to S., 37, 50, 59–60, 129, 138, 402

Rolle, Henry (1708–50), B. of Stevenstone, Devon., M.P., 51 n.; asked S. to send him Colonia's book, 81; compliments S. on his letters, 145; granted a living to E. Rolle, 32 n., 129; made a tour of Holland, 125; promised E. Rolle to take him to France, 59–60, 135; S.'s letters to, 24, 50–1, 61–2, 81–2, 125–6, 142–50; S. to meet him at Paris, 135; writes to S., 81

Rolle, John, of Stevenstone, 227 n.2

Rolle, Margaret (1709–81), Baroness Walpole, later Countess of Orford, 313; advice to S., 367 n.10; considers S. a philosopher, 328; met at Florence, 328, App. 1; on oppression of the court of Rome, 324

Rolle Walter, John (1714?–79), M.P., 51, 62

Rollin, Charles (1661–1741), historian: verses on death of, attributed to S., 412

Romagna, 99, App. 3

Romano. See Giulio Romano

Rome, 12, 13, 17, 61, 66, 67, 80–112 *passim*, 138, 151, 196, 242, 248, 262, 295, 296, 312, 314 n.2, 315, 330, 331–82 *passim*, App. 1, App. 5; arrival at, 94; blessing of beasts at S. Antonio Abbate, 344–5; Candlemass, 349; carnival and horse races, 352–3; consistory, 336–7; cost of lodging and coach, App. 3; effeminacy of modern Romans, 343,

349–50; flood at, 331–2, 333; gardens and vineyards, 114; 'greatness of things ... in such numbers', 13, 94, 117, 335; mala aria, 117; map of, 352, App. 11; operas, 12, 342–3; Pope Benedict XIV, *see* Lambertini; posts uncertain, 376; presence of classical past, 13, 115; Pretender at, 342; Tiber, *see separate entry*; transportation from London, App. 2; warm in December, 338

—structures and public places: Arch of Titus, 381; Campidoglio, 127 n.7; Capitol, 115, 125, 126, 291 n.7, 381; Colosseum, 115; Corso, 352; Esquilino, 344; Forum, 116 n.6; Lacus Curtius, 116 n.6; Mausoleum of Augustus, 13, 137; Monte Testaceo, 378 n.4; Palazzo Corsini, 127 n.7; Palazzo Farnese, 148, 382 n.7; Palazzo Lancilotti, 15; Palazzo Spada, 116 n.3; Palazzo Verospi, 133 n.2; Piazza di Pasquino, 127 n.7; Piazza del Popolo, 352; Piazza di Spagna, 332; Ponte Milvio, 332; Porta del Popolo, 103; Prata Quinctia, 115; Rotonda, 50, 115, 126, 332, App. 16; St. John Lateran, 374, 380, 381–2; St. Peter's, 100, 108, 114, 332; St. Theodorus, 115; S. Antonio Abbate, 115, 344–5; S. Maria Antiqua, 116 n.8; S. Maria Liberatrice, 115; S. Maria Maggiore, 115; S. Sabina, 116 n.11; Sublician bridge, 116 n.5; Tarpeian Rock, 115; Teatro Alle Dame, 342, 343 n.2; Temple of Diana, 344; Vatican, 114, 150

Roquelaure, Antoine-Gaston, D. of (1656–1738), 338 n.2

Rosalba. *See* Carriera, Rosalba

Rosenberg, Island of, 168 n.9

Rosicrucians, 304 n.5

Rospigliosi, Gianbattista (1646–1722), general, 353 n.4

Rossi, Alba Rasponi: at Bologna, 389

Rossi, Andrea (*fl.* 1727–75), engraver at Rome, App. 11, App. 16

Rotterdam, 178–9

Roubilliac, Louis-François (1705?–62), sculptor, 408 n.8

Rouen, App. 2

Rousseau, Jean-Jacques (1712–78), man of letters, 398 n.7

Rovero, Giovanni Battista (1684–1766), Bp. of Acqui, 319

Royden. *See* Rawdon

Rozelli's coffee-house, 178

Rubens, Peter Paul (1577–1640), Flemish painter

—general: 180; admired, 16; his 'Graces fat', 17

—paintings at Antwerp: 'Assumption of the Virgin' at St. Mary's, 427; 'Christ taken from the Cross' at ibid., 427; 'Cross taking down' at St. Vanburgius, 427; 'Dead Saviour' at St. Mary's, 427; 'Holy Family' at Mme de Wiet's, 428; landscape at Mr. Ferrari's, 428; 'Melchisedec's sacrifice' at Mme Lunden's, 428; 'Miracles of St. Francis' at Recolets, 428; 'St. Apollonia' at Augustins, 428; 'St. Ignatius' at Jesuits' Church, 427; 'St. Sebastian' at Augustins, 428; 'Saviour on the Cross and R.'s third wife' at Mme de Wiet's, 428; 'Saviour sleeping in the storm', unfinished, at ibid., 428; self-portrait with his three wives at St. Jacques, 428; 'Susanna and the Elders' at Mme de Wiet's, 428; three old heads and portraits? at M. de Leyck's, 429

—at Genoa: altar-piece at S. Ambrogio, 157

—at Lille: 'Beheading of St. Catherine' at St. Catherine's, 182; 'Fall of the Angels' at Église de l'Ange Gardien, 182

—at Modena: 'St. Jerome', 138

—at Paris: at M. Paris's, 188; at Palais Royal, 186; twenty paintings at Luxembourg Palace gallery, 185

—at Poggio a Caiano, 124

Rubicon, 99; how to see 'Puniceus Rubicon', App. 5

Russel, John (1710–71), 4th D. of Bedford, politician, 287 n.5

Russell, John (*fl.* 1740–50), painter: met at Rome, App. 1; quoted, 354 n.6

Ryswick, 168 n.6, 178

Sacchi, Andrea (1599–1661), It. painter: 'Dying Ann', print, App. 13; print of ?, App. 13; 'Romualdo', celebrated picture, 16

Sackville, Lady Caroline (d. 1775), sister of Lord George Sackville-Germain: met at Paris, App. 1

Sackville, Charles (1643–1706), 6th E. of Dorset and E. of Middlesex, Restoration poet and critic, 4, 7

Sackville, Charles (1711–69), styled E. of Middlesex, later 2d D. of Dorset, 33, 38, 47, 69, 72, 82, 84, 221, 386, 417; his character, 3, 4–5, 6 n.19, 7, 33, 37, 97, 221; does not accompany his family to Europe, 199; and establishment of masonic lodge at Florence, 5–6; on Italian character, 141 n.2; leading member of the Soc. of Dilettanti, 7; leases house outside Florence, 122, 126; looks like Louis XV, 184; masonic medal of, as 'Magister Florentiae', 5, 6 n.20; mock-encomium on S. commissioned by, 3–4; his passion for opera, 6, 84; patronage of Vaneschi, 6; and Amorevoli, 387 n.3; prolongs stay in Florence, 127, 128; pursues the Muscovita, 274 n.3; S.'s acquaintance with, at Oxford, 3, 34 n.3; S. asks him for a buck, 246; S. corresponds with him, 7, 209; subscribes for twelve copies of *Polymetis*, 10

Sackville, Lord John Philip (1713–65), M.P.: his character, 65–6; met at Geneva, App. 1

Sackville, Lionel Cranfield (1688–1765), 1st D. of Dorset, Viceroy of Ireland, 47; cr. D.C.L. at Christ Church, 3; offers S. deanry at Clogher, 10, 211 n.1; received by Louis XV at Versailles, 199

Sackville, Thomas (1536–1608), 1st E. of Dorset, dramatist, 4; *Gorboduc*, edited by S., 7, 204

Sainctot, Chevalier de, Master of Ceremonies, 200 n.6

Saint-Aignan, D. de. *See* Beauvillier(s), Paul-Hippolyte

St. Amand: abbey, 182

St. Anne: statue of, 43

St. Anthony, 91, 345; his tomb at Padua, 94 n.8

St. Anthony Abbot, patron of beasts, 115, 344–5

St. Bartholomew: picture of, in Milan cathedral, 78, 148

479

Spence, Joseph (*cont.*)

Lord Middlesex in satirical verse, 4, 7, 393; called 'my master in the antique' by H. Walpole, 354; has nothing to do with scandalous history, 6, 7, 357; had colds at Oxford, 35; helps young men to New College, 195, 199, 201; to a preferment, 416–17; to Winchester College, 45, 80; interest in luminaries of humble origin, 180, 181 n.7 (*see also* Joy, William; *Improvvisatori*); lack of worldly ambition, 10, 11, 198, 305; Latin panegyric on, 18–19, 280 n.7; learns to dance, 38; but not good at it, 80; passes for a grave thinking man of great solidity, 279; for a philosopher (with Lady Walpole), 328; for a poet, 245; his practice of benevolence, 417; sonnet addressed to S. by an *improvvisatore* appealing for help, 21

CEREMONIES OBSERVED: Benedict XIV takes possession of St. John Lateran, 381–2; Candlemass ceremony at Rome, 349; cattle blessing at S. Antonio Abbate, 344–5; consistory presided by the Pope, 336–7; coronation of new Doge at Venice, 395–6; Easter customs at Dijon, 42–3; Maundy ceremony, 281; nun professing at Lyons, 12, 54–6; at Venice, 87; processions in France, 42–3, 48; processions for rain at Turin, 284–5; royal marriage at Turin, 287–9

ON CONTEMPORARY EVENTS AND PERSONALITIES: arrest of Victor Amadeus II, 67 n.3, 74; Boerhaave at Leyden, 170–1; Cocchi at Florence, *see separate entry*; Colonia at Lyons, 71–2; court of Turin, *see* Charles Emmanuel III, Savoy, Hesse-Rheinfels-Rothenburg, Carignan; Don Carlos parting from Florence, 126, 127; effects of 1737 eruption of Vesuvius, 363–4; establishment of masonic lodge at Florence, 5–6; Ficoroni, 130; Horace Walpole at Reggio, 387–8; Lady Mary Wortley Montagu at Rome, 356–60; Le Sage at Paris, 21–2; Louis XV at Versailles, 184–99; Maffei at Verona, 80, 82; Old Pretender at the opera, 342; Pope Benedict XIV, 331–4, 336–8; Prince of Orange at Breda, 179–

80; recent excavations of Herculaneum, 372–4; Rosalba at Venice, 16; Turretini at Geneva, 70 n.5; for S.'s closer friends, *see also* Cartwright, Elizabeth; Downes, Robert; Holdsworth, Edward; Massingberd, William; Pitt, Christopher; Pope, Alexander; Rolle, Edward; Smyth, Arthur

FINANCIAL CONSIDERATIONS

—costs: Belloni's bill of credit, App. 10; Dijon less expensive than Oxford, 33; footman, valet, and tipping, App. 3; lodging and coach in Italy, App. 3; ought to get bill of credit four months before one needs it, App. 5; postage, 39, 41 n.1; preliminary short tour, 2; a tour, 1; transportation from London to Rome, App. 2; virtù, App. 11–13; wine, 46, 125

—income: has 'enough to live comfortably', 297; increase of stipend, 1, 60; stipend at Oxford, 1, 10 n.41; 'worth near £1000', 10, 207

GALLERIES AND COLLECTIONS VISITED

—Antwerp: Académie des Peintres, Mr. Clasen's, Mr. Ferrari's, M. de Leyck's, Mme Lunden's, Mme de Wiet's, App. 6

—Brussels: Town House, 30, 181

—Florence: Grand Duke's gallery, 142–50; Lorenzo Library, 340

—Genoa: Palazzo Balbi and Durazzo, 156

—Lyons: Jesuits' Library, 49

—Milan: Ambrosiana, 80 nn.2, 3; Count d'Arese's gallery, 78; Settala's gallery, 320

—Modena: Duke's Palace, App. 15

—Naples: S. Martino, 107

—Paris: Hôtel de Bourbon, 186; Louvre, 185; Luxembourg Palace, 185; Palais Royal, 186; Card. Polignac's, 186–8; Cte de Toulouse's, 188; Tuileries, 185; Versailles (picture gallery), 190

—Parma: App. 15

—Poggio a Caiano, 124

—Turin: Royal Palace, 275–8

—Venice: 89–92

—Verona: Bishop's Palace, 82; House of Bevilacqua, 82

GARDENING: Cascine at Florence, 133 and n.4; criticizes French gardens as

Spence, Joseph (*cont.*)

not natural, 417–18; criticizes regular Dutch gardens, 167, 169, 177; his garden at Birchanger, Essex, 175, 202, 215, 242, 265, 339, 393, 408 and n.8; 'Genius of the Apennines' at Pratolino, 329; Luxembourg gardens and Tuileries, 417–18; his MS essay on gardening, 15 n.63; prefers The Hague wood to regular gardens, 177; prefers little Trianon and woods at Chantilly to Versailles, 178 n.9, 197, 220; Prince of Orange's gardens at Breda, 180 n.4; the Tuileries, 194 n.3; Versailles, 184, 194–5

LITERARY INTERESTS AND AESTHETICS

—literary interests: *Anima Dannata*, account of performance, 231–3; annotated copy of, 233 n.3; asks Cocchi to translate *Crito* into Italian, 17; on Eastern manner of writing, 17, 120; on *improvvisatori* at Florence, 20–1; interest in the influence of Provençal poets on the Renaissance, 18; on Italian tragedies, 21; on Italians' regard for English writers, esp. Pope, 22, 88; Latin verses on the Bormida, 317 n.1; low comedy at Leghorn, 21, 118; on Molière, 18 n.79; on Pope's translation of Homer, 1, 18 n.79; project for a Poetical Dictionary, 18 n.78; his reading abroad, 18, 67 n.7, 120, 137, 272; receives Pope's verses from H. Walpole, 333, 354–5; saw Lady Mary's MSS at Rome, 361; saw MS account of Lord Sandwich's travels and urged him to publish it, 282–3; translated Cocchi on ethics, 17; translation from Dante, 121 n.4; treatise 'sul Rinascimento della Letteratura', 17; verse encomium on Swiss freedom, 70 n.4; verses on Lord Middlesex, 4–5. *See also* Cocchi, Dr. Antonio; Duck, Stephen; Maffei, Marquis Scipione; Montagu, Lady Mary Wortley; Pitt, Christopher; Pope, Alexander

—aesthetics: S.'s admiration of Raphael, 15, 188; aesthetics of *belle nature*, 15–17; on allegories in shop signs at Venice, 90, 92 n.3; concept of grace in motion, 17; method of comparing allegorical representations, 15, 135–7, 145, 146; prefers

ancient simplicity to modern multiplicity, 15, 82, 145–6

ON MANNERS

—Europe: difference between continental and English nobility, 113, 128, 168; on recent humanisation of war, 407

—France: coal pans under feet of women, 38; cuisine, 46, 269; fishing and water-coaches in the Saône, 58, 390; head-dress of women, 38, 48; hospitality, 55, 56, 64–5; painting and bawling of women at opera, 161; swallow fishing and ladies bathing, 58–9, 73; women compared with English women, 274 and n.4; women not pretty, 63–4

—Germany: character, 113

—Holland: bolder waggons and phaetons, 167, App. 5; cleanliness in, 167

—Italy: bandits and robbery, 102, 106, 113–14, 121–2; carnival at Florence, 140–1; at Rome, 352–3; at Venice, 94–6; character, 102, 141; *Corsa del Palio* at Siena, 117; head-dress of women, 77, 92, 117–18; horse races at Bologna, 99 n.8; at Rome, 353; noblemen's dress at Lucca, 124; at Venice, 87; number of spies there, 87; oppression of the court of Rome, 324; Romans now effeminate, 343, 349–50; royal trainoes at Turin, 240; theatrical style of preaching and lecturing, 18, 93; women kept indoors, 76; women at Venice, 255

MISCELLANEOUS: seasons in Italy, 101, 132; hailstorm at Blois, 191; thunderstorm at Turin, 296–7, 298; inundation at Rome, 331–2, 333; on seeing the cold, 247–8; nightingale and migrating quails at Turin, 297–8, 299; storks in Holland, 167–8. *See also* Antiques; Ballotting; Cities, city governments; Fortifications; Freemasons; Hospitals for foundlings

MUSIC: concerts at Dijon, 36; at Rome on Lincoln's birthday, 378 n.2; conservatorios at Venice, 397–8; gondoliers sing Tasso in Venice, 19; opera houses at Bologna, 390; at Lyons, 52; at Naples, 113; at Paris, 161; at Reggio, 386; at Rome, 342; at Turin, 234; at Venice, 84; at Verona, 21, 80; opera introduced

Spence, Joseph (*cont.*)

to Russia, 20; operas and castrati, 6, 84, 239, 342–3

ODDITIES: M. André, the adept, 302–4; Master Claude, the Piedmontese surgeon, 300–2; William Joy, the English Samson, 153–5; Quentin Metsys, the blacksmith turned painter, 180; Sir John Royden, the Irish inamorato, 245; Vaucanson's mechanical duck, 413

PERSONAL, WHILE ABROAD: advantages of becoming familiar with persons of high rank abroad, 11, 36, 356; associates with freemasons at Florence, 6; cheats Mrs. S. by misdating letters, 39–40, 166, 221 n.1, 223; on conversation with ladies, 2, 9–10; counts number of mules on way to Genoa, 399; dines with the Pomfrets at Rome, 377 n.2; falls into a tub of fermenting grapes, 133, 140; first letter from home, 37, 170; gloomy at Rome, 378 n.3; homesick, 152, 154, 159, 202, 208, 295, 297, 350, 417; hopes never to marry, 255; not a French girl, 53, indulges in 'pixie twaddle', 269, 393–4; infects whole Academy with walking, 241–2; keeps track of the English met abroad, 54, 152, 199, 209, 243, 246, 299, 325, 328, 332, App. 1; lazy and bored at Blois, 204, 208; learns conversational French with Mme Cotheret, 2, 38; his French master, 18 n.79, 38, 41, 42, 43, 192 n.5; his French themes, 17, 18 n.79; 'pain of talking French', 31, 41; life at Royal Academy in Turin, 226, 229–30, 234–7; long time without letters, 12, 61, 121, 129, 192, 347, 362–3, 376, 402; longs to be back with Mrs. S., 152, 175, 238, 245–6, 265, 273, 407–8; longs to be in Rome, 7, 66, 97, 208, 209, 242, 295, 313; at Lord Binning's assembly in Naples, 139; loses Christmas Day in crossing to France, 31, 41; meets ambassadors and politicians at The Hague, 179; musical, is a judge of music, 84; lover of the opera, 239; has a good singing voice, 296; sings while washing his head, 294, 296; not overfond of kings, 278; paces monuments, 82, 234; patriotic thoughts from abroad, 88, 125, 279; plays backgammon, 197; reads Shakespeare and Pope in chaise, 33; restless at Turin, 295, 297, 306, 310, 311; sea-sick, 29; never sea-sick?, 165, 209; takes siestas, 294; thoughts of old age and retirement, 12, 137 n.12, 265–6, 407; turned a fisher at Lyons, 52; walks at Dijon, 35, 38, 40; at Blois, 205; at The Hague, 177; at Lyons, 64; at Rome, 377; at Tours, 215; at Turin, 226, 227, 256, 296; walks behind the chaise, 405; 'would have nothing to say to' an actress who made advances to him, 232; writes 'like a traveller', 105, 195, 247, 249, 326, 414

RELIGION: acquainted with Jesuits, 43; brings A. Pope 'beads and medals that had been blessed at Loreto', 100; Cardinal Fini, 349–50; crypt of St. Bénigne, 44; describes gloomy life at Carthusian college, 40–1; describes performance of *sacra rappresentazione* at Turin, 231–3; English visitors not obliged to kiss Pope's slipper, 335; find plenty of meat at Lent, 353 n.1; on French nuns, 57; gets thirty-three years of indulgence for attending mass, 338; has no intention of offending Roman Catholics, App. 7; heathenish images in the Low Countries, 30; the hostie and ass worshipping it, 90; indulgences at Sens, App. 15; Italian criminals take refuge in churches, 121–2; keeping Sundays at Geneva, Lausanne, 71; in Holland, 170; lacks ecclesiastical ambition, 305; liberties of nuns at Venice, 87; monks at St. Rémy great lovers of champagne, 32; never quarrelled about religion, 66; Papists married by Protestant magistrate at Amsterdam, 173; penances at Dijon, 43; piety of common people, 42–3, 116; Pope Benedict XIV, 321–2, 323, 331–2, 337; purgatory pictures common after Milan, 79; relics, etc., 32, 44; on Samothracian mysteries, 292–3; theatrical style of Italian preaching, 18, 93; thoughts on religion, 41; transformation of ancient Roman cults into Roman Catholic ones, 108, 115–16; visits churches at Calais and Dijon, 29,

Spence, Joseph (*cont.*)

42–3; warns mother not to write on religion and politics while he is in Italy, 66, 75; wasteful splendour at Loreto, 98, 100. *See also* Benedictines; Carmelites; Carthusians; Ceremonies Observed *above*

RESIDENCE: Byfleet, 10, 262 n.3; Birchanger (cottage), 223, 224, 234, 269, 305, 336, 350, 405; London: Queen's Street, 12, 224, 239, 245, 261, 273, 336, 407; Stratton Street, 408 n.7; Suffolk Street, 169, 221, 414; Oxford, 2, 12, 21, 24, 33, 35, 37, 82, 112, 152, 294. *See also* Winchester *below*

ROMAN PAST: amphitheatre at Arles, 185; at Nîmes, 158, 401; at Verona, 82; Anxur, 106 n.1; asks H. Walpole to get a medal of Virgil, 347; buys an intaglio from the Mausoleum of Augustus, 13, 137; compares cascade of Terni with Virgil's description of it, 103 n.5; compares neighbourhood of Naples to Elysian Fields, 105; death of Maxentius, 332; describes eruption of Vesuvius A.D. 79, 373–4; 'divine enthusiasm for antiquity', 66, 252–3; 'enamoured of . . . this country of medals and statues', 135; Formiae, 107; 'greatness of things . . . in such numbers' at Rome, 335; heathen temple at Dijon, 44, 50–1; how to see the Rubicon, App. 5; inscription S.P.Q.A., 173; S.P.Q.G., 70; poses as cicerone presenting antiques, 142–50; prefers old Romans to modern effeminate Romans, 343; prefers Romans to old Gauls, 51; presence of ancient Rome, 114–16; records Holdsworth's remarks in interleaved Virgil, 14 n.53; Roman aqueducts near Lyons, 64; stay at Rome and Florence conducive to S.'s interest in the antique, 13; tauribolium at Lyons, 61–2; Via Latina, 104, 106 n.1; visited Grand Duke's gallery 'above hundred times', 142, 151; visits recent excavations of Herculaneum, 374–5; visits Virgil's tomb, 105, 109. *See also* Antiques; Works and Manuscripts, *Polymetis below*

SCENIC DESCRIPTIONS: Arno Valley, 121–2; Brussels to Paris, 183–4; Calais to Dijon, 33; cascade of Terni, 101–2; the Cascine at Florence, 132–3; crossing the Apennines, 101–2, 325–6; crossing the Channel to Holland, 166–8; Dijon to Lyons, 47–8; diversions on the Saône at Lyons, 57–9; excursion along the Brenta, 84, 390; excursion up Mount Vesuvius, 110–12; The Hague, 176–7; Luxembourg gardens and Tuileries, 417–18; Lyons to Geneva, 68–9; Marly and St. Germains, 198–200; passing of the Alps, 11, 71–3; range of houses and gardens belonging to the King of France, 193; road from Rome to Naples, 104–5; Rome to Leghorn, 117–18; situation of Venice, 391–2; 'travelling ground' at Acqui, 318–19; Trianon, 197–8; Venice to Loreto, 97–9; Versailles, 194–5

SECOND-HAND ACCOUNTS OF TRAVEL: Lady Mary on her stay in Turkey, 357–60; Lord Sandwich on his tour of the Middle East, 243–4, 248–9, 252–8, 263–4, 266–71, 273–4; Shaw on petrified town in Africa, 130–1; Shelvocke on his voyage round the world, 209–14; Tomlinson on his dangerous excursion to the top of Vesuvius, 151–2

SOUVENIRS: artificial flowers, 378–9, App. 11, 12; bay leaf from Virgil's tomb for Christopher Pitt, 109; an intaglio found in the Mausoleum of Augustus, 13, 137; lapis lazuli knives and forks for Mrs. S., 393, App. 12; list of virtù bought, App. 11–13; pictures of the towns he visited, 66; his portrait by Rosalba, App. 11, 12; presents for A. Pope, 22, 100; Raphael's pencil designs, 16, 261, App. 12; sends home box of books, 141; of virtù, 348, 377

WINCHESTER: helps Winchester youngsters to New College, 45, 80; Hetty 'my mistress' absolutely lost to me, 52–3; 'poser' at Winchester College, 200 n.1; saw eclipse of the sun as a boy, 325. *See also* Spence, Mirabella; and for S.'s acquaintances there, Bale; Ball; Barton; Belson; Bigg; Brewer; Burton; Cheyney;

—her acquaintances: associates with gentlemen of the Cathedral, 209; Betty, her housemaid?, 248, 295, 326; corresponds with Edward Rolle, 31–2, 34, 37, 45, 59, 203, 208, 214, 226; complains that he writes seldom, 138, 241, 330; offers him money after he was robbed, 402; knows Lady Shuttleworth, 53; proud of being related to the Neville family, 11, 29 n., 204–5

—her health: complains of a trouble, 336; ill with 'fits', takes sour wine as remedy, 203, 204; poor memory, 11 n.44; has trouble with her eyes, 83, 102, 175, 202

—as a letter writer: endorses S.'s letters, 11, 23, 25, her amusing endorsements, 79, 92, 104, 166, 198, 331, 342; has 'a particular good manner of writing letters', 11, 238; owns a number of franks, 224; writes in a small hand, 11, 175, 202; writes to Lord Lincoln on his birthday, 377; his reply to her, 409–10

—personal: an affair that involves double taxes, 117, 241; calls *The Faerie Queene* 'a collection of pictures', 198 n.4; excellent venison pasty maker, 245; her interests, 12; her love of cleanliness, 167; has a map of Italy, 76, 117, 295; and of Rome, 352; her race in the churchyard, 414; reading psalms and dropping spectacles, 293; has trouble with Count Hyems, 44; her 'vast folio of recipes', 269

—and J. Spence: asks S. about young D. of Savoy, 257; about altar 'To the Unknown God', 292; urges him to become a warden or a bishop, 11, 305; apologises for it, 323; tells him to air his nightcaps and stockings, 196; thinks that he has a knack of enlarging stories, 293

—S.'s affection for her, 11–12; 'fondled' her 'in imitation of Pope', 12; lies to her about his departures, 39–40, 166; obliged to her for his third tour, 262; offers her financial help, 204, 241; orders one of his books for her, 201; plans to settle down in London with her, 242, 261–2, 407–8;

on return will introduce her to friends he made abroad, 11 n.44, 261–2

Spence, Richard (1701–post 1757), S.'s brother, employed by the African Company, 24 n.5, 29 n., 39, 129, 155, 160, 224; corresponds with S., 37; forwards mother's letters to S., 36; forwards S.'s letters to Mrs. S. with postscripts, 47 n.4, 48 n.1, 165 n.4, 185 n.9, 196 n.8; and Job the Black, 175 n.3; 'money affair', 75, 79, 117; in touch with secretary of D. of Dorset, 47; wrote to Rolle, 45

Spence, William, secretary to E. of Argyll, 122

Spenser, Edmund (ca. 1552–99), poet, 11, 197

Spino, Marchioness of (d. 1733): helped Victor Amadeus II with his plot, 74

Spinola, Giorgio (1667–1739), cardinal: and Lambertini, 322

Spoleto, 101

Stafford (i.e., Strafford), Lord. *See* Wentworth, William

Stanhope, Philip Dormer (1694–1773), 4th E. of Chesterfield, 406 n.1

Stanhope, William (1719–79), later 2d E. of Harrington: proposed to Miss Dunk, 366

Stanislas I Leszczynski (1677–1766), K. of Poland 1704–9, 161

Steevens, Mr.,? member Soc. Dilettanti 1750: met at Rome, App. 1

Stevenstone, Devon., head. 50, 51 n., 60 n.3, head. 61, head. 81, head. 125

Stewart, William, member Soc. Dilettanti 1737, subscr. *Polymetis*: met at Rome, App. 1

Sticker's gardens, 178

Stilicho, Flavius (ca. 360–408), Roman general, 277

Stillingfleet, Benjamin (1702–71), naturalist, 240 n.2

Stone, Andrew (1703–73), secretary to the D. of Newcastle, M.P., 216 n.5, 260, 367, 384; forwards letter to Mrs. S., 237; S. corresponds with, 9, 224, 250, 370; S.'s letters to, 25, 309–10; *passim* in headnotes to *Letters 75–179*

Stosch, Philip von (1691–1757), Baron, art connoisseur and spy, 13, 347; advised S.

on medals, 14, 149 n.5; freemason, 6; on Provençal poets, 18 n.77

Strabo (ca. 58 B.C.–ca. A.D. 25), Greek geographer, 112

Strafford, Lord. *See* Wentworth, William

Strange, Lord. *See* Smith, Stanley James

Strode, William (1698–1776), Col., 62d Foot, Lt.-Gen. 1765, M.P., member Soc. Dilettanti: met at Florence, App. 1

Strowde, Mr. *See* Strode, William

Stuart, Mr. *See* Stewart, William

Stuart, Sir William (d. 1777): met at Lyons, 54, 56 n.2, App. 1; at Venice, App. 1

Sturgis, Rev. Samuel (ca. 1701–43), Lady Walpole's lover, 314 n.5, 390, 391 n.9; met at Florence, App. 1

Suares de la Concha, Francesco (1720–77), known as 'Cecchino': travels with H. Walpole, 390

Suetonius (ca. 75–ca. 160), Latin historian, 136

Sulzbach, Johann Christian, Pfalzgraf von, m. 1731 Eleonora-Philippina of Hesse-Rheinfels-Rothenburg, 75

Suza, 73 n.1, 227, 229 n.6

Suzon, the, 34

Swift, Jonathan (1667–1745), satirist, 19, 302 n.6

Swinny, Mr.: met at Venice, App. 1

Swinton, Mr.: met at Florence, App. 1

Switzerland, 47, 65, 66, 75, 339; goiters in the Alps, 72, 73 n.2, 236. *See also* Alps, the; Geneva; Lausanne

Syling, Mr.: met at Marseilles, App. 1

Syracuse: 'Dionysius's Ear', 253, 254

T., Mr., App. 5

Tacca, Pietro (1577–1640), It. sculptor: statue of four slaves, 1624 (Leghorn), 119

Tacitus, Publius Cornelius (ca. 55–120), Roman historian, 374 n.2

Tain, App. 4

Talbot, Sir Charles (1685–1737), B. Talbot, Solicitor-General, Lord Chancellor, 54

Talbot, George (1719–87), 14th E. of Shrewsbury: met at Florence and Paris, App. 1

Talbot, William (1710–82), B. Talbot of Hensoe: met at Lyons, 54, 56 n.3, App. 1

Tanaro, 312

Tanis. *See* Teniers, David II

Tarquinius, Sextus (d. 510 B.C.), 291

Tarquinius Priscus (616–579 B.C.), K. of Rome, 292

Tasso, Torquato (1544–95), It. poet, 19; *Gerusalemme Liberata* sung by gondoliers at Venice, 19

Taurus, Mt., 249

Tempe, valley in Thessaly, 68

Temple, Mr. *See* Grenville, Richard

Teniers, David II (1610–90), Flemish painter: 'Big-bellied Virgin' at St. Jacques (Antwerp), 428; smaller pieces by 'Tanis'? at Mme de Wiet's (Antwerp), 428

Teresa, singer at Venice, 397

Terni: cascade of, 101–2, 103

Terracina, 106 n.1

Tesi, Vittoria (1700–75), opera singer: at Reggio, 386

Thames, the, 47, 53, 58, 75, 399; frozen, 247; superior to the Seine, 192–3

Theodore, K(ing?), 173

Thompson, Rev. Anthony (d. 1756), British chargé d'affaires at Paris 1740–4, 410; met at Paris, App. 1

Thompson, Sir William, Recorder, 382 n.4

Thomson, James (1700–48), poet, 131 n.9; his intimacy with S., 56 n.3; met at Lyons, 54, App. 1; at Venice and Florence?, App. 1

Thouars, App. 4

Thynne, Frances (ca. 1699–1745), Css. of Hertford, 242 n.2. See also *Hertford Correspondence*

Tiber, the, 103, 115; overflown, 332, 348; statue of, 185

Tiberius (42 B.C.–A.D. 37), Roman Emperor, 99

Tilson, Christopher (1670–1742), M.P., subscr. *Polymetis*: met at Paris, App. 1

Tindal, Nicholas (1687–1774), historical writer, 339 n.4

Tintoretto, Jacopo Robusti (1513–94), Venetian painter
—paintings at Modena: *tondi*, 438
—at Paris: at Palais Royal, 186

—at Venice: 'Crucifixion' at S. Rocco, 91; 'Deliverance' at ibid., 91; 'Paradiso' at Great Council Hall, 89; 'The Plague' at S. Rocco, 91; 'St. Roc' at ibid., 91; 'St. Stephen' at S. Giorgio, 90; 'Salutation' at S. Rocco, 91; 'Venice besieged' at Great Council Hall, 90; 'Worshipper of St. Mark' at School of St. Mark, 91; several pictures, ibid., 91

Tiridates I (d. ca. A.D. 73), K. of Parthia, 92 n.2

Tirol, 339 n.2

Tisi, Benvenuto, styled Garofalo (1481–1559), It. painter, 262 n.3; 'Great Bacchanal' (Modena), 438; 'Mars, Venus(?) and Cupid' (ibid.), 438; 'Triumph of Ariadne' attributed to (ibid.), 437

Titian, Tiziano Vecelli (ca. 1487/90–1576), It. painter
—paintings at Milan: at the Ambrosiana, 80 n.3
—at Modena: 'Give to Caesar', 439; 'Madonna', 438; 'St. John bringing lamb to Christ', 438; ?'Titian (Veronese?) and his family', 438; 'Virgin' (Titian's wife), 438; 'Virgin and Bambino', 439; 'Woman taken in adultery', 438
—at Paris: at Palais Royal, 186
—at Parma: 'Magdalen's head', 439; 'Paul III', 439; portraits, chiefly of the Farnese family, 439
—at Venice: designs for mosaics in Church of St. Mark, 89; at Grimani's?, 91; 'Old Woman with Eggs' at Carità, 15 n.62, 92; 'St. Jerome in the Wilderness' at Barberigo's, 91; 'St. Peter the Martyr' at S. Giovanni e S. Paolo, 90; 'St Sebastian', unfinished, at Barberigo's, 91; 'Venus viewing her face' at ibid., 91; 'Weeping Magdalen' at ibid., praised by Rosalba, 16, 91, 188

Titus, Roman Emperor A.D. 79–81, 373, 381

Tomlinson, John (1663–1745), London physician: met at Florence (1733), 151–2, App. 1; at Paris (1737), App. 1

Torbia, 400 n.2

Tortona, 156, 398 n.1

Tortonese, the, 279

Toulon, App. 4; Caryatides' House, 157; port of, 157, 401; S. visits a French man-of-war at, 157

Toulouse, 403, 405 n.1, App. 4

Toulouse, Cte de. See Bourbon, Louis-Alexandre de

Tournai, 174; citadel and abbey, 182

Tournefort, Joseph Pitton de (1656–1708), French botanist, 258

Tours, 174, 205–15 passim, 247, App. 1, 4; 'garden of France', 207

Townley, John (1697–1782), or his brother Francis (1709–46), Jacobites: met at Florence, App. 1

Townshend, Lady Ethelreda, or Audrey (ca. 1708–88), née Harrison, m. 1731 Charles, 3d Visc. Townshend, 237 n.2

Townson, Rev. Thomas (1715–92), of Malpas, Cheshire: remarks on Virgil, App. 16

Trajan, Roman Emperor A.D. 98–117, 65 n.2

Transylvania, Princess of: accompanied Lady Mary to St. Sophia, 359–60

Trauttmansdorf (1462–1609), adept, 304 n.6

Travelling Jew, 301, 303

Trevisani, Francesco (1656–1746), It. painter: at S. Filippo Neri (Turin), 277

Trevor, John Morley (1717–43), M.P. for Lewes, 265; connected with the Pelhams, 7, 165 n.; elected M.P. for Lewes, 216; his Italian chaise for sale, 216 n.4; resolved to master French, 7, 174; S. accompanies him on second tour, 7, 165; subscribes for twelve copies of Polymetis, 10; unexpectedly recalled to England, 7, 216

Trevor, Richard (1707–71), Bp. of St. David's and of Durham: grants S. prebend at Durham, 10

Trevor, Robert Hampden. See Hampden-Trevor, Robert

Trianon, 12, 193, 195, 197–8, 199

Trinité, Count de la, 307

Tripland, Mr.: met at Rome, App. 1

Tromp, Cornelis (1629–91), Dutch admiral: his tomb, 178

Verona, 81 n.5, 84, 295, 398 n.1, App. 1;
amphitheatre, 82; antiques at Bishop's
Palace and House of Bevilacqua, 82;
Maffei, Teatro Filarmonico, 21, 80, 82,
83 n.5, 386 n.2

Veronese, Paolo (ca. 1528–88), It. painter
—paintings at Genoa: 'Magdalen washing
Christ's feet' at Durazzo Palace, 156
—at Modena: 'Adoration of the Magi',
438; 'Christ carrying Cross', 438;
'Marriage of Cana', 438; 'Painter and
family making vow to Virgin', 438
—at Paris: altar-piece at Collège des
Quatre Nations, 189; at Cte de
Toulouse's, 188; 'Two Vices leading
Young Man' at Palais Royal, 186;
'Virtue with Hercules' at Palais Royal,
186
—at Parma: 'Finding of Moses', 439
—at Turin: two paintings at Royal Palace,
277
—at Venice: 'Family of Darius' at Pisani
Palace, 91; 'Marriage of Cana' at S.
Giorgio, 90; 'Our Saviour with the
Publicans', copy, at Dominicans, 91;
'Pharaoh's Daughter' at Grimani's, 91

Versailles, 416 n.5; château and gardens,
178 n.9, 184, 193, 194–5, 197, 220;
court at, 416 n.5; display of fountains,
196 n.3, 199; picture gallery, 190

Ver Voort. See Voort, Michiel van der

Vesey, Agmodisham (d. 1785), Irish
politician and M.P., subscr. *Polymetis*:
met at Paris, App. 1

Vesuvius, 22, 104, 105, 108, 112, 138, 437
(195, mistaken for Aetna); eruptions in
A.D. 79, 373–4; in 1631, 111, 112; in
1648, 346 n.4; in 1737, 363–4; excursion
to the top of, 11, 109, 110–12; Dr.
Tomlinson's, 151–2; surroundings of,
see Naples, neighbourhood of

Vezey, Mr. See Vesey, Agmodisham

Via Appia, 1, 106 n.1, 113

Via Emilia, 99, 313

Via Flaminia, 1, 103, 106 n.1

Via Latina, 104, 106 n.1

Vicenza, 85 n.5, 394, 398 n.1

Vico, Lago di, 117

Victor Amadeus II (1666–1732), K. of
Sardinia 1718–30, 75 n.2, 83 n.3, 227

n.1, 274; his character, 278–80; as D.
of Savoy, 227; doubled his kingdom,
278–9; imprisoned for attempting to
resume the crown, 67 n.3, 74, 81;
neglected arts for war, 275; report of
his arrest, 69; at siege of Turin, 407

Victor Amadeus III (1726–96), styled D.
of Savoy, from 1773 K. of Sardinia,
287; 'beautiful child', 74, 290; Mrs. S.
asks about him, 257

Victoria Marghareta (1740–2), dau. of
K. Charles Emmanuel III, 292

Vienne, 159, App. 4

Vigan, 316 n.4, 399, 400, App. 1

Vignory, 34 n.1

Vijverberg, 178

Vilette, Marie-Claire Deschamps de
Marcilly, Marquise de (1675–1750): in
convent at Sens, 222 n.1; helps S. with
research on Provençal poets, 18 n.77

Villa, Dom, archivist at Royal Academy of
Turin, 235 n.5, 241, 278 n.1; Lowth's
account of in 1749, App. 14

Villaborgius (?van der Borcht *or* Burg),
Flemish painter: 'Venus stopping Mars'
at Shooters' Hall (Antwerp), 427;
'Vulcan arming a young person' at Mr.
Ferrari's (Antwerp), 428

Villani, Giovanni (ca. 1280–1348), Florentine historian, 18, 120

Villar, Cte de, App. 16

Villars, Mr. See Villiers, Hon. Thomas

Villeneuve le Roy, 222

Villettes, Arthur (ca. 1702–76), British
secretary at Turin 1723–41, resident
1741–9, 251; acquainted with Maréchal
Rehbinder, 303; introduced Lincoln to
the best company, 230; Lincoln inter-
cedes for him, 286, 316, 371, 372 n.4;
met at Turin, 225, App. 1; not allowed a
secretary, 286; recommends Lincoln a
surgeon, 300; recommends him to go to
Acqui, 309–10; S. writes to, 377

Villiers, Hon. Thomas (1709–86), M.P.
for Tamworth, later Visc. Hyde and E.
Clarendon, member Soc. Dilettanti: met
at Dijon, App. 1

Vincent, Rev., subscr. *Polymetis*: met at
Florence, App. 1

Vinci. See Leonardo da Vinci